EATING UP
ROUTE 66

T. Lindsay Baker

EATING UP ROUTE 66

Foodways
ON AMERICA'S
MOTHER ROAD

UNIVERSITY OF OKLAHOMA PRESS : NORMAN

This book is published with the generous assistance of the Wallace C. Thompson Endowment Fund, University of Oklahoma Foundation.

Library of Congress Cataloging-in-Publication Control Number 2022007569
ISBN 978-0-8061-9069-3 (hardcover)

The paper in this book meets the guidelines for permanence and durability of the Committee on Production Guidelines for Book Longevity of the Council on Library Resources, Inc. ∞

1 2 3 4 5 6 7 8 9 10

To Susan Croce Kelly and Michael Wallis,
who in 1988 and 1990
authored the books that began a revival of interest in U.S. Highway 66

CONTENTS

CHAPTER 5 **TEXAS** 155

CHAPTER 6 **NEW MEXICO** 175

CHAPTER 7 **ARIZONA** 209

CHAPTER 8 **CALIFORNIA** 242

ILLUSTRATIONS

RECIPES

PREFACE

Six years into active research on this book project it seemed important for me to drive Highway 66 as nearly as I could to the way old-time motorists experienced it. Others might say that my several 2,400-mile road trips in modern cars were arduous enough, but my mind became set. Eighty-five percent of the old pavement was still there, I had a willing sidekick, and I owned an appropriately basic antique car. We made the entire trip in both directions in a four-cylinder 1930 Ford station wagon with a varnished wooden body, waterproof canvas top, and snap-on window covers. In the heat of July 2017, we bounced from Chicago to California and back, the skinny tires thumping at every pavement expansion joint along the way.

Making about two hundred miles a day, we crossed and then recrossed the heartland in thirty-five-mile-per-hour "slow motion." Some days we ended up covered with dust, especially in the Southwest. When we halted each evening, weary from the constant shaking of the car, we wolfed down whatever a café offered, washed off the day's grime, and tumbled into bed. The next morning we rose before dawn, had a bite of breakfast, and set out again. Each time we killed the motor to add fuel or take a welcome break from the constant trembling of the little car, we never knew for sure how easily it would start again.

Why would anyone want to undergo this test of mind and body? College-student companion Chris Gillis and I wanted to recreate insofar as we could what road travel was like for pre–World War II motorists. To do this, we made "the California trip" in the type of vehicle for which Route 66 originally was designed and built. During the monthlong sojourn, we bunked down in multiple historic lodgings with squeaky bedsprings and took meals at many roadside eateries, some celebrated and others not. This experience made real for us the three elements of road travel that left perhaps the strongest impressions on motorists during first half of the twentieth century: bodily fatigue, physical discomfort, and emotional uncertainty.

The purpose of this book is to explore the eating encounters of travelers along U.S. Highway 66. The volume covers the road's entire length, from Chicago to the Pacific, from its initial designation in 1926 through its phased replacement by interstate highways, mostly constructed in the 1960s and 1970s. During this half century, both motoring and public dining changed dramatically. Vehicles evolved from the primitive, boxy, and sometimes temperamental Model Ts into streamlined, dependable motorcars with air conditioning that cruised along at seventy plus miles per hour. At the same time, Americans transitioned from eating primarily locally grown foods cooked from raw ingredients to dining on fare raised and processed in distant locales and often shipped pre-prepared to restaurants along roadsides. Some of the entrepreneurs along Highway 66 themselves played instrumental roles in helping transform how Americans nationwide ate. There was never one, single Route 66 eating experience. Instead, there were multiple, constantly varying ways that travelers found nourishment going from place to place. This book sets out to examine how roving wayfarers on the Mother Road ate while America changed.

ACKNOWLEDGMENTS

This book project was born when I suggested to Acquisitions Editor Charles E. "Chuck" Rankin from the University of Oklahoma Press that I thought it would be fun to write a book about roadside dining along Route 66. We chatted at a reception during the Western History Association annual meeting in San Diego, California, in October 2001. Since that time, Chuck, Editor-in-Chief and later Director John N. Drayton, Acquisitions Editor Jay Dew, Director B. Byron Price, and Editorial Director J. Kent Calder have all encouraged me to pursue this large and complex topic, and I sincerely appreciate their long-term moral support.

More than anyone else, my sweet bride, Julie P. Baker, has "lived" with Route 66 and its roadside eateries throughout this project. Not only has she served as my most brutal and most valuable editor, but she has bounced down the old pavement with me in two complete end-to-end research trips along Highway 66 as we sought out both existing historic eating places and the sites where former eateries served food and drink. Together, the two of us kitchen tested multiple historic recipes to come up with the ones selected as sidebars on these pages, and Julie's formal training in dietetics greatly facilitated our redrafting these instructions in ways that modern cooks can more easily understand.

Chris Gillis Jr. joined me for a sojourn by four-cylinder Ford the length of the Mother Road in both directions. Always in good humor, this college student put up with his septuagenarian travel companion's inscrutable ways for a full month on the road, while traversing parts of urban and rural America that he never imagined existed. Every time that the little car had mechanical problems, we pooled our combined know-how and ignorance to get it going again.

From the outset, experts on the history of Route 66 generously have imparted their knowledge to me. They have shared their own rare documents, photographs, and publications, and have directed me to the repositories containing even more. They likewise have suggested helpful people to interview. As the project drew to its close, a number of them critiqued parts or all of the manuscript. Among these generous and eminently knowledgeable colleagues have been David G. Clark, Chicago, Illinois; Dave Sullivan, Pontiac, Illinois; Dr. Terri Ryburn, Normal, Illinois; Bill Thomas, Atlanta, Illinois; Buz Waldmire, Rochester, Illinois; Joe Sonderman, Saint Louis, Missouri;

John F. Bradbury, Rolla, Missouri; Tommy G. Pike, Springfield, Missouri; Susan Croce Kelly, Lake of the Ozarks, Missouri; Michele Hansford, Carthage, Missouri; Michael Wallis, Marian Clark, and Rhys Martin, Tulsa, Oklahoma; Jerry McClanahan and Mariko Kusabe, Chandler, Oklahoma; Jim Ross and Shellee Graham, Edmond, Oklahoma; Bob Blackburn, Oklahoma City, Oklahoma; Delbert Trew, Allanreed, Texas; Frank Norris and Kaisa Barthuli, Santa Fe, New Mexico; Paul Milan and Steve Owen, Grants, New Mexico; R. Sean Evans, Flagstaff, Arizona; Jim Hinckley, Jan Davis, and Louise Benner Kingman, Arizona; David Knudson, Yucaipa, California; Albert Okura, San Bernardino, California; Morgan Yates, Los Angeles, California; and Scott Piotrowski, Glendale, California. Steve Rider and Mike Ward, known for their extensive private collections of Route 66 paper ephemera, generously shared copies of historic menus from roadside eating places during the early stages of this project and then toward the conclusion critically reviewed the manuscript.

Much of this book is drawn from materials preserved in libraries, archives, and museums along the length of the Mother Road. Professional staff members in these institutions made available often one-of-a-kind documentation, historic photographs, oral-history interviews, and scarce periodicals. Among the colleagues in these repositories who took particular interest in the project and who went the extra mile to make valuable materials available were Heather Johnson, Curt Teich Archives, Lake County Discovery Museum, Wauconda, Illinois; Heather Bigeck, Joliet Area Historical Museum, Joliet, Illinois; Karen Moen, Bloomington Public Library, and George Perkins and Bill Kemp, McLean County Museum of History, Bloomington, Illinois; Don Fink, Route 66 State Park, Eureka, Missouri; Mark Spangler, Route 66 Museum of Missouri, Lebanon, Missouri; Kathleen Seale and Carole Goggin, Rolla Research Center, State Historical Society of Missouri, Rolla, Missouri; Tracie Gieselman-France, Duane G. Meyer Library, and Konrad Stump, Springfield-Greene County Library District, Springfield, Missouri; Paula Scott, Will Rogers Library, Claremore, Oklahoma; Sheri Perkins, Tulsa City-County Library, Tulsa, Oklahoma; Larry Johnson, Oklahoma Collection, Metropolitan Library System, and Mallory Covington and William D. Welge, Research Center, Oklahoma Historical Society, Oklahoma City, Oklahoma; Donna Littlejohn, Amarillo Public Library, Amarillo, Texas; Warren Stricker, Panhandle-Plains Historical Museum, Canyon, Texas; Greg Smith, Texas Historical Commission, Austin, Texas; Nancy Brown Martinez, Audra Bellmore, Clare Lise Benaud, and Michael T. Kelly, Center for Southwest Research, University of New Mexico, and Eileen O'Connell, Special Collections Library, Albuquerque/ Bernalillo County Library, Albuquerque, New Mexico; R. Sean Evans, Cline Library, Northern Arizona University, Flagstaff, Arizona; Shannon Rossiter, Mohave Museum of History and Arts, Kingman, Arizona; Chris S. Ervin and Hugh E. Brown, Mojave Desert Heritage and Cultural Association, Goffs, California; Sue Bridges, California Route 66 Museum, Victorville, California; Sue Payne, California Room, Norman F. Feldheym Public Library, San Bernardino, California; Christie Kimsey, Richard Rocha, and Dan McLaughlin, Pasadena Public Library, Pasadena, California; Peter Blodgett, Huntington Library, San Marino, California;

Cynthia McNaughton, History and Genealogy Department, Los Angeles Public Library, and Marva Felchin, Autry Museum of the American West, Los Angeles, California; and Jim Balducki, Los Angeles County Library, Norwalk, California.

Route 66 experts and roadside businesspeople made available much of the essential data that went into creating this study of roadside dining along Route 66. Often, the most valuable information came from individuals who own, work in, or otherwise are connected to past and present eating places. I would like to thank in particular Patrick Rhea, Dell Rhea's Chicken Basket, Willowbrook, Illinois; Debby Funk, Funks Grove Pure Maple Sirup, Shirley, Illinois; Michael Higgins, Maldaner's Restaurant, Springfield, Illinois; Travis Dillon, Ted Drewes, Inc., Saint Louis, Missouri; Connie Echols, Wagon Wheel Motel, Cuba, Missouri; Marsha Paulus, Wilder's Steakhouse, Joplin, Missouri; Scott Nelson, Nelson's Old Riverton Store, Riverton, Kansas; Tom Clanton, Clanton's Café, Vinita, Oklahoma; Gene Waylan, Waylan's the Ku-Ku, Miami, Oklahoma; John Walden, El Rancho Grande Restaurant, and Georgia Econoomou Tsilekas, Coney Island Hot Weiners, Tulsa, Oklahoma; Dawn Welch, Rock Café, Stroud, Oklahoma; Bobby Lee, Big Texan Steak Ranch, Amarillo, Texas; Allen Ehresman, Texas Longhorn Café, Glenrio, Texas; Ed Pulsifer, La Fonda Hotel, and Deborah Potter, Five & Dime General Store, Santa Fe, New Mexico; Mona Duran, Duran Central Pharmacy, and Dimitrios Anagnostakos, Western View Diner and Steakhouse, Albuquerque, New Mexico;

Steve Gallegon, Joe & Aggie's Café, Holbrook, Arizona; Tina and Fred Wong, Grand Canyon Café, Flagstaff, Arizona; Amy Franklin, Hackberry General Store, Hackberry, Arizona; Tammy Rutherford, Rutherford's 66 Family Diner, Kingman, Arizona; Nancy Carmody, Honolulu Club, Yucca, Arizona; Susan Alexis, Wagon Wheel Restaurant, Needles, California; and Joe Bono, Bono's Italian Restaurant, Fontana, California.

The people who genuinely made this book possible were the entrepreneurs who recognized the corridor of consumption that Highway 66 created. These businesspeople invested their resources and their lives in creating enterprises that supplied travelers with food and drink. They made motoring across the continent possible while at the same time earning their livelihoods. In so doing, they made memories. Some travelers saw the chicken feathers wafting up in the breeze from the alley behind the Lewis Café in Saint Clair, Missouri, as kitchen workers plucked birds to cook for the day's diners. Others experienced their first enchiladas at El Rancho Grande Restaurant on Eleventh Street in Tulsa and thenceforth enjoyed the warming bite of red chili seasoning. Some who made it so far remembered the crisp breading around moist but firm whitefish fillets they munched over Pacific waters at Orie Bennett's Sea Food Grotto on the Santa Monica Pier. These remembrances made Mother Road sojourns unique experiences for each of the hundreds of thousands of Americans and overseas visitors who "made the California trip." Thanks for the memories.

U.S. HIGHWAY 66

1926 ·······
1939 ———

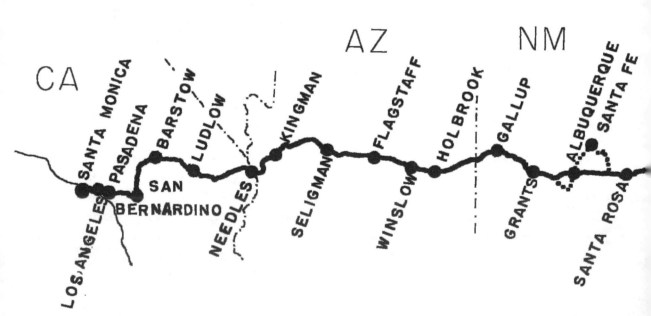

INTRODUCTION

Route 66 was a 2,400-mile road that in the mid-twentieth century connected a pair of sophisticated cities, Chicago and Los Angeles, across the heartland of rural America. It took drivers to the home turfs of cowboys, Native peoples, mobsters, and movie stars. Songs, books, movies, and television made this highway famous. The route lasted for nearly sixty years in some areas before being replaced by more efficient interstates. Travelers fell in love with the road's story, its colorful vistas, and the local people who welcomed them. Motorists first traveled its length in unreliable early automobiles, followed by military transports, buses, and ultimately modern air-conditioned cars. This book tells about those journeys and how the hot and dusty or cold and tired travelers kept going: they had to eat.[1]

The movement of people along Highway 66 created a long, narrow corridor where they found food, lodging, fuel, and auto repairs. From one end to the other, local residents turned entrepreneurs in responding to these travelers' needs. The roadside became a linear marketplace. The pages that follow explore how travelers ate their way across the nation while motoring on Route 66 in its heyday, a time when Americans were moving away from home-based local foods to publicly offered mass-produced fare.[2]

In the old days of animal-drawn transportation, states and counties were responsible for building and maintaining their roads and bridges. County commissioners or their counterparts used tax money to construct and repair this basic infrastructure. Because people used the roads primarily to visit their county seats to resolve legal matters, to buy and sell at local markets, and to attend social gatherings, the commissioners focused spending on the roadways leading to these towns. They gave little thought to travel outside the county; the farther a road was from the local courthouse, the less attention it received.

Into this mix of wagons and buggies entered bicycles during a great national fad in the 1890s, and their riders interestingly became the first significant promoters of good roads. After the turn of the twentieth century, automobile use proliferated, and drivers joined cyclists in demanding better avenues connecting towns. A number of state and regional groups organized to promote the construction of highways.

After long years of such promotion, the U.S. Congress in 1916 passed the Federal Aid Road Act, providing matching grants for states to build highways that would facilitate cross-country travel, beginning the first systematic road building in many parts of the country.[3]

As more and more Americans purchased cars, the number of drivers exploded during the 1920s. They demanded better highways, which at first had no pavement, shoulders, or even stop signs. To facilitate cross-country travel, the U.S. Bureau of Public Roads in 1926 began assigning numbers to existing roadways connecting two or more states, designating east-west thoroughfares with even numerals and north-south ways with odd numbers. "Good roads" promoters from several states compromised in assigning number 66 to a series of roadways that ran southwestward from Chicago through Saint Louis to Tulsa, Oklahoma, and then westward via Oklahoma City, Amarillo, and Albuquerque to Los Angeles. Route 66 was thus born, even though much of it in the rural Southwest was only graded dirt.[4]

After the United States fell into the Great Depression in 1929, the federal government provided funding for road construction as a means of creating jobs for unemployed people. The assistance enabled the last states to complete the paving of Highway 66 during the 1930s. This two-lane strip of hardtop became the most important avenue of exodus for thousands of farm families leaving Oklahoma and Arkansas for better lives in California during the waves of drought and dust that came in 1934, 1936, and 1939–40. John Steinbeck in 1939 brought the plight of these dust bowl migrants into focus in his novel *Grapes of Wrath* and, in the process, gave Highway 66 the sobriquet "the Mother

Road." After the United States entered World War II in 1941, the route carried heavy loads of war materiel. Peacetime then brought a deluge of motorists, revealing that the old roadway and similar highways were inadequate for such flow. This led to the 1956 creation of the interstate highway system. In stages over the next quarter century, states, with federal assistance, replaced the old 66 pavement with the newer freeways, either by overlaying the outmoded blacktop or by installing the new highway adjacent to the old roadway and downgrading the former route to secondary or tertiary use. The old road, however, did not die.[5]

No sooner was Highway 66 decommissioned in the 1980s than people began recognizing its historical significance. Starting in Arizona, grassroots groups organized state Highway 66 associations. They lauded remaining old-time restaurateurs and other roadside entrepreneurs, marked historic sites, organized tours, and encouraged the preservation of vintage buildings, bridges, and pavement. Remarkably, the love affair with Route 66 attracted heritage tourists from across the United States and abroad in increasing numbers to motor along the remaining 85 percent of drivable historic roadway. Their experiences encompassed patronizing old-time diners, restaurants, bars, and lodgings, in this way supporting preservation efforts. Today an avocational subculture of people devote themselves to driving, studying, photographing, and in other ways experiencing the old Mother Road.[6]

What was it like to set out on Highway 66 in the old days? How did it feel to bounce down concrete roadways that caused the car to joggle every few seconds when crossing an expansion joint? The cars of the 1920s and 1930s, built with buggy-style transverse springs and no shock absorbers, made the ride rough. Steering was mechanical. Drivers used their own muscle power to engage the brakes because stepping on a pedal in the floor pulled medal rods beneath the vehicle, which in turn expanded friction shoes inside the wheel hubs. No engines yet had pressurized cooling systems, so radiator water (or nonfreezing water and alcohol mixtures in wintertime) evaporated away, requiring frequent stops for refilling. Almost every traveler carried a supply of water. The major brands of petroleum products generally sold reliably clean gasoline, but many early travelers carried cheesecloth for straining fuel suspected of containing dirt, rust flakes, or other debris. No cars had air conditioning yet, and only the more expensive ones had at best inefficient heaters and windshield defrosters. Until the 1940s, tires and tubes were all made from natural rubber from the tropics, which wore away much more quickly than later synthetic materials; flat tires were an accepted part of driving. Because long-distance telephone calls were pricey and awkward to make, people had to make reservations for lodging only by letter or telegram, so most of them blindly advanced down the road in hopes of finding adequately clean and safe overnight lodging. They did not know what they might find. The hallmarks of road travel for just about everyone were bodily fatigue, physical discomfort, and emotional uncertainty.[7]

But what about the food? This is, after all, a book about eating one's way along Route 66. What did people encounter when they set out from the Great Lakes for the Pacific coast? They found meals prepared by caring grandmothers and inedible slop that barely merited

being called sustenance. Just about every road tripper began journeying with a supply of nonperishable provisions from home. In the wintertime the outside cold kept food somewhat fresh. African Americans could never predict what welcome, if any, they might find, and as a rule carried enough staple groceries to get them to their destinations. White travelers dined in every type of commercial eatery from quick-service lunch counters to sit-down, white-tablecloth restaurants. The pages that follow chronicle the choices white and Black travelers experienced as they made their way across the country. Driving their own vehicles gave motorists the convenience of dining at places off the main road, a distinct advantage over those traveling by train or bus or hitchhiking.[8]

Many travelers chose to feed themselves, and grocery stores were their primary source of foodstuffs. Small stores with unrefrigerated goods dotted the roadsides during the early years, gradually being supplanted by supermarkets as the decades passed. It was at one of these stores in Oklahoma City that the familiar modern-day wheeled shopping cart was invented in 1937. Roadside stands also served motorists, with fruit and juice kiosks springing up all along the road.[9]

Boardinghouses represented traditional eating places that white or Black travelers patronized in towns. These were multibedroom dwellings sometimes called "tourist homes," where residents and the public received family-style meals at set times. Cafés, grills, lunchrooms, coffee shops, and diners in time supplanted boardinghouses with quickly prepared dishes freshly made. Cooks of these latter eateries most often fried foods on grills or in reservoirs of hot fat. Frequently associated with them were sandwich shops and drugstore soda fountains, which flourished during the first half of the twentieth century. These establishments typically served sandwiches and light meals, often with ice cream and carbonated soda water–based beverages. During the 1930s, outdoor drive-in eateries spun off from these fast-service cafés, providing customers with freshly prepared food brought to their vehicles for in-car dining. By the 1960s, many popular eating places provided drive-up windows where customers received quick-service foods and drinks.[10]

True restaurants offered a wider variety in foods and preparations. In addition to frying, the cooks additionally employed baking, broiling, and stewing. Usually, customers were seated at tables, frequently with tablecloths and china dishes. Many restaurants began as hotel dining rooms, which had long offered similar meals. Cafeterias represented a separate class of enterprise in which customers selected from prepared foods and staff served it on plates and in bowls. Diners then carried meals on trays to tables. Truck stops were fueling stations for cross-country trucks where drivers and others dined on meals served cafeteria style or with table service. Professional drivers could eat while their rigs received service and repairs in the shop. Yet another variant on the restaurant, most common in Illinois among the Route 66 states, was the supper club. These provided high-end evening table service meals accompanied by entertainment and/or live music in settings that typically permitted patrons to bring their own alcoholic beverages.[11]

Some popular eating places operated outside of towns but near enough to be reached conveniently by car. Tearooms evolved in the 1910s and offered light meals and no alcohol primarily to middle-class white women.

These enterprises served foods for quiet repasts, celebrations of festive occasions, and regular gatherings for bridge clubs or other entertainments. Tearooms came and went from multiple locations along the Mother Road.[12]

Also outside towns, but catering to a different clientele, were roadhouses, alcohol-serving grill-style quick service establishments. They attracted male customers mainly, but both sexes could find food and drink there. Prohibition prevented the legal sale of alcohol from 1920 to 1933, but some roadhouses gained reputations as speakeasies where customers might find illicit booze. After 1933, legal sales of beer, wine, and other alcoholic beverages returned to areas that voted "wet" in local-option elections, permitting some of the old-time saloons to reopen as bars and taverns, while new ones sprang up where none had been before. Most of them served food.[13]

American eating preferences changed substantially during the half century from the 1920s to the 1970s. The middle-class diet by the 1920s already had become more standardized across the country as a result of many home cooks using the same recipe books, like the long-popular *Boston Cooking School Cookbook*. Their widespread use led to families eating essentially the same griddle cakes or corned beef and cabbage in all parts of the country. By the 1920s, many national brands marketed staple groceries like Snowdrift shortening and Post cornflakes in every state. Processed foods like Kraft Macaroni and Cheese dinners and Hostess Twinkies pastries became common in the 1930s. World War II slowed down this process, but it subsequently resumed with even more strength. Packaged processed foods abounded.[14]

Much of the increasing uniformity in American eating stemmed from the growth of franchised chain restaurants, and Route 66 entrepreneurs led part of the movement. In the mid-1930s Rubye and Beverly Osborne of Oklahoma City developed innovative ways to prepare fried chicken, and they created the earliest multistate group of franchised, individually owned cafes offering the same fried chicken product.[15] Edith and Gus Belt in Normal, Illinois, devised a system for upgrading the meat quality in hamburgers in order to justify selling at higher prices as Steak 'n Shake Steakburgers, and these spread across the Midwest during the depths of the Great Depression.[16] Brothers Richard and Maurice McDonald on Route 66 in San Bernardino, California, in 1948 developed a completely new method for mass-producing identical hamburgers, french fries, and malts that business partner Ray Kroc subsequently spread around the country in McDonald's restaurants.[17] Experimenters opened a frozen custard walk-up in an existing commercial building on the Mother Road in Joliet, Illinois, and in 1940 began the Dairy Queen firm that remains today one of the largest ice cream business in the United States.[18] Back in San Bernardino, Glen Bell replicated methods perfected at the Mitla Café to pre-fry corn tortillas into crispy U-shaped taco shells ready to receive savory fillings. In this way he founded the Taco Bell drive-ins, which widely popularized tacos introduced from Mexico earlier in the twentieth century. Today, the genius and hard work of these and other Route 66 entrepreneurs has touched the lives of virtually every person living in the United States.[19]

Grab your hat, and your pocketbook. These places might take cash only. Step behind the wheel of your imaginary Ford V-8 and head down the Mother Road. Together let's sample the down-home American cuisine that our traveling ancestors feasted on at the side of the road. Go ahead. Eat up Route 66!

....

ILLINOIS

Chicago

Many travelers began odysseys on Route 66 in Chicago. On the shores of Lake Michigan, it was the second largest city in the nation after New York. At the opposite end of the road, Los Angeles was growing on the Pacific, and between lay over 2,400 miles of the American heartland.

For over two decades Route 66 travelers arrived and departed downtown Chicago at the end of two-way East Jackson Boulevard. From 1953 onward, one-way eastbound Route 66 traffic flowed on Jackson Boulevard, while one-way westbound Route 66 traffic shifted to Adams Street, one block north. Within about fifteen miles, departing drivers reached the suburban outskirts with scattered green fields, having made their way out of the big city quicker and easier than they might have imagined. Not every traveler, however, wanted to leave immediately. Some preferred to see the sights and try the local fare.[1]

Highway 66 motorists generally ate in three types of places in the Windy City. Some chose ones that conveniently fronted on the highway or were within a block or so of its well-marked route. Others took meals in hotels where they were already staying or that they otherwise found convenient. A third group—sightseers—sometimes went farther afield to places they considered to be tourist attractions. Dining choices abounded right on the roadway along Jackson and Adams.

FRED HARVEY COMPANY RESTAURANT AND LOUNGE (BOWL & BOTTLE RESTAURANT AND LOUNGE)

Directly on Highway 66 stood the handsome Straus Building, on the first commercial block of the Mother Road in Chicago. Financier Simon Wilson Straus erected the thirty-story steel-frame skyscraper in 1924, and for a short while it was the tallest building in the city. The Fred Harvey Company, which operated hotels and eating places mostly associated with railway travel in the West, had offices just across Jackson Boulevard in the Railway Exchange Building, and its executives wanted a place nearby to show off the expertise of their chefs and bartenders. Coinciding with the start of the Century of Progress world's fair in Chicago, the Harvey firm in 1933 opened a high-class cocktail lounge on the top floor of the tower together with a restaurant at 71 East Jackson Boulevard on the ground level. This was the first Harvey food venture not connected with a railway company. It served customers until the firm encountered problems renewing its lease in 1941. A decade later, after Straus had bankrupted, in 1951 Harvey negotiated with new building owners to lease the street-level restaurant space, and there for two more decades the Bowl & Bottle Restaurant and Lounge served food and drink. The Fred Harvey Company operated eating places favored by well-heeled travelers scattered along Highway 66 all the way to California. This was just the first of many that drivers would pass.[2]

MILLER'S PUB / VANNIE'S / WABASH INN

As early as 1934 and the end of national Prohibition, Miller's Tavern opened at 23 East Adams Street, much of the time operating under the Miller's Restaurant and Miller's Café names. The prime location was just a block west of Michigan Avenue. Then, in 1950, four Greek-American brothers, Jimmy, Nick,

One of the dining rooms in the Fred Harvey Company's Bowl & Bottle Restaurant and Lounge at 71 East Jackson Boulevard in Chicago during the 1950s. This eating place, which additionally offered a moderately priced cafeteria-style snack bar, operated in the very first commercial block of Highway 66. Photograph NAU.PH.95.44.85.2 courtesy of Fred Harvey Company Records, Special Collections and Archives, Cline Library, Northern Arizona University, Flagstaff.

Old-Fashioned Navy Bean Soup, BOWL & BOTTLE
RESTAURANT AND LOUNGE, CHICAGO, ILLINOIS

Hans Mayr, the Fred Harvey Company's chef at the Bowl & Bottle in the first commercial block of Route 66 in Chicago, perfected this version of navy bean soup, which proved to be a customer favorite. Mayr provided the recipe for a cookbook published by his employer to publicize its food service.

Six servings

1 cup dry navy beans

1 quart water

½ cup diced cooked ham or a ham bone

1 small clove fresh garlic

¼ teaspoon salt

½ cup butter

3 slices of bacon (diced)

1 tablespoon fresh leek (finely chopped)

⅓ cup onion (chopped)

¼ cup carrot (chopped)

⅓ cup celery (chopped)

2 tablespoons all-purpose flour

1 cup fresh tomato (diced)

1 cup milk

¼ teaspoon black pepper

Wash the dry beans, removing any pebbles that might be mixed in with them. Soak overnight in 1 quart cold water.

Place beans and water in a pot with diced ham or ham bone, and cover both with a half inch to an inch of cold water. Cover and simmer for three hours, occasionally stirring.

As the beans approach the desired tenderness, separately crush garlic. In a separate skillet, melt butter and add garlic, salt, diced raw bacon, leek, and onion. Cook until the onions turn transparent and the bacon pieces become crisp. Add flour and cook mixture at low heat for two minutes, stirring constantly. Combine with beans, adding chopped carrots and celery, and cook an additional forty-five minutes. Add the chopped tomatoes during the last fifteen minutes. Just before serving, add milk and pepper. When done, add salt to taste if desired. Dip from the bottom of the soup pot when serving.

Original recipe from Atchison, Topeka and Santa Fe Railway Company and Fred Harvey Company, *Super Chief Cook Book of Famous Fred Harvey Recipes* ([Chicago]: Santa Fe Railway and Fred Harvey, [ca. 1955]), 15.

Van, and Pete Gallios, all of them veterans of World War II, joined in purchasing the popular eatery and running it as a tavern under the old café name. In 1962 they remodeled and enlarged the space, giving it a faux Bavarian façade and renamed it Miller's Pub. It operated alongside the old westbound alignment of Route 66 on Adams Street until 1989, when it suffered a fire, its ruins being replaced by a parking garage. The brothers rebounded by shifting Miller's Pub a few hundred feet around the corner to 134 South Wabash, where for about twenty years they also had managed Vannie's, a lesser-known Italian restaurant and bar. They renovated Vannie's into a new Miller's Pub, which today remains an eating and drinking destination. For years its specialty has been baby back ribs. The Gallios Brothers ran another eatery only a block away at 204 South Wabash, also just a few feet off Highway 66. Called the Wabash Inn, it served informal meals for over two decades starting around 1965. Because Miller's Pub stayed open until 4:00 A.M., for years it was a popular retreat for the late-night crowd, notably musicians who came there to nibble on supper after their nightclub performances had wound down. Many customers came there just to see celebrities like comedian Jimmy Durante and singer Tony Bennett. Miller's was so popular among athletes that at times it fed the entire Chicago White Sox baseball team.[3]

THOMPSON'S RESTAURANTS

As Route 66 motorists made their way west along Jackson Boulevard and, after 1953, on Adams Street, they passed through a network of reasonably priced lunchrooms interspersed with restaurants offering more pricey fare. Sometimes called "one-armed" cafés, they often were furnished with old-style wooden school desks that seated one person with a narrow tabletop on one side. A number of these everyday eateries were owned by John R. Thompson, who as a farm boy had come to Chicago in 1891, opening his first café downtown on State Street. By 1921 that initial eatery grew into a chain of 109 lunchrooms, 49 of them in Chicago, 11 in New York, and several elsewhere. By the 1930s, Route 66 travelers passed in front of or within a block

Clean-up time in the Thompson's Restaurant at North Michigan Avenue and Ohio Street in Chicago, July 1941. During the Great Depression, Route 66 motorists passed directly in front of, or within a city block of, five of John Thompson's reasonably priced eateries. Photograph by John Vachon, Office of War Information, call number LC-USF33-016151-M [P&P] LOT 1073, courtesy of Library of Congress, Washington, D.C.

of five Thompson's eateries at 12 and 801 West Jackson Boulevard, 214 South Wabash, 220 South Clark Street, and 300 West Adams Street. By no means just hamburger joints, these lunchrooms featured sandwiches like boiled ham, corned beef, and cold salmon on "Milwaukee rye bread" baked in the company's own commissaries. Remembered for more than their food, Thompson's restaurants were prominent in their refusal to serve African Americans until 1960s court decisions and statutes forced them to do so. The chain of diners persisted about as long as the Mother Road, being purchased by Green Giant in 1971.[4]

BERGHOFF RESTAURANT

A gastronomic landmark in Chicago, the Berghoff has served Dortmund-style beer and German food for well over a century. It began through the efforts of Herman Joseph Berghoff, a teenaged immigrant from Germany, in 1870. He established a small brewery in Fort Wayne, Indiana, producing a style of light beer he knew in the old country. Hoping to gain exposure for his product outside the Hoosier State, Berghoff applied unsuccessfully for a license to sell it at the 1893 World's Columbian Exposition in Chicago. Undeterred, he set up a stand outside the grounds and hawked his beverage to attendees coming and going. He then asked for a wholesale license to sell his Indiana-made beer in the city, but he could only get permission for retail sales. This meant that technically he had to operate a restaurant as an outlet, so in 1898 he opened the Berghoff Café in a building on what became Route 66 at West Adams and South State Street. Initially it was a men-only affair where customers purchased steins of brew and with each one received a free sandwich. The owner razed the building in 1913, so Berghoff reopened half a block away at 17 West Adams.

When enforcement of Prohibition under the Volstead Act began in January 1920, Herman Berghoff converted his brewery to produce nonalcoholic near beer and soda pop and expanded the food offerings in his Adams Street tavern to encompass a full range of German and American dishes. In 1931 local food critic John Drury characterized the Berghoff as a place where one could find "pig's knuckles and sauerkraut, Thueringer sausage and red cabbage and other such heavy Teutonic dishes." When Prohibition ended in 1933, eighty-one-year-old Herman received Chicago liquor licenses number one for his bar and number two for his restaurant. The busy downtown location that combined substantial meals with good service expanded in 1936 into a second storefront and then in 1950 into an adjacent four-story building, doubling its sidewalk-level dining area. Still, the customers kept coming. Local Chicagoan Kathy Scopelliti reminisced that in the 1950s, "It was a big deal to come downtown—wearing hats and gloves—and go to The Berghoff." Its wood-paneled bar long remained a male-only bastion, but in November 1969 several women members of the National Organization for Women barged in, approached the bar, and made history. Not long thereafter well-known New York feminist Gloria Steinem reputedly followed suit. When Herman's namesake grandson retired in 2006, the Berghoff temporarily closed, but only to reopen under the guidance of great-granddaughter Carlyn Berghoff, whose brother and successor, Peter Berghoff, has continued its long tradition of food and drink hospitality.[5]

Young employees from the Chicago Board Options Exchange enjoying beer and singing in 1990 on the sidewalk in front of the Berghoff Restaurant at 17 West Adams Street. It has served Dortmund-style beer and German food for over a century. Author's collection.

CHICAGO UNION STATION

A new Union Station for Chicago opened in 1925 at the site of a previous railroad station, and quickly many travelers adopted it as a convenient food stop. The architects designed the structure as the first railway terminal in the nation to accommodate automobile parking as well as trains, so the eating places inside served both rail and auto travelers. Ramps and lower-level passageways designed expressly for cars inside the north and south walls made it easy for people to be let out at the same level as the main waiting room and its choice of several restaurants. With Jackson Boulevard and Adams Street passing along two sides of the massive depot, Route 66 travelers found it surprisingly easy to drop in for convenient meals.

From 1925 through 1970, the Fred Harvey Company held the contract for all food service in Chicago Union Station. At the time of opening, the firm operated a formal restaurant, lunchroom, cafeteria, coffee shop, soda fountain, candy shop, and fruit stand. If this were not enough, the Harvey Company also ran all the newsstands, tobacco stands, barber shops, hairdressing salons, and a drugstore. Depression-era food writer John Drury described the formal restaurant as "one of the most elegant railroad terminal dining rooms in the country," though he personally preferred the lunchroom, which he described as receiving "heavy patronage because the service is quick and because it is open all night." The station was busiest during the World War II years, when as many as three hundred trains and up to 100,000 passengers passed through daily. After the war, business diminished at Union Station with fewer people traveling by rail. As part of a subsequent restructuring, in 1957 the Fred Harvey Company remodeled its main dining room into the Gold Lion Grill. Having an exterior entrance at West Jackson Boulevard and Clinton Street, the restaurant, with its deep red carpet, red leather upholstery, and gold appointments, attracted a high-end trade. Despite the appeal of the Gold Lion, the fortunes of the Fred Harvey Company declined with decreasing rail travel. The firm merged with Hawaii-based Amfac, Inc., in 1968, and by 1970 closed down all retail operations in Chicago.[6]

LOU MITCHELL'S RESTAURANT

Not quite a block beyond Union Station, Lou Mitchell's Restaurant has been serving up meals in the 500 block of West Jackson Boulevard since 1923—to rave reviews. Food editor Mimi Sheraton of the *New York Times* declared, for example, "If I were to recommend only one American coffee shop to a foreign visitor, it would be Lou Mitchell's." Louis W. "Lou" Mitchell's father, William, founded the eatery on the north side of the street in 1923, naming it after his son. It moved to the present location across the street at 565 West Jackson in 1949, when the former building was demolished. Lou inherited the business from his dad, and made it famous for a well-prepared basic menu, high-quality ingredients, and superb service. On most mornings, a line of breakfast customers waiting for seats extended out the front door onto the sidewalk, with Lou cracking jokes as he handed out fresh donut holes to all and

giving mini boxes of Milk Duds chocolates to the ladies.

Among the café's signature dishes were omelets and memorable French toast made using day-old Greek bread from its own in-house bakery. No matter what they ordered, all breakfast customers automatically received complimentary little white bowls with a clove-scented stewed prune and thin slice of orange. Mitchell called his restaurant a "complete process house," meaning that virtually everything served was made in-house from raw ingredients. For years the café opened only for breakfast and lunch, Lou quipping, "It's great to make money, but at the same time trying to corner every dime on Jackson Boulevard isn't worth it." The neon sign outside the restaurant declares, "Serving the world's finest coffee," a claim supported by its receiving the Golden Cup of Fine Coffee Making Award in 1959 from the Coffee Brewing Institute of America. On entering the front door, one of the first things a customer sees is a giant rectangular glass-sided reservoir displaying the crystal-clear water from which the java is brewed. Because of its location near Union Station, many savvy travelers made their way diagonally across Jackson Boulevard to dine at Lou's, piling stacks of suitcases just inside the front windows. Many customers recalled members of the waitstaff as vividly as their gregarious boss; a waitress explained, "You've got to make people want to come back to your restaurant." In 1992 restaurateur Heleen Thanasouras-Gillman and her family purchased the venerable eating place. She observed about the customers, "Some people have read about us in a book, and some have been coming here since they were born. Now they are sixty-five and they

Lou Mitchell's French Toast, CHICAGO, ILLINOIS

For decades, Lou Mitchell's Café at 565 West Jackson Boulevard in Chicago has served Route 66 travelers. Its French Toast was, and remains, a breakfast favorite. Lou himself shared these directions with *Chicago Tribune* food writer Phylis Magida in 1981.

Three or four servings

1 loaf white bread (unsliced)

2 cups (more or less) peanut oil

4 to 6 large fresh eggs

1 dash vanilla extract

3 to 4 tablespoons real butter (room temperature)

2 tablespoons powdered sugar

1 to 4 fresh strawberries (sliced)

Honey or maple syrup

Slice bread 1 to 1 ¼ inches thick, trim away the crusts, and cut in half to make rectangles.

Beat eggs until they are light and fluffy (well aerated). Add 1 drop of vanilla to eliminate any egg odor but not to add any flavor. Do not add any milk or liquid.

Heat sufficient peanut oil in a skillet to measure just over an inch deep. (Lou Mitchell heated the oil to 180°F, but the author's kitchen test showed that 350°F worked better in stove-top home preparation.)

Place half of the slices of bread into fluffy beaten eggs. Let the slices soak on one side for about a minute, and then carefully turn them over to soak the other side for an additional minute. Drain away any excess beaten egg. Place the batter-soaked slices into the hot peanut oil and fry for five minutes until golden on one side; then turn the slices to fry for another five minutes on the second side to the same golden color. Do not turn the cooking bread slices more than once, as they will become hard. Lou himself declared, "I can't repeat often enough that you must not turn the toast more than once. . . . Whatever you cook in life, don't turn it too many times." Remove from the hot oil using a slotted spoon and allow the slices to drain on paper towels. Immediately put a little real butter on top of each slice.

While keeping the completed pieces warm, repeat the dipping and cooking procedure with the remaining bread.

Sprinkle French Toast with powdered sugar and garnish with a few strawberry slices. Serve with honey or pure maple syrup.

Original recipe from Phylis Magida, "French Toast," *Chicago Tribune*, November 19, 1981, sec. 7, pp. 1, 3.

bring their grandkids." Heleen's heirs perpetuate Lou Mitchell's traditions of quality food, personal service, and good-natured fun.[7]

CHICAGO ART INSTITUTE CAFETERIA (MATHER TEA ROOM)

As part of their experiences in the Windy City, many travelers sought out meals in places they considered to be tourist attractions. One was the Chicago Art Institute, at the very head of the Mother Road where West Adams Street dead-ended into Michigan Avenue. At least as early as 1921 a small cafeteria-style lunchroom served convenient basic lunches for Institute staff and students in its art classes. Few people outside of the institution knew of its existence, but then in 1927 the museum opened the Mather Tea Room, which offered table service, and it began attracting outside customers including tourists. "Here you may dine with the embryonic artists, sculptors, decorators, and architects of the town," noted a local restaurant critic.

Food service at the Art Institute took a new turn in 1942 with the arrival of experienced cafeteria manager Mary Ann Warner. While keeping the inexpensive canteen, she added more elaborate meals in the tearoom as well as open-air dining in the nearby McClintock Court Garden. From three hundred customers daily, she increased patronage to three thousand a day by 1950. The Art Institute became a destination not only for lovers of fine art but also for those seeking moderately priced lunches. Journalist Elizabeth Rannells in 1955 penned with tongue in cheek, "Our favorite contemporary work of art by Warner is a luncheon of sliced breast of turkey with sugar cured ham in wine jelly, accompanied

by a fresh lemonade and followed by homemade frozen rum pie." When the American Library Association national convention met in Chicago in 1963, a member of its local arrangements committee recommended the Art Institute as a reliable place to find bargain lunches. Though Mary Ann Warner passed away in 1964, she made the Chicago Art Institute into a favored mealtime stop for travelers, a role it has maintained to the present day.[8]

Cicero

From the downtown area, motorists headed west, initially along West Jackson Boulevard from 1926 to 1953, and then along one-way West Adams Street to an intersection with West Ogden Avenue. Here, the streets angled to the southwest on four-lane Ogden and continued for eight miles through Cicero and Berwyn. Without noticing any city limits signs, travelers might have thought that they were still in Chicago. Cicero had two dubious distinctions: being the municipality that gangster Al Capone's henchmen took over and used as his headquarters in the 1920s, and as the first "sundown town" where African Americans could not safely stop overnight before the implementation of 1960s civil rights legislation.[9]

HENRY'S DRIVE-IN

Just after Mother Road travelers made their way beneath railroad tracks on West Ogden Avenue from Chicago into Cicero, they came to two notable hot dog stands, Henry's Drive-In and Bunyon's Restaurant. Robert B. Henry established his eatery in August 1952 on the southeast side of Ogden Avenue at 6031. It developed a reputation for its own modification of Depression-era hot dogs. Rather than having lots of garnish like some latter-day

Chicago-style dogs, Robert Henry made his with frankfurter, mustard, onion, pickle slice, and locally popular spicy-hot pickled sport peppers, but no relish. He piled french fries on top and wrapped everything in the same paper. Based on the generous portions, Henry's slogan early became, "It's a Meal in Itself." The stand had a special method of heating its precooked frankfurters in the ground-level kitchen, using the steam generated by the boiler in the basement. When an order came in, staff members flash-steamed the franks, heating them in just moments to ensure the freshest flavor. The sport peppers on Henry's hot dogs left the most vivid memories for Paul Lawrisuk, who started going there as a teenager with friends in 1953. He related, "We all had a hot dog with all the trimmings which included very hot peppers. One of the young children in my friend's family thought the pepper was a pickle and received a real surprise." For years Henry's has caught the attention of motorists with a giant three-dimensional hot dog perched atop its sign in front. In 2017 writer Tom Lohr identified Henry's Drive-In as one of the fourteen best places to eat hot dogs along the entire length of historic Route 66.[10]

BUNYON'S RESTAURANT

For years Robert Henry's friendly competitor was Hamlet Arthur "Art" Stevens's hot dog stand, about 750 feet farther along West Ogden Avenue at 6150 on the northwest side. The story of this eatery began when a lightning bolt struck a former tavern and used-car lot office, gutting the structure. Stevens acquired the property fronting on the busy arterial street and decided that there was enough traffic for him to enter the fast-food business selling hot dogs and Italian beef sandwiches. Erecting a new building in 1965–66, he ornamented its top with a nineteen-foot-tall fiberglass lumberjack figure he had purchased on a trip to California. Later moved to the ground in front, the statue looked like Paul Bunyan, so, using creative spelling, Stevens began calling the business Bunyon's Restaurant. He modified the figure to hold a giant hot dog instead of its original axe. The sandwich business proved good, and Stevens expanded his building in 1970. The owner stated, "When we opened at 11:00 A.M., 20 people would be standing outside the door," adding, "At midnight, we had a hell of a time closing the place." It is worth noting that Art was one of many Chicago-area restaurateurs to offer a regionally distinctive Lenten dish, the pepper and egg sandwich. Observant Catholics abstained from eating meat on fast days, such as Fridays and during Lent, and instead they sought nonmeat alternatives. Stevens's sandwich of eggs and bell peppers on bread satisfied that need, and Bunyon's typically made them available to customers during the weeks of penance and fasting preceding Easter. Stevens maintained his operation until 2003, claiming to have made twenty million hot dogs during his forty-year career. When he retired, the property and its giant fiberglass sculpture went on the market. The buyers, Andres Soto and Gabriel Soto, opened El Tio Loco taco restaurant, which continues preparing and vending quick-service meals.[11]

The story of Bunyon's doesn't stop right here. Historic preservationists in the Route 66 Association of Illinois feared that the iconic fiberglass Bunyon figure might leave the state. Although the Stevens family had received a significant cash offer to sell the statue, they agreed instead to donate it to be preserved

In the mid-1960s, Art Stevens purchased this nineteen-foot-tall fiberglass figure holding an oversized hot dog to attract motorists' attention to his Bunyon's Restaurant at 6150 West Ogden Avenue on the Mother Road in Cicero, Illinois, and it stood there until 2003. An unidentified person snapped this Polaroid picture. Author's collection.

by members of the organization. These volunteers found a new home for the fiberglass man in Atlanta, Illinois, a quiet farming community midway between Chicago and Saint Louis. After carefully protecting the sculpture, association members restored it in 2003. The giant was one of dozens made by the International Fiberglass Company of Venice, California, between 1964 and 1974 as advertising eye-catchers. Art Stevens himself rededicated the figure in a special ceremony in Atlanta in 2004. He used a paintbrush attached to the end of a long pole to daub mustard on its oversized hot dog in a symbolic christening. The sculpture remains there in open-air public display today.[12]

Berwyn

Drivers continued through Cicero, most of them unaware when they entered the next suburban municipality of Berwyn. Like Cicero, for decades Berwyn had a predominately Czech and Slovak population, many of the breadwinners working in industries like the giant Western Electric plant, where most landline telephones provided by American Telephone and Telegraph Company subsidiaries were made. Berwyn likewise was regionally known as a "sundown town" where African Americans were unwelcome as either homeowners or as transient overnight guests. Many others from the southwest side of Chicago experienced Berwyn from its half dozen blocks of Hamburger Row along West Ogden Avenue just before its intersection with Harlem Avenue. This Ogden Strip became a mecca for white teenagers, who flocked there in cars to consume hamburgers, hot dogs, and ice cream while courting members of the opposite sex and occasionally imbibing illicit alcohol.[13]

MAC'S DRIVE-IN

A favorite stop in the row was Mac's Drive-In at 7135 West Ogden Avenue. Food vending at this location began with ice cream when Genevieve and Redmon "Red" Clark in 1940 opened a walk-up/drive-up frozen custard stand offering curb service to motorists. The summertime-only eatery operated into the early 1950s, when new entrepreneurs acquired the old site.[14] Already in 1932 three brothers, Irvin, James, and Lucian Frejlach, had established their own ice cream company. The brothers were operating ice cream stands elsewhere in the suburbs, when in 1954 they took over the former Clark location. There, in June, the Frejlach Ice Cream Company opened Mac's Drive-In, featuring fifteen-cent hamburgers with ten-cent french fries, and, of course, ice cream. That fall, the Frejlachs introduced a special large burger they called the "Big Boy," which they described as having "a double cut bun, two patties of top quality ground beef, cheese and a special dressing." In light of the drive-in's name, they later renamed their double-decker the Big Mac. Always looking for ways to expand their business, the Frejlach brothers purchased for $5,000 an exclusive franchise covering Cook County, Illinois, from the successful McDonald brothers, the pioneers in inexpensive hamburgers in San Bernardino, California. After businessman Ray Kroc acquired rights

to produce McDonald's hamburgers from the two California brothers, in 1956 he wanted to begin erecting quick-service hamburger stands in metropolitan Chicago, his home. As he wrote, "The brothers had sold Cook County to the Frejlach Ice Cream Company," and "it cost me $25,000 to buy that area from the Frejlachs." Kroc also secured their permission to call his largest burger the Big Mac. James Frejlach and family members also acquired a franchise from Harlan Sanders for the sale of Kentucky Fried Chicken, and today a KFC outlet operates at the old drive-in site on Ogden Avenue.[15]

Lyons

Highway 66 motorists initially made their way from West Ogden in Berwyn along either Harlem Avenue or Lawndale Avenue into Lyons, where they proceeded southwestward toward Joliet. In the late 1930s, the main Highway 66 shifted westward to the town of Plainfield and then southward to connect with the older road below Joliet. Suburban Lyons, with mostly tree-shaded bungalow neighborhoods, had its own dubious side. If Berwyn had its teenage carousers along the Ogden Avenue strip, its arterial extension into Lyons in the mid-twentieth century gained a doubtful reputation from a garish collection of taverns and nightclubs together with a small red-light district.[16]

LYONS TOURIST HOTEL RESTAURANT (HOUDEK'S RESTAURANT, HOUDEK'S STEAK HOUSE, KAREN'S SMORGASBORD, TURN 'N TIME TAVERN)

On the south side of Lyons, Mother Road travelers came to Houdek's, an eating place that remained popular for decades. Longtime local resident Joseph Houdek and his son of the same name opened what they called the Lyons Tourist Hotel Restaurant in 1929 at the intersection of Lawndale Avenue and Joliet Road. There they offered meals, ballroom dancing, and a handful of rooms for rent. The menu featured chicken and steak dinners. The elder Houdek died in 1935, but his son continued running the family business, adding barbecue to his menu by 1939. In the 1940s, the family called the enterprise Houdek's Restaurant, and then Houdek's Steak House, though in addition to broiled steaks the menu offered "Chick-a-ninny Specials" comprised of panfried chicken, a tossed salad, a relish dish, and rolls. By 1950 third-generation restaurateur Joseph C. Houdek joined in the family enterprise, where he kept the kitchen open twenty-four hours for travelers. Joseph Houdek Jr. died in 1955, though son Joseph C. maintained the business for a while. The building later housed Karen's Smorgasbord and then the Turn 'n Time Tavern before being removed in 2004 to make way for redevelopment and a gasoline station.[17]

Behind Houdek's Restaurant, starting about 1929, was a tourist attraction unlike any other known along Route 66. The Whoopee Auto Coaster was a circular wooden roadway with undulating highs and lows, pitched curves, and a flimsy railing. For a fee of ten cents, customers could drive their own cars once around the track, experiencing the stomach-churning sensation of climbing uphill only to dip down and whiz around the banked curves at daring speeds. Lyons historian Gladys Yirsa explained, "You paid your admission and lined up to take your turn riding this hilly, wooden track. The old man let one car in at a time, and that car had to reach a certain point on the Whoopee Coaster before he'd let in another." By about 1938, the Whoopee Auto Coaster had closed, a victim of both the economic hard times during the Great Depression and increased weights of passenger cars.[18]

McCook
SNUFFY'S 24 HOUR GRILL (STEAK 'N EGGER)

Constructed of locally quarried limestone and doing business under several names, Snuffy's 24 Hour Grill has served meals to Highway 66 travelers and locals since about 1929. The industrial suburb of McCook, Illinois, where Snuffy's stands at 8408 Joliet Road, has always had an economy based on heavy industry—rock quarrying, diesel electric locomotive rebuilding, and petroleum reprocessing. At the time of this writing, it had just over two hundred actual residents but another estimated twenty thousand wage earners employed within its municipal bounds. Snuffy's is one of the handful of places to eat in this town of hardworking laborers, so it is easy to understand its long popularity. In addition to quick-service meals, Snuffy's for years offered an extra attraction for customers in the form of pinball machines set up for gambling. In 2011–12 the eatery closed and was listed for sale. A private buyer renovated the restaurant, making some additions and redecorating the interior. It then opened as a member of the Chicago-area Steak 'n Egger restaurants, a small chain that traces its beginning to 1955.[19]

Hinsdale (Willowbrook)
TRIANGLE REST (ROUND UP TAVERN, TRIANGLE INN, DELL RHEA'S CHICKEN BASKET)

About seven miles beyond Snuffy's outbound motorists on Joliet Road came to the first of several "chicken houses" that specialized in a great American favorite, fried-chicken dinners. Because the birds could be raised almost anywhere with a modest investment, eateries featuring fresh chicken abounded along American highways, as exemplified by those operating along Route 66. In the days before widespread mechanical refrigeration, birds could be kept alive until the day they were expected to be needed, when restaurateurs or their help could dispatch them, pluck and clean their bodies, and cook the fresh poultry.

Ervin "Irv" F. Kolarik began food vending alongside U.S. Highway 66 on the Triangle Goat Farm south of Hinsdale in 1927. Using an existing fruit orchard as his location, he set up a hot dog stand and a single gasoline pump with a few picnic tables, calling the enterprise the Triangle Rest. Proceeds were lucrative enough for him subsequently to erect a filling station building that over time included two service bays and a lunch counter. As soon as Prohibition ended in 1933, the grassroots entrepreneur added beer to his offerings and changed the business name to the Round Up Tavern, while maintaining his food service. It was about this time that two sisters living on a local farm came to the little eatery, sampled its fare, and told Irv that his meals could be improved. They offered to teach him how to prepare tasty fried chicken if he in return would buy fowls and eggs exclusively from their family farm. A deal was struck. The sisters' "secret recipe" is now known: sprinkle cut-up pieces of fresh chicken with salt and marinate in the brine overnight; then dredge the chicken in milk, flour, and fine bread crumbs and refrigerate for four to six hours before frying. People enjoyed the preparation so much that Kolarik expanded his food business into the two service bays of the station,

renaming the enterprise the Triangle Inn. The two women could not keep up with the demand for fresh birds, so the businessman started buying his chickens instead from farmer Stanley Helma, who had recently moved into the area. Irv Kolarik's lease on the Triangle Inn site ran out in 1946, so he purchased an adjacent tract at 645 Joliet Road and hired Chicago architect Eugene F. Stoyke to design a new single-story brick restaurant with a flat roof, which he named the Chicken Basket. It had big canted plate-glass windows so that customers inside could watch private aircraft taking off and landing across Highway 66 at the small Hinsdale airport.

Across Highway 66 another entrepreneur in 1943 bought the competing Woodbine Restaurant. Purchaser Delbert F. "Dell" Rhea had experience in the hospitality field from managing the huge Stevens Hotel on Michigan Avenue in Chicago and as the executive vice president of the Chicago Convention Bureau. His father-in-law was the very same Stanley Helma who had been providing poultry to Kolarik. Rhea farmed out the operation of the Woodbine to others, but his connections in the neighborhood meant that he was on hand when Irv Kolarik's business lagged with the construction of Interstate 55 in the early 1960s. The new expressway bypassed the section of old Route 66 in front of the restaurant. A banker informed Rhea that a financial institution was repossessing the Chicken Basket, so in 1963 the businessman was able to buy the floundering eatery for a modest price. Through hard work, attention to customers, and care in portion control, Dell and wife Grace resurrected the eating place, turning it over to their son, Pat, in 1986. Today Dell Rhea's Chicken Basket at 645 Joliet Road in Willowbrook is a culinary landmark on the old highway with a booming business. It is a frequent stop for both Chicagoland residents and Mother Road enthusiasts.[20]

Romeoville
WHITE FENCE FARM

Heading southwestward from McCook, midcentury motorists began feeling that they were finally getting into the country-side, although later suburban growth filled in many of the formerly open fields. It was here in the vicinity of Romeoville that coal magnate Stuyvesant Peabody developed a 450-acre horse farm in the 1920s. Because the neighborhood offered no restaurants he could recommend to his wealthy friends, he opened up a small private eating place on his own land just for them. The white-painted wooden railings around his estate gave it the name, White Fence Farm. Soon, other motorists came seeking refreshment, and the roadside stop began serving the public. Specialties of the house for about twenty years were hamburgers made using ground sirloin steak and ice cream sodas. Peabody passed away in 1946, and a series of other entrepreneurs with pockets shallower than his tried and failed to make the restaurant pay.[21]

Into the story came Robert Hastert Sr., with experience working at the Joliet Poultry Market. In the 1930s, he and wife Doris estab-lished their own chicken-processing plant in Aurora, just to the northwest. They succeeded beyond their expectations during the home-front meat rationing of World War II. Shortly after the conflict ended, the couple's poultry market evolved into an Aurora restaurant, the Harmony House. From the outset, they featured panfried chicken with a distinctive preparation. Son Robert Hastert Jr., who later

managed the family's eating places, explained their secret formulation this way. In the 1940s, while working in the poultry plant, Hastert Jr. delivered freshly cleaned fowl to restaurants around Aurora, including one called the Chicken Joint. There, he observed a young employee in its kitchen putting floured pieces of chicken into a pressure cooker and then a few minutes later transferring the mostly cooked pieces to a refrigerator. Then others would fry up the precooked chicken in hot fat for the last three minutes before serving. When his dad opened the Harmony House in Aurora, Robert Jr. paid the teenager two hundred dollars to work in the restaurant for a week, "so he came over and taught me and the other cooks how to do the chicken." The same basic preparation continues even today. Having mastered this method of frying lots of chicken quickly, the Hastert family then applied what they had learned on Route 66.

Bob Hastert Sr. explained the subsequent events this way: "One night in 1952, I was playing cards with a friend who owned a rundown piece of property called White Fence Farm." They discussed the tract on the Mother Road and Hastert offered to buy it, but they were unable to settle on a pur-chase price. Then the entrepreneur proposed, "Let's flip a coin. . . . Heads, White Fence Farm is mine for $50,000, tails $100,000." The coin went into the air, landed heads up, and Hastert bought the ramshackle country restaurant for fifty grand. It took two years to repair and renovate the eatery on the old Peabody property, but it opened in 1954 with three modest dining rooms and a porch for open-air dining.

Each year the Hastert family took advan-tage of the period of slow business in the depth of the winter to close operations so that they could undertake renovations and expansions in preparation for the coming year. Over time they created a facility capable of seating 1,200 customers with only modest wait times for their freshly prepared meals. For decades, its standard four-piece chicken dinner has come with family-style servings of kidney bean salad, coleslaw, cottage cheese, and pickled beets. Many diners come especially for the warm corn fritters rolled in powdered sugar. The historic restaurant at 1376 Joliet Road remains in business, as do several associated carryout stores around metropolitan Chicago.[22]

Joliet

Joliet, pretty or scruffy, was known for its steel mills, limestone quarries, and the Illinois State Penitentiary system. This largest city between Chicago and Bloomington grew from its strategic position on major railway lines and on the Illinois and Michigan Canal, connecting the Great Lakes with the Mississippi. With a multicultural population including many immigrants from eastern and southern Europe, it had 43,000 people in 1930 and 52,000 by 1950. It offered welcome breaks for white motorists who had made the thirty-five-mile drive from downtown Chicago, but it never had many places that advertised meals or lodging for Black travelers.[23]

THE FIRST DAIRY QUEEN

All along Highway 66, travelers enjoyed stopping at ice cream stands, but Joliet holds its own particular place in American ice cream history. At 501 North Chicago Street, motorists came to the birthplace of the genuine Dairy Queen soft-serve ice cream business. This modest, two-story brick commercial building fronting on the Mother Road had inexpensive rent that local ice cream retailer Sherb Noble could afford in 1940. It was here that he first sold soft-serve ice cream developed by father-and-son entrepreneurs J. F. and H. A. "Alex" McCullough, using a special freezing machine developed by a Wisconsin dairy equipment fabricator. The McCulloughs had learned through trial and error that the tastiest mixture for making soft serve had 5 to 6 percent butterfat, while the best texture, after being mixed with air in the machine, came from chilling the mix to eighteen degrees Fahrenheit. Noble hired Grace and Jim Elliott as managers, and they opened on June 22, 1940, selling cones, sundaes, pints, and quarts. By the end of the season, the Dairy Queen in Joliet had grossed $4,000, recouping most of the initial investment in machine, supplies, and space rental. Sherb Noble proudly reported, "We sold 2,170 gallons of mix for an average of $1.84 a gallon." From this initial outlet, which operated in the same location through 1950, the beloved Dairy Queens spread first across the Midwest and then across the United States, where they remain one of the largest ice cream franchises.[24]

Elwood

ABC RESTAURANT (BOB-O-LIN TAVERN AND RESTAURANT, TRADE WINDS, FOUR PALMS, THE OASIS, NEW MAVERICK)

Across Illinois, motorists on Route 66 encountered country taverns known regionally as roadhouses. These were establishments that served both alcoholic beverages and freshly prepared meals. Some closed during Prohibition, but many just stopped public sales of alcohol and emphasized food. Undoubtedly, many of them doubled as speakeasies and continued surreptitiously to sell beer, wine, and liquors despite the federal laws.[25]

Among the many country roadhouses was the popular Bob-O-Lin Tavern and Restaurant, which began during 1920s Prohibition as the ABC Restaurant. Together with six tourist cabins and a filling station, the ABC stood on the east side of the Mother Road in the dispersed Elwood community about five miles south of Joliet. Local residents remember the Chicago Cubs baseball team coming to the ABC, where they could find good food and clandestine alcohol. Doris and James McKean purchased the roadhouse in 1941, renaming it the Bob-O-Lin. When Highway 66 was widened into four lanes soon afterward, they moved the main building eastward out of the way and reopened. It was well worth their expense, for the Bob-O-Lin during World War II became a favored stop for commuters working at the Joliet Army Ammunition Plant. Parked cars belonging to customers frequently lined both sides of the road. In the mid-1940s, Stephie and Tom Tapella took over the Bob-O-Lin, adding musical entertainment. Old-time customer George Knoop remembered, "It was a nice place to go dancing, listen to music and have dinner." The Tapellas ran the roadhouse well into the 1950s before selling it to others, who less successfully operated the business first as the Trade Winds, then as the Four Palms and The Oasis, and finally as the New Maverick before it burned in the 1960s.[26]

Wilmington
DARI DELITE (LAUNCHING PAD)

Seven miles south beyond the Bob-O-Lin, motorists came to the town of Wilmington. Established in 1836, the town had offered respite to travelers at least since its founding

year, when its Eagle Hotel opened as a stagecoach inn. John and Bernice Korelc seemingly inherited the penchant for old-time hospitality. As early as 1952, they were operating the Dari Delite roadside stand at 810 East Baltimore Street. They sold a limited menu of hot dogs, soft drinks, and ice cream specialties, but earned enough money to expand. In 1965 they erected a new building offering a full range of quickly prepared sandwiches, french fries, and chili, as well as ice cream, signaling these changes by renaming their eatery the Launching Pad. At a National Restaurant Association convention in Chicago, John and Bernice visited a display by the International Fiberglass Company (the same firm that fabricated the Bunyon lumberjack figure for Bunyon's Hot Dogs in Cicero), which specialized in oversized sculptured figures as eye-catchers for business. The Korelcs ordered a huge male figure made up as an astronaut, complete with a helmet and rocket ship in his arms. When the sculpture arrived in Wilmington in three pieces hauled on two trailers, the couple sponsored a contest for local schoolchildren to name it, with the "Gemini Giant" winning the competition. The Korelcs operated the Launching Pad until their retirement in 1985, when they sold the business to their daughter and son-in-law. The eatery served ice cream and sandwiches into the early 2010s, closed for about seven years, and then reopened when Holly Barker and Tully Garrett returned it to operation in 2019. The green-painted Gemini Giant continues to greet visitors.[27]

1930s Alignment via Plainfield

In the late 1930s, the alignment of Highway 66 changed from Joliet Road via the city of Joliet to a new route by way of Plainfield that bypassed congestion in Joliet. This roadway became the main U.S. 66, with the older route through Joliet by 1940 being designated Alternate U.S. Highway 66. The two roadways came together again between the towns of Wilmington and Braidwood about thirty-five miles to the southwest. Today, Interstate 55 overlays much of this later 1930s alignment.[28]

WELCO TRUCKERS LODGE

The Wells Petroleum Company of Chicago was in the business of selling fuel, in particular diesel and gasoline to drivers of big-rig trucks. Its owners saw the intersection of U.S. 66 and U.S. 66 Alternate as the ideal place to create a combined rest stop and fueling station for trucks on the outskirts of the big city. In the 1930s, the firm created an unusual-for-the-time combined filling station, repair garage, restaurant, and barbershop with lounges and bunks for long-distance truckers. Drawing from the oil company name, the owners called it the Welco Truckers Lodge. Additionally, the company ran similar operations in Gibson City, Illinois, and Walkerton, Indiana. In 1950, after a fire destroyed the buildings at the Welco Truckers Lodge, the company promptly rebuilt.[29] It was about this time that Charlie Reid joined the Wells Petroleum Company. At first a chauffeur and assistant, Reid had such energy that eventually he became president of the firm. With earlier careers in both Montana ranching and the circus business, the Chicago-born entrepreneur liked to call himself "Montana Charlie." He had the Welco truck stop building north of Joliet painted plum and lemon yellow, and he garishly decorated the four corners of its roof with life-size black plastic Angus bulls. This was not enough. Reid purchased additional land immediately

south of the business and around 1970 created Montana Charlie's Little America Flea Market. There, he erected cheaply built, brightly painted buildings with signs identifying them with names like "Justice of the Peace" and "Miner's Supplies," while providing access for customers on avenues called "Frontier Trail" and "Indian Trail." The flea market outlived the Welco Truck Lodge, which closed after the construction of Interstate 55 left the fueling station without convenient semitrailer truck access.[30]

Gardner

As motorists in past years made their way southwestward from Chicago and reached Braidwood, they felt that they were entering an alien world where the focus of all activity was mining underground coal. A whole series of little towns like Godley, Braceville, and Gardner had prospered from extraction of this natural fuel in the 1890s and 1900s like other areas through which drivers would travel. Here, the mineral resources were depleted and communities retained only a tenth of the people who had resided there during the boom times. Underground excavations left the landscape pimpled with ugly piles of waste that the locals called "gob-heaps." Today, that material has mostly been removed and recycled for road construction and other purposes, leaving the landscape more pleasant than it was for midcentury motorists.[31]

RIVIERA RESTAURANT AND TAVERN

Two miles before they entered Gardner, travelers came to the Riviera Restaurant and Tavern. The roadhouse was the brainchild of James Girot of nearby South Wilmington. For years he eyed the property where the Mazon River flowed beneath Highway 66, and in 1927 he had the opportunity to exchange some investment stocks for just under two acres of wooded property on the east side of the crossing. Because of the economic decline of the surrounding former coal-mining towns, he then was able to purchase cheaply the disused payroll office from an energy company at South Wilmington and a two-story former Methodist church that had once doubled as a school in Gardner. Structural movers in 1928 relocated each of the two buildings to the new site on Highway 66, where Girot had excavated a basement set back from the road. Carpenters attached the two buildings over the cellar so that he could operate a restaurant in one area and live with his family in the other. After the stock market crash in October 1929, the securities Girot had exchanged for the land became almost worthless, so he thanked his good fortune for having made the swap when he did. The location on the Mother Road brought the enterprises he named the Riviera a steady stream of out-of-town business, not to mention local customers. When Prohibition ended in 1933, Girot opened a bar in the basement, the same year adding a separate filling station fronting on the highway. In time he developed a swimming hole in the Mazon River and even assembled a modest animal menagerie for customers' entertainment.

Food was a major attraction at the Riviera Restaurant and Tavern. Jim Girot and his wife, Rose, served up frog legs, chicken, and steaks. When Rose sold the property to Chicago saloonkeepers Bob and Peggy Kraft in 1972, the new owners maintained and even added to the appeal of the meals. Spaghetti at the Riviera with tomato-based meat sauce became famous all up and down

the old highway. The Krafts moved the dining area from the ground floor into the basement, where the temperature was naturally cool. The kitchen shifted upstairs, and a dumbwaiter connected the two work areas. In addition to transporting orders, meals, and dirty dishes between the floors, the dumbwaiter also became the hiding place for a revolver just in case of a ruckus.

For years, slot machines supplemented the income for operators of the Riviera. Multiple forces contended for control of these gaming devices, among them local political bigwigs, enterprising thugs, and others similarly motivated by greed. Violet Grush, Jim Girot's daughter, remembered from those days, "Me and my cousin were cooking frog legs one night, and all of a sudden there was this guy standing by the door." The unidentified hoodlum ordered, "Stay where you're at," and the women froze even though the frog legs were jumping in the skillet. She concluded, "We just stood there while they took the machines out."

The Riviera Restaurant and Tavern operated until owners Bob and Peggy Kraft reached their mid-eighties. When the business closed on January 1, 2008, the building fell silent. Though a real estate broker attempted to sell the eighty-year-old Riviera, no buyers were forthcoming, and a fire burned it to the ground in June 2010.[32]

STREETCAR DINER

By the 1930s, many cities were reducing or even eliminating streetcar lines as public transport, letting more flexible bus routes assume their roles. This happened in Kankakee, Illinois, where no-longer-needed streetcars were sold to the public. Twenty-year-old George Kaldem of Gardner learned of the

Spaghetti Sauce, RIVIERA RESTAURANT
AND TAVERN, GARDNER, ILLINOIS

Six cups

2 cups onion (chopped)

4 cloves garlic (finely chopped)

2 tablespoons shortening or oil

1 ½ pounds ground beef chuck

½ teaspoon salt

¼ teaspoon black pepper

3 eight-ounce cans tomato sauce

2 six-ounce cans tomato paste

3 large bay leaves

¼ teaspoon basil

½ teaspoon sugar

1 cup water

In a large pot, combine chopped onions and garlic with shortening and cook until onions are transparent. Add ground chuck and cook about ten minutes, stirring until meat has browned. Add remaining ingredients plus 1 cup of water. Simmer over low heat for three hours, stirring every twenty minutes and adding water if needed. The sauce should have a thick, not runny, consistency. When done, add more salt and pepper to taste if desired. Serve over freshly prepared hot spaghetti or other pasta.

Original recipe from Rose Girot Brooks in Route 66 Association of Illinois, Springfield, *The Route 66 Association of Illinois Preservation Committee "We Work for Food": A Collection of Recipes by Route 66 Association of Illinois* (Kearney, Neb.: Morris Press Cookbooks, 2003), 50.

sales and purchased an especially old trolley that had entered service as a horse-drawn car and later had been adapted to run on electricity. The utility sold the old car to Kaldem for three hundred dollars, not a small sum at the time, and he hired next-door neighbor Gordon Gunderson for another hundred dollars to move it from Kankakee to a lot on Highway 66 near Grundy Street in Gardner. The plan was for his mother, Minnie Springborn, to use the old streetcar as a roadside diner. The mover placed the metal and wooden trolley in its new setting on a footing of creosoted railway ties salvaged from a nearby mine. Kaldem in turn added a tiny, rectangular kitchen to one side, extended the roof outward to shelter the car from the elements, and created a driveway and parking area between it and the highway by laying down waste-coal cinders.

Through most of the Depression years, Minnie helped support her family by running a diner in the recycled streetcar. Gardner did not yet have a municipal water system, so Minnie and others had to haul in all the well water needed for cooking, drinking, and washing. Customers sat on five stools along a short counter or in four miniscule, hard-seated booths. Despite the crowding, the little roadside eatery gained a reputation for Minnie Springborn's tasty from-scratch cooking. Plate lunches comprised of meat, potatoes, vegetables, bread, and coffee sold for thirty-five cents. Open from seven in the morning to eight at night, the little diner served all three meals daily until 1939, when family illness forced Minnie to close the enterprise. Gordon Gunderson again moved the little streetcar, first to his own backyard as a summer house, and then to become a fishermen's cottage on the Mazon River behind

the Riviera Restaurant and Tavern. There, it eventually deteriorated and became a storage structure. Then in 2010, after fire had destroyed the Riviera itself, grassroots preservationists who had already been attempting to stabilize the streetcar relocated it to a park area in Gardner, where they restored the little diner to its 1930s appearance.[33]

Pontiac
LOG CABIN INN (OLD LOG CABIN); NEW LOG CABIN RESTAURANT (COUNTRY CABIN, PONTIAC FAMILY KITCHEN)

After motorists left Chicago and one hundred miles before they reached Springfield, they came to Pontiac, a natural place for Mother Road travelers to take a break. In this propitious location, by 1930 the town of eight thousand people offered travelers multiple places providing refreshment and sustenance. Among these establishments were the Old Log Cabin, established in 1926, and the New Log Cabin, opening in competition in 1955.

On the very year that Illinois State Highway 4 was designated as U.S. Highway 66 in 1926, two Italian-American brothers, Joe and Victor Selotti, erected a filling station and adjacent diner on the extreme north side of Pontiac. It faced the two-lane roadway that paralleled the railroad tracks headed into the county seat town. The thrifty Selotti brothers had an opportunity to purchase of a pile of used cedar utility poles, which they cut to length, notched, and assembled into a "log" building they called the Log Cabin Inn. They constructed a barbecue pit in an adjacent little shack, where Joe perfected his skills in cooking and smoking beef and pork, while Victor sold fuel and patched inner tubes. Joe's pet crow entertained and "talked" to anyone who chanced to saunter by. When

Highway 66 was widened into four lanes in the 1930s, the new pavement went past the rear of the eatery. The two brothers, never to be deterred, jacked up their building, turned it around, and adjusted it forward about fifty feet to attract the attention of travelers. This move gave them a chance to enlarge the dining room, which was crowded many of the twenty-four hours that it stayed open daily.[34]

By 1946 the building was owned by others, with well-known local restaurateur Paul Johnson managing the café. A decade later, local real estate promoters encouraged him to consider establishing a new restaurant as an anchor in a new shopping area under construction at the intersection of old Highway 66 and Illinois State Route 23, closer to the center of town. That eatery opened in 1955 in a gleaming glass-front building as Paul's New Log Cabin Restaurant and Lounge. Almost immediately, locals began calling the still-operating original enterprise the Old Log Cabin. The new restaurant introduced menus with prime rib, steaks, chicken, and seafood, together with occasional then-exotic offerings like lobster. Back at the Old Log Cabin, the regulars continued to enjoy more basic meals of barbecue, pork chops, beans, and corn on the cob. Though the New Log Cabin experienced damage from a tornado and two serious fires and later changed its name to the Country Cabin and then Pontiac Family Kitchen, it and its predecessor continued serving meals to locals and travelers at the time of this writing.[35]

Chenoa
ZIRKLE BROTHERS' CAFÉ (WAHLS' CAFÉ, STEVE'S CAFÉ)

To say that Steve's Café in Chenoa, Illinois, ten miles south of Pontiac, became an institution would be an understatement. In many ways, this Route 66 eatery became the emotional heart for generations in the town, not to mention becoming a culinary landmark for decades of Highway 66 travelers.

In 1924, when Illinois State Highway 4 was the main road from Chicago to Saint Louis, Tom and Charles Elliott erected a combined gas station, garage, and lunchroom at its side in Chenoa. They sold the property to Paul Lanterman, whose wife ran a tiny diner with counter space for nine customers plus a table for four. In the mid-1920s, Lanterman passed the property along to brothers Elmer and Orville Wahls, who in turn arranged with two other brothers, Clinton and Thomas Zirkle, to run the café. By 1934 the Wahls brothers took back the Zirkle Brothers' Café, adding a separate dining room. Steve Wilcox became the day chef at the twenty-four-hour eatery, and then in 1942 Wilcox and wife Helen purchased the business, renaming it Steve's Café. The name stuck for the next fifty years.[36]

Upon high school graduation in Chenoa in 1934, Don Schopp became a busboy at the eatery. He warmly remembered evenings when most diners had left the back dining room and teenagers came in for nickel Coca-Colas and dancing to big-band music on a coin-operated jukebox. Always a supporter of Chenoa High School athletics, Wilcox treated members of football and basketball teams that won championships for years to what the local press called "those inimitable steaks." The high schoolers in Chenoa felt such fondness for the restaurateur that the graduating class of 1955 dedicated its yearbook in his honor.[37]

The restaurant's broader reputation came from its steaks, considered by many to be the

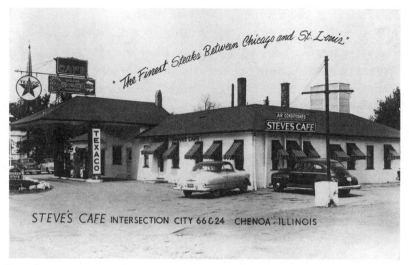

Steve's Café in Chenoa was a popular stop for steaks and pies on Highway 66 midway between Chicago and the state capital, Springfield, Illinois. A traveler mailed this photo postcard in July 1959. Author's collection.

best between Chicago and Saint Louis. Helen Wilcox's pies, however, vied with the steaks for praise. Many political bigwigs stopped off at Steve's as they motored between Chicago and the state capital in Springfield, telephoning ahead long-distance to reserve pies for the road. On one occasion, cook Howard Dill recognized at the counter a highway patrolman who doubled as chauffeur for the state governor. Dill quipped to him, "How's the Governor?" to which the officer replied, "Ask him yourself, he's sitting right here beside me."

Steve Wilcox, a disabled World War I veteran, died unexpectedly in 1958, mourned by neighbors and customers. Several different owners attempted to recreate the atmosphere Wilcox had fostered in the old eatery, including a volunteer group of Chenoa businessmen who ran it for six years. Finally, in 1975 Ken and Peg Sipe purchased the old restaurant, and it began to shine again as Steve's Café and Lounge. Even though the four-lane pavement

had long bypassed the eating place, customers eagerly sought it out, again reveling in steaks and homemade pies. As heritage tourists found the old Route 66 pavement, they flocked into Chenoa to have their own Steve's Café experience. One out-of-town enthusiast declared in 1991, "I'm a fanatic about Americana and great cheeseburgers," adding, as he lovingly patted the worn Formica top on the lunch counter, "Look at that. Isn't that beautiful?" The special magic persisted until 1994, when Ken Sipe lost his life in a single-vehicle auto accident in Bloomington. The restaurant closed and was sold at auction, and its building at the time of writing housed a residence.[38]

Normal and Bloomington

The adjacent towns of Normal and Bloomington became the place for many motorists to break their trips. The two communities offered travelers a wide range of food and lodging, including multistory hotels. The twin cities became seats of higher education, with Normal hosting Illinois State Normal University and Bloomington becoming the home for Illinois Wesleyan University. The Mother Road enabled many students conveniently to come and go from the campuses by automobile. ("Normal" at the time was the term used in referring to schools in which the emphasis was teacher training, and the name became attached to both the state university and the city.) Initially, Highway 66 coursed directly through both towns, skirting downtown Normal and going through the east edge of the Bloomington business district, but in the 1950s through traffic diverted to a beltway on the east and south sides of the two towns. In 1930 the combined communities had a population of roughly 37,000, which grew to almost 50,000 by 1950.[39]

SPRAGUE SUPER SERVICE (TRIANGLE CAFÉ, IRENE'S, LUSHER'S, ALENE'S, PINE STREET CAFÉ, CAKE GALLERY)

Local building and sewer contractor William Sprague saw the initial East Pine Street entry of Highway 66 into the north side of Normal as a logical place to invest money earned from other ventures. He purchased several lots on the south side in its 300 block in a neighborhood that was already developing as an "automobile row" dotted with filling stations and garages. In 1930 Sprague erected an impressive Tudor-Revival-style combined service station, garage, and café with two upstairs apartments, a large one for his own family and a smaller one for the station manager, who actually ran things. He envisioned his Sprague Super Service becoming a beehive of activity, but the onset of the Great Depression dampened enthusiasm. Nevertheless, the businesses opened,

the Greyhound Corporation for a while shifted its Normal bus station there, and Sprague's Café opened under management of the businessman's daughter, Pansy. As soon as Prohibition ended in 1933, the eatery started serving beer and, around that time, advertised chicken and frog leg platters at twenty-five cents apiece. Around 1937, Joseph E. Ruzic acquired the property, opening the Triangle Café in the restaurant space at the east end of the building and offering meals day and night. His eatery operated until 1941, when the entire facility became available in a fresh lease. This began its occupation by a series of tenants, during which time various individuals used the filling station to sell regional Zephyr gasoline as well as major brand Cities Service, Shell, Texaco, and Gulf products. The restaurant served meals off and on from the 1940s through the 1970s under such names as Irene's, Lusher's, Alene's, and the Pine Street Café. In 1974 Beverly Hodge rented the kitchen and dining room, where she opened the Cake Gallery catering business, which later expanded into a bridal shop, and constituted the last known use of the restaurant in commercial food service. In the 2010s local historic preservationist Terri Ryburn-LaMonte spearheaded efforts to restore the historic structure, which has been happily adapted to serve as a Route 66 visitors' center for the city of Normal.[40]

CHAT 'N CHEW

There were plenty of entrepreneurs in Normal and Bloomington who attempted to make a living providing food, fuel, and lodging to Highway 66 motorists, but this does not necessarily mean that all those needs were met. African American travelers typically experienced very different receptions than did their white counterparts. When Bessye Brown, her sister, and two brothers, both recently discharged from the military, arrived from Chicago in 1945, they stopped at the downtown Bloomington Woolworth's variety store for a quick meal. After they waited at the lunch counter for half an hour without being acknowledged, a white employee informed them that their patronage was unwanted. Angered by the blatant racial discrimination, Brown declared, "Now mind you that both these boys have seen service," but their status as World War II veterans meant nothing to the white managers. The four Chicagoans strode out of the store with empty stomachs.

African Americans on the road generally sought out the comparatively few businesses that welcomed Blacks, including one in Normal that Lutie Anson established in 1934 primarily to serve Black young people attending classes at Illinois State Normal University who, because of racial discrimination by whites, had to live off campus. This was just the type of local enterprise that African American travelers hunted. Anson, who was married to locally well-known postman Luther Anson, rightly felt that African American students needed a safe place near the school to congregate and socialize. Consequently, she opened a small grocery store, called the Chat 'n Chew, inside a little wooden building at 403 North Fell Avenue in Normal. The location was just a block north of what then was U.S. Highway 66 along Willow Street, providing easy access for Black motorists. A local resident explained the enterprise this way: "They . . . set it there for the Colored students to have some place to drink a milk shake, have a bottle of pop, a hamburger because every place else you had to take it outside in those days." He added,

"They had a little space to dance in there. Couple of booths. A little counter space. And that's the idea of the Chat and Chew—give them somewhere to go to hang out." Lutie Anson died in 1940 and others helped her husband run the neighborhood store, with Luther being joined by his second wife, Clara, in 1947. That same year the enterprise suffered a fire but continued in business for another decade until Luther's death in 1957. The estate subsequently sold the property at auction.[41]

STEAK 'N SHAKE

All up and down Route 66 entrepreneurs developed food service concepts that in time spread across the United States. One of these innovators was Augustus "Gus" Hamilton Belt, who with wife Edith moved to Normal in 1926, the year Highway 66 received its numerical designation. They saw others scrambling to earn their shares of the income to be made from providing services to automobile drivers, and Gus opened a series of filling stations in Normal and Bloomington that additionally sold and repaired tires and tubes. In May 1932, he added the Shell Inn at 1239 South Main in Normal, a former residence converted into a service station that had a short-order café on the side. While Gus sold gasoline and auto supplies, Edith fried up fish and chicken dinners and prepared sandwiches, after 1933 adding beer to the mix. When Normal residents voted their town "dry" in 1935, this decision stopped the Belts' beer sales, and the couple had to rethink their food service. This situation led them to fresh, new ideas.

Ordinarily, cheap hamburgers in the depth of the Great Depression sold for a nickel apiece, but Gus and Edith wanted to maximize their profits. Gus decided that if

The original Steak 'n Shake in Normal, Illinois, in 1940. The kitchen has large plate-glass windows on three sides exemplifying the company slogan "In Sight, It Must Be Right." Courtesy of McLean County Museum of History, Bloomington, Illinois.

they ground up steak meat to combine with other cuts, people would pay ten cents for what he termed a "steakburger." Gradually, the couple developed new concepts based on food quality, preparation speed, and low prices. They devised a strictly limited menu of hamburgers, french fries, and milkshakes, all selling for ten cents each. Employee Warren Chrisman remembered, "Everything was a dime, except cheeseburgers, and lettuce and tomato burgers, which were 15 cents." The sandwiches had pickles, but Gus insisted that they be sliced lengthwise, because, he stated, "You ought to be able to taste pickle in every bite." They offered the very first in-car service

for hamburgers in Normal. Teenaged Bob Rogers worked there in 1939, and recalled, "A drive-in with curb service was a novelty," and it attracted attention and business. Teenaged "curbies" took orders at the vehicles, carried them inside to cooks for preparation, and then delivered the food to the customers in their cars, handling all sales.

Seeking to increase revenues, Gus Belt began opening branches of his Steak 'n Shake drive-ins around Bloomington and Normal, expanding into larger towns like Champaign, Decatur, and Springfield during the late 1930s. In 1949 the firm began a long relationship with architects Bert and Jack

Luer, who collaborated in creating another new idea, a standard-plan design for Steak 'n Shake restaurants. They employed basic white and black glazed tile exteriors pierced by large windows to encase what they considered to be, in Jack's words, "a machine to produce food simply." The plate-glass openings showcased the kitchen areas so that customers could see for themselves their cleanliness. The edges of the flat roofs on the Luers-designed buildings bore boldly painted slogans like "In Sight, It Must Be Right," "It's a Meal," and "Takhomasak." By the time of Gus Belt's death in 1954, the restaurant chain had grown into such markets as Saint Louis and other midwestern cities, and by the year 2000 had over 350 branches spread even more widely. The original Normal store, at the site of the old Shell Inn, remained in use by Steak 'n Shake to the end of the twentieth century. The property then sold to become a Monical's pizza parlor, the new owners generally preserving the floor plan and basic design of the historic eatery.[42]

LUCCA ITALIAN RESTAURANT (LUCCA GRILL)

South on Highway 66 along Main Street at the northeast edge of the central business district in Bloomington, motorists came to Market Street and the Lucca Grill. After surviving a major fire in 1900, the city's central business district consisted of comparatively newer buildings. These included the two-story brick structure that housed the Lucca at the corner of Market and North East Streets, a block east of Main. In 1936 brothers Fred and "Uncle John" Baldini, whose family had emigrated from Lucca, Italy, established the Lucca Italian Restaurant (being called Lucca Grill by 1937), actually a combined tavern and café. In this former plumbing shop, they offered customers a special "tap room plate lunch" at twenty-five cents and "spaghetti and ravioli at all hours." When U.S. Army soldiers liberated Lucca during World War II in 1944, the brothers immediately put up a hand-lettered sign on the front of their building that read, "Lucca, Italy, is liberated. Thanks Americans."

Although other area businessmen had offered pizza baked in restaurant kitchens earlier, the Baldinis were the first in Bloomington to install a bona fide traditional pizza oven in 1953. Running the eatery until retirement, John and Fred in stages turned the business over to Fred's sons, John and Charles "Tot" Baldini, who together owned and ran the enterprise for two decades. John Baldini's son-in-law, Charles "Chuck" Williams, bought Charles's half interest in 1982. Then, when John retired a decade later, he sold Williams his half as well, making him the sole proprietor. Twenty-eight years later, he sold the Lucca to his longtime managers, John F. Koch and Anthony Smith, who currently run it much as their predecessors did. Over the years, the Italian bar and grill became a social institution in Bloomington, a favored haunt of college students and local residents alike. Journalist Ward Sinclair wrote in the *Washington Post* in 1980 that "in an era of plastic and cushions," the Lucca remained "decidedly old-timey, with austere furniture and a vast mahogany bar, sports pennants and political mementos." Little has changed, and it still serves notable dime-thin pizza from its almost seventy-year-old oven.[43]

Shirley
FUNKS GROVE PURE MAPLE SIRUP

Motorists heading southwest from Bloomington glanced out their car windows as they passed the impressive screen at the Phil Kron Drive-In Theater, opened in 1947, and at its adjacent Sinorak Cafeteria.[44] They proceeded out of town on Highway 66 paralleling the tracks of the Alton Railroad seven miles to the village of Shirley. By this time travelers realized that the surrounding vegetation had changed, and had changed drastically. From open prairie, motorists entered a geographical anomaly, a grove of bur oak, white oak, and sugar maple trees so dense that they obscured vision to either side. The phenomenon of a small, thick forest on the mostly treeless Illinois farmland resulted from terrain conditions along Timber Creek, a tributary of the Sangamon River, that over the millennia gave the trees a measure of protection from prairie fires. This special natural circumstance preserved the grove as an isolated "island" of timber many miles west of comparable stands of trees to the east in Indiana.

It was into this grove four miles south of what later became Shirley that Isaac Funk moved in 1824, hewing trees in order to create a pioneer farmstead. It was only after he had been there through a winter that he realized that many of the trees were not just maples, but also the valuable sugar maple variety. He could collect their sap, heat it in cauldrons, and, through boiling, concentrate it into maple syrup. Isaac procured a large iron kettle and began cooking down the natural sweetening for his family, selling or giving the excess to neighbors. Generations passed, with the Funks enjoying their natural bounty. Then, in 1891, grandson Arthur Funk began the first commercial sales of maple syrup and sugar from the family grove. In 1926 granddaughter Hazel Funk described the basic principles: "The best sap flow is where the change from winter to spring is slow; where the days are warm and sunny and the nights frosty." This flow generally began in the second or third week of February and lasted for four to six weeks. Fifty to sixty gallons of sap had to be collected from metal canisters hung on spouts driven into the trees to cook down into just one gallon of finished product. February and March were times of feverish work in gathering sap and boiling it down, but then the window of opportunity quickly closed. Later, syrup maker Mike Funk further explained, "Once the maple trees start to bud, a chemical change occurs in the sap giving it a bitter taste." During most of the early years, the Funk family contracted on the shares with neighboring farmers like Jim Moran and Samuel Spaulding to come onto their property, collect sap, and then process it into sellable sweet liquid.

By the time that Highway 66 opened through Funks Grove, the Funk family had begun more actively marketing their syrup. In 1934, for example, family members were selling syrup by the pint, quart, half gallon, and gallon. While the largest containers at the time went for $3.25, the Funks also reboiled some of the syrup into solid maple sugar, which they marketed in two-inch blocks for ten cents apiece. A journalist reported that many of the purchasers were "tourists passing through who see the camp and the sign and drive in to buy genuine maple syrup." After a hiatus occasioned by restrictions on sugar sales during World War II, in 1947 grove owner Hazel Funk Holmes (now married to Henry Holmes) encouraged her family members to take over all the aspects of syrup making. It was at that time when she began promoting the spelling of their product as "sirup," a designation meant to indicate that

Collecting sap from maple trees at Funks Grove using a horse and wagon in late winter–early spring ca. 1933. *At right*, firewood awaits use at the syrup house for boiling the sap down into maple syrup. Courtesy of McLean County Museum of History, Bloomington, Illinois.

their goods were made 100 percent from natural maple tree sap without the addition of any other sugar. Since that time, Funk family members have gradually expanded and modernized their maple operation, building a new sugarhouse and a shop for retail sales. They remain vendors at the side of old Highway 66 to the present day, and Funks Grove has become a flavorful attraction for modern-day tourists.[45]

Through Funks Grove

Not everyone who came to Funks Grove did so just to pass through on the highway or to buy maple syrup. During the decade of the 1920s, dancing to syncopated beats of jazz music became the rage for young Americans, and outdoor summertime dance pavilions proliferated across the nation, like Rossi's Ballroom up Highway 66 just outside Braidwood. The phenomenon exploded in central Illinois, with a dance platform amid the oaks and maples eleven miles south of Bloomington at Funks Grove Park becoming the end point for many couples' nights out. The pavilion there began attracting dancers arriving in automobiles as early as the First World War, and it remained popular for a decade. Tree-lined Illinois State Highway 4, later U.S. 66, through Funks Grove consequently became one of the fashionable stretches of roadway for nighttime "petting parties." Highway patrolman Chester D. Henry described the section as "a lover's lane, boy . . . they parked there thick on Friday night, Saturday night. . . . I'd like to have had the concession stand there." During daylight, this wooded stretch of roadway became one of his most fruitful locations for apprehending those who drove over the speed limit, Officer Henry noting, "We would . . . check the traffic going both ways."[46] The eight miles from Shirley took motorists through the grove and then back out onto the open prairie, where they came to the farming town of McLean.

McLean
SHIRLEY OIL AND SUPPLY COMPANY (DIXIE TRUCKERS HOME, DIXIE TRAVEL CENTER)

Today truck stops where drivers of big rigs and automobiles find fuel, food, and rest along interstate highways seem ubiquitous, but it was not always that way. These enterprises began appearing during the 1920s when certain operators of filling stations began trying out new ways of providing not just fuel but also repairs, tire service, and food to long-distance commercial drivers. One of these entrepreneurs was John P. Walters, who, with others in 1923, incorporated the Shirley Oil Company in little Shirley, Illinois, on the northeast side of Funks Grove. Their initial plan was to make money from delivering fuel, kerosene, and oil to rural customers from a bulk station near the railroad tracks in Shirley. Five years later they expanded their capital stock from $7,500 to $20,000 as the Shirley Oil and Supply Company. Seeing the proliferation of automobiles, they wanted to begin earning profits from commercial sales of highway fuels. The firm secured space for its first retail filling station in McLean, Illinois, inside part of an operating auto repair garage, and there in one corner the owners also created a tiny lunch counter with six stools. Within two years they were selling the Dixie brand oil and gasoline, which they

received from a subsidiary of Standard Oil of Indiana that distributed fuels wholesale to independent stations. By 1931 they even were sponsoring a local youth basketball team called the Dixie Oilers. Back in Shirley, the businessmen moved their earlier outlet into a new single-story brick building attached to a preexisting two-story frame house about 1934. Then on the morning of January 26, 1937, the Shirley station caught fire, destroying the buildings, including the café, but somehow avoiding igniting the underground gasoline tanks. The owners estimated losses at $10,000 but fortunately still had their retail outlet in McLean.[47]

Because the McLean filling station, garage, and café sold the Dixie brand oil and gasoline, customers began associating that trade name with the enterprise. John W. Geske, John Walters's son-in-law and a member of the firm, later explained, "There was a time in this part of the country when people thought if they went south they would find more hospitality, so we thought Dixie was a good name." By 1940 advertisements were calling the fuel stop the Truckers Dixie Home, which quickly became the more easily articulated Dixie Truckers Home. The owners discovered that they needed to offer around-the-clock services, so they expanded coffee, sandwich, and snack sales to all hours. "If you have coffee and sandwiches, pretty soon you have to have plate lunches, too," Geske elaborated. Food service became an important revenue stream for the Shirley Oil and Supply Company, with drivers beginning to plan their cross-country trips specifically to include stops in McLean. After he had run away from an adoptive home in Chicago at age thirteen in 1947, Brad Jay Bogart experienced his very first food on the road at the Dixie after a trucker picked him up as a hitchhiker on the outskirts of the Windy City. Bogart fondly recalled, "Pete bought me a hot beef sandwich, open style with hot brown gravy and mashed potatoes." The adolescent later remembered that when they left the truck stop, the waitress hugged him while saying, "God bless you, honey," and slipped two dollars into his hand. Many other wayfarers reported similar kindnesses from the staff at the terminal on the side of Highway 66 in McLean.[48]

The Shirley Oil and Supply Company suffered fire loss a second time on June 28, 1965, this time at the McLean facility. Grease ignited in the kitchen and flames quickly spread up wooden exhaust ducts. As in Shirley in 1937, the complex burned to the ground, though insurance and the deep pockets of the owners enabled the company to rebuild, larger and better than ever. The new 35,000-square-foot McLean facility that opened in 1967 had twenty double-sided fuel pumps, a 250-seat restaurant, a shop catering to long-distance drivers' needs, hot showers, and lounge and bunk rooms where truckers could sleep or relax watching television. There was even a single-chair shop for cutting hair. "I see more of Dixie than my own hometown," quipped one driver, "so I make this my regular barber shop." In 1990 the Illinois Route 66 Association placed its Hall of Fame

Nighttime at the twenty-four-hour Dixie Truckers Home ca. 1940. Courtesy of McLean County Museum of History, Bloomington, Illinois.

exhibits at the Dixie, where they remained until 2003. In this year the private owners sold the Dixie Truckers Home to an out-of-state corporate buyer, which redecorated the truck stop and continues its operation as the Dixie Travel Center.[49]

Atlanta
PALMS GRILL CAFÉ

Just four and a half miles down Highway 66 from McLean, drivers came to the little farming community of Atlanta. Today it is one of the showplaces of old-time Illinois prairie culture, with a treasure trove of vintage homes and businesses, an open-air farming museum, and multiple antique shops. One of its attractions is the Palms Grill Café, fronting on old Highway 66 in the tiny downtown. In 1909 John F. Adams purchased the two-story commercial space at 110 Arch Street, the north side of the 1867 Downey Building in Atlanta. He rented it to a grocer for years, eventually passing ownership to his son, James Robert Adams. A native of the area who, after service in World War I, settled in Los Angeles, son J. Robert dealt in California real estate and dabbled in music and drama. He renovated his Atlanta, Illinois, property into a modern eatery that opened in August 1934 as the Palms Grill Café, its new neon sign reputedly making it "the brightest spot on Route 66 between Chicago and St. Louis." For years local businessman Robert Thompson administered the commercial property for absentee-landlord Adams, with multiple managers operating the restaurant over the years into the 1960s. On a typical midcentury Sunday, February 23, 1947, the eatery offered a set-price one-dollar lunch that included a selection of either fried spring chicken or grilled pork chops with whole-kernel corn,

baked potatoes, hot buttered biscuits, and a choice of homemade pie or ice cream for dessert. Pies at the Palms immediately became popular after an unexpected visit there by boxer Max Baer just after the café opened. Cook Tina Shiflett had just taken several pies from the oven when the prize fighter asked for a slice of the coconut. Consuming it with relish, Baer got up and stepped into the kitchen. The celebrity gave every employee in the hot room a dollar tip and raved to Shiflett, "My gosh, woman, that's the best pie I ever ate."[50]

After serving meals into the late 1960s, the Palms closed and its space became a combined residence and small-engine repair shop. After the death of owner John Hawkins in 2002, his heirs donated the building to the Atlanta Public Library and Museum, which restored the entire Downey Building and returned the Palms Grill Café to operation as a full-service restaurant. It provided meals for modern-day diners who could look through its plate-glass front windows across the street to view a fanciful nineteen-foot-tall fiberglass John Bunyan figure holding a giant hot dog. Preservationists relocated the whimsical sculpture that originally stood at Bunyon's Restaurant in Cicero, Illinois, to a downtown lot opposite from the Palms Grill in 2004 as a monument to Route 66 popular culture.[51]

Lincoln
THE BLUE MILL (THE MILL)

When it first was designated a federal highway, the Mother Road came into Lincoln, Illinois, on North Kickapoo Street, took three ninety-degree turns, and exited town via Washington Street. Just before outbound drivers crossed railroad tracks on the way out of town, at 738 South Washington, they came to a long-standing eating and drinking place known as the Blue Mill. Paul Coddington erected the unusual-looking two-story wooden building in 1929, giving it the superficial appearance of an old-fashioned Dutch windmill with four big wood-slatted blades. With the end of Prohibition in 1933, the café began selling alcoholic beverages and transitioned into a tavern that served food. In 1945 Albert C. and Blossom E. Huffman purchased the location and business, shortening its name to The Mill. Soon thereafter they acquired and moved to Lincoln a surplus two-story barracks building from the World War II Camp Ellis army training base about sixty miles away. Attaching the addition to the rear of the structure, the Huffmans more than doubled the size of their combined tavern and restaurant.

Soon after Blossom and Albert took over, they introduced to the menu an Americanized version of German schnitzel, in reality a delicious breaded pork tenderloin. Their advertisements read "Schnitzel's, Schnitzel's, Schnitzel's," inviting customers to enjoy the entrées as part of larger meals or in sandwiches. After a number of years, the Huffmans turned the business over to their son, George E., whose own son, Dan, eventually helped manage the eatery. The latter Huffmans showed a boundless sense of humor as they decorated the dining and drinking areas with entertainingly costumed mannequins and even a blue-jean-clad mechanical leg that looked like it was poking through a ceiling. The popular Mill served food and drink until 1996, when it closed its doors. Though the city threatened to demolish the disused building, grassroots preservationists secured both local and outside funding to protect and eventually to restore The Mill to become a visitors'

center and gift shop catering to heritage tourists on Route 66.[52]

Broadwell
HARBOR INN (PIG-HIP RESTAURANT)

For more than five decades, motorists along the Mother Road stopped for fuel and meals north of Springfield at a roadside filling station and eatery that was the "brain child" of Ernest Leo "Ernie" Edwards. He had grown up in Illinois, graduating from high school in Lincoln. Casting about for what he should do with his life, in 1937 he decided to open a lunchroom on the northwest side of tiny Broadwell, a village bisected by Highway 66. He erected a tiny eatery, but at his mother's recommendation quickly added a modest wood-frame filling station with gas pumps in front. The enterprise immediately started earning the family income. Brother Joe Edwards ran the station while Ernie with his mother's assistance managed the lunchroom. Because he had found bargain wallpaper and curtains with pictures of ships, Edwards initially called the eatery the Harbor Inn.

In a story that he liked to recount, Ernie Edwards explained how the little lunchroom gained the moniker Pig-Hip around 1938. His mother, Naomi, had just taken a freshly baked ham from the oven and put it out to cool, when a local farmer came in famished, asking for a sandwich. When Ernie asked him what kind, the farmer gestured, saying, "Just give me a piece of that pig hip." Ernie thought that the name was catchy, so he started calling the sandwich and his café the Pig-Hip. The dish became the specialty of the house, being made from two ounces of thinly sliced uncured baked ham cut into quarter-sized pieces served on a buttered, grill-toasted bun dressed with lettuce and

Pig-Hip Sandwich Sauce, PIG-HIP
RESTAURANT, BROADWELL, ILLINOIS

....

Ernie Edwards prized this sauce, which he served for years on his notable thinly sliced baked ham sandwiches at the Pig-Hip Restaurant on the west side of Route 66 in little Broadwell, Illinois. Throughout his career, he kept the recipe secret, seeing it as the key to the flavor of his popular dish.

....

About three pints

10 ounces prepared mustard

20 ounces prepared tomato ketchup

22 ounces prepared salad dressing (not mayonnaise)

2 ½ ounces Worcestershire sauce

2 tablespoons black pepper

1 tablespoon seasoning salt (mixture of salt with garlic powder, onion powder, paprika, and black pepper)

Thoroughly mix ingredients in a large bowl and refrigerate for future use.

When assembling sandwiches, place thinly sliced pieces of baked ham (not cured ham) on a toasted bun, garnishing with lettuce, sliced tomato, and sliced dill pickle, topped with about 1 teaspoon of sauce.

From Sue and Jim Cable (Broadwell, Ill.), in Route 66 Association of Illinois, Pontiac, Ill., *The Route 66 Association of Illinois Hall of Fame and Museum Presents Kickin' in the Kitchen: A Collection of Recipes by Our Members* (Kearney, Neb.: Morris Press Cookbooks, 2016), 87.

tomato. As the finale, the sandwich received a dollop of Ernie's special sauce, reputedly concocted from ketchup, mustard, salad dressing, salt, and mystery seasonings. He never divulged the recipe. Always looking for more ways to earn income, Edwards in time opened the first of three successive tiny Tizit cafés in nearby Lincoln and for years served as the local justice of the peace.

Business continued prospering, but the United States entered World War II in December 1941, leading to changes even in tiny Broadwell. The next year the highway department added two more lanes to the existing two-way Highway 66 through the hamlet, and its right-of-way overlapped onto the Edwards family's enterprise. "They took out the original restaurant, and that [settlement payment] gave me a little nest egg," Ernie later recounted. He and his family consequently rebuilt both the filling station and the café a few feet farther back from the pavement. After the two brothers entered the armed forces in 1943, with Ernie serving as an army cook in the South Pacific, Naomi hired help to keep the station and lunchroom open. On return from the war, the two brothers resumed running their respective enterprises. Ernie added an apartment to the rear of the café, where he and wife Leota lived. About this same time, Ernie's sister and brother-in-law erected a row of cabins just to the northeast that they christened the Pioneer's Rest tourist court. By the early 1950s, Ernie was able to expand his original eatery into a larger facility with plate-glass windows facing the highway, a long counter with stools, and tables with additional seating. With the eatery in this basic configuration, he held sway in the Pig-Hip into the 1990s. Losing Leota and a then a second wife both to cancer, in 1984 he married

Frances Cook, a longtime waitress who had been a close friend. Together they ran the restaurant until it closed at their retirement on September 9, 1991. For a time thereafter, Ernie himself maintained a Route 66 visitors' center in the eatery building, but discontinued it after a fire in 2007. Ernest L. Edwards died on April 11, 2012, revered by friends and former customers.[53]

Springfield

From the Pig-Hip in Broadwell, the distance down Highway 66 was only twenty-three miles to Springfield, where many travelers took breaks from the road. The city was best known to the outside world as the home of Abraham Lincoln and as the state capital of Illinois. Both points of significance drew people to the town, which had been founded in 1821. Most of the early businesses surrounded the old state house, which in 1876 became the Sangamon County Courthouse, while hotels serving politicians, lobbyists, and out-of-state visitors mostly stood four to five blocks south and west in the vicinity of the current capitol building, built in 1888. Highway 66 initially passed north and south through this business district.

It was in one of the downtown hotels, the Leland Hotel, known as a retreat for Democratic legislators and their cronies, where one of Springfield's notable culinary creations, the horseshoe sandwich, was born in 1928. This flavorful concoction of toasted bread, grilled ham or other meat, and french fries, all smothered with a big dollop of sharp, cheesy rarebit sauce became known for miles around Springfield and still may be enjoyed in many of its down-home eating places. Springfield also gained a reputation as the flavorful seat of chili culture in Illinois, its downtown and surrounding neighborhoods being filled with multiple chili parlors, each with its own particular blend of spices and seasonings. Some of the decades-old enterprises still serve this toothsome delicacy, the best versions of which always leave a red rim of grease in the bowl.[54]

Not all travelers looked forward to arriving in Springfield, for the city simmered in its own midwestern stew of white racism. Even though Abraham Lincoln received acclaim during his lifetime as the great emancipator of enslaved Africans in the American South, the majority white people in "the home of Lincoln" saw Blacks as racially inferior. The city had about 48,000 inhabitants in August 1908, when members of its white population rose up in a riot that for two days raged in the predominately Black district. To cries of "Lincoln freed you, we'll show you where you belong," the mob looted and burned scores of homes and businesses, while it killed two innocent African Americans. From a total of 3,100 Blacks living in Springfield, an estimated 2,000 fled the town in fear, even being harangued out of surrounding all-white communities where they sought refuge. In later years a handful of lodgings and eateries served African American travelers who came to or passed through the state capital, though most of them were only boarding and rooming houses. Otherwise most eateries refused Blacks service until after passage of civil rights legislation in the mid-1960s.[55]

MALDANER'S RESTAURANT

When Route 66 was first designated, motorists came into Springfield on Peoria Road, zigzagged through a bungalow neighborhood, and dropped down into the business district on Sixth Street. There they came to Maldaner's Restaurant, one of the oldest eating places on the Mother Road still in business. John C. Maldaner came to Springfield in 1866, working for seventeen years in the kitchens of the Leland Hotel. He opened a confectionery shop on the east side of the courthouse square with Charles F. Frank in 1885, additionally providing high-class food preparation for off-site meals and banquets. At least as early as 1888, Maldaner had gained a reputation as far away as Chicago for being "Springfield's famous caterer." In 1898 the eatery moved a block south to 222 South Sixth Street, where it remains today. This site is diagonally across the street from the 1840s brick commercial building where Abraham Lincoln and William H. Herndon in 1843–52 shared an upper-story law office. John Maldaner's son, Charles J., joined him in the restaurant and catering business, eventually succeeding him and then taking Walter J. Tabor as a partner in 1922. Tabor's daughter, Betty Woods, remembered, "At that time, it was more of a fountain place with sandwiches, tea and ice cream, and they had a German baker who took orders in advance." She continued, "In the evening, lawyers would come in with the families and employees who worked downtown."

Maldaner's position fronting on an early alignment of Highway 66 along Sixth Street brought in considerable trade from motorists. From its early days, the eating place featured an old-time local specialty. This dessert adopted by Maldaner's was a special lemon cream sherbet, which had been served in 1842 at the wedding reception in Springfield for Mary Todd and Abraham Lincoln. John Maldaner himself received the recipe from a Lincoln cousin, and the restaurant still prepares the dessert but keeps the formula

Chef Joe Schweska's Original Cheese Sauce for Horseshoe Sandwiches, SPRINGFIELD, ILLINOIS

The horseshoe sandwich, one of the signature dishes of Springfield and surrounding Central Illinois counties, consists of a skillet-broiled ham steak served on toasted white bread topped with fresh french fries and then smothered in savory Welsh rarebit sauce made with sharp cheddar cheese. Chef Joe Schweska developed this specialty at the Leland Hotel in Springfield in 1928 and a decade later revealed his secret rarebit recipe in the Christmas edition of the *Illinois State Journal* newspaper. The key to successfully making these "horseshoes" is in concocting the sauce. While one cook is fully engaged in making the sauce, it is helpful for a second person to prepare ham steak, french fries, and toast.

Two quarts of sauce
½ pound butter
½ pound all-purpose flour
1 quart whole milk
1 pint beer
1 pound sharp cheddar cheese (grated)
1 teaspoon salt
⅛ teaspoon cayenne pepper
⅛ teaspoon dry mustard
1 tablespoon Lea & Perrins Worcestershire sauce

Melt butter in a large, heavy pan. Once the butter is bubbling, gradually stir in flour, mixing thoroughly, and cook about one to two minutes. Add milk, salt, cayenne pepper, mustard, Worcestershire sauce, and beer. Stir near continuously over medium heat to avoid scorching.

After the mixture bubbles, gradually add cheese, continuing to stir. (Some Springfieldians like to double the cheese and add a cup more of milk.) Cook the rarebit sauce until it thickens to the consistency of creamy salad dressing. Chef Schweska's 1928 sauce was thinner than what is served nowadays on horseshoe sandwiches.

To use this sauce for horseshoe sandwiches, place white toast on warmed platters. Remove bones from the pan-broiled ham steaks and lay atop toast. Cover with a layer of freshly cooked french fries and ladle cheese sauce on top. This recipe leaves plenty of extra sauce for more horseshoes later on.

Original recipe from Robert Woods, "Experience, Accuracy Basis on Savory Dishes, Say Chefs Who Give Favorite Recipes," *Illinois State Journal* (Springfield), December 25, 1938, pt. 2, p. 7.

secret. Maldaner's Restaurant continues to operate in the same location to which it moved in 1898, with culinary historian Marian Clark considering it to have "a history longer than almost any other eating-place along Route 66."[56]

DEW CHILLI PARLOR

In the years around the turn of the twentieth century, chili parlors sprang up in cities and towns across the United States. The spicy stew-like concoction of beef simmered with ground Mexican chiles and other seasonings originated in the border country of Texas and Mexico, though it is not known in the interior of Mexico. Entrepreneurs served the dish in simple "parlors," many of them just stand-up lunch counters in side streets. Newspaper columnist Dave Felts reminisced from his Springfield boyhood, "We ate a lot in the alleys, at such popular and well patronized downtown places as the Dew, the Fex and Paddy Healy's." The Dew actually had its beginnings at 607 South Eleventh Street, half a dozen blocks southeast of downtown, in 1909. There Joseph A. "Joe" Bockelmann and Thomas J. "Mickey" McNerney acquired a tavern, with Joe buying out his partner two years later. Soon thereafter he opened a Dew Chilli Parlor downtown in an alley at 606 Post Office Court. (Bockelmann liked to spell his product "chilli," and several other purveyors in Springfield followed suit.) The location was about midway along a passage that connected Sixth and Seventh Streets behind the main post office in Springfield, meaning that it was only a few feet away from what became Route 66. By the late 1920s, Joe had abandoned his initial parlor and expanded into a tavern-like facility at 720 South Fifth Street, just a block off Sixth Street and the Mother Road.

Then, in 1949, he erected a handsome brick chili parlor on the front of his residence at 1216 South Fifth, closing his earlier Fifth Street location. In 1955, after years of sating appetites in the downtown alleyway, Joe shuttered his Post Office Court location to concentrate his efforts on the location at Fifth.

According to Joe Bockelmann, "Most people don't like chili too hot and too highly spiced," so he consciously made it mild. "My chili is good because of what is left out," he declared. Still sold in Springfield, the dish can be ordered straight or with the addition of beans, chopped raw onions, or cheese, or served on top of spaghetti. Additional seasonings allow customers to spice up their bowls any way that suits their individual tastes. Springfield native Will C. Grant described Dew chili in 1952 when Joe Cooper was assembling materials for a first-ever book-length history of the dish. He wrote, "The Dew has a rich, palate-tickling blend of spices, suet, and high quality meat. I note he uses a little more suet than common. But no stretchers, such as flour." He then stated, tongue-in-cheek, that Joe Bockelmann had opened his 1216 South Fifth parlor "in the residential section so mothers will have this glowing pabulum handy for their growing babies." On Joe's death in 1975, the place of business passed by bequest to Rita Maurer Patton, who had worked at the Dew as a waitress for thirty-three years. Her successors, with a few interruptions, have continued to serve Joe Bockelmann's original recipe chili in Springfield up to the present day.[57]

THE MILL

Down Highway 66 from Chicago, travelers found opportunities to dine at establishments called supper clubs. (Earlier in their journey, for example, they could have nice meals at Frank Mangam's Chateau in Lyons on the southwest side of metropolitan Chicago.) Supper clubs were night spots where white people with at least moderate means went to enjoy the combination of food, alcoholic beverages, musical entertainment, and dancing. Most often associated with the Upper Midwest, Minnesota and Wisconsin in particular, goodly numbers of these supper clubs operated in Springfield, Illinois, from the 1930s into the 1970s. The typical evening consisted of guests arriving about four o'clock for cocktails in the lounge, then moving to a dining room for a sumptuous "supper," and then returning to the lounge or going to a separate performance area for a live musical revue. During the latter part of the evening, guests also could enjoy intervals of their own ballroom dancing. Some of the enterprises also had private gaming areas. The presence of large numbers of lobbyists who wined and dined state legislators only boosted the business for Springfield supper clubs. Motorists who wanted to enjoy nights on the town in the Illinois capital often sought the pleasures that these establishments offered.

One of the several supper clubs in Springfield was The Mill at 906 North Fifteenth Street. After U.S. Highway 66 was rerouted to bypass the central business district along Ninth Street in 1936, the nightclub was only eight short blocks to the east, adjacent to a large Pillsbury flour mill that gave the night spot its name. Owners Lewis and Herman Cohen first entered business as grocers until larger chain stores began moving into Springfield. During those days, however, their store already served meals at a fifteen-seat lunch counter. After the brothers sold their L. & H. Grocery business, in its building in 1933 they opened a tavern that catered to couples looking for good food, drink, and entertainment. Over time it grew and gained a statewide reputation from a menu that tempted diners with charcoal-broiled filet mignon and porterhouse steak, lobster tail, chicken dinners, and lamb chops with mint jelly. Sophisticated mixed drinks in the cocktail lounge were a particular draw. The business suffered two serious fires, the brothers rebuilding larger and more luxurious replacements each time until The Mill boasted five hundred seats in multiple dining rooms. In 1940 Ruth Hesse Koehler went to work as a waitress at The Mill at three dollars a week plus tips. She recalled from those days, "It was very elegant, high class. There were booths and tables and cloth tablecloths and napkins." She said, "You never saw anyone without hats and gloves and dressy dresses and the men wore suits and ties." Wanda and David E. Punch celebrated his safe return home to Springfield from the Korean War by heading to The Mill. After Herman Cohen learned of the special occasion, he announced to the guests that the club would be closing early at eleven o'clock, but he asked the Punches to linger. By the early closing time, the waiters had departed, but Herman, the orchestra, and the Punches remained. "The place is yours," he told the couple, "Order up . . . and dance away to your heart's content." They had the band and the giant dance floor to themselves. Many Springfieldians and old-time out-of-town visitors had their own particular memories of The Mill, which operated until 1971, its building burning a year later.[58]

COZY DOG DRIVE-IN (COZY DRIVE-IN)

When he returned from World War II, Illinois native Edwin S. Waldmire II brought an idea home he had seen during military service. He was drafted in 1945 and found himself at the Amarillo Army Air Field in Texas. On a short trip to Oklahoma to see one of his brothers, he had a meal that changed his life. Waldmire later recounted, "We stopped in a greasy spoon in Muskogee." Using a traditional waffle iron, "They poured batter in a trough, put in three wienies and baked it for 15 minutes." With time on his hands back on the base in Amarillo, Waldmire began experimenting with ways to shorten the cooking time for the unusual concoction of dough around a frankfurter. During this creative interval, he sought help from Donald Strand, an old fraternity buddy from Knox College in Illinois, whose father ran a commercial bakery. "I asked him to make a batter I could dip a wienie in and deep fry it like a doughnut." Ed, who already had experience running a successful short-order grill, experimented further, eventually perfecting the batter using his own combination of cornmeal, flour, baking powder, eggs, milk, and seasonings. He also concluded that the best way for a person to hold onto the creation was for the frank to be speared lengthwise on a slender wooden stick. (Other people elsewhere in the United States about the same time were developing their own similar batter-dipped and deep-fried frankfurters, usually calling them corn dogs.)

After Waldmire's return home, in summer 1946 he rented an open-air stand beside a swimming area on Lake Springfield, where he could cook up his dough-covered frankfurters on sticks. As he liked to say, "Things went like topsy" because business was so good that he had trouble keeping up with it. He later explained that during the preceding war years, "Gas, sugar and meat had been rationed for so long that everyone was dying to try something new. . . . We couldn't make them fast enough." This success led high-energy Waldmire to set up a stand at the Illinois State Fair later that year, followed by two subsequent seasonal stands on busy street locations in Springfield. He joined forces with businessman Gilbert Stein, an early Dairy Queen franchise holder. In 1949 they acquired a street corner fronting on Highway 66 in the 2900 block of South Sixth Street opposite from a big Allis Chalmers tractor factory. Then they jointly erected side-by-side walk-up food vending kitchens with a shared covered open-air seating area. Customers could buy Waldmire's "Cozy Dogs" on-a-stick at one side and purchase Stein's ice cream and beverages on the other. Eventually Ed and wife Virginia with partner Stein remodeled the building to enclose the breezeway and thereby create indoor seating. In these early years, trade was so strong that the Cozy Dog Drive-In was open twenty-four hours a day. Always inventive, Ed devised a special gadget that held several dogs in the hot fat to cook at the same time. Over the years Ed and Virginia had five sons. One of them, Bob, recalled, "My four brothers and me got to grow up in that restaurant. And my dad would pay us, a penny a fly, to swat flies, and two cents per table to clean the table."

While most white-run eating places in Springfield refused to serve African Americans before civil rights legislation was passed in the sixties, independent-minded Ed Waldmire decreed that his restaurant would seat and feed all hungry customers. Subsequently he was recognized by being appointed the first commissioner of human rights for the city of Springfield. Waldmire also openly opposed the U.S. war in Vietnam. On one occasion he closed the drive-in for two days to host a "peace write in" event with free donuts and coffee for anyone who would write letters of protest to their Congress members.

After Ed's retirement in 1976, son Edwin "Buz" Waldmire III assumed management of the family business with his wife, Sue, later becoming the sole owner. In 1996 the restaurant moved a couple of hundred feet north to a new building at 2935 South Sixth Street, when its earlier site was occupied by a Walgreen's pharmacy. It remains in operation as the Cozy Drive-In, serving the same basic menu of Cozy Dogs, hamburgers, french fries, and a variety of breakfasts. Since the 1990s the eatery has become a must-see attraction for heritage tourists traveling historic U.S. Highway 66. Its guest book is a place where customers record sometimes very personal remembrances like, "I've enjoyed [them] since 1950," "I've had one every year since 1970," and "It wouldn't be a trip home without you!"[59]

Original Alignment from Springfield toward Saint Louis, 1926–1930

When it first received designation as a federal highway, Route 66 generally overlaid the existing Illinois State Highway 4. The roadway twisted and turned over the Illinois prairie through multiple coal-mining areas south of Springfield as it passed through such towns and villages as Girard, Carlinville, Gillespie, and Benld. In 1930 Highway 66 shifted to the southeast to a route that connected Springfield with Saint Louis through communities that included Farmersville, Litchfield, Mount Olive, and Staunton, where the roadway merged with the earlier alignment.

Even though the original routing existed only for about four years, some motorists preferred it over the newer replacement, so many of the eateries that initially fed Highway 66 motorists in 1926–30 continued to serve later cross-country motorists. The strongest impressions that travelers took away from this generally level landscape was of beautiful farms interspersed with unsightly tipples and slag heaps left by underground mining. The mostly rural hinterland these two roads crossed already had a reputation for white racist hostility toward African American travelers, so these motorists generally tried to get across the hundred miles between Springfield and Saint Louis without tarrying along the way.[60]

Benld

COLISEUM BALLROOM

Ballrooms sprang up across the nation during the 1920s, but not many survived more than a few years. The Coliseum Ballroom in Benld was an exception, because it operated for decades. Brothers Ben and Dominic Tarro, known to law-abiding folks as local grocers, erected the huge structure with masonry walls and a gently curved bowstring-arch roof at the side of Illinois State Highway 4 in 1924. The Tarros had other business interests, however, the most lucrative probably being that of supplying raw materials to a huge illegal distillery east of town on Cahokia Creek. These profits, combined with purported funds invested by Chicago underworld figures, made it possible for Ben and Dominic to create the facility with a ten-thousand-foot maple dance floor and balconies on three sides together with concession stands and bars selling food and drinks. Local dance band leader Walt Schlemer described the Coliseum in the 1950s as "the largest ballroom in the state outside of Chicago." The location of the entertainment facility 250 miles south of Chicago and 50 miles northeast of Saint Louis enabled nationally known bands playing weekends in Chicago and Saint Louis to stop off for easy weeknight shows in Benld. Among the name entertainers who came there during the big band era of the 1930s and 1940s were Duke Ellington, Tommy Dorsey, and Lionel Hampton. After rock-and-roll grew in popularity in the 1950s and 1960s, the venue attracted shows from the likes of Fats Domino, Chuck Berry, and Ike and Tina Turner. After founder Dominic Tarro was slain in a gangland killing in 1930, his wife, Marie, assumed active management of the Coliseum, followed by her daughter, Joyce, who in 1976 also was murdered. The building then stood vacant until being converted into an antique mall in the 1990s, burning to the ground in 2011.[61]

Alignment from Springfield toward Saint Louis Starting in 1930

To eliminate slowed driving at multiple sharp turns, the route of Highway 66 from Springfield toward Saint Louis shifted southeast to a much straighter alignment in 1930. The new course bypassed several small towns, further expediting travel. Additional pairs of lanes were added to this stretch of highway by World War II, making it a four-lane paved motorway. Although this new road sped up the journey for travelers, it was lined by multiple places to eat, both stand-alone restaurants and cafés combined with filling stations and other services.[62]

Litchfield
ARISTON CAFÉ

Not very many restaurants can claim to have operated on two different alignments of U.S. Highway 66, but one is the Ariston Café, known best from its many years in Litchfield. It did not begin there, but rather on the 1926–30 route that followed Illinois Highway 4 through Carlinville. There, on the state route, Panos "Pete" Adam, a young immigrant from Greece, established a café in 1924 at the suggestion of a local banker, who backed him financially. He and partner Tom Cokinos called it the Ariston, which is anglicized from the word in Greek for "the best." When Adam learned about 1929 that Highway 66 would shift fifteen miles to the east through Litchfield, he leased an existing commercial building at the southeast side of the roadway junction with Illinois State Highway 16. The economic crisis following the October 1929 stock market crash, combined with the awkwardness of managing two geographically separated enterprises, eventually led Adam to close his Carlinville location to concentrate his efforts in Litchfield. The decision paid off, and in 1935 he was able to erect a handsome new brick restaurant across the roadway at 413 South Sherman Street still facing Route 66.

To enhance revenues, Adam installed a pair of gasoline pumps and underground fuel tanks in front. That same year Pete married a Greek widow, Emily Batzis, who brought two daughters into the home and the restaurant, and three years later the couple had a son, Nicholas. The family worked together making the Ariston a success by emphasizing quality of both food and service. Above the bar they placed a neon sign that still advises customers, "Remember where good food is served." Though the building has been enlarged on two sides since its initial construction, the main dining room remains mostly as it appeared during the 1930s. It has the original bar with stools on the right, six 1935 birds-eye maple booths on the left, and tables and wooden chairs purchased in 1938 on the main floor. On the fluted ends of the booths are matching historic art deco lamps sold by the Fitzpatrick Fixture Company in Springfield. The whole room is a marvelous time capsule from the Depression era.

In the 1940s Highway 66 rerouted one block west of the eatery, so Pete and Emily erected a new neon sign on that side of the building to continue attracting motorists. After they sold the restaurant to Gene Boyd in 1960, he introduced Mexican dishes to an already broad menu that emphasized steaks, chops, and seafood. Boyd ran the Ariston for six years but experienced financial difficulties and turned it back over to the founders. At that time their son, Nick Adam, with new bride, Demi, came back to Litchfield, where they assumed management of the restaurant until selling it to new owners in 2018. The white-tablecloth and napkin restaurant appeals to both local residents and travelers, and it has become a dining destination for Route 66 heritage tourists from around the world.[63]

Staunton
66 TERMINAL CAFÉ

Staunton, Illinois, was a convenient place for westbound long-distance drivers on Highway 66 to fuel up in Illinois before entering the congestion of Saint Louis, Missouri. It also made a welcome stop for eastbound drivers leaving the city to get out of their vehicles, walk around, and relax. This strategic position helps explain why Joe Roseman chose the eastern outskirts of the town as the place to build his 66 Terminal. He erected and opened this combined fueling station, garage, restaurant, and motel catering to truck drivers in 1940. John C. Meckles ran the station and garage, while Estell R. Felts managed the café. The restaurant earned a reputation up and down the highway for its fried chicken. The entire complex was constructed of brown-painted ceramic blocks and had a distinctive square decorative tower. A dirigible-shaped weather vane surmounted the tower, with both sides bearing the identifying words "66 Terminal." Joe Roseman's son watched construction and early operation of the enterprise. "I was made aware very quickly that the 66 Terminal name meant the highway and the [Phillips 66 brand] gas that we used," adding, "I felt a sense of adventure about being on Highway 66."

The truck stop at Staunton developed an unexpected source of income from buyers who drove new cars home from Detroit factories. These vehicles left the factories with special "break-in" oil to be changed after five hundred miles of use. Many of these drivers ate in the café and spent the night in the 66 Terminal motel rooms while the midnight crew in the garage drained out the used oil, refilled crank cases, and greased the fittings. John Meckles bought out Roseman's share of the business in 1952 and seven years later expanded the lodgings with a two-story motel building. His son, John D. Meckles, joined him in the business, which served the public until 1977, after the location was bypassed by Interstate 55. Many thousands of customers stopped at the 66 Terminal on the outskirts of Staunton.[64]

Edwardsville
CATHCART'S CAFÉ

Eighteen miles to the southwest of Staunton, Edwardsville tempted motorists as they approached Saint Louis congestion. With six thousand people in 1930 and eight thousand by 1940, the town offered several choices of food, drink, and lodging for white travelers. As westbound motorists came into town on Saint Andrew's Avenue and turned right onto East Vandalia Street, they crossed the railroad tracks and on the left saw Cathcart's Café. Tennessean George B. Cathcart had spent a number of years working as a coal miner at Thurber, Texas, and elsewhere before he came to the Edwardsville mines. In 1922 he and his wife, Clara, purchased an existing two-story home as a rooming house, the Cathcart Tourist Inn, while he continued mining. Two years later he erected a twelve-by-twelve-foot wooden hamburger stand on the corner of the lot near the house. As an attraction to customers, on the first day of business on May 8, 1924, the entrepreneur gave away ice cream to every child. The enterprise prospered, and in the next decade Cathcart expanded it six times to become a modern combined café, soda fountain, and grocery store that he called Cathcart's Café. The local newspaper asserted, "Many a traveler will pass up his regular meal hour just to reach Edwardsville and eat at Cathcart's."

Truck drivers likewise formed part of the trade, but their vehicles created complications. Several neighbors took George to court in 1928 complaining about "incessant parking of large noisy and foul smelling stock trucks in front of residences." George and Clara divorced in 1927, and agreed that he would retain ownership of the café and she

of the residential guesthouse. Having been an active union member as a coal miner, Cathcart strongly supported the efforts of President Franklin D. Roosevelt to bring the national economy out the Great Depression, even posting in the front window of the café a copy of a 1933 telegram of support that he had sent to the White House. When he planned retirement after twenty-six years in the mines and twenty-seven in food service, Cathcart attempted to sell his café, but he died on March 4, 1952, before realizing that goal. The restaurant building subsequently housed a cabinet-making shop and other businesses before being razed to make way for a modern financial institution. His and Clara's old two-story white Tourist Inn still stands next door.[65]

Mitchell
LUNA CAFÉ

Highway 66 passed through Mitchell, Illinois, from 1926 through 1965, when this stretch of roadway ceased to be part of the latter-day Bypass 66. Initially drivers went through on their way to bridges across the Mississippi farther south at East Saint Louis, Illinois. Then, in 1929, the Chain of Rocks toll bridge opened across the Mississippi River between Mitchell and the northern suburbs of Saint Louis, Missouri, enabling through travelers to avoid big-city congestion. Seven years later, in 1936, that same Chain of Rocks Bridge became the official Highway 66 route over the river. Among the numerous folk who opened businesses along the corridor of consumption that the Mother Road created were Irma and Herman Raffaelle. At least as early as 1926 the couple owned and operated a tavern on the north side of the highway at what today is 201 East Chain of Rocks Road in Mitchell. Their Luna Café was a simple two-story wood-frame affair with a gable roof and a false front. The downstairs housed a restaurant and public spaces, while the upstairs contained multiple bedrooms rented initially to transient railway workers. When Prohibition ended, the Raffaelles added beer, wine, and liquor, advertising "drink mixing our specialty." Their popular food items during the Depression era included steaks, chicken, and frog-leg dinners. The clientele at the Luna varied over time from elite Saint Louis diners to criminals and reputed prostitutes using the upstairs bedrooms. Irma and Herman ran the tavern until his death in 1937, when she assumed full management, later being joined in 1941 by second husband George Dee Jones. It is believed that it was about this time that a notable seven-color neon sign depicting a full cocktail glass with a red cherry was erected in front of the tavern. Irma owned or operated the roadhouse throughout all its years on official Route 66. Afterward the tavern ownership passed through Chester Whyers, Ray Herrin, Anita Bowman, Al Young, and Larry Wofford, who maintained continuous operation. Many heritage tourists intentionally make the Luna Café a planned destination as part of their experiences in traveling Old Highway 66.[66]

East Saint Louis
BUSH'S STEAK HOUSE

By the time westbound travelers reached East Saint Louis in Illinois, they generally were tired and wanted only to get across the Mississippi River into Saint Louis, Missouri. Similarly, drivers setting out northeast from Saint Louis rarely tarried in East Saint Louis, for they felt they had miles to cover before taking any rest stops. People living in or visiting in Saint Louis, Missouri, did, however, go across to East Saint Louis to eat and drink. When national Prohibition ended in 1933, Missouri passed legislation that prohibited the sale on Sundays of beverages with over 5 percent alcohol. Bars and nightclubs in Saint Louis, Missouri, consequently had to stop serving booze at midnight on Saturday and sell none until Monday. However, across the river in East Saint Louis there were no such restrictions on Saturday night or Sunday alcohol sales. As a result, considerable numbers of people in Saint Louis drove across the bridges into East Saint Louis for nightcaps on Saturday evenings. Columnist George Killenberg remarked in 1949 that each Saturday night there was "a mass exodus eastward across the Mississippi River bridges that some observers have compared with the frantic evacuation of Paris before the German blitzkrieg." The situation led to the establishment of multiple luxury restaurants, cocktail lounges, and nightclubs close to the Illinois ends of the bridges.

Brothers Ed and Jack English, veterans of the food and bar trade, and partner Marty Miller saw the Saturday night traffic jams on the bridges and decided to take advantage of partygoers' desires unobtainable in Saint Louis. Just beyond the Illinois end of the Eads Bridge, they opened up the two-story, four-hundred-seat Bush's Steak House in 1946. It featured some of the best food in Saint Louis or East Saint Louis, with showcase meals of steaks, chops, and seafood including lobsters. Musical accompaniment enhanced the atmosphere. In 1950 the owners added an intimate second-floor cocktail lounge to cater to the desires of patrons who a Saint Louis journalist characterized as "the late stayer-uppers from this side of the river." Business at Bush's Steak House remained strong through the 1950s, but declined as the urban core of East Saint Louis faded. The steak house closed in early summer 1961, and the building suffered a fire three months later. The once luxurious restaurant was not rebuilt, and its building was removed the next year.[67]

On into Saint Louis and Missouri

Mother Road travelers motored three hundred miles from the shores of Lake Michigan in Chicago to the banks of the Mississippi opposite Saint Louis. They made their way across the prairie heartland of America and were about enter the wooded and hilly Ozarks of Missouri. Before them lay Saint Louis, the largest city they would meet along the route until they reached Los Angeles and the Pacific. The metropolis on the Mississippi River would offer them more dining choices than they would meet anywhere else along their trek across North America. Even those who sped around the city on bypass routes would likely tarry long enough for a snack, and those who took their time would be rewarded with more meal choices than they could ever sample.

....

MISSOURI

After passing through a series of low-lying, gritty industrial towns in southern Illinois, motorists on Highway 66 entered Missouri by crossing the Mississippi River by bridge into Saint Louis. It was one of only three large urban areas the Mother Road traversed. The River City offered travelers perhaps more eating options than either Chicago or Los Angeles because the lengthy drive across the metropolis changed several times, carrying travelers through multiple distinct neighborhoods. Convenient dining choices abounded along each of these routes.[1]

Saint Louis

Saint Louis long prospered from a fortuitous position at the forks of the two great rivers of North America, the Mississippi and the Missouri. Consequently it became a figurative and literal gateway to the American West. It not only was a destination for steamboats plying the Missouri and Mississippi Rivers but also served as a starting point for wagon roads and railroads extending westward. Travelers funneled through Saint Louis because for years it was the southernmost point on the Mississippi where engineers could build permanent bridges. It was these bridges that shaped both the local history of Route 66 and the economic development of the city as a whole.[2]

Once across the river from southern Illinois, motorists traversed Saint Louis on a series of thoroughfares, some dictated by bridge locations and others by improved roads. Cross-country travelers often found these pathways confusing; one such group was the Aldrich family on a trip between Flint, Michigan, and California in March 1945. Peter Aldrich remembered from his youth, "Driving through St. Louis was a chore. It seemed like Route 66 turned left or right every few blocks." In the early years, drivers crossed either the McKinley Bridge or the Municipal Bridge into downtown. From there arterial streets took them westward to the area of Forest Park, site of the 1904 Saint Louis World's Fair, and from there south and west to Manchester Road and on out of the city through the little towns of Manchester, Pond, and Gray Summit. Street widening in 1933 created a new way southwest along Gravois Avenue, Chippewa Street, and Watson Road in the direction of Eureka and Pacific. This alignment came to be known as the City 66 route. The opening of the Chain of Rocks toll bridge over the Mississippi several miles upstream in 1929 diverted much of the through traffic from Illinois into Saint Louis's north side. From there the City 66 route passed down Riverview Drive and connecting streets to the central business district before cutting west. Then, in 1936, an alternate route around the city opened as Bypass 66. It took a lengthy but less congested course from the Chain of Rocks Bridge west and then south to intercept Watson Road on the far southwest side of the city. It was along these multiple streets, avenues, boulevards, and roads that motorists dined their way across Saint Louis as Route 66 alignments changed over time.[3]

JEFFERSON HOTEL / MAYFAIR HOTEL

The best-heeled travelers sought food and lodging in the fine hotels of Saint Louis. When Highway 66 motorists began arriving in the mid-1920s, these accommodations clustered either in the central business district or a short drive west in the area of Forest Park. There, in the Central West End, some of the wealthiest Saint Louisans made their homes in large, gated mansions. During the heyday of Route 66, the downtown Jefferson Hotel at 415 North Twelfth Boulevard was the premiere center-city hostelry. Erected in 1904 to house visitors attending the Saint Louis World's Fair, otherwise known as the Louisiana Purchase Exposition, it stood thirteen stories tall and received an adjacent thirteen-story addition in 1928. The hotel offered a wide range of dining choices from a coffee shop to a 1,200-seat banquet hall. Roast beef was a specialty of the house. Many people went to the Jefferson for evening dinner and dancing after enjoying performances at downtown theaters. One customer in 1946 commented that it had "good food with Rockaway oysters as a good choice," while another complimented its "excellent food, perfect service." Only about four blocks away at 806 Saint Charles Street, the Mayfair Hotel during these same years likewise offered multiple eating areas, among them the Hofbrau Restaurant featuring German-American fare. Specialties in the main dining room included "Mayfair chicken" and lamb chops.[4]

CHASE HOTEL / PARK PLAZA HOTEL

At the northeast corner of Forest Park in the Central West End, a pair of hotels hosted many Highway 66 travelers. Chase Ullman opened the Chase Hotel at the intersection of Lindell and Kingshighway Boulevards in 1922. Just to the north, Sam Koplar erected the Park Plaza in 1929, taking its name from Forest Park and the Savoy Plaza Hotel of New York. It gained fame for its food and celebrity guests, among them five U.S. presidents. In 1961 the Chase and the Park Plaza merged, with a new lobby and entrance connecting them. Saint Louisans still remember the Hunt Room at the Park Plaza for the first truly luxurious brunch in the Midwest.[5]

ATLAS HOTEL

Not all travelers could find food and shelter in the fine Saint Louis hotels. African American motorists, in fact, were barred by custom from the great majority of hostelries, which welcomed whites only. The options available to these travelers were in a handful of segregated hotels and boardinghouses. Perhaps the best known of these inns was the Atlas Hotel at 4647 Delmar Boulevard, half a dozen blocks north of the original

Route 66 alignment along Lindell Boulevard. The Atlas was the nicest among the choices Black motorists had in Saint Louis. Shortly after its 1946 opening, the local white press described it as "the new get-together place of the Negro community," adding, "It looks as if it might be located at Palm Beach." Operating until after the end of formal racial separation in the 1960s, the Atlas accommodated and fed such Black celebrities as boxer Joe Louis and singer Charles Brown. Many frugal African American travelers avoided the comparatively expensive rates at the Atlas and found more modest places like the Adams Hotel at 4295 Olive Street or Mrs. Ira Love's guesthouse on the near-north side at 4334 Ashland Avenue. Local Route 66 authority Joe Sonderman summarized the lodging and dining situation for African Americans, stating that if one were Black and visiting Saint Louis, "You'd just go to a certain part of town" to find a place to eat and stay.[6]

MISS HULLING'S CAFETERIAS

Among the most popular moderately priced eating places in all of Saint Louis, serving thousands of Route 66 travelers, were the two Miss Hulling's Cafeterias in downtown. Florence Louise Hulling came to the River City as a teenager from Mascoutah, Illinois, in 1911, and found employment as a waitress at Childs Restaurant in the business district. By 1930 she was its manager, but one of her regular diners prompted her to set her sights higher. With this encouragement, that same year she invested all her savings, six hundred dollars, in leasing a basement space where two preceding restaurants had already failed. There she began what became the first of a local chain of eateries featuring meals prepared

Three ladies dressed to share in a festive meal at the Atlas Hotel in the 1950s. For years starting in 1946, the Atlas was the finest hostelry catering to African Americans in Saint Louis. Author's collection.

from fresh ingredients in small batches at a time and strict attention to both cleanliness and flavor. In 1931 Hulling married Stephen R. Apted, the customer who had inspired her, and the couple combined her cooking abilities with his business acumen to make two downtown Miss Hulling's Cafeterias at 725 Olive and 1103 Locust into Saint Louis institutions. After World War II, they expanded the enterprise into several local eateries, which by the early 1960s fed 7,500 to 8,000 customers daily. Florence strictly supervised all the food

Glazed Strawberry Pie, MISS HULLING'S
CAFETERIA, SAINT LOUIS, MISSOURI

Motorists passing through downtown Saint Louis on the early Route 66 alignments often sought out Florence Hulling's two cafeterias at 1107 Locust and 725 Olive in the central business district. It was worth the expense and bother of finding street-side parking or of leaving one's car in a parking garage in order to dine there. Starting in 1930, Florence and her staff prepared the nearest to down-home meals that locals and out-of-town travelers could find, including her summertime Glazed Strawberry Pie.

One pie
1 quart ripe strawberries
1 cup water
¼ cup light-colored corn syrup
1 ½ tablespoons cornstarch
1 pinch salt
¾ cup sugar
1 teaspoon lemon juice
Few drops red food coloring
1 nine-inch baked pie crust in pan

Wash and stem the strawberries, taking out 1 cup of the small or less perfect berries. Crush the fruit, add water, and cook two to three minutes. Strain fruit and reserve the juice. Add corn syrup to the strained fruit. In a separate container, combine cornstarch, salt, and sugar and mix into the berry juice; then combine with fruit and corn syrup in saucepan. Stirring constantly, cook mixture until thick and clear. Remove from heat and add lemon juice and food coloring.

Fill the baked pie crust with the remaining whole strawberries. Over them pour the thickened sauce so that all the fruit is covered. Allow to cool completely and if desired top with whipped cream.

Original recipe from Florence Hulling Apted, *Miss Hulling's Own Cook Book* (Saint Louis: Miss Hulling's, 1962), 25.

service, maintaining her personal touch even as a silver-haired matron.[7]

EARLY PROTESTS AGAINST SEGREGATION

Most downtown Saint Louis eating places by custom served only whites. When members of the local Congress of Racial Equality (CORE) began efforts to open them to African Americans in the late 1940s, they first targeted lunch counters in variety stores and drugstores and tearooms in department stores. CORE members began protests as early as 1947, and by 1953 they succeeded in opening most lunch counters in the central business district to all customers. The tearoom at the Stix, Baer, and Fuller Department Store, a holdout against the pressure, eventually desegregated in 1954. Black residents and travelers through the city had to wait until passage of the national Civil Rights Act of 1964 for most other restaurants, cafés, and taverns to accept their patronage.[8]

FOOD FOR THE DOWN-AND-OUT

Some transients passing through Saint Louis could barely manage to pay for the cheapest meals. Throughout the years that Route 66 carried people across the city, travelers also included those who self-identified as hoboes, bums, and tramps, some riding on railway freight cars and others hitchhiking along the highway. They tended to congregate for company and self-protection in camps known as "hobo jungles," one for years functioning on the Mississippi riverbank beneath the west end of the Eads Bridge and another westbound out of the city at a former chicken farm on Manchester Road near Ballwin, affording convenient access to the Mother Road for thumbing rides. A journalist observed the transients in one of these camps

in 1937 as they "cooked and ate a mulligan stew in a large can," later sharing among themselves hunks from a twenty-cent slab of commercially baked cake. In 1932 Joseph Szalanski made his way through Saint Louis as a hobo, jotting in his journal, "Crossed the river into St. Louis[,] MO, walk around[,] take in all the sights, bummed a restaurant[,] got a good feed, came under the bridge again[,] went to sleep."[9]

PRETZEL VENDORS

A few steps, or perhaps several steps, up the social ladder from the hoboes were the people who, starting in the 1920s, peddled pretzels to motorists along arterial streets mostly on the south side of Saint Louis. Gravois Avenue, a Highway 66 alignment starting in 1933, became one of the favorite sales areas for these vendors. A local journalist in 1931 described the sellers as "mostly boys and old men . . . near the curb with a basket of pretzels." A year later another writer reported the cries resounding along Gravois Avenue as being, "Pretzels, pretzels, nice fresh pretzels here, folks. Five cents a bag. Who wants pretzels?" One of these sellers, Henry J. Fabricius, worked on Route 66 at the intersection of Gravois Avenue and Jefferson Street for fifteen years during the 1940s and 1950s, hawking many thousands of pretzels to passing drivers. Customers found the Saint Louis variety of pretzels to be thicker, with larger knots of twisted bread, than typically prepared elsewhere. At least half a dozen different firms baked the German-style treats during the 1930s, but by the time Mother Road traffic diverted to interstates the pretzel bakeries had shrunk to just two: Gus's Pretzel Shop and the Gingerich Pretzel Company. By then the number of regular street-side

A street-side pretzel vendor in downtown Saint Louis ca. 1930. Author's collection.

vendors likewise had dwindled to only about half a dozen.[10]

PARKMOOR DRIVE-IN

For many travelers, hamburgers were just above the level of foods sold by street vendors. By the time that Highway 66 began crossing the city, Saint Louis boasted of having dozens of stands selling the grilled ground beef patties served between two pieces of bread. A few of these enterprises became significant in national fast-food history, the most important being the Parkmoor Drive-In. This eatery at 6737 Clayton Road, opposite from the southeast corner of Forest Park on one of the earliest Mother Road alignments, was founded by William Louis McGinley. In 1924 he invented the lightweight door-mounted, collapsible aluminum trays on which carhops placed food for diners in their cars at drive-in restaurants. He and wife Ellen came to Saint Louis in the late 1920s to promote sales of their trays, but only a few restaurateurs showed any interest. To demonstrate how well the devices worked, McGinley himself built and opened

the Parkmoor, his own short-order café with curb service. The combination of tasty meals made from scratch with the choice of in-car or indoor dining at reasonable prices made the Parkmoor an instant success. Specialties of the house included hamburgers made from never-frozen ground beef, the "chickburger" (minced chicken sandwiches on buns), and homemade "all cream" ice cream. His commercial success led McGinley to open six more local outlets, two of them also fronting directly on Route 66 in Saint Louis. The Parkmoor restaurants operated through all the years that the old highway traversed the city, with the last one closing in 1999. His trays today are collectible antiques.[11]

EAT-RITE DINER

After the Municipal Bridge across the Mississippi started bringing Route 66 directly into downtown Saint Louis in 1929, the highway took motorists west on Chouteau Avenue in the direction of Forest Park. This alignment, used by some later travelers as well, passed directly by the present-day Eat-Rite Diner at

622 Chouteau on the south side of the central business district. A filling station occupied the site as early as 1921, but by 1936 the White Kitchen had appeared. An almost dazzling number of eating places followed, among them Spick's Grill, the Serv-Rite Sandwich Shop, the Regal Sandwich Restaurant, the Gateway Sandwich Shop, and from 1986 to 2020 the Eat-Rite Diner, which temporarily closed its doors during the coronavirus pandemic. The old-time slogan of the diminutive café, which specialized in short orders, was "Eat-Rite or Don't Eat at All."[12]

BUCKINGHAM'S

Westbound motorists on the earliest alignments of Highway 66 along Manchester Road found themselves proceeding out of the city along a former stagecoach road. It extended westward through the little town of Manchester, eventually reaching Jefferson City. Along this arterial street, they found multiple eating and drinking options. Here, for example, entrepreneur Mabel Ann "Trixie" Buckingham in 1942 opened a tearoom in a nine-room, two-story frame house at number 8945 Manchester Road. Her husband, Clyde, worked as the supervisor at the McKinley Bridge. Trixie's venture in the food business grew into a profitable enterprise she called Buckingham's, with such specialties as "delicious fried chicken, potatoes, fresh vegetables, apple sauce, relish, pickles, honey butter and hot rolls." When husband Clyde retired from work at the bridge in 1949, he joined his wife full-time in helping run the eatery, which that year attracted the attention of popular food critic Duncan Hines. Hines recommended Buckingham's as being "largely a chicken dinner restaurant . . . but they also serve T-bone steaks,

Swiss steaks and fried shrimp," also pointing out its homemade pies. The couple operated Buckingham's until 1963, when they retired, selling it to Sue and Bennett J. Barton, who continued dishing up meals under the same business name at least until 1967. Painted white and using the slightly altered 8949 street number, the handsome old home at the time of this writing housed an engineering firm that is proud of the heritage of the building.[13]

NINE MILE HOUSE (PORTA'S TAVERN, TRAINWRECK SALOON)

Proceeding west from Buckingham's, motorists traversed a slight left bend in Manchester Road just before coming to the Nine Mile House at number 9243. This was the first of several "mile houses" along the former stagecoach road that in its latter days carried U.S. Highway 66. These taverns were traditionally spaced approximately a mile apart on multiple dirt roads leading out of the city, among them Manchester Road. At least as early as 1876, the Nine Mile House operated here as a tavern, serving both food and drink. By 1890 the Reisenleiter family ran it in a two-story building with a welcoming porch across the front. Baptiste and Caroline Porta purchased the inn in 1932, changing its name to Porta's Tavern, eventually adding gasoline pumps, a barbecue pit, and an enclosed dance floor. Customers knew Porta's as much for its roast beef sandwiches as for its drinks. Sons Angelo and Joe took over the business after returning home from World War II. They eventually sold to George and Kris Hansford in 1982, who changed the name to the Trainwreck Saloon from its nearness to railway tracks, and it has operated since then under that appellation.[14]

BIG CHIEF CABIN HOTEL (BIG CHIEF DAKOTA GRILL, B. DONOVAN'S STEAKHOUSE, BIG CHIEF ROADHOUSE)

Motorists driving out beyond the little town of Manchester found mostly open countryside during the early years of Route 66, though the area gradually filled in with suburban sprawl as the years passed. The area around the little town of Pond, about twenty-five miles west of downtown Saint Louis, remained mostly rural until the 1929 opening of an impressive facility devoted to car users. The Big Chief Cabin Hotel was a complex consisting of sixty-two tourist court–style cabins positioned on three sides of a landscaped rectangular yard, the front of which was occupied by a two-story, full-service restaurant, filling station, and—after the end of Prohibition in 1933—a bar. The fashionable Spanish mission style structure with an ornamental bell tower had a stucco exterior, curvilinear parapets, and a red tile roof. Its location at Pond made it convenient for travelers who wanted to stay overnight in the quiet just a few miles outside the city, while at the same time giving the restaurant appeal as a "country" destination for urban dwellers seeking to enjoy a lunch or dinner. Big Chief advertisements extolled its chicken dinners, steaks, and sandwiches, noting that curb service was available for those who preferred to dine in their cars. The eatery operated at least into the World War II years, while the cabin customers gradually shifted from overnight guests in the 1920s and 1930s to weekly and monthly renters in the 1940s to 1970s. By 1990, when new owners began renovating the then-derelict restaurant building, all the cabins had been removed. Since 1995 the eating place has pulsed with renewed activity as the Big Chief Dakota Grill, B. Donovan's Steakhouse, and most recently as the Big Chief Roadhouse.[15]

WHITE CASTLE ON CHIPPEWA STREET

In 1933 improvements in arterial streets brought U.S. Highway 66 out of downtown Saint Louis a new way on Gravois Avenue, connecting with Chippewa Street and then Watson Road to carry travelers westward toward the towns of Eureka and Pacific. This realignment bypassed the initial route west and south on Manchester Road through Manchester, Pond, and Gray Summit. Just over four miles southwest of the central business district, U.S. Highway 66 traffic angled westward from Gravois onto Chippewa Street. From there, in two miles motorists on Chippewa came to a street-side food stand long popular among both travelers and budget-minded Saint Louisans.

The White Castle system of eateries of Wichita, Kansas, established in 1921, was expanding during the 1920s and 1930s. Its first bargain-priced hamburger kiosk to operate in Saint Louis stood near Union Station in 1925, with others popping up quickly across the city. On November 13, 1937, the company opened a white-painted walk-up outlet at 6000 Chippewa Street alongside its intersection with Hampton Avenue. The location became one of the busiest and most beloved of the hamburger chain's stores in Saint Louis, being remodeled in 1949, 1971, and 1974, and retaining curb service for motorists in their cars as recently as 1970. Visitors crossing the city seemed to enjoy White Castle burgers as much as locals. In 1978 long-distance truck driver Robert Farmer declared, "I usually stop in at White Castle whenever I pass through St. Louis," adding "They are real tasty with a flavor all their own." The Chippewa-and-Hampton store survived until 1983, when, despite local protests, it was razed.[16]

TED DREWES FROZEN CUSTARD

Chippewa Street carried motorists to one of the meccas for frozen custard lovers from across the United States. Frozen custard, a cousin of ice cream, differs through the addition of eggs to the regular ingredients of cream and sugar. Soft-serve machines add air to the liquid as it freezes, giving the otherwise dense ingredients a pleasing creamy texture. The treat became popular across the Midwest following its introduction at the 1933 World's Fair in Chicago. One of its early promoters in Saint Louis was a local tennis star named Ted Drewes. He discovered the dessert in 1929 while visiting with cousins who worked at a carnival in Florida. Taking advantage of his name recognition as a popular athlete, he opened Ted Drewes Frozen Custard at 1600 Natural Bridge Avenue in 1930. By the next year, he expanded to a walk-up stand still in business at 4224 South Grand Boulevard, in 1941 adding an outlet fronting on Highway 66 at 6726 Chippewa Street. Drewes's use of honey as a sweetener helped give his product a distinctive flavor. His stands served frozen custard only during the warm months, but the entrepreneur developed a lucrative sideline selling Christmas trees on his otherwise vacant parking areas during the winter. In time the elder Drewes turned the business enterprise over to his son and other heirs, who continue operating the stands on Grand and Chippewa.[17]

Ted Drewes Jr., son of the founder, was working in the summer of 1959 when a neighborhood teenager named Steve Gamber returned day after day to buy flavored malted milkshakes. Drewes remembered, "He was kind of noisy, always asking for a really super-thick malt and was never satisfied." To please the teenager, Ted made him a malt without any milk. "The malt was so thick," he said, "it wouldn't fall out of the cup," so he could safely turn the container upside down. "What do you call this," Steve asked, to which Drewes replied, "a concrete." Steve returned with his friends the next day, and they all ordered "concretes." Since that time the dish has become a specialty at Ted Drewes's that multiple other ice cream sellers across America have copied.[18]

Chain of Rocks Bridge

In the late 1920s a new bridge across the Mississippi River opened and gave motorists new options for entering or traversing Saint Louis. The 1929 Chain of Rocks Bridge allowed Illinois motorists to cross the Mississippi several miles upstream from earlier spans. From this point they had two options. Those with business or seeking lodging and food in the heart of the city itself could motor south on Riverview Drive and connecting streets to downtown Saint Louis. From the central business district, they then could continue west and southwest on the City 66 route or earlier alignments. Travelers who wanted only to skirt the urban congestion and move on down the road toward the west could choose a bypass route that officially opened on January 1, 1936. From the Chain of Rocks Bridge, it went west and then south through mostly rural, open country on Lindbergh Boulevard through Kirkwood and on to a juncture with the city route. It was at this intersection of Lindbergh with Watson Road (Bypass 66 with City 66) in 1932 that the Missouri Highway Department built the first cloverleaf highway intersection west of the Mississippi River. Travelers considered the interchange, constructed in pink granite, to be an engineering marvel. From this point U.S. Highway 66 continued on toward the towns of Eureka and Pacific.[19]

ROMINE'S SANDWICH SHOP (ROMINE'S RESTAURANT)

If travelers chose to take the City 66 route on Riverside Drive and its connecting streets from the Chain of Rocks Bridge to downtown, they traversed the Saint Louis north side. At 9053 Riverside they came to Romine's, one of the best-known Saint Louis chicken dinner houses. At least as early as 1930, Edith I. and John F. Romine operated a combined sandwich shop and barbecue stand in a white-painted building at 9051 Riverview. According to longtime waitress Rose Polster, the street was still gravel when the eatery opened, and when it was paved, Romine's supplied meals to the highway workers. When the census taker called on Mr. and Mrs. Romine on April 3, 1940, they were living next door at 9049 Riverview with her mother and three boarders who worked as waitresses in the café, which by this time was known as Romine's Sandwich Shop. In 1945 Elmer and Catherine Milke purchased the café, in time expanding it to include a dining room, bar, and take-out window. It became well-known for its fried chicken, potatoes prepared from scratch—mashed, baked, or fried—and house salads made with a special Mayfair dressing. (The dressing, originating from the Mayfair Hotel in Saint Louis around 1935, incorporated anchovies with cooking oil, garlic, mustard or horseradish, celery, onions, champagne, and black peppercorns.) As they approached retirement,

the Milkes sold the restaurant to their son, John Albert Milke and partner Ed Krueger. The two continued the food traditions until selling to Steve Schafermeyer, who had had the experience of working there as a young man. He ran Romine's Restaurant together with his own chain of Malone's Grill and Pub locations until 2006, when increasing crime in the neighborhood forced him to close the historic restaurant. At the time of this writing, some of the Malone's Grill locations continued to serve fried chicken and salads with dressings prepared using the old recipes made locally famous by Romine's.[20]

Kirkwood

SPENCER'S GRILL

The little town of Kirkwood, established in the 1850s, had its own identity separate from that of the nearby metropolis, though the Bypass 66 route passed straight through its business district. Travelers found several places to eat there, but one of the most popular was Spencer's Grill. (Local residents chose to keep the traditional name of their north-south main street Kirkwood Road when elsewhere most of Bypass 66 was renamed Lindbergh Boulevard in 1930.) The longtime grill had its origin in the activities of an Arkansan named Bill Spencer, who came to Saint Louis in the depths of the Great Depression. He got jobs at well-known White Castle hamburger stands, including the one fronting on the Mother Road 66 on Chippewa Street. Then, in 1941, he purchased Lee's Grill at 303 South Kirkwood Road in the business district of Kirkwood and renamed it Spencer's Grill, before being drafted into the army two years later and having to sell the business. On return from military service, where he saw action on Okinawa, in 1947 he purchased another existing café at 223 Kirkwood Road from Hugo Eberhart, renamed it Spencer's Grill like his old café, and ran the enterprise a quarter century until 1973. During much of this time, vehicle movement along Bypass 66 was so heavy that the diner stayed open twenty-four hours a day. Since the 1970s multiple owners have operated Spencer's Grill, but old-timers affirm that it maintains the same hometown atmosphere that they remember from years past.[21]

HOWARD JOHNSON'S RESTAURANT

As motorists proceeded southward from Kirkwood on Bypass 66, they saw increasing commercial activity near its intersection with City 66 along Watson Road. Motels and eating places abounded, with one of the enterprises being a Howard Johnson's Restaurant that opened in 1955, only two years after the chain's first outlet in Missouri had been established in another Saint Louis suburb. The single-story Kirkwood Howard Johnson's at 1130 South Kirkwood Road, like others spreading across the Midwest, had a distinctive bright orange low gabled roof surmounted by a stylized colonial-style cupola with a weather vane. Harry G. Giessow erected the restaurant, adding an adjacent motor inn in 1973, and he and his

Customers dining in Spencer's Grill at Kirkwood, Missouri, shortly after Bill Spencer purchased this location in 1947. Photograph 809.1574 (47) 1947 7187 courtesy of Francis Scheidegger Photograph Collection Addenda (S0809), State Historical Society of Missouri Research Center–St. Louis.

son operated them at a high standard until the family sold the property in 2001. As the Howard Johnson's chain faced stiff competition from others at the end of the twentieth century, it closed many of its restaurants. This eventually left the Kirkwood outlet as the last Howard Johnson's Restaurant west of the Mississippi, not to mention being the last along former U.S. Highway 66. Saint Louis historian Kip Welborn savored his meals there, reminiscing, "I filled my gullet with Tendersweet Clams over more than one lunchtime at the Howard Johnson's restaurant in Kirkwood, and on no occasion was I disappointed." The new owner, however, could not share his customer's nostalgia, and for lack of business closed the Howard Johnson's in Kirkwood on October 21, 2002.[22]

On Into Missouri beyond Saint Louis

By 1936 the two branches of the Mother Road, City 66 and Bypass 66, came together at the cloverleaf intersection of South Lindbergh Boulevard and Watson Road. Watson Road itself had been carrying the westbound flow from the city since 1932. Even though suburban sprawl continued southwestward along U.S. Highway 66, most motorists felt that they were leaving metropolitan Saint Louis once past this highway junction. Some would miss the good times, visits with friends and family, meals, and drinks they had enjoyed in the metropolis, but others felt just as pleased to leave behind the confusion and traffic, preferring the unpredictable open road to the complications of a busy city.

The road ahead was not necessarily the thoroughfare to which travelers driving from Chicago had grown accustomed. By the 1940s all of U.S. Highway 66 between the Windy City and Saint Louis had been improved into a four-lane paved motorway. From Saint Louis onward, motorists encountered primarily two-lane driving the rest of the way to California. As years passed, especially into the 1950s and later, significant western stretches also became improved into freeways, so that during the last years of Highway 66 travel it developed into a patchwork of two- and four-lane stretches.

Leaving the Mississippi River valley behind, the course of Highway 66 in Missouri crossed a domelike upland called the Ozark Mountains. Rather than having sharp peaks, these instead had gently rounded knobs, sometimes 1,100 to 1,700 feet above sea level, that were dissected by rivers, creating generally broad but sometimes steep-sided, winding valleys. Most of the region had forest cover, although farmers over the decades had cleared trees from much of the land level enough to raise crops. The area remained predominately rural, with the highway passing through a string of county seats and railroad towns. Some travelers familiar with the taller and more rugged Rockies could hardly believe that the smooth-edged knobs and ridges they found in Missouri were actually "mountains."[23]

Saint Louis Outskirts
SYLVAN BEACH RESORT

About a mile and a half west of the intersection of City 66 and Bypass 66 southwest of Saint Louis, travelers crossed the Meramec River. For years, this clear-flowing stream had attracted city dwellers seeking wholesome outdoor activities, albeit sometimes accompanied by a meal and a bottle of beer. Westbound motorists on the Mother Road would follow the valley of the Meramec toward its head for the next sixty miles, though from this point onward the river was mostly beyond view. Up and down this particular stretch of the watercourse close to Saint Louis, entrepreneurs ran low-budget resorts, often placing buildings on wooden stilts for protection from springtime flooding. Fred and Ethyl L. Wiemeyer owned the upstream east bank of the river where Highway 66 crossed. Here the channel had a natural gravel bar that sheltered swimmers from potentially dangerous currents in the main stream. In 1932 the Wiemeyers leased the property to Louis W. Peters to develop. He and his partners constructed a combined bar and restaurant, baseball diamonds, a swimming pool, picnic tables, stables, and bridle paths, calling the complex the Sylvan Beach Resort.

In 1934 the tavern burned, and this loss combined with the economic hard times of the Great Depression caused Peters and his backers to go bankrupt. In order not to lose everything to creditors, the Wiemeyers themselves took over operation of the recreational area in 1935 and began earning a profit. By 1936 they were advertising "St. Louis' most beautiful picnic grounds," offering a reopened restaurant and taproom, dancing, open-air swimming, horses for hire, canoe and rowboat rentals, a shooting gallery, and simple carnival-type rides. "Southern style" pork and beef barbecue topped the menu in the eatery. The next year chicken dinners became the attraction in the restaurant, but in 1940 it began advertising one-pound steak dinners "with salad bowl, french fried potatoes, [and] hot biscuits" for fifty cents. Automobile traffic along Highway 66 grew to the point that the restaurant by 1945 provided twenty-four-hour service, not to mention dancing

for customers in its Marine Room. Frank Daniel Sagehorn purchased the property in 1953, though construction of a new Meramec River bridge the next year encroached on the restaurant. Sagehorn continued operating Sylvan Beach and its tavern until 1962, when more of its grounds were taken for construction of Interstate 44. The remaining site now forms part of the Emmenegger Nature Park.[24]

Times Beach

Highway 66 motorists crossed the Meramec River a second time ten miles farther west. There tourists and pleasure seekers had been enjoying its clear waters for years. In 1925 owners of the *St. Louis Times* newspaper invested in riverside property and began an unusual real estate promotion at the place they aptly christened Times Beach. They offered readers the opportunity to purchase twenty-by-one-hundred-foot lots for only $67.50 at $10.00 down and $2.50 a month, provided that they maintained their newspaper subscriptions for at least six months. In order to erect a structure on any plot, buyers had to own three adjacent lots, but still the offer was enticing. Dozens of so-called summer cottages began appearing, with some of them becoming full-time residences, and by 1954 the village of Times Beach incorporated. Many of the houses stood atop wooden stilts above occasional high water, as the Meramec was prone to sudden rises. The location flooded repeatedly, with serious inundations to low-lying areas coming in 1950, 1957, and 1979. In the meantime the municipal government made arrangements with the Russell Bliss Asphalt Paving Company in the 1970s to spray waste oil on its unpaved streets to reduce dust. Unbeknownst to the town fathers, Bliss removed toxic wastes mixed with oil from industrial sites and then disposed of the poisonous sludge by laying it down on the streets of unsuspecting communities. The slurry deposited in Times Beach was laced with cancer-producing dioxin. In 1982 the nature of the pollution became known, and the federal Environmental Protection Agency declared that everyone would have to leave the town. Eventually the EPA purchased all the properties and undertook the systematic burning of over 250,000 tons of dioxin-contaminated soil. On completion of the massive cleanup, the agency transferred the site of the former town to the Missouri Department of Natural Resources, which adapted it to become the Route 66 State Park.[25]

STEINY'S INN / BRIDGE HEAD INN

Being a resort community, Times Beach never lacked for places to eat and drink. Among its watering holes offering food was Steiny's Inn, located at the west end of the 1930s Meramec River bridge. Brothers Edward and Dave Steinberg opened the tavern at least as early as 1941, with Ed doing the cooking and Dave the bartending. They lived upstairs in the wood-frame structure while serving the public downstairs. Then, in 1947, the building burned, and they had to either look for another location or to build anew. The scarcity of construction materials right after World War II complicated their quandary.

During this same time, another tavern, the much larger Bridge Head Inn, opened in October 1936 at the opposite end of the Meramec River bridge. Standing two stories tall on the south side of Route 66, it offered a spacious ground level with dining room and dance floor, coffee shop, bar, and long screened porch with views overlooking the river plus sixteen guest rooms upstairs. Quickly the Saint Louis press described the inn as "a Highway 66 merry spot," where "touring joy seekers" could find hot dance music together with eats and drinks. Its menu from Sunday, August 21, 1938, offered all-inclusive luncheons with an appetizer, au gratin potatoes, cauliflower, green peas, salad, and choice of desserts, to go with such entrées as prime rib au jus, sirloin steak, and stuffed green peppers at prices ranging from 85¢ to $1.25. After a few years, however, the restaurant gained a shady reputation for illegal gaming and illicit alcohol sales. Its fortunes had reached a low point in September 1947, when Ed and Dave Steinberg needed to replace their fire-destroyed Steiny's Inn at the other end of the bridge. For $30,000 the two brothers purchased the complex that a decade before had cost $58,000 to build. Their wisdom in making the purchase was confirmed by their next quarter century of steady trade for the restaurant and bar they renamed Steiny's Inn. It became noted among travelers and locals for its steak and chicken dinners and its "double decker" sandwiches. In 1972 the Steinberg family sold the property and business to William and Jeanette Klecka, who for the next decade ran it under the old name of Bridge Head Inn. James Kell purchased the property in 1982 and renamed it the Gallery West just in time to discover that dioxin had contaminated all of Times Beach. The Environmental Protection Agency later headquartered in the old tavern during its decontamination effort, which left the inn as the only surviving building from the former town. When the Missouri Department of Natural Resources received the site following the cleanup and adapted 424 acres to become

Customers and staff enjoying each other's company at the bar in Steiny's Inn, Times Beach, Missouri, in 1942. Photograph 809.388 (37) 1942 courtesy of Francis Scheidegger Photograph Collection Addenda (S0809), State Historical Society of Missouri Research Center–St. Louis.

the Route 66 State Park, the agency converted the historic tavern to become its interpretive center, which at the time of this writing was open to the public.[26]

Pacific

RED CEDAR TAVERN (RED CEDAR INN)

Travelers from Times Beach passed through Eureka and the small community of Allenton as they motored along the Meramec River valley toward Pacific. About a mile and a half before town, they came to the Red Cedar Inn. Two brothers, James Arthur "Jim" and Bill Smith, had supported themselves in the late 1920s and early 1930s by distilling and selling illegal liquor on their farm a little farther west

outside Villa Ridge, but as soon as Prohibition ended they entered the legal booze trade. After opening bars in Eureka and Fenton, they combined forces to erect a large roadside tavern on U.S. Highway 66 east of Pacific, just beyond a tall bluff known as Jensen's Point. Using timbers from cedar trees felled on the Smith farm, local craftsmen hewed and assembled them into a tavern building measuring approximately forty by fifty feet. The two brothers opened the doors of their Red Cedar Tavern in October 1934, serving alcoholic beverages and food and bringing in musicians for evening dancing. With some minor expansions to the facility, Smith family members remarkably owned and mostly ran the tavern for the next seven decades. About 1940 they changed the name to Red Cedar Inn to suggest openness to families as clientele. Come the customers did, enjoying meals of deep-fried chicken and catfish. A food critic declared chicken at the Red Cedar the best he could find anywhere in the entire Saint Louis metropolitan area, noting "The chicken here had a deep-brown, almost-cracker-crisp crust, giving way to exceptionally moist breast meat." It's no wonder generations of customers kept returning to the Red Cedar. The eatery served travelers and locals until 2005, after which time the property was acquired by the City of Pacific, which at the time of this writing was adapting the historic roadhouse to become a local Route 66 visitors' center.[27]

JENSEN'S POINT ROADSIDE REST AREA

Westward from the cloverleaf intersection of City 66 and Bypass 66, the highway right-of-way in the 1930s was landscaped with mostly native trees and shrubs as part of the Henry Shaw Gardenway. This pioneer parkway design and construction project connected the city with the Henry Shaw Arboretum, established on a 1,600-acre reserve in 1925 by the Missouri Botanical Garden outside Villa Ridge. When the alignment for U.S. Highway 66 relocated to the route through Eureka and Pacific in 1933, county, state, and federal authorities joined with private individuals to establish a nonprofit organization that planted and cared for ten thousand trees between the Saint Louis city limits and the arboretum. Starting in May 1935, men from the federal Civilian Conservation Corps began further improvements along the parkway, the most prominent effort being construction of a rustic stone and timber

lookout tower and picnic area atop Jensen's Point, a hundred-foot-tall sandstone bluff overlooking the Meramec Valley about two miles east of Pacific. The job entailed creating parking areas, hewing steps up the bluff, and hauling, cutting, and laying Bedford limestone walls, a courtyard, and a roofed vantage point. The end result in 1939 was a roadside rest area that served generations of Highway 66 travelers. It made an ideal location to uncork a thermos with hot tea or coffee and enjoy fresh pastries bought in the city. After cross-country traffic diverted to the interstate highway in the early 1960s, use of the picnic area sadly dwindled and vandals defaced the stonework. The Missouri Highway Department returned ownership to the original land donors, who fenced off the lookout and attempted to protect the site. Subsequently a grassroots effort led to the property being deeded to the City of Pacific, which, with assistance from others, restored the Jensen's Point picnic area and reopened it to the public in 2016.[28]

WILLIAMS SHACK

The modest community of Pacific, Missouri, had three important attributes. First, it stood on the banks of the Meramec River, meaning that nature placed it in a valley that formed a natural thoroughfare. Second, it lay at the foot of impressive sandstone bluffs that happened to be made of commercial grade silica, a necessary ingredient in glass making, which gave rise to a local quarry business. Third, it was situated where two railway lines intersected, which made it a good location for transshipment of cargoes and subsequent business activity.[29]

Multiple eating places came and went in Pacific. The Cave Tavern, Parrett's Restaurant,

Young people having a good time at Williams Shack in Pacific, Missouri, in 1942. Photograph 809.381 (37) 1942 courtesy of Francis Scheidegger Photograph Collection Addenda (S0809), State Historical Society of Missouri Research Center–St. Louis.

and Cottrell's Restaurant fed travelers for many years, but probably more memories were made at a low-budget ballroom called the Williams Shack. It appealed to people who drove Highway 66 to Pacific with things on their minds other than just getting down the road. The nearness of Pacific to Saint Louis, less than forty miles away, meant that the town could attract lots of people for boogying to live music. Brothers James G. "Jim" and Paul Joseph Williams, both in their twenties, pooled their resources at the end of Prohibition to open a tavern in a preexisting building beside the railroad tracks in Pacific. Their Williams Shack served as a combined music and drinking venue that also offered

sandwiches and snacks. For several years it featured live-music dancing on Saturday nights and melodies from disc recordings the rest of the time. Both brothers were draft age during World War II, and Paul went into the army on May 13, 1942. After basic training at Camp Wolters, Texas, he was shipped to the Pacific Theater of Operations, where, at age thirty-seven, he lost his life in combat on September 19, 1943. He became the first war casualty from the town of Pacific. Brother Jim Williams continued to operate the Shack for years. It not only served as a private dance hall, but also made space available for charitable fundraisers and political gatherings at least into the 1960s. By the 1980s, the building, with its wide-open covered dance floor, had been adapted to house antique auctions.[30]

Villa Ridge Vicinity
BANANA STAND (THE DIAMONDS, TRI-COUNTY TRUCK STOP)

Two miles beyond the town of Pacific, Highway 66 travelers passed the entrance to the Henry Shaw Arboretum of the Missouri Botanical Garden. Those with time on their hands could turn in to view not only nurseries for native trees and shrubs but also multiple greenhouses where staff tended orchids and other fragile plants for exhibition at the main botanical gardens in Saint Louis. Continuing another two and a half miles beyond the arboretum, the Mother Road came to an important intersection. Here the initial 1926 alignment of Route 66, which had exited Saint Louis along Manchester Road, joined the 1933 roadway. The alignments met near the top of a rise near Gray Summit that offered distant views of the Missouri, Meramec, and Bourbeuse river valleys. Spencer Groff inherited land in this neighborhood as part of his family's farm, and as early as 1919 he realized the significance of the location even when the roadways were still unpaved. According to stories still told, on the Labor Day holiday that year he saw motorists streaming past and he spontaneously started selling them locally grown plums that happened to be in season. This occasion proved to him that pleasure drivers would stop to buy the right goods. Next he started selling bottles of soda pop chilled in a tub of ice. On family property fronting on the Mother Road about two miles west of the junction, Groff shortly put up gasoline pumps and added hot dogs, fresh fruit, eggs, and cold

buttermilk to his offerings. He soon discovered what motorists wanted and what they did not. His stand grew from an umbrella over a chair to a shack covered with the thin metal top from a silo that he could "peel" on and off like the skin of a banana. A passing customer quipped to Groff that his enterprise looked like Adam's banana stand, and the name stuck—the Banana Stand—no matter what he sold.

It did not take long for Spencer Groff to outgrow the metal-sheathed wooden shack. With a pick he scratched on the ground his concept for a four-sided diamond-shaped building to be constructed on a triangular piece of land at a country crossroads. Erecting a white-painted, wood-frame building for this combined café and gasoline station, he called it The Diamonds but still painted pictures of bananas on the side so customers would associate it with the earlier stand. He opened the new food and fuel stop on July 3, 1927, the official date for the inauguration of the new U.S. Highway 66 through the area, which was just on the fringe of the little town of Villa Ridge. Groff targeted his sales to recreational drivers, but much of it instead came from through travelers and growing numbers of truck drivers. In 1928 Groff drilled a well, erected a water tower, and decorated it with an electrically lighted diamond-shaped sign that nighttime drivers could see as they approached.

Though he basked in the commercial success of The Diamonds, Spencer Groff had reached middle age and felt that he needed to let others manage his enterprise. About 1935 he sold the majority of the venture to his manager, Louis B. "Louie" Eckelkamp, and his partner, Noble Key. They further expanded the enterprise, made it into a Greyhound bus stop, and added tourist cabins and two swimming pools (one heated and the other cold). Local resident Bill Miller recalled, "As a boy, I remember what a delight it was to take an evening dip in The Diamond's icy-cold pool." During the Eckelkamp and Key ownership, The Diamonds suffered a devastating 1948 fire in which the main restaurant burned to the ground. Though he had just lost a thriving $100,000 complex, Louie Eckelkamp showed up at the site shortly thereafter, selling hot dogs, hamburgers, popcorn, and sodas to curiosity seekers who had come to view the still-smoldering ruins.

Sixteen months later Eckelkamp opened a new, $350,000 Diamonds with even more features than the first. Inside customers found a cafeteria, coffee shop, popcorn sales, gift shop, bus station, and travel bureau, with fuel sales outside. If this were not enough, he painted THE DIAMONDS in block letters on the flat roof so that it could be read from airplanes. It was at this time that Lou Kofton made a solo eastbound trip along Route 66 from California to join her husband at a military base in Virginia. She jotted in her trip diary on July 10, 1952, "When I got to Gray's Summit there was a restaurant that claimed it was the 'World's Largest Roadside Restaurant,' so I stopped for dinner, it WAS a big place. I think it was called Diamonds." The truly large travel center operated into the 1960s, even though it was bypassed in late 1959 by the new four-lane, restricted-access Interstate 44 highway that passed within nine hundred feet. The longtime owner quipped, "It may as well be nine miles." In response to the changes, Louis Eckelkamp erected a "New Diamonds" food, fuel, and lodging complex fronting on the interstate farther to the east at Gray Summit, across from the botanical

arboretum. Opened in 1969, it operated until 1995, after which it was demolished. Back at the earlier location, the 1949 fireproof Diamonds complex under new management in 1971 became the Tri-County Truck Stop, once more serving motorists until its closure in 2006. At the time of this writing, this building stood vacant on former U.S. 66 with its windows boarded up.[31]

KEY'S TWIN BRIDGE CAFÉ AND FILLING STATION

After leaving The Diamonds, drivers proceeded southwestward toward Saint Clair along the top of a low rise, offering impressive views of the Bourbeuse River valley. Originally a single two-lane bridge spanned the stream, but growing traffic created a bottleneck, especially in the wintertime when prudent motorists ventured out only if they had snow chains. The Missouri Highway Department added a second overhead truss Bourbeuse River bridge in the 1930s, giving the neighborhood the name, Twin Bridges, where 66 divided into two one-way paved roadways. It was here that Noble and Edna Key for decades operated Key's Twin Bridge Café and Filling Station. The Keys had worked earlier at The Diamonds for Spencer Groff and subsequently joined Louis Eckelkamp in purchasing the business about 1935. After a decade there, the husband and wife decided to retire early. Time lay heavy on the couple's hands, however, and in fall 1948 they purchased a café and filling station buildings at the Twin Bridges that John Kovak had erected three years earlier. Two side-by-side flat-roofed, concrete-block buildings housed the enterprise. From just a lunch counter, the Keys with sons Bill and Bob expanded the eatery into a restaurant that for years served short orders and meals around the clock. Noble Key also owned a vineyard near Steelville, Missouri, that produced grapes under contract to the Welch Grape Juice Company, leaving enough aside for Edna to use in canning grape jelly for the café and in baking special homemade grape pies.

The gas station catered to truck drivers in particular and had a contract to provide fuel to the Transcon Truck Lines. The café location at the end of the bridges became a popular stop for holiday makers from Saint Louis as they came and went to rivers and lakes in the area. A local journalist reported seeing "heavy traffic returning to St. Louis . . . with the peak about midnight" at the end of the Independence Day holiday in 1949. He added, "Mama and I stopped at the Twin Bridge café near the junction of Highways 50 and 66 to watch the large crowds refresh themselves with cold drinks and sandwiches." The Key family ran the Twin Bridge Café until the death of son Bob in 1977, after which time they leased it to others. At the time of this writing, only foundations remained at the site, but its key-shaped neon sign survives at the interpretive center for the Route 66 State Park at Times Beach.[32]

Saint Clair
LEWIS CAFÉ

From the handsome side-by-side twin bridges over the Bourbeuse River, drivers continued about eight miles on two-way pavement through a landscape of gentle, green hills with cultivated fields to Saint Clair. Established in 1859 and the site of a thriving local shoe factory when Route 66 arrived in 1926, by 1940 the community had about 1,400 inhabitants. Characterized by redbrick commercial buildings and rambling wooden residences, the town lay mostly southeast of the Mother Road. It was where Vergil Lewis, after fourteen years at the footwear plant, joined his brother, Ralph, in opening a confectionery and sandwich shop in the downtown business district in October 1938. After four years Vergil bought out his brother. In an old-time commercial building at 145 South Main Street, the Lewis Café became well-known for its fried chicken and homemade apple pies. Vergil initially bought his chickens live from local farmers and then killed, plucked, and butchered them behind the building. A local writer remembered, "A day with a low wind was a good day, as feathers from 24 fryers picked up on the breeze and sailing over to Dierking's Market was no asset to the scenery." The apple pies came "straight from fresh apples, peeled, quartered, cores removed, into the pastry." Dorothy O. Moore in 1953 saw local resident Ben Reed hauling "a huge bucketful of wild blackberries" into the eatery, where his wife worked. She washed them, dredged the berries in sugar, and baked them in pie dough for the pleasure of the day's diners. The Lewis Café doubled its size by expanding into an adjacent commercial building in 1961. Vergil Lewis sold the enterprise to his nephew, Fred W. Short, in 1973, who in turn sold the café to his son, Chris Short, in 1995. In a modest brick storefront, it continues serving diners today.[33]

Stanton
WURZBURGER'S RESTAURANT

After leaving Saint Clair on Highway 66 for Stanton, ten miles away, travelers passed more roadside enterprises where proprietors hoped they would pause long enough to spend some money. These included Benson's Tourist City and Ozark Rock Curios. Most drivers, however, pushed on to Stanton. Though it had only about a hundred people in 1940, this community was the turnoff point for an important Missouri tourist destination—Meramec Caverns. From Highway 66 a gravel road, later paved, wound its way three and a half miles south into the steep-sided valley of the Meramec River, where Lester Dill in the 1930s began developing the natural Saltpeter Cave into a significant attraction.

A small town filled with budget-minded parents looking for bargain ways to feed kids on vacation was not where one would expect a high-end destination restaurant serving gourmet meals, but Wurzburger's Restaurant played that role in Stanton for half a century. Effie and Louis Wurzburger married in 1915, about the same time purchasing property fronting on the Old Wire Road connecting Saint Louis with Springfield via out-of-the-way Stanton. Here they opened an eatery in their own home, using the two largest rooms to seat customers and serving on the front porch during the warm months. Effie raised their own "garden sass," or vegetables, but could not find all the ingredients her taste demanded locally. Every Tuesday she and Louis traveled the sixty-two miles into Saint Louis for grocery shopping, in the early years doing so on the train. The couple had been serving meals at the crossroads in Stanton for a decade when the gravel way in front of their business was designated as U.S. Highway 66 in 1926. Lester Dill's opening of the nearby cave to the public in 1933 only added to the Wurzburgers' business, though the couple preferred guests who made advanced reservations and came for leisurely meals. One local remembered, "Tourists asking for sandwiches

were given Mr. Wurzburger's salt-and-pepper retort that no sandwiches were served." The specialties of the house included Ozark trout, steak, and chicken dinners, with seasonal braised guinea hens prepared with a special sherry sauce starting in October each year. Among the distinguished diners who sought out Wurzburgers in little Stanton were author Robert Ruark and journalist Bob Considine. After Louis Wurzburger's death in 1960, Effie continued running the modest restaurant known for its sumptuous meals until she passed away five years later.[34]

Cuba

After departing Stanton, motorists followed the 66 Highway another twenty-three miles through gently rolling wooded Ozark hills and the Bourbon community to the little town of Cuba. According to stories still told, two of the settlement's founders gave the town its unexpected name from their recent experiences on the Caribbean island as they returned by ship from the California gold rush. Laid out alongside expected railroad tracks in 1857, businesses faced the steel rails along Main Street until Highway 66 came through a block northwest on Washington Street. The town grew from 750 people in the mid-twenties to about 1,200 in 1946, when travel writer Jack Rittenhouse observed, "Cuba is now an important highway town." Many travelers saw Cuba, Missouri, as the real gateway into the Ozarks. When Viola Van Koevering passed westbound through the area on Highway 66 on November 1, 1934, she penned in her trip diary, "From Cuba to Lebanon—about 90 miles—we went over the Ozark Mountains. Practically all we saw was hills, valleys, and trees."[35]

Lemon Cheesecake, WURZBURGER'S
RESTAURANT, STANTON, MISSOURI

Effie and Louis Wurzburger developed this lemon cheesecake, which pleased customers for decades on the Mother Road in Stanton, Missouri. Like many preparations in the mid-twentieth century, it calls for raw eggs as an important ingredient. Make certain of the freshness of your eggs and be aware of diners' food allergies and preferences in deciding to recreate this vintage dessert.

Eight servings

For crust:
1 ⅓ cups finely crushed dry zwieback bread or graham crackers (Effie used zwieback.)
6 tablespoons butter (melted)
1 cup sugar
1 teaspoon cinnamon

For filling:
2 cups ricotta cheese (dry cottage cheese)
1 cup heavy whipping cream
4 egg yolks beaten
1 ¼ cups sugar
¼ teaspoon salt
3 tablespoons lemon juice
Grated rind of 1 fresh lemon
½ teaspoon vanilla extract
4 egg whites
2 envelopes (¼ ounce each) unflavored gelatin

Combine finely crushed zwieback or graham crackers with melted butter, sugar, and cinnamon. Firmly press mixture into the bottom and sides of a well-buttered metal spring form pan 6 ½ to 7 inches in diameter and 3 inches tall. Bake at 375° F for eight minutes. Set aside to cool.

Rub ricotta or dry cottage cheese through a wire sieve. Add 4 beaten egg yolks, 1 cup sugar, salt, lemon juice, and grated lemon peel. Cook the mixture in a double boiler for about five minutes, stirring constantly, just until thoroughly heated but not overcooked. In a saucepan heat ½ cup water and add gelatin, stirring until dissolved, and gradually add to the mixture.

In a separate bowl, whip the cream until it makes stiff white peaks, adding vanilla extract. (To make whipped cream from scratch, it helps to chill the bowl and the whisk or beater in the freezer for about twenty minutes and to make certain the liquid cream is absolutely cold.) In another bowl, beat egg whites until they are fluffy, adding the remaining ¼ cup of sugar. Gently combine the whipped cream and egg whites, lightly folding them into the lemon and gelatin mixture without puncturing their air bubbles. Once mixed and smooth, pour the mixture into the prepared crust. Refrigerate for six hours before serving.

Original recipe from "Favorite Recipes of Famous Taverns," *Ford Times* (Ford Motor Company, Dearborn, Mich.) 45, no. 11 (November 1953): 58–59; and "Let Them Eat Cheesecake," *Evening Sun* (Baltimore), November 14, 1979, sec. F, pp. 1, 4.

LAZY Y CAMP

On the north side of the Mother Road in Cuba, just before it forked at a Y intersection between the old road on Main Street and the newer 66 alignment on Washington Street, stood the Lazy Y Camp. Henry Nobbe and his family started the combined filling station, cabins, and eating house around 1926, being succeeded the next year by Mr. and Mrs. R. J. Horsefield. By the early 1930s, Harry and Jennie Comfort, with their children, assumed management. The cabins offered clean bed linens and towels but no running water, with showers and toilets available in separate buildings, all for a dollar for cottages with one bed or a dollar and a half for those with two beds. Jennie prepared meals on a wood-burning cast-iron cook stove, serving dinners of chicken, ham, or roast beef with potatoes, vegetable, salad, biscuits, and a dessert for sixty cents. Daughter Emma Comfort Dunn remembered, "We kept chickens in a pen and my dad Harry butchered a dozen at a time." Jennie could purchase ground beef for twenty cents a pound from a local butcher, Emma recalled, and for hamburgers, "we made our own patties and froze them in the ice cream box." Raising as many vegetables as they could, "during the summer every sandwich plate was garnished with a big slice of tomato from our garden." Summertime brought plenty of trade, but the Comforts found winter to be just the opposite. Emma reported, "Nights went by when none of the cabins were rented. An occasional traveler came in for hot chili or a sandwich, but few asked to see a dinner menu." Some destitute travelers offered to exchange clothing, watches, and other personal belongings just for food or gasoline. The Comforts and their customers all struggled to make it through the Great Depression. Mr. and Mrs. Byron Boss purchased the Lazy Y in 1939, and were running the camp when the last known newspaper articles showed it operating in 1940.[36]

WAGON WHEEL CAFÉ

The Wagon Wheel Café, which operated in conjunction with the Wagon Wheel Cabins and filling station on the immediate east side of town, offered travelers the perhaps highest quality dining in Cuba. In 1934 owners Margaret M. and Robert W. Martin acquired two adjacent tracts of land on the north side of Highway 66. The next year they hired mason Leo Friesenhan to erect a masonry café building with a filling-station sales counter inside, followed by over a dozen Ozark stone cottages with steeply arched gable roofs, all completed by 1936. An actual gasoline station came in the mid-1940s. Joe and Clara Slowensky managed the restaurant and station for the first seven years, with owner Margaret Martin taking over in 1943. For most of the subsequent decades, the restaurant/filling station operated separately from the tourist court.

Mary H. and R. J. Lewis purchased the station and café in August 1947, bringing the Wagon Wheel to its height of popularity as an eating place, even drawing customers from Saint Louis. The menu featured fresh trout raised locally, as well as pies with "mile-high" meringue. Waitress Millie Gahr remembered, "We served a lot of trout from Hoppy's, the fish hatchery in Steelville. . . . I would get several requests to bone it out at the table." She added, "I had a knack for it and could pull the bones out in one piece." A seven-year veteran of the waitstaff, Wilma Grayson Becker, recalled, "The Wagon Wheel was too expensive for most people; it was for doctors and lawyers, with white shirts and ties, the women wore hats and gloves. The local yokels went to the Midway to eat." Work hours were long, with Becker noting, "Had to be there at 7 am and worked until after supper but we got big tips." Sadie May Pratt and husband William followed as café owners in 1950, later opening a new Wagon Wheel Restaurant two miles west of Cuba in 1956 to be closer to four-lane traffic on a recently completed bypass. The old café building then housed a series of non-food enterprises, while the Pratts served meals in the newer location until they retired in 1975. In 2009 preservation-minded entrepreneur Connie Echols purchased the entire old Wagon Wheel property, which already had become recognized as the oldest continuously operating motel on Route 66. She restored the cabins as well as the filling station and café buildings, returning the complex to active use as a hostelry catering to heritage tourists.[37]

Rosati
ROADSIDE GRAPE VENDORS

Travelers started seeing carefully tended grapevines alongside Highway 66, but the concentration grew most dense along a three-mile-long natural rise around the rural community of Rosati, six miles beyond Cuba. Italian immigrant farmers, who earlier had settled in Arkansas, began moving to the area in 1898. These Italian families planted their own modest vineyards for home wine production, but within a decade a commercial market grew for their grapes in places along the railroad like Saint Louis, Rolla, and Springfield. Other local farmers adopted the new crop, and, together with the Italians, in 1920 they organized a cooperative to bargain with bulk buyers, in 1922 signing the first of multiple annual agreements with the Welch Grape Juice Company. Even though the farmers contracted all their production to the firm, the arrangements allowed them to sell 1 percent of their crops directly to private individuals. Dozens of families erected inexpensive roadside stands, where in late August and September they peddled grapes to motorists. Robert Magnin's father planted a half-acre vineyard, and during the 1930s the children sold the fruit. "This was accomplished by lining the kids along Highway 66 a hundred yards or so apart and when a car appeared we stood as near to the highway as we dared and held up our baskets." He explained further, "There were often three, four, or five of us there so we got a lot of cars to stop." The children sold the fresh fruit for twenty-five cents per small basket. Magnin remembered that when drivers complained that the price was too high, he and his siblings would reply, "'20 cents without the basket,' and we usually made the sale." To the present day, travelers through Rosati see farmers raising and harvesting grapes, some being used in local wine production; a handful of farmers still operate seasonal late-summer roadside stands fronting on the historic pavement of old Route 66.[38]

Saint James
COMMERCIAL CAFÉ (ROSE CAFÉ, MARY'S CAFÉ, JOHNNIE'S BAR)

Half a dozen miles farther southwest from the Rosati vineyards, travelers came to the little town of Saint James. A number of eating places served travelers in this community that claimed 1,800 inhabitants by 1940. Frequently Highway 66 ran the length of the main commercial arteries in towns, but Saint James was just the opposite. The Mother Road along

James Street intersected Jefferson Street, the principal business thoroughfare, at a right angle. At the southwest corner of the stoplight junction stands an unassuming, flat-roofed, five-bay commercial building that for nine decades housed a series of cafés, stores, and taverns serving travelers and locals alike. The enterprises began around 1928 as the Commercial Café. On March 1 of that year, the eatery hosted the organizational meeting for the Saint James Chamber of Commerce. John F. and Mabel Rose were owners and proprietors, later giving the business its second name of Rose Café. Their menu featured steaks, "milk-fed" chicken dinners, and daily plate lunches. After John's death in the 1940s, Mable rented the building to several tenants, among them Mary Atkins, who ran Mary's Café within its walls. By Atkins's tenure, the enterprise was doubling as the local bus station. Over time, the facility housed a grocery store and additional cafés until 1960, when John Bullock became the tenant and opened Johnnie's Bar. Later purchasing the property, he filled the taproom with mounted animal heads, antique firearms, and prehistoric stone tools, creating a virtual museum. He made Johnnie's famous for the hamburgers prepared on its grill and promoted the bar as a retreat for heritage tourists who, by the late 1980s, had begun driving old Route 66 just to seek out such old-time places. At the time of this writing, a second generation of Bullock family members continued to own the tavern, which remained easy to recognize from its obsolete neon Stag Beer signage.[39]

KOZY KOTTAGE KAMP / ROCK HAVEN COURT

Just after crossing Jefferson Street, motorists on James Street entered a two-block-long oasis of green that dates back to the initial paving of Highway 66 in Missouri. In selling land along the alignment that was paved about 1929, the property owner insisted that it have two separate lanes and an avenue of trees. Locals helped pay for this short but attractive boulevard, which, according to local tradition, was the first four-lane segment of Route 66 in Missouri. It survives to the present day. Just three blocks beyond the now-mature elms, motorists came to the first of two cabin camps that offered both lodging and food, the Kozy Kottage Kamp and, farther on, the Rock Haven Court. (The substitution of Ks for Cs in the names of public accommodation, mirroring the letters in "Ku Klux Klan," made it clear that only white trade would be welcomed.) Few lodgings or eating places in small Ozark towns before the 1960s invited Black customers. The Kozy Kottage Kamp, starting at least as early as the 1930s, provided lodging in several wood-frame cabins arranged in a semicircle behind a combined filling station/store/café that also served as the home for the managers. Though the Kozy Kottage had long ceased renting accommodations, some of its individual cabins survived into the early 2000s.[40] The Rock Haven Court provided lodging, fuel, and meals another mile and a half southwest of Saint James on the north side of Highway 66. It opened at least as early as 1941 and by 1949 consisted of six single and two double cabins, gasoline pumps, and an office/manager's residence that later expanded to house a full-service restaurant. Meals offered during the postwar years were so nice that the Ozarks Dental Society met there on November 20, 1951, for a full turkey dinner. As its name suggested, many of the buildings consisted of native Ozark stone. The complex remained active at least into the late 1970s, when it operated as the Rock Haven Nightclub, a rural roadhouse.[41]

Rolla

Leaving Saint James, drivers came to Rolla in eight miles. With over five thousand in population in 1940, it was home to the Missouri School of Mines. Some travelers lingered in the town to attend activities at the college, to see family members attending classes, or to visit the on-campus Mineral Museum. Highway 66 merged with U.S. 63 about two miles north of Rolla, and the two continued together on the same streets through the college town until the Mother Road veered to the west on the south side. With lots of auto traffic, a number of hotels, tourist courts, and campgrounds catered to travelers' lodging needs, while a wide range of eating places competed for their appetites.[42]

PENNANT HOTEL AND TAVERN

For decades the Pennant Hotel and Tavern was the most prominent purveyor of food and lodging to travelers in Rolla. The complex came into existence as part of a plan of Edward D. Levy, president of the Saint Louis–based Pierce Petroleum Corporation, to create a regional network of high-class hotels and restaurants comparable to the Fred Harvey Company's hostelries serving railway travelers. In 1929 Rolla and Springfield boasted the first such facilities. Levy envisioned opening service stations with adjacent modern hotels at 125-mile intervals along major highways across the scenic Ozark Mountains. The Great Depression ended the ambitious project, with the financially troubled Pierce enterprises being taken over by the Sinclair Consolidated Oil Corporation. The four-story, white-painted wooden Pennant Hotel stood at the top of a high hill on the north side of Rolla just east of U.S. Highways 66 and 63, while the nearby three-story frame tavern and service station lay slightly lower and closer to the road. After Sinclair's takeover, it eventually sold the facilities to private owners, who for decades maintained and operated them as profit-making enterprises under a variety of names.[43]

BELL CAFÉ

With traffic from U.S. Highways 66 and 63 merged onto the same pavement just north of Rolla, this section of roadway through town became a prime location for entrepreneurs to attract motorists and their pocketbooks. In town the highways angled to the right for a few blocks before turning south again on the northwest side of town. It was on this diagonal stretch between Oak and Elm Streets in 1929 that auto dealers Robison and McJilton erected a new masonry Buick showroom and garage. They had hardly completed the new facility when Mr. and Mrs. Robert Bell occupied and adapted the structure instead to house their Bell Café. The eatery became a Rolla institution, with thousands of travelers dining there for about a quarter century. Competition among bus companies was spirited in Rolla before and during World War II: the Pickwick motor coaches stopped at the Pennant Tavern, but the Bell Café—at least by 1941—became the official stop for the contending Greyhound and Missouri-Kansas-Oklahoma bus lines. A modern station and café were erected next door to the old eatery in 1947. In the newer facility, the Bell continued serving meals into the 1950s, while its adjacent former building subsequently housed a college fraternity, a children's day-care center, and a flea market before being razed in 2002. At the time of its demolition, the old Bell Café was described as the last surviving commercial building erected to serve historic Route 66 travelers still standing in Rolla.[44]

ZENO'S MOTEL AND STEAK HOUSE

Just past the central business district, U.S. Highway 66 forked to the west, leaving U.S. 63. Development of facilities catering to motorists on Rolla's west side lagged behind that on the north side. Fred and Vernelle Gasser, who operated a motel west of Rolla, saw the potential for a restaurant on the less congested west side, and they contacted friends Loretta and Zeno Scheffer. The latter couple had run a vending machine business in Saint Louis for several years, but they relocated to Rolla and pooled resources with the Gassers in 1957 to erect a twenty-room motel on the south side of Highway 66 catering to eastbound motorists just coming into town. They quickly made money from the venture, and two years later they added a sixty-seat restaurant, calling the combined enterprise Zeno's Motel and Steak House. They featured slow-cooked steaks and prime rib, seafood, pasta, and salads. Business continued to grow, and the entrepreneurs added an annex with twenty-eight guest rooms in 1978 and expanded the restaurant with more seating and rooms for special events. Three generations of Scheffer family members eventually participated in motel and restaurant management before Zeno's dream venture closed in fall 2011.[45]

Centerville (Doolittle)

As traffic proceeded generally westerly from Rolla, in about six miles it came to the community of Centerville. Rather than being clustered around a crossroads, it stretched out along two miles of Highway 66 on either side of its intersection with a country road that led southward to Newburg. Centerville's name came from its position about midway between Rolla and Newburg. The neighborhood boomed during World War II from its proximity to Fort Leonard Wood, its tourist courts filling every night. After Lieutenant Colonel James N. Doolittle's widely publicized 1942 "thirty seconds over Tokyo" aerial bombing raid on Japan, local residents chose to rename their town after the gutsy war hero. He visited there after the war in October 1946 to thank the residents for the honor. In the open-air event, he and about four thousand members of the public "feasted on squirrel and rabbit from the Ozark hills and fish from the nearby Gasconade River." The community prospered modestly until the late 1950s, when it was bypassed by a new four-lane U.S. Highway 66.[46]

BENNETT'S CATFISH CAFÉ

Probably the best-known resident of Doolittle was preacher and restaurateur Paul Bennett. Growing up in the Lebanon, Missouri, area, Paul became adept at hunting and fishing. His father had owned property at a magnificent natural spring which later became Bennett Spring State Park. At age nineteen young Paul felt the call and became a minister in the Church of God, and by the mid-1920s was founding congregations for that denomination. At least by 1941 he had moved to Centerville (Doolittle), opened a roadside eatery, filling station, and tourist camp with cabins, and used the profits to finance travels across the United States as an evangelist. Then about 1945 Bennett erected an open-air tabernacle adjacent to the campground. When he dedicated the facility, he advertised that he had made arrangements for "over 1500 lb of live fish" as well as "chicken and some country ham" to "feed Camp Meeting attenders at the regular prices" of his restaurant. Saving souls and selling catfish seemingly went together. Business at Bennett's Catfish Café boomed as locals, travelers, and revival attendees made it regionally famous. Newspaper editor Edward W. Sowers later reminisced, "My, how I and my family did enjoy those catfish dinners, complete with slaw and cornbread sticks." The tabernacle attracted large crowds to hear nationally known preachers and singers like the Blackwood Brothers Quartet. At age fifty-five, in 1951, Paul Bennett unexpectedly suffered a fatal heart attack, but his wife, Gladys, long a partner in the food business, continued the eatery. When Route 66 became a four-lane thoroughfare and shifted north of Doolittle in 1952, she moved the restaurant alongside farther west, but when the road moved again in 1966, becoming Interstate 44, she retired and closed down the catfish house.[47]

ELDOMAR RESTAURANT

Over the years a number of cafés, tourist courts, and filling stations came and went from Doolittle. We know more about Emma W. and Henry Nollau's Eldomar Restaurant than many others because their daughter, Elsie Nollau Hudgens, shared remembrances of growing up in the eatery with local historian John F. Bradbury Jr. The Nollau family moved to Rolla from Affton in Saint Louis County in September 1946 and later purchased property with highway frontage in Doolittle. Operating with wife Emma as the legal owner of the business, the family erected a restaurant on the south side of Highway 66 in the little town. Once the building was up, an uncle who was talented in woodworking constructed the counters and tables, trimming them with wild cherry wood harvested from the property. The Nollaus named their café Eldomar from

Paul Bennett (*standing at left*) with diners in Bennett's Catfish Café in Doolittle, Missouri, ca. 1945. Bennett helped finance his travels as an evangelist with earnings from this eatery. Courtesy of John F. Bradbury Jr. Files, State Historical Society of Missouri, Curtis Laws Wilson Library, Missouri University of Science and Technology, Rolla.

the first letters in the names of their three daughters, Elsie, Dorothy, and Marie, opening it in 1948 and building a solid clientele. Elsie remembered, "Mother was well known for her good Hamburger[s], Chicken Dinners . . . Ho-Made Pies [and] Cakes." Mother Emma earned additional income by catering meals for outside groups. The enterprise did well until 1952, when U.S. Highway 66 shifted to an alignment just north of Doolittle, taking away the cars and their drivers' trade. The Nollau family had little choice but to close and sell the business.[48]

Arlington

The Little Piney Creek flows into the Gasconade River in a scenic Ozark valley through which both Highway 66 and the Saint Louis Southwestern Railway passed. Named Arlington as early as 1869, the scattered community has attracted nature lovers since its founding. The paving of U.S. Highway 66 across Missouri in 1931 substantially increased the number of people who made their way into this area of the Ozarks for recreation. In 1933 George Grant Prewitt and his son, Vernon, took advantage of their already owning the huge Stony Dell artesian well just west of Arlington and constructed an impressive open-air swimming pool complex. Two-lane Route 66 bisected the site, with the 44-by-100-foot pool on the south and tourist cabins and picnic grounds to the north. Inside the pool area, a café offered short-order meals for bathers, though many people preferred to bring picnic baskets. In 1935 the local press described the poolside restaurant as having "elegant highly polished cedar tables and booths" and offering "delicious meals and sandwiches . . . served in most tempting style." After Fred and Esther

Widener purchased the complex in 1954, the eatery became known for its steaks and seafood.[49] Because Stony Dell attracted so many summertime customers, sometimes parking their cars a quarter mile on either side of the pool, a number of additional eating places sprang up in the Arlington area to cater to their tastes. Over the years these enterprises included Vernelle's Restaurant, the Beacon Hill Restaurant, the Country Village (also known as the Truckers' Home), the Happy Hill Restaurant, Granny's Vittles, and the Powellville Café. Stony Dell pool drew summertime bathers to the Gasconade Valley at Arlington until construction of four-lane Interstate 44 in 1967 took the entire pool area, leaving behind only a handful of smaller stone buildings.[50]

Clementine (Basketville)

Around the Phelps and Pulaski county line about four miles beyond Arlington, drivers came to another attraction. At the scattered rural community of Clementine, as many as nine Ozark folk basket makers erected craft shops. From their products, locals knew the vicinity as Basketville. Brightly painted signs and rows of handwoven baskets on the ground, on shelves, and suspended from ropes and wires drew travelers' attention. The selections included shopping baskets, egg baskets, firewood carriers, and even baby cradles typically woven from long strips of thin wood split from native white oak trees. Most vendors offered shoppers welcome refreshment with tubs of iced sodas to eke additional nickels from tourists who tarried to look at the wares. The craftspeople at Clementine not only sold at their stands but also wholesaled their baskets to other roadside vendors.[51]

As they made their way on the narrow concrete roadway past the collection of basket stands, drivers passed through the nearby community of Hooker, where the highway grades through tree-covered Ozark hills grew steeper. This rural community offered more refreshments and food at Charley Ray's Store and Camp, the Fancher Store, Odell's Grocery and Lunch Room, the Valleyview Store, and Veterans Bar-B-Q.[52]

Devils Elbow

Beyond Hooker the twisting two-lane 66 led to the Devils Elbow crossing of the Big Piney River. The site received its name long before from lumberjacks who cut local timber for making railroad crossties and floated the logs downstream tied together in "rafts" to a sawmill at Jerome. Often the timbers annoyingly snagged at this sharp bend, giving rise to its name. An impressive iron truss bridge on tall concrete piers spanned the river here in 1923, and when the road became part of U.S. Highway 66 in 1926, the link became part of its cross-country network. The steep roadways in the area created real problems, especially for truck drivers pulling heavy loads. Local pirates were known sometimes to crawl surreptitiously into the rear of struggling motor trucks, tossing boxes of goods onto the road once the drivers had started uphill; the thieves knew that the drivers could not stop once they started creeping up the steep grades. Car drivers likewise dreaded the sinuous, winding roadway. Remembering childhood trips, Bill Roseman recalled, "Devils Elbow was supposed to be the death's corner of the world," giving his dad "white knuckles ten minutes before we'd go through."[53]

DEVILS ELBOW CAFÉ

Drivers and passengers found respite in a handful of eating places at Devils Elbow, which in the 1920s developed as a minor resort destination in this scenic corner of the Ozarks. About 1932 Vernon Prewitt, who also undertook and supervised the stonework at Stony Dell for his father, erected a combined café, filling station, and store for Dwight Rench, a locally noted fishing guide. Called the Devils Elbow Café, the structure,

After traveling by train from Oregon to Detroit to pick up a new Plymouth sedan at the factory, an unidentified couple drove it via Highway 66 on a trip to the Grand Canyon on their way home. Along the way in Missouri, they stopped for lunch at the Devils Elbow Café in early December 1938 and were so intrigued with its Ozark rock construction that they took this and several other pictures. Author's collection.

with pointed stones along its entire cornice, was one of the most imaginative of all the vernacular Ozark stone commercial buildings. Through the Depression years, it served sandwiches for ten cents and plate lunches for a quarter dollar. When Rench placed the business for sale "at the end of bridge on Big Piney River and Highway 66" in 1942, he advertised that it had a large dining room, a separate café room, modern toilets, and living quarters. Other owners continued operating the restaurant for years, with the building surviving until it was destroyed by fire in the 1970s.[54]

MUNGER-MOSS SANDWICH SHOP (ELBOW INN)

Because of its natural tourist appeal, the area around the elbow bend of the Big Piney River supported a number of additional eating and drinking places. As early as 1930, for example, Nelle and Howard Munger opened a modest resort just downstream from the bridge. After Howard's death, Nelle married Emmett Moss, and in 1936 the couple opened a sandwich shop beside the bridge that they aptly called Munger-Moss. All through the Depression years, they ran the eating place specializing in "Old Kentucky Barbecue" in the out-of-the-way fishing camp fronting on the highway. By the early 1940s, the couple sold their popular eatery to a pair of former Saint Louis saloon operators, Jessie and Carl G. "Pete" Hudson, who continued the business throughout the World War II years. As was the case at other restaurants, customers carried away their own recollections of the sandwich shop beside the Big Piney. In September 1939, for instance, Mrs. Perle Lorts and her daughter, Gladys P. Robinson, of Rolla found quiet time together more memorable

than food. They were regular members of a local bridge club, but on what would have been one of their regular nights out with card-playing friends, they went instead "to Munger-Moss' at Devil's Elbow," where they dined and had "a delightful evening of 'just talk.'" Doris Witt of Springfield reported her own experiences at the eatery overlooking the scenic river: "It was a small place," she noted, but she best remembered the "fairly treacherous downhill path to the outhouse."

The Hudsons sold the sandwich shop to Nadine and Paul Thompson in 1945 and opened another barbecue restaurant in the much larger town of Lebanon. Because the Munger-Moss reputation was so well established, they took the business name with them. Back in Devils Elbow, the Thompsons changed the restaurant sign to read Elbow Inn, and they ran the enterprise into the 1960s. Subsequently the building served as a residence and stood vacant. Then after thirty years it reopened as the Elbow Inn tavern in the 1990s, becoming a favorite haunt for motorcyclists and heritage tourists driving the old pavement of Route 66. It still sells beer and barbecue.[55]

Hooker Cut

The volume of auto and truck traffic at the Devils Elbow dropped dramatically in 1945. The change took place indirectly because of the construction and then operation of Fort Leonard Wood, a huge U.S. Army training facility located about five miles toward the west. The need for easier road communication between the base and Saint Louis led the Missouri Highway Department with federal financial assistance to construct a four-lane segment of Highway 66 to avoid the bottleneck created by the restricted roadway, steep grades, and narrow bridge at Devils Elbow. As part of this bypass route, engineers supervised digging of the largest roadway rock cut ever undertaken in the United States up to that time. Excavation of the Hooker Cut removed 300,000 tons of dolomitic limestone, most of it dislodged with dynamite blasts, to create a gash ninety-three feet deep and eighty-six feet wide, a remarkable feat still visible today. To reduce the likelihood of rocks tumbling onto the roadway, engineers terraced the rock wall back to create fifteen-foot-wide horizontal "shelves" every thirty feet. The new roadway stretched about eight miles from the entrance of Fort Leonard Wood almost to the Pulaski-Phelps county line at Clementine. Later bypassed by Interstate 44, the now historic four-lane concrete pavement remains in service as Missouri State Highway Z. The project spelled the doom of the scattered roadside Hooker community, just west of Devils Elbow, where mom-and-pop businesses like Veterans Bar-B-Q had served travelers.[56]

Saint Robert

In 1940 the War Department, in anticipation of possible overseas conflict, conceived plans to create a large army training camp to serve the American Midwest. It contemplated a site in Iowa, but on December 3, 1941, announced that it would build Fort Leonard Wood in the comparatively undeveloped Ozarks near Waynesville, Missouri. The location was just south of Highway 66 near the tracks of the Saint Louis–San Francisco Railway, popularly called the Frisco Line. Local entrepreneurs immediately scrambled to rent, buy, or build facilities along the highway and in nearby Waynesville to house, feed, and entertain construction workers and then later armed service members and their families. North of the new post was a small Catholic church named in honor of Saint Robert, so the newly built-up area took that place-name. Within weeks the scattered community became a boomtown of bars, dance halls, cafés, tourist courts, and places of entertainment. Typical enterprises that came and went through the years at Saint Robert were listed in a 1957 publicity magazine. The publication promoted businesses serving soldiers and their families such as the Silver Star Restaurant, the Hi-Ho Club, Page's and Mooney's grocery stores, the Wagon Wheel Night Club, the 509 Tobacco Store, Tut's Café No. 2 (later Oakwood Café and then Sunshine Café), the Park 'n Eat Restaurant, service stations, used car dealers, and insurance agencies. At the time of this writing, the role of Saint Robert in serving military personnel stationed at Fort Leonard Wood has continued, with the area abounding with motels, eating places, nightspots, bars, liquor stores, and used car lots.[57]

Waynesville

Waynesville, four miles west of the main entrance from Highway 66 into Fort Leonard Wood, received the greatest infusion of people, money, and associated vice from the thousands of construction workers and subsequent soldiers at the post. Prior to the start of the training camp, the quiet little Ozarks town nestled in the valley of Roubidoux Creek had fewer than five hundred souls. Route 66 passed through the heart of the modest business district, its motorists bringing much of the outside income to the community. Things changed dramatically with the infusion of people in 1940, so that two years later a journalist asserted, "A great part of Waynesville just now is geared to the job of providing entertainment for soldiers." The military personnel were almost all young men, some of them away from home for the first time, and all looking for ways to enjoy themselves when they received leaves from duty. The reporter observed "a dozen or so beer parlors" quenching the thirsts of soldiers, selling them fifteen-cent bottles of beer that ordinarily cost only ten cents elsewhere. Waynesville became a boomtown based substantially on sating the thirsts and appetites of the military trainees, with its population doubling by 1950 and doubling again by 1960, as Fort Leonard Wood became a permanent training facility. From 1940 onward Route 66 travelers had to shoulder themselves through the press of humanity that sought diversion on the northern fringe of a garrison comprised of tens of thousands of men and a few women. In time Waynesville became a more stable community with paved streets, sanitary sewers, and modern schools, but its "scabtown" reputation dating back to World War II has been hard to shake.[58]

TOURIST INN (OLD STAGECOACH STOP) / BELL HOTEL

In the days before the wartime influx of people and money to Waynesville, Highway 66 motorists had a choice of two places to stay, both of them providing what travel writer Keith McCanse in 1929 described as "meals family style." The older was the Tourist Inn, a two-story wooden pre–Civil War stagecoach stop and tavern on the north side of the courthouse square. It began as a two-room dog-trot log cabin that received a wood-frame second floor and porch galleries in the 1880s. By the time that motorists began taking the Mother Road through Waynesville in the mid-1920s, the venerable

hostelry was operating as a boardinghouse offering rooms and simple meals shared by diners sitting elbow-to-elbow at big tables. It served travelers into the 1950s, but after falling into disuse and neglect, it was restored in the 1980s as the Old Stagecoach Stop local museum. The second lodging house affording food to motorists passing through Waynesville opened about 1925. It was then that Robert A. and Eva Bell expanded their home to start providing rooms to travelers coming to Waynesville for business or pleasure. Eventually their Bell Hotel grew to occupy a three-story wood-frame structure with cabins at the side. It became a destination for locals and out-of-town folk who came for chicken dinners served both at noon and in the evening. After a fire in January 1942, damage was repaired and the Bell Hotel continued operating for decades until its building was adapted to become part of a funeral home during the mid-1970s.[59]

Hazelgreen
GASCOZARK STORE (SPINNING WHEEL TAVERN)

When drivers came to the Pulaski-Laclede county line about fifteen miles southwest of Waynesville, they found Hazelgreen, a rural community scattered for about a mile along the road. On the right was a combined store, café, and filling station with the unusual name of Gascozark. In the early 1930s, Frank A. Jones purchased the property that already had a modest building. He made several additions, but the structure ended up with an unattractive irregular front. To even things up, in 1939 a stonemason "rocked" the exterior with a veneer of Ozark stone, giving the building a unified appearance. Jones already owned a small nearby resort on the Gasconade River, and he coined the business name as a combination of the words "Gasconade" and "Ozark." Over the years several people, including Rudy and Clara Schuermann, operated the eating place. By the 1950s it had become the Spinning Wheel Tavern, serving that role into the next decade before becoming a residence. At the time of this writing, the architecturally interesting building stands unused.[60]

EDEN RESORT

Crossing an iron-truss bridge over the Gasconade River in Laclede County, the two-lane brought motorists to Eden Resort, probably the most luxurious fishing lodge anywhere directly on the Mother Road. Saint Louis businessman Stanley M. Riggs sought to invest in a high-end Ozarks resort and reputedly searched the region for a location that had good fishing and a forest setting that also was easy for motorists, bus travelers, and railroad passengers to reach. The banks of the Gasconade River just beyond Hazelgreen met all these requirements, including a location fronting on Highway 66 for drivers and bus riders and convenient access for train passengers at stations in both Lebanon and Richland, Missouri. After purchasing the site, Riggs set about erecting a large central lodge building, two shower houses, and multiple brown-painted wood-frame cottages with one to five rooms each. Daily rates in the 1930s were comparatively expensive at three dollars per person or eighteen dollars a week. Riggs's managers served meals in a screened dining room the length of the main lodge, which also had indoor seating, a fireplace, and space for dancing. Highway signage advertised deluxe chicken dinners and thick, tender steaks, with cocktails

available legally after the end of Prohibition in 1933.

In 1942 Walter and Helen Dickinson became managers of Eden Resort and, after four years, purchased the property from Stanley Riggs. By the early 1950s, Eden was enlarged to about two dozen accommodation units with food still served in the main building. A local writer in 1952 described the lodge as "where fine meals are served and square dancing takes over in the evenings." The conversion of U.S. 66 into a four-lane freeway in 1956 dramatically impacted the Eden, cutting the resort off from the main highway and making it reachable only by service road. This handicap eliminated most drop-in business, though old-time customers continued returning. Son Dan Dickinson declared, "It wound up being a fishing camp." Even so, Walter and Helen continued to run the business until after Walter's death in 1971, with the widow staying on a couple of years before she closed things down. Today only overgrown ruins and foundations remain from some of the buildings, the glamorous hospitality long gone.[61]

Hazelgreen to Lebanon

All along Highway 66 through the Missouri Ozarks, motorists drove past multiple roadside businesses from tourist courts and filling stations to taverns and fishing camps. Many of them offered food ranging from groceries to full-service meals. Southwestward from the Gasconade River bridge and across Laclede County to Lebanon, for example, they came to a rock Red Ball gas station about nine miles out of Lebanon begun by a Mr. Brockman around 1933 and then purchased in 1947 by John and Ruth Riley of River Forest, Illinois. The couple expanded the station to include tourist cabins and a short-order café, operating the enterprise for almost twenty years as Riley's Court and Snack Bar. Five miles farther on, travelers came to the 4 Acre Court, another grassroots local business, which friends Ray Coleman and Blackie Waters established in 1939. The partners put a filling station, office, and café on the ground level of a two-story masonry building that had living quarters upstairs and erected a row of stone cabins behind. They served travelers for about two decades. Other such enterprises along this same fourteen-mile stretch of roadway over the years included the Blue Moon Camp, the Harbor (later Geno's) Tavern, the Skyline Café and Motel, the Vesta (later El Rancho) Court, and Scotty's Tourist City. Perhaps the best remembered eatery along this section of roadway was the Satellite Café and Truck Stop five miles northeast of Lebanon and near the Sleeper community. Known as "the Space Station," the enterprise in the 1960s and 1970s was a collaboration of Norman and Loren Alloway, who owned and operated the eatery, and LeRoy Hawkins, who ran the adjacent Phillips 66 station. In its heyday Kirk Pearce enjoyed eating at the Satellite, which he later described as "a little bitty tiny place" that had homemade pies. In his mind was stuck the image of its "kind of space ship sign" that resembled a stylized rocket.[62]

Lebanon

Lebanon was the largest inhabited place between Rolla and Springfield, with 5,000 inhabitants in 1940 and 6,800 by 1950. Highway 66 passed northeast/southwest through town on Elm Street, missing the main commercial district by about five blocks. This roadway alignment gave entrepreneurs both

space and comparatively affordable land for creating businesses to meet the needs of travelers. Although other towns like Waynesville were closer to Fort Leonard Wood, Lebanon, at thirty-five miles' distance, likewise profited from expenditures by the War Department and by military personnel associated with the post. This meant that after the Second World War many locals had money available to invest in providing food, lodging, and services to the growing numbers of Mother Road travelers. By the time that a city directory was issued for Lebanon in 1953, for example, it listed thirty-one cafés and four taverns serving Missouri foods.[63]

CHICKEN SHANTY CAFÉ (MUNGER MOSS DINING ROOM)

One of the best known of the Lebanon eating places had its beginning when Jessie and Pete Hudson sold the Munger-Moss barbecue and sandwich shop in Devils Elbow on the Big Piney River in 1945. Taking the proceeds to Lebanon, the pair used this nest egg to purchase the Chicken Shanty Café and four acres of land on Highway 66 just outside the northern city limits near several tourist courts. Because they had kept the already-established business name, Jessie Hudson reported, "We changed the name of the café from Chicken Shanty to Munger Moss, and we put in a barbecue." Quickly the eatery gained popularity among locals and travelers. Missourian Kirk Pearce became a regular customer. From those days he remembered, "Munger Moss had a Black man that barbecued for a long time. He was wonderful—it was the best barbecue you could ever ask for." In time the Hudsons expanded both the facilities and the meal choices, with the Munger Moss Dining Room offering a full daily menu as well as banquet service. While building their restaurant trade, Jessie and Pete Hudson erected multiple tourist cabins near the eatery, eventually having seventy-one units in their Munger Moss Motel. They sold the restaurant in the 1970s, but subsequent owners found themselves less able to maintain the former level of quality and service. Eventually the eating place closed and its building was removed. At the time of this writing, lodgings at the Munger Moss Motel remained a popular overnight stop for tourists traveling old Route 66.[64]

WRINK'S FOOD MARKET

Just two blocks farther down Highway 66 was Wrink's Food Market, a grocery store that became a long-favored provider of supplies to travelers. The Wrinkle family ran a resort on the Gasconade River into the 1920s and in 1929 moved to Lebanon, where they purchased the downtown Jefferson Hotel and Café. Son Glenn E. Wrinkle grew up in the hotel eating its fare, which he described as "all home-cooked." After service in the Pacific during World War II, Glenn returned to Lebanon and worked at the Jefferson. His father, however, had begun building a projected two-story hotel on the northern outskirts of town but in 1948 became ill and unable to complete the job. "I was only making $30 a week working at the Jefferson and I wanted to have some kind of business on Route 66," Wrinkle said. In 1950, with only three hundred dollars' worth of stock and no grocery experience, Glenn opened Wrink's Food Market in the uncompleted one-story brick building shell his father had erected. "I started it, and it almost ended me," he later declared. Initially Wrinkle received substantial trade from Highway 66 motorists, but that dwindled after the construction of a freeway bypass around Lebanon. Gradually the town grew northward toward his store and increased his customer base. The growing appeal of heritage travel on the former 66 Highway in the 1990s brought more out-of-town trade. Wrinkle personally managed the grocery until his death at age eighty-five in 2005. After brief unsuccessful efforts by others to reopen the store, its final contents sold at auction in 2009. Today inside the former food market, the founder's granddaughter operates an antique and specialty store with a sandwich shop in the back.[65]

ANDY'S STREET CAR GRILL

Realizing that many streamlined and narrow diners were actually adapted from former railway dining cars, Andrew Liebl of Lebanon conceived the idea of transporting two disused streetcars from Springfield to serve the same purpose. In 1946 he had the cars placed end-to-end on footings at 333 East Elm Street in Lebanon. Inside he installed kitchen equipment, counter, tables, and seating, and here operated Andy's Street Car Grill until 1961. Although Liebl served all types of sandwiches and plate lunches, the specialty of the house was his "fried domestic rabbit." Historian Kirk Pearce knew Andy's Grill when it was in operation and explained that the proprietor served only "tame rabbit," which was supposedly fatter than the wild variety. An automobile repair garage currently occupies its site.[66]

Phillipsburg
UNDERPASS CAFÉ

About twelve miles beyond Lebanon, Highway 66 passed beneath the tracks of the Saint Louis–San Francisco Railway just before coming into the hamlet of Phillipsburg. Drivers decelerated to go beneath the underpass and then bear to the left, leading local entrepreneurs Edward Lawson and O. E. Carter to erect a prefabricated filling station in 1941 just where the cars slowed down. They added the Underpass Café in 1950. The popular little eatery fed travelers and locals in the town of 170 people until the opening of a new four-lane Highway 66 bypass in 1957 diverted traffic. By the time that travelers reached Phillipsburg, they realized that they had emerged from the hilly Ozarks. In a typical observation, Viola Van Koevering jotted in her trip diary in November 1934, "From Lebanon on, we saw more farms," adding "Country quite level the remainder of the way through Missouri." Most drivers would describe the landscape as gently rolling.[67]

Conway
HARRIS CAFÉ

Quickly travelers came to a onetime culinary landmark about two miles northeast of the little town of Conway. In 1929 Marie and Byron "Barney" Harris chose this place to open a hometown café that became known up and down the Mother Road as the home of the little round pies. "They had little bitty pies. I remember them," reminisced Kirk Pearce, further recounting that they were "raisin, gooseberry, all kinds. And that brought a lot of people up there, to buy these little pies." On a trip to California, Marie had seen small meat pies and decided to copy the idea with fruit filling. And pies were by no means all that Marie prepared in this general roadside eatery, which fed customers breakfast, lunch, and dinner for decades. Oral traditions even relate that gangsters Clyde Barrow and Bonnie Parker were counted among the Harrises'

1930s customers. Byron and Marie remained in food service until retirement in 1967, but the little round pies continued, locally at the McShane Café in Conway and about seven miles down the road at the Garbage Can Café on U.S. 66 north of Marshfield. The small pastries put this area on the map.[68]

Conway to Marshfield

When the newer four-lane U.S. Highway 66 opened between Lebanon and Springfield in the second half of the 1950s, it bypassed several towns and some long stretches of the older two-lane roadway by as far as four or five miles. The newer road skirted not only Conway but also the village of Niangua and the larger town of Marshfield. All these communities had hosted eating places, filling stations, garages, and tourist courts. From the 1920s into the 1950s, the Abbylee Court and Café; the Rockhaven Service Station, including a restaurant and tavern; and Carpenter's Camp, later Oakvale Park, all offered prepared meals in Niangua. Once travelers reached Marshfield on the two-lane, they had choices of eating at Mother's Café operated for twenty years by Mary and Presley L. Bresee; the Sinclair Tourist Camp known for its pies baked by Pearl Bell; and the Skyline Café, taking its name from being built at the reputed highest elevated point for nine hundred miles along Highway 66. Half a dozen more miles down the road, motorists came to meal options at the Red Top Court Café and across the pavement at Otto's Steak House in the little Northfield community. The profusion of dining choices in Missouri must have befuddled eastbound travelers who had crossed the desert Southwest, where frequently they had driven miles and miles between places to eat.[69]

GARBAGE CAN CAFÉ

Marshfield, with almost two thousand people in 1950, offered multiple dining choices. One of the most fondly remembered local eateries, however, was actually outside of town on the 1950s four-lane U.S. Highway 66 bypass. Here Letha and Kermit Lowery opened the Garbage Can Café and adjacent Phillips 66 service station in 1952. The restaurant became a landmark from its unusual name, its wastebasket-shaped neon sign, and its homestyle food, especially its small from-scratch pies. Letha had inherited the recipes for the little, round pies from the Harris Café that had made them famous in Conway. "We baked three to four hundred pies a day," she remembered, noting that she regularly made up her pie crust dough twenty-four hours in advance to give it a crispier consistency. John Sellars, as a college student who drove between Springfield and Lebanon, frequently stopped off at the Garbage Can during its heyday. He reported, "It was a great place to eat." During the 1960s the wayside café was one of the earlier Missouri Route 66 eating places to desegregate. African American traveler Homer Boyd remembered, "Two little ladies . . . ran that place, and everything was homemade. . . . They were really nice, and the food was excellent. And you had to be very particular about where you ate because [if you were Black] you couldn't eat every place." Kermit Lowery died in 1966, but family members continued operating the Garbage Can until 1972.[70]

Springfield

As they made their way southwesterly along the Mother Road, travelers began seeing signs that they were approaching Springfield, the second largest urban center that they would encounter in Missouri. In 1950 the city boasted almost 67,000 inhabitants. Established in the 1830s, occupied by both Union and Confederate forces during the Civil War, and prospering after the arrival of important railway lines in the 1870s and 1880s, Springfield steadily grew in importance. Notably it was the location where officials from Missouri and Oklahoma in spring 1926 agreed to propose that the newly designated highway between Chicago and Los Angeles should receive the number 66. Over time several alignments of that roadway traversed the city, creating corridors of consumption that served travelers for decades as they crossed the United States. J. N. Darling passed through Springfield pulling a travel trailer in December 1936, describing the handsome city as having "a well-designed courthouse dome dominating the skyline" and business district crowded with shoppers. He contrasted it with "the tumble-down cabins on lean-looking soil which had bordered the highway."[71]

In addition to having the most people along Highway 66 in Missouri outside Saint Louis, Springfield also had the most African Americans. Originating from enslaved Africans, the Black population increased as substantial numbers of freedmen came there following the Civil War. In 1906 the city experienced a brutal lynching of three Black men followed by threats and intimidation against others. An estimated half of the African American inhabitants fled the city. The core of Black families who remained in Springfield ultimately provided welcoming lodging and food for African American travelers who otherwise likely would not have been able to stay overnight or eat in the town. These hostelries and eating places operated until the passage of federal civil rights legislation in the 1960s prohibited racial segregation of public accommodations.[72]

STEAK 'N SHAKE

The Mother Road originally turned south onto Glenstone Avenue at the northeast side of Springfield, and this thoroughfare became a prime location for erecting motels and eateries. The alignment then turned west on Saint Louis Street on its way toward the central business district, and it was on this latter artery that a notable Steak 'n Shake opened in 1962. The Steak 'n Shake restaurants came into existence on Highway 66 in Normal, Illinois, in 1935, and by 1948 their owners had expanded the hamburger and milkshake chain into metropolitan Saint Louis. By the early 1960s, the firm wanted to move farther toward the south and west, so it chose Springfield as a place for expansion. In December 1961 the company purchased a large lot at the southwest corner of Saint Louis Street and National Avenue on the City 66 route, razing the older structures there, and began construction of a rectangular, flat-roofed white-and-black masonry and glass drive-in restaurant. The company topped the standard-plan building with a two-sided bulb and neon sign reading "Steak 'n Shake" and "It's a Meal." As people attended a grand opening on June 21, 1962, they read in painted and neon lettering on the roof overhang corporate slogans like "We Protect Your Health" and "Grinding Only Gov't Inspected Beef for Steakburgers." Customers had the option to dine inside, to pick up food at a drive-up window, or to park at the side for personal ordering and carhop delivery. Sales at the initial Springfield Steak 'n Shake and another that opened farther south on Glenstone Avenue disappointed corporate directors, however,

and in 1972 they permitted longtime company employee Herb Leonard to purchase them. He invigorated both stores, making them profit leaders. A son, Gary Leonard, succeeded his father in running Steak 'n Shake restaurants in Springfield, consciously preserving the historic 1962 look of the two. With Leonard's cooperation, the store at Saint Louis and National was placed on the National Register of Historic Places in 2010. It is almost a time capsule from 1962.[73]

KENTWOOD ARMS HOTEL

Westbound half a mile on the City 66 alignment toward the central business district, motorists came to the six-story Kentwood Arms Hotel at 600 East Saint Louis Street. Erected by local business promoter John T. Woodruff in 1926, the hostelry always catered to Highway 66 travelers. Woodruff himself served as the first president of the U.S. Highway 66 Association, organized in 1927. When the Automobile Club of Southern California published its earliest guidebook to driving the Mother Road in 1932 to coincide with the Los Angeles Olympic Games, the Kentwood Arms placed an advertisement to attract trade from those traveling to the international sporting event. The Kentwood Arms was one of several multistory hotels in and around downtown Springfield during the first three-quarters of the twentieth century, others including the Colonial, the Ozarks (later Moran and then Downtown Motor Inn), and the Sansone. All of them provided food service for guests and locals, with several also offering bars and cocktail lounges. Because they were conveniently located near multiple business houses, these hostelries tended to be favored by commercial travelers over the more widely scattered tourist courts. The hotels' proximity to the 1923 Shrine Mosque Auditorium also attracted both performers and out-of-town visitors visiting Springfield for musical and dramatic entertainments.[74]

Through the middle years of the twentieth century, the Kentwood Arms was the most exclusive eating place in Springfield. Its Crystal Room was so formal that gentlemen were required to wear coat and tie for dinner. Joseph Jefferson worked as a waiter at the Kentwood Arms and later candidly stated, "It was classy because only rich people went there." In the days before air conditioning, the sixth-floor terrace garden caught even the lightest breezes, making it appealing for drinks and more casual meals. Food critic Duncan Hines endorsed the Kentwood Arms from the 1930s to the 1960s. In 1939 he advised, "If you are on your way west, better enjoy a dinner here for you will soon be in the wide-open spaces," and then in 1945 he particularly recommended its steak, Ozark rainbow trout, and braised guinea hen. The hotel provided lodging to travelers until 1968, after which time it converted to become apartments and then starting in 1983 housed students as a dormitory for Southwest Missouri State University.[75]

The Kentwood Arms Hotel became the first prominent lodging and food service in Springfield to end racial segregation. Although Missouri had passed no laws separating Blacks from whites in public accommodations, white Missourians separated themselves from Blacks by custom. Irv Logan, a Black man who grew up in the community and who had African American friends who worked at the Kentwood Arms related, "You could go to work there, but you could not lay your head down in there." A Springfield Chamber of Commerce survey of eating places in 1958 showed that of 116 eateries, only 3 run by Blacks and 26 owned by whites, many of them drive-ins without indoor seating, served African Americans. A handful of other locations would provide Black customers with food but "only in the back" or "only in one certain booth." Local white journalist Sarah Overstreet remembered the racial separation during her own childhood: "My parents and I ate at Red's Giant Hamburg on Chestnut Expressway all the time. It was a tiny hamburger joint. . . . They didn't serve Blacks." The story was the same all across town. When Vice President Richard M. Nixon's presidential campaign committee began making plans for him to speak in Springfield in mid-September 1960, they learned that the Kentwood Arms Hotel would accommodate all his entourage except for two members of the press corps who were African Americans. Local Republican leaders feared that Nixon might cancel his appearance altogether if his entire party were not allowed to stay overnight under the same roof. Consequently hotel owner Earl Moulder publicly acknowledged that segregation had caused hardship "for a great number of fine people" and stated that he would make his hotel and its eating places open to all people without regard to race. At the very same time F. W. "Bill" McClerkin, president of Heer's Department Store, officially made his entire store on the public square "open to all." His decision included Heer's exclusive sixth-floor Garden Room tearoom, for decades a popular destination for white ladies shopping downtown and theretofore inaccessible to Black customers. It would be several more years, however, before all Springfield merchants, hoteliers, and restaurateurs would cease separating the races.[76]

GRAHAM'S RIB STATION

Railroad tracks paralleled Highway 66 about three blocks north of the central business district, and during the heyday of the Mother Road most African Americans in the town resided beyond these steel rails and east of Jefferson Street. Black motorists turned north the short distance into this neighborhood in search of places where they would be made welcome for food, lodging, and automotive services. One of the reliable destinations for these otherwise shunned travelers was Graham's Rib Station at 540 East Chestnut Avenue, half a dozen blocks north of downtown. African Americans Zelma and James M. Graham opened their barbecue stand at this site in 1932, ten years later purchasing the lot. Their specialties were slow-cooked, smoked ribs, prime rib, beef, pork, and ham. Daughter Elaine remembered going to the packinghouses with her father, where "he was very particular about the quality of the meat." By the 1940s the Grahams offered inside service at a counter, tables, and booths as well as a walk-up window and, for a while, curb service. James even built an outdoor table around a hickory tree on the grounds. The eatery location made it convenient for many lunchtime customers, both white and Black, to walk to the Rib Station from the central business district. Elaine Graham reported that, according to her dad, "Everyone should be served. And the service was not separated. . . . They could sit together." For years Graham's was one of the few genuinely racially integrated eating places in Springfield.

Because Springfield offered few overnight accommodations for Blacks outside of private homes, in 1945 James and Zelma Graham erected a string of six Ozark stone cottages in a half circle behind the Rib Station. Over the years, using their counter as a registration desk, the husband and wife housed thousands of travelers from all over the United States in Graham's Modern Tourist Cabins.

The dining room filled with customers at Graham's Rib Station, Springfield, Missouri, in the 1940s. Photograph MOU-SP-2005-020_0019, courtesy of Katherine G. Lederer Ozarks African American History Collection M35, Department of Archives and Special Collections, Duane G. Meyer Library, Missouri State University, Springfield.

James and Zelma operated their barbecue restaurant from 1932 to the late 1950s, when Chestnut Street was widened into the Chestnut Expressway. The project displaced their original building, leading to a replacement concrete-block building farther back on the same lot. James suffered a fatal heart attack at the restaurant on November 28, 1957, but Zelma continued operating it for another decade, producing and bottling her late husband's popular barbecue sauce even longer. The newer building remains at the site, currently housing an Asian restaurant, and one of the 1940s tourist cabins survives nearby as a storage structure.[77]

ALBERTA'S HOTEL AND SNACK BAR

Other African American entrepreneurs saw the need to provide meals and lodging for Black travelers in Springfield. Margie Alberta Northcutt Ellis similarly realized that she could both provide a service and earn income by making clean and secure rooms available to Blacks and serving them reasonably priced meals. With a reliable income earned as a maid for Southwestern Bell Telephone Company, in the early 1950s she purchased a disused two-story wooden hospital building at 617 North Benton Avenue, a block west of Graham's Rib Station and six streets north of Route 66. By 1953 she adapted the former medical center to house a series of ten to fifteen guest rooms, a dining room, the Rumpus Room teenagers' club, a detached café, and support areas, calling the complex Alberta's Hotel and Snack Bar. Eventually she added a barbershop and a ladies hairdressing salon.

Always looking for avenues to meet the needs of her African American customers, Ellis for a while promoted and backed operation of the Crystal Palace music club.

She regularly advertised in Victor H. Green's guidebooks for African American travelers, ensuring that any Black motorists headed toward Springfield would know that they would receive a welcome in her lodgings and eateries. In time the businesswoman developed an overflow lodging facility on a ten-acre "farm" fronting on Highway 66 on the extreme west side of town, which also supplied fresh produce and eggs to the hotel and café. Because of its proximity to the Shrine Mosque Auditorium, Alberta's Hotel was able to make accommodations available to many of the Black musicians and other entertainers who came to Springfield, among them Ray Charles, Stevie Wonder, and the Harlem Globetrotters exhibition basketball team. Ellis's grandfather, an army cook during the Spanish-American War and World War I, supervised the kitchen, where guests enjoyed breakfast as part of their overnight stays. The separate café, known as Alberta's Snack Bar, faced Clay Street in its own building and served meals to both overnight guests and the general public. Homer Boyd and George Culp became regular customers, with Boyd best remembering eating beans and cornbread there, and Culp fondly recalling the chicken sandwiches and slices of apple pie. Alberta Ellis operated her hotel and café until after the passage of the 1964 Civil Rights Act, which legally ended the need for businesses like hers that catered exclusively to African Americans. She passed away in Springfield shortly thereafter in 1966.[78]

CASPER'S

The central business district of Springfield provided many customers to its downtown eating establishments like hotels, restaurants, and food vending stands. One of the

Alberta Ellis standing in front of the Snack Bar short-order grill at Alberta's Hotel in Springfield, Missouri, ca. 1960. Photograph courtesy of Ora "Cricket" Logan Collection, Accession No. SP-2017-006 (unprocessed collection), Department of Archives and Special Collections, Duane G. Meyer Library, Missouri State University, Springfield.

longest-lived of these enterprises was a chili parlor known since its founding as Casper's. The eatery began when Casper C. Lederer in August 1910 succeeded Louis Rebori in operating a fruit and confectionery shop at 213 East Walnut Street. There he specialized in fresh fruits, ice cream, candies, tobacco, and, by 1917, quick-service lunches. Since the shop was typically open until midnight and was one of the few late-night food stands in Springfield, a popular slogan became, "We can always eat at Casper's place." The confectionery and sandwich shop operated on East Walnut Street, two blocks south of the central square and Route 66, into the World War II years. Then, about the time the conflict ended, Casper relocated it for a couple of years to a site on the extreme west side of the city directly on U.S. Highway 66. In 1948 Lederer secured a lease to use a wartime surplus Quonset hut on City 66 at 1916 South Glenstone Avenue. There Casper's continued to sell sandwiches, hamburgers, and increasingly popular chili served in bowls full to the rim. Casper's followed the general custom of white-owned eating places in Springfield, and it was on the 1958 Chamber of Commerce list of eateries that refused to serve African Americans inside. After Casper Lederer died in 1972, his artist son, Charles, assumed ownership of the established café, where he had assisted his father. In 1985 the landlord at the Glenstone location announced plans to demolish the building, so Casper's relocated to another Quonset hut at 601 West Walnut, only a few blocks west of its original 1910 location. Charles Lederer died in 1985, but subsequent owners have maintained the old family recipes and special ambience of the down-home chili parlor. Many heritage

Barbecue Sauce for Spare Ribs, ALBERTA'S
HOTEL, SPRINGFIELD, MISSOURI

Alberta Ellis owned and operated Alberta's Hotel and there provided food and lodging for African Americans traveling through Springfield, Missouri. She also had a day job as a maid for the Southwestern Bell Telephone Company. When local employees of the firm compiled a cookbook in the early 1960s, she submitted the recipe for the sauce that her husband, Robert, used when grilling spare ribs at the hotel. It makes a savory but thin sauce applied to the meat "using a swab made by wrapping a clean cloth around the end of a long stick."

About a quart of sauce

1 large onion

1 clove garlic (more if desired for individual taste)

1 green bell pepper

¼ cup margarine

1 eight-ounce can tomato sauce

1 cup water

1 cup vinegar

½ cup tomato catsup

2 tablespoons Worcestershire sauce

1 teaspoon salt

Chop onion, garlic, and bell pepper. Sautee in margarine until the onions start to become transparent. Add tomato sauce, water, vinegar, catsup, Worcestershire sauce, and salt, simmering the mixture on low heat for twenty minutes. Add salt to taste if desired. Refrigerate until needed.

Robert Ellis's favorite cut of pork for grilling was spare ribs, which come from the belly area of a pig. In kitchen tests, the author found that four pounds of these raw ribs comfortably feed eight people. In cooking the meat on a grill, turn and baste the ribs with the sauce every ten minutes until browned and done at 195° F, about an hour. This internal temperature will ensure that the collagen in the meat will have begun converting to gelatin, giving ribs the desired tenderness. Once cooked, cut the ribs apart, slicing lengthwise between the bones.

Original recipe from Southwestern Bell Telephone Company, *A Direct Line to Our Favorite Recipes*, rev. ed. (Springfield, Mo.: Southworth Printing Company, 1961), 99, Special Collections, Michigan State University Library, East Lansing.

tourists consider a bowl of red at Casper's to be an essential part of experiencing historic Route 66.[79]

RED'S GIANT HAMBURG

Julia and Sheldon "Red" Chaney's colorful personalities enhanced the appeal of their forty-year hamburger stand on the highway. Popular among locals, Red's Giant Hamburg became a notable destination for travelers as interest revived in historic U.S. Highway 66 during the 1980s. The simple café with a drive-up window had its origins in entrepreneurial activity by the couple after Sheldon returned home from service in Europe as an army medic during World War II. His parents felt that their son needed to "shake off the dust from the Army," and they took him and his young bride on an overland trip from Illinois to Colorado and back. During the whole sojourn, Sheldon and his dad, Alfred C. Chaney, looked at various towns where they might want to start a small business. Springfield in the scenic Ozarks was their choice. In 1946 Alfred purchased three lots fronting on Route 66 on the western side of Springfield in the 2800 block of West Chestnut Avenue that already had a Sinclair filling station, a residence, and a three-unit tourist court. His plan was to run the cottages while his son and daughter-in-law operated the gas station, which had a small lunch counter inside.

Red Chaney had studied business administration at Bowling Green State University, and he understood the basics of running commercial ventures. He had an outgoing temperament and athletic abilities perfected on the school's tumbling team. When he came to Springfield to stay in 1947, Sheldon never hesitated to put on a show for the entertainment of customers. With wife Julia running the kitchen, Chaney became the front man. Many people remembered him wearing gym shoes and bounding over the counter to slide across the floor to tables bearing trays laden with food. He soon closed the filling station, removing a partition wall to create more space inside for diners. Even so, the eatery never had but just a few seats. When a friend began experimenting with a postwar intercom system, Red installed one so that customers could place orders from their cars and then pick up the prepared food from a window in the side of the building. He did everything possible to speed up service, during the noon rush tossing payments into a cardboard box rather than counting it into a cash register and clipping five- and ten-dollar bills with clothes pins on a wire so he could grab them to make change faster. All this took place while loud rockabilly music resounded through the tiny dining room.

From his university study, Sheldon Chaney realized that he needed to learn from experts about how to maximize his food-vending profits. He attended national and regional restaurant conventions in Chicago, where he learned that consistent profits in the hamburger business came from using high-quality ingredients and strictly maintaining portion control. Throughout the four-decade operation of the Chaneys' food business, the couple ground their own meat from all the normal beef cuts, to which they added kidney suet, described by Red as "a storehouse for minerals and vitamins." He proudly stated, "I trim and grind all the meat, and use all the fat. . . . I ball the burgers with a hand dipper because you can't run kidney suet through a machine." Also from the experts, he discovered that the best grill for hamburgers at the time was one with a nickel-plated surface. On its top Julia cooked five sizes of burgers: junior, giant, senior, jumbo, and "sooper," the last consisting of two patties on a five-and-a-half-inch bun. Sheldon also learned at the meetings which types of deep-fat fryers to use. Julia remembered, "He spent a fortune that time he went up to the restaurant convention, but it paid off in a short time." On another occasion she declared, "We could make more money than some of the big steak restaurants."

Red Chaney understood that publicity was another key to earning profits. Just after he opened the gas station, he parked an army surplus jeep in front and decorated it with a shiny whirligig that spun in the wind. The parked cars over the years changed, but he always maintained some type of movable eye-catcher. Chaney erected a tall, cross-shaped wooden sign that was intended to read "Giant Hamburger" but discovered it was too tall to clear overhead power lines. Not to be deterred, he simply cut off the bottom two letters so that the placard henceforth would read "Giant Hamburg." The name stuck, and from that time onward identified the eating place. When customers began backing their cars into the sign, he protected it by parking an inoperable pale blue-green 1955 Buick between its base and the front of the building. Inside Chaney painted the eatery according to his own tastes, making the ceiling light blue because "flies won't land on it." He covered the walls with white tinted with peach, made the seating green, and painted the floor "as much like dirt as possible" to give the décor colors people might associate with picnics. "It stimulates the appetite and people enjoy it," he quipped in the 1980s to journalist Susan Croce Kelly.

As Julia and Sheldon Chaney aged, they decided to close down their eating place. "When I get to be eighty, I'm going to walk out that door," declared Sheldon. That time came in 1984. On the last day of business, Red's cooked 721 hamburger patties while customers stood in line for their last "sooper" burgers. The buildings stood for a few years until they were razed in May 1997, just two weeks before Red Chaney himself passed away.[80]

DAIRY TOWN

Just about every substantial town through which Highway 66 passed had one or more places that specialized in hamburgers. Only a handful, however, became as well-known as Red's Giant Hamburg. Less than a mile west of Sheldon and Julia Chaney's establishment, Glen R. and Johanna N. Eicher owned and operated the Dairy Town at 3500 West Chestnut Avenue for a decade. It was one of the thousands of lesser-known hamburger stands. The Eichers moved to Springfield from Great Bend, Kansas, about 1948, and purchased a three-acre tract fronting on Highway 66 where the Cordova Motel was already operating. As a teenager, Sarah Overstreet sometimes helped the Eicher daughter, Karen, in cleaning guest rooms, and she remembered the Cordova as being a "little group of white stucco cabins with tiny radiators and Venetian blinds." In the early 1960s, Glen Eicher purchased a drive-in restaurant building and had structural movers relocate it to the corner of his motel property facing Route 66. Then, on July 12, 1964, he opened the Dairy Town drive-in, which featured hamburgers, french fries, and soft-serve ice cream. "From that time on, I had a standard forty-hour shift there," remembered daughter

Karen. She continued, "It was open until about midnight or one or two. His theory was, when the customers stopped coming, then it was time we closed." There were no regular hours in this family-run enterprise. Karen remembered, "If a football team came through town on a bus and they were hungry, you know we unlocked those doors and started working." The Eichers operated the Dairy Town until 1973, when they retired and sold the property.[81]

Springfield to Carthage

From Springfield, U.S. Highway 66 proceeded in a westerly direction just under sixty miles to the next good-sized town, Carthage. Along the way it passed through a number of small towns and villages as well as scattered rural places of business, many of which at one time or another offered food, lodging, and fuel services to motorists. These communities in order of westbound travel were Halltown, Paris Springs, Spencer, Heatonville, Albatross, Phelps, Rescue, Plew, and Avilla. Though some of them were incorporated, none of these towns had as many as two hundred residents anytime during the operation of Route 66.

Paris Springs
GAY PARITA STORE, CAFÉ AND STATION

Among the communities between Springfield and Carthage was Paris Springs, twenty-three miles from the former. It originated in the development of a mineral spring discovered in the 1850s, which in 1872 became the site of a two-story wooden hotel. Health seekers traveled to the spring's reddish orange waters seeking cures for bodily ailments. After U.S. Highway 66 was routed about half a mile south of the built-up community, people

began erecting homes and businesses at its intersection with the unpaved road north. Called Paris Springs Junction or Gay Parita, the crossroads hamlet never grew to more than a few dozen people. Around 1930 Gay and Fred Mason erected a wood-frame, white stucco store and café combination on the south side of the highway and a similarly designed white stucco filling station with cabins and a garage on the north side of the road. Both the store and the station had graceful front parapets with gently curved cornices and rectangular corner posts. The gasoline station burned in 1955, and in later years property owners Gary and Lena Turner reconstructed a replica 1920s filling station at the site of the original, now preserved by later owners, which has become an attraction for heritage tourists. The Gay Parita store and café building, for many years a residence, still stands across the road.[82]

Carthage

The generally westbound two-lane Highway 66 curved to the southwest as it approached the wooded valley of the Spring River and the outskirts of Carthage. Crossing the river on a concrete viaduct, travelers found an especially attractive town that had ten thousand to eleven thousand inhabitants throughout the period of the Mother Road. As early as 1920, a substantial flow of motorists passed through Carthage, which stood at the intersection of the Ozark Trail and Jefferson highways. These later became U.S. Highways 66 and 71 when the federal Bureau of Public Roads began numbering thoroughfares in 1926. This important road junction created a business environment that supported more tourist courts, eateries, filling stations, and auto and tire repair shops than the town otherwise might have had. This economic boost was so important that the local chamber of commerce began touting the community as the "Crossroads of America." Carthage, however, was already a well-to-do town. It was the home to many capitalists and others grown wealthy from the Tri-State lead and zinc mines located just to the southwest. Highways, railways, and an electric interurban connected the town full of gleaming mansions with the gritty mining district around Joplin and beyond, which at one time produced one-fourth of the zinc consumed by the entire world. It was claimed that Carthage in its heyday had more millionaires per capita than any other town in America.[83]

BOOTS DRIVE-IN

The junction of U.S. Highways 66 and 71 in Carthage also proved to be a magnet that attracted entrepreneurs. One of these transplants was Arthur Boots, a farm implement dealer from Independence, Kansas. His brother had prospered running a motel at Eldon, Missouri, despite the economic depression of the 1930s, and Arthur dreamed of repeating that success. Later his son, Robert Boots, related, "I remember him studying a map on the kitchen table. He was looking for two long highways that joined and run together for a certain length of time, and . . . he found it in Carthage." Arthur, wife Ilda, and son Robert relocated to Carthage, where in 1938 the couple purchased a town lot at 107 South Garrison Street, just feet away from the 66 and 71 intersection near the central courthouse square. Arthur first erected a filling station, and, using its profits, constructed the first four units of a self-built, white stucco Streamline Moderne

tourist court in 1939, later adding more rooms under the same flat roof. In time he closed the gasoline station and converted it into a motel office, calling the complex Boots Court. Not all, however, went as planned. Arthur's sunny hopes became clouded when the couple divorced in November 1940, with Ilda receiving the motel as part of her settlement.[84]

Arthur Boots ran the nearby Red's Café in Carthage for a while but in 1945 began construction of a new eating place directly across the street from his former tourist court, deciding to call it Boots Drive-In. As with the motel, he chose the still-stylish Streamline Moderne architectural style, which emphasized smooth lines and curved surfaces. Son Robert remembered, "There were never any plans or never an architect. . . . He had it in his head." The eating place opened in 1946. A few months later journalist Al de Buhr from Washington, Missouri, ate at the drive-in, which he subsequently described as "the most modern and efficient restaurant I have ever seen." He depicted the eatery as being shaped like "a rather square oval," noting that the wall surface "from three feet to the ceiling is glass, showing entire kitchen, fountain, stools and all the dispensing equipment." The efficiency inside impressed de Buhr as much as the architecture outside: "Arthur Boots, the operator and designer, shares ownership with three other men, who take over the actual operation of three eight hour shifts to keep the place a going concern 24 hours a day." De Buhr also pointed out that, as a manager, Boots understood that portion control was an important key to profits in food service: "Every piece of meat for a hamburger, or a ham and eggs plate is measured by scale." In the immediate post–World War II years, donuts became an unexpected profit center

The Boots Drive-In on Highway 66 in Carthage, Missouri, ca. 1950. Arthur Boots came to the southwest Missouri town in 1938, built Boots Court, and then operated eating places there for the rest of his life. Courtesy of Steve Rider.

for the drive-in. Sugar remained rationed when it opened in 1946, but son Robert Boots explained, "Being a veteran, I had a sugar allowance." With his ration certificates he legally purchased the sweetening, which the café staff sprinkled on hot donuts fried in a special machine. "Lord, we sold donuts till I couldn't stand the sight of one. Really. It was just phenomenal."[85]

Boots Drive-In provided more than food as the location for remote broadcasts of a live radio program most mornings. Lee Crocker, formerly an aircraft mechanic for Trans World Airlines, came to Carthage in 1947 as the manager and on-air announcer for local station KDMO. He devised the concept for a live broadcast each morning at eight o'clock from the crowded counter inside Boots Drive-In. He called it "Breakfast at the Crossroads of America." Robert Boots remembered, "He had a mellifluous voice, a deep bass voice, and he would get on the radio, and, man, he'd talk to these people from far away, and they just really loved it." Crocker, according to Boots, "was kind of a slender guy and [had] a big Adam's apple and a lovely voice." The program continued about ten years, and proved to be a boon to business at the drive-in. After just a few years, Arthur Boots sold his shares in the restaurant, and son Robert and his uncle purchased the enterprise, running it for several years and even employing Ilda, Robert's mother, as a staff member. The busy little eatery eventually left family ownership but continued in business until 1970. In the meantime Arthur Boots remained in the restaurant trade in Carthage, owning and operating the Frosty

Mug Drive-In at 315 East Central Avenue and then the Burger 'n' Shake at 411 West Central Avenue, both on old Route 66. The distinctive 1946 Boots Drive-In building still stands, currently housing the Great Plains Federal Credit Union at 120 South Garrison Street across the street from the now beautifully restored Boots Court.[86]

Carterville and Webb City

In the half dozen miles from Carthage to Carterville, the Missouri landscape changed dramatically. Green trees, fields, and pastures surrounding the former town gave way to lead and zinc mines, great piles of grey "chat" debris from underground, and smokestacks. The mining district through which Highway 66 would pass for the next fifty miles had operated since the 1870s, but exceptional demand for metals during World War I created a temporary boom during which thousands of workers and others flooded into the area. Following the war, prices plummeted for lead and zinc, closing mine after mine, leaving the broad streets of Carterville, Webb City, and Joplin seemingly deserted. The population of Carterville, for example, dropped from an estimated twelve thousand during the boom to only about a thousand in 1940. By this time, travelers saw not the hustle and bustle of former days, but instead desolate streets, smokeless chimneys, and grimy-looking buildings with boarded-up storefronts. Webb City, two miles beyond Carterville, survived the decline of the mines somewhat more successfully than its neighbor, though its population dropped as well. Even at the time of this writing, the community had approached but not regained the eleven thousand inhabitants it had in 1910. Many Route 66 travelers remembered Webb City for two sharp ninety-degree turns in the center of its business district. African Americans knew of Webb City as one of the many sundown towns along Highway 66, where Blacks were unwelcome after dark.[87]

MONTIE'S KREAMY KUP (BILL'S DRIVE-IN)

On the way out of Webb City, motorists turned south from West Broadway onto South Madison Avenue. Where it intercepted West Thirteenth Street was a long-popular ice cream, hotdog, and hamburger stand that fed many travelers. A fifty-four-year-old widow, Montie Benintendi, conceived the idea of erecting a soft-serve ice cream kiosk on Route 66 at the south side of Webb City in 1954. Her husband, Clem, had died three years before, and she tired of her long-term job as a presser and finisher at a laundry and dry cleaning shop. In April 1954 she applied to Webb City authorities for a zoning permit to build an eighteen-by-twenty-four-foot "ice cream store" at the intersection of South Madison and Thirteenth. Before officials granted permission, Benintendi had to secure consent from the majority of her prospective neighbors, with the city council giving the authorization in October. Contractor Henry F. Armstrong of Joplin proceeded to put up the concrete-block structure at 1229 South Madison, which Benintendi named Montie's Kreamy Kup. Janice Thornton, who knew Benintendi at the time, characterized Montie as a feisty woman who "wasn't scared of nobody," and who she remembered tapping on the plate-glass windows and shaking her finger at misbehaving teenaged customers in the parking lot. Montie ran the Kreamy Kup until about 1965, when she sold the business to Bill and Virginia Thornton. By this time the store occupied a rectangular building with two walk-up windows. After their purchase, the Thorntons changed the name to Bill's Drive-In, added a kitchen, enlarged the menu to include hot foods, and eventually erected an enclosed dining room with eleven booths and two ceiling fans. The specialty of the house was foot-long Coney Island–style chili-cheese hot dogs. One customer remarked, "You can get a hot dog on a bun anywhere, but it's the chili that makes it. . . . It's the best of Joplin and Webb City." In 1975 the Thorntons sold the drive-in to their son, also named Bill, and he ran the eating place for the next two dozen years, eventually closing the eatery and retiring in 1999. At the time of this writing, a Wendy's restaurant operates at the site.[88]

Joplin

Only five miles separated Webb City from the central business district of Joplin, the economic heart of the Tri-State mining district. The town came into existence after the 1870s discovery there of lead and zinc deposits on the ground's surface. Railway connections made it the major shipping point for smelted metals coming from the mines located along an arc from Missouri across part of Kansas and down into Oklahoma. As typically took place in areas of mining, the town initially attracted a high proportion of unaccompanied men together with entrepreneurs eager to sell them lodging, meals, alcohol, and good times. The most storied early eating and drinking place in Joplin, founded about 1890, was the three-story House of Lords at 319 Main Street. Its ground level housed the finest restaurant in the city; its second floor, a casino with high-stakes gaming; and the third level, a luxurious bordello. National Prohibition laws in 1920 forced the closure

of the House of Lords, but for decades other establishments satisfied the same appetites. The 1941 city directory listed 111 restaurants and cafés, as well as 28 bars and retail liquor outlets in a city of about 37,000 people. Kansas by its constitution was for decades a "dry" state, and Joplin, just across the state line in "wet" Missouri, became a destination for thousands of Kansans thirsting for alcoholic beverages and seeking other pleasures.

Joplin was one of the few places in southwestern Missouri where African American motorists could reliably find overnight accommodations. The choices, however, were limited to a handful of privately owned guesthouses, many of which also served meals. The lynching of a Black man in 1903 cast a long shadow over the African American community in Joplin. Following the killing, a white mob raged through Black neighborhoods attacking residents and burning their homes, even cutting the hoses of fire fighters so that they could not put out the flames. An estimated half of the Black residents fled the town entirely, leaving a remnant that constituted only about 2 percent of the general population. Until after the passage of civil rights legislation in the sixties, Black motorists passing westward through Joplin could find services but not so many as they had been able to obtain in places back up the road like Springfield and Saint Louis.[89]

DICK AND JOHN'S BAR

As a mining center, Joplin developed a reputation as a place for hard drinking and good times. Over the years it had hundreds of bars, many of them along or near Route 66. Sale of alcoholic beverages became illegal for thirteen years starting in 1920 due to national Prohibition, though many evaded the law.

After the ban ended in 1933, bars, taverns, roadhouses, and lounges reopened almost overnight in all the areas of the country, like Joplin, that did not have local proscriptions. A typical example on the Mother Road at 636 South Main Street in downtown Joplin was Dick and John's Bar. A partnership between tavern keepers John Davenport and Dick Metsker, it opened in 1936. The co-owners advertised the saloon, located in a narrow commercial building with tall windows and doors at the front, as "Swell," though they offered customers, in their own tongue-in-cheek words, "bad drinks, terrible foods, poor service, [and] rotten music." Although they did not advertise this offering openly, Davenport and Metsker also made gaming available; each plead guilty to charges of operating a "gambling house" in March 1937. Within a year of opening Dick and John's, Davenport had moved on to run John's Bar at 213 West Fourth. For a quarter century, he remained in the tavern business in Joplin, owning and operating such local drinking establishments as the Victory Bar, 2 Johns Bar, the Ringside Tavern, the Broadway Bar, the Pla-Mor Bar, John's House of Lords, the Kum-Bak Bar, and Mom's Rainbow Tavern.

Interior of Dick and John's Bar in Joplin, Missouri, packed with customers not long after it opened in 1936. Photograph from Production File D4757 courtesy of Lake County (Illinois) Discovery Museum, Curt Teich Postcard Archives.

The building that housed Dick and John's Bar was razed during urban renewal in the city center during the 1960s.[90]

SOUTHERN BUFFET (WILDER'S BUFFET, WILDER'S RESTAURANT, WILDER'S STEAKHOUSE)

Just five blocks south of the intersection of Main Street with West Seventh, where Route 66 turned west, stands Wilder's Restaurant, where travelers and Joplinites have gone for fine food and drink for decades. The eating place at 1216 South Main Street had its origins in the activities of a family of three ambitious pharmacists: Charles H., Jay L., and Verne Kirby Wilder. As druggists, they had legitimate access to alcohol that most other people could not legally purchase during Prohibition, and press accounts of Jay's and Vern's activities indicate that they sought ways to enhance their incomes through its illicit sales.[91] In 1930 Charles and Jay opened a branch drugstore at 1216 South Main, calling it the Southern Pharmacy. At least by 1933, Verne was working at the Southern Pharmacy; as soon as Prohibition ended in March of that year he added beneath the same roof a legal saloon also serving food called the Southern Buffet. It was here that he made the transition from pharmacist to restaurateur. Wilder's establishment became a popular resort for eating, drinking, and wagering on sports events. Verne even hired a Philadelphia Phillies baseball pitcher, Al Gerheauser, to work during his "off season" one winter in his South Main Street bar and grill. Evidence shows that the best was never too good for Verne Wilder, with his longtime chef, Bill Saulbeamer, remembering that "only the finest ingredients were used, regardless of price." Kitty Leavitt waited tables for Verne

for twenty-seven years and observed, "He was awful picky with his waitresses. Their character, manners and appearance were of utmost importance." After the U.S. Army established the Camp Crowder military training center twenty-seven miles south of Joplin near Neosho during World War II, hundreds of servicemen flooded into Joplin on weekends, seeking food, drink, and entertainment. Wilder's Buffet could always provide the first two of the three, and business flooded in. A menu dated May 30, 1942, listed T-bone, sirloin, and tenderloin steaks; chops; cutlets; fresh- and saltwater fish; multiple egg dishes; salads; and homemade pies. The bar offered customers a full range of cocktails, fizzes, sours, cognacs, rums, wines, champagnes, liqueurs, sherries, and port. The back of the menu advertised that Wilders, as the "sporting headquarters," made available the results of all major athletic events "by direct wire" in real time.[92]

Wilder's had a shady side that only some of its customers knew. For the majority of people, it was "one of the best restaurants in town," but this activity was on the ground level. Upstairs, on the private second floor, Vern Wilder operated a casino room for years, which was a publicly known secret. The game room was an on-and-off operation that was "on" most of the time but conveniently "off" whenever the police might happen to raid. George Turner of Springfield gamed in the casino in 1957 and described how he got inside. Access was via the Southern Cigar store, adjacent to the restaurant. According to Turner, "I . . . went behind the cigar counter through a door, then down a long corridor to a door with a buzzer," which was controlled by an employee back at the cigar counter.

"After entering this door you continue down the hall to the stairs that wind up to the right to a steel door, which was opened. The stairs turn toward the street and at the top of the stairs you open a door into the gambling room, which has a small bar at the left." Here, for years, the high rollers of the Tri-State mining district enjoyed choosing among multiple games of chance. The direct wire with athletic game scores, advertised on the back of the restaurant menu, actually existed to facilitate betting on the sporting events. This upper floor was the scene of a still-unsolved gangland bombing about eight o'clock on the night of Thursday, September 3, 1959. Unknown parties detonated an estimated five sticks of dynamite on the roof above Verne Wilder's office, injuring six people and killing a restaurant employee. No one was ever indicted for the blast. In time, gambling at Wilder's came to an end, but its legacy remains a topic of interest to Joplin historians.[93]

Spending approximately $50,000, Verne Wilder enlarged and remodeled his popular restaurant and bar in 1946. He accomplished the goal by expanding into adjacent buildings, creating an eating place with banquet facilities that reputedly could seat as many as 750 people. During this time he renamed the business Wilder's Restaurant. The former pharmacist ran the eating place into the 1970s, when he retired. Others continued the operation until Marsha and Mike Pawlus purchased it in 1996, renaming it Wilder's Steakhouse. Marsha's father, Kenneth Smith, had worked there years before. "My father peeled shrimp in the alley," she said, adding, "and ran it up to the gamblers." The restaurant still is known as the one of the premiere eating places in Joplin and is a destination for

many modern motorists making the Route 66 trek.[94]

STATE LINE MERCANTILE (PADDOC LIQUORS)

Heading out of downtown, drivers proceeded westward on West Seventh. Locals knew the immediate neighborhood along Seventh as "The Strip" from its many bars and nightspots, though the thoroughfare also was home to many of the motels and other businesses serving motorists. Continuing on, the travelers passed the 160-acre Schifferdecker Park, donated to the city by mine owners in 1930. The urban landscape opened up briefly before becoming congested again as the roadway approached the Kansas state line. The constitution of the Sunflower State for years prohibited the sale of alcoholic beverages. Since bars and stores on the Missouri side of the boundary were the nearest places where many Kansans could buy beer, wine, or liquor, a number of enterprises sprang up and thrived in this neighborhood informally called Central City. The neighborhood is so quiet and out-of-the-way today, it is difficult to imagine its former role as a hot spot for drinking, eating, and partying.[95]

Congregated in the small area just east of the Kansas-Missouri state line, interspersed with residences, are the mostly disused buildings that formerly housed such enterprises as the State Line bar and grill, Harry's Super Station, and Gillead's Barbecue. Best preserved among these historic business places is the State Line Mercantile. The liquor package store was actually founded in 1925 as a combined gasoline filling station and grocery store by Harry Gray and Fred Archer, owners of the nearby Oasis Night Club. As soon as Prohibition ended in 1933, they speedily added sales of retail liquor, which represented the bulk of business. Across the entire west end of the rectangular wood-frame building, facing Kansas, large block lettering read, "STATE LINE MERCANTILE" and "PACKAGE LIQUORS." Conrad L. Ricker and two Army Air Corps buddies from the Chicago area were recently discharged from the armed forces in Amarillo, Texas, in October 1945, when the three piled into a 1940 Ford and headed home to the Windy City, taking turns driving around the clock. Ricker recollected, "We crossed into Missouri at Joplin and spotted a large beer sign that covered a tavern's entire outside wall. Being thirsty and a little hungry, we couldn't resist stopping for refreshments." One can only speculate that the State Line Mercantile may indeed have been where they paused. As early as 1952, the store came to be known as Paddoc Liquors, taking the name from the nearby Paddoc Stables, and it continued operating in the same structure under that name until closing recently.[96]

On into Kansas

Just beyond the bars, package liquor stores, and clubs, the surface on two-lane Highway 66 changed from concrete to asphalt. The differences in paving marked where Missouri road maintenance ended and Kansas highway upkeep began. The Sunflower State lay just to the west, where drivers quickly crossed a small concrete culvert. Ahead of them lay the prospects of good eating in Galena, Baxter Springs, and at the Spring River Inn outside tiny Riverton.

....

KANSAS

The Sunflower State of Kansas boasted just thirteen miles of U.S. Highway 66, but it offered travelers views that ranged from the dirty, dusty, and polluted landscape of lead and zinc mines to green woods and the clear-flowing Spring River. In 1926 transportation planners routed federal highways along preexisting paved roadways where possible, and the mining activity in the Missouri-Kansas-Oklahoma Tri-State district had already led to constructing the desired pavement across the southeastern corner of the state. This meant that the area saw heavy cross-country traffic on the Mother Road until 1957, when a new four-lane highway connected Joplin, Missouri, with the Will Rogers Turnpike in Oklahoma, bypassing Kansas entirely.

As old-time drivers rolled from the concrete pavement in Missouri onto the black asphalt of Kansas, they entered more of the eerie moonscape created by lead and zinc mining that they had already traversed on the east side of Joplin. When Ellen and Herb Tappenbeck drove on Route 66 in 1947, she penned, "What I saw of Kansas I didn't like. Too barren and the towns are so dismal looking." From the state line to Galena, about a mile and a half, the couple passed through an industrial environment of mines, piles of waste, ore processing mills, and terrain denuded of trees used as timbers to prop up underground tunnels and workings.

Galena

Motorists westbound into Kansas came first to Galena, named for galena lead ore. They turned south onto the main street at the north end of the commercial district. The community had boomed from the 1870s until after World War I, when dropping prices for lead and zinc coincided with exhaustion of the richest deposits. From an estimated thirty thousand people during its heyday, the population dropped to about four thousand by 1940, with even fewer today. Because the earth beneath the town had been honeycombed with tunnels from mine workings, some no more than fifty to sixty feet underground, property throughout the built-up area of the town occasionally sank slowly into the ground without warning. The semi-abandoned community, lined with formerly occupied homes, became a shell of its former self. Eastern motorists saw what must have resembled the set for a Hollywood western movie, with a main street lined with mostly unoccupied false-front buildings, their tops frequently ornamented with decorative sheet-metal cornices.[1]

GREEN PARROT INN (NINA'S GREEN PARROT)

Travelers found a handful of eating and drinking places in Galena, one of the longest lasting being the Green Parrot Inn. The abundance of disused commercial buildings fronting on Main Street during the middle years of the twentieth century made it comparatively easy for entrepreneurs of limited means to open businesses. James Vernor Thomas was one of these enterprising individuals. The Kansas state constitution of 1880 outlawed the production, transportation, and sale of all alcoholic beverages, but a new law in 1937 defined beer with 3.2 percent alcohol or less as being a cereal malt beverage and thus legal. Thomas applied for and received a legitimate license for the sale of 3.2 beer and in 1942, inside a two-story, fifty-year-old brick building at 317 South Main Street, opened the Green Parrot Inn. The tavern sported not only a live parrot but also a pet monkey that drank beer right out of customers' mugs. The bar offered more than lightweight beverages. For regulars the proprietor also had a private back room where they could imbibe illegal hard liquor. The owner's nephew, Jerry Thomas, remembered car trips to Joplin: "We loaded cases of whiskey, gin, and vodka into the spacious trunk and back seat of Uncle Vern's LaSalle and transported the load back across the State Line." Young Jerry at the time asked his uncle how he finagled the illicit sales, to which he candidly replied, "I made substantial contributions to the Sheriff's election campaign, and I make regular monthly payments to the Police. They look the other way; they don't bother me."

After a few years, James Roy Green and wife Nina purchased the tavern, with Nina becoming full-time manager after her husband's death in 1952. She ran the taproom until selling the enterprise in 1981. The barroom made the widow more-than-modest profits because it unexpectedly became a destination for college students from neighboring states. They flocked to her strategically located barroom in the southeastern tip of Kansas because the legal drinking age for beer there was only eighteen, whereas in both Missouri and Oklahoma it was twenty-one. The Green Parrot remained in business until 2006, during its last ten years being the only tavern left serving the public in Galena. The next year it achieved momentary national notoriety when, over a twenty-four-hour period in July 2007, its building slipped into a sinkhole created by the collapse of an underground mine tunnel. Local authorities filled the hole with bricks and other remaining rubble, leaving the site a vacant lot.[2]

Riverton
SPRING RIVER INN

At the south end of the threadbare commercial district of Galena, travelers turned west. For a while they left behind the cinder-covered wasteland of mines and ore reduction mills, driving about three miles into the alluring wooded valley of the Spring River. Unlike most watercourses in the state, which ordinarily ran muddy, this stream flowed over a rock bottom that made for clear waters. Highway 66 crossed the waterway on a multiple-arch reinforced-concrete bridge. For years the timbered valley had attracted summertime pleasure seekers, including some who erected substantial homes like that of B. F. Steward on the west bank in 1902. Three years later he sold the property to become the Country Club of Joplin, Missouri, and for a quarter century the site became one of the elite social centers for the entire Tri-State region. The Great Depression forced closure of the club, with the big house again becoming a private residence. In 1952 June and Gates Harreld purchased the property, conveniently just a quarter mile north of Highway 66. They converted the large dwelling into a restaurant and event center with six private dining rooms, calling it the Spring River Inn. The Harrelds were succeeded in 1970 by Judy Birk and then in 1994 by Dewayne and Lavern Treece and their daughter and son-in-law, David and Kay Graham. A popular stop for many cross-country motorists, the inn became noted for its almost overpowering thirty-five-foot-long buffet table loaded with homestyle foods and desserts. Especially remembered was its cinnamon pull-apart bread. The restaurant served meals until 1996, burning to the ground two years later.[3]

WILLIAMS' STORE (EISLER BROTHERS' OLD RIVERTON STORE, NELSON'S OLD RIVERTON STORE)

Less than a mile west of the Spring River on Highway 66, motorists came to another type of food-vending enterprise, one more suited to less well-heeled travelers. Here the Riverton Store sold groceries and cold-cut sandwiches to generations of locals and travelers. The enterprise sprang to life on the north side of the old two-lane about 1920, when Lora Leona Williams and husband Leo opened a small diner and filling station on the east-west roadway through Riverton. A tornado destroyed the place of business in 1923, and thereafter the Williamses erected the current flat-roofed, hollow ceramic tile store with an open-sided canopy and gas pumps in the front. The sales area occupied the east half of the structure, and living quarters took up the west side. In 1933 Leo and Lora enclosed the front, creating a protected breezeway for selling fresh produce, being one of the last structural changes to the facility. The roadside enterprise became known as a reliable stop for groceries, sandwiches, and soda pop for decades. The Williams couple jointly operated the business as well as other local ventures until Leo's death in 1948. Lora then assumed full management until retirement in 1970, with family members maintaining operation until Joe and Isabel Eisler bought the enterprise in 1973. Their nephew, Scott Nelson, assisted, and he purchased the business in 2010, continuing its operation as Nelson's Old Riverton Store at the time of this writing. Visitors find their senses almost overpowered as they push open the screen door, walk into the emporium, and see traditional groceries and merchandise on all sides while breathing in the aromas of fresh bread, cheese, vinegar, and smoked meats. It is no wonder that virtually every foreign tourist driving the Mother Road includes a stop for the old-time country store experience in Riverton.[4]

Baxter Springs

From Riverton motorists drove west and then south six miles into Baxter Springs, the last town they would see in Kansas. Most of the way they saw fields and woods, crossing two small streams on single-span arched reinforced-concrete bridges. The town of

Baloney and Cheese Sandwich,

OLD RIVERTON STORE, RIVERTON, KANSAS

For decades staff in the Old Riverton Store made custom sandwiches from ingredients in its refrigerated meat and cheese cooler, but then the practice waned after the mid-twentieth century. Owner Scott Nelson resumed sandwich making in the 1980s and told the author, "I have been selling baloney and cheese sandwiches to some of the same customers for over thirty years." The secret to this popularity is freshness. He explained, "We don't cut anything until we receive an order."

One sandwich
2 slices white bread
4 or 5 thin slices baloney (bologna) (freshly sliced)
2 medium-thick slices of American cheese (freshly sliced)
1 teaspoon Miracle Whip salad dressing

Using a disc-style cutter, carve off 4 to 5 thin slices, about 2 ½ ounces, of baloney (bologna) from its tube-like sausage. (Do not preslice this lunchmeat, because exposure to the air alters its taste.) Using a similar slicer, cut 2 medium slices of American cheese.

Spread Miracle Whip on 1 slice of white bread. Place sliced baloney and cheese on the bread, putting the second piece of bread on top. Insert the completed sandwich into a paper sack and serve with a prepackaged bag of commercial potato or corn chips and a bottle or can of an alcohol-free beverage.

Imagine that you are seated in summertime shade at one of the tables beneath the canopy at the front of the Old Riverton Store on a Wednesday, when baloney and cheese sandwiches typically sell at a special reduced price.

Original recipe from Scott Nelson, owner of the Old Riverton Store, in oral history interview with T. Lindsay Baker, July 24, 2013.

about four thousand people welcomed travelers with tree-shaded residential streets and a busy commercial district. The Civil War history of the area included a massacre of several dozen Union troops by William Quantrill's irregular Confederate partisans in 1863. The incident likely seemed foreboding to many Black motorists, who knew they would soon cross the state line into Oklahoma only a couple of miles beyond Baxter Springs. There the customary racial segregation in eating and lodging they had experienced crossing Illinois, Missouri, and Kansas would become separation of the races reinforced by state law.

PORTLAND CAFÉ (BLUE CASTLE CAFÉ)

The Portland Café, later known as the Blue Castle Café, served locals and travelers in Baxter Springs as early as 1918. Charles Beavers founded the eatery, which operated for years at 1109 Military Avenue. George Lewis purchased the Portland in 1920, and he and wife Loretta ran it for over two decades. Then Frank VonArx acquired the business in 1946, renaming it the Blue Castle Café. He quickly sold to Frances and Ralph Adams, who became the second set of longtime wife-and-husband owners. Under their guidance, the Blue Castle became an important stop for diners who sought meals like hamburgers, fried shrimp, and special deep-fried boneless turkey strips prepared similarly to modern-day "chicken tenders." During the early years, however, the Adamses struggled to make ends meet, relying on the proceeds of their pinball machines, which allowed wagering to help earn necessary revenues. Ralph remembered, "Those machines helped a lot during the lean times. They helped us get through those first years." After a decade in 1957, the couple had saved enough money to purchase and renovate the old Ritz motion picture theater just down the block at 1145 Military Avenue. They converted the two-story building into a new Blue Castle with forty street level seats in the front and forty-eight more spaces in the rear, used mostly for luncheon and dinner meetings. A menu from the mid-twentieth century shows fried chicken, catfish, and pork chops together with sandwiches, salads, and desserts as typical fare. In 1980 Frances and Ralph Adams retired, and their location in the former Ritz Theater again became a venue for screening motion pictures.[5]

On into Oklahoma

From Baxter Springs it was a mile to the state line with Oklahoma. Drivers exiting town reentered another area of visible lead and zinc mining activity punctuated with dusty "hills" of piled-up waste "chat" excavated from underground. For years the boundary with Oklahoma could be spotted from a distance by a little "State Line" filling station and a few threadbare shacks where vendors sometimes peddled local mineral specimens. A change in the pavement and a white wooden sign with black lettering marked the actual boundary.[6]

CHAPTER 4

OKLAHOMA

When travelers arrived in Oklahoma from Kansas, they entered a still-quite-young state, having joined the union in 1907. Outsiders often felt that Oklahoma retained some of its rough edges from frontier days, a sense reinforced by its wide-open spaces. The region had come to the United States in 1803 as part of the Louisiana Purchase, and within three decades its eastern areas had become known as the Indian Territory reserved for Native Americans. It opened to non-Indian settlement starting in 1889 but grew slowly and had barely two million people by the mid-twentieth-century heyday of the Mother Road. Except for areas around Tulsa and Oklahoma City, the route motorists took on Highway 66 was thinly populated by descendants of Native tribes and by both white and Black residents.

Highway 66 took drivers from the extreme northeast corner of Oklahoma southwestward to Tulsa, a known petroleum production hub and its second-largest city. From there the two-lane continued westward to Oklahoma City, the state capital and principal population center. The journey thus far passed through gently rolling occasionally wooded areas, but then it headed westward onto the semiarid, grass-covered plains. Travelers saw trees decrease in size and number until the landscape became open undulating prairie with mostly grass. Farms and ranches noticeably grew larger where the increasingly semiarid land became less productive. The farther motorists proceeded, the fewer people they saw. During the 1950s the four-lane Turner and Will Rogers Turnpikes between Missouri and Oklahoma City bypassed the old road, later becoming designated Interstate 44. Subsequently Interstate 40 in stages replaced Route 66 westward to the Texas state line.[1]

In Oklahoma travelers encountered legalized separation of the races, the first they experienced along the route. The initial session of the new Oklahoma legislature in 1907 began passing laws to ensure that whites and Blacks were kept apart, and within eight years it expanded the statutory division to include schools, public transportation, restaurants, and even hospitals. African American motorists already were aware of discrimination in lodging and dining in Illinois, Missouri, and Kansas, but in Oklahoma the separation was by state

Family of Oklahoma migrants eating lunch on the roadside in June 1939 while they studied maps showing the way west. Photograph by Russell Lee, Farm Security Administration, call number LC-USF33-012276-M5 [P&P] Lot 524, courtesy of Library of Congress, Washington, D.C.

mandate. Westbound travelers also found similar statutes in Texas, and only escaped Jim Crow segregation laws when they passed into New Mexico. Many Black visitors from the East already had traversed communities where African Americans were not allowed to stay overnight, and these sundown towns abounded across Oklahoma. A Black Missourian who traveled the Mother Road during these days cautioned, "You don't want to go into Oklahoma and stop."[2]

Kansas State Line to Commerce

From a filling station and modest wooden sign marking the Kansas-Oklahoma state line, drivers continued south and west to the village of Quapaw. Noted for its historical association with the Quapaw Indians of the Mississippi Valley, the predominately non-Indian town was organized in 1891. It experienced short-lived prosperity during the World War I era from nearby lead and zinc mines, reaching a population high of 1,400 people in 1920. The figure dropped to fewer than a thousand by 1950. For a time the community offered lodging in the modest Gateway Hotel. Breadwinners for local families during the Great Depression sought work in the intermittently operating mines, supplementing their earnings by farming the thin soil. In July 1939 writer Ned DeWitt observed, "Those families who are unable to obtain work . . . place signs in the windows of their homes . . . 'Homemade Pies and Cookies,' and the like," in hopes of making sales to passing motorists.

A young black man drinks from a racially segregated water canister at the streetcar station in Oklahoma City in 1939. Photograph by Russell Lee, Farm Security Administration, call number LC-USF33-012327-M5 [P&P] Lot 540, courtesy of Library of Congress, Washington, D.C.

The roadway in this first stretch of the Mother Road in Oklahoma created memories for many motorists. Viola Van Koevering drove this way in a Model A Ford on November 2, 1934, jotting down, "Roads were quite bad for about the first 50 miles in Oklahoma. We could not drive much faster than 25 miles per hour and sometimes not that fast." That very same autumn, however, Zephine Humphrey and her husband also motored the Mother Road southwestward from Kansas, and they saw things differently. She penned at the time, "People had told us that we would find Oklahoma monotonous . . . but it did more to refresh us than any State we had yet seen." She reported how the pavement became arrow-straight, in her words, "an immeasurable bee line humming away from beneath our wheels to a couple of vanishing points on the horizon before and behind." A dozen years later Jack D. Rittenhouse scratched out on a yellow pad as he drove 66 across northeastern Oklahoma, "The road for the next 100 miles is good; with wide shoulders, generally grassy," adding, "The hills are low, the countryside almost flat and with patches of wood."[3]

Commerce

Like many other towns in the Tri-State lead and zinc mining district, the town of Commerce was already suffering economic decline by the time Highway 66 was routed through its center. The population reached 2,608 in 1930, but seventy years would pass before it again achieved that level. Baseball great

Mickey Mantle grew up in Commerce and gave it notoriety through the middle years of the twentieth century, even though its businesses mostly withered.

BLACK CAT CAFÉ

About 1925 Commerce local Dorothy Saffell opened the Black Cat Café on the main street and ran it for years, later passing the business to her son, Riley, and daughter-in-law, Edna. Like thousands of other main street cafés along Highway 66, the eatery featured three meals a day as well as plate lunches and short-order sandwiches. In 1933, years before common use of air conditioning, Riley added an open-air dining area "in order that his customers may enjoy the cool of summer evenings." For much of its early history, the Black Cat catered to night motorists, serving meals around the clock or at least late into the evening. As a teenager, Mickey Mantle enjoyed hanging out at the Black Cat in the late 1940s, remembering, "I used to spend my Saturday nights there, watching the tourists go in and march out. It was the only joint in town that had a neon sign." In 1954 Riley Saffell advertised, "Black Cat Café in Commerce for sale or trade for acreage," adding "Selling on account of health." Operations passed to Margie and Glenn Dawson, with the eatery remaining in business at least into the 1960s, after which it burned.[4]

Miami

Miami (pronounced "My-am-uh") marked the end of the Tri-State lead and zinc mining district. A writer in 1936 noted, "Tourists are attracted by the mountains of chat, large piles of rock and . . . cave-ins visible from U.S. Highway 66." The town came into existence in the 1890s and boomed from mining. That prosperity brought a population of eight thousand people by 1930, plus seven hotels, some of them multistory, as well as a magnificent vaudeville and motion picture showplace, the Coleman Theater. When lead and zinc mines began shutting down, Miami escaped the depopulation experienced elsewhere by the 1945 opening of a massive B. F. Goodrich tire plant that buoyed the local economy for another forty years. During this time, between 1954 and 1962, Miami curiously became known as a "marriage mill." Oklahoma allowed immediate weddings after the issuance of marriage certificates, whereas Missouri, Arkansas, and Kansas all required three-day waiting periods. With Miami positioned in the extreme northeastern corner of Oklahoma close to the other three states, it became a destination for thousands of couples seeking to wed quickly. Most of them came to its courthouse, justices of the peace, and wedding chapels by automobile. The Mother Road traffic passed through the center of town until the opening of the four-lane Will Rogers Turnpike from Missouri to Tulsa in 1957. The two-lane road retained the official U.S. Highway 66 designation until it was decommissioned and the newer expressway was renamed Interstate 44.

Miami was not welcoming to Black motorists. It was the first of several sundown towns in the state where the white inhabitants prohibited African Americans from staying after dark. No hotels or tourist courts provided accommodations for Blacks. After the opening of the Will Rogers Turnpike, Joseph Jefferson, an African American traveler from Springfield, Missouri (where he had worked at the Kentwood Arms Hotel), experienced the misfortune of having car trouble just outside town, where he knew "[you] didn't let the sun go down and catch you." Jefferson managed to find a ride back to Joplin, Missouri, where he found lodging, while he left the vehicle in the hands of white mechanics in Miami overnight. He reported, "I had it fixed there, and went back, rode the bus back to get it" and continued his journey.[5]

THE KU-KU (WAYLAN'S THE KU-KU)

In the mid-1950s Ray Kroc proved that profits could be made through assembly-line preparation and sale of inexpensive hamburgers when he franchised the methods developed earlier by the McDonald brothers. His success convinced entrepreneurs across the nation that they, too, could do the same. Among these businesspeople was Arthur E. Bradley of Salina, Kansas, who in 1964 chartered The Ku-Ku, Inc., and that year began selling franchises for The Ku-Ku fifteen-cent hamburger drive-ins. In time about fifty distinctive multigabled eateries sprouted across the central Great Plains and Midwest, each one with a giant fiberglass bird that regularly through loud speakers cried "coo coo." One of these stores opened in 1965 at 915 North Main Street on the old Highway 66 business route through Miami. Inside were hamburgers for fifteen cents, french fries for fifteen cents, and milkshakes for twenty cents. In time The Ku-Ku chain collapsed, but in 1973 Gene Waylan purchased the Miami drive-in and since that time has operated it as Waylan's The Ku-Ku. Although the oversize Ku-Ku bird no longer sounds his cry, he still perches on the front beckoning to heritage tourists who consider the drive-in to be an essential stop as they make their way along old Highway 66. This survival is the last intact Ku-Ku drive-in in the country. Owner Gene Waylan proudly declared, "About every day someone is taking pictures of the place."[6]

Afton

BUFFALO RANCH

In the early days of Highway 66, motorists exited Miami taking a series of zigzags south and west through the countryside. The roadway was paved in 1922, but to quite different standards than those of today. The surface consisted of a reinforced-concrete base nine feet wide with curbs on each side, the middle being filled in with rock asphalt. Known as the "sidewalk highway," the narrow track carried Mother Road traffic until it was replaced in 1937 with a standard twenty-foot-wide concrete roadway along a more direct route. Two miles before reaching Afton, from 1953 to 1997 drivers passed a tempting roadside attraction called the Buffalo Ranch.

In the early 1950s Kansas transplants Aleene and Russell Kay entered what they termed the "tourist business." They considered four potential locations, deciding on the area south of Miami where U.S. Highway 66 came together with U.S. 59, 60, and 69. The location had lots of traffic. The gimmick that would bring them customers would be bison. They purchased seven head from a Texas breeder and erected a curio stand as the first of an eventual four buildings. Big black-on-yellow painted signs read, "Buffalo Ranch." The Kays sold Wild West novelties in the shop, but viewing the bison was free. "We opened with the idea that we wouldn't charge to look at the animals because if people had to pay, too many children wouldn't be able to see them," Aleene later explained. Over time they added a western wear store, the Chuckwagon Barbecue restaurant with family-style meals, and the Dairy Ranch ice cream and sandwich stand. Russell died after a decade, but Aleene continued to run the attraction on her own, later remarrying Leo Albro. Betty Wheatley purchased the Dairy Ranch, operating the seasonal drive-in eatery serving regular hamburgers, buffalo burgers, soft drinks, and ice cream. The Buffalo Ranch closed in 1997, and, after half a dozen years, a new owner bulldozed the old buildings and in their place opened a large truck stop/convenience store under the same Buffalo Ranch trade name.[7]

Vinita

GRAND CAFÉ

If African American motorists entering Oklahoma had not yet experienced institutional racism, they felt it as they approached Vinita, fifteen miles southwest of Afton. There, at the side of the Mother Road in the late 1930s and 1940s, octagonal signboards patterned after stop signs beckoned to the Grand Café just ahead, proclaiming, "Eat N[—] Chicken." According to a menu used in the eatery, this dish was a fried half chicken served with fried potatoes, fresh roll, butter, and honey. (The combination was likely copied from the contemporary "Chicken in the Rough" dinners already popularized in Oklahoma City by restaurateurs Beverly and Rubye Osborne.) Dripping with condescension, the menu read, "When Colored folk eat chicken . . . they avoid bother with silver service—they eat as nature had intended, and is most practical, with the use of the hands," so the restaurant served this chicken meal without utensils. By state law in Oklahoma, the restaurant separated the races, so it invited only whites into the dining area.

The Grand Café fed generations of white diners at the side of Highway 66. It opened around 1912, about the same time that Walter E. and Ella Updegraff came to Vinita from Arkansas and purchased the competing Boston Café. After running it about three years, in 1916 they sold the Boston to purchase the Grand at 117 East Illinois Avenue. The enterprise prospered, but Walter passed away in 1922 at age forty-six. His death left Ella to supervise everything in the restaurant. She developed her own reputation not just for

A crowd of all-white diners enjoying a meal at the Grand Café in Vinita, Oklahoma, ca. 1960. Courtesy of Eastern Trails Museum, Vinita, Oklahoma.

her coordination of the business activities but also for her mastery of commercial cooking, especially pies. In addition to sales in the restaurant itself, Ella baked pies she packed for Frisco Railway dining cars stopping at Vinita. On July 10, 1933, the Ripley's Believe It or Not newspaper column featured a drawing of Mrs. Updegraff and a brief description of her preparation of a reported sixty pies every day in just forty-five minutes. During most of these years, the Grand Café served the public around the clock, doubling as the Greyhound bus station. Menus show that it sold the offensively named chicken dinners at least between 1938 and 1952. (It was in 1942 that dramatist and cinematographer J. Richardson Jones photographed the racially derogatory roadside advertising, and in 1943 he forwarded prints to the National Association for the Advancement of Colored People in Washington, D.C.) Ella Updegraff retired in 1947, turning the Grand Café over to her children. Ownership passed through two other owners by the early 1950s, when Archie and Lanoe Wilson purchased the eatery, running it for another eighteen years. In about 1969 the café sold to the first of another three sequential owners, after which it closed, and its contents were dispersed at auction in the 1970s. In 1989 the block of commercial buildings across from city hall where the Grand Café had operated was razed to make way for a new McDonald's fast-food eatery.[8]

CLANTONS CAFÉ

Clantons Café at 319 East Illinois Avenue in Vinita is the most recent of several Clanton family-run eating places in the town. The eateries began in 1927 when Grant "Sweet Tator" Clanton opened the Busy Bee Café. His grandson, Tom Clanton, explained to the author, "He couldn't make a living farming, so he took a skillet and opened a place on the main street on 66." Clanton continued, "My dad started his own [café]. I had two aunts that had restaurants. They had two here and one in Claremore." By 1930 there was a bona fide eatery named Clantons Café in Vinita, and in 1946 family members shifted it to the current location, the next year erecting a new structure. Though remodeled after a 1998 fire, the historic 1947 building remains the core of the existing restaurant, marked by a historic neon sign with the one word "EAT" in block letters. Through the years Clantons Café gained a reputation not only as a place to find good cheeseburgers and chicken-fried steak, but also as a destination featuring calf fries, which are breaded and deep-fried cattle testicles. This food specialty has been showcased at an annual festival in the town since 1979. At the time of this writing, Grant Clanton's great-granddaughter and her husband, Melissa and Dennis Patrick, constituted the fourth generation of family members continuing old-time food traditions in Vinita.[9]

GLASS HOUSE

The four-lane Will Rogers toll road between Joplin and Tulsa opened in June 1957. Even as the turnpike was under construction, officials in the state capital contemplated how to welcome motorists to Oklahoma with something more than just toll booths after the Missouri state line. Highway authorities employed architects Hudgins, Thompson, and Ball to design for a site at the southeast side of Vinita the first-ever restaurant to be built over a super highway. The plans called for a giant reinforced-concrete arch one hundred feet long and seventeen and a half feet above the pavement to house a restaurant with gasoline stations at ground level on both sides. No one anywhere had ever erected such a structure. The Continental Oil Company built the striking building and thereby received a lease to operate its commercial outlets for twenty-five years. Construction began in 1956, and on January 31, 1958, the unusual facility opened with Conoco filling stations at each end and the Glass House restaurant on the upper level with automobiles zooming beneath. International Host held the initial food service contract from 1958 to 1974, followed by the Howard Johnson Company for the next decade. The eating place featured sit-down meals, but, as a local resident remarked, "People wanted to eat and get the hell down the road." They did not come to Vinita for leisurely, table service meals. By 1987 it seemed that no firms were interested in contracting for the space where predecessors had lost money. The McDonalds Corporation, however, saw dollar signs where others could envision only losses. Its executives viewed the arched structure over what had been designated Interstate 44 as a spectacular setting for selling bargain-priced hamburgers, french fries, and other fast foods. In 1988 the firm took over, creating what at the time was the world's largest McDonald's restaurant. The exceptional building aged and gradually began looking worn, and the Oklahoma Turnpike Authority consequently began major renovations in 2011. With new convenience stores/filling stations at each end and the upper-level open space housing a gift shop and multiple fast-foot kiosks, the facility reopened in 2014 as the Will Rogers Archway.[10]

Claremore

Westbound motorists departing Vinita on old 66 drove thirty-seven miles to the next county seat at Claremore. They passed by the edge of Chelsea and drove through the tiny communities of Bushyhead, Foyil, and Sequoyah, generally not pausing except for necessities. A few tourists turned east the four miles from Foyil down a county road to view the Totem Pole Park, a garden of folk art concrete sculptures that Ed Galloway created between 1937 and 1961. Regular drivers in the 1930s and 1940s, however, knew to pay particular attention to something different at Foyil. A long stretch of straight pavement led into the village, where a curve carried the road through the built-up area. Local resident Norman R. Martin remembered, "This was an excellent place for a speed trap," a fact that all local residents recognized.[11]

Claremore, with just over four thousand people in 1940, had two major claims to fame. The first was mineral water. After the discovery of highly mineralized groundwater in 1903, the community became a center of healing in the years before people began understanding that germs caused infectious illnesses. The town filled with bathhouses, hotels, and boardinghouses to accommodate cure seekers. By the time that Route 66 was designated in 1926, it teemed with entrepreneurs offering food and lodging. Claremore's second claim to notoriety came as a complete bonus as the home of humorist Will Rogers, who became a star first in vaudeville and later in motion pictures. Frequently he referred to the community as home in his syndicated newspaper columns and later in a coast-to-coast live Sunday evening radio show. After the entertainer's death in a plane crash in 1935, the state of Oklahoma erected the impressive stone Will Rogers Memorial museum and mausoleum on a hill overlooking the town about a dozen blocks northwest of Highway

66. When Lucille Byerly Lackore made a trip to California in a Model T with three girlfriends in 1932, they were impressed when "we saw a large water reservoir on which the words 'Claremore Hometown of Will Rogers' were painted."[12]

HOTEL WILL ROGERS

Taking the name of Claremore's favorite son, the Hotel Will Rogers opened on Highway 66 in early 1930. The six-story buff-colored brick structure housed seventy-five guest rooms, each one decorated differently, an elaborate coffee shop just off the lobby, and a bathhouse for health seekers on the top floor. Although he had no financial connections with the enterprise, entertainer Will Rogers liked to stay there and brought the hotel free publicity. In his newspaper column on February 17, 1930, for example, he declared that the facility was the "most up-to-date hotel in the Southwest" and boasted that its six stories made it "higher than any hotel in London." He added, "It's got more baths in one room than Buckingham Palace, where the King lives." What Rogers failed to mention was that whenever people stepped inside, they were greeted by gentle wafts of hydrogen sulfide gas with the odor of rotten eggs given off by the distinctively brownish-colored mineral water that attracted many of the ailing customers. Some hotel guests came for multiday mineral-water bathing treatments, the management offering them special all-inclusive weekly rates for accommodations, three meals daily, plus baths and massages.

To serve its guests, as well as local customers and passing motorists, the coffee shop opened early in the morning and served food well into the evening hours, providing breakfast, lunch, and dinner as well as meals for groups. A menu from 1940 offered typical midcentury steak, chicken, and fish plates, a range of salads, sandwiches, and desserts, with the unexpected notation, "We have a splendid and very capable chef, and any item of food desired and not listed on this menu will gladly be prepared on request, if available." After World War II, Americans began seeking more sophisticated medical treatments, especially antibiotics, and with those changes the fortunes of the Will Rogers Hotel declined along with the other mineral baths in the town. From an estimated 125,000 mineral baths given in Claremore annually during the 1920s, the numbers dropped until the old Hotel Will Rogers was the last place in town offering the treatments. It closed to the public in 1991, and two years later the Rogers County Historical Society purchased the disused building in hopes that at some future date it might be rehabilitated.[13]

Claremore to Tulsa

Twenty-seven miles on Highway 66 separated Claremore from Tulsa, the second largest city in Oklahoma, with 142,157 people in 1940. Even after the Will Rogers Turnpike opened in 1957, the official Highway 66 continued as it had to make its way past the little town of Catoosa over a hilly terrain of farms and pastures with trees clumped around homes and along stream courses. At Catoosa the roadway bypassed the old part of town in 1942, a writer about that time noting that "a new settlement has sprung up to the south of the road." This in fact was a scattering of filling stations, eating establishments, and country stores. Catoosa prospered after it became the terminus for the McClellan-Kerr Arkansas River Navigation System in 1971. This waterway enabled barges to connect downstream with the Mississippi River and thence the Gulf of Mexico. Most Tulsa-bound motorists sped past the village, although some riding the old pavement in the 1960s tarried at Wayne Henry "Wolf Robe" Hunt's Catoosa Indian Trading Post, where knowledgeable buyers found high-quality Native-made silver jewelry, paintings, and other artwork. Still others lingered across the road at Zelta and Hugh Davis's Natures Acres wildlife park; there in the 1970s Davis sculpted a giant concrete whale. After proceeding southward two miles from Catoosa, the old two-lane Highway 66 at a place known locally as the "Dead Man's Curve" made a ninety-degree, sharp turn to the west. Lloyd A. Gilbert Sr. grew up in this rural neighborhood and remembered, "Many motorists failed to make the turn and would crash into the filling station or wind up in Mr. Gallo's pasture," the accidents sometimes taking place two or three times in a given night. From here drivers proceeded westward along an extension of Eleventh Street into Tulsa.[14]

Tulsa

Many Highway 66 motorists paused at least for fuel and food in Tulsa even if they did not spend the night. Starting in 1901, multiple oil discoveries made Tulsa a center of the American petroleum industry for many years, giving it comparative prosperity through the Great Depression. The money that oil brought to the city helped fund an impressive downtown commercial district and appealing suburbs, as well as two major art institutions, the 1939 Philbrook Museum of Art and the 1949 Gilcrease Museum. From its earliest days, Tulsa had a substantial African American population that many whites wished lived elsewhere. Such intolerant attitudes in 1921

led to a massacre considered to have been the worst instance of racial violence in the history of the United States. At least thirty people, and likely far more, lost their lives when mobs of whites burned down thirty-five blocks of Black-owned businesses and homes. Despite the devastation, many African Americans stubbornly rebuilt their lives in a north-side ghetto, where they continued to live in a racially segregated society. It was here in the neighborhood that survivors reconstructed after the carnage that entrepreneurs provided food and lodging for Black travelers making their way along the Mother Road.[15]

OLD ENGLISH INN

Until 1959 Highway 66 entered Tulsa from the east along West Eleventh Street. In the early years from 1926 to 1932, the federal highway jogged north on Mingo Road to Admiral Place, where it turned back westward into the city. Traversing the business district, the route zigzagged southwestward on several congested streets to reconnect with Eleventh and exited the city over a bridge across the Arkansas River. At the place where the 1926 alignment turned west on Admiral Place from Mingo Road on the extreme northeast side of Tulsa, drivers passed a handsome Tudor Revival–style restaurant/tavern called the Old English Inn, which had an adjacent filling station and tourist cabins. Neither the enterprise nor the highway location were accidents. The rural property at this strategic intersection belonged to Cyrus Avery, the very same good-roads promoter who in 1926 played an instrumental role in bringing U.S. Highway 66 through Tulsa and across Oklahoma. The entrepreneur established the business in 1921 on farmland that he already owned in hopes that a future roadway would bring customers. His plans reached fruition with the opening of Highway 66 five years later. As increasing numbers of women began driving, his restaurant became a favored tearoom destination for genteel luncheons and bridge parties. Despite criticisms that Avery had used his influence to route the federal highway past his farm, the Old English Inn earned profits until it was removed in 1943 to make way for a new traffic circle at the Mingo Road–Admiral Place intersection.[16]

IKE'S CHILI

One of the oldest among the eating places in Tulsa was a family-run chili parlor established by Greek immigrant Ike Johnson. This downtown hole-in-the-wall café served meals to generations of locals and travelers alike, its setting near hotels, parking garages, and public buildings making it easily convenient to customers seeking hearty, inexpensive fare. Johnson came to Tulsa from Texas after the start of the oil boom, in 1907 opening a chili parlor called Ike's in an alley off Second Street between Main and Boulder Avenues. His nephew, Ivan O. Johnson, came to help him the next year, with Ivan's brother, Bill P., joining the two in 1916. From the early days, the Johnsons offered their diners chili three ways: chili only, with beans, and with both beans and spaghetti. Customers learned that at Ike's they could eat as many crackers as they wished so long as they paid for their chili. This policy led to the café reputedly becoming one of the largest individual soda cracker customer accounts of the National Biscuit Company. "One part of the fun at Ike's," wrote a journalist, "is to doctor your own bowl of chili to taste," the tables being supplied not just with salt and pepper but also with hot pepper sauce, Louisiana hot sauce,

chili powder in tin shakers, and vinegar. She described Ike's chili as being "rather greasy, not too spicy and thoroughly enjoyable." Over the years the café shifted to other rented spaces including 117 South Boston Avenue, 115 North Boston, 312 South Main Street, 20 West Third, and eventually to 712 South Boston, all in downtown and none more than four blocks from the original alignment of Highway 66. Other branches came and went elsewhere in the city. Ike's customers remained loyal year in and year out, one remarking in the 1960s, "When you mention Ike's, you are mentioning the prize place in downtown Tulsa." Ike Johnson passed away in 1928, his nephews carrying on the business. The next generation of offspring argued over the rights to the Ike's Chili trade name and operated competing eateries, but they all offered good food. Most recently, in 2014, Ike's Chili moved to 1503 East Eleventh Street, on the old 1933–59 alignment of Highway 66.[17]

CONEY ISLAND HOT WEINERS / CONEY I-LANDER

Ike's Chili was not the only place in downtown Tulsa where Mother Road travelers found good value for their money. The very same year that the roadway received number 66 in 1926, Christ Dimitri Economou opened a hot dog stand at 311 South Boulder Avenue in the central business district. An immigrant from Greece, he had worked in the hot dog trade in McKeesport, Pennsylvania; Lincoln, Nebraska; and Dallas, Texas, before coming to Tulsa in hopes of opening a stand there. The Oil Capital was booming, and the thirty-five-year-old decided it was the right place to sink his roots. Economou introduced his sandwiches as being made using the "Coney Island System," referring to preparation in the authentic manner of vendors at Coney Island, New York. (Ironically the "Coney Island System," also known as the "New York System," was developed by other Greek restaurateurs in Rhode Island.) These East Coast–style hot dogs in the early twentieth century typically were made using mixed beef, veal, and pork frankfurters served in steamed white bread buns garnished with yellow mustard, chopped onions, celery salt, and a chili-like meat sauce characteristically seasoned with chili powder, paprika, cumin, and allspice. The five-cent sandwiches proved to be popular among customers, and the stand operated in downtown Tulsa for over nine decades. When the *Tulsa World* newspaper needed to build a new press room, it purchased the Coney Island's space, which then moved half a block to 108 West Fourth Street. Later the shop moved across the street, only to return to 108 West Fourth, before a final move in 2015 to 107 North Boulder Avenue. Son James Economou assumed active management of the eatery in the late 1960s, but his brother-in-law, Charles Kingsley, felt that the enterprise should expand. While James continued to operate the old-style downtown stand, Kingsley, with others, created a separate Coney I-Lander brand and opened several drive-in-style branches in and around Tulsa, some of which remain. In the meantime James Economou's daughter-in-law, Vicki Economou, succeeded him in 2010 in managing the old-time downtown eatery.[18]

BISHOP'S RESTAURANT

Not everyone who passed through downtown Tulsa was looking for cheap eats like chili or hot dogs. The city had prospered since the early-twentieth-century oil discoveries, and even through the hard times

of the Great Depression many people still earned enough disposable income to dine out. Goodly numbers of them brought their hunger and pocketbooks to Bishop's Restaurant, or its quick-service branch, Bishop's Driv-Inn. The restaurants sprang from the collaboration of William W. "Bill" Bishop and Joseph H. "Harry" Powers. The entrepreneurs had operated eating places in Missouri before relocating to the Drumright, Oklahoma, oil boomtown in 1913. There they opened the short-order Kansas City Waffle House. Relocating to Tulsa three years later, they launched another hash house called the Kansas City Waffle House No. 2 at 121 South Boston Avenue. Over the next decade, they opened more waffle houses, with No. 5 in Oklahoma City in 1925 and others as far west as Santa Fe, New Mexico. Tulsa, however, is where the partners focused their efforts most intently, in 1930 expanding one of their short-order outlets at 510 South Main Street in downtown to become the two-story Bishop's Restaurant.

For the next three decades, Bishop's reigned as the culinary standard in Tulsa, many travelers scheduling cross-country trips to coincide with its mealtimes. Highway 66 passed only a block and a half south. The ground floor offered a coffee shop with a large U-shaped bar as well as a sit-down dining room. Upstairs, diners found a buffeteria with tables groaning with a remarkable spread of prepared foods. Bishop's became a social center for Tulsans, the type of place to which one brought out-of-town guests and visiting business colleagues. Many deals were agreed upon there. Among the petroleum magnates who regularly dined at Bishop's were millionaires J. Paul Getty, Josh Cosden, William Skelly, and Harry Sinclair. A writer in 1936 commented, "Bishop's is a favorite rendezvous for after theater crowds and midnight parties." Trade was so good, even during the hard times of the thirties, that in 1936 Bishop and Powers erected a modernistic art deco Bishop's Driv-Inn with curb service at the intersection of Tenth Street and Boston Avenue, directly fronting on the new 1933 alignment of Highway 66. Hexagonal in shape, the gleaming white building supported a towering central spire.

The best remembered Bishop's food specialty was its Brown Derby, named after the famous contemporary Hollywood restaurant fifteen hundred miles to the west near the terminus of the Mother Road. The dish consisted of a hamburger steak topped with Bishop's distinctive Diablo Sauce and grilled onions, served with french fries, scalloped potatoes, or deep-fried onion rings and hot rolls. The chef's salads at the restaurant could be ordered with a special house-prepared "wine oil" dressing that was so good that customers bought it by the pint to take home. After the Oklahoma City oil field began active production, in 1933 entrepreneurs Bishop and Powers converted their existing Kansas City Waffle House No. 5 at 113 North Broadway in the capital city to become a full-fledged Bishop's Restaurant as well. Their Tulsa drive-in, however, never prospered as well as the sit-down Bishop's, and it closed in 1942. The two flagship restaurants in Tulsa and Oklahoma City both prospered into the 1960s, when they suffered from the economic declines of the central business districts. The Tulsa location closed first in 1966, with the Oklahoma City eating place following three years later. Many old-time customers lamented the passing of Bishop's. Mary Lou Marcy of Edmond, Oklahoma, reminisced three decades later,

"In my mind, I can still taste their chocolate eclairs—real pudding filling, dark chocolate icing and a cherry on top."[19]

Like most white-run eating places in Tulsa, Bishop's Restaurant refused to seat African Americans in its dining rooms until after the passage of civil rights legislation. Prentice Gautt, the first Black football player for the University of Oklahoma, felt the sting of its discrimination on the evening of November 1, 1956. After the OU team had completed a game in Tulsa, their bus pulled up to Bishop's for a prearranged postgame meal. Gautt was the only Black member of the team. After the players filed into the dining room, where plates of food were waiting, the restaurant assistant manager, referring to Prentice, announced, "We can't serve that guy." The ballplayer sat down with his fellow team members anyway, and the manager rushed over to him saying, "Sir. It's our policy, not anything personal, but it's our policy that we can't serve you. We've got a place for you downstairs." Having heard this patter before in other segregated eateries, Gautt got up and quietly returned to the bus, his stomach growling and feelings riled. Only moments later his team members, two or three at a time, began filing out of Bishop's and back onto the bus. Not one of them had eaten, and the driver took them on to another restaurant on the outskirts of Tulsa where the management would welcome the whole team. Prentice recalled, "And, we ate until we were stuffed."[20]

EL RANCHO GRANDE RESTAURANT

As mid-twentieth-century motorists made their way across the heartland on Route 66, they began to come upon Hispanic foods with which they were unfamiliar. Although

Brown Derby, BISHOP'S RESTAURANT, TULSA, OKLAHOMA

Taking its name from the nationally known Brown Derby Restaurant at the far end of the Mother Road in California, the Tulsa Brown Derby was a carefully seasoned and grilled hamburger steak covered with grilled onions and a savory Diablo Sauce served with french fries, mashed potatoes, or deep-fried onion rings. A beloved downtown restaurant just a block off the Mother Road, Bishop's opened in 1930 and served this specialty until it closed in 1966.

Six to eight servings

For sauce:
1 quart chicken stock
1 ½ cups tomato ketchup
¾ cup Heinz (or comparable) chili sauce
1 teaspoon Liquid Smoke
1 teaspoon A-1 steak sauce
1 teaspoon Worcestershire sauce
½ teaspoon salt
½ teaspoon black pepper
½ cup margarine
8 tablespoons flour
½ cup sweet pickle relish
¼ cup parsley (chopped)

For hamburger steaks:
2 pounds ground beef
2 eggs
1 ½ teaspoons dry mustard
1 teaspoon prepared mustard
½ teaspoon Liquid Smoke
1 teaspoon salt
1 teaspoon black pepper
1 ½ teaspoons Worcestershire sauce
½ medium onion (sliced to make rings)
2 tablespoons cooking oil

In a large saucepan, combine first eight sauce ingredients (chicken stock, ketchup, chili sauce, liquid smoke, A-1 steak sauce, Worcestershire sauce, salt, and pepper) and bring to a boil. In a small pan, melt margarine and gradually add flour, stirring together for about two minutes, and then add to the sauce mixture to thicken it. Allow to stew gently. Just before serving, add pickle relish and parsley

While the sauce is simmering, combine all the hamburger steak ingredients, mixing well. Shape into six to eight patties. (Bishop's used quarter pound–sized servings.) Grill over charcoal or cook on a stove top using a skillet at medium heat to your desired doneness.

As the meat cooks, place sliced onion in a skillet and sauté in oil until the onions turn light brown.

Serve beef patty covered with grilled onions and topped with Diablo Sauce.

Original recipe from Suzanne Holloway, *The World's Finest* ([Tulsa]: World Publishing, 1983), 39.

there had been Mexican cafés in Chicago as early as the 1920s, the dishes travelers first encountered on 66 were the regional Tex-Mex variety. These were foods that evolved among Mexicans living in Texas along the state's border with the Republic of Mexico, typified by chili con carne, enchiladas, and tamales. For years the first known such eating place directly on the Mother Road that westbound travelers encountered was El Rancho Grande Restaurant at 1629 East Eleventh Street in Tulsa.

Ruby A. Rodriguez, the wife of a Saint Louis–San Francisco Railway worker, entered the restaurant business in 1951. With the assistance of Cecilia Neito, she opened a café she called El Rancho Grande at 621 South Boulder, just steps away from the earlier alignment of Highway 66 through downtown and only three blocks north from the 1933 route. She undoubtedly took the business name from the phenomenally successful 1949 Mexican motion picture, *Alla en el Rancho Grande* (Out on the Big Ranch), which popularized the ranchero song of the same name. In 1953 Rodriguez relocated her business to rented space on the ground floor at 1629 East Eleventh, facing Mother Road traffic. In the early 1970s, real estate investor Jeff Walden Sr. purchased the two-story brick building, which had four apartments on the upper level. In time Ruby's daughters, Martha and Judy, took over restaurant management, while their mother's main cook, Inez C. "Larry" Lara, continued running things in the kitchen. Then, in 1984, a time when the Oklahoma petroleum industry was in a slump, the Rodriguez family experienced cash flow problems. They stopped paying certain taxes as well as rent. The business eventually sold at auction, with landlord Jeff Walden purchasing

as much of the food service equipment as he could afford. Keeping Larry Lara on board as cook, he and his sons reopened El Rancho Grande. Lara eventually spent forty-six years working in the same kitchen, and in the process he made El Rancho into a legend among restaurants specializing in Tex-Mex cuisine. When author Gustavo Arellano wrote a history of Mexican food north of the border in 2012, he identified Lara's "Nighthawk Special" as one of the five top dishes in all the Mexican restaurants in the United States. The meal consists of two cheese and onion enchiladas centered between swirls of queso cheese sauce on one side and chili con carne on the other. The Walden family still owns and operates El Rancho Grande. Though it occasionally bows to fashion and offers more trendy dishes, Larry Lara's recipes still reign supreme among its customers. John Walden, Jeff's son, explained to the author, "We sell a lot more cheese enchiladas than anything."[21]

Sapulpa

Motorists proceeded southwest out of Tulsa, crossing the Arkansas River on an impressive reinforced-concrete arch bridge constructed in 1916. Once over the river, the highway paralleled the tracks of the Saint Louis–San Francisco Railway about ten miles to Sapulpa, the seat of Creek County. Travelers passed through a seemingly continuous sprawl of petroleum-related industrial plants, tank farms, and roadside businesses all through West Tulsa and Red Fork. From childhood car trips with his family in the late 1940s and 1950s, Lloyd "Shorty" Smith remembered that the "smell of oil refineries burning off the gasses was a shock to the senses." Despite the odors, Sapulpa prospered from the early-twentieth-century oil boom that likewise had contributed to the growth of Tulsa, and it offered motorists most services they might expect. The population of the town grew steadily from about ten thousand in 1930 to over fourteen thousand by 1960. Following the Second World War, many travelers paused in Sapulpa to visit the sales rooms of the Frankoma pottery works, established by John and Grace Lee Frank, which for decades produced distinctive ceramic dining ware, vases, and statuettes.[22]

NORMA'S DIAMOND CAFÉ

For half a century starting in 1950, Norma Lee Hall owned and operated Norma's Diamond Café on the side of Highway 66 at 408 North Mission Street across from the cemetery in Sapulpa. The same year her husband, Bob Hall, opened the Diamond Truck Stop next door, selling fuel and providing services to truckers and motorists alike, with both enjoying meals at the adjacent café. Norma gained a reputation up and down the Mother Road for her special breakfasts served on locally produced Frankoma pottery dishes. The "Red Top" was a favorite midday feature during the wintertime. It was a bowl filled halfway with beef stew and then topped with a thick layer of hot chili served with cornbread, all made from scratch. The preferred dish for Tulsa author Michael Wallis, however, was cornbread served with ham and beans, which, he declared, "can make a grown man weep with joy." Norma's Diamond Café became subject matter for several documentary films on Route 66 during the 1990s, spreading her renown far beyond Oklahoma. Long after the 1953 opening of the turnpike past Sapulpa deprived his truck stop of much of its former through traffic, Bob decided to retire and close it down after thirty-six years. Norma,

however, persisted running the café until 2000, the year she passed away.[23]

Stroud

Westbound motorists followed the two-lane forty-seven miles from Sapulpa through the sleepy village of Kellyville, the onetime oil boomtown Bristow, and quiet Depew on the way to Stroud. Along the way travelers realized somewhere around Bristow that the color of the soil had dramatically changed. All the way from Illinois, cross-country travelers had observed cultivated fields in shades of brown and black, but in Oklahoma they turned distinctively red. During a 1941 westbound journey, Irene M. Roberti penned in her trip diary that she saw "miles and miles of red earth . . . [that] continued on thru Oklahoma and into Texas." Six years later, in 1947, Ellen Tappenbeck jotted down from her travels, "The soil is so red that you wouldn't think that anything could grow here." Jack Rittenhouse alerted 1940s motorists to take care in highway construction diversions in Oklahoma because, in his words, "Detours are quite difficult in wet weather if you are routed over a dirt road of this red earth."[24]

During the years that the Mother Road traversed Stroud, on brick paving through the business district, its population gradually grew from about 1,500 to 2,500 inhabitants, almost all of them either white or Native American. As part of a violent racial incident in 1901, angry whites drove all African Americans out of Stroud, giving the community the reputation of being a sundown town where no Blacks were welcome after dark.[25]

ROCK CAFÉ

To this day heritage tourists flock into the Rock Café at 114 on the south side of West

Main Street in Stroud. There it is as common to hear foreign tongues spoken as English. Many travelers from the East experience their first southwestern-style "chicken fried steak" here, though in its heyday the Rock was best known for its greasy hamburgers. The story of the eating place begins in 1936, when local entrepreneur Roy C. Rives bought six and a half lots in the downtown area. Then, in 1939, for five dollars he purchased stone, from which he would construct his café. The brown sandstone chunks came from a road cut excavated along Highway 66 near Kellyville, about thirty miles to the east. When the time came to lay the concrete foundation, workers trundled the slurry from the cement mixer one wheelbarrow at a time. Eventually the walls went up and a galvanized steel roof covered the top. The eatery opened in August 1939 with Miss Thelma Holloway managing. The effects of the Great Depression were waning and Prohibition was over, so the Rock Café experienced strong demand for its hamburgers, plate lunches, beer, and soda pop. Later owner Ed Smalley remembered things being so busy that "there were trucks parked up and down the highway and around the building." Several managers followed Holloway, with Mamie Mayfield assuming the duties in 1959. She kept the doors twenty-four hours a day and, by the time she retired in 1983, had given the Rock a reputation up and down the Mother Road as a good place to stop. Even after the 1953 opening of the four-lane Turner Turnpike, many drivers preferred instead to use the old "free road," so the eatery continued to feed many motorists. After Oklahoma oil prices slumped in the 1980s and its economy sagged, the fortunes of the Rock Café declined, but in 1993 new owner Dawn Welch recharged its prominence. Her purchase coincided with a revival of interest in old Route 66, leading increasing numbers of heritage tourists to the landmark eatery. Disaster struck in 2008, when a fire gutted the historic stone structure. With outside assistance, Welch rebuilt the café, reopening the next year. The original 1939 grill survived the fire, was refurbished, and, at the time of this writing, was still in service cooking the Rock Café's signature greasy hamburgers.[26]

HOWARD JOHNSON'S TURNER TURNPIKE RESTAURANT

When the Turner Turnpike opened in 1953 between Tulsa and Oklahoma City, it had a midway rest area and restaurant for travelers going both directions. Because of its central location, Stroud became the site for this facility. The Phillips Petroleum Company was the successful bidder to provide fuel and food to motorists along the eighty-eight-mile restricted-access super highway, and it funded construction of a modern restaurant on the south (eastbound) side of the freeway. An enclosed elevated "skyway" enabled westbound travelers to climb a set of stairs from a westbound parking area, safely walk fifteen feet above speeding traffic to the other side, and then descend into the restaurant. Because the Howard Johnson Company received the contract from Phillips 66 to operate the eateries on the Turner Turnpike, architects designed the 150-seat restaurant to specifications set out by the food service firm. This meant that it had a coffee-shop area with counter and table service where customers could buy breakfast and short-order meals as well as soda fountain specialties made using the company's twenty-eight flavors of ice cream. The Stroud facility also had a more formal dining room

A cook in the kitchen of the Rock Café in Stroud, Oklahoma, in 2017, preparing food on the grill that survived a fire that gutted the building in 2008. Author's collection.

featuring steaks, seafood, poultry, salads, and desserts.

The position of Stroud halfway between Tulsa and Oklahoma City made the turnpike Howard Johnson's a desirable setting for lunch and dinner meetings of state organizations, such as the representatives of the nineteen firms comprising the Oklahoma Dental Laboratories, who gathered there in October 1953. The restaurant operated several years before the Oklahoma legislature passed laws ending racial segregation in eating places, but, because it was on the turnpike funded substantially by the national government, it followed federal antidiscrimination guidelines and from the outset served African

Americans. The Phillips 66 agreement with the Oklahoma Turnpike Authority lasted twenty-five years and was extended five more. In the mid-1980s the authority planned major changes in the midpoint rest area, which involved closing the Howard Johnson's Restaurant, shifting the existing two roadways slightly northward, and erecting new food and fuel facilities on the median between the thoroughfares. People who had grown fond of the pedestrian "skyway" lamented its loss, together with its signs bearing in large letters the slogans, "You're Doin' Fine, Oklahoma" eastbound and "I'm on to Oklahoma" westbound. In 1987 the Oklahoma Department of Human Services moved its offices from cramped quarters in the Lincoln County Courthouse into the former restaurant, where the organization operated several years before the aging structure was razed. Today the site is occupied by an industrial facility bordering on the south side of the freeway, with its concrete foundations still visible from the air.[27]

Wellston

Wellston lay twenty-six miles farther down the two lane from Stroud, a dozen miles beyond the Lincoln County seat in Chandler. Wellston held the dubious distinction of having been one of the first communities in the Sooner State bypassed by the Mother Road. When U.S. Highway 66 initially came into being, it consisted of preexisting roadways connecting Chicago to Los Angeles. The local road west from Chandler, at the time unpaved, looped northward through the commercial district of Wellston, which had about six hundred people. The state government committed itself to pave the way through the town, but in 1932 the U.S. Bureau of Public Roads insisted that, if it

The elevated "skyway" that, starting in 1953, enabled westbound travelers safely to cross over nonstop freeway traffic to reach the Howard Johnson's Restaurant on the eastbound side of the Turner Turnpike at Stroud, midway between Tulsa and Oklahoma City. Author's collection.

were to provide matching paving funds, the federal highway should instead continue straight toward the west and avoid the extra distance and slower speeds required to go through the community. Bureaucrats argued for months, but eventually the federal agency prevailed. When the new pavement was laid in 1933, it bypassed Wellston, a decision local residents have resented ever since. The state itself had to fund paving a connecting loop up through the town, which became the first U.S. 66 Bypass anywhere along the route.[28]

PIONEER CAMP TAVERN BARBECUE (BUTCHER BARBECUE STAND)

At the point where the original Route 66 angled northwestward toward Wellston, the Pioneer Camp, a roadside campground with one-room cabins, opened in 1929. Facilities like this typically included not only simple cabins but also gasoline stations, basic grocery stores, and often short-order cafés. In addition to these amenities, the Pioneer Camp became known for its barbecued meats. Lloyd Swisher initially owned and

operated the enterprise. Mr. and Mrs. Chris Osterman succeeded him in 1934, running things for over a decade, followed by others into the 2000s. Journalist Susan Croce Kelly stopped here in the early 1980s, describing the Pioneer Camp Tavern as "a treat, a place in mostly dry Oklahoma where you can get delicious barbecued rib dinners and a cold beer." In 1995 the Bouska family purchased the country tavern and operated its barbecue pit until a 2007 kitchen fire gutted the building, closing the old-time business. Later, in 2015, grandson Levi Bouska opened a new Butcher Barbecue Stand adjacent to the old Pioneer Camp Tavern, using, adapting, and updating the family's time-tested meat cooking methods.[29]

Luther
THREATT STATION

Most of the filling stations, lodgings, and eating places along Highway 66 belonged to white Americans, leaving Black travelers to wonder what types of reception they might find. Their constant fears were of embarrassment, rudeness, or, even worse, hostility. Scattered along the thoroughfares, however, they found occasional enterprises run by Black entrepreneurs like Allen Threatt Sr. After the stress of driving through well-known sundown towns like Stroud and Miami to the east, and Edmond to the west, African Americans could pull into the Threatt's filling station, and, as his grandson Edward explained, "They could exhale and relax and not have to worry about anything." It was in 1915 that Allen Threatt opened his roadside enterprise on the south side of Oklahoma Highway 7, which in 1926 became the Mother Road. He chose a location at the junction with local Pottawatomi Road, which ran north and south along the boundary between Lincoln and Oklahoma Counties three miles east of the little town of Luther. In addition to selling fuel, making light repairs, and patching punctured tires and tubes, Threatt maintained a stock of basic groceries. Not very much is known about the chronology of the existing stone, cross-gable filling station building, but a group of local African American businessmen in a report dated May 9, 1939, wrote, "Mr. Allen Threatt and his son, Ulysses, operate a service station, just east of Luther and have just completed a spacious native-stone building in connection," adding, "They also have an amusement park, which is the scene of various public gatherings."

Threatt Park adjacent to the station was the setting for many social functions organized by members of the Black community living in and around Luther. At least as early as 1935, open-air dances; church, club, and family picnics; Black Democratic Party rallies; Easter egg hunts; and local baseball games were taking place there. Participants

sometimes included liberal-minded whites. In conjunction with the filling station and the park, Threat family members constructed a free-standing barbecue pit and stand, with notices of gatherings sometimes bearing announcements like, "There will be plenty of Barbecue." The events could run well into the evening as the Threatts strung wiring for incandescent lights over picnic tables where guests ate and drank during the programs. Younger family members looked forward to these outdoor crowds, especially the dances, because they set the stage for "treasure hunting" the next day. Allen Threatt III, a boy at the time, later remembered, "They were jitterbuggin' at the dances and all the change in their pockets would fall out. I would come out early next morning and pick up the change— we'd have a pocketful." In addition to his roadside enterprises, in 1937 Allen Threatt opened a rock quarry on his nearby farm for sales of building materials and then in 1948 erected a commercial building on Second Street in Luther. There for a while an eatery called the Luther Café served the public. The filling station later opened a small tavern and snack bar, operating into the 1970s. The original stone structure survives and in 1994 was placed on the National Register of Historic Places.[30]

Arcadia
WHITE GOOSE CAFÉ

Arcadia, a hamlet of two hundred to three hundred people midway between Luther and Edmond, is best known today for its restored 1898 round hay barn, now a museum. In the days of the Mother Road, it was a threadbare rural community in which half the small business district had burned in 1924. A few energetic entrepreneurs worked to earn livelihoods selling fuel and food to passing motorists, but the proximity to much larger Edmond meant that these locals only eked out a living. The Tuton Drugstore a block off Highway 66, for example, added a soda fountain with food service in 1909, but the whole store closed in 1941, stood vacant all through World War II, and subsequently housed a modest grocery store. An exception to the seeming stagnation was the White Goose Café, built by Jim Crabb in the mid-1920s shortly after Highway 66 was routed past the south side of the village. Longtime resident Perry Rogers ate there while he was growing up in the 1920s and later recalled, "It looked sorta small from the outside, but was big enough for a small counter with stools, and I think 3 tables with chairs that didn't match, and of course the kitchen." Rogers fondly reflected that he usually ordered the twenty-five-cent plate lunch, which consisted of meat with two vegetables. The cook, a Mrs. Brown, he remembered, "was more than generous with the servings," and she gave customers as much bread and water that they wanted. Ample roadside parking outside the White Goose made it a convenient stop for truck drivers, helping it maintain a strong trade until after the Second World War. The eatery closed in the early 1950s, about the same time that the Turner Turnpike took away much of the traffic from the old two-lane 66 Highway past the town.[31]

Edmond

Six miles west from Arcadia westbound travelers came to a Route 66 landmark before arriving in Edmond. Here southbound U.S. Highway 77 merged with the Mother Road and for a few miles the two ran along the same pavement. Known as the Bradbury Corner, the junction took its name from Everett Marvin Bradbury's filling station, where, from 1923 to 1953, motorists purchased fuel and downed sodas and snacks. The site today is obliterated, having become part of the modern interchange of Oklahoma Highway 66 with Interstate 35 and U.S. Highway 77.[32]

Edmond sprang into existence during the 1889 land run into the Oklahoma Territory, and by the time Highway 66 received its numerical designation in 1926, it had about three thousand people. In 1891 it became home to the Territorial Normal School, a teachers' college that today is the University of Central Oklahoma. That same year the first African Americans began moving to Edmond, but they failed to create a self-sustaining community and it dwindled away, leaving only whites in the town. Subsequently it became a sundown town, where Blacks were unwelcome. Royce B. Adamson, a former editor of the *Edmond Enterprise* and founder of Route 66 eatery the Royce Café, promoted the town on one of his restaurant's advertising postcards. Issued around 1940, the front of the card touted the community as "a good place to live" with "6,000 live citizens" but "no Negroes."[33]

HIGHWAY CAFÉ (WIDE-A-WAKE LUNCH, WIDE-A-WAKE CAFÉ)

When westbound Mother Road travelers reached the center of Edmond, the combined U.S. Highways 66 and 77 turned ninety degrees to the south onto Broadway and in the direction of Oklahoma City. In the first block of this route, on the right side stood the Wide-A-Wake Café for over fifty years. As its name suggests, the eatery offered hot food around the clock no matter when a hungry traveler might appear at the door. The café with the notable name actually succeeded an earlier diner at the same 213 South Broadway location, the Highway Café, which had opened at least by 1929. In 1931 Essie Maye Noe took over the earlier business, renaming it the Wide-A-Wake Lunch, offering inside dining and curb-service meals that included sandwiches, other short orders, plate lunches, and what she publicized as "real coffee." By the next year, she was advertising, "You'll certainly like our . . . barbecue pork or beef" at her Wide-Awake-Café. The business proved to be so strong that Essie Maye's husband, Eugene Weldon "Gene" Noe, joined her, as did his brother T. Crawford Noe and wife Cleo. It became a real family enterprise. When Edmond received a short-term economic boost in 1930 after a modest oil field opened just to its west, the Wide-A-Wake did all it could to attract oil workers by advertising, "We serve BIG HUSKY MEALS for hard-working men" and inviting, "You're just as welcome here in work clothes as Sunday duds." Even though Gene Noe left the café for military service during World War II, other family members maintained the business through price controls and food rationing that accompanied the conflict. Operating at the side of the important roadway, the restaurant became a regular stop for many travelers and long-distance truck drivers, who left notes and pictures on its public bulletin board. By the early 1960s, both brothers had passed away, but widow Cleo Noe continued running the Wide-A-Wake Café for another decade until it closed in 1972. This Edmond institution was one of the few eating places along U.S. Highway 66 to have become the setting for a novel, with Curt Munson publishing his fictional *Tales of the Wide-A-Wake Café* in 2004.[34]

ROYCE CAFÉ

In the depths of the Great Depression in 1933, newspaper editor Royce B. Adamson sold his half of the *Edmond Enterprise* to his partner and invested the proceeds in a restaurant on Broadway a block and a half south of the Noes' Wide-A-Wake Café. Using variegated brown local stone for the exterior, in 1934 Adamson with wife Neva built the first phase of what eventually became a multiroom dining emporium that served generations of travelers and locals. Seating customers at tables, in booths, and on stools along a counter, the Royce Café began by offering round-the-clock meals, reduced operating hours due to staff shortages during World War II, and then returned to twenty-four-hour service in peacetime. In 1942 Royce Adamson died unexpectedly at age fifty. Widow Neva continued operating the café with son-in-law James Tindall as manager for another decade and a half. The Royce was the only restaurant in Edmond to receive endorsement from national food critic Duncan Hines. The culinary authority in 1941 reported that the Adamsons had successfully "made this place in a small town well known" even in other states and recommended its waffles, steaks, hot bread, and twenty-two varieties of sandwiches. For a few years, Tindall also operated a satellite Royce Café in Oklahoma City. Desiring to retire, in 1958 Neva sold the Edmond eating place to Jim Mills, and it subsequently passed through other hands until closing in 1970. Adapted to alternative uses, the now-painted stone-faced building at 402 South Broadway remained standing at the time of research.[35]

Oklahoma City

The distance from Edmond to Oklahoma City was only about eleven miles, bringing travelers into the largest city in the Sooner State. For all the early years, Highway 66 carried motorists directly south to the state capitol building, where the roadway turned west. By 1931 a bypass route took travelers around the areas of heaviest congestion. The highway always passed north of downtown Oklahoma City, where the large hotels and multiple eating places served businesspeople and shoppers. This meant that much of the higher-class dining lay well beyond the Mother Road. Nevertheless, Highway 66 travelers found a considerable selection of convenient places to eat.[36]

African American travelers could breathe sighs of relief on coming into Oklahoma City. Like Tulsa, it had a substantial Black population and entrepreneurs who ran lodgings, eating places, and automobile services eagerly seeking their trade. Most of these were in the Deep Deuce neighborhood in the vicinity of Northeast Second Street, with the Black population and its businesses gradually expanding and moving northward into the area just east of the state capitol, closer to the Mother Road. Until efforts by civil rights activists like Clara Luper in midcentury, most white-owned and -operated lodgings and restaurants in Oklahoma City strictly served only whites until after 1964.[37]

One of the strongest impressions that visitors took away from Oklahoma City between the 1930s and 1950s was of its oil well drilling rigs, hundreds of them. Drillers discovered the Oklahoma City Oil Field in late 1928, and, within a few years, wells and latticed derricks covered the southeast side of the city, gradually expanding into additional areas.

They even dotted the grounds of the state capitol building and governor's mansion. The petroleum industry helped fuel population growth, which rose from 98,000 in 1920 to more than double that figure at 204,000 in 1940. Visiting Russian journalists Ilya Ilf and Eugene Petrov in the mid-1930s observed, "In private yards, on sidewalks, on streets, opposite school buildings, opposite banks and hotels—everywhere oil was being pumped." When writer Ernie Pyle from Albuquerque approached the city at night around the same time, he thought to himself, "Why, it looked like the New York sky line, only the buildings all seemed about the same height." Then he realized, "Those weren't buildings all lighted up. They were oil derricks . . . right in the city." In 1941, after they had slept overnight at the Alamo Plaza Motor Court, Irene M. Roberti and three of her girlfriends from Massachusetts headed west on Highway 66, but not before taking "pictures of the oil wells clustered about the eastern and southern ends of the city." Almost all of the former derricks now have been removed, so it is difficult today even to imagine how they looked to former travelers.[38]

MITCHELL'S OAK CLIFF NIGHT CLUB (SILVER CLUB, KENTUCKY CLUB, RAMADA CLUB, COUNTY LINE BARBECUE, GABRIELLA'S ITALIAN GRILL AND PIZZERIA)

As travelers on Highway 66 made their way southward from Edmond to Oklahoma City, after eight miles they came to an eating place that under several succeeding names fed generations of diners. There, on a rise three miles north of the state capitol building, they were still in partially wooded rural country well outside any city limits. The restaurant and nightspot became known not just for fine dining and dancing but also for substantial sums changing hands at its illegal gaming tables. W. Earl and Grace Mitchell, former tavern owners, moved to the wooded site in 1929. They named their new roadhouse Mitchell's Oak Cliff Night Club, offering chicken dinners, clandestine alcoholic beverages, and a ballroom floor with music. The location at 1226 Northeast Sixty-Third Street, just four blocks east of the Mother Road, made it convenient to motorists but somewhat hidden from prying eyes. After a few months, a fire destroyed the first structure, but the Mitchells rebuilt the profitable establishment within six weeks. In addition to purveying nighttime frolic and indulgence, the couple cleverly masked the illicit evening pursuits by proffering after-church Sunday afternoon chicken lunches. During the muggy summer, they promoted the club as "Cool! Breezy! Invigorating!" with "30 buzzing fans" enhancing the patrons' comfort. After squabbling with a silent partner over beer sales following the end of Prohibition, the Mitchells closed the nightclub in winter 1933–34 but reopened it the next summer as the Silver Club, "catering to those who enjoy good music—excellent dinners and a smooth dance floor."[39]

The nightspot next became the Kentucky Club in 1938, taking this name from the Kentucky Jockey Club, which scheduled the dates for horse races at Churchill Downs in Kentucky. The enterprise featured chicken and steak dinners together with dancing to live orchestras, all under the ownership and management of Anthony A. "Tony" and Winnie Marneres. The venue burned in December 1945, with fifty guests and employees safely escaping the flames. Tony rebuilt, creating a dance floor surrounded by thirteen booths made to resemble stalls in a racing stable. Each one took the name of a different Kentucky Derby winner. With fine food and chic dance music, the Kentucky Club became a place where wealthy Oklahomans retreated for high-dollar illicit gaming. Burgundy velvet drapes and tuxedoed bouncers guaranteed privacy for clients inside the booths, as did secluded game rooms upstairs. The venue gained notoriety from press reports and rumors of occasional gunplay, robbery victims tied to trees, and surprise raids on high-stakes wagering. John William Bell, Winnie Marneres's brother, came to the Kentucky Club in 1946, eight years later becoming its principal chef. He fondly remembered, "I made 700 to 800 biscuits a day," along with from-scratch apple butter. By 1946 lamb fries (breaded and fried lamb testicles), a specialty from the Bluegrass region of Kentucky, became a prominent menu item. John Bell declared, "The guests liked lamb fries; they had them for a main dish, they had them for hors d'oeuvres. Always lamb fries."[40]

In August 1954 the Highway 66 Bypass for Oklahoma City shifted to Grand Boulevard, now Interstate 44, just south of the Kentucky Club, increasing traffic flow and greatly enhancing land values. The next year the Cowboy Hall of Fame and Museum opened a quarter mile to the east, also on Northeast Sixty-Third Street, bringing thousands of tourists to the immediate area. Tony Marneres contracted with others to rename his nightspot the Ramada Club in 1961 and make it part of a million-dollar Ramada Inn motel complex. The nightspot operated under this name until it reopened under its old Kentucky Club identity in 1979–81. The 1946 building then was renovated to become the County Line Barbecue, serving very popular barbecued meats until 2010, being succeeded two years later by Gabriella's Italian Grill and Pizzeria.[41]

CHICKEN IN THE ROUGH (BEVERLY'S DRIVE-IN)

Beverly Osborne was a go-getter. Born in 1896 to a sharecropping family on a farm outside Marlow, Oklahoma, he quickly learned that to get ahead he had to work hard but also to achieve tangible goals. His first job at age eight was as a shoeshine boy and then at age ten as a cook and soda jerk in small-town drugstores. His later success was intertwined with wife Rubye Aileene Massey. As a young married couple, in 1921 they chanced into Oklahoma City's Hunt's Waffle Shop at 209 West Grand Avenue (later Sheridan), wedged between the Colcord Hotel and the Orpheum Theater. They saw the tiny six-stool diner as an opportunity. Using all their savings, borrowing on their car, and pawning Rubye's diamond ring, the Osbornes raised enough money to purchase the already-operating eatery, reopening it as Osborne's Waffle Shop on December 7 of that same year. Through long hours, irrepressible attitudes, and assistance from Beverly's two brothers as night managers, they made a profit and expanded their original waffle shop into eight short-order diners by 1931. The Great Depression took its toll, and within four years they retreated back to just the one downtown waffle shop.[42]

Still hoping to find a "big idea" that would bring long-term success, the couple took a motor trip to California in 1936. Their goal was, in Beverly's words, "to see what the big restaurants were doing" and thereby discover an innovation they could bring home to Oklahoma. To their surprise, somewhere along the way in the vicinity of Amarillo,

Texas, a bump in the road gave them the hoped-for flash of inspiration. With Beverly at the wheel and Rubye at his side, he hit a rough place in the pavement and bounced pieces of a chicken dinner from her lap onto the seat. With a smile, she quipped, "This is eating chicken in the rough!" Already this expression had become a slang term for consuming handheld pieces of fried chicken, but as he drove along Beverly cleverly connected it through word play with the "rough" outer areas of golf courses. Soon he envisioned a cartoon character rooster carrying his own set of playing clubs. On the West Coast, they undoubtedly visited fried chicken houses where operators at the time were already serving their specialty without any flatware. Consequently Beverly and Rubye combined a mascot stogie-smoking chicken golfer with the idea of selling complete meals of cut-up fried half chickens with french fries, hot rolls, and little jugs of honey for an even fifty cents.[43]

On their return to Oklahoma City, the Osbornes purchased an existing restaurant building at 2429 North Lincoln Boulevard. The eatery fronted on Highway 66 just two blocks north of the Oklahoma State Capitol—close enough for bureaucrats and their office personnel to walk over for meals. Opening formally on September 5, 1936, Beverly's Drive-In offered the choice of curb service or inside dining, featuring chicken dinners, barbecue, and sandwiches. Within about six months, the eatery was advertising "Chicken in the Rough" and boasting that "it has made us famous." The dish did indeed earn a fortune for the Osbornes, for they expanded their base into a chain of eight Oklahoma City restaurants and spread their special flair for hospitality. Journalist Max Nichols later

Beverly and Rubye Osborne with five of their employees standing proudly in front of their flagship Beverly's Drive-In at 2429 North Lincoln Boulevard in Oklahoma City, ca. 1952. Photograph from Production File 2C2270 courtesy of Lake County (Illinois) Discovery Museum, Curt Teich Postcard Archives.

reminisced that the establishment on Lincoln Boulevard "was more of an institution than a restaurant," adding, "We met there after any kind of event, from a movie to a formal dance." He continued, "Almost any evening, and every Saturday night, we could find high school and college friends in the restaurant . . . plowing through Six-by-Six hamburgers and baskets of Chicken-in-the-Rough." The Osborne's dream had arrived.[44]

With others, Beverly developed a special four-foot-long grill that used minimal amounts of grease while successively steaming and frying cut-up pieces of chicken. The device gave the same highly desirable flavor and texture of stove-top iron-skillet frying and could handle 150 pieces at a time, giving economies of scale. By the latter 1930s, the Osbornes were placing ads around the country selling franchises, including leases of their specialized cookers and permission to advertise using the copyrighted cigar-smoking rooster Chicken in the Rough trademark. As many as 350 restaurateurs signed up from the Atlantic to the Pacific and even in Hawaii and overseas. Franchisees paid royalties of two cents per chicken order or 2 percent of their incomes based on sales taxes. This was one of the earliest national franchises of owner-operated restaurants in the United States. By the 1950s Beverly and Rubye Osborne were reputedly earning a remarkable $2 million annually.[45]

Beverly's Drive-In on North Lincoln Boulevard prospered until 1960. The State of Oklahoma then purchased its site as part of a plan to erect more office buildings and land-scape the capitol grounds. The old original restaurant downtown lasted until 1972, with the Osbornes selling the franchise business in 1969 and then the remaining Oklahoma City restaurants to their longtime manager a decade later. One last Beverly's restaurant still serves the old-time Chicken in the Rough in a comparatively new building at 3315 Northwest Expressway, where the special taste can still be found.[46]

FLORENCE'S RESTAURANT

When African American motorists pulled into Oklahoma City, they knew that they would not be welcomed in most of the white-owned eating places. They typically headed to the segregated Black neighborhood of Deep Deuce along and parallel with Northeast Second Street just east of downtown. It was here in 1952 that Florence Kemp established her café, which has thrived since that time. Growing up in the all-Black Oklahoma town of Boley, her mother took her along on her jobs as a maid. After graduating from high school in Boley, Florence made a trip to visit family members in California. There she glimpsed a world she could only have imagined at home in Oklahoma, one filled with a wide range of businesses and entertainment venues owned and operated by African Americans. Inspired by her experi-ences, twenty-one-year-old Florence started

her own café at 916 Northeast Fourth Street on a shoestring. It was a gutsy ambition for a young Black woman in 1950s Oklahoma City. "When we first opened, everything I had was secondhand, including the pots and pans, and the stove," she remembered. Kemp made a success of the enterprise, but, after about fifteen years, her location was threatened by urban renewal. African Americans had already started moving into a dusty, semi-industrial area a dozen blocks east of the state capitol, and in 1969 she relocated her eatery to 1437 Northeast Twenty-Third Street. There the café became a haven for homestyle pork chops, meatloaf, and fried chicken served with fresh green beans, sweet potatoes, and buttered corn. Local food critic Dave Cathey described the eatery as a place where he sought good company and "communion with homemade corn muffins sopped in gravy." Now operated by Kemp's daughter, Victoria, Florence's Restaurant at the time of this writ-ing remained a destination for those with a taste for genuine, old-time scratch cooking.[47]

DOLORES SANDWICH MILL (DOLORES RESTAURANT AND DRIVE-IN)

Amanda and Ralph A. Stephens ultimately found financial success in food service in Oklahoma after several disappointing false starts. After the stock market crash in 1929, they came to the Oklahoma City, starting three downtown cafés that also folded one after the other. Years earlier in Hannibal, Missouri, however, they had acquired a recipe for special barbecue sauce from an Illinois pit master, and they served it at a new Oklahoma City eatery named after their daughter. This was the Dolores Sandwich Mill at 33 North-east Twenty-Third Street, which opened on April 15, 1930. This time persistence paid off.

The combination of friendly service with skillfully prepared meals, notably including the Kum-Bac barbecue sauce and Amanda's from-scratch pies, proved to be the keys to triumph.[48]

The Stephenses built the Dolores in the middle of the block on busy Twenty-Third Street, which carried Route 66 traffic. Their eating place, by 1939 called the Dolores Restaurant and Drive-In, was roughly between the state capitol building and the fashionable Paseo shopping and entertainment district just to the west along Twenty-Third—near-perfect for an eating place. The Dolores was different from most of its competitors. First of all, it served only nonalcoholic drinks, and second, it skipped the breakfast hours, opening only for lunch and dinner. The front of the building had a residential look, but regulars knew to drive around back to the parking and curb-service areas. There they likewise found the main entrance and an open-air patio. Inside were two dining areas, the Old English Room and the Monterrey Room, which had then-popular Spanish Renaissance Revival architectural touches. It must have been in this latter space that Irene M. Roberti ate on a 1941 cross-country trip, after which she commented, "The dinner we had at the 'Dolores' was rather too spicy, yet quite in keeping with the place." The menu initially featured hamburgers, sandwiches, salads, and Amanda's homemade pies, but it soon expanded to include steaks and other dishes. National food critic Duncan Hines chanced to stop at the Dolores on a western road trip in 1939, and he recommended its meals. Later he wrote, "I enjoy eating here, especially their steaks and Suzi-Q potatoes and barbecued ribs." More than anything else, though, Hines enjoyed the hot biscuits, describing them as "the best biscuit I have found anywhere in America, made by Neal, a colored woman, who does not use a recipe, but has a remarkable sense of feel, which tells her when the mixture is right."[49]

The Suzi-Q potatoes that Hines enjoyed were a genuine contribution to American food culture. Both Amanda and Ralph were keenly interested in potatoes and their preparation. In the late 1930s, Ralph experimented with special utensils for slicing spirals of potato rather than straight-cut pieces for french fries. They placed the corkscrew-like fries, called Suzi-Q potatoes (also spelled "Su-Z-Q"), on the menu in 1938, and the idea caught on. The couple then carried the concept to California in 1945, when they opened the first of several Dolores Drive-In eateries in metropolitan Los Angeles. The specialty spread to all corners of the United States as "curly fries," and the dish remains on menus of many fast-food establishments to this day. Amanda retained her interest in preparing potatoes, and in 1941 she amazed her peers at a potato-peeling competition staged at a meeting of the Oklahoma Restaurant Association. There she successfully stripped the skins from two of the tubers using a simple paring knife in just thirty seconds.[50]

Amanda and Ralph were eager for their employees to make favorable impressions on customers. Even during labor shortage days during World War II, they strictly adhered to using adolescent boys and young men as their "curbies" or carhops. In 1937 they told potential applicants for these jobs to expect "small pay until you are some account." The Stephenses felt that looks were important, and when they sought a hostess their ad stipulated, "Need attractive lady." In seeking a cashier, they stated, "Must be alert &

Gumdrop Fruit Cake, DOLORES RESTAURANT
AND DRIVE-IN, OKLAHOMA CITY, OKLAHOMA

Amanda and Ralph A. Stephens built a prosperous business at the Dolores Restaurant on Twenty-Third Street in Oklahoma City based on good food and superlative service. The eatery is known as the birthplace of curly fries in 1938, but food critic Duncan Hines really enjoyed Amanda's creative gumdrop fruit cake. Accordingly, he placed its recipe in every one of his annual cookbooks issued from 1940 to 1960.

One large or three small cakes depending on the size of pans (tube, loaf, or round)

1 cup butter (room temperature)

2 cups sugar

2 eggs (beaten)

4 cups all-purpose flour

1 teaspoon ground cinnamon

¼ teaspoon ground nutmeg

¼ teaspoon ground cloves

¼ teaspoon salt

1 ½ cups drained applesauce

1 teaspoon baking soda

1 tablespoon hot water

1 teaspoon vanilla extract

1 to 2 pounds gumdrops (cut into quarters)

1 pound white or golden raisins

1 cup pecans (chopped)

Cream together butter and sugar. Add beaten eggs.

Sift together flour, cinnamon, nutmeg, cloves, and salt. Set aside ½ cup for coating raisins, nuts, and gumdrops.

Place prepared applesauce in a wire strainer to drain away excess liquid, leaving 1 ½ cups of applesauce pulp.

Add the remaining flour mixture to creamed butter, sugar, and beaten eggs, alternately with applesauce pulp. Mix everything thoroughly. Dissolve baking soda in 1 tablespoon hot water and stir into the dough mixture. Add vanilla.

Sort the gumdrops to remove any black candies. Using scissors, cut each remaining gumdrop into four pieces. Toast the chopped pecans in a little butter until slightly browned. Dredge the pecans, cut gumdrops, and raisins in the reserved flour mixture. Turn into batter and stir well.

Line metal pans with greased parchment paper, pour in dough, and bake at 300° to 325° F for 1 ¼ to 2 hours, or until a tester comes out clean and cakes are golden brown. Take care not to overbake. Remove from oven; cool on a rack for ten minutes before removing from the pan to continue cooling. Serve sliced warm or cool.

Original recipe from Duncan Hines, *Adventures in Good Cooking and the Art of Carving in the Home*, 2nd ed. (Bowling Green, Ky.: Adventures in Good Eating, 1940), unpaged recipe 366.

The front of a menu from the Dolores Restaurant of Oklahoma City, featuring a plate of its signature Suzi-Q curly french fried potatoes ca. 1940. Dolores owners Amanda and Ralph Stephens invented special cutting implements to slice potatoes into spirals, making this dish possible in the late 1930s. Courtesy of Oklahoma Image Collection, Metropolitan Library System of Oklahoma County, Oklahoma City.

quick thinking. Prefer around 30 yrs., under 140 lbs." Waitress applicants needed to be between eighteen and thirty-five years of age and "Must be neat & have nice personality." Frequently they stipulated the race for job applicants, placing whites in front areas dealing with customers and relegating Black employees to the kitchen. In a representative instance on August 27, 1958, they placed side-by-side advertisements in the local newspaper for "White girl for fountain work" and "Colored girl for dishwashing machine." After

the passage of civil rights legislation in the mid-1960s, they tempered the ads specifying Black employees; in 1966, for example, they sought "Lady from East side for salad department."[51]

Amanda Stephens died in 1966, and Ralph continued to run the Dolores until 1970. The Southwest Restaurant Association, Inc., then managed the eating place for four more years, but it was never quite the same. Today a Sonic Drive-In operates in the same general area where the Dolores once was "the Unusual Sandwich Mill."[52]

STANDARD FOOD MARKET

Today, the dozen blocks along the Twenty-Third Street corridor westward from the state capitol area through a 1920s commercial strip does not seem like a hotbed for food-vending innovation, but that is just what it was during the Great Depression. Not only was it the general neighborhood where Beverly and Rubye Osborne developed new ways of cooking and franchising fried chicken dinners and where Ralph and Amanda Stephens invented curly fries, but it also saw the introduction of a first-ever innovation for retail food buyers—the grocery shopping cart. Oklahoma City grocer Sylvan Nathan Goldman, the son of Lithuanian Jewish immigrants, made public this invention in 1937 at the ten stores he and family members owned in the city, including one at 2416 North Walker Avenue, just half a block north of Route 66 along Northwest Twenty-Third Street.

On January 18, 1932, in Oklahoma City, the native of Ardmore, Oklahoma, together with uncle Henry Dreyfus and brother Alfred D. Goldman, formed a legal partnership called the Standard Food Markets. The family had long been in the grocery trade, but the economic upheaval of the Great Depression turned the retail world upside down. In an effort to jump-start their business enterprise, their new grocery effort began purchasing and then operating existing food stores around Oklahoma City. Only days after the family organized the new company, it acquired the existing Sunshine Food Store at 2416 North Walker, giving it the new Standard identity.

For years Sylvan Goldman had pondered that his customers only purchased as much food as they physically could carry in tradi-tional handheld shopping baskets. Muscular oil field workers, for example, could buy and tote a lot more than aged widow ladies. As he sat at his desk one evening in 1936, the grocer spied an everyday folding chair. He thought to himself that if he raised the seat a few inches and then installed another seat close to the floor, the pair of platforms could support two ordinary wire shopping baskets. Quickly he envisioned adding two wheels at the rear and two swivels on the front. A shopper could unfold the hinged carrier, thereon rest two plain shopping baskets, and then wheel them through a store without needing to carry any-thing. Goldman then sent for Fred Young, who worked for him as a carpenter and main-tenance man, and the two men perfected the shopping cart concept by trial and error over the next months. On June 4, 1937, the Stan-dard Food Markets advertised the sensation of "no more baskets to carry" at its outlets, including the one just off Route 66 on North Walker Avenue. Customers hesitated to use the wheeled carts, so Goldman hired several men and women of varied ages to push carts filled with groceries around each of the stores to demonstrate their convenience, and the idea took off with flair. Customers quickly

recognized the advantage of not having to lug heavy purchases through the store. Shortly thereafter, Goldman organized the Folding Basket Carrier Company of Oklahoma City to manufacture the carts, which he sold to other retailers. The first out-of-state buyer was on Route 66 in Amarillo, Texas. From the proceeds of selling his carts around the United States and other later investments, Sylvan Goldman became a millionaire known for his philanthropy.

The Standard Food Market at 2416 North Walker Avenue remained in Goldman com-pany hands for decades. It was a regular stop for some Route 66 travelers who preferred to prepare their own picnic meals in their cars rather than spend money in restaurants. In 1961 its name changed to Humpty Dumpty Supermarket, a chain also owned by the Goldman interests. The store continued selling groceries into the 1980s, after which time its building was adapted to other uses including a storefront church.[53]

TRIANGLE BARBECUE (CLASSEN FRUIT MARKET, TRIANGLE GROCERY, MILK BOTTLE GROCERY)

One of the most distinctive buildings along Route 66 alignments crossing Oklahoma, the Milk Bottle Grocery provided fresh and staple foods to travelers traversing the city for much of its history. It is known equally from its diminutive triangular footprint and from the oversized milk-bottle-shaped advertis-ing sign mounted atop its roof. The three-sided plot of land where the building stands resulted from the construction of the early twentieth-century Belle Isle streetcar line, which cut diagonally northwestward across the north-south/east-west orientation of most Oklahoma City streets. As the community grew, Classen Avenue, parallel to the streetcar line, carried increasing volumes of vehicular traffic, including that of Highway 66 during its early years. This swelling flow of motorists converted the otherwise negligible wedge of land at its intersection with Twenty-Fourth Street, just thirty-nine by thirty-two feet, into valuable real estate.

The visual landmark now known as the Milk Bottle Grocery came into existence at 2426 North Classen Boulevard as a flat-roofed, three-sided brick commercial building erected by general contractor John J. Gordon about 1924–25. Early on, it housed Cooper Cleaners and Hatters, and later H. J. Cook's Triangle Barbecue. Oral traditions connect it to purported illicit alcohol sales during national Prohibition. By 1936 the property became the office of the Oklahoma Realty and Investment Company run by D. T. Covington through the rest of the 1930s. It next housed Ben Hammon's Classen Fruit Market, and then, after the Second World War, the Triangle Grocery. In 1948 property owner Leonard E. Cantrell, possibly tired of repeated armed robberies at the site, sold to Wayne D. Purcell.[54]

It was about the time of the 1948 ownership change that that Steffen's Dairy contracted to rent advertising space atop the pocket-sized store. A sheet-metal crew then constructed a custom rooftop steel framework for an oversized milk bottle. Skilled workers pieced together long, narrow strips of sheet steel into the shape of an eight-foot-diameter round bottle with a smooth-edge base, tapered neck, and rimmed top. They even created the crenelated appearance of the folded paper caps that once closed milk bottles. Painted white, it advertised the Steffen's Dairy that leased the rooftop space,

and the owner adapted his business name to become the Milk Bottle Grocery. Later the three-dimensional, disproportionally large sheet metal bottle advertised Townley's Dairy and currently Braum's Ice Cream and Dairy Stores.[55]

Topped by the extra-large milk bottle signage, the little building continued to house a succession of varied businesses. From Milk Bottle Grocery and Market into the 1970s, the subsequent lessees included Kalikow's Flavored Popcorn, the Beer Box, T. Krepps Floral, the Rib Shak, the Hop Ky Restaurant, the Saigon Baguette Sandwich Shop, Prairie Gothic souvenirs, and offices of Laud Studio landscape architects.[56]

Warr Acres, Bethany, and Yukon

From the 1920s through mid-1950s, U.S. Highway 66 entered Oklahoma City from the north, dropped down to Twenty-Third Street, proceeded westward to a point where it turned north to Northwest Thirty-Ninth Street, and then exited the city westward on Thirty-Ninth. Subsequently newer four-lane freeways connected Highway 66 more directly across the northern side of the city and were built on top of or parallel with Thirty-Ninth to head on west. Drivers all saw that the landscape west of Oklahoma City was becoming more level and that they were entering wheat-raising country. Coming from staid Connecticut in 1934, motorist Lewis Gannett was really impressed by signage as he left Oklahoma City, which, with informal hospitality, read, "So long, hurry back."[57]

Throughout these years, westbound motorists passed through the modest town of Bethany, about five and a half miles west on Thirty-Ninth Street. The town began as an enclave of Nazarene Church adherents, who named it for a biblical village outside of Jerusalem. The 1909 establishment of Oklahoma Holiness College, now Southern Nazarene University, marked the beginning of the community. In 1930, when Bethany had only about two thousand inhabitants, it experienced a powerful tornado that killed twenty-three. Most Highway 66 motorists knew the community marked by storm damage mainly as a place where, due to religious proscriptions, they could not purchase alcohol or cigarettes and where all the places of business closed on Sundays. Much to the chagrin of the socially conservative residents, after enjoying three decades "being left alone" in comparative isolation, in 1937 real estate developer Clyde B. Warr laid out a new residential development he called Warr Acres next door between Bethany and Oklahoma City. By 1948 the newer suburb grew into a legal municipality, which, in the 1970s, gained a dubious reputation as a retreat for gambling parties in private homes. Eventually inhabitants of adjacent Bethany and Warr Acres became reconciled, and later merchants from both even joined the same combined chamber of commerce.[58]

Beyond Bethany, crossing a 1924 through-truss bridge over the North Canadian River alongside Lake Overholser, drivers came to Yukon after seven miles. By day the 140-foot-tall concrete Yukon grain storage elevators standing above the horizon showed drivers that the town lay ahead, while at night, starting in 1930, a rotating electric beacon atop the milling facility beckoned them toward the community. Later, "Yukon's Best Flour" signage in neon was added. Established in 1891, the community began attracting large numbers of Czech immigrants from the Habsburg Empire around

1898, and since the 1960s their descendants have staged a popular cultural festival. With roughly 1,500 residents counted in 1930 and 1940, Yukon gave white motorists a welcome place for food, fuel, and lodging from the earliest days of Route 66. Black motorists, however, did not find the same hospitality, with a local writer in 1936 advising, "All the people belong to the white race. No Negroes are allowed to spend the night here."[59]

SANITARY CAFÉ (NEWKIRK'S CAFÉ, BELISLE CAFÉ)

Charles A. "Charley" Newkirk established his eatery, the Sanitary Café, in 1912 inside an existing building. Then, in 1931, he relocated to 422 West Main Street and changed its name to Newkirk's. In 1928 Benjamin Lee "Bud" Belisle, a local star basketball player for Yukon High School, "started in school at Oklahoma University . . . but very quickly decided he would rather help Mr. Newkirk." The good-looking young man never returned to classes and stayed for over a decade. A menu printed about 1940 shows a full range of breakfasts, hot and cold sandwiches, and main courses, including pork chops, ham, and steak, together with eggs scrambled, fried, or as omelets. It was about this time that Bud enlisted in the U.S. Army in April 1941, where he became a mess sergeant serving in both Europe and Panama. Following his discharge at the end of 1949, the veteran returned to cooking in Yukon for his old boss. The editor of the local newspaper quipped that he "didn't get in enough cooking in his nearly 10 years in the Army, so when he came back home he had to get into the café business." After about a year, Belisle leased the existing Pete's Place hamburger café, but three years later, due to illness, Charley Newkirk put his restaurant up for sale. His longtime former employee acquired the business and, despite the distractions of serving as the mayor and the head of the chamber of commerce for Yukon, Bud ran the eating place as the Belisle Café for another decade until 1963.[60]

El Reno

Highway 66 headed west as straight as an arrow ten miles from Yukon to El Reno, the seat of Canadian County founded in 1889. The community had a steady population of about nine thousand to eleven thousand people from the 1930s to the 1960s, including a substantial African American minority. Black owners operated the Morocco Hotel and a number of eating places that served African American motorists traveling on the Mother Road. Until civil rights legislation of the sixties, most white-run eating places provided meals to Blacks only at the rear entrances. Willie Miner, who came to the town in 1920, remembered, "We couldn't eat in no restaurant unless we ate in the kitchen and then we had to go to the back door. We'd pay the same price but we didn't get the same service." This county-seat town in wheat-raising country offered eastbound hitchhiking travelers on Highway 66 a welcome respite from thumbing rides. Starting in 1911 and through 1946, they could ride an electric interurban railway that connected El Reno to Oklahoma City and then another electric rail line north to Edmond, speeding them at modest cost thirty-seven miles across the largest city in Oklahoma to a point where they could more easily catch rides farther along the road toward Saint Louis and Chicago.[61]

In the last half century, El Reno has become connected with a traditional sandwich known as the onion fried hamburger. Some writers have claimed that the dish originated in the town. The local delicacy consists of an otherwise regular hamburger in which sliced, raw onions are pressed into soft ground-beef patties when first placed on a grill so that the onions sauté and become caramelized inside the meat as it cooks, imparting a particularly savory flavor. Since 1989 the community has celebrated an annual Onion-fried Burger Day in which nowadays volunteers prepare and cook an eight-and-a-half-foot diameter "largest hamburger in the world" to sate the appetites of celebrants.[62]

HAMBURGER INN

The Hamburger Inn at 106, and later 110, West Wade Street holds the distinction of being the first grill in El Reno to prepare onion fried burgers. It opened under the shared ownership of H. W. Davis and his son-in-law, E. C. Cannon, with son Ross Davis later taking over. Longtime El Reno resident Marty Hall knew the proprietors, and he explained the origin of the special sandwiches this way: "It was back in the twenties, back during the Depression. Onions were cheap then, and hamburger meat was expensive. Same as it is now." Hall reported that it was in the Hamburger Inn that the cook "came up with this idea of adding onions to the burgers and smashing them into the meat with the back of his spatula." This not only made the meat go farther but also made the burger appear larger. Hall concluded, "And then he'd reach for an old coffee can from the edge of the griddle and pour on a little bacon grease from breakfast," explaining, "You can't cook an onion without grease." The Hamburger Inn remained in business for decades, appearing in El Reno city directories as recently as 1975.[63]

BOB'S WHITE ROCK (ROSS'S GRILL, ROBERT'S GRILL)

Robert's Grill, in a small, flat-top, white-painted concrete-block building at 101 West Wade Street in El Reno, is the least changed of multiple diners specializing in hamburgers at El Reno. In 2008 food writer George Motz reported, "Robert's is a perfect example of what all hamburger stands looked, felt, and smelled like in the 1920s." So impressed was Motz that he declared, "Robert's is, historically speaking, one of America's most important treasures." Fourteen stools stand at an L-shaped counter overlooking a flattop grill and a wall of stainless steel. The eatery opened in 1926 across the street from the Hamburger Inn, where the onion fried hamburger of El Reno was born. Initially it operated as Bob's White Rock, then Robert's Grill, and for a while in the 1950s and 1960s as Ross's Grill. Current proprietor Edward Graham went to work at the diner in 1979 and purchased it a decade later. Robert's offers a limited menu of breakfasts, hamburgers, french fries, tater tots, and Coney Island hotdogs served with chili sauce and slaw. National food critic Michael Stern reveled over the cooking skills he observed at the grill, writing, "It is a joy to sit at the counter and watch him [Graham] slap a round of beef on the grill, top the beef with onions, then use his spatula to mash the patty into a juicy round as it cooks."[64]

JOHNNIE'S GRILL

Johnnie's Grill is another hamburger outlet that served many thousands of Highway 66 travelers who drove the brick streets through El Reno. John "Johnnie" Siler opened the diner at 311 South Rock Island Avenue in 1946. He adopted the onion fried hamburger techniques that his predecessors had perfected, and proudly cooked up the sandwiches with fries and other short-order fare until retiring in 1967. Otis Bruce then assumed the reins at Johnnie's, continuing the same cooking methods. The founder taught Otis the importance of properly seasoning the grill, coming back to the café to instruct him. "I was pretty skeptical," Bruce said, "but we burnt the ingredients into it, and it worked." Snow caused the roof to collapse into the original Johnnie's building in 1986, but Otis simply moved the business across the street to 301 South Rock Island, and continued there until selling it to Steve Galloway in 1995. The latter expanded the eatery in 2005, and it remains a destination for heritage tourists traveling old Route 66. Galloway reported that he was still maintaining the original gas-fired grill for use outdoors during the annual Onion-fried Burger Day.[65]

Across the South Canadian River

When the U.S. Bureau of Public Roads began assigning numbers to routes connecting the states in 1926, it essentially pieced together existing roadways. In the country from El Reno westward toward Hydro, only one reliable bridge crossed the South Canadian River. This was a privately owned toll bridge near Bridgeport erected in 1921 by businessman George Key. Because this suspension span, for which drivers had to pay a one-dollar fee to cross, offered the only secure way over the river in times of high water, Highway 66 was laid out via roads that looped up through the towns of Calumet and Geary to Bridgeport in order to use this particular bridge before continuing on to

Onion Fried Hamburger, JOHNNIE'S
GRILL, EL RENO, OKLAHOMA

Johnnie Siler opened a grill fronting on the Mother Road in El Reno, Oklahoma, in 1946, and from the outset offered customers a distinctive sandwich for which the town was already known—the onion fried hamburger. Cooks like Johnnie used their spatulas to mash raw onions into uncooked ground beef patties on the grill so that the onions caramelized as the meat broiled, imparting a particularly savory flavor. In the hands of his successors, Johnnie's Grill still serves onion fried hamburgers and is where the author observed the preparation of this house specialty.

One burger

2 ⅓ ounces ground chuck beef (90% lean, 10% fat)

¼ white onion sliced (not chopped)

1 dash salt

1 dash black pepper

1 large hamburger-style white bread bun

¼ ounce prepared yellow mustard

2 partial leaves iceberg lettuce

1 large slice of fresh tomato

6 thin slices of dill pickle

With damp hands, form a ball of fresh, raw ground beef and drop onto a hot griddle or skillet. Press the ball into a patty about a half inch thick. Completely cover the top of the meat with slices of white onion. With a spatula, mash the onion pieces into the soft meat. (Historically, cooks at Johnnie's at this point sprinkled the meat with salt and pepper, which today diners may add from shakers.)

Cook both sides of the patty until brown and the onions soften. Split the bun and place both halves (crust up) onto the cooking patty with edges overlapping onto the grill to warm and toast.

Dress the bottom half of the bun with mustard, lettuce, and a thick single slice of tomato. Place the cooked patty with any loose meat crumbles and grilled onions onto the dressed bun. Top with the remaining half bun and wrap the completed sandwich in a large square of white paper. Serve with half a dozen thin slices of dill pickle as garnish.

Original recipe from oral history interview with Sam Kann and Beth Mulinax at Johnnie's Grill, El Reno, Oklahoma, July 17, 2014.

Hydro. Many individuals living along and near this 1926 alignment saw its designation as U.S. 66 as a golden opportunity to sell goods and services to motorists. In 1930 and 1931, for example, local farmer and lumber dealer Henry Breeze of Calumet erected first a filling station and then expanded it into a store, while his wife added tourist cabins, expecting the traffic to pass their location for years to come. The state purchased Key's suspension bridge in 1930, making if free to cross, but already its engineers were considering how to shorten the route by constructing a completely new, more direct road with a modern permanent bridge over the South Canadian between El Reno and Hydro. Completed in 1933, this remarkable bridge was the longest in Oklahoma. Consisting of thirty-eight one-hundred-foot steel Warren pony trusses on substantial concrete piers, it created an elevated roadway twenty-five feet wide and three-quarters of a mile long. At the time of this writing, this crossing remained in service carrying mostly local traffic that still bypasses the three towns. Calumet and Geary continued to receive at least some motor traffic from other thoroughfares, but Bridgeport, well off the beaten path, withered away. In 1938 its postmaster reported, "There are so many empty business places you feel as though you were entering a ghost town," noting that the "very nice large bank building" had "windows knocked out and partly boarded up, empty and dust-covered."[66]

LITTLE'S CAFÉ, STATION, AND MOTEL

Just a couple of miles beyond the west end of the bridge over the South Canadian, U.S. Highway 281 forked south from the Mother Road toward the little town of Hinton and points beyond. This "Hinton Junction"

became the site for a roadside picnic area and a string of ever-changing filling stations, eating places, and tourist courts. Among the entrepreneurs who made this their home were Ann and W. Leon Little, who had married in western Oklahoma in 1932 and who ran a simple filling station on the original alignment of Highway 66 near Bridgeport. When Mother Road traffic shifted southward to the new roadway, they opened a new station near the end of the new bridge. Quickly the enterprise expanded to include Little's Café, with Ann in charge of the eatery and Leon running the station. A row of tourist cabins followed. Some of the most memorable dust storms of the Great Depression years occurred about this time. Ann recalled, "I would fix lunch, and. . . . I'd put the plates on the table and . . . I'd cover them with two thicknesses of cloth to keep the dust off." Despite her efforts, "I would have to fold back the cloth at the corners to lift it off, and the dust would be thick on it." In fall 1939 a customer came into the café/station reporting, "There's a movie company down at the head of this bridge makin' a picture." Two or three of the young women employees from Little's Café went down to investigate, finding that the crew filming John Ford's motion picture adaptation of John Steinbeck's novel *The Grapes of Wrath* were shooting the scene portraying the burial of Grandpa Joad at the side of the road. The Littles observed 1950s construction of four-lane freeways supplanting the old road between Oklahoma City and the Missouri state line. They realized that inevitably these changes would come to the western part of the state as well. Consequently they made alternative plans and moved to nearby Hinton, where Leon secured appointment as postmaster in

1962. Only ruins remain of their roadside enterprise.[67]

Hydro
DITMORE SERVICE STATION (PROVINE SERVICE STATION, LUCILLE'S ROADHOUSE)

In 1941 Lucille Ione and Carl Robert Hamons used money that he had inherited from his parents to purchase an existing filling station about a mile southwest of little Hydro, Oklahoma. The location, however, had its own interesting history prior to their arrival. Carl Ditmore purchased the land there alongside U.S. Highway 66 in December 1928 and erected a two-story wood-frame filling station/store with living quarters upstairs. He leased this Ditmore Service Station to the Transcontinental Oil Company but, within just a few months, sold it to George Carlisle "Carl" and Glada Faye Ethel. The Ethels began selling Phillips 66 gasoline, a business arrangement that persisted into the 1970s. In June 1934 W. Oscar and Ida F. Waldroup purchased the property from the Ethels, rechristening it the Provine Service Station, from a place-name already associated with the rural neighborhood. At some point in time, the Waldroups or earlier owners added a four-unit row of tourist courts to the enterprise, setting up the property as Lucille and Carl Hamons found it in 1941. They later erected a modest neon sign reading Hamons Court. The Hamonses earned their family income by providing fuel, overnight lodging, groceries, and short-order meals for travelers. Lucille later noted, "I . . . made hamburgers, sandwiches, and breakfast for tourist[s] upon request." Carl earned a little extra money hauling hay for farmers. Lucille reported that during World War II she had many customers who lacked money to pay,

so she "would feed them and give them gas in exchange for some appliance or other articles of value they might have." Occasionally during wartime she even purchased travelers' broken-down vehicles "and then they would catch the bus and head on West looking for work." She hired local teenagers to strip down the cars for usable parts and tires, which she then resold at a profit to other motorists.

On her own after Carl's death in 1971, Lucille continued to run the station and courts. That same year Interstate 40 construction cut off the station's direct access to the new thoroughfare, with the old highway becoming only an access road. Lucille then added beer sales, subsequently developing a lucrative trade by supplying the beverage to students who drove to her store from Southwestern State College in Weatherford. It was about this time that people began calling the old Provine Service Station Lucille's Roadhouse. With a revival of interest in historic U.S. Highway 66 during the 1990s, heritage tourists discovered Lucille's roadside enterprise. She and her filling station/store became the subject of nationwide newspaper articles and other publicity, the property being placed on the National Register of Historic Places in 1997. Hamons passed away in 2000, with title to the property passing through her heirs to a sensitive private owner who has carefully preserved the station and adjacent tourist court.[68]

Clinton

Nine miles beyond Hydro, drivers came to Weatherford and then, after fifteen more miles, arrived in Clinton. Both were substantial towns with several thousand residents during the heyday of Highway 66, and they abounded with accommodations in hotels and tourist courts. During concert tours, Elvis Presley occasionally chose the Trade Winds Motel in Clinton for nights of quiet rest between performances in larger places where passionate fans gave him little peace.[69]

BRADFORD CAFÉ (POP HICKS CAFÉ, POP HICKS RESTAURANT)

For decades travelers recommended the Pop Hicks Restaurant up and down the Mother Road. In addition to providing the usual public services, Ethan Edwin "Pop" Hicks was one of the earliest restaurateurs in western Oklahoma to offer private meeting and banquet rooms. These facilities attracted large numbers of out-of-town customers, many of them driving via Route 66. Although the eatery became well known among Mother Road diners, its origins are murky. E. E. Hicks had come to Clinton at least by 1930, working there as a welder. During this time he became acquainted with William Thurmon Bradford, operator of Bradford Café, but the two did not hit if off well. On the night of Friday, July 24, 1936, they got into an argument at a filling station. Bradford approached Hicks in what seemed to be a threatening manner, and the latter shot him dead with a .32 caliber pocket pistol. The county attorney declared the shooting to be in self-defense. In a comparatively short time, Hicks was managing his victim's café, which he later renamed the Pop Hicks Café, and here the scandal seemingly ended. Years later Hicks's daughter remembered that this original diner had "three small booths and three or four bar stools, and a lean-to . . . on the back as a kitchen." At this site, 223 West Gary Boulevard, E. E. gradually added larger

dining and food preparation areas, eventually expanding into an adjacent building. The business profited from 1950 onward from the Glancy Motel being constructed immediately next door. By 1960 Hicks had become so well respected in regional food circles that his peers elected him president of the Oklahoma Restaurant Association. His eating place in socially conservative Clinton gained notoriety in the 1950s and early 1960s for welcoming African American diners at a time when segregation remained the rule across the state. One of his employees later declared, "Pop was one of the first to open his front doors to Black people." E. E. Hicks retired in 1968, his enterprise eventually passing into the hands of Howard and Mary Nichols. It continued to serve meals under the Pop Hicks Restaurant name until fire destroyed the building on August 2, 1999.[70]

Canute

Named for an ancient Norse king, the village of Canute became a place where visitors tarried because of the appeal of life-sized sculptures in its roadside cemetery just to the east. With a population heavily comprised of immigrants from Central Europe, the predominately Catholic residents led by a local priest created an artificial earthen mound of red soil atop which they placed a life-size figure of Christ on the cross surrounded by other biblical characters. Into the man-made hill, the faithful excavated a re-creation of the holy sepulcher complete with a figure of Jesus. For visitors with more earthly concerns, Canute itself in the mid-1930s offered food from four grocery stores, three cafés, and a drugstore. One of the historic buildings that survives today began in 1936 as a roadhouse and dance hall, to which a service station was later added. The Canute cotton farmers and their families did enjoy kicking up their heels; in 1932 they even organized an open-air dance in the bottom of a railroad underpass at the west end of the community to celebrate the completion of paving on two-lane Highway 66.[71]

Elk City

It was only seven miles farther west to Elk City, a substantial town founded in 1901 with roughly five thousand people in the 1930s and 1940s. Traces of petroleum were first found near the town in 1924, other discoveries followed, and since that time the community experienced economic booms and busts associated with the industry. Through the years motorists on Highway 66 provided another stream of income to Elk City, which hosted multiple service stations, lodgings, and eating places. The business district gained its own reputation for the seemingly random manner in which people parked their vehicles. Viola Van Koevering made her way through town on November 3, 1934, and with tongue in cheek noted in her trip diary: "Parking problems are managed very efficiently in Elk City. Cars are parked in the middle of all streets. Angle parking at each curb is also practiced. The result is that you have to go about 10 miles per hour in order to keep from hitting some other car."[72]

CASA GRANDE HOTEL

The four-story, buff brick Casa Grande Hotel visually dominates downtown Elk City, and for decades stood as the largest hostelry between Oklahoma City 130 miles to the east and Amarillo, Texas, 150 miles to the west. Edward Merton Woody chanced to recognize the strategic position of Elk City when he stopped there in 1927 to have a flat tire repaired at the M&M Oil Company. Already experienced in the hospitality trade and always looking for new opportunities, he took advantage of the trip delay to assess places in the town where a hotel might be erected, and he liked what he found. Woody subsequently contacted old business colleagues in Bristow, Oklahoma, and later made new contacts in Elk City to raise the funds to erect a state-of-the-art hotel and dining facility at the corner of Highway 66 and Third Street in downtown. Oklahoma City architects J. W. Hawk and J. O. Parr, known for their designs elsewhere in the state, planned the modern, new hotel in Spanish Eclectic style to include a coffee shop at the rear of the lobby, a separate dining room, and more private banquet space, plus sixty guest rooms and merchandise display areas for salesmen. The hotel opened in 1928 and hosted a national Highway 66 Association meeting three years later. For years the Casa Grande provided the highest status dining in Elk City. A journalist from Oklahoma City ate there in 1950, reporting that "the sirloin steaks were thick and juicy and originated in Elk City territory but came through Kansas City." To remain competitive, in 1957 the owners redecorated the coffee shop and dining room, while converting the banquet facility into the redesigned Green Room, offering dinners and dancing with live music on Friday and Saturday evenings. Tastes in lodging changed over time, the Casa Grande declined, and in 1985 it became the now-shuttered Anadarko Basin Museum of Natural History, as well as providing a limited number of apartment rental units. All motorists taking the old pavement of the Mother Road drive directly past this impressive edifice.[73]

Sayre

Cross-country travelers motored west out of Elk City, passing an impressive petroleum refinery, and, after a few miles, angled southwest to reach Sayre after about seventeen miles more. Travelers observed the landscape growing progressively drier, with fewer and fewer full-height trees except in towns, as they made their way farther into Great Plains country. Here they began to see yucca and greyish green sagebrush growing at the roadside. In this semiarid environment, Sayre grew as the seat of Beckham County, experiencing an oil boom in the 1930s that boosted its earlier 1920 population of 1,703 to 3,157 a decade later. The boom played out, though, and the number remained about three thousand for the rest of the Route 66 period. Filmmaker John Ford felt that Sayre sufficiently fit the stereotypical dust bowl Oklahoma town enough that his crews filmed the fictional Joad family driving past its courthouse in a scene for the 1940 feature film *The Grapes of Wrath*. In 1930 Sayre received an employment boost when the United Carbon Company constructed a carbon black plant about four miles west of town. Here vast amounts of natural gas were burned to create the soot-like black substance sought after by vehicle tire makers. Carbon black not only turned natural rubber dark in color but also imparted toughness and durability to tires of the day. As far away as twenty miles, hundreds of thousands of Route 66 motorists viewed the black industrial smoke drifting upward from this facility for two decades, becoming an identification mark for Sayre. A 1936 writer described how "when the wind comes from the south or southwest great clouds of black smoke are wafted over the town."[74]

OWL DRUGSTORE

The Owl Drugstore at 101 West Main Street was already an institution in Sayre when U.S. highway 66 first passed it in 1926. The brick building, erected about 1901, may indeed have been the oldest masonry structure in the town. Here Prentice Rogers rented space for an Owl Drugstore as early as 1908. Not long thereafter property owner E. K. Thurmond sold the building to brothers Luther and Russell Randle, both pharmacists, who continued the Owl Drug name. Luther and wife Louise assumed active management until his death, and she operated the store through the end of 1957. A soda fountain appeared inside early in the business's history, and the Owl Drug became a popular hangout for Sayre teenagers for years. Although subsequent owners gave the drugstore interior and exterior facelifts, the fountain and lunch counter remained essentially unchanged, serving meals, snacks, and ice cream to residents and travelers alike until closing finally in the 2000s.[75]

Erick

Just over fifteen miles southwest of Sayre, drivers came to Erick, the last substantial town they would see in Oklahoma. It was along this roadside that they saw the red Oklahoma soil start turning more brownish. Like many other communities in western Oklahoma, Erick was established by townsite promoters at the turn of the twentieth century. The area experienced an oil play during the 1920s that bumped the population up to 2,231 by 1930, but it never again even approached that figure. It was during this same period on the night of July 13, 1930, that, in a sudden maneuver, whites drove out all of the African Americans residing in Erick and the nearby smaller community of Texola, rendering both sundown towns. When Jack Rittenhouse passed through Erick in 1946, it reminded him of the set for a Western movie from "its wide, sun-baked streets, frequent horsemen, [and] occasional sidewalk awnings." The community subsequently became known as a home of singer-songwriter Roger Miller, whose recording of "King of the Road" about the daily life of a hobo pulsed on travelers' car radios for months in the mid-1960s.[76]

BEE CITY (HONEY FARM)

Some roadside entrepreneurs were not even looking for the businesses that they eventually ran. This was the case of farmers Olin and Maxine Wilhelm, who raised crops just west of Sayre, an area of cotton, alfalfa, and clover hay production. Around 1953 Olin's father gave the couple thirty-five hives of bees. The young couple gratefully accepted the gift, gradually added more hives, and made arrangements with their farming neighbors to distribute the bee colonies around their fields in exchange for shares of the honey. Local crops and wildflowers provided nectar for the bees. Initially the Wilhelms sold their product only to local consumers and to occasional Route 66 motorists who saw a homemade "Bee City" sign marking the unpaved sandy road to their farm. Eight years later, about 1961, the couple realized that their 150 hives were earning more income than their farming. In 1964 Maxine recounted, "We sold our cattle, dropped our cotton allotment, and went into the bee business in earnest." They created a sales shop, added candle making, and began bulk sales of honey. Over time, the farm became a destination for tourist buses and school groups. The notoriety of the Bee City apiary prompted the chamber of commerce in Erick to start

an annual honey festival in 1983 that continued for over a decade. In 1990 new owners purchased the apiary, and their successors operated it into the 2000s on the west side of Erick.[77]

Texola and on into Texas

When westbound Route 66 drivers arrived in Texola, seven miles beyond Erick, they reached the end of their passage across Oklahoma. The Texas state line lay just beyond the little town, which reached its peak of population at 581 in 1930 before drought in the following years decimated its surrounding dryland farms. Today the community has perhaps three dozen residents. During the early years of Highway 66, however, a modest hotel and multiple cafés served meals to Mother Road sojourners. Among these eateries were the DeLuxe Café, the City Café, and D. C. Campbell's Café, offering "ice cream, cold drinks and everything good to eat." More than a stopping point for food, Texola in the 1930s and early 1940s developed a dubious reputation as a speed trap for motorists. There, according to the state attorney general in 1941, "The mayor acts as the police judge and the city marshal, who has been appointed by the mayor, is the arresting officer in all cases." The marshal stopped tourists almost exclusively, and the mayor as judge typically assessed them fines of $6.50, considered at the time to be excessive.

Some travelers stopped in Texola voluntarily. In summer 1932 Lucille Byerly Lackore and three girlfriends on a California-bound trip by Model T took a lunch break there. She penned in her trip diary after their meal in a drugstore, "I played 'Whiz Bang' for about half an hour with a young man while Hazel scribbled some cards to send back home." The mechanical game was a version of pinball introduced that very year and had already reached the little town on the Oklahoma plains. Ahead for the four girls and the many motorists both before and after them lay the Lone Star State of Texas—famed in Western movies but looking pretty windswept and austere from the pavement of the Mother Road.[78]

CHAPTER 5

TEXAS

The wide Texas sky beckoned as drivers crossed into the Lone Star State. They had entered the Great Plains in western Oklahoma, but soon they would advance onto the eerily flat Staked Plain (or Llano Estacado), a semiarid and treeless land where short grasses formed the only natural vegetation. Population was sparse, distances between towns grew, and the only city along the way, a modest one, would be Amarillo, a hundred miles west. The region formerly was the home to the Comanche Indians and the bison off which they lived. These southern plains began receiving Euro-American ranchers and their herds of cattle in the 1870s, with farmers following them twenty years later. In 1930, the year of the first census after the designation of Highway 66, the eight Texas counties the Mother Road traversed or even touched claimed just over a hundred thousand people. Ten-year-old Peter Aldrich from Michigan was not very impressed when his parents in March 1945 drove with him across the state. "The novelty of the 'wide open spaces' in the Texas Panhandle quickly wore thin," he later wrote, adding, "It was hard to believe that there could be so few trees." The seemingly level Texas prairies, however, created their own special travel memories. On August 12, 1938, Evelyn Tucker and a girlfriend departed Tulsa on a vacation to the Pacific coast, driving straight through the first night. Pressing westward from a midnight coffee break in Shamrock, Texas, the women munched on pieces of fried chicken they had brought from home. From the front seat, Evelyn observed, "There was a beautiful moon and the road shined like a piece of ribbon in the night." She remembered that along the way, "we were entertained by huge jackrabbits, attracted by our headlights, which would jump up and run alongside the car for a short distance."[1]

Once across the state line from Texola, Oklahoma, motorists saw only open fields and pastures. As part of the Texas centennial celebrations in 1936, the state's highway department erected an art deco masonry boundary monument at the side of Highway 66, later replacing it with a fossilized limestone marker in the shape of the state silhouette. It was at this point westbound by the 1930s that travelers encountered an official state-line inspection station. There, uniformed personnel queried travelers about fresh citrus fruits they might be transporting and examined the titles to their motor vehicles to deter automobile theft. Just beyond the state border, for several years Oldham's State Line Texaco Station sold oil, motor fuel, soda pop, and snacks. The enterprise began on one side of the roadway, but then the states of Texas and Oklahoma made the short stretch of Highway 66 straddling the state line into a divided four-lane motorway. The second pair of lanes was laid on the opposite side of the station, enabling owner Ralph W. Oldham to add more pumps and from the center median sell fuel from both sides of his boxy little facility. This profitable arrangement lasted until later road improvements encroached onto the business's space and forced its removal.[2]

Heading west over gently rolling prairies, travelers felt the elevation gently rise as they drove the roughly dozen miles to Shamrock. To the right they could look down gullies and valleys leading toward the North Fork of the Red River in the distance. In July 1941, Irene M. Roberti penned in a trip diary, "We followed mile upon mile of very straight road—straight and with gradual up-grades. The vegetation is so very different here." The Mother Road across Texas roughly paralleled the tracks of the Chicago, Rock Island and Gulf Railway, a subsidiary of the larger Chicago, Rock Island and Pacific, as highway builders realized that the early-twentieth-century railroad survey crews had already picked out the easiest route toward New Mexico. English driver Mark Pepys in fall 1935 observed, "The railway track ran alongside" and "Three times in the morning, we saw trains making their long transcontinental trek." Two transported passengers and one was "made up of many khaki-coloured refrigerator trucks carrying fish and fruit eastward from the coast of California."[3]

When African American travelers on the Mother Road crossed from Oklahoma into Texas, they simply passed from one state with legalized racial segregation into another. The one place in the Texas Panhandle where they could reasonably expect to find sit-down meals and lodging was Amarillo, and these were mostly from Black entrepreneurs. The separation likewise extended to bus travel, with African Americans sitting in the rear of motor coaches and surrendering their seats to whites to stand in the aisle if the vehicles became full. Route 66 Greyhound driver Howard Suttle, a white man, remembered that in Texas, "At every station, there were 'white' and 'colored' drinking fountains and restrooms. Every rest stop or bus station had a place for colored people; usually a small table in the rear of the kitchen." Although not mandated by state law, discrimination often extended as well to Hispanic Americans. Joseph P. Sánchez remembered from a 1958 road trip from New Mexico to Texas the emotional sting he felt in seeing handmade signs in Amarillo restaurant windows and doors reading "No Mexicans Allowed." These situations persisted until civil rights legislation was passed in the mid-1960s.[4]

Soon the roadway led travelers into the town of Shamrock, with a population of two thousand to three thousand souls during the Route 66 years.

Shamrock
U-DROP INN (NUNN'S CAFÉ, TOWER CAFÉ)

When Highway 66 received its numerical designation in 1926, it zigzagged across the eastern side of the Texas Panhandle on existing unpaved roads. It made multiple ninety-degree turns at north-south/east-west survey corners while roughly paralleling the Rock Island tracks. It entered Shamrock on East Railroad Avenue in the heart of what then was a modest business district. Over the course of the next half dozen years, state highway engineers and the Wheeler County commissioners straightened the roadway, shifting its entry to town northward a dozen blocks, creating fresh economic opportunities in a heretofore underdeveloped area.

Local retired rancher Lackington Randall Clay Sr. owned all four corners of the road junction where Twelfth Street (relocated Route 66) intersected with North Main Street, already carrying north-south U.S. Highway 83. He owned a filling station on one of the corners that started earning substantial profits as soon as the new 66 alignment opened to traffic, but the conservative stockman refused to sell any of the other valuable property. In 1933 Clay died, bequeathing the property to his wife, and this set the stage for investment opportunities. Amarillo businessman James M. Tindall approached Clay's daughter, Beatrice "Bebe" Nunn, and her husband, John Lawson Nunn, with a proposal they found too good to refuse. The investor offered to build for the couple on one corner of the intersection any kind of commercial building they might want if in exchange Bebe would convince her mother to sell to the promoter some of the other strategically located property. She recalled, "So my husband picked up a rusty nail in our yard and drew up just what he wanted," a stylish combined service station and restaurant. The deal was struck with the outlines scratched in the dirt. The Nunns got their building, and Tindall acquired the desired corner real estate.

Construction progressed through 1935 and into 1936 on a fanciful beige and green concrete, brick, and tile structure, which became a memorable stop for travelers on Route 66. It consisted of a gasoline station with garage and twin canopies on the west end ornamented by a large four-sided Portland cement obelisk topped by a stylized tulip. The richly ornamented east end of the complex housed a full-service commercial restaurant. Amarillo architect Joseph Champ Berry designed the building in Art Deco style, featuring geometric patterns, strong vertical elements, and sculptural ornamentation. Fashion at the time might instead have suggested smoother Streamline Moderne lines, but clearly Berry followed the Nunns' own aesthetic preferences. Green and vermillion neon bedecked the exterior, with Bebe Nunn fondly reminiscing, "Back in the '30s, neon was all the go. Our sign and tower was all bordered in green and red neon. It shined so bright that you could see it from way back past McLean," twenty miles west.

The projected new restaurant did not yet have a name, so John and Bebe Nunn offered fifty dollars to whomever in the public might propose the best moniker. A local boy suggested U-Drop Inn and received the prize, which was considerably more than the weekly wage for a waitress. After its opening on April 1, 1936, the round-the-clock restaurant gained a wide reputation for its steaks, with John Nunn purchasing entire sides of beef at eleven cents a pound and hanging them in a special cooler. Bebe remembered, "He cut all our steaks—and we had a great number of steak eaters—so they knew they could ask for a certain thickness and get it." After a few years, the Nunns turned the restaurant over to others, but then in 1950 resumed its management under the Nunn's Café name. Other operators included Grace Bruner, who purchased the restaurant in 1960, making it the Greyhound bus stop in Shamrock. "We had about ten [bus] schedules a day. We kept sandwiches made up and put them on the counter before a bus was due, as there wasn't time to order from the kitchen. . . . We also kept plenty of pies and apples. Of course, candy, cookies, chips and gum," she remembered. The iconic eatery and service station remained in business into the 1990s, after which time the City of Shamrock acquired the landmark and restored it to become a handsome tourist travel information center.[5]

McLean

Drivers coursed westward along Highway 66 twenty miles from Shamrock to McLean. After half a dozen miles, they passed through the crossroads community of Lela, where they could pause for limited services. The roadway remained unpaved into the early 1930s, making the way difficult during wet weather. At McLean travelers found a town of wood-frame and masonry homes and commercial buildings, the most prominent being the two-story brick Hindman Hotel, where meals were served. The two-lane Mother Road initially passed along First Street until 1951, when the state highway department reduced congestion by converting First Street into two lanes westbound and making Railroad Street, just a block south, into two lanes eastbound. Eventually nineteen gasoline stations operated up and down these two thoroughfares, one being a fine cottage-style 1929 Phillips 66 fuel stop that is preserved today. For years farmers around McLean raised watermelons as a sideline, shipping out twenty-eight railway carloads of them in

just a single day in 1937. On a cross-country trip a decade later, Ellen Tappenbeck jotted in her diary on the hot last day of August 1947, "Stopped in McLean for cold water and cold watermelon, eaten outdoors." The roadway through McLean was the last portion of old Highway 66 in Texas to be supplanted by Interstate 40. In 1982, not long before these changes, motorist Roy Blount Jr. passed that way. He reported his surprise when, "All of a sudden the speed limit was 45 and then 35 and . . . by cracky there was a crossroads! A red-light! The Interstate Highway System had somehow not gotten up to bypassing McLean yet." The transfer of traffic to the freeway came just two years later in July 1984. Today, McLean's population has dwindled to less than eight hundred, half its 1930 total.[6]

Alanreed and the Jericho Gap

Between McLean and Groom, travelers ascended through roughly broken country onto the nearly flat and treeless Staked Plain, a geographical subsection of the larger Great Plains. Since passing through western Oklahoma, motorists had paralleled the tracks of the Chicago, Rock Island and Gulf Railway. After 1938 the drive over the two-lane Mother Road from McLean via the little town of Alanreed to Groom was just a matter of proceeding thirty miles at highway speeds. Prior to this time, however, the trip took a slow, circuitous route over unpaved roads because the roughness of the topography prevented them from following the railway tracks as closely as on smoother terrain. From McLean the way dropped a mile and a half south and then turned west to proceed through the settlement of Alanreed and the scattered Jericho rural community almost thirty-five miles to the larger town of Groom. Seventeen miles of this road through sparsely inhabited ranch country in the northern edge of Donley County was the last section of the Mother Road in Texas to be paved, with the blacktop not reaching it until 1936. The initial mostly dirt track, impassable after heavy rains, generally followed existing north-south and east-west unpaved county roads that alternated with meandering lanes that sometimes approached the railroad tracks. Along the way travelers passed (and sometimes stopped at) such modest eating places as Shirley Faye's Diner at her husband's Texaco service station in tiny Jericho. Eventually old-time motorists zigzagged their way back onto pavement east of Groom, breathing sighs of relief that they had made their way across the Jericho Gap.[7]

Groom

GOLDEN SPREAD GRILL

In 1956 entrepreneur Pete Ford erected the Golden Spread Motel at 407 Front Street on Highway 66 in Groom. Four months later he opened an adjacent coffee shop called the Golden Spread Café. The appellations originated from a mid-1950s economic booster promotion of the Texas Panhandle being a "golden spread" of productive farms and ranches. Ruby Denton of Groom went to work for Ford on February 9, 1957, the day the eatery opened, and in time she herself purchased the enterprise. For forty-five years she worked in and managed the restaurant, which served many thousands of meals to Route 66 travelers and locals. Business boomed alongside the roadway, with Ruby providing jobs for as many as twenty full-time employees and her menu each day attracting up to four hundred vehicles bearing diners. In addition to its food, the Golden Spread became known as a reliable source for road condition information in bad weather. During a 1971 blizzard, for example, Ruby reported a "full house" of stranded travelers in her dining room, noting, "They are bringing people in. . . . People are still getting stuck." After the 1980 diversion of cross-country traffic away from the old road to Interstate 40, the motel closed but the Golden Spread Grill continued serving meals. In the latter years, one of its regulars, Jack Bivens, generally came in twice a day. "I start out with coffee in the morning," he reported in 1993, adding that for lunch, "On Mondays I eat Mexican food" and "On Tuesdays, I eat beans and greens." One reason for this level of customer loyalty was that everything in the kitchen was made from scratch. Denton declared to journalist Susan Croce Kelly that most successful café operators were women. "I'll tell you why," she explained. "Most men don't like to work that hard and don't like to take the guff." Veteran restaurateur Ruby further elaborated, "When you operate a café, you don't travel—you stay home and tend to business. The café business is fun if you like it, and I like it." She managed the Golden Spread Grill until the age of eighty-two in 2002. For a time afterward, the Route 66 Steakhouse occupied its building, to be succeeded in 2009 by the Grill, which still serves homestyle food beside what once was the Mother Road through Groom.[8]

Conway

From Groom onward the old-time highway returned to paralleling the Chicago, Rock Island and Gulf tracks fifteen miles to Conway and thence another twenty-eight to Amarillo. Among the Texas towns that motorists passed, Conway was one not to have been spawned by railway construction. Instead the dispersed rural community started growing about 1892 around the Lone Star country school. It never was more than a hamlet, though it boasted of trackside grain-handling facilities, filling stations, and a simple wood-frame four-unit tourist court, filling station, and café combination. Longtime Conway resident C. M. Hudson owned the modest complex as early as 1945 and was followed by other proprietors. The eatery known as the Conway Café and later as Buddy's Café served travelers and local residents as recently as 1969, when it hosted a morning "coffee" for campaigning U.S. senator Ralph Yarborough. During a winter blizzard in February 1980, a fire swept through the facility, leaving only ruins of some of the buildings, which by the 2000s had been removed.

Because of its location in sparsely settled, often barren country, Conway residents each winter inevitably found themselves sheltering motorists who unexpectedly became stranded by winter snow and ice. This happened to Delbert Trew, who grew up in the 1930s on a ranch in the area. On return from pasturage in New Mexico in a Ford farm truck, he and his party learned that the Mother Road east from Conway was so drifted with snow that no vehicles were getting through. They trooped into the still-standing little gasoline station at the crossroads to discover twenty more storm victims. Women and children found refuge in the owner's home, while the men crowded into the station. "We took turns sleeping on the floor, ate everything edible, chewed all the tobacco, smoked all the cigarettes, cleaned out the house and all the neighbors in about 20 hours." Reflecting on the experience of being snowed in, he concluded, "I'll bet the owners were glad to see that storm let up."[9]

Amarillo

Amarillo was the only true city that Mother Road travelers found in Texas. It came into existence in 1887 at the side of the tracks of the Fort Worth and Denver City Railroad, which strategically helped link Denver, Colorado, with the Gulf of Mexico. The city prospered from wheat and cattle raising even before an oil boom grew its population from 15,494 in 1920 to 137,969 by 1960. Amarillo offered food, lodging, and virtually any services that a traveler might seek. Many cross-country motorists left the city telling stories of being overcharged for vehicle repairs, with expensive "generators from Amarillo" becoming almost proverbial up and down the highway. On the other hand, travelers did generally find safe, quiet, and comfortable beds in a profusion of hotels and motels there, together with meals ranging from short-order hamburgers to lobsters flown in for freshness.

The alignments of Highway 66 through Amarillo remained more stable than in many other places along the route. Throughout the period motorists entered the city along Northeast Eighth Avenue, renamed Amarillo Boulevard in 1963. Travelers proceeded through an increasingly dense commercial strip, eventually intersecting North Fillmore Street. Here they turned south and drove just over a dozen blocks into the heart of the business district. Just as they passed the Potter County Courthouse, drivers along 66 made a ninety-degree turn west, this time onto Sixth Avenue. After two blocks they crossed over busy Polk Street, the "main street" of downtown, and proceeded westward on Southwest Sixth Avenue to the outskirts. Between the 2700 and 3900 blocks of Southwest Sixth, they passed through the still mostly preserved 1920s San Jacinto district, a bungalow neighborhood filled with popular eating places and nightspots. During the 1950s, Southwest Eighth Avenue became a new four-lane U.S. 66 bypass westward from Fillmore Street to the extreme west side of the city, where it curved down to join the earlier alignment. The more congested older route via downtown along Fillmore and Sixth then became known as Business 66.[10]

BIG TEXAN WESTERN STYLE CAFETERIA (BIG TEXAN STEAK HOUSE, BIG TEXAN STEAK RANCH)

Northeast Eighth Street, later renamed East Amarillo Boulevard, became the most densely packed concentration of motels and restaurants in mid-twentieth-century Amarillo. Tourist courts, cafés, bars, dance halls, filling stations, and repair garages all lived from trade that came to them on rubber tires. When the Underwood's Barbecue Cafeterias of Brownwood, Texas, began expanding after World War II, the firm opened a branch at the northeast end of the Amarillo motel district at 4515 Northeast Eighth in 1956. It operated there in a purpose-built beige brick facility, but, after seven years on February 21, 1963, the restaurant moved closer into the city. This relocation created a business opportunity for a midwestern newcomer.

Robert James "Bob" Lee was born in Kansas City, Missouri, in 1929. As a young man, this son of a restaurant operator served as a mess sergeant in the air force. He then earned a degree from the University of Missouri in home economics because that was the only department in the school at the time where he could study professional food service. In 1955 Lee married South Bend, Indiana, nurse Mary Ann Prcygocki and went to work for the Marriott Hot Shoppes, Inc. For this national corporation, he first helped manage restaurants in multiple locations throughout the northeastern states but later wound up in Dallas, Texas. By this time Bob and Mary Ann had decided that they wanted to settle down in one place, so he began looking for airport restaurant management contracts that might be available. In 1959 The city council of Amarillo accepted his proposal to administer its air terminal meal services, so later that year the Lees moved to the city on Route 66. After five years Lee tired of dealing with municipal bureaucrats, so in early 1964 he opened his own Big Texan Western Style Cafeteria in the facility fronting on the Mother Road that Underwood's had recently vacated.[11]

Bob and Mary Ann Lee's new eating place initially met only indifferent success. He even advertised the property for sale on the real estate market in the spring and summer of 1964. Genuine modern-day cowboys, however, saved the business. The Big Texan was five minutes by pickup truck from the Amarillo Livestock Auction, and its stockyard employees started driving over to the convenient eatery, especially on Fridays after work. Other customers, many of them out-of-state Mother Road travelers, found the cowmen's clothing and demeanor bizarre but fascinating. Lee started cashing the cow punchers' paychecks and offering them beers for twenty-five cents apiece as encouragement to hang around the dining room and offer local color. Then one day one of the cowboy's horses escaped from a trailer in the parking lot, and the man ran out, got the animal under control, and returned it into the trailer. "There were people running into each other on Route 66, pulling off the road with their cameras," son Bobby Lee later reported. In this moment his father realized that travelers from back east genuinely wanted to see real cowboys. He approached one of the auction workers and proposed, "Look, you come back tomorrow. I'll pay you twenty-five bucks just to sit on your horse and wave to people." The young man thought that the out-of-state restaurateur had lost his mind, but he did return. Remarkably, diners started pouring into the formerly quiet cafeteria, and it soon converted to become the western-style Big Texan Steak House. Lee even dressed up his waitstaff in cowboy attire with toy six-guns. Next he hired two extra-tall male basketball players from nearby West Texas State University to dress up like ranch hands to greet guests at the door. Live fiddle and guitar music followed. In every way the businessman tried to help tourists to experience the Hollywood fantasy of the Wild West.[12]

The stockyards employees gave Bob Lee his greatest gimmick. Son Danny Lee remembered the occasion this way: "The cowboys from the stockyard always caused a stir in the place. They were such pigs when they ate." Bob never ceased to be amazed at how much food they could put away. He proposed to his regulars, "I'll tell you what. Next Friday night, when you guys get paid, everybody come up here and put up $5. I'm going to serve you one-pound steaks for one hour, and who ever eats the most gets all the money in the pot." He announced the competition to the media and created a buzz about the steak eaters. On the evening of the contest, one man got ahead of all the others, and he gloated, "Well, bring me a salad too. What else you got there? Bring me a shrimp cocktail and bring me a roll." In the end, the auction cowboy consumed four and a half pounds of steak with the trimmings. Danny Lee remembered his dad declaring at the time, "From this day forward, anybody who comes in here and eats a seventy-two-ounce steak, complete with side orders, will get it for free." Since that time the offer has stood, with several people on most given days taking up the seventy-two-ounce-steak challenge. Only some succeed.

On November 15, 1968, Interstate 40 opened through Amarillo and traffic flow diminished to a trickle on the old Highway 66. Business for the steak house plummeted. Bob and Mary Ann Lee spent most of their savings purchasing 9.7 acres of land along the interstate on the far eastern side of the city. They salvaged materials from several disused wooden barracks at the former Amarillo Army Air Field and, with the lumber, erected a new and much larger restaurant on the freeway. On April 30, 1970, they closed the doors at the eating place on the old road and reopened the next day on the interstate as the Big Texan Steak Ranch. The popular restaurant thrived in the new location and continues each year to serve steak dinners to thousands of travelers, many from overseas.[13]

DING HOW RESTAURANT

Throughout the United States, Chinese entrepreneurs established eating places that typically served both American food and variants of Chinese fare to mainly American diners. Many such businesses sprang up along Highway 66, but the Ding How in Amarillo stood out visually. Joe Suey Woon, the mastermind behind the restaurant, had a long history in Amarillo. He arrived about 1924, working at the Chinese-run Empire Café and then for years as a part owner of the downtown Canton Café at Fifth and Taylor, only a block off Highway 66. In 1957 he left his former partners and erected his own restaurant, Ding How, at

2415 Northeast Eighth Avenue specifically to cater to the Highway 66 trade. The rectangular, single-story, flat-roofed structure had a cream-colored stucco front ornamented with red tile at its cornice and along a front canopy. Patrons made their way inside through a circular-shaped, covered brick entry and a pair of large red doors. At the front of the parking lot stood one of the most elaborate multicolored neon signs in Amarillo. Shaped like a four-tiered Chinese temple, it announced the Ding How, which is a transliteration of the Chinese words meaning "very good" or "well done." In 1957 twelve-year-old Ben Fong-Torres traveled to Amarillo with his father, who was one of the initial cooks at the new enterprise. They lived with other employees in a two-bedroom house behind the restaurant. Ben later remembered, "To give Ding How's visitors a sense of the Orient, our waitresses, none of them Asian, wore red satin blouses with mandarin collars, and black slacks." The menu offered a range of Americanized Chinese dishes like chop suey and moo goo gai pan, as well as steaks, Virginia ham, and fried chicken. Souvenir merchandise in glass cabinets at the cashier's stand attracted adolescent Ben's attention more than the food. "Ivory chopsticks, back-scratchers, plastic Chinese soup spoons, folding fans, and wisdom hats" all stuck in his mind, as did "a rack of postcards, both naughty and nice." The restaurant served meals at least into the 1990s, and its disused building and still-readable neon sign remained at the site at the time of this writing.[14]

LONGCHAMP CAFÉ (LONGCHAMP DINING SALON, RICE'S DINING SALON)

Seemingly born to be a salesman, F. Homer Rice of Amarillo knew how to make money.

During the 1930s and early 1940s, as a young man, he worked as an agent selling Wilson and Company meats, later dealing in used cars and running service stations, most of the time in the neighborhood where Highway 66 along Northeast Eighth Avenue turned south on North Fillmore Street toward downtown. Homer paid attention when, in 1943, Amarillo newcomer Harry G. Kindig opened up a new fish restaurant called the Longchamp Café in an existing building at 803A North Fillmore at the northwest corner of the strategic intersection. By the start of 1945 and despite wartime food rationing, Kindig was earning enough selling fish dinners that he could advertise for an experienced cook to take over his kitchen, stating, "salary no object if you are the right man." Later that year Kindig moved his eatery into new quarters in a purpose-built cream-colored Streamline Moderne–style facility with plenty of parking space; it was only four blocks away at 705 Northeast Eighth, still on the Mother Road. In spring 1947 Homer Rice purchased Kindig's already-established fish place, and grew it into a powerhouse among Amarillo eateries. Using clever advertising, he invited customers to a general restaurant he called the Longchamp Dining Salon, which showcased fresh seafood despite being landlocked hundreds of miles from any ocean. Among his special dishes were salmon, Gulf shrimp, Texas flounder, Florida pompano, and Colorado trout. "It if swims we have it," he widely advertised, though he also offered non–fish eaters government-graded steaks and fried chicken. Perhaps feeling that some potential diners might feel put-off by a restaurant featuring fish, in about 1953 Homer further broadened his menu and renamed the popular eatery Rice's Dining Salon. He still proffered lots of seafood but considerably expanded the general choices. By 1955 food critic Duncan Hines could advise, "Here there is a varied menu, but the emphasis is on very good T-bone steaks which have been making the traveling man happy for years and years." By 1963 Homer opened an adjacent Rice's Motor Hotel, which only increased the restaurant sales, but five years later Interstate 40 opened, siphoning away the traffic that had created the boom around the junction of Northeast Eighth and North Fillmore. By this time Homer Rice was aging, so he brought in outside managers for the motel and restaurant, which limped along into the 1980s before they closed. Today no evidence of either can be seen at the site.[15]

TEXAS BARBECUE PIT (TOM'S PLACE)

When African American travelers arrived in Amarillo, they knew the Lone Star State had strict customary racial segregation backed up by statutes. Even the local dining facilities of the Fred Harvey Company, generally open to all except in the Deep South, separated the races in Texas. Many of the Black wayfarers carried Victor H. Green's annual *Negro Motorist* guides to identify providers of lodging, food, and vehicle services who would welcome them. These paperback compendia recommended the Watley and Tennessee Hotels in Amarillo for lodging. Starting in the late 1940s, the guides endorsed Tom's Place at 322 Northwest Third Street as a reliable destination for tasty meals.[16]

The Longchamp Dining Salon at 705 Northeast Eighth Avenue in Amarillo, Texas, two years after Homer Rice purchased it in 1947. Rice touted, "If it swims we have it." Photograph from Production File 9BH686 courtesy of Lake County (Illinois) Discovery Museum, Curt Teich Postcard Archives.

Texas-born restaurant proprietor Thomas Jefferson Hughes came to Amarillo in 1923, working at a number of different jobs and about 1930 married Georgia Warr. About 1939 the couple opened the Texas Barbecue Pit at 218 North Van Buren Street, soon moving it to 322 West Third Avenue. Both addresses were in the Flats section, the oldest segregated Black area in the city, situated north of the railroad tracks and downtown. It was only four blocks west of the Highway 66 alignment along North Fillmore Street. The venture operated as a barbecue stand until 1947, when it expanded to become a full-service, sit-down restaurant known as Tom's Place. About this time the "Green Book" guides began listing it annually. Hughes, as the president of the Negro Business League, and later his son David W., as a civil rights activist, made the eatery a center for community involvement in Amarillo. As early as World War II, for example, it was one of four locations "in the colored section" where people officially purchased war bonds. By 1948 David Hughes, while working at the restaurant, unsuccessfully encouraged the city administration to employ African American police officers to serve Black neighborhoods, and then argued before the city council to open municipally owned golf courses to all citizens. In 1951 he was one of the activists who successfully desegregated the two-year Amarillo College and then five years later served as the spokesperson for the local civil liberties group that ended separation of the races in the Amarillo public schools. In 1956 David Hughes was one of the early African Americans to serve on an area grand jury. All this time the restaurant continued serving many thousands of locals and travelers from Highway 66, with one Amarillo old-timer remembering that Tom's Place had "some of the best barbecue you ever ate in your life." Georgia Hughes died in 1952 and Thomas followed four years later, but David W. Hughes continued the business after his father's death with the assistance of Mrs. Johnnie Warner. About 1959 David relocated to Lubbock, Texas, but Warner managed the restaurant until 1967. The next year George L. J. Fenley opened the Fenley Café in the same space, but it closed in the early 1970s. A bare vacant lot behind a chain-link fence marks the site today.[17]

THE ARISTOCRAT CAFÉ

All up and down Route 66, women entrepreneurs owned and operated successful eating places. Myrtle Mickey Wood was one of these self-motivated businesspeople. As early as 1946, she was operating Mickey's Café in rented space at 114–16 Southwest Sixth Avenue, directly on the Mother Road and just around the corner from Polk Street, the main commercial thoroughfare of Amarillo. The next year, in 1947, she moved into finer quarters that included air conditioning, unusual at the time, on the ground floor of a two-story commercial building across the street at 119 Southwest Sixth. There, on September 1, she formally opened the Aristocrat Café. Trade from working people and downtown shoppers combined with travelers from Highway 66 supported the enterprise profitably for about a decade. It gained a reputation for homemade baked goods, especially pies, and for its "tempting variety of fresh vegetables prepared to retain all of their natural flavor." Not long after the opening, Myrtle married Tillman H. McCafferty, and together they comanaged the restaurant for about three years, after which she assumed full supervision and Tillman's name disappeared from city directories. Customers seem to have really enjoyed her cooking. The local press reported that members of "the motoring public" were known to plan travel across the Texas Panhandle just so that they would "reach the Aristocrat Café for their luncheon or dinners." The restaurateur appears to have envisioned greater things, for in 1952 she opened a short-lived Mickey's Club tavern near the eastern end of the tourist strip of Highway 66 motels and restaurants at 4936 Northeast Eighth Avenue. She conducted her downtown eatery until about 1956, and afterward remained in the food trade. She subsequently ran the diner at the Amarillo Market Truck Stop on the south side and then in the 1960s and 1970s operated another Mickey's Café "with home-cooked foods you will like" at 2103 Southwest Seventh Avenue, only a block south of the U.S. Highway 66 business route.[18]

CALF STAND / PIG HIP / MUSICAL PIG / ROYAL PIG

It seems ironic that Amarillo, in the center of cattle-raising country and offering some of the finest-quality beef in America, would become an incubator for pork sandwich makers. This is just what happened in the 1920s and 1930s. For decades cross-country travelers stopped in the city for sandwiches made using generous portions of specially seasoned, thinly sliced baked pork. The multiple roadside eateries seemed to originate from the humble Calf Stand Barbecue, which Henry L. and Florence M. Hines opened in the San Jacinto district at 501 Georgia Avenue, a block south of the Mother Road, the year the roadway received its designation in 1926. Two years later the owners moved to

larger quarters directly facing the highway at 2704 Southwest Sixth Avenue. The couple seemingly did so well that their barbecue and sandwich business attracted competition. In 1931 Obie R. and Cora A. Tingley opened the Pig Hip, selling the same basic food selections across the street at 2705 Southwest Sixth. Henry and Florence held onto their trade at the Calf Stand until 1934, when they sold the business to Glen F. and Baby Jo Miller. The new owners renamed the short-order drive-up café the Musical Pig Sandwich Shop, a title that stuck. The eatery subsequently passed into other hands, serving food into the late 1940s. Forrest Willard "Fist" Ansley, onetime president of the National Route 66 Association, was the most colorful of several owners. Later, in the 1950s and 1960s, he created and operated the Prairie Dog Town tourist attraction on the east-side approach of Highway 66 into Amarillo.[19]

In 1931 Hugh H. and John C. Dinsmore, brothers from Alton, Illinois, opened their own Pig Hip Sandwich Shop at 501 South Pierce Street, in the central business district only a block southeast of Highway 66. Three years later, Obie and Cora Tingley closed their San Jacinto neighborhood shop and bought out the Dinsmores. The couple ran the curb-service diner for over a decade, while starting a modest chain of satellite Pig Hip sandwich shops in surrounding communities. Their slogan was, "They made their way by the way they're made." With the passage of time and passing into the hands of other owners, the downtown Pig Hip became the longest continuously operating drive-in in the city. Into the mid-1970s, it fed fresh pork sandwiches to generations of locals and Mother Road sojourners.[20]

Yet one more enterprising Amarillo couple sought riches through shaved pork sandwiches. As early as 1933, Gladys and Houston S. "Chisel" Benton were operating a short-order café called the Paramount Lunch four blocks south of Route 66 in the central business district at 914 South Polk Street. They secured a franchise for Maid-Rite crumbled beef hamburgers as well as producing their own Royal Pig shaved pork sandwiches served on special buns. A laudatory writer in 1937 reported that Chisel "says his special formula for making the Royal Pig sandwich . . . makes them so delicious and juicy that his own mouth waters every time he makes one for a customer." About 1946 the entrepreneurs opened the Royal Pig Café at 112 East Tenth Avenue, farther from the Mother Road; later, under other owners, it shifted to shopping center locations, where the restaurant name survived into the 2010s.[21]

GOLDEN LIGHT CAFÉ

To be significant, historic eateries do not need to be physically impressive or exotic looking. Because of its longevity, the humble Golden Light Café at 2908 Southwest Sixth Avenue is recognized as the oldest continuously operating eating place in Amarillo though many might consider it to be only a hole-in-the-wall "greasy spoon." Others, however, extol it as a place of pilgrimage.

Chester B. "Pop" Ray and wife Louise established the Golden Light Café in 1946, but they were not the first food vendors on this site at the north side of the Mother Road. As early as 1938, an eatery named Scott's Drive-In was selling diminutive hamburgers there for a remarkably cheap fifty cents a dozen. In 1939 Howard Martin took over the enterprise, renaming it Martin's Drive-In, and operating

the short-order food stand until his death in 1941, when his widow took over for about a year. Five years later Chester Ray established the next known eating place in this location as the Golden Light Café. Oft-told stories relate that Ray became ill when the time came to open the business and that his son and daughter-in-law had to take his place until he recovered. Chester and wife Louise ran the humble café with plywood seating and a natural gas-fueled grill until 1957. The Sanborn fire insurance map of Amarillo issued in 1955 shows the little diner occupying a rectangular stand-alone wood-frame building covered with asbestos siding. According to city directories, Ralph C. and Evelyn Boyd assumed the reins at the Golden Light in 1957, followed by Joe P. and Ollie Anna Crawford in 1960, and by other successors who maintained the ambience of the old-time bar and grill. With an exterior brick veneer; indoor booths, tables, and counter; open-air dining beside the rear parking lot; and an adjacent cantina offering live music in the evenings, the modest little eatery continues to serve the same old-style short-order foods that make it, in the words of one admiring writer, "one of the great diners of all time."[22]

BRADFORD GROCERY

Many Highway 66 travelers picnicked and cooked meals in tourist camps and along the side of the road. This meant that they became frequent customers at grocery stores, where they could purchase the bread, cold cuts, and tinned foods that became their staples. Some of these motorists started from home with victuals they had prepared in advance, but once they started eating them up they had to buy more. Lloyd "Shorty" Smith's family made multiple trips between Illinois and

Arizona by way of Amarillo in their Pontiac during the 1950s, and he reported, "We often stopped at grocery stores along the way to replenish our supply." He fondly recalled, "We frequently bought Vienna sausages; a perfect road trip fare, as they did not require refrigeration." As a girl in 1946, Marisue Pickering made the overland trip with her family from Texas to Arizona, and she reminisced about their meals "along the road or in our motor court rooms." She particularly remembered "my mom handing me the peanut butter jar and a spoon when I became hungry between meals." Because many African American travelers sought to avoid the embarrassment of patronizing segregated restaurants, where they were served at the rear kitchen doors, they frequently bought food at grocery stores and ate in their cars. Larger chain food stores generally treated Black customers with more courtesy, so these full-sized enterprises frequently received proportionally more trade from African American motorists.[23]

From the late 1920s to the mid-1940s, married couple Cecil Vincent and Lena Mae Bradford operated one of several grocery stores along Southwest Sixth Avenue, at the time carrying all the Highway 66 traffic through Amarillo. It is remembered for one of Cecil's novel marketing ideas. He started the business in 1927 as a corner store in part of a residence in the San Jacinto district just a block north of the Mother Road at 500 Virginia Street. By the next year, he moved to an improved facility in an existing flat-roofed commercial building at 3018 Southwest Sixth. There he and Lena ran their enterprise until his death in 1946, after which she managed it for about another year. During the depths of the Great Depression in 1932, Cecil and Lena faced competition from half a dozen other food stores in the twelve blocks of Southwest Sixth through the San Jacinto neighborhood. This meant that, on average, there was an eager grocer trying to attract business every two blocks. To make his and Lena's store stand out from the others, Cecil decided to start giving away chickens—live chickens. He climbed up onto the roof of the Bradford Grocery at a set time on certain Saturdays. From that elevated point, he tossed down a limited number of fluttering birds that customers and potential customers scrambled to chase down and catch at street level. To say that this created a commotion would be an understatement. Most of Cecil's shoppers had grown up in homes where their mothers had their own chicken yards, so they thought little of the need to dispatch and clean the live birds in order to cook them up for dinner. Highway 66 writer Tom Snyder described these "chicken follies" in his pioneering guide to Route 66 in 1990, and local historian and journalist Mary Kate Tripp, through her own contacts, confirmed their having taken place. Mary K. Holly reported to Tripp that she and her husband, Anderson C., had operated a fruit market only a block away and that she was well aware of the ruckus created by Cecil's aggressive marketing antics just down the street. Longtime Amarillo resident Syble Bradford (unrelated to the grocers) remembered that her family lived on the east side of the city but drove across town to Bradford's store on Southwest Sixth because it was a cash-only enterprise where "we could save a little money." At the time of this writing, a barber shop was operating at the site of the store that formerly offered free-fall, squawking poultry giveaways.[24]

As travelers headed west from Amarillo, all who had tarried there took away their own memories of the stops. Ruth and Lewis Gannett passed through the city on the way from New York to Los Angeles in a snazzy Ford V-8 in the summer of 1933. The next year he reminisced, "We shall not soon forget the melting T-bone steak that went with a thirty-five-cent three-course lunch in a café opposite the Ford service station in Amarillo." Not all the food experiences were so positive. In 1945 eleven-year-old John DiPonzio rode California-bound with his parents and brother in a 1939 Plymouth. "When we got to Amarillo, Texas, we stopped at this restaurant and sat at the counter," he reported. His father looked over the menu, but when the waitress came to take the order, he shook his head and told her, "We can't eat here; we can't afford it." Years later John reflected, "I always remembered the sad expression on my father's face."[25]

Vega

Westward from Amarillo, drivers traversed the most sparsely settled country that they had yet encountered. The land was seemingly flat and treeless with diminishing wheat fields interspersed with range land. On the outskirts Amarillo, they passed by two landmarks, a multistory Veterans Administration hospital established in 1940 and a processing plant opened in 1929 by the U.S. Bureau of Mines, which at one time supplied half of the helium gas in the world. Down the road, parallel to the rails of the Rock Island Line, motorists drove through the little towns of Bushland and Wildorado to reach Vega after thirty-six miles. This seat of Oldham County took its name from the Spanish word for "meadow" when it was established in 1903 alongside the newly laid steel rails. Vega was never a big town, but on the thinly populated western

side of the Texas Panhandle its five hundred to eight hundred people during Route 66 days made it a comparative metropolis. With a stable economy based on ranching, it offered travelers modest choices among a handful of service stations, lodgings, and eateries.

JERRY'S CAFÉ (KRAHN'S CAFÉ AND TRUCK STOP, ROBINSON'S ROUTE 66 CAFÉ, ANITA'S LONGHORN GAS AND CAFÉ, OLD 66 CLUB TAVERN)

At least as early as 1946, Boots and Dorothy Bruce were operating Jerry's Café at the side of the Mother Road in Vega. Although it did not seem that way, the level-appearing plains over which travelers had been passing actually tipped gradually upward toward the west, so drivers reached an elevation just over four thousand feet at the little town. This comparatively high elevation gave the whole western side of the Panhandle heavier snow than areas to the east. Consequently Jerry's Café on many occasions found itself providing shelter and meals to snowed-in motorists. On February 12, 1948, the Amarillo press reported the eatery that morning was full to overflowing. "Mrs. John Hohenshelt, the manager, said the cook let some of the early-bird strandees into the café at 5:30 o'clock," the *Amarillo Daily News* reported, adding that when she arrived half an hour later, "the place was packed." In 1950 Don and Ann Krahn purchased the existing café at 504 East Vega Boulevard, renamed it Krahn's Cafe and Truck Stop , and quickly thereafter constructed an adjacent Texaco truck stop. They ran the eating place and truck service center, with Don from his auto racing expertise becoming known regionally as "the Flying Dutchman." Subsequently owners operated their own eating places at the location under such names as Robinson's Route 66 Café, Anita's Longhorn Gas and Café, and the Old 66 Club Tavern. At the time of this writing the building stood vacant.[26]

Adrian

The two-lane road crossed the treeless plains fourteen miles from Vega to the little ranching community of Adrian. Its peak population, counted in 1960, was only 258 people. Highway 66 provided several families with their livelihoods, many of them having members who worked in service stations, garages, and cafés.

KOZY KOTTAGE KOURT (66 SERVICE STATION AND CAFÉ, BENT DOOR CAFÉ, TOMMY'S CAFÉ)

Born in Oklahoma, Manuel Freeman Loveless came to Adrian in 1935 as a transient aboard a Rock Island freight car. He dropped off the train because the town looked prosperous, not realizing that he had chanced to arrive when it was full of temporary workers during the wheat harvest. Even after the field hands left, he saw Highway 66 traffic continuing to pour through the little community twenty-four hours a day and he decided to stay.

Among the motorists was Montana-born Claudia Roberta Bruce, who met Manuel when she stopped for car service at the Collier Garage. In time they became husband and wife and together built the Kozy Kottage Kamp, tourist cabins combined with a filling station and café that subsequently became known as the 66 Service Station and Café. (White owners of roadside enterprises who wanted to avoid serving African American travelers were commonly known to spell their business names substituting Ks for Cs to mimic the Ks in "Ku Klux Klan.") The complex burned in 1947, leaving only a few of the cottages.

Local resident Bob Harris, who grew up in Adrian and as a teenager, worked for Manuel Loveless, returned home from World War II, and worked several jobs. In 1947 his family purchased the property where Loveless's old café and filling station had formerly stood. On the site he began erecting a new café and filling station. About this same time, the federal government was selling off excess property at military bases no longer needed after the war. Bob went to a sale seventy-five miles away at the old Dalhart Army Air Base,

Travelers on a road trip in an almost new but dusty 1934 Ford pause to purchase fuel and refreshments at the Adrian Mercantile Company in Adrian, Texas. A handwritten note on the back of the photo reads, "On way home—Sat. Aug 10th '35." Author's collection.

where he purchased elements from a metal and glass flight control tower. Hauling the parts and pieces back to Adrian, he incorporated them into the restaurant end of a new combined café and Phillips 66 service station. To reduce eye glare for air corps personnel in the original control tower, the upper parts of its windows had been canted outward, as was the doorway that led from inside to an outer gallery. Harris incorporated this unusually shaped doorway as the restaurant entry, giving the eatery the name, Bent Door Café. Old-time entrepreneurs Manuel and Claudia Loveless leased the building from Harris and operated both the diner and the station for twenty years. Their son, Tommy, so greatly enjoyed hanging out in the place that they eventually renamed it Tommy's Café. When the teenager grew old enough, he himself started working there. He would take the night shift in the kitchen from 4:00 P.M. to 6:00 A.M., while his mother took the days. Business boomed at the diner and service station so long as Mother Road sojourners funneled back and forth through Adrian. Then in 1968 the traffic flow diverted to newly completed Interstate 40. The eatery cut back its hours from round the clock to just breakfast, lunch, and dinner, but still could not reduce expenses enough to stay open. Both enterprises closed in 1970, and brothers Tommy and Larry Loveless opened a new café/filling station on the freeway, which in the hands of others has remained in business to the present day as a convenience store with self-service fuel pumps.[27]

ZELLA'S CAFÉ (JESSE'S CAFÉ, ADRIAN CAFÉ, MIDPOINT CAFÉ)

In the mid-1940s, Jeanette Vanderwork hired a local man to erect a building for a café on the south side of Highway 66 at the extreme west end of Adrian. It was a simple concrete-block structure with a hard-packed earth floor, but despite its crudeness and its north-facing entry, the simple one-room building offered enough protection from the cold Panhandle winds for Zella Crims to lease it for her Zella's Café. Several other tenants followed, as did more proper flooring. In 1956 Dub Edmonds and former navy messman Jesse Fincher purchased the property, which the former described as "an old building a cowboy built of cinder blocks." They remodeled and added onto the eatery, retaining the original one room and constructing an A-frame apartment space above an updated dining room and kitchen on the east side. Just to the west they operated a Humble filling station. Inside Jesse's Café, Fincher created a reputation for fresh-baked pies that are remembered to the present day. Edmonds recalled, "He would bake pies and set them on the counter and most of them were sold before they got cold." The business was so good that the entrepreneurs opened a satellite called Jesse's Café #2 in Wildorado, some twenty-eight miles to the east. Fran Hauser purchased the property in 1990, renaming it the Adrian Café, but then changed it to the Midpoint Café after she learned that Adrian was mathematically equidistant 1,139 miles from both Chicago and Los Angeles. Her friend Joann Harwell added her own twist to the pie traditions in the diner with her own handmade "ugly crust" version of cream and fruit pies baked each evening. Owned by successors, the Midpoint Café remains in business beside the old pavement in Adrian, where it has become almost a pilgrimage site and most certainly a photo stop for heritage tourists driving the old roadway.[28]

Basic Cream Pie, MIDPOINT CAFÉ, ADRIAN, TEXAS

In 1956 Jesse Fincher joined Dub Edmonds in purchasing an eatery in Adrian, Texas, known today as the Midpoint Café. Fincher was a former navy messman who specialized in baking; he made the eatery famous for his pies, which reputedly sold out before they were cool. Later cooks like Joann Harwell continued this tradition. In the 1990s, she created a sensation at the Midpoint with her "ugly crust" pies, and to this day travelers flock into the eatery to savor its fresh desserts.

One pie

3 tablespoons cornstarch

2 tablespoons all-purpose flour

²/₃ cup sugar

½ teaspoon salt

¹/₃ cup light-colored Karo brand corn syrup

3 cups milk

3 egg yolks (beaten)

2 tablespoons butter or margarine

1 ½ teaspoons vanilla extract

1 nine-inch baked pie crust in pan

In a large saucepan, combine cornstarch, flour, sugar, salt, syrup, and milk, mixing thoroughly. Bring to a boil, stirring constantly, and gradually add egg yolks, butter (or margarine), and vanilla. Continue cooking while stirring until the mixture thickens and starts to boil.

Pour the hot mixture into baked and cooled nine-inch pie crust. This recipe makes a generous amount of cream pie filling. Top with whipped cream or meringue.

To make a chocolate cream pie, add 2 to 3 tablespoons of Hershey's powdered cocoa to the mixture during cooking. For a coconut cream pie, add ¾ to 1 cup of packaged shredded coconut to the filling after it has been removed from the stove and mix thoroughly.

Original recipe by Joann Harwell from Cheryl Berzanskis, "Desserts Key to the Holidays," *Amarillo Globe-News* (Amarillo, Tex.), November 15, 2006, sec. B, pp. 1, 3.

Glenrio

As motorists proceeded westward from Adrian, it seemed as if the level, treeless plains might extend all the way to California, but the landscape deceived them. Only about five miles west of town they descended from the pancake-flat prairie downward into the eroded valley of the Pecos River. The elevation dropped more than two hundred feet in just over a mile as they advanced deeper into the valley of the Pecos, which they would not actually reach for a hundred miles at Santa Rosa. Vegetation immediately changed at the escarpment edge, and they started seeing lots of yuccas, cholla cactus, and thorny mesquite scrub brush. After eighteen miles without any services, travelers came to the little town of Glenrio, which lay astride the Texas–New Mexico state line. For years the Lone Star State had the advantage of one-cent-per-gallon-cheaper gasoline taxes than the Land of Enchantment, with filling stations in Glenrio mostly clustered on the Texas side of the boundary. When gasoline cost fifteen or twenty cents a gallon, a penny made a big difference to many customers. On the other hand, voters in Deaf Smith County, Texas, had voted to remain dry after the 1933 end of national Prohibition, meaning that all the bars and a dance hall in Glenrio operated on the wet Quay County, New Mexico, side of the line. The community came into existence, as had many others alongside the Mother Road, when the Chicago, Rock Island and Gulf laid rails across the Texas Panhandle to connect western Oklahoma with Tucumcari, New Mexico. Glenrio sprang up in 1907 and, though it probably never had more than a hundred people, it functioned as a significant rail-based cattle shipping point long before

Highway 66 was routed this way in 1926. The hamlet quickly assumed an increasing role as a fuel, food, and lodging stop for motorists. As a young U.S. marine, Michael Wallis hitchhiked through carrying his seabag during the 1960s and remembered that, after miles and miles of nighttime darkness along the desolate Mother Road, the electric lights of Glenrio made things so bright that "it'd look like two in the afternoon. There were trucks and babies nursing and GIs and tourists and cattle trucks," not to mention booze in the bars on the New Mexico side. The little village maintained this busy roadside life until Interstate 40 bypassed it in 1975, when the community began withering away into a ghost town.[29]

BROWNLEE'S DINER (LITTLE JUAREZ CAFÉ)

Observing the east-west traffic flowing across the state line, Joseph Brownlee and wife Lillian settled at Glenrio in the 1930s. Years later structural movers relocated a wooden bungalow as their home from Amarillo to the north side of Highway 66 at the east end of town, and in front of the dwelling the couple with son Joe erected a concrete-block Texaco service station in 1952. Two years later they added a Streamline Moderne–style concrete-block diner, painted white with green striped trim to match the color scheme of the service station, and it fed years and years of motorists as Brownlee's Diner and later as the Little Juarez Café.[30]

STATE LINE CAFÉ AND SERVICE STATION (TEXAS LONGHORN)

Homer and Margaret Ehresman were also drawn to business opportunities they saw in Glenrio. They relocated to the state-line community in the 1930s, with Margaret being appointed the postmaster by 1937 and Homer selling gasoline. In 1953 they erected the still-standing State Line Café and Service Station. Constructed with concrete blocks, the single-story main building had a gabled roof and housed a restaurant, a Phillips 66 filling station, and a small repair shop. Two years later the Ehresmans built the adjacent State Line Motel, consisting of two wings constructed of stucco-covered adobes (dried earthen bricks) and concrete blocks. About this time they renamed the whole enterprise the Texas Longhorn. Out front a tall illuminated sign on the west side read, "First Motel in Texas—Café," while the reverse side read, "Last Motel in Texas—Café." The tourist court, filling station, and eatery served travelers until 1976, the year after the interstate bypassed the town, by which time the Ehresman family had opened the Texas Longhorn 2 (TL²) Truck Stop on the interstate just to the west near Endee, New Mexico.[31]

On into New Mexico

The pavement changed from concrete to asphalt at the state line in Glenrio, marking where Texas and New Mexico highway departments provided roadway maintenance. Across the line in New Mexico stood a further scattering of bars, a dance hall, and a few more filling stations. Beyond this point drivers left behind the bright lights and hot food as they headed into sparsely inhabited ranch country where cattle outnumbered the few people.

CHAPTER 6

NEW MEXICO

The state of New Mexico officially began calling itself the "Land of Enchantment" in 1938, but Highway 66 motorists had known of its many charms for years. At least since the days of the Santa Fe Trail in the 1820s, New Mexico had beckoned to traders and travelers from settlements in Missouri and beyond. Then the Santa Fe Railway and the Fred Harvey Company famously promoted and developed it as a destination inside the United States where tourists could experience the diverse cultures of Native American and Hispanic people, many of them living in the very same areas they had occupied for centuries. New Mexico became safely "exotic."

If cross-country motorists knew that they had traversed a young state in Oklahoma, they found that New Mexico and Arizona were newer yet. The Sooner State had entered the union in 1907, but its two mostly arid southwestern counterparts became full-fledged states only in 1912. The populations were thinly scattered and the road networks sketchy when the Mother Road received its numerical designation fourteen years later in 1926.

Out-of-state travelers found four basic groups of people living in New Mexico, most of them quite different. The earliest residents were Native Americans from several distinct cultures, the largest three that Route 66 motorists encountered being Navajos, a variety of Pueblo peoples, and Apaches. They spoke their own languages and had dissimilar religions, making them as different from each other as Italians are from Russians. The second ethnic group encountered were descendants of early Hispanic settlers, who moved up the Rio Grande valley from Mexico starting in the 1500s. Newer immigrants from Mexico formed the third cultural group; many of them came northward into the state as they fled violence during the Mexican Revolution in 1910–20 and stayed. Though these Mexican newcomers spoke Spanish like the earlier arrivals, their culture had developed separately from that in the isolated Hispanic communities long in New Mexico. Anglo Americans, African Americans, and Europeans formed another group of newcomers. Most of them relocated there after the 1846–48 Mexican-American War that led to the region transferring from the Republic of Mexico to the United States. To say that these groups of people got along happily would be an exaggeration, but for the most part each group tolerated the others. In driving across New Mexico, motorists generally consumed foods that originated from one or more of these cultural groups, creating potential for memorable meal experiences.

Travelers from the East had already passed through a variety of striking landforms, including the eroded Ozark Plateau and flat and treeless Great Plains. In New Mexico they encountered three more distinct geographical regions, each one creating its own driving experiences. Near the state line, drivers dropped off the edge of the smooth plains into about a hundred miles of uneven ranch land eroded over eons by the Pecos River. After crossing the Pecos at Santa Rosa, they entered a basin-and-range plateau marked by multiple north-south trending valleys interspersed with ridges and ranges of the southern Rocky Mountains. Beyond the Rio Grande and continuing into Arizona, they traversed an intermountain plateau characterized by impressive flat-topped sandstone mesas and masses of igneous rocks including lava flows. The New Mexico landscape presented a continuously changing spectacle.[1]

Glenrio

Westbound travelers entered New Mexico at Glenrio, a little railroad town bisected by the state line. Quirks of political decisions separated the community into two halves. When Prohibition ended, for example, voters in Quay County, New Mexico, decided to permit the sale of alcoholic beverages, while those across the line in Deaf Smith County, Texas, opted to remain dry. This meant that for years all the bars and liquor stores in Glenrio lay west of the line. Through another governmental twist, the New Mexico legislature voted to levy tax on retail gasoline sales at a rate one cent per gallon higher than lawmakers in neighboring Texas, so most of the Glenrio filling stations sprang up on the east side of the boundary. With motorists stopping more often for fuel than for alcoholic beverages, most of the cafés and tourist courts consequently opened in the Texas section with the filling stations, where the railroad depot likewise stood.

Glenrio came into existence in 1907 when the Rock Island Railroad built across the state line in connecting the Texas Panhandle with a rail junction at Tucumcari, New Mexico. The siding here became a significant rail shipping point for locally raised cattle. The trackside community received a post office in 1908, almost twenty years before U.S. Highway 66 was routed through the village. The arrival of cross-country motorists seeking fuel and food brought new employment opportunities to the hamlet shared by two states. Daily traffic counts in the border area grew from 211 in 1928, to 300 in 1936–37, and to 970 in 1941, demonstrating how the flow of vehicles increased.[2]

STATE LINE BAR

John Wesley Ferguson came to Glenrio in 1924 as the railroad stationmaster. Shortly thereafter he started buying up property on the immediate north side of town, opposite the tracks and the parallel unpaved east-west roadway. There, in about 1925, he erected a Texaco filling station immediately west of the state line using sun-dried mud adobe bricks covered with protective stucco. After the end of Prohibition in 1933, he enlarged the adobe station to house the State Line Bar and erected the adjacent adobe and wood-frame State

Line Motel. During these years the post office in Glenrio, New Mexico, operated inside the Dewees General Merchandise Store, but that facility burned in 1937. The loss gave Ferguson the opportunity to erect a modest wooden addition to the west end of the State Line Bar, which he made available to the Post Office Department for a number of years. The combined State Line Bar/Texaco filling station with attached post office operated until about 1960, when the facility was completely remodeled. With a concrete-block veneer on the front, it subsequently served its postal role exclusively for least another decade. The wives of local entrepreneurs often received federal appointments as Glenrio postmasters, among them Margaret Ehresman and Lillian S. Brownlee, both of whose husbands operated service stations and cafés on the Texas side of the line. The taverns in Glenrio occasionally became scenes of alcohol-related violence, including a gruesome knife murder of fifty-eight-year-old State Line Bar manager Dessie Leach in 1973.[3]

Endee, Bard, and San Jon

Geological conditions frequently combine with the push and pull of local politics to complicate otherwise straightforward road placements and subsequent improvements. Both of these factors came into play along the forty-two miles connecting Glenrio with Tucumcari, the first good-sized town travelers met in eastern New Mexico. The way between the two points descended from the edge of the nearly level Great Plains downward into the valley of the Pecos River through strata comprised mostly of sand and caliche, a low-grade cousin of crumbly limestone. The area had virtually no naturally occurring gravel from which to build roadbeds. The caliche packed down when moistened, but in dry weather it created billowing clouds of dust, while summertime convectional rainstorms made its surface deceptively slippery. When this length of roadway finally was paved in the late 1930s, much of it had only an inch or so of asphalt laid directly on a caliche base, so the weight of trucks quickly mashed the

The State Line Bar and Texaco filling station just on the New Mexico side of the state boundary at Glenrio. The photographer wrote in fountain pen ink on the reverse side of the snapshot, "4/16/49 Gasing up at Glen Rio [sic] on borderline of Tex & N. Mex." Author's collection.

blacktop into ruts and potholes that required repeated maintenance. As if these conditions were not enough, a wet-weather temporary lake just east of Tucumcari often overflowed from rains, flooding the roadway. As decades passed, segment after segment of old Highway 66 was replaced by four-lane interstate, but the forty-odd miles between Glenrio and Tucumcari remained a narrow two-lane that locals called the "Bloody Alley." Many travelers lost their lives there, often in one-car rollovers when the caliche roadside gave way. Local politicians in San Jon, a highway-dependent community located between Glenrio and Tucumcari, effectively delayed the necessary surveying and the construction of a replacement freeway in fear that it would divert the business that Mother Road drivers brought to the tiny community of two hundred. Finally, in 1981, this last section of Interstate 40 in New Mexico opened between the Texas state line and Tucumcari. The old two-lane "bloody alley," crossing arroyos on timber bridges, remains drivable as a county road, though its thin, potholed asphalt topping was scraped away years ago. The caliche road base is still as slippery after rains as it was eighty years ago.[4]

Motorists passed multiple small eating places in the dusty little towns along the original alignment. Endee, Bard, and San Jon were never more than villages, their economies based mostly on cattle raising. Endee stood for the ND Ranch, while Bard took its name from the Bar-D Ranch. San Jon (pronounced "San Hone") developed a scattered two-block-long strip of businesses catering to auto travelers. Among its eating places over the years were the California Café, the Circle M, Smith's Café, the Silver Grill, the Mint, the White Café, and, in latter days, the Rustler Café.[5] The neighborhood also offered a favored stop usually called the Monument Rock. This naturally formed erosional remnant with a profile reminiscent of an apple core on end remained at the side of a gully about four miles west of San Jon. For decades motorists stopped for rest breaks within sight of the oddity, frequently picnicking near its base, until the two-lane was rerouted slightly, forcing travelers to walk farther overland to reach the natural curiosity.[6]

Tucumcari

Located at a railway junction where the Rock Island Railroad coming from Kansas met a branch of the Southern Pacific Railroad from the south, Tucumcari owed its 1901 founding to transportation. Six years later it became the western terminus for another Rock Island rail line across the Texas Panhandle and eastern New Mexico that the Mother Road had paralleled for over two hundred miles. Further enhancing Tucumcari's strategic location, U.S. Highway 54 came into town from the northeast. That roadway passed through downtown along Main Street and then exited southward on First Street to intersect east-west Highway 66 on Gaynell Boulevard, later known as Tucumcari Boulevard. In time much of the downtown commercial activity shifted southward to the growing east-west corridor of traffic along the Mother Road.

Local leaders bet that the economic future of their town would lay in serving the needs of traveling motorists. In the 1950s they launched a "Tucumcari Tonite!" publicity campaign to attract cross-country travelers to sleep and eat in their town. Boasting of over two thousand motel rooms along its commercial strip, Tucumcari became for many visitors the town "two miles long and two blocks wide." Many thousands stopped there, and the town abounded with places to eat. Lucille Byerly Lackore and three girlfriends from Iowa drove a Model T on a summer trip to California in 1932, and like many others they tarried long enough for lunch. "It was near noon when we arrived at Tucumcari, New Mexico, and we were, as usual, hungry. As we enjoyed a good noon meal, the waitress reminded us to set our watches back an hour," for they had crossed from the Central into the Mountain time zone. The 1962 Tucumcari telephone directory listed thirty-nine restaurants, cafés, or drive-ins in this community of eight thousand residents, and restaurateurs imaginatively sought ways to differentiate themselves from other contenders for travelers' dollars.[7]

PAP'S LUNCH (HARRY'S LUNCH)

Harry Elmer Garrison was a natural-born showman whose irrepressible bombast tended to obscure his business acumen. Born in Bells, Texas, in 1909, he relocated to Tucumcari by 1945 and opened a diner he called Pap's Lunch at 102 East Railroad Avenue, around the corner from the downtown train station. He renamed the diner Harry's Lunch and moved it across the street to a storefront at number 105. In steam-locomotive days, train crews changed at Tucumcari, and passengers temporarily left the rail coaches to grab hasty meals. Many stepped into a quick-service restaurant in the depot, but Harry himself made a point of meeting many trains dressed in a Hollywood cowboy getup, wearing fancy yellow and black boots, a Stetson hat, and a pair of pearl-handle six-guns. He rounded up interested passengers and led them on foot to his eatery, where he, wife Opal, and

employees speedily served meals. Train crews often dined there too. A longtime local resident remembered that Garrison typically fried up bacon, eggs, and pancakes for breakfast with hamburgers and chicken-fried steak following at lunch and dinner. Signage on the front advertised hot and cold sandwiches and Folgers brand coffee. Although Harry made himself the self-appointed goodwill ambassador of Tucumcari to the world, fellow professional restaurateurs recognized his accomplishments in making the diner a profitable business. In 1968 they elected him president and principal spokesperson for the New Mexico Restaurant Association.[8]

Unknown to Harry Garrison, one of the train passengers he escorted to his diner was hit parade songstress Dorothy Shay. Known on the nightclub circuit as the Park Avenue Hillbilly, the novelty vocalist was impressed by the entrepreneur's dress and demeanor, and she scribbled down her impressions. Based on this chance encounter, she created the lyrics for a popular song about falling in love with a cowpuncher from Tucumcari. Columbia Records released the disc in April 1948, and soon "Two Gun Harry from Tucumcari" was playing on radios across the nation. Consequently many Route 66 motorists pulled over for breaks in the town because they felt like they already knew something about it. Garrison never let anyone forget how he had advertised the town's name across the country. Dorothy Shay continued her career in music, later entering acting, while Harry remained in Tucumcari running his diner. As he planned retirement, he opened a furniture and secondhand store. About 1973 he moved the merchandise into his former café building, where a thrift shop continued operating at the time of this research.[9]

Montoya, Newkirk, and Cuervo

Motorists drove about sixty-four miles on the old 66 Highway from Tucumcari to Santa Rosa, the next good-sized town. As they headed west, some tarried for picnics or dips in an impressive open-air swimming pool at the Tucumcari Municipal Park, later called Five Mile Park, constructed by the Civilian Conservation Corps in 1940. Travelers gradually descended into the broad valley of the Pecos, crossing multiple intervening wet-weather drainages, until they came to the river itself at Santa Rosa. The country looked different from anything that first-time visitors had ever seen. "The bare rocks—they didn't have them back east," quipped restaurateur Ronald P. Chavez. Along the way drivers passed through a significant cultural divide as well, leaving the dominant white Protestant culture of eastern New Mexico behind and entering an area where people were predominately Hispanic and Catholic. Soon travelers found themselves meeting people who spoke Spanish as their native tongue and who may only have learned English in school or not at all. Chavez continued, "They heard people talk Spanish, and they found out what chile was." The seemingly alien landscape was semiarid ranch country with vegetation consisting of scrub brush, cactus, and sparse grass, where typically forty-five or more acres of land were required to sustain each individual cow. Most of the way the two-lane from Tucumcari hugged the south side of the Rock Island Railroad tracks, diverting away for the last twenty miles. With rail sidings and livestock loading facilities, the trackside villages of Montoya, Newkirk, and Cuervo barely clung to life until Highway 66 for a while brought them additional income. Today these communities have withered away after experiencing economic changes beyond the control of their residents. They are ghosts of their former selves with more ruins than occupied homes.[10]

Santa Rosa

U.S. Highway 66 crossed the Pecos River at the town of Santa Rosa. Hispanic rancher Don Celso Baca settled there in 1865, subsequently erecting a modest stone chapel to Saint Rose of Lima, the first canonized Catholic saint from the New World. Substantial town growth, however, awaited the 1901 arrival of the Chicago, Rock Island and Pacific Railroad, which soon linked to the larger Southern Pacific system. When Highway 66 arrived in 1926, the community had just over a thousand inhabitants; the total doubled by 1940 but thereafter remained stable throughout the Route 66 years. Although motorists coming from any direction got there by crossing semiarid, sometimes windswept country, they found a different environment along the Pecos River. With a limestone base, the subsurface strata had underground aquifers that created several natural lakes. The most notable among these anomalies was the Blue Hole, a natural sinkhole eighty feet deep and filled with crystal-clear, sixty-two-degree spring water. Nearby the Works Progress Administration created the twenty-five-acre Park Lake municipal recreation area with its own spring-fed reservoir between 1934 and 1940. From the earliest days, these and other bodies of water attracted travelers, including later motorists, who camped, swam, fished, and picnicked in the unexpected oasis-like setting.[11]

CLUB CAFÉ

Some eating places along Route 66 became beloved institutions, among them the Club Café in Santa Rosa. It created memories for many thousands of diners who for a half century passed east and west through the town where the pavement crossed the Pecos. Lou Kofton treasured her experience there in July 1952, when she drove solo from California to Quantico, Virginia, to rendezvous with her military husband. As she headed eastbound across New Mexico, Lou began noticing some of the twenty-six wooden advertising billboards featuring the rotund face of a fat man grinning with satisfaction. The signs led her to pull into the big parking lot on one side of the Club Café, where another of the beaming faces smiled down. Inside the air-conditioned restaurant, filled with red plastic upholstered seating, she struck up a conversation with members of a big Italian American family headed the other direction toward Los Angeles. "They ... were concerned about my driving all this way by myself, but I told them I was 'OK.'" The friendly exchange continued through a tasty meal. Still concerned, the family "ended up buying my dinner and wishing me well on the rest of my trip." Almost as a postscript, she jotted down, "The Club Café was rather large and nice with good food."[12]

Originally the Mother Road entered Santa Rosa from the southeast, but in the mid-1930s the New Mexico Highway Department rerouted it to a more direct course through town on Parker Avenue. This change opened opportunities for local entrepreneurs to purchase affordable business properties along the new alignment, including widow Mary Belle Epps. With the assistance of sons Charles Curry Epps and Nute Henry Epps, in the third week of November 1936, she opened a modest eatery with eight tables plus a counter on Parker at South Sixth Street. She gave it the then-fashionable name of Club Café. (At the time many ordinary Americans viewed exclusive members-only country clubs as being elite institutions patronized by the privileged, so they in turn gave ordinary cafés the "club" name to make them seem more alluring than they otherwise might be. The United States subsequently became dotted with eateries christened with the Club Café moniker.) The Epps family ran the roadside restaurant for the next five years. Longtime Santa Rosa businessman Adolph Serrano was there at the time, and he said, "I remember that they had very good hamburgers and pie, and the pie was 10 cents a slice!"

Two young men from Texas arrived separately in Santa Rosa during the 1930s. Floyd Shaw came first about 1933. With several engineering classes completed at Texas Technological College, he became a surveyor laying out and then helping build the improved Route 66 on either side of Santa Rosa. "I started surveying twelve miles east of Santa Rosa, went on through town and then went west," he later reported. Shaw liked the town with the multiple lakes and stayed. Philip Neil Craig came along shortly thereafter and struck up a friendship with fellow Texan Shaw. Each of them at times earned extra money working in the kitchens and sculleries of local eating places including the Nu-Way Café, the Cattlemen's Club, and the Rio Lounge. By the end of December 1936, Craig had wed Ruby Mae Epps, whose family ran the Club Café. Founder Mary Belle Epps was already in her mid-fifties and she found

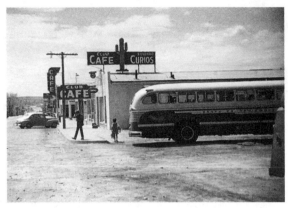

The Club Café eatery and bus station on Highway 66 in Santa Rosa, New Mexico, ca. 1946. By the 1980s, it claimed to have sold two million special sourdough biscuits. Author's collection.

managing the restaurant demanding, so in about 1941 she and her sons sold the business to Philip and Ruby Mae Craig and their friends, Floyd C. and Geraldine Shaw. Philip, Ruby Mae, and Floyd took active roles in running the enterprise, while Geraldine brought in separate income by directing the local library. The Craigs and Shaws built up the Club to perhaps its apex as an eating place. In stages they expanded its size and food selections, making it preeminent among Santa Rosa sit-down restaurants. "Club Café men know their beef steaks," proclaimed a mid-1950s menu, which featured three particular "Club '16' Steaks," each one weighing a full sixteen ounces. Sourdough biscuits freshly made using leavening of fermented dough saved back from previous bakings became so popular that eventually the Club claimed to have sold over two million of them.[13]

Ronald P. "Ronnie" Chavez in the 1950s was one of the many Santa Rosa teenagers who worked at the restaurant. He remembered, "The Club Café was a jumping son of a gun." Starting out polishing shoes near the entrance, he progressively worked his way up from busboy to dishwasher and eventually to

fry cook. Phil Craig took a particular interest in the teen. Chavez fondly recounted that the co-owner "taught me how to make sourdough biscuits and pies and cinnamon rolls. . . . He took me under his wing. I learned the food business and how to deal with people." Chavez, like many other young people who grew up in small towns, sought greater opportunities. He left the state and spent eighteen years working in California meat markets in Los Angeles and Monterey. In the meantime Interstate 40 bypassed his hometown, the Craigs and Floyds sold the old eatery, and others tried and failed to weather the loss of drive-by traffic. Chavez returned to New Mexico in 1973, purchased the floundering restaurant, and revived its fortunes for another eighteen years. He even broadcast a live radio program on KSYX AM radio just before mealtime at 6:30, 11:30, and 4:00 to lure motorists from the freeway onto old 66 and his eating place. Finally in 1992 the Club closed in part because the interstate drained away its customers and partly because reduced business led to deferring maintenance to its aging physical plant. Ronald Chavez moved to retirement at Taos

Red Chile Salsa, CLUB CAFÉ, SANTA ROSA, NEW MEXICO

Ron Chavez worked as a teenager at the Club Café in Santa Rosa before enjoying a career in California food service. When opportunity came, he returned as owner and manager of the Club, where he developed his own red chile salsa that many customers still remember.

About two and a half cups
¼ cup dry red New Mexico chile peppers (coarsely ground)
¼ cup onion (chopped)
¼ teaspoon oregano (ground)
¼ teaspoon dry cilantro (ground)
¼ teaspoon black pepper
¼ teaspoon powdered garlic
¼ teaspoon coriander seeds (ground)
2 eight-ounce cans Hunt's brand tomato sauce

Combine ingredients and mix thoroughly. Refrigerate until served.

Original recipe from Ronald P. Chavez, *Talkin' Chile Here* (n.p.: privately printed, 1997), 17, booklet in Center for Southwest Studies, Zimmerman Library, University of New Mexico, Albuquerque.

in northern New Mexico, where he entered a new career writing poetry and prose in both English and Spanish. In the meantime New Mexico Highway Department crews sawed down the last of the old Club Café billboards, and the fat man smiled no more.[14]

The "Dog Leg" to Santa Fe

When the U.S. Bureau of Public Roads approved the path for Highway 66 from Chicago to Los Angeles in 1926, its engineers essentially "pasted together" available roadways to create the cross-country route. At that time there was no functioning road connecting Santa Rosa directly with Albuquerque, just over a hundred miles to the west and the largest city in New Mexico. Consequently the planners routed the new federal way over the existing roads that that first went north and then west to Santa Fe, the state capital, and next dropped back down the Rio Grande valley south to Albuquerque. This was about a hundred miles longer than the distance a crow could fly between the two points. It was only in the mid-1930s that the New Mexico Highway Department laid out and constructed an all-weather two-lane highway that crossed over the Manzano and Sandia Mountains and descended the Tijeras Canyon to link Santa Rosa directly with Albuquerque. Consequently this chapter will explore first how travelers ate their way along the Santa Fe Loop from 1926 to 1937, and then how they munched on quick-service foods and other fare as they cut straight across after the Santa Rosa Cut-Off opened as Highway 66 in late 1937.

From the Pecos River crossing in Santa Rosa, the Mother Road in 1926 initially proceeded fifty-five miles northwesterly through sparsely settled ranch country to the intersection with U.S. Highway 85 at little Romeroville. This junction was only half a dozen miles south of Las Vegas, New Mexico, then the second-largest city in the state. Though Las Vegas was not on the 66 Highway, many motorists opted to drive the short distance to take advantage of its convenient overnight lodgings, groceries, hot meals, and selection of campgrounds. From the Romeroville road junction, travelers continued on sixty-six miles as they climbed into the Sangre de Christo Mountains, reached the summit at Glorieta Pass, and then dropped back down through rough country to Santa Fe itself.[15]

Glorieta Pass

From the Romeroville road junction, the original Highway 66 route meandered generally westward to Santa Fe, traversing the southern end of the Sangre de Christo Mountains and crossing the 7,500-foot Glorieta Pass. Much of its path lay along the nineteenth-century Santa Fe Trail and for forty miles paralleled the tracks of the Santa Fe Railway. (From this point westward, Route 66 intermittently paralleled these steel rails all the way to Los Angeles.) Because it traversed mountainous terrain, this route for years held the reputation for being one of the roughest along all of the entire Mother Road. Frequently early motorists encountered washed-out roads and even missing bridges. When they climbed to the gap at Glorieta, they found themselves at a historic Civil War site where Unionist miners from Colorado had pushed back a Confederate invasion of New Mexico in 1862. Along the way travelers passed the villages of Tecolote, Bernal, Pecos, and Cañoncito, where they usually could find emergency assistance, basic groceries, and soda pop but not much more.[16]

OLDEST WELL IN THE U.S.A. (OLD PIGEON RANCH)

Though the roadway between Las Vegas and Santa Fe might leave something to be desired, the visual appeal of the mountain scenery with its tall pine trees prompted many travelers to pause. Overheated non-pressurized radiators prompted others to stop for water refills after the climb. Showman Thomas Lacy Greer observed motorists taking breaks, and in 1926 he purchased 160 acres straddling a level stretch of the highway near the Glorieta Pass summit. In the 1850s Alexander Pigeon had operated a "road ranch" at the site, providing food and lodging for teamsters and others on the Santa Fe Trail, and his home was alternately occupied by soldiers from each side in the 1862 Civil War battle. Greer, who with his father had operated a rodeo to entertain American tourists in Juarez, Mexico, patched up the adobe Old Pigeon Ranch house, advertised it as an "Old Indian and Spanish fortress," and, for twenty-five cents, offered tours of his museum with curio sales inside. Were the actual history of the site not already enough, Tommy Greer promoted an admittedly old hand-dug well on the other side of the Mother Road as more eye candy for tourists. He called it the "Most Historic-Wonderful Old Indian Spanish American Well Nearly 400 Years Old" and Oldest Well in the U.S.A., inventing a Native legend to justify its fictional antiquity. In 1935 Russian writers Ilya Ilf and Eugene Petrov stopped at Tommy Greer's on a ten-week auto tour of America for the *Pravda* newspaper in Moscow. Above the well they saw a placard reading, "Your grandfather drank water here on his way to California for gold." They noted, "Beside the historical well a man sat in his little booth and sold colored post-cards with views of the same well." Promoter Greer operated his tourist trap into the 1960s. Today the adobe ranch house and the well, separated from each other by New Mexico Highway 50 just as they were by the Mother Road, are protected within the Pecos National Historical Park.[17]

Thomas Greer's Oldest Well in the U.S.A., one of the attractions at his combined rest stop and curio shop bisected by Highway 66 near the crest of Glorieta Pass between Las Vegas and Santa Fe, New Mexico, ca. 1935. Author's collection.

Santa Fe
LA FONDA HOTEL

Travelers on the Mother Road roughly followed the former wagon track of the Santa Fe Trail from Glorieta Pass twenty miles into the heart of Santa Fe. There the narrow, twisting streets and earth-colored mud-brick buildings made deep impressions on first-time visitors like motorist Lewis Gannett. In 1934 he wrote, "In Santa Fe, for the first time as you travel West, you feel a sense of the continuity of American history." He realized upon entering the city, founded by Spaniards in 1610, that he had driven into a place of true antiquity. College Street (now called Old Santa Fe Trail) led Route 66 downtown to Water Street, just a block from the central plaza and rear of La Fonda Hotel. This innermost area had hosted fondas or inns for three hundred years, and lodgings known variously as the Santa Fe House, the U.S. Hotel, and the Exchange Hotel had in turn occupied the southeastern corner off the square. In 1919 entrepreneurs collaborated to replace the outdated Exchange with a first-class, up-to-date hostelry in the Santa Fe architectural style. (It was about this time that local people began acknowledging the beauty and grace of old-style Pueblo and Spanish Colonial adobe mud-brick buildings. They embarked on preserving historic examples and erecting modern structures that mimicked them.) The new four-story La Fonda Hotel opened in 1922, but four years later the company that built it went into receivership. The Santa Fe Railway purchased the property at a bargain price and in 1926 leased it to the successful Fred Harvey Company, which already operated multiple hotels, restaurants, and lunchrooms along its lines. The luxurious La Fonda soon became headquarters for Harvey-operated Indian Detour motor coach and limousine tours that took rail-based eastern tourists to Native villages, prehistoric ruins, and scenic destinations.[18]

Food at La Fonda became a major attraction. German-trained chef Konrad Allgaier is credited with introducing gourmet dining to New Mexico. After working in eastern restaurants, he joined the Harvey organization in 1923 and in 1930 was transferred to La Fonda, where he remained for two dozen years. The German chef wedded classical kitchen training to traditional Native and Hispanic cuisine of New Mexico. At La Fonda he created such memorable dishes as Chicken Lucrecio—cooked chicken seasoned with ground chile, simmered in a cumin gravy, and sprinkled with toasted almond flakes. In 1938 food critic Duncan Hines encouraged his readers that La Fonda was "worth seeing even if you can't afford to stay, and worth loosening up a bit to dine."[19]

Besides being packed with "detourists" and other travelers, the hostelry became the social center for the elite living in and visiting Santa Fe. Albuquerque-based Ernie Pyle wrote for the Scripps-Howard newspapers, "You never meet anybody anywhere except at the La Fonda. You never take anybody to lunch except at the La Fonda." He went on to recount, "Life among the upper crust centers by daytime around the La Fonda Hotel. . . . You go there any time of day and see a few artists in the bar . . . or see an Indian that some white woman loves, or see a goateed nobleman from Austria, or a maharajah from India, or a rich New York broker, or an archeologist, or some local light in overalls and cowboy boots." La Fonda's bars and restaurants also attracted highway

Chicken Lucrecio, LA FONDA HOTEL, SANTA FE, NEW MEXICO

German-born chef Konrad Allgaier of La Fonda Hotel holds a special place in the food history of Santa Fe from his combination of European training with the indigenous Indian and Hispanic cuisine of New Mexico. For two dozen years starting in 1930, he created such memorable dishes as the popular Chicken Lucrecio, enjoyed by thousands of visitors to "the City Different."

Four servings

1 four-pound whole raw chicken

8 tablespoons flour

4 ½ tablespoons ground dry chile (chili powder)

½ cup olive oil

1 clove garlic (finely chopped)

1 teaspoon cumin (finely ground)

1 ½ to 2 quarts water

1 teaspoon salt

⅛ teaspoon black pepper

3 ½ tablespoons butter

2 tablespoons almond slices

Cut the chicken into four large pieces. Mix flour with 2 ½ teaspoons of ground dry chile (chili powder) and roll the chicken parts in the mixture. Fry the chicken in olive oil until golden brown, adding chopped garlic and cumin as the pieces cook.

Cover the cooked chicken with water, adding salt and pepper. Simmer for about two hours or until chicken is very tender. Remove chicken from liquid and keep warm. Strain the gravy. Add 3 tablespoons butter and reserved ground dry chile, stirring until smooth. Toast almond slices in remaining butter. Pour the hot gravy over the chicken and sprinkle with toasted almonds to serve.

Chef Allgaier recommended accompanying Chicken Lucrecio with New Mexican *posole* (a regional hominy stew) as its side dish.

Food critic Duncan Hines received a Chicken Lucrecio recipe from La Fonda Hotel, perhaps personally from Konrad Allgaier, in the 1930s, and after kitchen testing he placed it in his annual cookbooks from 1939 to 1960. His preparation was essentially the same as Allgaier's with the exception of his omitting the 2 tablespoons of ground chile in the final gravy mixture, which made the Hines version considerably less spicy.

Original recipe in "Fred Harvey Recipes from La Fonda Hotel[,] Santa Fe, New Mexico," mimeographed copy on legal-size paper, [ca. 1940], 11 lvs. unpaged, Fred Harvey Company Collection, series 4, box 12, folder 301, Special Collections, Cline Library, Northern Arizona University, Flagstaff; "Chicken Lucrecio," type-script, [ca. 1940], box 1, notebook II, unpaged, Duncan Hines Collection, Division of Rare and Manuscript Collections, Cornell University Library, Ithaca, New York; and Duncan Hines, *Adventures in Good Cooking and the Art of Carving in the Home* (Bowling Green, Ky.: Adventures in Good Eating, 1939), unpaged recipe 200.

contractors, many of whom built and maintained Highway 66. During the 1930s and 1940s, they gathered each month at the state capitol to submit bids at scheduled "lettings" for roadwork contracts, afterward heading as a group on foot to the fashionable La Fonda watering holes just five blocks away. There, salesmen for road construction equipment regularly wined and dined them in hopes of making sales. The Harvey Company operated La Fonda until 1968, and it remains a premiere lodging and eating place in "the City Different."[20]

WOOLWORTH'S LUNCH COUNTER

When Guy K. Austin and his family motored to Santa Fe in 1934, he knew that they would not be able to afford any meals at the La Fonda, speculating, "We could have obtained a snack lunch at this hotel for around $5 a head." Instead they walked through the sumptuous public areas in the hotel to gawk at no cost, and then, as he wrote, they exited and went around the corner where they "had a large and satisfying lunch at a delightful restaurant for the total cost of $1.80." We do not know where the Austins dined, but one of the most fondly remembered reasonably priced eateries that catered to tourists and locals alike was the Lunch Counter inside the F. W. Woolworth's variety store. It stood only a block down the sidewalk from La Fonda opposite the southwestern corner of the historic Plaza. The F. W. Woolworth Company began in Utica, New York, in 1879, selling discounted general merchandise at fixed prices, usually five or ten cents. This was one of the first retailers in the country to place goods on counters where customers could pick up and handle things before buying them, and the concept exploded in

popularity. By 1929 over 2,250 Woolworth outlets were vending "five-and-dime" goods across the country, with the outlet at 58 San Francisco Street on the Plaza in Santa Fe opening in 1935. It offered everything from cheap straw hats to bars of soap, and from the outset its soda fountain served short-order fare and ice cream specialties. In 1939 the store expanded into an adjoining store space, and architect John Gaw Meem redesigned the front in the increasingly popular Santa Fe style. The enlarged facility boasted a new luncheonette with an expanded menu, including roast turkey plate lunches, ham and cheese combination sandwiches, and jumbo banana splits. A later 1960s expansion increased counter space from twenty-two to eighty-four seats. Bargain food prices made the store a popular draw in a downtown full of otherwise generally expensive eating places.[21]

Although it appeared on the menu at the Santa Fe Woolworth's Lunch Counter only in the 1960s, long after Highway 66 had realigned away from Santa Fe in late 1937, the Frito chili pie prepared at its lunch counter gained wide renown. It consisted of freshly made New Mexican–style chili con carne ladled into the open top of a treated paper bag containing Fritos-brand corn chips and topped with chopped onions and shredded cheese. (The distinctive chips had been invented in 1932 by Texas entrepreneur Charles Elmer Doolin, who perfected a process for deep-frying extruded whole cornmeal.) In 1983, Santa Fe Woolworth's cook Carmen Ornelas, a fifteen-year veteran of the same lunch counter, explained how she created the memorably flavorful chili: "I put in about five pounds of ground beef, with a little water and salt and cook it 'till

The F. W. Woolworth's store on the Plaza in Santa Fe in 1939, just after it expanded into an adjoining building and architect John Gaw Meem redesigned the front in the fashionable Santa Fe style. For over four decades, locals and travelers dined at its popular lunch counter. Slightly retouched photograph from Production File 9A-H2390 courtesy of Lake County (Illinois) Discovery Museum, Curt Teich Postcard Archives.

it's well-fried. Then I add 13 ounces of flour and eight ounces of chile Caribe and garlic salts." The results became legendary. Generations of Santa Fe residents and their guests relished the experience of eating the savory concoction with plastic spoons directly out of the little paper bags while seated on shady benches in the Plaza. Store assistant manager Dennis Baca reminisced, "People used to drive by the front of the store and drop off their friends for a Frito Pie. Then they'd drive around the Plaza and pick them up." The Santa Fe Woolworth's closed when the parent corporation shut down its retail outlets in 1997, but a new Five & Dime General Store almost immediately occupied its old space and at the time of this writing was still serving the ever-popular Frito chili pie.[22]

Santa Fe to Albuquerque

From Santa Fe old Highway 66 proceeded southwestward over gently rolling semidesert to La Bajada. The place-name originated from the Spanish word meaning "the Descent," and justly so. Here, in just two miles, the unpaved roadway plummeted down a basalt escarpment into the valley of the Rio Grande five hundred feet below. Following the 1846 American military occupation of New Mexico during the Mexican War, the U.S. Army constructed a wagon road with multiple switchbacks and grades as steep as 28 percent up and down the drop-off. By 1926 the territory and the state of New Mexico had rebuilt the way several times, reducing the slope to an average of 5.5 percent, but going either up or down still challenged many drivers' abilities and nerves. Vernon McGill took the plunge in 1921, afterward reporting, "From top to bottom the descent is very rapid. It is more than quick. One feels as if the car were going to fall over into the curve in the road below, but one is out of this curve and into the next one so quickly that no time would be gained by falling." He concluded, "The road winds down the mountain side in a series of hairpin curves and looks like a snake in motion."[23] At its base motorists could settle their frazzled composure with soda pop and snacks at the Walden Brothers' service station and tourist cabins. Kansan Wallace Eugene Walden had moved to New Mexico by 1917, and in 1925 his brother and sister-in-law, Herbert C. and Marjorie Walden, joined him in establishing the business, which operated at the foot of the daunting incline until 1932, when the New Mexico Highway Department rerouted the roadway several miles to the east to go around La Bajada and thus avoid the switchbacks. From the base of the "hill," the southbound highway initially proceeded six miles to the Domingo depot on the Santa Fe Railway and nearby trading post, both about two and a half miles east of the Santo Domingo Pueblo itself.[24]

Drivers continued southwestward through more desert scrub from Santo Domingo, gradually approaching the edges of bright green irrigated fields immediately along the Rio Grande. It was through miserably hot summertime weather that James Albert Davis made the drive in the 1920s. He characterized the route between La Bajada and Albuquerque as being "a small desert to cross," complaining that "the heat was something terrible, [with] nothing but deep sand most of the way. . . . It almost made me

do the 'shimmy' to keep the car in the road as we did considerable skidding."[25]

Albuquerque

Albuquerque as a community was founded in 1706 by Spanish colonists in an area along the Rio Grande where there were already multiple Pueblo villages. The Santa Fe Railway laid rails two miles east of the sleepy little Hispanic settlement in 1880, when it had only 2,315 people. Platted alongside the tracks in 1885, a new Albuquerque became the commercial and population heart of the present-day city with about twenty thousand people when Mother Road travelers began arriving. Southbound motorists proceeded down Fourth Street through town and jogged across the river and then back again in traversing about two dozen miles along the Rio Grande to Los Lunas. There they crossed over the Rio Grande a third time to take a preexisting roadway westward to climb out of the valley.

It was not until 1937 that the route across New Mexico changed. In that year a new, more direct highway, cutting off the extra hundred-mile loop through Santa Fe, opened to traffic. It coursed almost due west over arid prairies from Santa Rosa, through the Manzano and Sandia Mountains down the Tijeras Canyon, and into Albuquerque. Thence drivers proceeded across the city on Central Avenue, over an almost new 1931 bridge spanning the Rio Grande, and up the Nine Mile Hill to exit the city. This new highway alignment changed the orientation of population growth and economic development for Albuquerque from north-south along the railroad to east-west along Central Avenue. The immediate pre–World War II change led to an explosion of business enterprises providing food, lodging, and services to people passing through the city in cars. Because this largest city in New Mexico supplied travelers' needs in country where often multiple miles separated sources of assistance, Albuquerque became an overnight destination for many motorists. Others who were "making time" to reach more distant points only tarried briefly, like Mark Pepys in 1935, who penned, "A need of sandwiches and gasoline accounted for half an hour's pause in Albuquerque."[26]

RED BALL CAFÉ

The original alignment of the Mother Road through Albuquerque proceeded southward on Fourth Street, across Central Avenue, and out of the city into irrigated farmland along the Rio Grande. In less than a mile from downtown, it passed a two-story home at 1303 South Fourth, where the Abel Padilla family had resided since the early 1920s. Around this time son Nestor Rube Padilla entered the food business, selling hamburgers first from a pushcart and then from a little space on the ground floor front of the dwelling. The business grew, mother Pilar Padilla died in 1944, and Nestor and his sister inherited the property. She sold her share to her brother, who, with wife Aurora, expanded the downstairs space into a larger, sit-down café while still residing upstairs. A popular comic book character of the day was the penurious hamburger-eating J. Wellington Wimpy in the Popeye cartoons, and during the 1930s Nestor applied his name from popular culture to the Wimpy Burgers sold in his eatery.[27] Its proximity only two blocks away from the Santa Fe Railway shops, the largest in New Mexico, undoubtedly led to the café's Red Ball moniker. Since the turn of the twentieth century, the railroad company had designated its crack freight trains, like those carrying vegetables on ice from California, as its high-priority "Red Ball Freight."[28]

The café became known up and down Fourth Street for the creamy chile sauce Nestor used on buns for his specialty sandwiches, although his eatery offered a broad range of menu choices. The hamburgers remained a principal draw for many Red Ball customers. "You could have lived on those hamburgers," reminisced longtime neighborhood resident Zeke Duran in 1989, adding, "They weren't like the ones you get now. Those were real hamburgers." Despite the realignment of Highway 66 away from Fourth Street to Central Avenue in 1937, trade for the café remained strong for over forty years. Nestor and Aurora and their heirs ran the Red Ball until 1979, by which time the Barelas neighborhood had entered an economic decline. In 1997 a new owner purchased the disused structure, initiating a multi-thousand-dollar rehabilitation and return to operation. With intermissions, that revival has continued, and at the time of this writing the eating place was a popular destination for New Mexican–style breakfasts and lunches, and, of course, the still-famous old-time Wimpys.[29]

ICEBERG CAFÉ (MAC'S ICEBERG, ICEBERG INN, ICEBURG CAFÉ)

In early November 1937, Mother Road travelers began taking the new course across Albuquerque. Officially designated on January 1, 1938, it carried them into the city directly from Santa Rosa, avoiding the extra hundred-plus miles of the loop through Santa Fe. This realignment brought streams of automobiles the full length of Central Avenue, forever altering many formerly sleepy neighborhoods. In 1935, for example, there were only three tourist camps on the avenue, but by 1941 the number exploded to thirty-seven.[30] Travelers soon were able to find abundant places to sleep and eat, including the Iceberg Café. Until one examined it up close, the structure looked as if it consisted of two giant chunks of ice sticking out of the ground.

Entrepreneur Carl Armstrong McAdams pondered how to create a café and filling station that would attract motorists' attention. In 1931 he acquired 3017–23 Central Avenue East, and, following plans that were only in his head, he constructed two small buildings to house an eatery and a gasoline station. On the outside he stretched netlike chicken wire over a fanciful wooden framework, smearing viscous concrete stucco on the outside, and painted everything dazzling white. From a distance the glorified huts simulated the appearance of jagged, ocean-eroded icebergs. He opened the venture called Mac's Iceberg on Wednesday, May 27, 1931, offering short-order sandwiches, frozen custard, and soft drinks both indoors and curbside. He declared in an advertisement, "We grind our own hamburger . . . and give you a generous portion of meat with good old onions, pickle and all the trimmings that make up a delicious sandwich." For the next seven years, the Iceberg sold quick-service food and gasoline at this location, though its ownership and management periodically changed. Because a later landowner negotiated to erect a more sophisticated service station on the same ground, he sold the two buildings to be removed. The buyer shifted them about twenty blocks east to 5319 Central Avenue East, on the corner with San Mateo Boulevard. There business resumed, with rental tenants running the café and filling station, but spelling its name "Iceburg" starting in 1947. By 1949 early TV broadcasts were being aired in Albuquerque, and the café manager advertised that evening customers could not only enjoy Mexican dinners, seafood, steak, and chicken but also watch "television nightly." In summer 1952 the Shaw Motor Company moved into the increasingly threadbare looking buildings, inviting people to buy, sell or trade cars "at the Iceberg." The next spring, in May 1953, a new landowner sold the two buildings to I. A. Boren, who hired a structural mover to relocate them to a site fifteen miles north in the town of Bernalillo. There, as the Iceburg Café and Truck Stop, the resilient little buildings returned to commercial life at least until 1960.[31]

ALVARADO HOTEL

From the original Iceberg, motorists drove along Central Avenue past the campus of the University of New Mexico and into downtown Albuquerque. This commercial strip contained some of the most impressive 1930s and 1940s Streamline Moderne and Spanish Pueblo Revival architecture in the city. Entering the central business district after passing via an underpass beneath the mainline tracks of the Santa Fe Railway, travelers came to the Alvarado Hotel, where for years they found the premiere lodging and dining in the city. In about 1893 the railroad erected a single-story wooden "eating house" for rail employees and travelers in Albuquerque. As part of its efforts to develop the American Southwest as a tourist destination, in 1902 the railroad company replaced the inadequate old facilities with a luxurious new complex consisting of a new passenger depot, a hotel with restaurants, and the Indian Building, where employees of its caterer, the Fred Harvey Company, showcased and sold Native American arts. Although it had a wooden framework, the entire complex was sheathed in rough stucco with simple ornamentation typical of the fashionable Mission Revival style. Paralleling the tracks south from Central Avenue, the buildings stretched two hundred feet, all connected by covered open-air trackside arcades.

Inside the Alvarado several distinct food services sated the appetites of those

A couple enjoying ice cream cones just outside the Indian Building arts and crafts sales venue operated by the Fred Harvey Company at its Alvarado Hotel in Albuquerque, New Mexico, ca. 1945. Author's collection.

who arrived by train as well as locals and out-of-town customers coming in automobiles. There they found high-quality meals and beverages in a formal dining room, a counter-style lunchroom, a club room for group meetings, and (both before and after Prohibition) a succession of bars. Because the Harvey Company operated food services all up and down the Santa Fe tracks, as its business partner, the railroad provided fast and convenient delivery of raw ingredients from wherever they were of the highest quality at the cheapest price. As elsewhere, in Albuquerque the company hired personable young women known as Harvey Girls as servers, and their presence inevitably attracted male customers. Lodging and food service continued at the Alvarado until AMFAC, the successor to the Fred Harvey Company, closed down operations on January 2, 1970. Before the end of the year, the grand railroad hotel was completely razed. A later intermodal transportation center at 320 First Street SW was constructed on part of the site.[32]

CENTRAL DRUG STORE (DURAN CENTRAL PHARMACY)

Pharmacist Pedro G. "Pete" Duran was born in 1897 only a few streets away from the two-block section of Route 66 along West Central Avenue in Albuquerque, where, for decades, the lunch counters in his drug stores prepared celebrated New Mexican–style foods. Tracing family roots to Albuquerque's eighteenth-century Hispanic founders, Pete attended local Catholic schools, Notre Dame University, and pharmacy training in Denver. He worked off and on for twenty years at Bernard Rupe's downtown apothecary before opening his own enterprise, the Central Drug Store, at 1823 West Central Avenue in

1942. This location was about eighteen blocks northwest of the downtown Alvarado Hotel. It is uncertain whether Duran's initial store offered food service, but when he moved the business a block west to 1929 West Central four years later it definitely did. In the early 1950s, the enterprise gradually came to be known as the Duran Central Pharmacy. Because of pavement widening along Central Avenue, the business relocated around the corner to 119 San Pasquale SW in 1959, remaining there for sixteen years. During this time Pete Duran retired, selling the business to his employee and colleague, Robert N. Ghattas, who wisely expanded the food service begun by his predecessor. In 1975 the pharmacy moved to the current location at 1815 West Central Avenue, only a few feet away from its original site.

Both Albuquerque residents and visitors in-the-know recognized the soda fountain at the Duran Central Pharmacy as a reservoir of traditional homestyle New Mexican cookery. Its location on Highway 66 made it easy for travelers to stop off for quick but memorable meals. The Duran bowl of chile, made with red or green chile, beans, and either beef or chicken, was especially popular. Although the antiseptic atmosphere of the dispensary made an odd-seeming setting for first-time diners, Duran's was almost always packed with patrons enjoying short-order fare, enchiladas, and huevos rancheros (fried eggs with chile sauce on top and a hand-rolled flour tortilla on the side), sometimes combined with sodas and milkshakes. Food critics Jane and Michael Stern discovered the Duran Pharmacy as early as the 1980s, and they described its fountain as "one of the most remarkable drug-store lunch counters in America." Their assessment was well founded.[33]

LA PLACITA DINING ROOMS

By the time that travelers reached Pete Duran's Central Drug Store, they found themselves at the edge of Old Town Albuquerque. Bypassed almost two miles by the railroad in 1880, this Spanish Colonial heart of the city survived into the twentieth century as a run-down neighborhood built around a central plaza. On one side stood the San Felipe de Neri Church, begun in 1793 and the oldest in the city. Otherwise the area was filled with generally neglected homes and businesses, built by elites in a bygone era, that were now accessed by dusty or alternately muddy unpaved streets. The Old Town looked pretty desolate. In the late 1920s, socialite and arts promoter Nelda Sewell saw the ill-kept quarter as a prime location for an arts district. To begin the process, in 1930 she purchased the Ambrosio Armijo House and surrounding seven-eighths acre directly on the square. She repaired and adapted the large residence at 208 San Felipe Street NW to become studio apartments together with a handful of shops and galleries rented as outlets for New Mexican arts and crafts. As early as 1931, a small eatery began intermittent operation in a ground-floor room with an interior patio. Within two years Inez B. Westlake was running the diminutive bistro, calling it La Placita Coffee Shop, *placita* being the Spanish word for "little square" or "small plaza" in reference to the courtyard.[34]

In December 1940 Marie and Cyrus F. Brown, newcomers from Illinois, opened a full-fledged restaurant—also called La Placita—in one part of the Casa de Armijo. It gradually grew to occupy most of the venerable complex, including the attractive open-air patio. La Placita offered both American and New Mexican fare, but the latter eventually took over most of the menu. A mid-1940s customer wrote to *Gourmet* magazine reporting that the restaurant offered "Native and 'arty' atmosphere that is enjoyable," noting specifically that it was "a good eating place specializing in fried chicken and Mexican dishes." Tourists filled the tables for lunch and dinner from June through August each year, leaving local diners to pick up the slack in business during the rest of the year, when only evening meals were served. Cyrus Brown passed away in 1944, and his son, Wentworth C., and sister-in-law, Vivian G. Brown, took over. Because landlord Nelda Sewell claimed exclusive ownership of the La Placita name, the Browns renamed their enterprise La Hacienda Dining Rooms in 1951. The next year they purchased an

adjacent former residence facing the plaza, the Blueher Mansion, which came with 2.3 acres of land. After a major rebuilding project, they shifted their restaurant operation there on June 8, 1954. Despite a fire in 1981, a restaurant using the La Hacienda name at the time of research was still operating in the space at 302 San Felipe Street NW.[35]

Texas-born Elmer D. and Rosalee Elliott had already come to Albuquerque in the 1940s, and Elmer prospered there as co-owner and operator of the downtown Court Café. The couple saw an opportunity when the Browns moved their eatery out of the old Casa de Armijo. They leased the restaurant portion of the building from Nelda Sewell, renovated the facility, and opened it in January 1955 as La Placita Dining Rooms. The Elliotts covered the open patio, but the

The open-air courtyard at the La Placita Dining Rooms in Albuquerque in the early 1940s. Subsequent owners covered the patio, but the same venerable forked tree remained growing upward through the later roof. Author's collection.

handsome cottonwood tree that grew at its center was allowed to extend upward through an opening in the roof to reach fresh air. Members of the Elliott family into the third generation continued to operate La Placita until it closed its doors during the Covid 19 pandemic in 2020.[36]

DESERT VU CAFÉ (WESTERN VIEW DINER AND STEAK HOUSE)

As motorists proceeded westward through Albuquerque on Central Avenue, they passed some of the newest districts of the city. The Sandia Reservation on the north and the Isleta Reservation and Kirtland Air Force Base, both on the south, blocked suburban growth in those directions, while the rugged Sandia Mountains stopped expansion eastward. This left available only the mesa on the west side of the Rio Grande, where, following World War II, the newest motels, restaurants, and other services sprang up to attract customers. Among these "west side" entrepreneurs was Jerome Henry Unser, who from the 1930s onward operated automobile garages and towing services fronting on the Mother Road at 5226 and later 7700 West Central Avenue. The "old man" encouraged his son Jerry Jr. to build and race hot rod cars, beginning a family dynasty of competition drivers who eventually earned nine Indianapolis 500 victories.[37]

Another enterprise that opened along the commercial strip of Central Avenue west out of the city was the Desert Vu Café at number 6411. It sated appetites on the north side of what used to be Highway 66 up Nine Mile Hill, at this point a gentle rise overlooking the Rio Grande Valley. At nighttime during the mid-1940s, people looking from this vantage point would see the twinkling lights concentrated along the river and down Central Avenue that marked Albuquerque, then a city of perhaps forty thousand to fifty thousand people. (Later unban growth added massive numbers of additional lights.) It was a perfect location for an eating place on the way into or out of town. Oral traditions indicate that an eatery served food here as early as 1937; however, its site was outside the area covered by city directories so we know few details. Early owners included husband and wife Harry C. and Tasia Pappas, both Greek Americans, as were most later proprietors. Known documentation for the Desert Vu starts in 1957 with newspaper advertisements seeking dishwashers. Restaurateur Steve Kourkoumelis assumed management in December 1969, taking advantage of the setting to rename it the Western View Diner and Steak House. The round-the-clock eating place gained a reputation among Burqueños and Mother Road regulars for its carefully prepared steaks, Greek specialties, and freshly prepared desserts, not to mention its interpretations of New Mexican fare. Peter I. Kellis and Stavros Anagnostakos each took turns running the restaurant. With booths, tables, and an L-shaped counter; plate-glass windows; and original neon sign, the eating place represents a time capsule of mid-twentieth century dining. Today it is easily found at the north end of a recently erected "Route 66 Gateway" neon arch spanning Central Avenue. Just beyond the Western View Diner and Steak House on the West Mesa at midcentury were areas covered with low hills and sand dunes that likewise overlooked the city. One old-timer reminisced, "That was the place to go if you were a young couple in love and had a car. It was a place to neck and cuddle. . . . It was so romantic to be surrounded by the darkness with the town shining away below."[38]

Santa Rosa to Tijeras Canyon

Until 1937 there had never been an all-weather roadway directly connecting Santa Rosa with Albuquerque, roughly 120 miles to the west. The sparsely inhabited, semiarid ranch country between the two places had far more cattle than the handful of people needed to tend them. As soon as the New Mexico Highway Department opened the roadway to passenger cars in autumn 1937, local residents began to envision heretofore unimagined ways to enhance their families' incomes by providing food, lodging, and auto services to travelers. Among these entrepreneurs were Roy and Daisy Cline.

CLINES CORNERS / FLYING C RANCH

Roy E. Cline, born on an Oklahoma farm in 1891, first came to New Mexico in 1918 and tried several different ways to earn a living. He farmed, he managed a hotel, and he operated a country post office, always hoping to find an easy source of income. His son, Roy Jr., remarked that his dad "never did want to work too hard." The father's opportunity came in 1934, when a trickle of auto traffic began flowing along a new but yet unpaved New Mexico State Highway 6 west from Santa Rosa toward Albuquerque. Learning where it would likely intersect another state roadway, son Roy leased eighty acres of public land at the expected junction point. Roy Jr. remembered, "He used my money to get the lease, and then we came over and bought five hundred [dollars'] worth of lumber and started building the place." It began as a filling station and repair shop called the Cline Garage, fifty-seven miles west of Santa Rosa

and sixty-two miles east of Albuquerque. At the time it was considered to be in the middle of nowhere. The roads shifted position at least a couple of times, and on each occasion Roy Sr. adjusted the location of the station, adding food service in a café he called Clines Corners. He had begun selling Conoco gasoline and oil products, and shrewdly he induced the petroleum company to identify his filling station on its complimentary highway maps. Soon thereafter Rand McNally and Company added the Clines Corners place-name to its annual road atlases, undoubtedly prompting thousands of customers to plan fuel stops at Roy Cline's "wide spot in the road."

The elder Cline seemed always to look for greener pastures. Son Roy Jr. declared, "Dad was making a better living than he ever did before," but in 1939 Cline decided to sell out and try his luck in the motel business in Flagstaff, Arizona. Buyer S. L. "Smitty" Smith purchased the enterprise, keeping the existing name, reconstructing the station in Streamline Moderne style with a distinctive square tower, and adding a bona fide sit-down restaurant. Becoming a scheduled rest stop for long-distance buses brought in even more business. Racks and shelves of southwestern curios followed, tempting travelers like Lou Kofton in 1952. "At Clines Corner[s]," she wrote, "there were all kinds of things to buy, but I just had some coffee and a doughnut and drove on." Although the interstate bypassed Clines Corners in 1960, subsequent years added newer and larger buildings and covered fueling areas, with the cafeteria inside the complex in the 1980s reputedly serving a thousand meals on some busy days. Clines Corners remains a frequent stop for many modern-day travelers.[39]

In 1945 Roy E. Cline Sr. returned to the semiarid ranch country where he experienced his first real financial success. He acquired a Highway 66 location just sixteen miles east of his old Clines Corners, where he erected a filling station and café he called the Flying C Ranch. Within five years he had added a garage, wrecker service, and bus stop. By 1955 the café grew into a full-fledged restaurant with a liquor license. Next came a twelve-unit motel. As U.S. Highway 66 was replaced by Interstate 40 during the 1960s, the Flying C retained its lifeline to auto traffic with its own exit from the freeway. As he contemplated retirement, Roy E. Cline sold the Flying C Ranch in 1961 to a New Mexico–based corporation associated with Stuckey's Pecan Shoppes. Three years later old-time competitors Claude M. and Willa Bowlin, who operated similar roadside enterprises across New Mexico and Arizona, acquired the business. A fire burned the buildings in 1976, but Bowlins, Inc., rebuilt the station and erected an adjacent Dairy Queen soft-serve ice cream and hamburger store, both of which at the time of research were still serving the public.[40]

CHERRY HILL CIDER STAND

By the time westbound drivers were passing through Moriarty, two dozen miles west of Clines Corners, they already had begun seeing hand-painted signs advertising cherries and glasses filled with iced red-colored beverages. About five miles out of town, they came to the crest of Cherry Hill, where for forty

Roy Cline's Flying C Ranch café, service station, and garage on Highway 66 between Moriarty and Santa Rosa, New Mexico, during the early 1950s. A summer thunderstorm threatens in the background. Author's collection.

years Frank Adams operated summertime roadside stands where motorists could cool down with the cherry cider depicted in the pictures. A regular customer remembered, "When you pulled up at the stand, got out of your car, and got your money out, they served the stuff to you in a glass, not a paper cup. You had to stand there and drink it and give them back the glass." Frank Adams, however, was not the person who conceived the idea of selling New Mexico cider along the road. Edna Clara Schierenberg, who in the 1920s moved to the apple-raising Ruidoso Valley west of Roswell, deserves this credit. A public health nurse from Missouri who saw army hospital duty in Europe during the First World War, she relocated to New Mexico by 1928 and during the 1930s started selling "cherry cider" from her home at Glencoe. By 1935 husband George S. King was assisting in the venture by recruiting others as roadside dealers for her shop-made product. Within five years he was in Edgewood advertising for "married couple or single woman to operate King's special cherry cider stands on 66 highway," stating that "$200 will stock you with cider and pay your rent for a year" in what he temptingly described as a "very pleasant and profitable business." It did not take vendors long to figure out that they did not have to drive to Glencoe to stock up on the special cider. They could mix it up for themselves. A recipe published in the local *Santa Rosa News* in midcentury demonstrated that it was common knowledge that one could prepare the concoction easily using apple cider combined with brown sugar, cloves, allspice, cinnamon, and a grating of nutmeg. Only red food coloring was needed to make it "cherry."[41]

Beyond the Cherry Hill Cider Stand, drivers passed through little Edgewood and

Barton and climbed Sedillo Hill. From its seven-thousand-foot summit, travelers began a winding descent through the sometimes steep Tijeras Canyon fifteen miles into the outskirts of Albuquerque, with Highway 66 becoming Central Avenue all the way across the city. The scenic canyon offered a number of bars, nightspots, and other diversions, but most of them catered primarily to clientele driving out from Albuquerque rather than travelers just headed into the city.[42]

Laguna Pueblo and Its Satellite Villages

The 1926 and 1937 alignments of U.S. Highway 66 came together about thirty miles west of Albuquerque. The earlier alignment passed southward (downstream) on the Rio Grande to Los Lunas, where, using a preexisting road, it cut west and then northwest toward a desert hamlet called Correo, Spanish for "mail." The later 1937 highway climbed the Nine Mile Hill out of the Rio Grande Valley from Albuquerque, crossed the Rio Puerco on an impressive overhead truss bridge, and dipped and rose all the way also to Correo. This wide place in the road had a couple of taverns and a tourist court but never much more. Because it was easily accessed from the Isleta and Laguna Pueblo Reservations as well as the Cañoncito Navajo Reserve, young people from all three Native American enclaves gravitated there to buy alcohol they could not legally purchase on tribal lands. The Anglo barmen bastardized the Correo place-name into "Korea," in reference to the Korean War. John Atkinson, son of a business owner, declared, "It lived up to its name. The fights out there were brutal."[43]

The Laguna Pueblo Native American community lay forty miles west from

Albuquerque. Its Keres-speaking inhabitants traditionally practiced irrigated agriculture, and the tribe governed activities on its reservation. Piety and interest in historic architecture both brought visitors to Laguna, the religious to worship in its 1699 Spanish Colonial Saint Joseph's Church and students of vernacular buildings to study and admire its traditional adobe houses. In this stretch of roadway westward from Albuquerque, travelers passed from what geographers call the Basin and Range Province to the Intermountain Plateau. All the rest of the way into Arizona, the land was dominated by sandstone mesas and masses of igneous rocks, creating dramatic backdrops to the roadway.

The Laguna tribe regulated business activities on its lands, authorizing only a handful of entrepreneurs to serve travelers. On the way into the reservation, for example, motorists could buy meals or stay overnight in cabins at the Laguna Camp in an outlying area called Mesita. Once travelers reached the Old Laguna village, the heart of the reservation, they could purchase supplies from an official trader who operated a general mercantile store. Just outside the bounds of the reservation, on the west side at the Paraje satellite village, Hugh Crooks operated the Paraje Trading Post for a quarter century, where he sold fuel, groceries, and hardware. It was probably here that Route 66 bicyclist Raymond G. Allen Jackson found shelter for the night on May 17, 1948: "The kind storekeeper allowed me to sleep in his chicken feed bin.... It was really good sleeping, no wind, no rain, and on four sacks of chicken scratch . . . my blanket furnishing the necessary warmth to top off a fine night's slumber."[44]

Budville and Cubero

After Paraje the two-lane entered a 7.6-mile stretch of non-tribal lands. Here non-Native Americans could legally own real estate and operate business enterprises. From the earliest days of the Mother Road, entrepreneurs took advantage of this situation and opened filling stations, garages, towing services, overnight cabins, bars, and eating places. In the mid-twentieth century, nineteen separate tourist-related businesses operated in this short distance.

OLIVIA MERCANTILE COMPANY (BUDVILLE TRADING COMPANY)

Olivia Grace Rice was one of the entrepreneurs who saw opportunity in the strip of roadway just west of the Laguna Reservation. She had accompanied her husband, Roscoe, in moving to the Southwest in 1919 when he took a job for the Bureau of Indian Affairs. While working on the Acoma Reservation, he erected a two-story adobe home on private property in the village of Cubero. Already by 1922 the couple converted part of the dwelling into a combined grocery store and post office, with Olivia herself serving as the postmaster. Quickly the enterprise took the Olivia Mercantile Company name. The Rices' 1936 divorce coincided with highway department plans to shift the Mother Road to a more direct route that bypassed Cubero proper a year later. Olivia Rice moved her grocery store to a new location on the blacktop about two miles east. By this time her sons had grown old enough to play an active role in selling gasoline and servicing cars. During World War II, son Roscoe Rice Jr. fought in five battles in the Pacific as a marine. This trauma was likely the cause of his unfortunate suicide on return home in 1946, followed by his mother taking her own life by gunshot three months later. These twin deaths left the roadside enterprise in the hands of thirty-three-year-old son Howard Neal "Bud" Rice. He continued operating the store and service station but expanded its outreach to run one of the most profitable towing services in the state. Within a year he renamed the business after himself as the Budville Trading Company and in 1951 became the local justice of the peace. Working with members of the Valencia County sheriff's department and state police officers, he oversaw the movement of motor traffic on "his" stretch of the Mother Road, accused by some drivers of converting it into a "speed trap." During a store robbery in 1967, an assailant tragically shot and killed both Bud and a houseguest, leaving his widow, Flossie, to run the business. About the same time, Interstate 40 replaced the old two-lane Highway 66, so the enterprise closed for lack of customers. At the time of this writing, the white-painted, disused store and an adjacent collection of abandoned vintage trucks and cars remained a popular stop for evocative photographs by heritage tourists.[45]

Grants

In the twenty miles from Cubero into Grants, part of it through the reserve of the Pueblo of Acoma, motorists could pause for cold drinks and groceries at a handful of filling stations. There were few sit-down eating places other than the modest Ramsey's Café in the hamlet of San Fidel. About ten miles outside of Grants, the roadway cut across an area covered by an ancient flow of volcanic lava that solidified in place. Locals called this phenomenon the malpais, from the Spanish for "evil country," for it was almost impenetrable on foot or horseback.

Grants came into existence in 1882, when the Atlantic and Pacific Railroad (later Santa Fe Railway) was building westward across New Mexico. Three brothers named Grant were among the construction contractors, and they called their local delivery point for supplies at the end of the track Grant's Camp. The railroad accordingly called its station Grants, and the name stuck. Because only a narrow strip of land was available between the rail line and basalt bluffs to the north, by the 1940s the community became known as the "the longest town in the United States for its width." A 1926 railway spur into the Zuni Mountains to the south accessed pine forest lands, with Grants sawmills processing the lumber. As these timber resources diminished, in the late 1930s cultivation of irrigated vegetables, particularly carrots, expanded for a time just west of Grants in the Bluewater area. Even so, the town had only about two thousand residents in 1950 until Paddy Martinez, a Navajo stock raiser, that year stumbled onto a deposit of high-grade uranium. The discovery led to a quarter-century mining boom that within a decade boosted the Grants population to ten thousand.[46]

WHITESIDE HOTEL AND CAFÉ

Sometime after 1910 Lucy Jane Whiteside and husband David B. Whiteside moved from their home in Joplin, Missouri, to work on a ranch in the Zuni Mountains south of Grants. Things went well for them until March 1919, when, following an argument, an assailant took David Whiteside's life by gunshot. In mourning, Lucy Jane and two children relocated from the ranch to Grants, where members of the local Masonic Lodge recognized her destitute situation and, at their own expense, erected the first phase of the Whiteside Hotel boardinghouse across the highway from the Santa Fe Railway depot. "Mother Whiteside" became a fixture in the community as operator of the hostelry and as a midwife over the years, delivering 479 babies. Her Whiteside Hotel and Café on Highway 66 at the east side of Grants became a favored destination for overnight stays and meals for both motorists and out-of-town railroaders. A local writer in 1953 remembered that "trainmen . . . always found a light in the window, a big pot of coffee on the stove and a roast in the oven." If the proprietress already had retired for the night, "travelers served themselves and left the correct change on the sideboard in the dining room." In 1929 the *Mohawk Hobbs Grade and Surface Guide* to the Mother Road advised that drivers could find "good 50¢ meals at Mrs. Whiteside's." In 1952 Lucy Jane Whiteside rebuilt her old boardinghouse and renamed it the Cactus Inn but, after a few months, sold it and relocated to live in retirement with a daughter in California. So beloved was the longtime restaurateur and midwife that town residents, old-time railroaders, and a Texas oilman she befriended pooled their donated resources in 1954 to erect the Mother Whiteside Memorial Library as the first public library in Grants. The building now houses the local historical museum.[47]

Continental Divide

Since leaving the Rio Grande Valley at Albuquerque, motorists climbed in altitude. From 4,953 feet elevation on the river, they ascended to 6,641 feet in Grants, and continued climbing toward the Continental Divide thirty-five miles ahead. Vehicles overheated as drivers struggled to make some of the uphill grades; the heat generated evaporated water and anti-freezing water/alcohol mixtures from their cooling systems, so drivers regularly stopped to refill them. The higher elevations naturally had slightly lower natural atmospheric pressure, and this lowered the boiling point for coolant liquids, further complicating overheating problems. If they did not carry water bags or other containers, travelers typically relied on refilling radiators at roadside gasoline stations.[48]

Were it not for signs, many early motorists would have crossed the 7,263-foot Continental Divide without recognizing it. When he made the trip about 1926, Dallas Lore Sharp jotted down, "We could not see the altitude, though we could hear it in our ears and feel it in our tingling blood. So Continental in its proportions here is this Continental Divide that the traveler by automobile can scarcely realize that he is going over it." It did not take long for enterprising businesspeople to realize that motorists would, however, pause at the summit where precipitation on the east flowed to the Atlantic and on the west ran to the Pacific.

TOP OF THE WORLD (TOP-O-THE-WORLD HOTEL AND CAFÉ)

The first known roadside entrepreneur at this point on the Continental Divide was Alma Blanche Gaines, who as a single woman in the 1920s acquired a section (640 acres) of land on either side of the Santa Fe railroad tracks just at the crest of the divide. It was her good fortune that U.S. Highway 66 was routed directly across her property, creating opportunities for her not only to open roadside businesses but also to sell parcels of what had become desirable commercial real estate. It was about this time that Alma married Joe Rosenberg, and together they opened what they called the Top of the World filling station and camp. This, however, was just the start, with a café, tourist cabins, and a 30-by-30-foot open-air dance hall quickly following. Alma and Joe divorced in 1938, but she had already connected with her next husband-to-be, Lewis N. Crow. The local press reported in 1942 that the Crows were "steadily improving their place at the Top of the World." By 1946 W. S. "Lee" Neal bought out the husband-and-wife team and began advertising the enterprise as the Top-o-the-World Hotel and Café, which offered a restaurant, bar, and filling station and meeting rooms, guest rooms, and detached tourist cabins. Portions of the business survived at least into the 1960s.[49]

Among those who purchased plots of land from Alma Gaines was B. D. "Dee" Westbrook. A Texan whose brother already was running a New Mexico trading post, he too sought his fortune in the Land of Enchantment. Around 1935 he opened a bar and café at the Continental Divide. After trying his hand in staging weekend dances to bring in alcohol and food business, he moved into selling souvenirs to tourists attracted by a free animal menagerie. Multiple other enterprises came and went through the 1930s to 1960s, among them the Continental Divide Camp; the Continental, the Great Divide, the Buck & Squaw, and the Distant Drummer trading posts; the Big Horn and B & G cafés; and even a latter-day Stuckey's Pecan Shoppe.[50]

A business traveler, who in the mid-twentieth century frequently drove back and forth over the divide, observed the constantly changing flow of activities in its half-mile-long strip of tourist traps, bars, cafés, motels, and dance halls. He liked to eat at the Top-o-the-World Café, recalling, "They had pretty good food there, steaks and such," noting that some customers drove in all the way from Gallup to enjoy meals and good company. He remembered, "It wasn't bad as places go, not a family place, but not too rough either." His strongest memories, however, were of the female taxi dancers who earned money working the crowd in the adjacent hotel bar. They skillfully charmed male customers into letting them play dance music on the jukebox, pocketing the money the men gave them, and then feeding the machines with their own color-coded, fingernail polish–painted coins. At the end of each day, the proprietor returned the marked silver, but jukebox change was not the young women's only income. After spins around the dance floor, the girls begged their companions for bar drinks. "The barman would serve the client a cocktail and the girl a coke and then charge you for two cocktails," the extra profits on the beverages later being split between the dancers and the house.[51]

Gallup

From the crest of the Continental Divide, motorists proceeded gradually downward in elevation just under thirty miles west to Gallup. They left pine trees behind in the mountains and reentered arid red rock country that reminded them of the landscapes they had seen around Laguna Pueblo. Along the way they passed Fort Wingate, a nineteenth-century military post that housed much of the U.S. War Department stockpile of high explosives including TNT and Dunnite during Route 66 days. As they approached Gallup, from Prewitt onward, these same travelers could look northward across the shallow, sandy bed of the Rio Puerco of the West to see one giant red-colored sandstone cliff succeeding the other. Some motorists were reminded of scenes from Western movies because these very same bluffs had served as backdrops in more than twenty Hollywood features filmed in the area. Once travelers arrived in Gallup, they found it to be another long, narrow ribbon of a town that reminded them of Grants. The Santa Fe Railway tracks, the Mother Road, and the community were all squeezed into a three-quarter- to mile-and-a-quarter-wide strip of land along the Rio Puerco, with difficult slopes on either side hindering development.

Gallup had an economic and social life quite apart from the Mother Road. Spawned by construction of the Santa Fe Railway in 1881, it housed substantial rail-repair facilities. Needing coal as locomotive fuel, the railroad encouraged others to explore for that resource, leading to the opening of nearby bituminous coal mines that operated for seven decades. As the demand for coal decreased, mining for another resource, uranium, took its place in the 1950s. Geography placed Gallup at the edge of the Navajo Reservation, the largest and most populous Native American community in the country. Three-quarters of the reserve was over the state line in Arizona, but most of its population was concentrated in its southeastern corner near the railroad town. Gallup accordingly grew into the largest trading center for Native-made arts and crafts in the entire American West. In 1922 it became the location for an annual intertribal Indian ceremonial, a combined rodeo, powwow, and fair celebrating Native American culture, which soon attracted

thousands of visitors each year. The railroad, the mines, and the American Indian trade all contributed to make Gallup a place where many people continuously came and went. Consequently it offered cross-country motorists an unexpectedly sophisticated range of choices in eating and sleeping.[52]

EL RANCHO HOTEL

Businessman Rupert Earl Griffith was a movie afficionado, but did not make or act in films. Instead he and his two brothers made their fortunes in operating motion picture theaters. By the mid-1930s, they owned scores of show houses across Oklahoma, Texas, and New Mexico, including the Navajo Theater on Highway 66 West in Gallup. Rupert had greater ambitions than just running movie houses. He wanted to try his hand at hotels and resorts.[53]

Having discovered Gallup through his theater business, Griffith became impressed with the assets he found; for him the community was a diamond in the rough. He believed that the visual appeal of the surrounding red rock country, the cultural draw of Native Americans, the near-complete paving of cross-country Highway 66, and easy access for train passengers and freight on the main line of the Santa Fe Railway combined to make Gallup the prime location for a substantial hotel. Half a mile from downtown, at 1000 East Route 66, he erected a fanciful three-story western-style luxury hostelry. He called it El Rancho Hotel, "the world's largest ranch house." Following its opening in November 1937, guests entering the lobby saw a soaring two-story roof supported on giant varnished pine tree trunks, a massive lobby fireplace flanked by rustic stairs, and a four-sided mezzanine filled with comfortable seating. The whole place was impressive. Guests could enjoy meals in a formal dining room, a coffee shop, or a bar. The chef prepared menu choices that diners might expect on either coast, ranging from fresh oysters on the half shell to roast prime rib of beef au jus. For their convenience and pleasure, overnight guests found a hairdressing salon, barbershop, and, behind closed doors, game rooms. When Armand Ortega first visited El Rancho as a teenager in 1941, he saw that "they had a casino in that big banquet room, and they had two dice tables, two twenty-one tables, a roulette wheel, and they had 16 slot machines in the middle." There was something for everyone.[54]

Because he was focused on further building his movie house empire and opening additional resort venues, Rupert Griffith farmed out daily operation of El Rancho to several of his close family members. His aunt and uncle, Mr. and Mrs. E. W. Turner, managed the hostelry proper, while his sister-in-law, Mabel Heath, oversaw the lobby curio shop. Supervision changed after Griffith's untimely death by heart attack in Beverly Hills in 1943. Ownership over the years passed through several out-of-state investors and then in 1961 to a consortium of local businesspeople. The level of service remained high for a quarter century.

Beginning in 1940 a series of Hollywood motion picture producers began filming outdoor scenes for Westerns and other motion pictures in the red rock country around Gallup. They typically headquartered at El Rancho. The stars lodged in luxury suites while production crew members occupied more prosaic quarters. Actors discovered that in Gallup they could let down their guard. A regular guest at the time reminisced, "You could go into the lobby of the El Rancho and it would be full of those Hollywood people. They would be laughing and talking and planning things. . . . They would talk to you, drink with you, dance with you." The brick-floored lobby and bar became neutral ground for all.

Public tastes in lodging changed as years passed, and by the late 1960s newer motels drained away the old hotel clientele. El Rancho began advertising the availability of cheap rooms for daily, weekly, and monthly rentals, becoming little more than a flophouse. Finally the complex came up for sale in a bankruptcy auction in 1987. Local Indian arts and crafts trader Armand Ortega (the former teenager who had first visited El Rancho many years before) purchased the entire facility and began what became a multiyear endeavor to return it to its former glory. Thanks to his efforts and those of others, again visitors can stay in and dine in this remarkable place.[55]

EL NAVAJO HOTEL

Travelers on the Mother Road had a choice of two first-class hotels in Gallup. Westbound drivers from 1937 onward arrived first at El Rancho, but those heading east initially came to El Navajo Hotel. The latter hostelry was already offering food and lodging when the U.S. Bureau of Public Roads designated Highway 66 as a cross-country artery in 1926. It stood between the tracks of the Santa Fe Railway and the 100 block of East Railroad Avenue (later East Route 66). Like the Alvarado Hotel in Albuquerque, it was erected by the Santa Fe Railway to plans prepared collaboratively with the Fred Harvey Company, which subsequently ran the combined hotel and restaurant. The facility served two roles: providing shelter and food for general travelers while at the same time feeding wholesome and timely meals to passengers on Santa Fe trains during thirty-minute refreshment stops before the company began using rolling dining cars.

Mary Jane Colter was the principal architect for the Fred Harvey Company from 1902 to 1948, and the El Navajo complex in 1916 was her first truly large undertaking. American entry to World War I in 1917 interrupted construction, but when the hotel opened in 1923 it looked different from any other such facility in the country. For several years architects in Santa Fe had been designing buildings with stylistic elements drawn from Pueblo and Spanish Colonial construction, but Colter for the first time combined this southwestern theme with the newly fashionable art deco style that was taking Europe by storm. The latter emphasized geometric shapes like zigzags, trapezoids, and circles. Later dubbed Pueblo Deco, this blending of the two schools of design became more widely known from the slightly later KiMo Theater in downtown Albuquerque. Architect Colter filled the hotel with fine Native American pottery, baskets, and weavings. Its interior was the first public space in the country where leaders of the Navajo Nation permitted display of images drawn from their ceremonial sand paintings. El Navajo provided upscale food and lodging until 1957, when it was razed as part of a widening of Highway 66.

When Englishman Mark Pepys visited El Navajo in the fall of 1935, he was less impressed with its architecture than by the egalitarian atmosphere found in its lunchroom. He wrote that Gallup "boasted a most excellent Fred Harvey house ... [with] a menu of amazing variety." The traveler continued, "Everyone sat along a huge counter: workmen, clerks, a cultured half-breed and tourists like ourselves. I like this. Had the governor of the State walked in, or the president of the whole country, I felt that both would have received the same service and no one would have looked more than twice at them." The overseas guest, who held a noble title as the Sixth Earl of Cottenham, had trouble believing the social equality exhibited by the diners that chance had tossed together in the coffee shop located between the railroad tracks and the Mother Road in Gallup.[56]

RANCH KITCHEN

The Ranch Kitchen was born over a hundred miles north of Gallup in the northwestern corner of New Mexico at Farmington. Its founders were two married couples, Helen and Earl Aaron Vance and Jean and Alexander C. "Buzz" Bainbridge, all of whom had worked in the hospitality trade for others. They longed to run their own business and decided that a homey restaurant with a western atmosphere would become their key to success. As its location in 1953, they chose Farmington, where at the time development of natural gas deposits was dramatically boosting population. The new eatery rode on the crest of this economic boom. Then, within months, a real estate promoter told them about the new Thunderbird Lodge motel being built on the west side of Gallup. To the four entrepreneurs, the steady flow of motorists on Route 66 seemed to be an even more reliable source of hungry diners than they had in Farmington.

The couples divided their efforts, with Earl and Helen moving to open a second Ranch

Kitchen in new quarters at the Thunderbird in June 1954. Within a year the Vances and Bainbridges went their separate ways, with the latter remaining in the older location. Meanwhile the new Ranch Kitchen at 1805 West Route 66 in Gallup prospered while becoming known for its limited but high-quality menu. For a dozen years, Swiss-born Erica Habluetzel ran food-service operations for the Vances and earned the Ranch Kitchen a reputation for strict standards of quality and service. "If the waitresses came into work without having pressed and starched their uniforms, they were sent home," a family member remembered. After thirty years ownership of the motel changed, and Earl and second wife, Beverly, lost their lease on the restaurant space. After pondering their options, in 1984 they decided to erect a new Ranch Kitchen farther out of town at 3001 West Route 66. This placed it nearer to an exit on newly opened Interstate 40. They and stepson John Marbury continued to operate the business until after Earl's death in 2004.[57]

The Ranch Kitchen was one of the early general restaurants to adopt a locally evolved entrée that later exploded in popularity across the American West. This dish was the Navajo taco, which combined white-flour-based Indian fry bread with savory toppings commonly associated with Mexican-style tacos. Native Americans have a love-hate relationship with fry bread that dates back to the years when they first were forced onto reservations. One of the easiest ways they could use their limited rations that included flour, baking powder, and lard was to prepare starchy and greasy "bread" from balls of dough made from flour, leavening, and water dropped into skillets of hot fat. By the 1960s

newspapers began reporting special events and fundraiser gatherings for schools in Arizona and New Mexico in which mothers and others prepared traditional fry bread as the base for Navajo tacos, which typically had chili con carne, beans, diced onions, lettuce, tomatoes, and shredded cheese somewhat precariously piled on top. As early as 1977, the Ranch Kitchen was advertising Navajo tacos as a regular menu item, later even printing color picture postcards showing the dish. About the same time, other restaurants likewise began adopting the specialty so that today Navajo tacos are served all across the American West, not just in the Navajo country around Gallup.[58]

On into Arizona

Highway 66 continued westward from Gallup about twenty miles to the Arizona state line. Motorists passed more tall red sandstone bluffs, sometimes driving near the bases. Along this stretch of roadway, a handful of trading posts sold gasoline and some groceries as well as Native American arts and crafts, but there were no sit-down places to eat until travelers came to a modest café called the State Line Station, just barely inside the New Mexico boundary. As part of efforts to promote New Mexico as a tourist destination during the 1930s, the state erected a wooden archway over the two lanes of traffic, greeting new arrivals with the words "Welcome to New Mexico." Those heading farther west could look up to read, "Come Again" on their side while contemplating Arizona pleasure stops ahead at the Petrified Forest and Painted Desert. Some of the others behind steering wheels instead were likely dreading the difficult climbs ahead over the San Francisco

Mountains near Flagstaff and the Black Mountains outside Kingman. Travelers who could afford the luxury could look forward to tasty meals served by attractive "waiter girls" at four more Fred Harvey Company hotels along the 66 roadside in Arizona, while others of lesser means might be sating their hungers with crackers, cheese, and water as they counted their coins in hopes of buying enough gasoline to reach their destinations.[59]

ARIZONA

Continuing down the valley of the Rio Puerco of the West from Gallup and still paralleling the Santa Fe Railway, Route 66 crossed from New Mexico into Arizona at the foot of huge red sandstone bluffs. Just about every Mother Road traveler had his or her own idea of what to expect in the Copper State. On a winter 1926–27 trip west with wife Daphne, Dallas Lore Sharp wrote that they approached Arizona expecting some unknown excitement, "as if we might be met by giant-armed cacti, Gila monsters, alkali flats, Apaches, and . . . poison springs." They then reported, "Instead it was more snow, identical with the snow of New Mexico." The landforms and diverse population that motorists had met already in some ways readied newcomers for the mountains, deserts, canyons, and people that they found. Even so, many travelers were still not fully prepared for the extremes that Arizona sometimes presented.

Heading west into Arizona, travelers found the same Intermountain Plateau region that stretched all the way from the Rio Grande Valley in New Mexico. Here it went by the name Colorado Plateau, from the Colorado River (and Little Colorado River) that traverse it. The landscape was generally level semidesert between five thousand and eight thousand feet in elevation, dissected by erosion-cut canyons. About two-thirds of the way across the state, motorists transitioned into a Basin and Range Province in which north-south trending mountain ranges alternated with long strips of desert plains. Each of these physical regions presented its own particular problems to road builders so that much of Highway 66 across Arizona remained unpaved until well into the 1930s.

Along with New Mexico, Arizona became a state in 1912. Its territorial and state governments had done their best to encourage counties to build and improve roadways, an effort assisted with federal matching funds starting in 1916. Even so, in 1926, when Highway 66 received its numerical designation, most roads in Arizona were still barely improved. Because it was expensive to build bridges and to fill in low places, most of these tracks followed the twisting contours of the land. Yet Arizonans in increasing numbers purchased automobiles, with ownership increasing from 34,000 in 1920 to 82,000 in 1927, and tax-paying drivers demanded highways better suited to cars. In 1933 the state received $5 million in Depression-era national recovery highway funds, most it going to complete paving projects that had been initiated but not completed. This played an important role in making Route 66 the first completely paved transcontinental highway in the country in 1938. It was estimated in the mid-1930s that 65 percent of the westbound traffic in the United States at some point passed over the Mother Road.[1]

In order to protect agricultural crops from insect pests and plant diseases, the Arizona state government set up official ports of entry on its highway borders with other states. Legislators knew their citrus raisers were particularly vulnerable, so state inspectors required travelers to give up any fresh fruits in their possession that had been grown outside the state. At the same time, they examined the ownership titles of any "foreign" (out-of-state) motor vehicles as a means of deterring interstate auto theft or illegal efforts by individuals to sell vehicles without paying in-state taxes. During the Great Depression, some of the border station personnel also were known to turn back

obviously destitute travelers who lacked the financial resources to support themselves should they become stranded. The Highway 66 inspection station for the Arizona state line operated initially at Lupton and then later twenty miles inside the state at Sanders.[2]

When African American motorists headed into Arizona before the mid-1960s, they did not know what reception might be awaiting them from businesspeople along the road. The Copper State had no legally mandated separation of the races in lodging, restaurants, and other public services, but many white owners and managers refused to admit Blacks. Unless they used special *Negro Motorist* guidebooks, out-of-state travelers did not know which eating places would serve them and which required that any Black customers go to the kitchen door to order, pay for, and receive food. A reader wrote columnist Johnny Otis at the Black-run *Los Angeles Sentinel* newspaper in 1960 that he and his wife were planning a road trip across the Southwest. He then queried, "Which route would present less prejudice at motels and restaurants . . . Highway 66 or the Southern route through Texas?" Realizing that his reader would undoubtedly encounter

State agriculture department plant and fruit inspection station at Lupton, Arizona, ca. 1950. Author's collection.

some racial discrimination wherever he went, the journalist responded, "Flip a coin."[3]

Lupton to Painted Desert

The first forty-five miles of the Mother Road in Arizona crossed sparsely inhabited desert and semidesert from the village of Lupton on the state line to the Painted Desert, where some limited facilities existed for travelers. An Arizona highway engineer in 1926 accurately observed, "From this point [Lupton] . . . there are no towns of any consequence but numerous trading posts." This was a fair assessment, for the entire thinly populated roadway linked one dispersed crossroad community with the next, each one with its own general store serving local Indian families and offering curios to travelers. None of the communities along this stretch of Highway 66 ever had very many people, with Lupton having only 33; Sanders, 88; and Chambers, 59 in the mid-1940s.

The greatest concentration of these mercantile enterprises clustered on either side of the New Mexico state line around Lupton. There, for decades vendors took advantage of the dramatic natural setting of red sandstone bluffs combined with an Arizona state port-of-entry station that slowed down vehicular traffic. Enterprising businesspeople sold tourists not just fuel and auto requisites but also genuine Native-made arts and crafts together with inexpensive lookalikes produced elsewhere. Some of the dealers were Native Americans, like several successive generations of the Yellowhorse family, but others were born elsewhere in the United States and abroad. Savvy managers almost always kept stocks of cold soda pop and packaged snacks to sate the appetites of customers. Among the Lupton-area enterprises that

came and went over the years were the Box Canyon Trading Post, Yellowhorse Trading Post, Cave of the Seven Devils, Lupton Café, Indian Trails Trading Post, Lupton Trading Post, Tomahawk Trading Post, and State Line Trading Post. Although it is hard to tell where they stopped around Lupton on August 26, 1947, Ellen and Herb Tappenbeck may have found more excitement than they expected. She penned at the time, "Had lunch on the Arizona border. They had a row of slot machines right in front of the door as you came in. Lively joint."[4]

During the drive through desert country, down the valley of the mostly dry Rio Puerco of the West, the landscape became less rugged but remained mostly barren and arid. Motorists passed scattered flocks of sheep belonging to Native American families, many travelers wondering where the animals found enough grass and water to sustain themselves. Increasingly they spotted the distinctive multisided, log-and-earth hogan lodges of Navajo families.

Ahead on the Mother Road, drivers came to scatterings of houses that had sprung up alongside Santa Fe Railway sidetracks and livestock loading facilities, each of them forming the nucleus for little crossroads communities. They passed by Allentown, Houck, Querino, Sanders, Chambers, and Navajo. Each of them at one time or another had a general mercantile store, usually called a trading post, where an entrepreneur extended credit to Navajo families, taking payment once or twice a year when they sold sheep wool or lambs. These same shopkeepers attempted to garner additional income from travelers by selling souvenirs, Native arts and crafts, fuel, groceries, and sometimes even quick-service meals.[5] At Houck an

A motorist enjoying a cantaloupe in the front seat of his car in the mid-1950s. Author's collection.

incongruous wooden-stockade Fort Courage succeeded the earlier White Mound Trading Post in 1967. The theme of the tourist attraction came from the 1965–67 *F Troop* television comedy program, which was set on the Great Plains but was filmed mostly at the Warner Brothers studios in Hollywood. Including a large gift shop, an ice cream parlor, and a sit-down café, Fort Courage managed to keep its gates open into the mid-2010s.[6]

Painted Desert and Petrified Forest

Two of the natural wonders of the American West lay ahead of westbound motorists on the Mother Road—the Painted Desert and the Petrified Forest. Travelers came first to the Painted Desert, natural badlands comprised of eroded layers of Triassic-era mudstone, siltstone, and shale in multiple colors originating from natural iron and manganese compounds. The highway offered multiple vantage points where travelers could pause and admire the spectacle and where adept businesspeople set up a filling stations, stores, and curio stands. Among those who did so were Dotch Windsor at his roadside

Painted Desert Trading Post and Harry E. "Indian" Miller and his sister, Julia Grant Miller, at their Painted Desert Park and Mountain Lion Farm. For travelers who were better heeled, there were both food and lodging at Herbert David Lore's Painted Desert Inn, which later the Fred Harvey Company operated.

Once tourists reached the Painted Desert, those who had time often looped down five miles south through Adamana to drive through the Petrified Forest. Designated a national monument in 1906, the reserve gradually expanded in size to encompass the Painted Desert as well and became a national park in 1962. Many travelers paused for picnics, including Zilpha Pallister Main, who in the 1920s wrote, "We reached the Petrified Forest in time for lunch, and used a big [mineralized tree] stump for a table and two smaller ones to sit on." Once they drove through the marvel of prehistoric trees turned to stone, motorists had to make a decision. They could double back on the park road to Route 66 and proceed on to Holbrook that way, or instead they could make their way about the same distance to the same town from the south gate of the park via U.S. Highway 260 (now U.S. 180).[7]

Holbrook

As early as the 1870s, Mormon agriculturists from Utah were establishing farms along the Rio Puerco and the Little Colorado near what later became Holbrook. Then, in 1881, the Atlantic and Pacific Railroad laid track through the valley, later selling an unbelievable million acres to Boston investors, who organized the Aztec Land and Cattle Company. For a quarter century, the town, as the headquarters for its Hashknife Ranch, earned a persistent reputation for being a rough place, receiving its first church only in 1914. When Herb and Ellen Tappenbeck drove through on August 27, 1947, she jotted down in her trip diary, "Went through Holbrook. . . . They actually go around with six shooters just as they do in the movies. . . . We didn't stop to see how tough it really is." In part because the Atchison, Topeka and Santa Fe Railway, successor to the Atlantic and Pacific, established major repair shops in Winslow, thirty-three miles to the west, even as the seat of Navajo County, Holbrook seemed never to prosper so well as its nearby competitor with an industrial base. In 1920, 1930, and 1940, the Holbrook population hovered around just 1,200 people, only increasing to 2,300 in 1950. Consequently trade with Route 66 motorists played a genuinely significant role in the economic life of the town.[8]

CACTUS CAFÉ (JOE AND AGGIE'S CAFÉ)

José "Joe" and Aggie Montano met at a dance in Holbrook in the 1940s. He was a local guy, and she came from the Concho Valley in eastern Arizona, where her New Mexican Hispanic family had settled in the nineteenth century. Joe had worked in a mercantile store in the commercial district south of the Santa Fe tracks, where he had begun developing personal relationships with his Native American customers. In 1943 the couple opened their own hole-in-the-wall café in the modest downtown area with help from Aggie's sister, Annie Gabaldon. Most of the out-of-town traffic then bypassed this neighborhood by heading west on Highway 66 along the north side of the railroad tracks. In 1953 the couple purchased Thomas Smithson's existing Cactus Café on the Mother Road at 120 West Hopi Drive, where they hoped to attract more hungry motorists. The decision proved to be sound, and in time they expanded the facility as Joe and Aggie's Cafe. Subsequent generations of diners have enjoyed their distinctive New Mexican–style fare, prepared using recipes from the kitchen of Aggie Montano's mother, Aurelia B. Tafoya. After thirty years, Joe and Aggie decided it was time to retire, and in 1978 they sold the eatery to their daughter, Alice, and her husband, Stanley Gallegos. As a popular barber, Stanley had gained notoriety helping organize a local Hubert H. Humphrey for President Committee in 1968. While the couple ran the restaurant, Stanley also cut hair on the side and for a while ran a modest tortilla factory. When Interstate 40 skirted the commercial district of Holbrook, old Joe Montano's long-standing connections with Native Americans helped keep the restaurant doors open. Grandson Steve Gallegos explained, "The café survived from Indian trade after the 1978 bypass," taking up the slack in business until a revival of heritage tourism along the Mother Road brought in more customers. Since that time Joe and Aggie's Café has prospered, and today the third generation of the family follows the same recipes prepared in some of the same historic cast iron cookware.[9]

Winslow

Across eastern Arizona, the Mother Road followed the valley of the Rio Puerco of the West. Just above Holbrook it flowed into the Little Colorado River, and drivers continued along the right bank of the latter stream another thirty-three miles to Winslow, passing through little Joseph City. Engineers laying out the old Atlantic and Pacific Railroad identified this route along the two river valleys as having the gentlest grade, so the tracks of the subsequent Santa Fe Railway remained within motorists' sight much of their way. It was the railroad that gave birth to Winslow in 1882. By the late 1920s, its industrial shops for repairing locomotives and rolling stock reputedly had a payroll totaling $200,000 monthly. The routing of Highway 66 through Winslow in 1926 added to the thriving economy, ensuring that it remained the most populous Arizona town on the Mother Road through the 1920s and 1930s with just under four thousand residents. Dry, dusty, and hot in the summertime, Winslow offered all the services that motorists might seek during their cross-country journeys.[10]

LA POSADA HOTEL

The Santa Fe Railway collaborated with its food contractor, the Fred Harvey Company, in erecting a two-story trackside dining and lodging facility at Winslow in 1897. Because the railroad did not yet provide dining cars on its trains, it scheduled short meal stops. Travelers hastily detrained, gobbled down plated or counter meals, and clambered back aboard in just half an hour. These establishments also provided lodging and meals to motorists like Caroline Rittenberg. She penned in a trip diary on July 10, 1925, "We motored on to Winslow and stayed in a Harvey House . . . [where] we were sure of the best service, delicious food, the most comfortable beds, and clean rooms."[11]

As a strategic division point on the Santa Fe Railway, Winslow was where two operational sections joined, making it the place where train crews changed and repairs were made. The town also happened to be roughly midway between tourist attractions along the Rio Grande in New Mexico and at the Grand Canyon in Arizona. By the 1920s the railroad and the Fred Harvey Company mutually promoted tourism to easterners to visit the picturesque Southwest, and they envisioned profits being made at a resort hotel alongside the tracks in Winslow. Such a hostelry would provide a base for motor coach and limousine tours east toward the Petrified Forest and north to the Hopi villages, as well as an overnight rest stop for travelers on the way west toward the Grand Canyon. The Harvey Company called on its primary architect and interior designer, Mary Jane Colter, to design a combined rail station and hotel with restaurant, coffee shop, and space for a bar. She envisioned a complex styled after an imaginary 150-year-old Spanish Colonial ranch headquarters fictionally named La Posada, meaning "the resting place." She wanted the newly built facility to look like the former home of a wealthy don that had survived for decades and then had been converted into a hotel with its historic furnishings and grounds intact. Two stories tall and with an adjacent depot, multiple landscaped courtyards, seventy guest rooms, five suites, and choices of dining areas, it was

Cheese Crisps, JOE AND AGGIE'S CAFÉ, HOLBROOK, ARIZONA

For years the Cheese Crisps have been a popular appetizer at Joe and Aggie's Café on the Mother Road in Holbrook. The finger food is their version of tostados consumed throughout the Southwest. The preparation is easy for home cooks to recreate.

Serving for two
1 large (burrito-size) flour tortilla
3 ounces Longhorn-style yellow cheddar cheese (grated)
Prepared red or green chile salsa to taste

Sprinkle grated cheese on top of tortilla in a flat pan. Place in oven at 350° F just long enough to melt the cheese. Remove from oven and cut into wedges. Top with either red or green chile salsa to taste.

Original recipe from Marian Clark, *The Route 66 Cookbook* (Tulsa: Council Oak Books, 1993), 168.

an opulent showplace that in pre-Depression days cost an immense $1 million. This last of several great Fred Harvey hotels opened on May 15, 1930, seven months after the great stock market crash.[12]

Food was a particular draw at La Posada, and its principal role was to feed train passengers. Verna Northcott Welsh remembered that during her Harvey Girl days waitressing in Winslow in 1937–41, "It was quite an experience to serve people in just 30 minutes." She reported that the La Posada kitchen prepared approximately 2,800 preordered meals for passengers arriving on seven different trains each day. These rail-based diners had only a short time to eat, while other guests took their leisure. For these less hurried patrons, a menu from 1940 listed meals of sea bass, breaded veal cutlet, roast young turkey, prime ribs of beef, or cottage fried steak; choice among three potatoes and either green beans or corn on the cob; lettuce and tomato salad; fruit, pudding, or sherbet; and coffee, tea, or milk, all priced between sixty-five and ninety cents per person. This is not to mention a la carte choices like fried half chicken or sirloin steak for two. The repasts were not cheap even then, but they were high quality.[13]

La Posada survived the Great Depression, though some questioned whether it would. Its employees subsequently fed meals to many thousands of soldiers and sailors on troop trains during World War II. By the 1950s most American travelers were abandoning rail travel and preferred private automobiles or airplanes. In 1956 the Harvey Company discontinued the Winslow food service and three years later closed the hotel doors. The grand and lovely facility was converted into offices for the Santa Fe Railway and then became vacant when those functions shifted elsewhere. Local volunteers continued to maintain the gardens as best they could. Then, in 1997, developer and preservationist Allan Affeldt purchased the historic hostelry at 303 East Second Street and began a multiyear restoration, which resulted in its room-by-room return to public service with its own chef-operated restaurant, the Turquoise Room. La Posada welcomes guests again.[14]

FALCON RESTAURANT

Mid-twentieth-century travelers knew that quality food service in Fred Harvey restaurants like La Posada was more expensive than in smaller eateries. Consequently Winslow abounded in lower-priced options, many offering satisfying repasts. When James Albert Davis drove through in July 1921, he exhibited his racial chauvinism when he commented, "Every lunch room in this town of 5000 is run by Chinamen." Nevertheless, he acknowledged, "They serve good meals and their prices are very reasonable." Later in the decade, a state business directory listed five cafés in the community, four of them operated by individuals with Asian names.[15]

The most notable long-term locally owned Winslow eating place traced its beginnings to immigrants not from China but from Greece. Two teenaged friends, Nicholas Demotien "Nick" Kretsedemas and George T. Cheros, decided to seek their fortunes in the United States in 1907. Landing first in Boston, they took food service jobs in several places around the United States. In 1928 Nick decided to return home, but George remained in America, in time locating in Winslow. By 1931 he had saved enough money to join with another Greek, Gus Thomas, in opening the Coney Island Café at 111 West Second Street.

Blueberry Muffins, LA POSADA HOTEL, WINSLOW, ARIZONA

La Posada Hotel, opened in 1929 by the Fred Harvey Company between the pavement of Route 66 and the tracks of the Santa Fe Railway, served memorable meals to travelers for a quarter century. Customers sang the praises of its blueberry muffins for miles either side of Winslow. Because perishable fresh blueberries were unavailable year-round during the heyday of Mother Road and rail travel, cooks at La Posada used frozen fruit, so to recreate the historic taste, color, and texture accurately, thaw and use the deep-freeze variety.

About fifteen to twenty muffins depending on size

$2/3$ cup sugar

$1/3$ cup shortening

2 eggs (beaten)

2 cups all-purpose flour

4 teaspoons baking powder

$1/2$ teaspoon salt

$2/3$ cup milk

1 cup frozen blueberries (thawed)

Cream together sugar and shortening. Add beaten eggs and mix thoroughly. Sift together flour, baking powder, and salt. Add the dry mixture alternately with milk to the creamed sugar and shortening and stir together. Gradually blend in blueberries and their thawed juice. Pour dough into full-size greased muffin pan(s), filling the cups half full. Bake at 400° F for fifteen minutes.

Original recipe from Atchison, Topeka and Santa Fe Railway Company and Fred Harvey Company, *Super Chief Cook Book of Famous Fred Harvey Recipes* ([Chicago]: Santa Fe Railway and Fred Harvey, [ca. 1955]), 21.

This was a twenty-five-foot-wide, hundred-foot-deep brick storefront that faced Highway 66 traffic passing through downtown. Its specialties were "sandwiches of all kinds" and bowls of chili. Securing an alcohol license after the end of Prohibition, in 1934 the partners advertised, "Drop in anytime for a Coney Island Sandwich and a glass of good old Budweiser Beer." After a decade George merged his business with George Stathis's White Café, a block away at 114 East Second, operating the latter eatery into the mid-1950s. In his early sixties, Cheros decided that the time had come for him to expand, and in 1954 he began planning the brand-new full-service Falcon Restaurant to compete with La Posada for the higher-end highway food trade.[16]

While George T. Cheros was building his restaurant business in America, his old friend Nick Kretsedemas had returned home to Greece and married, had four sons, and enjoyed a good life until war broke out in 1939. The family survived the German occupation, but Nick and one son died during the subsequent Greek civil war. After their father's passing, the surviving three sons delved into his old papers and discovered to their surprise that their "papa" had become a naturalized American citizen in the 1920s and that they were likewise eligible to live in the United States. Between 1947 and 1949, they settled in Alabama, where their father had lived two decades earlier. Out in Arizona, when childless George Cheros began planning his new $43,000 Falcon Restaurant at 1113 East Second on the Mother Road, he contacted his old friend's sons with a proposal that the three of them manage his enterprise. In this way the Kretsedemas brothers, Panagiotis Nicholas "Pete," George N., and James, came to Winslow in 1955 and collaborated for years

in operating and eventually purchasing the Falcon.

In 1956, the year after the Falcon opened, the old La Posada food service shut down and quickly the Greek-owned startup became "the place" to eat, drink, and meet friends in Winslow. In 1959 the Kretsedemas brothers acquired the state liquor license from the erstwhile bar in the former Harvey hotel and even purchased its vintage cash register for their new Falcon Cocktail Lounge. The combination of local trade with that of Route 66 motorists led to decades of prosperity for the brothers. Pete fondly remembered, "There would always be a line out the front from 6 P.M. to 9 P.M.," adding, "Most of the time you would be lucky to even see a license plate from Arizona in the parking lot." Famous for its from-scratch cooking, the Falcon remained in Kretsedemas family hands at the time of this writing.[17]

Meteor Crater
METEOR STATION (RIMMY JIM'S TRADING POST)

Heading westward from Winslow toward Flagstaff, sixty miles away, motorists passed an exceptional natural phenomenon, a giant meteor crater. The indentation in the desert floor, three-quarters of a mile across and 560 feet deep, came from the impact of a fireball believed to have been 160 feet across that fell from the heavens about 50,000 years ago. About twenty miles west of Winslow, Route 66 passed north of the remarkable site. The dirt road that led half a dozen miles to the marvel gave rise to and supported several sequential filling station, lunchroom, and general store operations.

Harry William and Hope Locke opened the first known Meteor Station crossroads store and fuel stop as a byproduct of Harry's all-consuming personal interest in the crater. In the mid-1920s they homesteaded land that encompassed the junction of Highway 66 with the road south leading to the remarkable depression. At the crossroads they sold gasoline and groceries while Harry showed travelers meteorite fragments and regaled them with stories about the natural wonder. In 1933 they erected a "meteorite museum" to the east and leased and eventually sold the store and station to a former rancher, James "Rimmy Jim" Giddings, who added a lunch counter and liquor sales. Through an irrepressible sense of humor, Jim made the stop known up and down the Mother Road. Behind the building, for example, the jokester set up fake tombstones to mark imaginary graves of salesmen he pretended to have dispatched. The former cowboy ran the enterprise until a heart attack took his life in 1943. For a time Winslow bartender Charles Harp operated a tavern in Jim's old place. Then, in 1948, Flagstaff businessman William H. Swizer, who inherited the property from Giddings, transferred its ownership to his daughter and son-in-law, Ruth and Cyril Brown "Sid" Griffin. For the next quarter century, the couple managed the lunchroom, store, and station as Rimmy Jim's Trading Post. When the alignment of U.S. Highway 66 shifted slightly north in 1949, they relocated some of the old structures and erected some new, maintaining the roadside enterprise until they sold it in 1970 to become right-of-way for Interstate 40.[18]

Over Canyon Diablo and into the Mountains

Motorists drove forty miles from the Meteor Crater junction to Flagstaff, but, within a short three miles, they unexpectedly crossed a bridge over a dramatic hundred-foot-deep chasm called Canyon Diablo. There, from the 1920s to the 1970s, a succession of entrepreneurs ran filling stations, stores, and tourist cabins, sometimes with menageries, under names like Canyon Lodge and Two Guns Trading Post. Motorists then passed through more parched desert for another dozen miles before they came to a second impressive gorge, Canyon Padre. On the horizon the San Francisco Peaks loomed upward, as westbound travelers gradually gained elevation amid scattered pine trees around little Winona and then later a bona fide ponderosa pine forest around the intersection with U.S. Highway 89. Mother Road travelers veered southwestward on 66 into Flagstaff, which by 1940, with five thousand people, took from Winslow the distinction of being the largest Arizona town on Route 66. The community prospered from lumbering, the Northern Arizona State Teachers College (later renamed Northern Arizona University), and the main line of the Santa Fe Railway, plus U.S. Highway 66. The Mother Road passed down the main street through the town, which was sandwiched between the mountains and the bottom of a valley. At just under seven thousand feet in elevation, the area vied with the Continental Divide and Glorieta Pass in New Mexico for being the highest point along the roadway connecting Chicago with Los Angeles. James E. Cook grew up in Flagstaff, and from his adolescent years after World War II he remembered hanging out in downtown cafés: "We'd sit in a booth . . . watching the world pass. . . . In summer cars were bumper-to-bumper on the narrow street: lots of older cars, of course, but also the boxy post-1949 Fords, bullet-nosed

Studebakers, Buicks with portholes, Cadillacs with fins." He commented that sometimes the eateries were "so crowded with travelers that the management didn't appreciate teenagers ogling the tourist girls."[19]

Flagstaff

MUSEUM CLUB

During the first twenty years, Route 66 motorists approached Flagstaff from Winona on what today is Townsend-Winona Road. Still in the pine forest, the road made a T intersection with U.S. Highway 89. Westbound travelers turned southwest toward town, where, after three miles, they came to the Museum Club, a tavern that in later years became noted for the musicians it attracted. The impressive two-story building constructed from pine logs was never intended to become a roadhouse. Instead taxidermist Dean M. Eldredge built it as a museum to exhibit exotic animal specimens and interesting artifacts he had gathered. It doubled as the office and workshop where he met with hunters and other clients seeking his professional services. Eldredge was born in Waterloo, Iowa, in 1888 and received notable press exposure from his animal-collecting exploits in the West and in Mexico. Deciding in his forties to settle down in scenic Flagstaff, in 1931 he acquired a tract of wooded land beyond what was then the northeastern edge of town and hired unemployed local lumberjacks to cut multiple sixteen- to eighteen-inch-diameter pines and deliver their logs to his site. There, with others' help, he hewed the logs and assembled them into what he termed "the biggest log cabin in Arizona," erecting it around five intact ponderosa pines, branches and all. After a community-wide opening reception in June 1931, the Dean Eldredge

Museum admitted guests for twenty-five cents apiece to view the proprietor's personal assemblage of preserved animal specimens, antique firearms, and Native arts and crafts. At the pinnacle of Eldredge's career, however, cancer struck. His health failed and the mastermind returned home to the Midwest, where he died in 1937.[20]

Local saddlemaker and noted fiddler Emmett Guy "Doc" Williams then purchased the imposing log structure. The taxidermist's family sold most of the collections to pay Eldredge's debts and funeral expenses, giving the new owner an open space where he opened Doc Williams' Museum Club. There he offered Dutch oven cowboy-style meals and dancing to live music Wednesday through Sunday nights. The facility passed through several other hands but always remained a bar and grill with a dance floor. Over the years the establishment went by such names as the Mount View Museum, Frank's Museum Club, Quirk's Museum Club, and Barker's Village Museum Club, though locals mostly nicknamed it "the Zoo" from the days when it was filled with Dean Eldredge's animal mounts. Through the years it was known for its charcoal-broiled steaks, fried chicken, shrimp, oysters, and Mexican dishes. Thorna and Don "Pappy" Scott acquired the roadhouse in 1963, and, through Don's personal connections with artists in the Nashville music scene, they made it a popular stopover point for country and western performers traveling to or from shows in Las Vegas. The Museum Club in Flagstaff became a venue where locals sometimes got to see and hear the likes of music greats Hank Thompson, Waylon Jennings, and Willie Nelson. Following the deaths of Thorna and Don in 1973 and 1975, local investors Paul and Martin Zanzucchi purchased and for years ran the roadhouse, which remains a still-active enterprise at 3404 East Route 66.[21]

GRAND CANYON CAFÉ

Santa Fe Avenue, taking its name from the adjacent railroad, carried westbound motorists toward downtown Flagstaff, and its north-side storefronts opposite from the tracks became prime real estate. In the mid-1930s widow Mariana Herman invested earnings from other ventures in erecting a connected row of four twenty-five-foot-wide rental buildings in the 100 block of East Santa Fe. Over the years they housed multiple enterprises, but the Grand Canyon Café at 110 remained for decades. George J. Dokos partnered with George L. Holt in opening the eatery in spring 1939, selling it to Ed Spaulding, manager of the nearby Weatherford Hotel, in 1942. Two years later Albert D. Wong moved to Flagstaff from Durango, Colorado, and by 1945 he purchased the café, bringing in brothers Edward F. and Alfred Wong and eventually nephew William "Bill" Yee as partners. For decades they operated the restaurant, open from early morning to midnight, featuring "American and Chinese Dishes." In 1950 the Wongs acquired an adjacent twenty-five-foot-wide building, doubling the size of their enterprise. Fred Wong, Albert's son, started working in the Grand Canyon Café as a boy, growing up in its kitchen and dining room, and as an adult he purchased the business from his relatives in 1980. He operated it with wife Tina until selling to other homegrown entrepreneurs in 2016. The buyers renovated the café, retaining many of its historic fixtures but completely reconstructing the kitchen. Under their

management, the new Grand Canyon Café opened the next year but struggled to retain old customers while attracting new ones. It closed in summer 2018.[22]

For almost eight decades, the old Grand Canyon Café was a cultural landmark in Flagstaff. Locals and out-of-town customers knew its workingman-sized breakfasts, its old-time merchants' plate lunches, and, during Fred Wong's years as owner, its chicken-fried steaks. Many diners sought out the Wong family's interpretation of Americanized Chinese food, the old-time neon sign outside announcing that within its walls one could find chop suey, the ultimate pseudo-Chinese dish invented in America. This author especially enjoyed the café's oversized pork egg rolls. Some employees themselves became veritable icons in Flagstaff, like waitress Julia Ann Sartor, who, for fifty-three years, from 1946 to 1999, waited on tables in the Grand Canyon. Even before the term "homeless" came into common parlance, the Wong family served free Thanksgiving Day lunches to everyone who came through the doors whether they could pay or not. As if this were not enough, on the other days of the year the Wongs made sure that whenever a person who was hungry and without a job sat down, he or she would receive a big bowl of thick, filling soup with crackers at no charge. As local writer Malcolm Mackey said, "If they were sober, they were fed."[23]

SPANISH INN (EL CHARRO CAFÉ)

Highway 66 originally turned south from Santa Fe Avenue (now renamed Route 66) onto San Francisco Street, crossed the main line of the Santa Fe Railway, and then immediately turned west on West Phoenix Avenue to head out of town. This initial alignment took it through the edge of the working-class Southside neighborhood where most Hispanic and African American residents lived. It was here that travelers seeking Mexican-style food headed. Four blocks south of the Mother Road, at 409 South San Francisco Street, in 1942 Maria Louisa Fajardo opened a café she called the Spanish Inn at a boarding house that belonged to her sister-in-law Dolores Montoya Montez and brother-in-law Santiago Vidaurri "Monte" Montez. In 1945 Dolores and friend Elsie Mondragon purchased the business, with the former taking over the enterprise. She prepared Tex-Mex dishes that evolved along the borders of Texas and Mexico, including chicken enchiladas, tamales, chile rellenos, and tostados, as well as "American food" like T-bone steaks with french fries.[24] While she and Santiago remained the property owners, they subsequently leased the Spanish Inn space to other proprietors, among them Alice Macias and Vera N. and Ernest A. "Ernie" Castro (who were the sister-in-law and brother of Raul Castro, the Arizona governor in 1975–77).[25]

In the meantime New Mexico–born Demetrio B. "Dan" Castillo made his way to Flagstaff, working for nine years as a cook in the downtown Monte Vista Hotel. There he decided he wanted a restaurant of his own. In 1946 Dan learned that space was available in a commercial building at 111 South San Francisco, and there he opened his own El Charro (meaning "the Cowboy") Café, offering what he termed "Spanish and American dishes." In 1956 Dolores and Santiago Montez placed their Spanish Inn property at 409 South San Francisco on the market, and, without delay, Dan and Clara M. "Clarita" Castillo initiated efforts to purchase it. Almost immediately the Castillos shifted their focus to the new

location and revised its business name from Spanish Inn to El Charro Café. For the next decade and a half, they operated the popular eatery, expanding the facilities and rebuilding parts of it following a 1965 fire. It was during this time that author and artist Bob Boze Bell, then an Anglo teenager from Kingman, Arizona, experienced his first Mexican-style meal at El Charro. "I was so naïve I tried to take the 'wrapping' off my burrito," he remembered, explaining, "I thought it was some sort of thick paper." After Dan Castillo's 1970 death, Clara continued managing the restaurant for three years until turning it over to Dan's nephew, Gilbert Lomeli Montoya, and his wife, Carlotta. Retaining many of the old-time recipes, they gave flair to the menu by adding several Sonoran-style dishes and preparations. The Montoyas continued the traditions of El Charro another four decades until 2013. Since that time at least two other eating places have occupied the historic building.[26]

TONY'S STEAK HOUSE (SPORTSMAN'S STEAK HOUSE, LUMBERJACK CAFÉ, GRANNY'S CLOSET)

In the early 1930s, the Arizona Highway Department and the Santa Fe Railway collaborated in constructing a two-lane underpass for Mother Road traffic beneath the main east-west railroad line through Flagstaff. From this time onward, Mother Road traffic proceeded west on two-lane Santa Fe Avenue to a left curve onto Sitgreaves Street, where it went under the tracks. The roughly 2,100-foot stretch of South Sitgreaves between the passageway and the junction where the road forked, west on 66 and south toward Prescott, became a prime setting for tourist courts, filling stations, and eating places. After a new four-lane underpass replaced the congested former passageway in 1958, the property fronting on this short sweep of pavement became even more desirable.[27]

Among those who realized the potential for profits along this upper end of South Sitgreaves were Anthony H. "Tony" and Alma Mae Souris. Greek-born Tony met Alma in Albuquerque, New Mexico, where, during the early 1920s, she worked as a Harvey Girl waitress in the Alvarado Hotel. Tony's experience began as a cook's helper on a passenger-carrying steamship during World War I, and he stayed in the food business for decades. In 1938 the couple moved to Flagstaff, where they opened the Holsum Coffee Shop. In October 1946 they launched the new $50,000 Tony's Steak House in a purpose-built forty-by-seventy-foot concrete-block structure at 218 South Sitgreaves. Reflecting 1940s tastes, the press reported that "attractive fluorescent lighting lends quiet and subdued beauty to the environment" inside the restaurant serving "steaks, chops, fowl and fish." After a decade Tony and Alma Souris sold their restaurant in 1956 to John and Dolly Mills from Williams, Arizona, who renamed it the Sportsman's Steak House. For three more years, they maintained it as one of the top meal destinations in Flagstaff. The restaurant even hosted a political luncheon featuring U.S. senator Barry Goldwater just before the November 1956 general elections.[28]

Robert O. and Violette M. Morison next purchased the restaurant in October 1959. Due to its proximity to the campus of Arizona State Teachers College and its Lumberjack athletic teams, they rechristened the eatery the Lumberjack Café. It thrived on trade from local customers, college students, and auto travelers. In May 1963 Bob attended the annual National Restaurant Convention in Chicago, where he learned about oversize fiberglass human and animal advertising sculptures used as eye-catchers for auto dealerships and eating places. He ordered a twenty-foot-tall Paul Bunyan–like lumberjack complete with a giant axe to position next to the entrance into the café. Steve Dashew, who about this time acquired the Ventura manufacturing plant that made the sculptures, later identified Morison's as the first of hundreds of giant "muffler men" that his International Fiberglass firm sold over the subsequent ten years. The figure attracted so much attention in Flagstaff that in 1966 Bob and Alma ordered a second lumberjack to be erected at the north end of the restaurant facing oncoming Route 66 traffic. Both statues appeared in a scene in the 1969 *Easy Rider* motion picture, in which actors Dennis Hopper and Peter Fonda rode motorcycles past the café. The Lumberjack became a favorite eating place for many latter-day Route 66 travelers like John Kofton, who reminisced, "They had good food and we always stopped there for eats when passing through." The obligations of daily operations, however, weighed heavily on the Morisons as years passed, and they transferred most management responsibilities to son Paul.[29] Then, in the summer of 1974, they sold the property and business to local entrepreneurs Paul and Patrick Zanzucchi. In honor of their grandmother, Ermelinda Zanzucchi, they renamed the restaurant Granny's Closet, even using her photograph in advertising. They donated the two twenty-foot fiberglass lumberjack figures to Northern Arizona University, where they remain at its Skydome arena. For the next forty years, members of the Zanzucchi family owned and managed

Granny's Closet, feeding two more generations of diners, before closing the enterprise in 2016.[30]

Williams

Westbound Route 66 proceeded thirty-three miles from Flagstaff to Williams. It passed the still-operating Kit Carson Camp and, on its earliest alignment, climbed and descended two inclines up to 7,410 feet in height. Only Glorieta Pass, New Mexico, at 7,500 feet, was higher in elevation along Route 66 as originally designated. Motoring through a scattered summer resort community at Parks, travelers continued through more forests as well as open mountain meadows. Occasionally they glimpsed trains of the Santa Fe Railway a little to their left. Williams, at elevation 6,762 feet, had come into existence in 1881 as a railway siding and shipping point for lumber, cattle, and sheep. Its fortunes changed in September 1901, when the railroad completed a sixty-four-mile spur to the south rim of the Grand Canyon. Thereafter thousands of pleasure seekers annually poured through Williams, making it the tourist gateway to this natural wonder and in time a regular stop for motorists along Route 66. Many stopped there for meals or snacks, like Jack Raymer with a group of Boy Scouts headed home to Los Angeles from camping at the Grand Canyon in April 1930. He reported that they paused at Williams, where "after tanking up on milkshakes and water we departed." In 1984 Williams was the last city on the Mother Road to be bypassed by an interstate highway.[31]

FRAY MARCOS HOTEL

While the Santa Fe Railway was making plans to construct a branch line from Williams northward to the Grand Canyon, it worked with its food and lodging contractor, the Fred Harvey Company, to build facilities to feed, house, and entertain the tourists it hoped to carry to the giant cleft in the earth. Accommodations at the canyon would eventually include the internationally known El Tovar Hotel and later the Bright Angel Lodge. Not all the east-west Santa Fe trains stopped in Williams at convenient times for travelers to make rail connections up to the canyon. This situation led the railroad to erect a modest trackside hotel in Williams in 1908 that the Harvey firm operated for years. It took its name from Fray Marcos de Niza, who in 1539 explored areas north of Sonora, including modern Arizona and New Mexico. The hostelry had three dozen guest rooms plus modest quarters for railroad crew members sleeping between trains and for hotel employees. Located in a two-story, reinforced-concrete Mission Style building just west of a connected depot, the Fray Marcos offered meals in a quick-service lunchroom as well as in a sit-down, white-tablecloth dining room. Though the Harvey Company maintained its high standards of service everywhere, all knew that the Fray Marcos functioned only as a layover point for travelers passing through Williams. Irene M. Roberti and three friends motored on Highway 66 to Williams on July 22, 1941, spending the night at the Fray Marcos, but they were not overly impressed with their evening meal. She jotted down in her notes, "We ate at a Harvey place in the RR station, but it was nothing to write home about." As elsewhere on the Santa Fe system, the hotel staff also provided thirty-minute-turnaround meals for train passengers during crew changes and locomotive watering in Williams, this role continuing into the early 1950s. Then, with the increased use of diesel power and more rolling dining cars on Santa Fe trains, the Fray Marcos became less needed and closed on January 31, 1954. (The railroad ended its passenger service to the Grand Canyon fourteen years later in 1968.) The old hotel stood mostly disused for three decades until the Grand Canyon Railway acquired the abandoned Santa Fe track from Williams to the canyon in 1988, began running its own trains on the line, and rehabilitated portions of the old Harvey House to form part of a new hotel and entertainment complex.[32]

ROD'S STEAK HOUSE

Although Rodney Eldrich "Rod" Graves was born in Maine in 1906, he grew up in California and discovered Arizona as a young man working for the U.S. Geological Survey. In his twenties he tried unsuccessfully to run an Arizona cattle ranch during the Great Depression, relocated to Seligman in 1935, opened the Corner Café, and in 1938 married local schoolteacher Helen Eugenia Baker. The next year the couple relocated to Williams, where they purchased and operated the Grand Canyon Tavern on Route 66 at 138 West Bill Williams Avenue. In late 1945 they sold the bar and used the proceeds to help erect a purpose-built, twenty-five-foot-wide, concrete-block restaurant building on Slagle Street between Bill Williams Avenue and Railroad Avenue. At the time this neighborhood, on Highway 66 just east of downtown, had the densest concentration of tourist courts and campgrounds in Williams. The eatery opened memorably on August 23, 1946, during a town-wide electrical power outage with unplanned lighting from candles. From the outset the restaurant emphasized steaks

prepared from high-quality beef, initially grilled over oak and juniper charcoal and later over mesquite. A silhouette of a Hereford steer became the trademark for Rod's Steak House, with steel cut-out signs dotting the sides of Route 66 as far away as Gallup, New Mexico. Many hundreds of scrapbooks across the world became home to similar die-cut cardboard Hereford-steer-shaped menus from Rod's, a reporter in 1948 explaining, "Customers may have the menu and [an] envelope for mailing it out." They went around the globe. Staff members gave away some three hundred of the clever bills of fare on particularly busy days. Rod and Helen ran the steak house until they retired in 1967, selling the enterprise to Jim Pickens. In the meantime Lawrence Sanchez before and after military service worked at Rod's for both of these owners. When Pickens decided to step down in 1985, Lawrence and wife Stella Kathleen Sanchez purchased the restaurant, which, at the time of this writing, they still owned and managed.[33]

SULTANA POOL ROOM (SULTANA BUFFET, SULTANA BAR)

The Sultana Bar had its beginning in 1912, and it holds the oldest continuous liquor sales permit in Arizona. A. R. Bolin erected the flat-roof, concrete Sultana Building on a quarter city block at 301 West Bill Williams Avenue. People at the time considered it to be "the finest building in Williams." The structure originally housed a motion picture theater (for silent films and then talkies), a pool room offering beverage service, a dance floor, and rental spaces for stores and offices. At one time or another it housed municipal offices, the local newspaper, a delicatessen, and even the court chambers for a justice of the peace.

A woman hugging the neck of a metal steer advertising Rod's Steak House in Williams, Arizona, ca. 1955. Author's collection.

All these years, however, the Sultana Pool Room remained a place where enthusiasts of billiards could find tables, balls, and cues. After enforcement of national Prohibition began in 1920, legal sale of alcohol ended for the next thirteen years. Building owner Charles M. Proctor applied for and received a state liquor license in time to sell 3.2 percent beer on April 7, 1933, the very first day of sales after Prohibition ended, and his successors at the Sultana Buffet and then the Sultana Bar renewed that authorization without break. The Beer and Wine Revenue Act of 1933 stipulated that beer could be sold by the drink *only* in bona fide restaurants, hotels, or incorporated social clubs, and this technical requirement explains why many vintage tippling houses like this one called themselves "buffets." Updated by renovations in 1929 and

1941, the traditional Sultana has kept much of its historic atmosphere, and, at the time of this writing, it remained a destination for heritage travelers seeking to experience an old-time western watering hole. The tavern is easy to spot from its 1950 neon sign featuring a martini glass with a red cherry.[34]

Ash Fork

Taking its name from three branches of Ash Creek is the town Ash Fork. Like so many other Route 66 towns, it began as a rail siding, in this instance in 1882 on the Atlantic and Pacific Railroad (later Santa Fe Railway). The town grew in importance with the construction of a connecting rail link southward to Phoenix in 1895. The community at the rail junction never numbered over a thousand people, though it served travelers' needs for food, lodging, and repairs. Drivers heading west into the town descended 1,600 feet in elevation from the lofty pine trees at Williams to scrubby cedars on the flats around Ash Fork. Before the Arizona Highway Department widened the road in 1955, the nineteen-mile stretch from Williams provided entertainment for generations of adolescent drivers like James E. Cook, who grew up in Flagstaff during the 1950s. "When the perpetual teen-age boredom became unbearable, we would drive to Ash Fork . . . for coffee," he fondly recounted. "The last few miles were a long grade called Ash Fork Hill, and we would kick the car out of gear to see if it would coast all the way into downtown Ash Fork." In 1960 the Santa Fe Railway relocated its main east-west rails ten miles north of the community, which entered a decline that became more pronounced when Interstate 40 skirted past its south side in 1979. Fires in 1977 and 1987 destroyed many of the historic commercial buildings that formerly stood in the town.[35]

ESCALANTE HOTEL

The rail junction at Ash Fork was the most important on the Santa Fe system in Arizona. Here a branch led south from the main east-west line to Phoenix, the capital and largest city in the state. Because train schedules did not always coincide with connections for passengers, the railroad and the Fred Harvey Company opened a modest lodging and eating house to accommodate travelers at Ash Fork in 1895. It burned in 1905, and soon work began on a replacement two-story, L-shaped, reinforced-concrete hotel, curio shop, and depot complex. Railroad company president Edward Payson Ripley named it the Escalante, after eighteenth-century Spanish priest-explorer Silvestre Vélez de Escalante. Opening in March 1907, the hostelry offered overnight accommodations for the next forty-six years, and became a haven for many early motorists along the National Old Trails Road and later Route 66. Jeanie Lippitt Weeden, who stayed at the Escalante, observed, "These Harvey Houses are the greatest boon to us motorists and we leave each with great regret, even if we know another will be at the end of our day's journey; each one as it came seemed to us the best of all." Driver Vernon McGill reported after his stay in Ash Fork, "It is remarkable to find such a luxurious hotel with every city accommodation and service in this outpost of human occupation."

Like the other Harvey Company lodgings alongside the Santa Fe, the Escalante Hotel fed train passengers during scheduled thirty-minute stops while steam locomotives refilled with fresh water after or before taking on the 1,600-foot elevation change between Ash Fork and Williams. The hotel also provided meals for others including motorists in both a quick-service coffee shop and a more formal dining room. A typewritten lunch menu from August 29, 1940, offered entire midday meals of roast sugar-cured ham, breaded veal cutlets, or "pounded" round steak, chilled nectarines, grapefruit juice, a selection of soups as appetizers, mashed or new potatoes, peas, tomatoes, and choice of pie, bread-and-butter pudding, or vanilla ice cream for dessert. These set lunches together with choice of beverages at the time cost seventy-five cents. A la carte options included fried halibut with lemon butter for fifty-five cents and pork chops with country gravy and fried apple slices for sixty cents. The lovely Escalante closed its rooms and food service in 1953 because it was no longer needed for feeding and lodging train passengers and because of competition from newer tourist courts and eateries. The obsolete complex sat mostly disused for twenty years and was razed in 1973. At the time of this writing, the Ash Fork Route 66 Museum operated inside a former warehouse near its site.[36]

Seligman

Another town that had 1880s beginnings alongside the Atlantic and Pacific Railroad, Seligman was named for of one of the company's investors, New York financier Jesse Seligman. Because of its nearby junction with an earlier branch line southward and a dependable water supply, the town became an operational division point on the later Santa Fe Railway. This meant that trains stopped here to "water" steam locomotives, change crews, and give passengers half-hour meal stops. As early as 1897, an eating house run by the Fred Harvey Company relocated there from Williams. In the 1910s the National Old Trails Road passed through, followed by Highway 66 in 1926, bringing motorists' trade. In time the town of under six hundred souls offered motorists not just a Harvey House but also several tourist courts, cafés, and bars. Travelers remembered Seligman mainly as the point where they changed their watches from Mountain to Pacific time zones just as driver W. C. Clark did in 1925, noting that his party "stopped at Seligman for lunch" and "set our watches." The money spent by drivers brought much of the economic life-blood to the town, and it impacted peoples' lives in unexpected ways. Angel Delgadillo grew up there in the 1930s. "I remember as kids my brothers and sisters would watch for the headlights of the cars at night," he reminisced. "We would run out and make our shadows on the buildings from those headlights."

The railroad and the highway gave purpose to Seligman but then took it away. The town received double blows when the interstate bypassed the community in 1978 and when the Santa Fe Railway discontinued it as a division point where train crews changed in 1984. Facing the prospect of economic stagnation or worse, in 1987 barber Angel Delgadillo encouraged a group of mostly local businesspeople to meet in Seligman to discuss the future. He envisioned potential salvation for the town and others like it by encouraging heritage tourism along the old Mother Road. At that gathering, the attendees organized the Historic Route 66 Association of Arizona, which became the first of eight such state organizations in the country. Its activities and those of others contributed substantially to reviving nationwide interest in Route 66 and consequently fostering

business activity along its length. Because of its relative closeness to large population centers in Southern California, Seligman has become a destination for lengthy day-trip motor coach tours operated from the West Coast, which enable domestic and foreign tourists to experience visiting a little-changed desert town on the old 66 Highway.[37]

HAVASU HOTEL

A billboard on Highway 66 advised drivers that it was only "3/4 mile to Seligman, Ariz." and the Fred Harvey Company's Havasu Hotel, where "Harvey House meals cost no more." For decades, drivers first on the National Old Trails Road and then on the Mother Road stopped for lodging and meals at this hostelry erected between 1905 and 1909 by the Santa Fe Railway and managed by the reputable Harvey firm. Its name came from the nearby Havasupai people. The handsome L-shaped, two-story masonry and wood-frame structure with a red tile roof featured a rectangular sheltered, tree-shaded garden. In its heyday, this was the only green, manicured lawn in all of arid Seligman. The main purpose for the Havasu was to feed passengers on Santa Fe Railway trains. Being informed in advance by telegraph how many customers were aboard individual trains, the kitchen staff and the pert Harvey Girl waitresses managed to feed entire trainloads of travelers in the half hour allotted for servicing locomotives and changing operating crews. A mid-twentieth-century breakfast menu from the lunch counter in the Havasu presented passengers on the tight thirty-minute schedule the following choices: either kippered herring with scrambled eggs or bacon with oven-baked shirred eggs, together with cottage fried potatoes; rolls, muffins, or toast with jelly; and coffee, tea, or milk (and orange juice included with both options), all for a dollar. Frances Hansen Coffey worked as a server at the Havasu in the 1930s, and she later remembered that fourteen to sixteen trains arrived daily and that the waitresses had to serve, clean up, and reset the places for these passengers in just thirty to forty minutes.

Seligman became a popular morning stop for many eastbound California drivers by the 1930s. Like trucker Lee Griffin, they would head out from Los Angeles about sunset, cross the Mojave Desert during the cooler nighttime hours, and then "wait until we got to Seligman to eat breakfast." The Havasu also provided the most comfortable lodging in Seligman. The 1929 *Mohawk Hobbs* guidebook for this stretch of Highway 66 described the Harvey hotel as having twenty-two guest rooms, doubles renting for $3.50, or $5.00 with a private bath—expensive for the day. In contrast the best other overnight stays in town were at the Hotel Johnson, which had doubles for $2.50 to $3.00, but all bathrooms were shared "in hall." The replacement of trackside dining with rolling railway dining cars halted the role of the Harvey hotel in feeding train passengers. This occurrence

This 1940s billboard on Route 66 outside Seligman, Arizona, advertised to motorists that "Harvey House Meals Cost No More" at the Havasu Hotel in town. Photograph NAU.PH.95.44.59.2 courtesy of Special Collections and Archives, Cline Library, Northern Arizona University, Flagstaff.

combined with changes in travelers' lodging preferences to spell the doom for Seligman's Harvey House. The food service ended in November 1954, followed by lodging closing shortly thereafter. The railroad company gutted much of the old building in 1955 to reuse it as offices, but these moved out in 1988. The firm then offered the old building to the local historical society with the provision that it be moved away from the valuable trackside location. The tiny community could never afford such a large preservation effort, so the Havasu was dismantled and removed in 2008.[38]

DELGADILLO'S SNOW CAP

The United States experienced an explosion of new roadside soft-serve ice cream stands in the years following World War II. Best known among the franchises was the Dairy Queen, born on Route 66 in Joliet, Illinois, in 1940. Arizona had its own homegrown facsimile of the DQ, the Snow Cap Ice Cream Company founded in Phoenix. As early as 1951, it advertised to prospective entrepreneurs, "Everybody loves ice cream!" tempting them with the prospect of a Snow Cap outlet grossing an operator from six thousand to fifteen thousand dollars in sales yearly with "no royalties." Snow Cap explained that the ice cream equipment alone cost $4,800, roughly the equivalent of $46,000 in 2021 buying power, but the appeal was strong, and locals on Route 66 in both Williams and Winslow opened their own Snow Cap drive-up stands.[39]

In Seligman, Juan Delgadillo, brother of barber Angel Delgadillo, had been working as a machinist for the Santa Fe Railway for thirty-five years. It was a good job, but the World War II veteran could foresee that the

gradual replacement of steam engines with diesel locomotives would eliminate maintenance positions like his. Through the early 1950s, he stockpiled salvaged building supplies on a vacant lot at 301 East Chino Street, since 1933 on the alignment of Highway 66. He tried unsuccessfully to purchase a Dairy Queen franchise and instead in 1953 negotiated an agreement with the Snow Cap firm in Phoenix. With his father's and brothers' assistance, Juan and wife Mary erected a modest flat-roof, rectangular walk-up ice cream and hamburger stand. Juan's serious focus on business brought a warning from his physician that the resulting tension could likely lead to an early death. According to Delgadillo, a fuzzy-shelled coconut resolved the problematic situation. The entrepreneur, with tongue in cheek, declared that the coconut told him, "Hang me up in a tree . . . and you will feel better." Juan followed the directive and concluded that the exotic nut was correct. He did feel good after doing something silly, so he went further. Next, he strung up more coconuts in the elm trees around the eatery. Customers chuckled so much that he followed with a deluge of toy rubber snakes, and then a profusion of displaced porcelain toilets. Diners promptly used them as improvised outdoor seating. The Snow Cap became a home for madcap humor, with decoy doorknobs on the hinged sides of entrances and ridiculous questions about whether customers wanted cheese on their cheeseburgers. With a smile on his face, Juan Delgadillo returned to health, the Snow Cap earned profits, and he presided there until his death at eighty-four. Today his heirs continue to run the walk-up roadside eatery with alfresco dining that still features tasty hamburgers, hot dogs, "dead chicken," and ice cream, all served with doses of slapstick humor.[40]

Grand Canyon Caverns

From Seligman motorists continued twenty-two miles northwestward along the two-lane to the Deer Creek Lodge, a roadside filling station with tourist cabins where Stan Wakefield served cold drinks, snacks, and some simple foods by 1939. His location was the near a cave found by a railroad woodcutter named Walter Y. Peck. Calling his discovery Yampai Caverns, Peck began letting tourists down into the opening using a rope and windlass. Later they clambered down on wooden ladders and rudimentary stairs. Everyone thought that the natural phenomenon, by 1936 being called Coconino Caverns, offered the prospects of making money, but they had trouble figuring out how to do it. By the 1940s and 1950s, two adjacent landowners, each owning part of the cave, vied for control. Whenever visitors drove up, each of them tried to sell them underground tours. Then, in 1957, two businessmen, Tom Moran and Herb Miller, formed a company to develop the site, changing its name to Dinosaur Caverns. Near the mouth of the cave, about a mile south of Highway 66, in 1961 they erected a handsome architect-designed visitors center, which included the Juniper Room, a table-service restaurant with a cocktail lounge. Former waitress Josephine Tapija described it as having "a real fancy dining room with dark green goblets . . . cloth napkins and all of that." Two years later, the investors added a motel on the highway known as the Caverns Inn, with its own coffee shop. Drivers passing through saved time by eating in the motel café, but those preferring leisurely meals chose instead the Juniper Room. During

this time the operators gave the attraction its fourth name, Grand Canyon Caverns, which it has retained. Business withered after an interstate bypass drained away traffic in 1978, and, in the mid-1980s the two eating places consolidated into the one off the highway at the cavern entrance. New owners acquired the property in 2000, and with fresh approaches they have worked successfully to revive the enterprise, with the restaurant in the visitors center resuming operation.[41]

Peach Springs
QUMACHO INN (QUMACHO CAFÉ)

Peach Springs today is the administrative center of the Hualapai Tribe. It came into existence as a railroad town when the Atlantic and Pacific Railroad built its way across Arizona in 1883. That same year U.S. president Chester A. Arthur recognized the Hualapai Tribe, which resulted in an inevitable land dispute between the railroad and the Native inhabitants. By the 1910s the National Old Trails Road passed through the quiet little community, followed by Route 66. An old-time Peach Springs Hotel, more like a boardinghouse, fed many early motorists, but by 1936 Yee Chee opened the Qumacho Inn, which became for twenty years the travelers' reliable stop for meals. Bion A. Elliott took over in 1939, gradually expanding the eatery to include adjacent tourist cabins. Ethel Jane and Guy Rutherford became owners in 1947, employing Wilbur "Bud" Lutte and his son-in-law, Jimmie Goree, as cooks. Not long after that, when Raymond Gabriel Allen Jackson made a round trip by three-wheel bicycle between Texas and California, he received an up-close view of the café operations. The Rutherfords' indigenous Hualapai dishwashers had asked for five days off to attend an

Independence Day powwow, and Jackson and another fellow hired on temporarily in 1948 to take their places. Jackson observed that the Native Americans made efficient kitchen help but that "they will not be rushed." A year later the Qumacho Inn gained valuable publicity after appearing in E. V. Durling's On the Side syndicated newspaper column. The popular commentator wrote that the "Cattleman's Morning Diet" at the eatery was the largest breakfast regularly served in a hotel or restaurant anywhere in the United States. The repast, priced at $2.75, consisted of a half dozen eggs cooked any style, a ham steak, a half loaf of bread toasted, potatoes, and "Java till the pot runs dry." In 1952 the Rutherfords divided their efforts to assist with the opening of the Copper Cart Restaurant in Seligman while running the Peach Springs restaurant for a few more years. Guy served as president of the Arizona Highway 66 Association. In later years Clara E. Linn operated the enterprise as the Qumacho Café at least as recently as 1973.[42]

Truxton
FRONTIER CAFÉ

Unlike most of the Arizona towns through which the Mother Road passed, Truxton was comparatively young. Although there had been a nearby railroad siding called Truxton since 1883, no town developed for decades. Then, in the late 1940s, the U.S. Bureau of Reclamation began seriously considering construction of a dam and hydroelectric plant at the Bridge Canyon rapids on the Colorado River to the northwest. It would have flooded part of the Grand Canyon. On the expectation that the highway turnoff to the projected dam site would become a rewarding place to make money, a number of investors including Donald Dilts and Clyde McCune erected service stations, cafés, and motels around the intersection. Although the dam was never built, the position of Truxton at the crossroads on Highway 66 just before Crozier Canyon, nine miles from Peach Springs and forty-two miles from Kingman,

The Qumacho Café in Peach Springs, Arizona, as it appeared during Clara Linn's tenure as operator in the late 1950s. Author's Collection.

meant that it received a steady flow of travelers, many of whom paused to eat.

According to stories still told, a Californian named Alice Valentine received a windfall inheritance in the late 1940s. Not knowing what to do with the unexpected wealth, she consulted a fortune teller, who advised her to drive four hundred miles and build a café. This was what the woman did, and, according to the reports, Truxton was where she stopped. There Alice constructed the Frontier Café and Motel, hiring sign maker Jack Wright to erect a tall, composite neon sign comprised of several older ones already in his shop yard. The heiress and the sign man fell in love, married, and ran the enterprise until his death from lung disease. Thereupon she sold the property and business around 1957 to Oklahomans Ray and Mildred Barker, who ran a nearby filling station. Until this section of Route 66 was bypassed by the interstate in 1978, its roadside businesses teemed with activity. Frontier Café employee Jerry Hughes reminisced that on Sundays during the heyday of the old road, local residents would see "a solid string" of big-rig trucks passing through town "bumper to bumper" that were loaded in Oklahoma and due in Los Angeles by Tuesday. The beginning of summer holidays 360 miles away on the West Coast made for a remarkable scene: "On June the 10th at midnight, you'd see a mass of lights comin' up over the hill there when the schools let out in California and everybody'd leave on vacation." Truxton was a good place to be. Together the Barkers operated the café and motel until Ray's death in 1990. With the assistance of others, Mildred ran it another twenty-two years until her passing in 2012.[43]

Through Crozier Canyon and Valentine

After Truxton the drive grew rugged for the next sixteen miles. It wound through Crozier Canyon past the historic Crozier Ranch and a government school for Hualapai and Hopi children in the village of Valentine. The three miles nearest to the Crozier Ranch, squeezed into a narrow space between the Santa Fe Railway tracks and Truxton Wash, comprised the last section of Route 66 in Arizona to be paved in 1938. From the days of the National Old Trails Road in the 1910s, at the Crozier Ranch the Carrow family conducted a general store and filling station, renting rooms to travelers first in the ranch house and later in tourist cabins. In the 1920s they added a snack bar and a modest open-air swimming pool for summertime guests, with the store and station becoming the local bus stop. The roadside enterprise prospered until flooding damaged some of the facilities in 1939 and 1940. As Route 66 drivers approached Hackberry, eight miles beyond the ranch, the canyon widened and its steep sides receded, allowing travelers to see the town nestled in a stream valley at the foot of the Peacock Mountains.[44]

Hackberry
HACKBERRY GENERAL STORE

Hackberry sprang up in 1875 following a rich silver discovery the year before in the Peacock Mountains. The mine operated off and on for decades, eventually producing about $3 million worth of silver. In 1883 the town moved four miles to be next to the steel rails of the Atlantic and Pacific Railroad. Originally the National Old Trails Road and then U.S.

Highway 66 passed through the streets of Hackberry, but this route required two separate fords of occasionally flooded Truxton Wash combined with two grade crossings over the railroad tracks. To avoid these hazards, the Arizona Highway Department improved Route 66 in 1933 by shifting its position to higher ground west of the tracks and skirting the town. Within a year three separate combined filling station/general stores opened along the new alignment. Positioned on a long curve, they became known as the South Side Grocery, the East Side Grocery, and the North Side Grocery. The North Side store, also known as the Hackberry General Store, sold three successive brands of gasoline products before closing in 1978. A dozen years had passed when itinerant Route 66 artist, ecologist, and preservationist Bob Waldmire acquired the disused property, rehabilitating it into what he called the International Bioregional Old Route 66 Visitor Center. With reinstalled vintage fuel pumps and historic signage, it became a de rigueur stop for all heritage tourists driving the mother road. Here, for four years, Waldmire promoted preservation of the old road, environmental awareness, and tolerance of others. Seeking a more secluded life, Bob sold the store in 1998 to John and Kerry Pritchard, who added their lifetime collection of American memorabilia to become permanent fixtures. In 2016 Amy Franklin bought the store to protect its tradition as a historic Route 66 curio and souvenir shop frequented by travelers from around the globe.[45]

Kingman

Once drivers passed by Hackberry and its three store/filling stations fronting on the road, it was only thirty miles farther into Kingman. The first third of the way was gently up and down followed by a long, straight stretch across a desert plain into town. About nine miles outside the community, travelers passed the entrance into the Kingman Army Air Field. During World War II, it served as a major training center for aircraft aerial gunners, but afterward it became one of five major storage facilities in the country for surplus military aircraft. In summer 1947 two married couples from Clinton, Missouri, went on a cross-country vacation trip that took them right past the Kingman base, where they were amazed to see thousands of obsolete war planes "stacked wing to wing, fuselage to fuselage, close as they could be packed" awaiting scrap dealers' furnaces. Traveler Irving Nagel reported to his hometown newspaper that the four Missourians "clocked the multiple rows for a solid five miles." Other drivers had their own memories of this stretch of road. Mary Lou Leichsenring Herridge and her husband made multiple eastbound trips in their 1946 Dodge sedan to visit family in Indiana. She recounted that on every return journey, "When we left Seligman, there was a big bump which separated two sections of road. When we hit the bump, we knew we were almost to Kingman." Like so many other Route 66 towns, this one was laid out along the Santa Fe Railway tracks. Though it never had more than five thousand people during the heyday of the Mother Road, the town prospered as a supply center for ranches and multiple mining districts, while profiting from the trade the highway brought. Motorists could satisfy just about any need or desire in Kingman, which road guides described it as supporting "many garages [that] carry big stocks and are well equipped to handle serious mechanical trouble."[46]

WHITE HOUSE CAFÉ (JADE RESTAURANT)

During the early days of motoring along Route 66, the highest status dining options in Kingman were a Fred Harvey Company eating house at the Santa Fe Railway depot or, alternately, at the three-story Beale Hotel. Chinese immigrant restaurateurs, however, competed actively for the attention of cross country motorists, operating the majority of the local cafés. Among these businesspeople was Lum Sing Yow, known locally as "China Jack." Though he was born in California in 1884, as a young man he had sailed to China to find a bride. Then, in 1922, he returned to the United States with two preadolescent sons and that year opened the White House Café at 403 East Front Street in Kingman. Son Charlie Lum grew up working in the eatery but in 1943 relocated temporarily to San Francisco, where he worked in the shipyards and then became part owner in the Club Shanghai restaurant there. Investing the proceeds from the sale of his share in the California bistro, in 1951 Charlie returned to Kingman, where the next year he built and opened his own Jade Restaurant. It was the first eating place in town to serve Asian food as a specialty, with all the previous Chinese-run cafés in the town offering mostly American-style meals. (If a customer at the old White House Café did indeed want an Asian meal, the manager invited him back into the kitchen, where the staff offered to serve him the same foods that they were eating.) The Jade Restaurant at 937 East Front Street (after 1955 renamed Andy Devine Avenue) later expanded to include meeting rooms and a cocktail lounge, becoming known up and down Route 66 as a favorite dining spot. Charlie Lum retired in 1978, transferring his business to his daughter and son-in-law. To this day he is remembered in the Arizona town for his public-spirited generosity. The entrepreneur contributed substantially, for example, toward the construction of a Little League baseball field, where one of the outfield fences bore a painted advertisement for his restaurant. "If you hit a homerun over that sign," remembered Bob Boze Bell, who in the 1950s as a boy played on the field, "you got a free meal" at the Jade courtesy of Charlie Lum.[47]

DENNY'S COFFEE SHOP NO. 96 (SILVER SPOON FAMILY RESTAURANT, RUTHERFORD'S 66 FAMILY DINER)

Exuberantly designed California coffee shops exploded from the West Coast across the United States during the years following World War II. These establishments were family restaurants that served no alcohol and that attracted diners for sit-down meals often accompanied with soda fountain desserts. The bold designs, which spread eastward, typically featured oversized roofs, eye-catching profiles, walls seemingly built solely from plate glass, and bright colors inside and out. Many originated from the Los Angeles architectural firm of Armet and Davis, and these inspired others. This new generation of coffee shops followed what were called "the ABCs of good design," meaning that they were created to be "Always Beckoning Customers."

Among the family restaurants that grew exponentially during the 1950s and 1960s was the Denny's Coffee Shop franchise. Harold Butler and Richard Jezak opened their first Danny's Donuts in Lakewood, California, in

1953, but after Jezak left the partnership, in 1956 Butler expanded the menus, shifted to round-the-clock service, and changed the name to Danny's Coffee Shop. Two years later Butler began working with the architects Louis L. Armet and Eldon C. Davis, who developed for him memorable designs employing oversized roofs with boomerang-shaped profiles. Historian Philip Langdon described walking into one of these Armet and Davis restaurants as "entering under a log canopy and then finding the space exploding upward to a high sloped ceiling and then back down to a lower scale at the counter area." The architects redesigned counter seating, mounting it above the floor and fitting it with padded bottoms and backrests. While he was beginning to expand his chain across the Southwest, Butler sidestepped confusion with the Los Angeles–based Coffee Dan's eateries in 1959 by renaming his growing business Denny's Coffee Shops, later cutting the title to Denny's. The business was eminently successful. At the time of this writing, approximately 1,700 Denny's coffee shops operated in the United States.

Don Yakel negotiated a franchise to build Denny's Coffee Shop No. 96 at 2011 East Andy Devine Avenue in Kingman around 1964. By June of the next year, he was advertising for a fry cook, requiring that applicants be "experienced and fast." He ran the twenty-four-hour coffee shop in the motel district on the east side of town for three years, before turning its management over to Jim Waters by 1968. Others subsequently ran the Denny's beneath a prominent, oversized projecting roof for a quarter century. By the 1990s new owners changed the name to become the Silver Spoon Family Restaurant, but they prudently preserved the well-designed and durably built exterior and interior features. In the 2000s

the historic coffee shop became Rutherford's 66 Family Diner, still maintaining a traditional coffee shop menu and preserving its now highly valued 1960s atmosphere.[48]

Sitgreaves Pass

For almost thirty years, Highway 66 took motorists over the barrier of the Black Mountains by way of a steep, sinuous climb to the 3,586-foot summit of Sitgreaves Pass and then down an even steeper twisting downslope into the gold-mining town of Oatman. So intimidating was the drive that locals hired themselves out to take the wheels of vehicles for white-knuckled motorists who felt too intimidated to pilot themselves over the hairpin turns and past the unprotected drop-offs. The fact that many early automobiles were underpowered, tended to overheat from their non-pressurized engine cooling systems, and had only mechanical brakes complicated the maneuver. The roadway not only frightened adults but left its marks on children as well. As a girl, Evangeline Hoerner McCoy passed over the Black Mountains as a passenger several times starting in 1926, and she remembered her fears: "Meeting cars on the road to Oatman was the worst experience of the entire trip. As a kid I was terrified as I looked over the edge of the precipitous cliffs and down the canyons. With each subsequent trip that we made in later years, whether driving east or west, the Sitgreaves Pass was my undoing." U.S. Highway 66 traffic passed over this tortuous way until the Arizona Highway Department opened a more direct route over desert flats by way of Yucca in 1952.[49]

COOL SPRINGS

Drivers leaving Kingman proceeded southwestward past a roadway north to Las Vegas and crossed an open desert flat toward what seemed to be an impenetrable wall of mountains. Though at first the road seemed to go nowhere, it led up and into those crags to cross Sitgreaves Pass after twenty-four miles. The uninviting desert elevations surprisingly held natural water seeps that made possible unexpected human activity. One of these trickles supported the small King's Dairy, and starting in 1927 a two-mile iron pipe carried its excess flow to the site of a new roadside filling station. Kingman entrepreneur N. R. Dunton conceived the idea of erecting the building partway up the Sitgreaves grade, twenty-one miles from town, knowing that the engines on many vehicles would overheat and require radiator refills to make the climb. If drivers stopped, they would likely spend money on other things, and, if not, then they could pay for any water they needed. To Dunton the name Cool Springs seemed appealing. In June 1936 the businessman sold the precariously situated filling station on the drop-off side of the road to Mary and James Walker of Indiana. They added a café, bar, and basic tourist cabins, calling the stop the Cool Springs Camp. Together they further developed the enterprise by raising poultry and offering special fried chicken dinners on weekends. They advertised in 1937 that their chicken was so tender that "no knives are served." The Cool Springs location, however, seemingly was not conducive to matrimonial bliss. The couple divorced, James left, and Mary and four children remained at the remote place of business. Then, in 1939, Mary remarried to produce deliveryman L. Floyd Spidell, but then she left him. Floyd subsequently had several more wives while he remained running the isolated station. When the federal highway shifted to the Yucca bypass road in 1952, trade diminished at Cool Springs, but Spidell's niece, Nancy Schoernerr, and her husband, Charles, kept the doors open until at least 1964. In 1991 the remaining buildings at the site became the backdrop in filming a scene for the motion picture *Universal Soldier*, resulting in the destruction of most of what had survived. A decade later Route 66 enthusiast and preservationist Ned Leuchtner acquired the property and began restoring the ruins at Cool Springs. As reconstructed, at the time of this writing, it housed a roadside stop for cold drinks, packaged snacks, and curios.[50]

SNELL'S SUMMIT STATION

The Sitgreaves summit loomed only three and a half miles beyond Cool Springs on the twisting road up and into the Black Mountains. There, as early as 1928, Osmon Snell and his English-born wife, the former Alice M. Burgoyne, operated a filling station, ran a beer tavern, and, of all things in such a remote desert setting, managed an ice cream parlor. The availability by the late 1920s of kerosene-fueled, gas-absorption ice-making machines made it possible for highway merchants to keep foods chilled in desert locations without electricity. When the U.S. government census taker visited the Snells' roadside stop on April 24, 1940, he found Osmon and Alice, nephew Charles Walz as filling station attendant, and employees Claude and Jane May Gault helping run the enterprise. A former miner who had long been exposed to dust underground, Osmon died at age fifty-six from silicosis on February 23, 1942. Alice continued running Snell's Summit Station and during this time was elected to the board of the Arizona division of the national Route 66 Association. Just beyond the Snell station was a broad pull-off area, where many motorists cooled overheated engines and took in the views. Alice was running the remote station when author Jack Rittenhouse passed through in 1946, but it was gone when Raymond Gabriel Allen Jackson camped out at the crest on his cross-country bicycle trip in 1948.

The panorama from the top, over the crags toward the valley of the Colorado River, was among the most spectacular on the entire Mother Road. Scenery, however, was not the only thing that stuck in peoples' minds. As a six-year-old, Kara Hewson Nelson made the trip over the pass with her parents and two-year-old sister as they drove from Los Angeles to Fayetteville, Arkansas, in 1942. Their 1930 Buick overheated on the climb up the Sitgreaves grade, and it was "blowing steam" when they reached the highpoint. She remembered, "What good fortune we had! There was a filling station at the top." While she and sister Katie looked over the precipice from the edge of the blacktop, her father filled the car radiator and cleared imbedded insects. Once the motor cooled down, "Daddy bought a Coke for Katie and me to share," after which her mother washed off their hands and faces with "the same hose Daddy used to flush out the radiator." Three decades passed by the time that Kara vacationed with friends near Bullhead City, Arizona. Like so many other modern-day tourists, they visited the old Oatman ghost town and headed up the road to where they heard was a beautiful lookout point. Once there, Kara somehow felt that she recognized the place, and she walked over to kick around with her shoe at some remnants of asphalt and fragments of building foundations. Then she spied a piece from an old gasoline advertising sign, and it opened the floodgates

of her memory: "I suddenly was six years old and the building was in place, the cars were there, the water and bugs and bees were all running over the asphalt." She then told her companions, "I've been here before. . . . It was a long time ago."[51]

Oatman

Just past the crest of Sitgreaves Pass, drivers descended as steep a stretch of U.S. Highway 66 as they would traverse anywhere along its length. The route dropped seven hundred feet in elevation in just two miles of tightly winding westbound roadway leading to the gold-mining village of Goldroad. There, N. R. Dunton of Kingman for years ran a towing service, and employees were hired to pull vehicles up this steepest portion of the eastbound grade. Onward from Goldroad the westbound road dropped, twisting and turning, sometimes with sheer drop-offs, until it wound its way into Oatman. The town owed its existence as a mining camp to a 1902 discovery of gold. Starting in 1913 it was the scene of the last gold rush in Arizona, when it ballooned to an estimated 3,500 inhabitants. By the time that the major mines closed down in 1942, it had produced an estimated $13 million worth of minerals. Daphne and Dallas Lore Sharp drove through in 1926, and Dallas reported that Oatman was "not a traveler's town," but rather it was "developed by gold miners for gold miners." Some drivers decided to spend the night in the rough-and-tumble mining town, but most chose not to tarry. They were more like eastbound motorist James Albert Davis, who reached there in late afternoon, August 2, 1921. "After refreshing ourselves with some ice-cream sodas and filling the radiator," he penned, "we pushed on over the mountains."[52]

Yucca

HONOLULU CLUB

The twisting way up and over Sitgreaves Pass daunted drivers for decades. Consequently some truckers and others with especially large or heavy loads opted instead to make their way to the crossing into California over a dirt track that roughly paralleled the Santa Fe Railway from Kingman to the Colorado River bridge at Topock. The desert along this route was so sparsely peopled that the only settlement passed was tiny Yucca. The barely improved fifty-six-mile route preceded the later paved two-lane highway bypass that the Arizona Highway Department built in 1951–52 to connect Kingman with Topock. Looping around the mountains, and thus avoiding steep grades, this roadway supplanted the earlier alignment as the official U.S. Highway 66 in 1952. After gold mines at Oatman closed in 1942, business from Mother Road drivers kept the town alive for a decade. As soon as traffic diverted away in 1952, however, most of the merchants, restaurateurs, bartenders, and innkeepers who depended on out-of-town money abandoned the community, some of them following the line of taillights to Yucca.[53]

One of the notable Oatman enterprises that made the move to Yucca was the Honolulu Club, a drinking and eating emporium that dated from the glory days of the old gold-mining camp. James Powell "Jim" Boyd, born in Hawaii in 1884 to an islander father and a Portuguese mother, made his way to Oatman by 1916. With wife Dorothy Mable "Dot" Boyd, he operated a series of taverns, cafés, and dance halls. Artist James Montgomery Flagg encountered Jim at Oatman on a cross-country auto trip in 1925, reporting, "At the bottom of a steep hill was

a camp for tourists run by a Hawaiian, a shiny black-haired smart Aleck, who drew Coca-Colas for us in the drinkorium by the roadside." This was not all, for Flagg insightfully added, "He chafed the natives with easy insolence and good English." In addition to the Oatman businesses, the entrepreneur, who spoke both English and Hawaiian, also led his own Honolulu Jim Boyd Dance Band, which, at least between 1929 and 1938, performed both in public venues and for private parties. Jim sang and played the ukulele. Though the Great Depression slowed the general economy, his Honolulu Club seemed to prosper. Ray Shaw moved to Oatman in 1934, and he later remembered that at the time, "There were so many people on Main Street on Saturday that you had to fight your way through the crowd to get to the Honolulu Club for a drink of bootleg whiskey and a game of poker." In about 1937 Alonzo "Bud" Williams acquired the Honolulu Club, by then housed in the three-story Walsh Building at the east end of the main street. Jim and Dorothy Boyd moved to California, where he spent the rest of his working career in food service. Like others in the old mining camp, Alonzo Williams knew that when work began on the Highway 66 bypass around the bottleneck at Sitgreaves Pass, its opening would cause otherwise isolated Oatman to wither away. He sold the business to Juan and Mary Rodriquez, who erected a brand-new concrete-block Honolulu Club tavern on the west side of the new road in Yucca. Bill Freiday was there at the time, putting up his own service station, and he remembered, "He just moved the license stuff there to Yucca to be on the main highway." Until recently the seemingly incongruous, blue-and-white-painted Honolulu Club bar and grill remained in business until it closed during the Covid-19 pandemic.[54]

Topock
TOPOCK STORE AND CAFÉ (CRINKLAW TAVERN, BLUE ROOM)

No matter which road travelers chose, over the Black Mountains via Oatman or skirting around the south end of the peaks via Yucca, they all found themselves at Topock, a village on the Arizona bank of the Colorado River. The Santa Fe Railway spanned the river here on its 1890 Red Rock Cantilever Bridge, leaving early-day motorists to cross on a precarious cable ferry. The state line ran down the middle of the watercourse. Then, in 1916, Arizona and California, in conjunction with the Bureau of Indian Affairs, erected the steel-arch Old Trails Bridge, which carried vehicular traffic into the Golden State for decades. It was this graceful structure that movie audiences saw in the 1940 *Grapes of Wrath* Hollywood feature. Because both the railroad and the highway served Topock, it always offered basic travelers' services with modest boardinghouse-like "hotels" and cabins for lodging, one or two stores, filling stations, some with minor auto and tire repairs, and stands offering quick-service meals.

Leslie A. Crinklaw was one of the entrepreneurs drawn to the Arizona side of the Colorado, where, as early as 1937, he ran a combined store, filling station, and café initially called the Topock Store and Café. For decades he and his employees provided fuel, basic groceries, and short-order meals. By 1942 he added a tavern. Though law-abiding sorts did not hesitate to patronize the store, station, and café, the Crinklaw Tavern gained a reputation as a place that attracted he-men customers undaunted by occasional

Sign identifying the building at the east end of the main street in Oatman, Arizona, housing Jim Boyd's Honolulu Club in the 1930s, which enticed customers with cold beer, mixed drinks, and dancing. Photograph neg. no. 5181 courtesy of Mohave Museum of History and Arts, Kingman, Arizona.

fisticuffs. A glass-sided terrarium became home to several impressive rattlesnakes that became stars in an occasional competition. The proprietor would drop a hard-boiled egg into the reptile cage with the challenge that if anyone could retrieve it without a snakebite, the house would give everyone a free round of drinks. Leslie Crinklaw ran the Topock enterprises until he was accidentally killed by a Santa Fe passenger train in 1950. His son, Jack, assumed management for another two decades, rebuilding the bar as the Blue Room following 1958 fire damage. It dispensed beverages until the Arizona Highway Department blocked vehicular access as part of making improvements to Interstate 40, the old tavern building being razed in 1973.[55]

On Into California

Once motorists reached Topock, it was only a few hundred yards to the California state line near the middle of the Old Trails Bridge. As the third-longest steel arch highway bridge in the United States, the drive across this span gave pause to motorists who feared heights. The initial wooden decking consisted of lengthwise runners spiked onto cross members with gaps between. People could look straight down between them to the muddy river water far below. Motorists had to steer their cars carefully to keep their wheels on the plank strips. This worked fine for passenger cars, but when Russell Byrd made his first cross-country trip driving a Yelloway bus in 1927, no one warned him that "The parallel planks on the bridge . . . would not fit our coach." The wheels on one side could roll on the decking, but not on the other. "I was reluctant to bump from rafter to rafter with the other wheels," he remembered, but there was no choice. "Very slowly and with a thump of my heart at each thump of the coach, I crept . . . across the bridge." Once over the Colorado River, the Golden State lay ahead.[56]

CALIFORNIA

When motorists made their way across the Colorado River bridge, at the middle they saw signs welcoming them to the Golden State, but what they found there was not necessarily what they expected. As a teenager in the 1950s, Bob Boze Bell pumped gas on Highway 66 in Kingman, Arizona. There westbound out-of-state drivers often asked him, "How far is it to California?" These travelers seem to have been envisioning surfers lounging in cool Pacific breezes. Young Bob told them that the border was only sixty-two miles farther but rarely warned that they were "about to descend into the blasting furnace" of the Mojave Desert. Once over the state line, drivers crossed over two hundred miles of barren desert to reach the Cajon Summit before finally entering semitropical, tree-filled metropolitan Los Angeles. Getting there required traversing one of the hottest places in the United States, where summer temperatures could exceed 120 degrees Fahrenheit and winter nighttime lows occasionally hit freezing.[1]

Early motorists met their own particular problems crossing the Mojave Desert. The roadway between the Colorado River and the Cajon Summit remained mostly dirt and gravel into the early 1930s. In places, drivers made their way through deep sand and stretches of sharp lava rock that abraded away tires. This was in addition to the effects of extreme summer temperatures on autos and on the humans who drove them. Hoffman Birney made the trip in 1929, writing that once motorists crossed the Colorado River into California, "Good road ceases at the boundary." He further quipped, "The Golden State reserves her concrete highways for her more western sections." Improved roads, however, were on the way. When Lewis and Ruth Gannett drove Highway 66 across the desert in 1933, he described the newly paved route in glowing terms: "You can see the ribbon of concrete stretching five or ten miles ahead of you" inviting the motorist to "open up your throttle and hold the car above sixty miles an hour." Even so, crossing the desert still exhausted motorists like musician Glen Campbell, who in 1960 drove a 1957 Chevrolet on which he "tied water bottles to the grill" for refilling the radiator.[2]

California did not necessarily welcome all motorists. Unlike Arizona and New Mexico, which had only become states in 1912, it had been in the union since 1850 based on the major influx of fortune seekers during the gold rush the year before. Economic development exploded after the state's connection by railroad with the rest of the United States in 1869. The predominately white population warily accepted the nineteenth-century arrival of Chinese and other Asian immigrants as laborers, treating them as members of an ethnic underclass. Attitudes toward African Americans mirrored those in many other parts of the country. Discriminatory clauses in deeds excluded them from owning property in many areas while white-only sundown towns dotted Highway 66 as far west as South Pasadena. Black, Asian, and Latino motorists all felt the brunt of discrimination as they sought food and lodging on the road, never knowing how they might be received by white businesses owners. During the depths of the Great Depression, large numbers of farm families fled drought and poverty on the Great Plains and in the South, taking to the road in ramshackle cars and trucks to seek new lives in California. As they passed through state-run agricultural inspection stations along the highway, they had to prove ownership of their vehicles and often show sufficient resources to avoid becoming financial burdens on the state before being allowed to enter. Even when laborers were demanded by West Coast defense industries during World War II, many Californians skeptically mistrusted newcomers and treated them as late-coming interlopers. Only after the passage of major civil rights legislation by Congress in the mid-1960s did all outright separation of the races in meals and lodging come to an end.[3]

Needles

Needles, the first California town to which westbound motorists came, owed its existence

to transportation. First, in the early 1880s, it was a steamboat port on the Colorado River, with the jagged Needles peaks seen downstream. Next came the Southern Pacific Railroad, which arrived from the Pacific coast in spring 1883. After the Atlantic and Pacific Railroad completed laying its tracks westward across Arizona, it erected a bridge across the river into the Needles area in fall of the same year. The A&P then purchased rights to the Southern Pacific line to Los Angeles, operating trains there as did its successor, the Atchison Topeka and Santa Fe, after 1897. The latter company made the old steamboat landing into a major rail stop. In 1914 the National Old Trails Road was routed through Needles, initially crossing the river on a ferry and then from 1916 over an impressive steel-arch bridge downstream. It was followed by U.S. Highway 66 in 1926. The Mother Road, which roughly paralleled the steel rails of the Santa Fe through half of New Mexico and all of Arizona, continued next to them across the Mojave Desert and down the Cajon Summit all the way into Los Angeles. In the 1920, 1930, and 1940 censuses, Needles had about three thousand people, but that number temporarily ballooned during operation of the nearby U.S. Army Desert Training Center during the Second World War, with the number hovering around four thousand through the rest of the Route 66 period. Though never large, Needles was important to westbound auto travelers, as it constituted the jumping off point into the Mojave Desert.[4]

EL GARCES HOTEL

In the early days of railroading, trains did not have rolling dining cars. At meal times trains stopped and passengers poured into trackside hash houses to gobble down quick meals. Unlike its competitors, the Santa Fe Railway from 1876 onward collaborated with English-born food and lodging vendor Fred Harvey to provide its customers with convenient, wholesome meals at jointly operated eating houses. The railroad added a second story above its Needles depot to house one of these dining facilities in 1898, but then the whole building burned eight years later. In 1908 the Santa Fe erected a two-story, fireproof, reinforced-concrete hotel, dining room, and lunchroom complex for the Fred Harvey Company to operate in conjunction with its station in Needles. The hostelry took its El Garces name from eighteenth-century Spanish missionary Francisco Garcés. Its location at 950 Front Street on the early alignment of Highway 66 through town helped make it the favored destination for well-heeled auto travelers to eat and sleep. Because of extreme summer temperatures in Needles, architect Francis W. Wilson designed the structure with a "floating" roof structure supported above the main building, permitting the wind to blow between the two to avoid trapping daytime heat. Wide colonnaded porches shaded the guest rooms and public areas on all four sides, further mitigating desert heat.

Food for train passengers was the main reason for building the elaborate, neoclassical El Garces complex. During thirty-minute stops, while crews serviced and watered the locomotives, passengers headed inside the hotel to enjoy a limited menu of set meals. Overnight hotel guests and others enjoyed far wider range of food choices. The November 26, 1939, menu for these more leisurely customers, for example, listed multiple meals with main courses like smoked Alaska cod with melted butter and panfried pork chops with applesauce. These and other entrees came with a choice of potatoes; green peas, carrots, and cauliflower; fruit salad; and a selection of rice pudding, pie, or ice cream for dessert together with coffee, tea, or milk, for seventy-five cents. On the occasions when road travelers were dining when a train arrived, they witnessed the crush of passengers trying to eat in just half an hour. This happened to American painter James Montgomery Flagg, who was seated at the El Garces Hotel lunch counter when "a seething mass of people" rushed in from a newly arrived train. "There were more people than stools, and we had the second layer of them leaning on our backs as we tried to eat our ham and potato salad." A child from the train pushed his way up to the counter next to Flagg to grab "the stiffening remains of an order of macaroni" that a previous diner had left behind. Despite such occasional confusion, for four decades the El Garces remained the best place in Needles to eat, closing in 1949. After housing railway company offices for a while, its building fell vacant, and then in 2014 was renovated to become the El Garces Intermodal Transportation Center, a role it continues to serve.[5]

LYNN'S BROILER (GARRETT'S RESTAURANT, WAGON WHEEL RESTAURANT)

By no means could every traveler afford the pricey meals served by attractive Harvey Girl waitresses in the El Garces Hotel. Most of them, in fact, sought far less expensive fare, which in the early days of the Mother Road in the desert Southwest often was found at Chinese-run eateries. As early as summer 1919, for example, motorcyclist C. K. Shepherd stopped at one of these. "After disposing of a steak at a Chinese restaurant," he took a siesta in the shade of a palm tree in the park area outside the El Garces before moving on. In October 1934 Guy K. Austin's family likewise dropped into a Chinese café in Needles, where chow mein with noodles struck their fancy. A 1927 business directory listed five eating places other than the Harvey House in Needles, and four of them had owners with Asian names.[6]

One of the favorite eating places for price-conscious motorists operated on the far northern side of town in the 2400 block of West Broadway. It was here on the Mother Road that local restaurateur and real estate investor Jack C. Richey erected Lynn's Broiler in 1956. For years Margaret J. "Marnie" Bemish managed the restaurant, but trouble struck in 1968. Construction of the new four-lane highway overlay parts of Needles, and its west-side interchange threatened several businesses, including Lynn's Broiler. Litigation over land use continued for two years, but in 1970 Jack Richey lost his entire rear banquet room and much of the main dining space to a projected exit ramp. He adapted the remaining lunchroom area into a coffee shop and creatively modified what was left of his building to house part of a new dining room. In about 1972 Billie J. and Dennis H. Garrett purchased the business and property, renaming it Garrett's Restaurant and offering a similar menu of steaks, seafood, and chicken but adding homemade bread and pies. After half a dozen years, the Garretts sold to James Ray "Jimmy" Jackson and Kenneth Clyde Wetmore, both of Needles, who maintained about the same bill of fare but changed the name to the Wagon Wheel Restaurant. That very year, 1978, a kitchen fire swept through the facility, gutting the interior. Jimmy Jackson and wife Cleo rebuilt,

and within a matter of months were back in business for another decade. The Wagon Wheel became just as popular among locals and travelers as the old Lynn's Broiler had been. Then, in 1988, the Jacksons sold the enterprise to John F. Rutan, whose son with others managed the enterprise, being succeeded about 2002 by new owner Susan Alexis. The Wagon Wheel Restaurant is one of only a handful of restaurants along the old highway that continues offering a classic mid-century road-food specialty, the egg-batter dipped, deep-fried Monte Cristo–style ham, turkey, and cheese sandwich sprinkled with powdered sugar and served with strawberry jam.[7]

Across the Mojave Desert

After leaving Needles, first-time westbound motorists headed into the most dreaded stretch of highway—the sparsely populated wastes of the Mojave Desert. One hundred sixty-five miles lay between them and Barstow, the next place with any substantial population. When writers for the Works Progress Administration of the late 1930s prepared a guidebook to California, they characterized the route as "passing through widely spaced 'towns'—mere groups of tourist cabins about gas stations and lunch rooms." This was not an exaggeration. The route traversed one of the hottest, most desolate parts of America. The motorists drove miles and miles between tiny, scattered crossroads communities, where they found high-priced gasoline, sometimes inflated auto repairs, and simple groceries or short-order meals. In many places they had to pay for water, the typical price in the 1940s being ten cents a glass for "clean" to drink or ten cents a gallon of unfiltered for refilling vehicle radiators. The very remoteness, lack of residents, and heat all combined to make the Mojave the ideal location for the Desert Training Center, planned and initially commanded by General George S. Patton during World War II, though travelers rarely saw many of the thousands of widely dispersed soldiers.

As motorists gradually made their way out of the valley of the Colorado River at Needles, after about seventeen miles they passed the Arrowhead Junction and the road north to Las Vegas, Nevada. They instead proceeded westward another fourteen miles to the hamlet of Goffs. Like most of the other desert stops they would pass, Goffs began in 1883 as a siding on the Southern Pacific Railroad. Intermittently the community supported stores, filling stations, cafés, and, for a time, even cabins, but business dwindled when U.S. Highway 66 was rerouted away in 1932 to a more direct alignment. From the crossroads most motorists continued on seventeen miles through little Fenner to arrive in Essex.[8]

Essex

WAYSIDE INN

The best known of the motorists' stopping places in Essex was the Wayside Inn, which actually had its beginnings in Goffs. At least as early as 1925, the enterprise was serving roadside meals in the former community. Eastbound motorist Paul E. Vernon stayed in a cabin there in 1928, commenting that "we had a good meal in an all-night restaurant." He added that the proprietor made space in his icebox overnight for some bunches of "Thompson white seedless grapes" on which his party had snacked all the way from San Bernardino. A fire believed to have started in a stove at the restaurant kitchen in February 1929 burned down not only the Wayside Inn

but also other businesses.[9] With the rerouting of Highway 66 away from Goffs three years later, the Wayside Inn sprang up again in Essex, where Mother Road traffic continued to flow. C. E. Wiley rebuilt the enterprise by 1932 to include a store with a filling station, an auto garage, a café, and a roadside camp with twelve individual cabins. The complex operated into the 1960s, suffering major fires in 1944 and 1958 but being rebuilt each time. Wiley's daughter and son-in-law, Marguerite and Fred E. Miller, became the next owners, succeeded among others by Oliver Bowen "O. B." and Helen Maxine Chambers, Richard C. and Florence Hebert, Charles D. and Margarite M. Finzel, and John R. Bentley Jr. Remnants of the mid-twentieth-century Wayside Inn still stand disused at the side of the old pavement in Essex.[10]

CADIZ SUMMIT STATION, CAFÉ, AND CAMP

Cadiz Summit was never a town. Instead it was a roadside stop strategically located at a 1,250-foot pass where, after a long climb, Highway 66 surmounted the Marble Mountains about nineteen miles west of Essex. Entrepreneur Thomas R. Morgan recognized early-day autos' tendency to overheat on the long ascent when he opened the first filling station at the apex of this rise in 1928. Using any building materials he could scrounge, he put up a rudimentary roadside station, café, and auto repair shop at the crest that he and wife Frances dubbed Cadiz Summit after the nearby Cadiz railroad siding. Life in this lonely setting beside the Mother Road was spartan at best. It had no drinkable groundwater, with every drop of potable water being hauled in, and, further, it only received electric power after forty years in the 1960s. Most owner-operators lasted about

The Wayside Inn as rebuilt by C. E. Wiley at Essex in the Mojave Desert of California ca. 1932. An anonymous customer mailed this photo postcard on October 16, 1944, writing, "We stayed here over night in Camp #5[,] 2 room and bath. It is nice and warm here." Author's collection.

six to eight years before tiring of the isolation and oppressive summertime heat.

Following the Morgans at Cadiz Summit came George and Minnie Tienken in 1936. They made the complex into a less rustic stop that many travelers remembered from the Mexican green parrot there, owned by the Tienkens' daughter. Former customer Cenovia Martinez Navarro fondly recalled, "You could stop and eat and they had a parrot . . . and the bird would say, 'I want a cracker,' 'I want a cracker.'" From these restaurant days in the 1930s, daughter Winnifred Tienken recounted, "Mom made fresh bread about twice a week. . . . She cooked a lot of beans and because of the problem keeping fresh meat we used canned corned beef, canned salmon, and canned pot roast." For people who lived scattered across the surrounding

desert, the Summit became a popular gathering place for informal Saturday evening dances during the Tienkens' management, the concrete foundations from the original garage erected by Tom Morgan becoming a modest open-air dance floor. Local musicians brought their own instruments and talent. The remote location seemed appealing to Clint and Dorothy Hunt, who purchased it in 1944. Five years later the couple sold to Jim and Mae Flannagan, who for a time ran the eatery and station with Jim's sister, Marie, and her husband, George Sterling. The Cadiz Summit Restaurant then consisted of two rooms, one with a double-door entry, booths, tables, and a counter with a soda fountain in front of the kitchen along the back wall. Above the fountain Jim displayed his prized collection of polished desert rocks. A large second room contained a jukebox, two pool tables, and a dance floor. During the summertime, when many people crossing the desert opted to drive during cooler nighttime hours, the restaurant stayed open around the clock. In about 1960 fire swept through the complex, but Jim Flannagan stayed on by himself for a while in what was left, selling gas and fixing cars, but his heart was not in it. Dick and Nadine Cruse leased the remnant of the popular old business in 1965, mainly providing fuel, towing, and minor repairs. When Interstate 40 opened in spring 1973, it diverted virtually all the former through traffic, and the Cruses had no choice but to shut down. Since that time the site has been abandoned. A few walls and foundations covered with graffiti still remain and are photographed by heritage tourists.[11]

Chambless

CHAMBLESS CAMP

James Albert "Jim" Chambless established the Chambless Camp, a combined filling station, store, and tourist cabin complex, on the old unpaved U.S. Highway 66 about three and a half miles west of Cadiz Summit. This Spanish-American War veteran had come to the Mojave country at least as early as 1921, and, six years later, he formally secured a federal homestead for a tract of desert land that encompassed the intersection of the highway with an unimproved dirt track to a mine. He and wife Fannie erected a service station, but shifted it half a mile south after the roadway was realigned during 1932 paving. By the end of the decade, the Chambless Camp consisted of cabins, a filling station, a café, and a general store with its own drilled well for water and a generator driven by a Chevrolet auto engine producing electricity.

The business thrived from trade brought by Mother Road travelers, but not everything went smoothly. On Monday, October 11, 1937, for example, driver Toby Melillo from Connecticut pulled into the camp for fuel, but when it was time to pay he instead poked a .22 caliber pistol into Jim Chambless's ribs and then, without paying, drove off toward the east. The unfazed station owner dashed into his office for his own gun, fired a few rounds at the departing vehicle, and then set out in hot pursuit in his own car while taking pot shots out the window. As events would have it, the highway was blocked for pavement resurfacing ten miles ahead, where Chambless himself apprehended the twenty-year-old thief. A sheriff's deputy took charge of the miscreant, and, a week and a half later, a court sentenced him to five years in the California penitentiary.

In 1940 Jim Chambless passed away, with widow Fannie and the children running the camp four more years before selling to William Edward and Wilhelmina Riddle. They and their offspring operated the multifaceted enterprise for two more decades, adding to and upgrading the facilities. The acacia trees that Fannie Chambless planted and nurtured and that the Riddles watered grew to maturity around the cabins and adjacent picnic grounds, so that by 1946 writer Jack D. Rittenhouse could describe the camp as "one of the few shady spots in the entire desert route." Steve and Lorraine Stephens purchased the business in 1965 and kept its doors open until 1991. Subsequently others attempted to resurrect the café and campground, but limited traffic flow on the old roadway led to their disappointment. Today the surviving buildings slowly deteriorate behind protective fencing.[12]

ROAD RUNNER'S RETREAT

Just a mile and a half west from Chambless, truck driver and heavy equipment operator Roy Hulbert Tull and wife Helen opened an imposing truck stop to serve traffic midway between Needles and Barstow in 1963. The complex consisted of an up-to-date, flat-roofed restaurant and a midcentury modern service station with an upswept canopy. From the popular appeal of roadrunner birds among southwesterners, they named their stop the Road Runner's Retreat. An impressive neon sign simulated the movement of one of the birds running across the desert floor. For a while Roy continued driving trucks as well as bulldozing naturally occurring salt at mining claims on the Cadiz Salt Lake. This left Helen mostly on her own to manage the twenty-four-hour eatery with lessees operating the gasoline station and auto repair shop. Eventually Roy joined Helen full-time at the stop, but the couple thereafter retired to Daggett, California, leasing the facility to Duke Dotson. Behind the retail operation, a number of employees lived in a scattering of mostly preowned mobile homes. The Road Runner's Retreat operated at least into 1972, but the next year Interstate 40 opened to the north, siphoning away almost all the truck and car traffic. Today the truck stop's fire-scarred and sun-bleached ruins lie at the south side of the road.[13]

Amboy

Like Goffs and Essex, Amboy began as a siding on the Southern Pacific Railroad in 1883. Decades passed before people moved to its arid surroundings, with railroad track workers and prospectors being some of the earliest. After the turn of the twentieth century, the Consolidated Pacific Cement Plaster Company opened a gypsum mine near there. Employees shoveled the mineral into furnaces to expel moisture and then ground it to powder to be shipped out by rail as plaster of paris. In 1914 the National Old Trails Road was routed through Amboy, leading a number of savvy businesspeople to recognize that money could be made providing services to motorists here in the middle of the Mojave Desert. Next came U.S. Highway 66 in 1926. Three years later, the Mohawk Hobbs road guide advised motorists: "This is one of the driest and hottest places on the whole route; a temperature of 120° is often exceeded in the summer. Recently no rain fell for over one year." Motorist James Albert Davis stopped about five o'clock P.M. for supper in Amboy on a cross-country trip in August 1922. He jotted down, "It surely was some hot weather to be sure, and my eyes burned something awful. It was so hot that you could not hold your hand on any part of the car." Despite the summer heat and the fact that all drinking water had to be hauled there in railway tank cars, about two hundred people lived in Amboy year-round in the 1930s and 1940s. The little community supported two cafés, three filling stations, three tourist courts, and four auto repair shops. After Interstate 40 opened in 1973 and diverted traffic away, however, most of the residents moved elsewhere and the location became one of the best-known ghost towns in California.[14]

BEN BENJAMIN'S CAFÉ AND GARAGE (BENDER'S ONE STOP SUPER SERVICE STATION, CONN'S SERVICE STATION AND CAFÉ, FROSTY SNACK BAR)

The Benjamin and Bender families were living in Amboy before U.S. Highway 66 first routed through the community. G. M. "Ben"

Benjamin owned land on both sides of the highway, and he sold tracts on the north side to Roy Crowl and Bill Lee. Oral tradition says that he used the proceeds from land sales to build parts of his own garage, where by 1923 he sold fuel and repaired motorists' vehicles, later adding a lunch counter and ten wood-frame cabins. He called it Ben Benjamin's Café and Garage. In the meantime brothers Martin "Mart" and Joseph M. "Joe" Bender and Joe's wife, Lucy, opened their own general store, selling to both residents and travelers. By 1932 the two brothers bought out Ben Benjamin, renaming the concern Bender's One Stop Super Service Station, gradually expanding amenities and even adding the local post office partitioned off in one corner of the store. Following the end of Prohibition in 1933, they began selling beer as a profitable adjunct to other foods and beverages.

By the mid-1940s Lillian and Constantinos "Conn" Pulos purchased the enterprise. It consisted of a store, café, bus stop, filling station, and about a dozen cabins. Some of the cottages provided overnight shelter for travelers while others housed employees. Cold beer remained a real draw in the middle of the desert. A motorist penned a postcard mailed in Needles on August 23, 1953, reporting, "I drove to Amboy while the wind blew through the car like a breath from a blast furnace. Beer at Amboy! Oboy, Oboy, Oboy." Employees at Conn's Café, however, had to be careful about giving customers beverages that were too cool. Della Foulenfont Inglis's mother worked in the café at the time, and later Della recalled, "Lillian Pulos cautioned my mother not to put ice in the water glasses in mid-summer in the middle of the day 'cause it was not unusual for these people to get off the busses and be overheated and she said it

would cause them cramps." Conn's Service Station and Café operated until 1964, when a fire gutted its main buildings. Lillie and Conn retired in San Bernardino after selling the charred site to Luther Friend, who, by 1966, rebuilt the station and café. He called the eatery the Frosty Snack Bar, and it featured malted milkshakes and hamburgers. Then, around 1970, Friend sold to Leonard Purdy, who maintained the business until the bypassing of old Highway 66 by Interstate 40 in 1973 led to closure of the business. Today only the concrete-paved apron leading south from the old highway into the station area and scattered foundations mark the site.[15]

ROY'S CAFÉ

Roy Irvin Crowl came to the Amboy area in 1927. He found work at a local surface salt mine and occasionally drove groceries into the surrounding mining camps. Observing the increasing traffic along Highway 66, Crowl left these earlier jobs to run a garage for Ben Benjamin. Then, in 1940, he and wife Velma purchased land on the north side of the road and opened their own auto repair shop, adding gas pumps and, in 1945, Roy's Café. Soon a string of tourist cabins sprang up that eventually became Roy's Motel. In the late 1930s, Herman Bazzell "Buster" Burris made his way to Amboy, not expecting to stay long but taking a job in Roy Crowl's garage. He turned out to be a good hand who stayed around, became indispensable to the business, and ended up marrying Velma and Roy's daughter, Betty. The years following World War II brought boom times to the two couples, who eventually employed ninety people to work full- and part-time. Velma and Betty supervised the motel and twenty-four-hour restaurant, while Roy and Buster ran the fuel and repair business. Buster explained how things worked this way: "We had four or five guys at the station, two or three girls [in the café], two or three cooks, and we'd rent out our rooms two times a day for people crossing the desert at night and in the daytime. . . . We rented them day and night." Roy and Velma retired in 1959, with Buster and Betty taking over full operation. They then sold the enterprise to James Arthur Parker and Lowella Anne Parker in 1965, who prospered a while but then were unable to maintain payments after Highway 66 traffic diverted to Interstate 40 in 1973. Buster and Betty came back and resumed management even though the heady days of the old Mother Road were long past.[16]

The hazards of crossing the Mojave in the summertime brought much of the trade to Roy's. When a car engine completely overheated and ruined its internal bearings, it often was less expensive to have Roy's mechanics install a rebuilt engine from his waiting stockpile than to pay towing charges to either Barstow or Needles just to have similar work done there. It is important to realize that cars, however, were not the only sufferers in the Mojave. Lowella Parker described the impact of the heat on travelers who came from more temperate parts of the country. "Many of those ladies from New York and New Hampshire, up in that area, they would . . . want to come in the restaurant and have a cold glass of water." She knew that people in frail health who were overcome by the heat could injure themselves by quickly downing a chilled drink. Parker continued, "What we would do is to take them out and set them in a chair in the shade . . . where we had the awning . . . in front . . . and get 'em a hot cup of tea and cool it down just a little bit and let 'em

sip that for a little bit and then they'd regain their senses." Then the travelers could come inside the café for the cold drink they initially had wanted plus perhaps something to eat.[17]

As early as 1975, Buster Burris, who over time had purchased many properties from people leaving Amboy, decided to sell out, but it took him a long time to find a buyer. He intermittently ran the café and filling station through the 1980s and 1990s when heritage tourists began driving the old Mother Road in increasing numbers. Almost all of them stopped at Roy's Café in Amboy. Buster's storytelling abilities made him one of the most frequently interviewed people along the old thoroughfare, with his grizzled visage appearing on newspaper pages and television screens across the nation. In 2005, after three decades of effort, Burris successfully sold the Amboy site to fast-food entrepreneur Albert Okura of San Bernardino, who today ably oversees preservation of the historic Route 66 ghost town.[18]

Bagdad
BAGDAD CAFÉ

From Amboy, motorists could look westward toward a remarkable geological feature, the easily recognized cone of an ancient volcano, the Amboy Crater. Many, however, in a hurry to reach their next stop, rushed past the solidified lava around the base of the eminence. In about seven miles, they came to Bagdad, a desert community that thrived because of its position on an 1883 railway siding, which was comparatively close to nearby mines producing gold, silver, and other metallic ores. The town persisted into the twentieth century despite that all the drinking water had to be brought in by railway tank cars. The groundwater was undrinkable. For a number of years, the Fred Harvey Company operated a trackside eating house for Santa Fe Railway employees, though motorists were welcome. Not all those coming to Bagdad, however, could afford to pay for food. This was the case of Joe Szalanski as a teenaged hobo in 1932. From a boxcar on the Bagdad rail siding, he called out to a local boy and asked him to tell his mother, "There is a boy in the car that didn't eat for three days." Dutifully the child complied, and "When he came back, he had a big bowl of cornflakes and hot milk[,] some kind of Mexican biscuits, cup of coffee and a saucer" not to mention a "bag full of dates." When Szalanski returned the dishes to the house, the mother obviously took pity on him and gave the young transient another "bag of biscuits" for good measure.

Gradually most of the business activity in Bagdad shifted a quarter mile south from the railroad tracks to the Mother Road in the 1930s, and there on the north side of the pavement stood the Bagdad Café with an adjacent service station and motel units. Among its owners were Bob Ragland, Ruth and Lee Baber, Alice Lawrence, and finally Carol and Charles "Buddy" Slusher. When they foresaw the completion of Interstate 40 about fifteen miles to the north, knowing that Bagdad would be bypassed, the Slushers closed down in 1972. Subsequently a pipeline company used the townsite for a temporary pipe storage yard, bulldozing all the remaining buildings. Unexpectedly German movie director Percy Adlon appeared on the scene in the mid-1980s to make the motion picture *Bagdad Café*, but, since the actual eatery no longer survived, he used the Sidewinder Café fifty miles down the road at Newberry Springs as its film reincarnation.[19]

Ludlow
DESERT INN CAFÉ AND HOTEL

Motorists could breathe a sigh of relief when they pulled into Ludlow, nineteen miles west of Bagdad. During the early years of the Mother Road, it had about three hundred residents, making it the largest populated place between Needless and Barstow. In late 1882 the Southern Pacific Railroad established a siding here, and subsequently short-line railways connected it both north and south to serve mining districts. As in Amboy and Bagdad, all water was hauled in by the railway. First, the National Old Trails Road around 1914 and then the Mother Road in 1926 were routed through the town. Trade from motorists helped sustain the community beyond the middle of the twentieth century. Many who stopped were like Roberta Ramsdell, who quickly jotted down in a trip diary in June 1935, "Ate lunch at Ludlow." In 1972 the new Interstate 40 was completed just north of the village, which received an exit, making it easy for tourists to turn off to visit what had mostly become a ghost town.[20]

A number of families earned comfortable livings providing food, fuel, repairs, and lodging to motorists the highways brought to Ludlow. Among them were Lee Yim and his Chinese-immigrant wife, Ginswa.[21] Born in San Francisco in 1884, Lee came to the desert community at least as early as 1916, when press reports show he was already in the restaurant trade. By the 1920s he opened the wood-frame Desert Inn Café and Hotel, a café with hotel rooms upstairs, together with a separate adjacent pool hall. A modest grocery store followed. Covered porches on the southeast sides of his buildings faced the main street and the railway tracks, giving customers welcome shade during hot summertime afternoons. Behind the hotel the couple kept a poultry yard with chickens, geese, and even pigeons. Granddaughter Stephanie Lee Jordan, who as a little girl spent holidays at the restaurant and hotel, remembered Lee saying, "Oh, we're having chicken tonight and whop . . . [he] cut the head off a chicken" for supper. She also fondly recalled stacks of Chinese-language newspapers at one end of the counter in the eatery."

Lee Yim had a secondary business that at times proved to be lucrative. From his store he provisioned prospectors in the area around Ludlow. In exchange for the grubstakes, recipients agreed to share anything of value that they might find. Among these prospectors was Billy Wheeler, who in early 1933 found a promising show of gold ore about four miles south of town. He divided the mineral claim with Lee fifty-fifty. Soon rail carloads of its ore were shipping out to a smelter in Salt Lake City, Utah, with the Lee family receiving far more in income than anyone anticipated. The Lees had multiple children who grew up in Ludlow, with six of their sons serving in the American armed forces during World War II. Building on the financial security made possible by their parents' hard work and prudent mining investments, a number of the children were able to attend colleges and universities and

Lee Yim's Desert Inn café, hotel, and pool hall fronting on Highway 66 in Ludlow, California, in 1926, the year the Mother Road received its numerical designation. The children in front of the porch are two of the proprietor's grandchildren. Photograph from Production File 112576 courtesy of Lake County (Illinois) Discovery Museum, Curt Teich Postcard Archives.

consequently find careers and lives away from the heat and dust of the Mojave Desert. Lee Yim himself lived in retirement in South Pasadena and passed away there at age eighty-four in February 1969.[23]

Hector Siding
MOJAVE WATER CAMP (POE'S CAFÉ, DESERT OASIS)

For years no one knew of any drinkable well water anywhere in the ninety miles between Danby, just west of Essex, and Newberry Springs. This was a long, dry stretch to which all potable water had to be hauled. Into this setting entered Mabel and Oscar Louie Hoerner with their three children from Kansas. Coming from the treeless, semiarid Great Plains, where almost all water lay underground, they were familiar with well drilling. In 1926 Mabel's aunt and uncle, Jo and Charles Van Dorn, who lived in Newberry Springs, recommended that they homestead land on the rutted dirt road in the bare, dry section east of the town. There they could drill a well and open a filling station and café. The Kansans seemed undaunted by the fact that no one had ever successfully sunk a fresh-water well in the area, so they took on the task.

Oscar filed paperwork to acquire 160 acres of federally owned desert land straddling what later that year would become Route 66. The site on the original alignment was adjacent to the Santa Fe Railway tracks just west of its Hector siding, roughly twelve miles east of Newberry Springs. Oscar rented a well drilling rig and, with his two teen-aged sons, began the quest for groundwater. Daughter Evangeline recounted, "What do you know, they hit water thirty feet down!" The liquid was impregnated with natural soda, but despite its odd taste was completely drinkable. Mabel and Oscar felt that their future had been secured with their possession of the only potable water on the ninety-mile stretch. They had their own private oasis. Using materials they scrounged or bought cheaply, including worn-out, creosoted railroad crossties, they erected a combined filling station, café, and residence, together with three little one-room tourist cabins. Although their Mojave Water Camp never had electricity or telephone service during their tenure, it successfully offered fuel, short-order meals, and car parts; rudimentary tire and motor repairs; and basic groceries. Daughter Evangeline and her mother used a kerosene range to cook for hungry travelers. A Crosley Icyball refrigerator, also fueled by kerosene, provided a small supply of ice so that they could squeeze seasonal, inexpensive lemons for fresh lemonade to sell at ten cents a glass. Using eggs from their own flock of laying hens, the mother and daughter made and served what Evangeline described as "scrambled eggs and Vienna sausage sandwiches by the dozens." Because Oscar controlled the only source of water for miles around, he could instruct motorists to "get your water where you buy your gas." He sold his soda-tainted water by the glass or by the bucket for auto radiators unless drivers filled up with his gasoline, when it was free.

Living conditions were hard at the Mojave Water Camp, though the Hoerners made a comfortable living. Then, in July 1929, a major problem arose: Oscar suffered a broken arm in crank-starting a customer's vehicle, and the local physician ineptly set the fracture. To remedy the medical blunder, Oscar sold the Water Camp to one of his brothers, and the whole family took the long-shot gamble to travel by car cross-country for treatment at the Mayo Brothers Clinic in Rochester, Minnesota. With their father's arm reset, the Hoerners returned to California by auto, this time in the dead of winter. In the interval brother Harry had moved the buildings comprising the Mojave Water Stop a short distance south to an adjusted alignment of Highway 66. He took out homestead papers for the new site, but he was so tired of the service station business that he sold everything back to Mable and Oscar on their return for a single dollar. The family resumed selling fuel, preparing roadside meals, and renting tiny one-room cabins for another four years, but then their fortunes took an unexpected turn. In May 1928, well before his injury, Oscar had discovered in the nearby lava flows around Mount Pisgah a whitish clay that stuck to his boots, and he wisely filed mineral claims to the surrounding 1,400 acres of federally owned land, not really understanding what the substance was. He later learned that the suspicious "goo" was bentonite, a nonmetallic clay comprised of volcanic ash capable of absorbing large amounts of water. In 1932 he sold his mineral property to the California Talc Company, the successors to which mined the bentonite for decades. This income enabled the hardworking family to relocate to much more pleasant Newberry Springs.[24]

The old Water Camp well, providing groundwater where none other existed, made their station property desirable. The Hoerners sold it to a Shell oil distributor in 1934, and a family named Shores assumed its operation. The station, snack bar, and garage transitioned through a number of operators but continued to be called the Mojave Water Camp as recently as 1939. Edgar Allen "Ed" Poe was the best remembered of the later owners for his efforts in the late 1940s to transform the outdated old stop into a modern filling station with an adjacent new Poe's Café, both of which were flat-roofed and painted white. Operating at times under the Desert Oasis name, the stop remained in existence at least until 1974, by which time its section of old Highway 66 had long been bypassed by Interstate 40.[25]

The Road to Newberry Springs

During the years before the Mother Road was paved across the desert, westbound motorists dreaded the ten to fifteen miles into Newberry Springs. There the roadway skirted through the edge of the prehistoric Mount Pisgah lava flows, where millennia before molten lava poured out onto the surface of the land. Gas bubbles had formed in the igneous mass as it solidified. When modern-day people constructed an east-west roadway parallel to the railroad tracks, they inadvertently created several miles of razor-sharp rock fragments as their iron-tired wagon wheels broke open the ancient gas bubbles. Sometimes a layer of protective soft dirt blew over the jagged surface, but when winds whipped away the soil, the remaining sharp stones chewed up old-time natural-rubber automobile tires. Daphne and Dallas Lore Sharp drove across the Mount Pisgah flows and observed that "blistered, blown-out, disemboweled tires told an awful story of . . . the eviscerating lava rock." They found the way littered not only with cast-off rubber tires but also by whole abandoned vehicles: "Unhallowed as junk, protruding from the drifting sand, or prone where they had fallen, lay the bones of every known species of car."[26]

Newberry Springs

CLIFF HOUSE

After westbound drivers made their way through the hostile lava-flow environment around Mount Pisgah and the Mojave Water Camp, they ironically came to the tree-shaded oasis of Newberry Springs, where groundwater naturally came to the surface at the base of a picturesque mountain. Here they found a world of willows, alders, and cottonwoods unlike any vegetation seen since Needles. As early as 1923, the Cliff House, named from the rock face of the Newberry Mountains, offered travelers a combined filling station, grocery store, garage, short-order café, campground, and, of all things, swimming pool. On road trips from Arizona in the late 1920s, sisters Betty Clack Grounds and Ollie Clack Bond remembered, "After crossing the hot desert, we kids always enjoyed stopping at Newberry Springs." They recollected a particular family picnic beneath the trees when their parents drove their grandmother back home to California in a Model A Ford. "For our picnic lunch, Mom and Grandma fixed fried chicken, potato salad and ginger bread with whipped cream." The ladies managed to keep the thick cream cool enough beneath a moistened dish towel for whipping. "We can still see Grandma bringing out an egg beater and whipping the cream!"

Motorists stopped to swim at Newberry Springs at least as early as 1923. In the 1930s Cliff House owners Doris and Marion J. Sischo rebuilt and expanded its pool, opening up an unknown spring outlet that produced such a gush of water they had to cap the flow to control it. The pool now measured ninety by thirty feet and had a diving board over the nine-foot-deep end. The Cliff House served many roles in the community, being the regular polling place during elections, housing the local post office, and, for years, having the only telephone in the village. As if being an oasis in the desert were not enough to distinguish it, the Cliff House owners created their own unique waymark in the form of a wooden telegraph pole mounted vertically in the ground. Whenever a motorist came into Newberry with a tire that had blown out in the desert, he could try to toss it up and onto the spike-like pole; by 1924 the stack of rubber casings reached the top. The enterprise remained in business as a campground, pool, and store into the 1960s. By this time others in the area began impounding the natural spring fountain in their own excavated ponds to create fishing and swimming attractions, bringing new generations of water lovers to Newberry Springs. The old Cliff House building today houses the local chamber of commerce at 44544 National Trails Highway.[27]

Daggett

Daggett clings to life alongside the Santa Fe Railway tracks and old Highway 66, though its handful of present-day residents belie a significant history. Like so many other towns across the Mojave, the town was spawned by a humble railroad siding, but, at about the same time it was settled, mineral prospectors made a strike half a dozen miles north at Calico. The latter community ballooned to 1,200 people, and almost everything they needed passed through the Daggett railroad siding. Eventually the mining camp became the most productive silver district in California, producing $20 million in precious metals. As the mines played out, shipments of calcium borate (borax) from area deposits for a time cushioned Daggett's decline. Never incorporating, the community survived as a supply point for miners, ranchers, and a few farmers who tried to irrigate crops from the Mojave River, becoming a stop for motorists in need of food and services on the Mother Road.[28]

CALIFORNIA STATE FRUIT INSPECTION STATION

Fruit raising played an integral role in the California economy, leading the state's department of agriculture to establish inspection stations on incoming highways. The purpose was to prevent introduction of plant diseases or parasites in fruits, vegetables, and cotton originating elsewhere. This meant, for example, that travelers would have to turn over any oranges purchased in Arizona to avoid bringing potential pests to California orange groves. In part because the summertime heat in the Mojave Desert around Needles was so great, the state placed its Highway 66 inspection station well west of there in a location about four miles outside Daggett, where it would be easier to staff and operate. Authorities erected a gable-roof, wood-frame station in 1930, adding a second flat-roof canopied wooden building in 1944. These functioned until 1953, when a larger steel-frame, metal-roof facility took their place, serving until 1967. Almost every westbound Mother Road traveler after 1930 had his or her own memory of surrendering fresh produce and live plants at the side of the road in the desert just east of Daggett. Peter Aldrich was only ten years old in 1945, but years later he begrudged, "We were asked to turn in our Michigan apples at the California Agriculture inspection station." Agents likewise inspected car and truck ownership titles in efforts to counter interstate auto theft.

Californians as a group resented paying taxes to support welfare disbursements to indigent people coming from other states, and, at times during the 1930s, agricultural agents refused entry to travelers unable to prove they had the financial means to avoid becoming burdens on the state. When Kansan Alan Staller hitchhiked to the Golden State in 1938, for example, an inspection officer asked him, "You got a job in California?" When Staller replied that he expected to find one, the agent responded, "We have enough unemployed men in California. Go back!"[29]

Barstow

Travelers saw the character of the Mojave Desert change as they drove the eight miles westward to Barstow. They noticed more homes across the arid lands and along the intermittent Mojave River, which supported scattered irrigated farming. Though still dusty and mostly barren, the desert showed more frequent splotches of green than travelers had seen anywhere in the 150 miles since leaving Needles. At Barstow the main line of the Santa Fe Railway forked southwest to Los Angeles and west toward San Francisco, and this important rail juncture brought growth to the town, which Highway 66 only further enhanced. By 1950 the community had grown to 6,135 people and a decade later had almost doubled that number.[30]

CASA DEL DESIERTO HOTEL

Barstow's strategic position at a major branch of the Santa Fe Railway lines meant that travelers could find food and lodging. The railroad was already stopping its trains here to water and service steam locomotives and to change crews, so it made this the place where passengers received thirty minutes to leave the cars for hasty trackside meals. In 1897 the Fred Harvey Company began managing food and lodging services here, but a major fire in 1908 damaged both maintenance and passenger facilities. Consequently the railroad erected a near-palatial two-story combined depot, hotel, and restaurant, the Casa del Desierto, Spanish for the "House of the Desert" in 1909–11. The National Old Trails Road initially brought early motorists to the doors of the Harvey hotel. By the time that Highway 66 was routed through Barstow, the main route had shifted to the south side of the tracks onto Main Street all the way through town. This alignment left access to the Casa del Desierto via North First Avenue, initially over a bumpy grade crossing and then, after 1930, on a two-lane steel bridge spanning the multiple tracks.

In spring 1929 Letitia Stockett and two young women friends made a round trip by Chrysler automobile from New England to the Pacific coast, during which they stayed overnight in the Barstow Harvey House. Fatigued from travel, they nevertheless pinched their pennies to eat their evening meal in the lunchroom rather than in the more expensive formal dining room. Letitia recounted, "There was an immense circular counter, very large, very scrupulously clean. In the hollow circle were shining nickel-plated contraptions, some to keep food cold, some to keep it hot. Large urns, presided over by brisk and smiling girls, dispensed coffee and tea." She continued, "We were the only women in the restaurant, but we felt perfectly at home, [and] enjoyed our supper hugely." The Casa del Desierto fed and lodged both rail and highway travelers until the Santa Fe Railway gradually placed rolling dining cars onto its trains in the 1940s and 1950s. The

building closed in 1959, at which time Evelyn F. Pattison leased portions of it, where for another dozen years she ran what she called the Harvey House Restaurant. During the 1990s the City of Barstow with others restored the large masonry structure at 681 North First Avenue to house an intermodal transportation center, offices of the local chamber of commerce, rental space for private businesses, the Western America Railroad Museum, and the Route 66 Mother Road Museum.[31]

Up the Mojave River Valley

For the next thirty-six miles to Victorville, motorists drove southwest and south up the immediate valley of the often elusive Mojave River. In most places its course appeared to be a dry bed, although it had considerable water percolation beneath the surface. This shallow underflow allowed enterprising farmers to irrigate a few crops, raise chickens and turkeys, and water livestock. The roadway ascended about seven hundred feet in elevation, transporting motorists into the High Desert environment, unlike the seemingly absolute wasteland they had already crossed. In the valley green spots stood out where scattered cottonwoods, tamarisks, and willows grew along the banks of the Mojave, while upland areas began supporting bizarre-looking Joshua trees with spiky leaves. Four modest roadside communities punctuated the drive: Lenwood, Hodge, Helendale, and Oro Grande.[32]

Victorville

Drivers realized that they were approaching a place with more human activity as they observed increased irrigation along the Mojave River, two big concrete plants, and a large electric power switching station coming into view. Then, after 1930, they crossed the river, usually a sluggish flow, on an unusual steel overhead truss bridge. Still in use today, it spans the stream at an angle. Victorville lay just ahead. Here a stratum of rock created a safe crossing point for mid-nineteenth-century teamsters driving wagons across the river. The arrival of the California Southern Railroad in 1885 ensured that a settlement would remain at the ford. Victorville, however, grew slowly until it was discovered by urban dwellers from metropolitan Los Angeles, about a hundred miles away. During the 1920s and 1930s, its environs became a convenient location for Hollywood-based motion picture crews to film open-air scenes for Westerns. At the same time, the Route 66 highway link encouraged proliferation of dude ranches catering to movie stars and other city folk. Subsequent traffic congestion on the arterial

streets in Victorville led Highway 66 traffic to shift from its original alignment through town to a four-lane freeway as early as 1957. Since that time, community planners have boosted the town's heritage connections with the Mother Road, with Victorville becoming the home for the California Route 66 Museum in 1995.[33]

HOLLAND BURGER CAFÉ (EMMA JEAN'S HOLLAND BURGER CAFÉ)

On the northeastern edge of Victorville, motorists came to an eatery that was long popular with those who regularly drove the road—the Holland Burger Café. In 1947 Robert "Bob" and Catherine L. "Kate" Holland opened this simple concrete-block diner with plate-glass windows on the southwestern side of the Mother Road. Across the highway a truck stop called the Cottonwood Springs Café competed for the highway trade, but Bob

Washington Pettit washing dishes in the waters of the Mojave River after roadside camping outside Victorville, California, ca. 1932. Author's collection.

Holland's burgers were so tasty that his establishment outlived his friendly rival. Holland placed the café on the market after a decade, and ownership passed through several hands until Richard and Emma Jean Gentry purchased the business at 17143 North D Street in 1979. It subsequently became noted not just for its hamburgers but also for Emma Jean's freshly baked pies. The Gentrys' son, Brian, and his wife, Shawna, took over the eatery, which had become known as Emma Jean's Holland Burger Café. At the time of this writing, the pale green painted diner continued serving memorable breakfasts and lunches daily except Sundays.[34]

MURRAY'S DUDE RANCH

More than a dozen dude ranches hosted guests in the scenic High Desert country around Victorville in the 1930s to 1960s, almost all admitting only white guests. Lela and Nolie B. Murray followed a different course at their place outside of town. From 1937 to 1955, they invited people of any race to the only African American–owned and –operated dude ranch in the country. The couple purchased forty acres about five miles northeast of Victorville in the Apple Valley rural community in 1922, seeing the land as a quiet country retreat in an area that already had a handful of Black homesteaders. Nolie had prospered from running a successful billiard parlor and cigar shop in downtown Los Angeles, but Lela envisioned creating a haven where she could help troubled or sickly children find respite and rejuvenation. For fifteen years she invited and housed young people at her Victorville farmstead, where they rode horses, swam in a pool, and ate wholesome meals of fresh garden produce and poultry that she herself raised. Boxer Joe

Louis heard about the couple and, with their permission, came to their country place in 1937 to train for upcoming bouts. The press consequently discovered "Murray's Ranch," an estimated ten thousand people flooded in to see the champ, and Lela and Nolie realized that they could expand their home for children into a guest ranch patterned after the many whites-only facilities around them. By a quirk of coincidence, at this same time editors of nationally read *Life* magazine sent a journalist and a photographer to cover a nearby rodeo, and they came to the ranch to interview and take pictures of Joe Louis. The subsequent article gave the facility high-profile publicity from coast to coast. Murray's Dude Ranch opened to the public, with food being one of its major attractions. Chef Malcolm Keys from Riverside, California, prepared meals from 1938 into the mid-1950s. Customers raved over his chicken dinners. Leona Thomas Griner worked as a secretary for Lela during these times and later reported that, for most resident guests, "chicken wasn't really that high on the list, because there were stews . . . home-cooked meals," adding, "He did a lot of hamburgers, because people would come in and order a hamburger and go back to the swimming pool. He loved dill pickles."[35]

Over the years thousands of African American guests stayed and dined at Murray's Ranch because they were denied such pleasures elsewhere. One potential customer wrote to Lela and Nolie that he enjoyed riding horseback and expressed, "I always wanted to spend a few weeks on a dude ranch. Being colored, I doubted that I would ever have the chance. . . . Please let me know the cost of a vacation with you." Each Easter the Murrays organized and sponsored a special

Two guests enjoying the desert sun at Murray's Dude Ranch outside Victorville, California, ca. 1950. On the reverse side, one of the women penned in ink, "Elease & me sitting on the corral at Murray's ranch." Author's collection.

Victorville in 1939, and in a typical instance the white director, producer, and stars Jack Benny, Andy Devine, and Phil Harris all stayed at the exclusive Yucca Loma Dude Ranch, while the film crew members slept at the white-run Green Spot Motel and other similar local white-run lodgings. Edmund Lincoln Anderson, the African American actor who played Jack Benny's valet, Rochester van Jones in the production, as well as other Black film crew members, had no choice but to stay with other segregated African Americans at Murray's Ranch.[36]

During World War II, jazz singer Pearl Bailey performed at a United Service Organization (USO) show at the Victorville Army Air Field and learned about Murray's Ranch. She and husband Louis Bellmon returned a decade later and were impressed with what they saw. By this time, however, Lela had passed away, and Nolie and second wife, Calie, were struggling to maintain operations. Bailey purchased most of the ranch, converting it into a personal retreat, where she hosted friends as guests. In time the star tired of the responsibilities and sold the property, which deteriorated with limited maintenance. Finally, in 1988, several local fire departments burned the surviving buildings as part of a training exercise.[37]

Across the High Desert

Southwestward from Victorville, over the course of eighteen miles, drivers gradually climbed upward about 1,600 feet in elevation to the summit of a pass that would lead them down into metropolitan Los Angeles. They reached it by traversing what Californians called the High Desert, a wide-open landscape with dispersed shaggy Joshua trees. Motorists observed increasing numbers of

open-air sunrise worship service, followed by a country breakfast at the ranch dining hall. In some years as many as a thousand people of all races came for the gatherings; nevertheless, the stigma of discrimination remained. Whenever a white stranger arrived at the train depot in Victorville and sought a ride to Murray's Ranch, cab drivers continued to ask, "You know you are going to a Negro ranch?" Paramount Pictures filmed the movie *Jack Benny Rides Again* outside scattered cabins and travel trailers that were intermittently occupied by urban dwellers who sought escape from the city at least on weekends. Though the rainfall here was still only about six inches annually, many sojourners agreed with 1929 motorist Hoffman Birney, who quipped, "You leave the desert behind at Victorville." It was somewhere in this visually appealing area in the 1920s that James Albert Davis's party paused on the roadside for a break after "we stopped in Victorville and bought a watermelon." Cajon Summit, the high point at 4,260 feet, had become a southeastern gateway between the San Gabriel and San Bernardino Mountains into Southern California in the 1830s. By the time Highway 66 was designated in 1926, the pass carried not only automobiles but also transcontinental trains, and it retains that same strategic importance today.[38]

SUMMIT INN

The modern-day improvement of pressurization of auto motor cooling systems, which permits the coolant liquid to circulate at higher temperatures without boiling, did not become widely adopted by carmakers until the 1940s. Before this time motorists dealt with engine overheating and radiator coolant loss as expected events in cross-country travel. Consequently the crests of long ascents like the Cajon Summit became optimum locations for gasoline stations; potential customers often had to pull over to add water to their radiators even if they did not need fuel. At least by the time that the National Old Trails Road opened across Southern California in 1914, canny businesspeople had established roadside service enterprises at the pass. By 1920 a "Summit Station on [the] main road" was sufficiently well known to become a landmark for giving directions to other area locations.[39]

By 1923 M. R. and C. T. Whitlock were running the Summit Station, within three years adding a lunch counter serving short-order meals. Then, when Route 66 took the place of the National Old Trails Road over the pass in 1926, the California Highway Commission reconstructed portions with a wider thirty-foot roadway. The press reported that the new alignment led "directly through the

A well-dressed couple and their two Boston terriers enjoy a roadside picnic with tablecloth, china, and napkins in the High Desert of Southern California while the trunk lid of their car provides protection from the wind, ca. 1950. Author's collection.

site now occupied by the Summit Inn," so the owners had to adjust their location back from the road. This they did, and the station and café prospered, adding five cabins. By 1932 it became a scheduled stop for cross-country buses. Despite the 1926 widening, the Mother Road twisted and turned as it made the three-thousand-foot slope between the crest and San Bernardino, frequently with steep drop-offs along its outer edge. There were only a limited number of places to safely pull over to change a flat tire or stretch one's legs. Consequently the Summit Inn became an increasingly desirable business property. By 1938 ownership of the land and money-making enterprise began passing through a series of real estate firms and individuals, including Robert J. Hart, Lois and John R. Browning, and Rex E. and Jack Booth. Despite the sometimes nerve-racking climb up from the city, the restaurant became a destination for motorists seeking change-of-pace family-style Sunday lunches during the late 1930s. The repasts featured baked ham, pork loin, fried chicken, or beef prime rib with vegetables, desserts, and soft drinks for sixty cents a person. Because it had to be hauled in for years, diners had to request drinking water.[40]

Dorothy J. and Burton H. Riley purchased the property in 1952, just in time to experience a move like the Whitlocks before them. A new four-lane U.S. Highway 66 realigned across the pass, leaving the old business behind, so the Rileys rebuilt their Summit Inn and service station near a new exit on the highway. The couple liked reliable, mature workers, even going so far as to advertise locally for waitresses aged "30 years or over." German-born Hilda Fish, already an experienced server who met the age requirement,

applied, was accepted, and started on a very hectic Memorial Day in 1960. "Is this place going to be this busy every day?" she asked herself, but the Summit Inn turned out to be such a rewarding place to work that she commuted up and down the grade to her job for the next thirty-five years. Customers looked forward to Fish's smile, her good humor, and her signature beehive hairdo. In 1966 Cecil A. Stevens purchased the enterprise and, just like his predecessors, benefitted from its advantageous geographical location. In the late 1960s, construction of Interstate 15 barely missed the eatery, though Stevens had to adjust the position of his service station. Motorists continued to consider the crest of the Cajon Summit as the logical place to take a break, fuel up before going into the desert, or enjoy a burger and a signature fresh apple tart with a cup of coffee. Over the years the Summit Inn survived several nearby brush fires, including one in 1959 started by a three-year-old boy playing with matches, but it was not so lucky in 2016. The Blue Cut Fire burned it to the ground, leaving only foundations behind.[41]

Down the Cajon Grade

In the days of mechanical vehicle brakes and non-synchronized transmissions, drivers shifted to lower gears to let their idling engines help slow the plunge their vehicles took downward three thousand feet in elevation from the Cajon Summit in twenty-one miles of roadway into San Bernardino. Motorists found the change in landscape eye-popping. From the sparse High Desert on the north side of the mountains, travelers found themselves in an Eden of citrus groves, eucalyptus- and palm-lined avenues, and irrigated subtropical plantings. Vernon

McGill made the descent in the 1920s and reported, "The scenes changed abruptly at every turn. Cactus and sage brush were left behind, and . . . it seemed as if we had dropped into another world." Miles of orange and lemon orchards common to California caught the attention of most new arrivals. "All the groves were neatly cultivated and the trees evenly trimmed until each was just alike," wrote an impressed Evelyn Tucker on a 1938 California trip from Tulsa. James Albert Davis could not resist the urge, recounting "I stopped the car several times and got out and picked some oranges off the trees, but I always took care there was no one looking."

As an important agricultural market and railroad center, San Bernardino had 37,481 people in 1930 and 63,058 by 1950, so it was a substantial small city during the heyday of Highway 66. Here the roadway turned west and proceeded fifty miles through a series of smaller communities to Pasadena, at the edge of Los Angeles proper. Mother Road travelers saw the population grow more dense as they progressed westward through the mostly rural areas filled with citrus groves, vineyards, and other intensive farming. They enjoyed an idyllic landscape until the urban sprawl of subsequent decades took over virtually all the land that at one time supported what historic motorists saw as an agricultural paradise.[42]

San Bernardino
MCDONALD'S DRIVE-IN

Motorists had two choices for their entry to San Bernardino. Those headed farther west typically chose the main alignment southeastward down Cajon Boulevard to veer south on Mount Vernon Avenue to Foothill Boulevard, which took them west toward Pasadena and Los Angeles. Those headed to downtown San Bernardino instead took the City 66 alignment southeast on Kendall Drive to North E Street, leading to the central business district. It was at 1398 North E Street, fronting on the Mother Road, that two brothers, Richard J. and Maurice James "Mac" McDonald, developed innovative new efficiencies that changed how Americans eat.

The McDonald brothers came to California from New England in the 1920s, and they tried lots of different ways to make their living. By 1937 they erected an octagonal wooden building at 742 East Huntington Drive in Monrovia. There, on U.S. Highway 66, the McDonalds sold hot dogs and bargain-priced orange juice made from fruit that prematurely fell from local trees. The enterprise succeeded, and three years later they secured financial backing to erect a larger venue. Selling the old site, they cut the stand in half and relocated it forty miles east to a new city lot at 1396 North E Street, the City 66 route leading to downtown San Bernardino. Employing young women as carhops to take orders and payments and to deliver food to customers in their cars, the McDonald's Drive-In offered customers a choice of barbecue, fried chicken, hamburgers, and "delicious homemade pie."

The financial success the brothers found encouraged them. They tired of the inefficiency and cost of using carhops, but, more importantly, they had never-tested ideas they wanted to try. Consequently, in fall 1948, the McDonalds completely rebuilt the inside of their eatery. Their goal was to sell only identical fifteen-cent hamburgers made with 3.5-inch buns, 1.6-ounce beef patties, quarter-ounce portions of onions, ketchup, mustard, and two slices of pickle, together with ten-cent french fries, twenty-cent sixteen-ounce milkshakes, a choice of three ten-cent cold drinks, and coffee for a nickel. This was the complete menu. These prices collectively undercut virtually every local competitor. The brothers dismissed the twenty carhops and most of the other employees, converted the food pickup windows into openings where customers could place and collect their own orders, and completely revamped the kitchen into one unlike any other in the country.

In the custom stainless steel work space, a "grill man" prepared the burgers, and a "shake man" mixed the milkshakes, while a separate "fry man" cooked the freshly sliced french fries. In the meantime, in assembly-line fashion, "dressers" prepared the buns with toppings and assembled the burgers, while counter staff received orders, took payments, wrapped food, and handed it through the windows to buyers. The McDonald brothers eventually had so much business that they purchased eight, five-spindle Multimixer milkshake machines, enough to blend forty shakes at a time. This use of so many mixers drew the attention of Illinois-based Ray Kroc, who sold the Multimixer. While on a sales trip to California in 1954, he made a business call at the McDonald brothers' operation. There he quickly recognized that he was seeing a truly new development in volume food sales through quick preparation paired with self-service. Kroc and the two brothers subsequently negotiated a contract for the former to become their agent for sales of franchises. This and later agreements laid the foundation for Ray Kroc and his successors to spread McDonald's hamburger restaurants across the United States and abroad. Although the original building was removed in 1972, San Bernardino food-service entrepreneur Albert Okura has preserved a later structure on the site as an unofficial McDonald's museum.[43]

MITLA CAFÉ

The main Highway 66 alignment down Mount Vernon Avenue, west of the San Bernardino central business district, passed through a predominately Mexican neighborhood. There local residents, among them Lucia Montaño, operated a wide variety of grassroots enterprises. Montaño sought extra income to help support her family and in 1937 invested a small nest egg to open a hole-in-the-wall Mexican eatery at 602 North Mount Vernon. She named it the Mitla Café in honor of a pre-Spanish cultural center near her Mexican birthplace. Customers liked Lucia's food and trade grew, but then the next year, in 1938, husband Vicente died. As a widow, Lucia carried on by herself, in 1941 marrying Santa Fe Railway worker Salvador Rodriguez. Eventually he gave up his good job as a mechanic's helper to help manage the family restaurant that over the years grew to occupy most of the city block.[44]

Among the dishes that Lucia and Salvador promoted at the Mitla were tacos. Comprised of flatbread tortillas folded to hold meat, beans, or other foods, tacos originated in Mexico City in the second half of the nineteenth century. Thousands of people fled violence in Mexico during its revolution in 1910–20, and these immigrants helped introduce tacos to places like California, Arizona, and New Mexico, where at the time they were mostly unknown. Typically people made tacos using fresh, soft tortillas, but Salvador was one of several innovators in the late 1940s who devised ways to fry U-shaped crispy corn tortillas in advance so that kitchen staff needed only to add spicy beef, onions, cheese, and additional savory fillings. Other contemporary experimenters went so far as to patent their utensils for deep-frying tortillas. In San Bernardino the Mitla's tacos stood out from all the others.[45]

TACO BELL

San Bernardino was an incubator for new food-vending ideas, and the Mitla Café stood only about two miles away from the McDonald's Drive-In. Young entrepreneur Glen Bell was inspired by what he saw the McDonald brothers doing at their remarkably efficient hamburger stand, and he hoped that he himself might achieve similar success. In 1951 he opened a tiny hamburger and hot dog stand on Highway 66 at 596 North Mount Vernon, directly across the street from the venerable Mitla Café. In the evenings after closing, he sometimes dined on the other side of the street at the Mitla, where he enjoyed the distinctive crispy tacos. The enterprising Anglo concluded that, if he could find out how the cooks fried the corn flatbread tortillas so crunchy without scorching them, he might be able to adapt the "hard taco" concept to fast-food production. Irene Montaño's in-laws ran the Mitla, and she remembered, "My father-in-law would say Mr. Bell kept asking about the tacos, how he made them, and so my father-in-law finally invited him into the kitchen to teach him." Based on what Bell learned from Salvador Rodriguez, the young entrepreneur developed a way to fry multiple crispy taco shells before they were needed. Refining the idea, he began a succession of food chains, Taco-Tia in 1954 and El Taco in 1961. He finally reached what he considered to be perfection with Taco Bell in 1962. To appeal to non-Hispanic clientele,

each of the early stores looked like a fanciful Spanish mission with a curvilinear cornice, a fake tiled roof, and a mock bell tower. The concept of quickly preparing tacos and other simple Mexican dishes took off, and by the time Glen Bell approved a merger with the PepsiCo beverage giant in 1978, his Taco Bell chain had over eight hundred outlets across the nation. Today over six thousand continue to sell the crispy tacos that Glen Bell replicated from those he enjoyed at the Mitla Café on Route 66. The Mitla, a culinary institution in San Bernardino, continues serving traditional Mexican meals in its original location.[46]

Fontana

After drivers turned onto Foothill Boulevard in San Bernardino, they headed westward with little deviation for fifty miles through citrus orchards and vineyards to Pasadena. Much of this farmland was lined with avenues of trees. Daphne and Dallas Sharp made the drive in 1926, and he poetically penned that "by the Foothill Boulevard we drifted from San Bernardino through a dreamland—shade of eucalyptus, shade of pepper trees, shade of tropic palms across our way." Every five or six miles travelers passed through or skirted the edges of towns with one thousand to three thousand residents. In later years these areas grew to become suburban hubs for residential developments that eventually gobbled up almost every acre of farmland. The little communities included Rialto, Fontana, Cucamonga (now Rancho Cucamonga), Upland, Claremont, La Verne, San Dimas, Glendora, Azusa, Monrovia, and Arcadia. When Evelyn Tucker made the trip west in August 1938, she observed, "As we drove further into the valley, there seemed to be little towns scattered along the highway, a mile or so apart." The blatant self-promotion of signs identifying these places annoyed Los Angeles–bound Hoffman Birney, who in 1930 complained about "Chamber-of-Commerce advertising signs of a host of small towns, each sign interesting only for new superlatives and a candid striving to out-ballyhoo the press agent of the neighboring community." One of these towns was Fontana, initially surrounded by citrus orchards, vineyards, and poultry farms. During the 1940s Henry J. Kaiser erected a huge plant here to supply steel to World War II industries, transforming the rural community into an industrial center that nowadays serves as a center for trucking based enterprises.[47]

BONO'S HOBBY NOBBY MARKET (BONO'S ITALIAN MARKET, BONO'S RESTAURANT AND DELI, BONO'S ITALIAN RESTAURANT)

Near-ideal conditions for raising grapes under irrigation attracted many Italians to Southern California, including Frances and James Bono and James's father, Sicilian-born Joseph Bono. Already familiar with viticulture, they came to Fontana in the 1920s to raise grapes commercially. The Bonos themselves tended the vines and then brought in extra labor to pick the crops. After loading the harvest into railway boxcars, one or two family members typically accompanied the grapes to market to handle the eventual sale, usually in Chicago. Even though the extended clan provided most of the labor, the family still found it hard to make a living raising grapes that sold to wholesale buyers for only about seven dollars a ton in the 1930s.[48]

Taking her cues from other farmer neighbors, Frances Bono launched an open-air roadside stand she called Bono's Hobby

Nobby Market at 15395 Foothill Boulevard in July 1936, where she sold fresh produce and freshly squeezed orange juice for ten cents a glass. "Back then, it was pretty hard," she told Route 66 food historian Marian Clark. Her children would come to her and ask for nickels to buy school lunches, but Frances frequently did not have them to spare. Her stand initially offered juice, oranges, lemons, and grapes for both eating and wine making. Father-in-law Joseph Bono made weekly trips to a wholesale grocer in Los Angeles who handled imported foods, and he brought back extra Italian specialties like spices and pasta to sell at the stand. These additions prompted Frances to rename the venture Bono's Italian Market. Then they started making their own table wine, sold to buyers who brought in their own jugs. Next they began grinding and curing homemade Italian sausage. An influx of Italian American workers to the Kaiser steel plant at Fontana increased demand for ethnic foods, and Frances began baking breads and cakes. In 1943 the Bonos expanded the rudimentary produce stand into an enclosed food market that could exclude the elements and provide better after-hours security. Mechanical coolers refrigerated specialty cheeses and meats. Then, in 1957, Frances began offering simple hot meals, like a "heaping platter full" of spaghetti with sauce for forty-nine cents. Again the name changed to Bono's Restaurant and Deli. More elaborate family-style evening meals that required reservations followed until her death at age eighty-three in 1994. Her son Joseph Anthony "Joe" Bono, by this time a lawyer working for the San Bernardino County district attorney, closed the operation after her passing. It subsequently operated intermittently until 2013, when structural movers shifted the entire building back as part of street widening. In 2019 a lessee reopened the long-popular eatery as Bono's Italian Restaurant.[49]

GIANT ORANGE

At one time scores of fresh orange juice stands dotted California roadsides. Fruit that prematurely dropped from trees in commercial orchards sold cheaply, while it cost little to put up an open-air kiosk. A highway or a busy arterial street was all that was needed for a person with limited resources to go into business. Individuals began almost all the initial juice stands, yet a handful of entrepreneurs erected multiple outlets in order to profit from economies of scale in purchasing bulk oranges and in buying simple squeezing implements. Among these entrepreneurs was Frank E. Pohl of Richmond, California, whose Giant Orange Company had sixteen outlets in the 1930s, each spherically shaped and painted orange to simulate the appearance of a mammoth fruit. Flagstaff, Arizona, native Lorraine Bellwood Hunt remembered California trips with family members in their 1935 Studebaker. Once they reached the Golden State, "We stopped at a roadside stand that was round in shape with a little window. It was painted bright orange, just like a real orange!" Journalist Bob O'Sullivan reported that stopping at an "All-You-Can-Drink-10-Cents orange juice stand" was a tradition in his family's 1930s road trips from Denver to Los Angeles, relating, "My mother bought orange juice for my sister and me." In time the proliferation of fast-food eateries and convenience stores serving iced carbonated beverages diminished the appeal of orange juice, while post–World War II inflation raised the sales price at most

stands from a dime a glass to forty cents. State legislation in the 1970s governing variances to permit commercial activity on land zoned for agriculture further impeded juice stand operators, and most of the roadside kiosks disappeared during the decade. A handful of the "giant orange" shaped stands have been preserved, including a seven-foot-tall example relocated to Bono's Italian Market in the 1990s. Preserved but not in use, it may be viewed on the south side of the old Mother Road adjacent to the landmark eatery at 15395 Foothill Boulevard in Fontana.[50]

Rancho Cucamonga
SYCAMORE INN

Standing in a grove of sycamore trees fed by natural springs at the base of the Red Hill eminence, the present Sycamore Inn is the fourth hostelry to serve travelers in this location. As early as 1848 Billy Rubottom constructed a simple stop for stagecoaches being driven to and from Los Angeles. Two successors likewise served food and drink in horse-drawn days at the grove, which became popular for local gatherings. During the early twentieth century, several local businessmen saw increasing numbers of people moving into the citrus- and grape-raising country between San Bernardino and Pasadena and chose the Sycamore Grove, already on the National Old Trails Road, as an ideal setting for creating a European-style country inn. They formed the Sycamore Park Corporation, purchased five acres encompassing the best of the shady area at the foot of Red Hill, and broke ground in December 1920 for a recreational Sycamore Inn venue that the following year offered a restaurant, overnight accommodations, tennis courts, a dance pavilion, and a feature they called the "hot water plunge." John Klusman, the treasurer for the company, became the initial manager, making the Sycamore Inn a popular destination for music, food, and festive gatherings. During Prohibition from 1920 to 1933, its location twenty-five miles away from the county seat in San Bernardino enabled the managers to purvey illicit alcoholic drinks far from the prying eyes of sheriff's deputies. Owners of the Sycamore Inn expanded its facilities, notably in 1939 and 1954, but the two-story main building at 8318 Foothill Boulevard in Rancho Cucamonga retains its historic character with dark paneling, a giant mirror behind the bar, and deep, cushioned booths and chairs. It remains a mecca for diners who favor traditional steak and potatoes.[51]

Duarte

SPORTSMAN'S TAVERN

The visual paradise of orchards and vineyards continued as old-time drivers made their way westward from San Bernardino. Along the way, almost like pearls on a necklace, charming communities offered food, fuel, and respite. The stops that some travelers considered were in Upland, Claremont, La Verne, San Dimas, Glendora, Azusa, and, after just twenty miles, Duarte. Eateries along the way vied for motorists' appetites as they gradually made their way toward the metropolis.

Among the choices in Duarte was the Sportsman's Tavern, a long-standing woman-owned business enterprise in Duarte. In spring 1932 Ohio-born Ethel May Maskey drove her aunt on a visit to relatives in Southern California. They took Highway 66 past a four-acre orange grove for sale east of Monrovia in the then-unincorporated community of Duarte. Having enjoyed wild game in France as a Red Cross worker during the

First World War, Ethel aspired to run her own restaurant specializing in the sorts of exotic fowl she had developed a taste for in Europe. She purchased the tract at 1452 East Huntington Drive and erected the first building as the brasserie itself. Behind it she constructed pens and coops for raising exotic birds as well as ponds for propagating frogs and terrapins. Fresh trout regularly came from the Azusa Angling Club. From the outset the Sportsman's was an upper-tier restaurant offering carefully prepared fresh foods served in a quiet setting with white tablecloths. Diners could always rely on finding chicken, steak, and ocean fish choices, but the Sportsman built its reputation on reservations-only wild-game dinners. Sharon Thoreau, food editor for the Automobile Club of Southern California's *Westways* magazine, reported in November 1935, "At this season you may dine on pheasant, quail, Guinea fowl, wild duck, wild turkey or freshly caught brook trout." She then suggested when diners telephoned in advance, "You might mention what you yearn for—be it young pigeon, venison, or diamond-back terrapin. If it is seasonable and possible to procure[,] you may have it cooked to order to suit your taste."[52]

One Monday in 1937, two sisters, Adeline E. "Patsy" Baker and Lillian Marie "Lallie" Wadsworth, who already had a decade of experience as partners in Southern California food service, walked into the four-year-old Sportsman's Tavern. They liked what they saw in Ethel Maskey's dining room and kitchens, and within twenty minutes the pair placed a deposit to purchase the entire establishment. The two sisters ran the restaurant jointly until Adeline's death in 1949, when Lillian's daughter and son-in-law joined her in managing the Sportsman's for another thirty years. In

1978 they sold the longtime culinary landmark, by that time surrounded by other commercial enterprises, to Anna Marie and Louis C. Petrie, who for another half dozen years operated the eatery as the Way It Was Restaurant. Disappointingly, today the site is occupied by a financial institution and its adjacent parking lot.[53]

Arcadia

VAN DE KAMP'S COFFEE SHOP (DENNY'S COFFEE SHOP)

In 1915 Theodore J. Van de Kamp, a new arrival to California from Wisconsin, had begun wholesale production and sale of potato chips. When his brother, Lawrence L. Frank, asked to invest two hundred dollars in the venture, Theodore suggested that he start retailing the product. This began a decades-long family venture. The brothers erected street-side outlets in prefabricated wooden miniature Dutch windmills fitted with serving windows. They cleverly staffed them with pretty girls wearing blue and white costumes. Quickly the enterprise transitioned to marketing baked goods, becoming known as Van de Kamp Holland Dutch Bakers. The family expanded operations to encompass sales counters inside grocery stores and drive-in-style coffee shops offering quick-service meals and oven-fresh cakes, pies, and breads. One of these restaurants opened on the Mother Road in Pasadena as early as 1935. By the Second World War, Van de Kamp outlets could be found scattered up the West Coast from California to Washington. The trademark remained the Dutch windmill and personnel dressed in blue and white.[54]

In 1967 Van de Kamp Bakeries secured the strategic northeast corner of Huntington Drive (Route 66) and Santa Anita Boulevard in Arcadia. The location was just six miles west of Duarte. The grocery store that had occupied the space since 1950 was removed, and construction began on a roughly circular sixteen-sided Van de Kamp's Coffee Shop. Big plate-glass windows afforded generous views of the adjacent auto-filled street intersection. Surmounting everything was a two-story simulated Dutch windmill with four rotating, illuminated blades. The company began seeking employees for the Arcadia restaurant in June 1967, and Sandra Harris became one of the early waitresses. "It was really busy. Lots of traffic passed," she fondly remembered. Fortunes for the company eventually waned, and the bakery and restaurant divisions split in 1979. Then, a decade later, Denny's Coffee Shops acquired the Arcadia location, and has operated it ever since. In 1999 the company threatened to remove the iconic Van de Kamp Dutch windmill from the roof in Arcadia, but local preservationists and Route 66 enthusiasts protested in person, carrying "Save the windmill" placards. The restaurant chain not only relented but also repaired the windmill, installed new lights, and returned its blades to rotating in 2019. The eatery at 7 East Huntington Drive remains popular among heritage tourists.[55]

Pasadena

MOTHER GOOSE PANTRY

Half a dozen miles beyond Arcadia drivers came to Pasadena, by the 1920s and 1930s a substantial suburb of Los Angeles. Incorporated in 1886, it developed as a well-to-do residential community. Because steam railways enabled people comfortably to cross the country at will, many wealthy families from the northeastern states built or purchased second homes in Pasadena, where they could exchange cold and icy winters for the warmth of California sun. There they could enjoy the Tournament of Roses Parade, begun in 1890, and the Rose Bowl football game, started in 1902. With just 9,117 people in 1900, the local population exploded to 45,354 by 1920 and 81,864 by 1940. When Guy K. Austin drove into the city in late October 1934, "An eighty-foot boulevard led us through Pasadena" while "Stately royal palms lined the shopping thoroughfares." The city never competed with Los Angeles and Hollywood for entertainment, but a 1955 tourism magazine touted, "What it lacks in night life and revelry, Pasadena makes up in eating places." There were so many places to eat that some local restaurateurs vied with each other in coming up with the wackiest visual appeal, as did J. W. Beasley and George M. Wiley in creating the Mother Goose Pantry.[56]

These two California businessmen envisioned an entire chain of fairy tale–themed cafés, each one housed inside a gigantic, two-story high-top shoe. The dining room occupied the larger downstairs area, its linoleum floor serving as an oversized insole, while the kitchen functioned upstairs in the ankle area. Beasley, Wiley, and other investors

The Mother Goose Pantry shortly after J. W. Beasley and George Wiley constructed the café on Colorado Boulevard in Pasadena, California, in 1927. Author's collection.

incorporated Mother Goose, Inc., in November 1926. Then, in the spring and summer of 1927 at 1949–59 East Colorado Boulevard in Pasadena, they fabricated their first giant shoe, using a wood frame, poultry netting wire, and stucco more commonly employed in erecting more prosaic buildings. (This was the same construction method used four years later in creating the similarly fanciful Iceberg Café in Albuquerque.) A parking area occupied the space adjacent to the shoe, while in back two long, narrow buildings with multiple rounded openings housed an arcade of specialty grocers called the Mother Goose Market. Opening on September 1, 1927, the Pantry advertised ice cream, toasted sandwiches, "Texas tamales," and frozen orange juice as the house specialties. Because there was such limited headroom inside the shoe, the managers hired only diminutive waitresses who stood no taller than five feet two and who weighed no more than 112 pounds. In the meantime the grocery outlet attracted business by telling customers that there would be "great fun for the kiddies while mother and dad shop," adding, "Park close to Mother Goose's big shoe."[57] Although the dreams of multiple Mother Goose Pantries failed to materialize, the prototype survived the 1929 stock market crash and served meals at least into 1936. The owners then offered the property for lease, with several more short-term eateries coming and going until 1945. Then the unique structure began housing first the Tiny Tot's Shoe toy store, followed in 1949 by the Big Shoe Toyland, which lasted until the Christmas season of 1952. The giant shoe disappeared, and by 1953 a motorcycle shop operated at the site, where today visitors find a Taco Bell drive-in restaurant.[58]

South Pasadena
RAYMOND PHARMACY (FAIR OAKS PHARMACY)

The original alignment of Highway 66 turned south on Fair Oaks Avenue from Colorado Boulevard on the east side of the Pasadena central business district. From there it proceeded across the separate municipality of South Pasadena and then angled southwestward on Huntington Drive and Broadway Avenue to terminate where it met U.S. Highway 101 on Seventh Street in downtown Los Angeles. (In 1936 the highway was rerouted and extended to Santa Monica.) For nearly a decade, Fair Oaks Avenue carried cross-country motorists directly past one of the notable soda fountains in Southern California.

In 1909 Thomas Edward Barrett opened the Raymond Pharmacy in a commercial storefront at 1520 Mission Street, just around the corner from Fair Oaks Avenue in South Pasadena. A year later he sold the enterprise to another druggist, William A. Sloane, who had come to California from New York. For a decade the latter ran the pharmacy, at least as early as 1913 using a soda fountain described as having "12 syrups, 2 creams, [and] 3 draught arms." He very obviously realized that food service combined profitably with purveying medications. In the meantime Gertrude Ozmun, a locally known real estate investor, acquired the corner lot at Mission and Fair Oaks just east of the drugstore. In 1913 she hired an architect, razed the existing corner structure, and, in summer 1914, erected a new brick commercial building as investment property. Sometime during these months, Ozmun and Sloane agreed that once she had completed construction, he would shift his Raymond Pharmacy into this prime

Chocolate Ice Cream Soda, FAIR OAKS
PHARMACY, SOUTH PASADENA, CALIFORNIA

The Fair Oaks Pharmacy returned to its Edwardian splendor in the 1980s, maintaining its long-standing reputation for making some of the best ice cream treats along old Route 66. It has served fountain specialties at least since 1913, and many heritage tourists including the author choose to celebrate completion of their trips along the Mother Road with its ice cream sodas.

sixteen-ounce chocolate ice cream soda
1 scoop firmly frozen chocolate ice cream
3 ounces sweet chocolate syrup
10 to 12 ounces carbonated water (club soda or seltzer water)
2 to 3 scoops firmly frozen vanilla ice cream

Place one scoop of hard-frozen chocolate ice cream in a sixteen-ounce soda glass. Add 3 ounces of chocolate syrup and, with a long-handled utensil, cut and stir the two together until the ice cream becomes soft and mushy. (Staff at the pharmacy often accomplish this by using a dull butcher knife.) Fill to within 1 ½ inches of the top of the glass with bubbly unflavored soda water. Top with two or three heaping scoops of vanilla ice cream.

Original recipe in the author's manuscript notes from observing staff prepare chocolate ice cream sodas at Fair Oaks Pharmacy, South Pasadena, California, on July 23, 2017, in author's collection.

corner location at 1526 Mission Street. This he did the next year, making 1915 the date that later owners would designate as marking the drugstore's founding.[59]

The preparation of sandwiches and ice cream specialties formed an integral part of the new Raymond Pharmacy business plan. Although ownership and management of the sideline soda fountain changed over time, it regularly served both locals and motorists stopping off along Highway 66. In 1950 the drugstore became the Fair Oaks Pharmacy, connecting its name with that of the major arterial street through the heart of South Pasadena. Not long thereafter Harry C. and wife Gen Libby assumed operation of the lunch counter, which they advertised as the Fair Oaks Pharmacy Coffee Shop. In 1961 drugstore owners Harry Cherniack and Beryle Kremer remodeled the entire building interior, adding air conditioning. They lowered ceilings, laid new linoleum on the floors, and replaced most of the interior furnishings. The fountain services continued under the supervision of David MacDonald as the Skewer & Skillet Coffee Shop, by 1968 becoming the Fair Oaks Fountain Lunch.[60] In the late 1980s, pharmacy owners Michael and Meredith Miller decided to restore the vintage atmosphere customers formerly enjoyed at the Fair Oaks, and they purchased interior fixtures and furniture from a closed historic drugstore in Joplin, Missouri, a town also on Route 66. In 1991 the Millers completed a full interior renovation of the facility, with customers today still relishing many of the same foods that preceding generations likewise enjoyed inside the same space. The author especially enjoys its ice cream sodas.[61]

It happens that this mecca for ice cream lovers, along with other nearby businesses, was for years off-limits to nonwhites. South Pasadena was the last sundown town (communities where African Americans and members of other stigmatized ethnic groups were prohibited from staying overnight) that Highway 66 traversed from Chicago to Los Angeles. In South Pasadena, municipal ordinances required that, on purchasing any property, the buyers had to sign restrictive covenants included in deeds stating that they would prevent any nonwhites from living on the property. The discriminatory statutes persisted until civil rights legislation of the mid-1960s. For decades most local residents made it clear that, unless people from the outside were white, they would be considered unwanted.[62]

Los Angeles
CASA LA GOLONDRINA

Out-of-town visitors longed for entertaining experiences in semitropical Los Angeles. Movies like *Zorro*, set in California's Spanish colonial and Mexican past, led many travelers who had time and money to visit some of the celebrated old mission churches. Others went no farther than Los Angeles itself. The original Hispanic core settlement of 1781 around which the city grew was located only a couple of blocks east of the original Route 66 alignment into downtown, making it easy for guests to visit the historic plaza, the Church of Our Lady Queen of the Angels, and the nearby preserved and enhanced Olvera shopping street, which ran for a block north of the square. If the buildings were not genuinely old, during a major 1928–30 renovation, they were made to look vintage and Hispanic. Concurrent with the conversion of Olvera Street from a neglected urban slum into a fashionable open-air pedestrian market, it became the home to one of the best-known Mexican restaurants in the city.[63]

As a young woman in her twenties, Consuelo Castillo de Bonzo opened her first eating place, La Mision Café, at 148 North Spring Street on the immediate north side of downtown in 1924. It happened that the building stood where a new Los Angeles city hall would be built, so she shifted a block south to a former tobacconist's shop at 132 South Spring. As events turned out, this site became the location for the steps that eventually would lead into to the new public edifice, so she again needed a different location. Simultaneously a public-spirited preservationist, Christine Sterling, was spearheading efforts in 1928–30 to adapt the nearly forgotten Olvera Street into a tourist attraction. She made arrangements with de Bonzo to open a Mexican restaurant inside the 1850s Pelanconi House, reputedly the oldest brick structure in the city. The young entrepreneur found financial backers, organized La Golondrina, Incorporated (named from a popular Mexican song about swallows returning to their birthplace), and, on April 19, 1930, opened Casa la Golondrina. The high-class eating place featured Mexican cuisine served in a lower-level wine cellar, in an upper-level dining room, and in an open-air patio. In 1940 California magazine editor and food critic Phil Townsend Hanna strongly recommended Consuelo's enterprise to out-of-town guests, calling "La Golondrina . . . perhaps the city's most heavily patronized Mexican-Spanish restaurant," featuring "tacos, chiles rellenos, Arroz con Pollo and other native delicacies." With the meals came music and entertainment: "Mexican troubadours entertain luncheon guests from noon to 2 P.M., and dinner guests from 6–8 P.M. Thereafter the musicians go upstairs to the fiesta room, where there is dancing and a lively Mexican floor-show until 2 A.M." It is easy to understand the restaurant's popularity with tourists. Casa la Golondrina has maintained this appeal over the decades, and currently is in the hands of its founder's granddaughter, remaining a destination for those seeking a taste of Old California.[64]

CLIFTON'S CAFETERIAS

As motorists made their way down Broadway Avenue toward the original 1926–36 end of Route 66 at U.S. Highway 101 on Seventh Street, in the very last block of the Mother Road at number 648, they came to Clifton's Brookdale Cafeteria. This establishment was a monument both to good eating and to the Golden Rule. Clifford Clinton, scion of a family of San Francisco restaurateurs, sought his own fortune by moving to Los Angeles in 1931. He and wife Nelda leased a building 618 Olive Street, where a venerable Boos Brothers' Cafeteria was failing, and there opened his own buffet only two blocks off the Mother Road. Their first self-service restaurant made money, so four years later in 1935 the couple opened a second cafeteria right on Highway 66 at 648 Broadway Avenue.

Clifford Clinton spent part of his boyhood in China, where his father was a missionary, and there he saw grinding poverty up close. From the outset he and Nelda followed the principle of turning away no person who was hungry regardless of ability to pay. An information sheet they distributed in the 1930s explained, "Our cashier will cheerfully accept whatever you wish to pay—or you may dine free." The flyer then further emphasized, "Our cashiers will not act snippy—and will graciously and unquestionably receive what you feel you wish to pay."

In 1939 the Clintons redecorated their Broadway Avenue eatery, hiring Hollywood set builders to recreate the forest environment of the Brookdale Lodge in the Santa Cruz Mountains. Crews hollowed out entire redwood trees to encase vertical pillars in the dining room, while the designer from the Club Trocadero created an interior waterfall with giant boulders. Customers flocked in, so much that business suffered two blocks away at the earlier Olive Street location. Subsequently Clifford Clinton's imagination went wild in creating in that restaurant a simulated South Seas paradise. Crews covered the front of the four-story building with trees and plants on either side of a full-height flowing waterfall. Inside the Pacific Seas Cafeteria, guests found more tropical flora, murals, and twenty-foot steel and neon lilies, hibiscus,

and palm trees. In both cafeterias, customers had access to public bulletin boards where they could leave messages; a vintage Los Angeles guidebook noted, "There are always notices about people driving, east, west, north and south, and advertising for passengers to go along." Perhaps because of the spectrum of social classes they served, Clifton's Cafeterias always seemed to attract members of the literati. Author Ray Bradbury was a regular attendee of the restaurant's mealtime meetings of the Los Angeles Science Fiction Society and chose the Brookdale branch as the venue for his eighty-ninth birthday celebration. Novelist Charles Bukowski in *Ham on Rye* wrote, "Clifton's Cafeteria was nice. If you didn't have much money, they let you pay what you could." The Pacific Seas Cafeteria on Olive Street closed in 1960 when the Clinton family lost its lease, but the Brookdale on Broadway remained in business

Customers enjoying a musical performance while dining at the foot of the Aloha Stage in Clifton's Pacific Seas Cafeteria in downtown Los Angeles during the 1940s. Author's collection.

until 2011. Then a new owner completely renovated the historic eatery, reopening it in September 2015 with a spectacular recreation of Clifford Clinton's 1939 redwood forest interior. It is no accident that today's neon lighting on the front spells out the words "living history."[65]

RED POST CAFÉ (RED POST COFFEE SHOP, FORMOSA CAFÉ)

During the 1920s worn-out streetcars were sold as surplus property when replaced and generally were cheap to buy. A former boxer named Jimmy Bernstein purchased one in 1925 and moved it to 7180 Santa Monica Boulevard on the southeast corner with North Formosa Avenue in the Hollywood district of Los Angeles. This location was directly across the street from the Warner Brothers motion picture studio, so it was a busy neighborhood. With the addition of a grill, an icebox, and reconfigured seating, the eatery became an almost instant success known at the time as the Red Post Café, and sometimes as the Red Post Coffee Shop. Over the years new kitchen and seating areas were added, but the old trolley car remained a dining room. Because the location was adjacent to one movie studio and close to three others, customers packed it during lunchtime. One midcentury reviewer described it at midday as "jammed with actors in costume—some famous and some who would like to be." Needless to say, it became an autograph hunter's paradise. In 1945 Lem Quon, who grew up in a family that ran other Los Angeles restaurants and who cooked in the military during World War II, returned home to join Bernstein as a partner, later quipping, "I ran the kitchen and he ran the front." It was about this time that the restaurant name changed to become Formosa Café, and its street number adjusted to 7156 Santa Monica Boulevard. All through the years, it served both Chinese and American fare. On Bernstein's death in 1976, Quon became the sole owner, later passing the business to a son and grandson. In the late 1980s, Warner Brothers acquired the real estate encompassing the Formosa and in 1991 threatened to raze the building and replace it with a five-story parking garage. Preservationists intervened, and then, in 2017, the 1933 Group, a hospitality firm with a track record in safeguarding historic resources, signed a long-term lease for the restaurant. It then undertook a tasteful restoration of the Formosa Café, including its streetcar dining room, and returned it to serving food and drink.[66]

West Hollywood
BARNEY'S BEANERY

John Elwyn "Barney" Anthony was in his twenties when, in 1920, he opened a male-only café and student gathering place called Barney's Beanery at 2231 Telegraph Avenue, outside the Sather Gate into the University of California, Berkeley campus. He was fresh out of World War I service as a navy cook. The retreat became known as an anything-goes hangout, though national Prohibition narrowed his customers' drinking options. Locals knew it as "where college long hairs are wont to gather." Military hero William F. Dean remembered that, as a poor college student, he and his friends were unable to get tickets to the 1921 Rose Bowl football game, so "We waited around for news of the outcome in Barney's Beanery." Owner John Anthony's name frequently showed up in the local press because of his generous support for youth athletic teams. He was comfortably situated, but after seven years he answered the beckoning call of potential trade in metropolitan Los Angeles.[67]

John and wife Catherine "Kate" Anthony opened a new Barney's Beanery in 1927 in a repurposed wooden bungalow at 8447 Santa Monica Boulevard. The thoroughfare would not become designated as U.S. Highway 66 until 1936, but in 1927 it already carried substantial auto traffic from Los Angeles to the beaches at Santa Monica. When looking at the urban setting today, it is hard to imagine its appearance when the venture opened for business in rural country surrounded by cultivated fields of poinsettia plants. The couple ran their eatery, serving both women and men twenty-four hours a day, and it quickly gained a reputation for attracting motion picture and entertainment personalities. Hollywood columnist Jimmie Fidler reported, for example, "After all the swankeries are closed, you'll find the big stars spooning onion soup at Barney's." Food writer Phil Townsend Hanna seconded the observation by saying the combined restaurant and bar never closed and was "popular from 2 A.M. until dawn with entertainers, musicians, writers and yes, even chefs, employed in Hollywood night spots." The passage of time brought changes in clientele, with the beanery becoming an insider's hangout for rock-and-roll artists in the 1960s. Singer Janis Joplin, for example, was a regular and downed two vodka and orange juice screwdriver cocktails in her favorite booth before heading to the Landmark Hotel, where later on the evening of October 4, 1970, she died from a drug overdose. Now sharing the block with other businesses, Barney's Beanery remains open daily into the wee hours of the morning after almost a century.[68]

Beverly Hills
BROWN DERBY

According to the stories, three good friends, film producer Herbert K. "Herb" Somborn, movie theater owner Sid Graumann, and screenwriter Wilson Mizner, sat around the dinner table at the Ambassador Hotel in Los Angeles one evening in 1925. Their conversation made its way to the subject of the city needing a restaurant where Hollywood types could gather comfortably. Mizner offhandedly stated that if the food and service were really good, "people would probably come to eat it out of a hat." Herb Somborn took the remark as a challenge, and the next year built and opened a bowler-hat-shaped eatery at 3427 Wilshire Boulevard, across from the Ambassador. He called it the Hat and later the Brown Derby. Herb hired a Montana restaurateur, Robert Howard "Bob" Cobb, to be his general manager and could not have made a better choice. For the next half century, the latter made the eating place a dining destination for the movers and shakers of Hollywood filmdom. As such, quite naturally, it attracted fans who wanted to see the stars. The latter group included tourists who had motored to California over Route 66.

The original 1926 Brown Derby, the only one actually shaped like an oversized hat, grew so busy that Somborn moved it half a block to 3377 Wilshire Boulevard a decade later to gain more space on its corner with South Alexandria Avenue. The location allowed the addition of outdoor dining. Business was so good that he created a second Brown Derby restaurant at the corner of Hollywood and Vine, 1628 North Vine Street, opening it on Valentine's Day 1929. Its nearness to Hollywood motion picture studios attracted filmmakers and actors. Out-of-town visitors enjoyed its hundreds of framed caricature drawings of Tinseltown notables. Beverly Hills had become a popular home for movie stars, so in 1931 Somborn established a third Brown Derby there at 9537 Wilshire Boulevard and Rodeo Drive. Over the years this branch consistently generated revenue as Rodeo Drive increasingly became the exclusive shopping street for metropolitan Los Angeles. Herb Somborn passed away in early 1934, but Bob Cobb continued management of the restaurants, paid off his old boss's debts, and opened a fourth eatery at 4500 Los Feliz Boulevard in 1941 in the well-heeled Los Felix neighborhood near Griffith Park. Of all the Brown Derbies, the one most convenient to Highway 66 motorists was the one in Beverly Hills, only two and a half blocks, or four minutes, away from the Mother Road by car.

Though many customers gravitated to the Brown Derbies in hopes of seeing their favorite screen stars, most diners came because of Robert Cobb's interpretation of classic American fare. Some of its dishes came into existence by accident. Late one night the restaurateur was putting together a salad for himself using chopped-up leftover

Col. Verena Zeller (*left*) with friend Frances Sully enjoying a meal at the Hollywood Brown Derby. After wartime and peacetime duty in the U.S. Army, Zeller became the first chief of the Air Force Nurse Corps in 1951, about the time that this official army photograph was made. Author's collection.

Cobb Salad, BROWN DERBY, BEVERLY HILLS, CALIFORNIA

The story goes that the well-known Cobb Salad came to existence one evening when several of Robert Cobb's friends dropped into his kitchen at the Brown Derby as he was putting together a salad dinner for himself using cut-up leftover chicken and chopped cold ingredients. The restaurateur enlarged the dish for all five guests, and when they subsequently returned as paying customers, they asked for the "Cobb Salad." With the Brown Derby's distinctive French dressing, the salad spread not only up Route 66 but also around the world.

Cobb Salad for four to six

For salad:
½ head iceberg lettuce
½ bunch watercress
1 small bunch chicory
½ head romaine lettuce
2 medium-sized tomatoes (peeled)
2 breasts of broiled chicken
6 strips crisp bacon
1 avocado
3 hard-boiled eggs (shelled and diced)
2 tablespoons chives (chopped)
½ cup Roquefort cheese (finely grated)

For dressing:
1 cup water
1 cup red wine vinegar
1 teaspoon sugar
juice from ½ lemon
2 ½ tablespoons salt
1 tablespoon black pepper
1 tablespoon Worcestershire sauce
1 teaspoon dry English mustard
1 garlic clove (finely chopped)
1 cup olive oil
3 cups salad oil

For salad, finely cut washed and drained iceberg lettuce, watercress, chicory, and romaine lettuce and arrange in serving bowl. Peel tomatoes, remove seeds, and finely dice, arranging in a strip across the greens. Dice cooked chicken breasts and arrange over the greens. Chop the bacon into small pieces and sprinkle over the top. Peel avocado, cut into small pieces, and arrange them just inside the edge of the serving bowl. As decoration, sprinkle chopped eggs, chives, and grated Roquefort or similar blue cheese.

For the dressing, combine all the ingredients except the oils and mix well. Add olive and salad oils and mix well again, chilling before serving. The author's kitchen tests showed this dressing to be somewhat salty for some present-day tastes. Makes about 1 ½ quarts, so store excess refrigerated for future salads. Just before serving, shake and carefully pour 1 cup of Brown Derby French dressing over the whole salad.

Original recipe from *The Brown Derby Cookbook* (Garden City, N.Y.: Doubleday, 1949), 22, 68–69.

chicken and other cold ingredients close at hand when four of his friends barged in after a movie preview. They invited themselves to join him in a salad supper, and, when they subsequently returned, the same friends asked for the "Cobb Salad." This dish, made with chopped chicken breast, iceberg and romaine lettuce, watercress, chicory, tomatoes, avocados, crumbled bacon, boiled egg, and Roquefort cheese, served with Robert's own homemade French dressing, spread around the world in popularity. Few people today think of the Cobb Salad as Route 66 road food, but that it was. Because he desired always to offer freshly baked apple pie, the indefatigable restaurateur spent a reputed ten thousand dollars in experiments over the years to find out how best to premake and freeze apple pies, so that all four of his restaurants could serve the same perfectly baked fruit dessert around the clock. Finally Cobb developed a preparation using Jonathan or Winesap apples, sugar, cinnamon, nutmeg, and butter in his own flaky pastry, which he then dubbed the Ten Thousand-Dollar Apple Pie. With such dishes as these, it was no wonder that people kept coming back to the Brown Derby. The food was just that good. The four restaurants operated into the 1970s and 1980s, by which time tastes in dining were changing and, one by one, they closed. The domelike upper structure of the original 1926 eatery survives today on the roof level of the two-story shopping center at 3427 Wilshire Boulevard that took its place.[69]

Santa Monica

Angelenos' beloved ocean beach at Santa Monica was among the most accessible because of easy streetcar and auto access from metropolitan Los Angeles. In 1936 the California Highway Department rerouted U.S. Highway 66 to bypass downtown congestion and follow Sunset Boulevard and then Santa Monica Boulevard through Hollywood and Beverly Hills to Santa Monica. Once there, the official route turned south on Lincoln Boulevard for three blocks to meet U.S. Highway 101 Alternate at Olympic Boulevard, half a dozen streets shy of the Pacific shore. Most tourists continued southwest on Santa Monica Boulevard to the traditional end of the Mother Road on the cliffs above the Pacific at Ocean Avenue. There, a 1952 a bronze plate set in concrete marked its western terminus as the end of the Will Rogers Highway.[70]

BELLE-VUE FRENCH RESTAURANT

Anne and James John Wallace chose this unofficial end of the Mother Road on Santa Monica Boulevard at Ocean Avenue as the place to establish their Belle-Vue French Restaurant in 1937. It was just a year after Highway 66 extended to Santa Monica, and, despite the Great Depression, the couple's good food, careful management, and strategic location overlooking the sea made the upscale French-style bistro a long-term success. The fact that James was born in Rennes, France, to American parents gave the Belle-Vue a seeming authenticity that diners appreciated.

The Belle-Vue earned a distinguished reputation for its French culinary interpretations of poultry, beef, and pork, but it was seafood that that brought customers back time after time. For years the Wallaces and, after 1963, their successors, Stella and Eddie Pilloni, had a Friday-only luncheon featuring bouillabaisse, a French deep-sea stew made with shrimp, lobster, clams, scallops, and whitefish, all seasoned with wine and served with rice, garlic roux, and toasted bread. The big bowls came to the tables with bibs to protect the diners from spotting their clothes while cracking open the lobster claws. One loyal customer during the late 1960s claimed to have consumed 250 bowls and was looking forward to more. After Eddie Pilloni's death in 1976, his son and daughter with Stella's assistance continued the Belle-Vue until 1993, when it closed. Since then other restaurants have occupied the distinctive two-story pale-pink-colored building.[71]

BENNETT'S SEA FOOD GROTTO

Many cross-country motorists who made their way down the Mother Road wanted to go as far west as they could. This meant that they turned south on Ocean Avenue two blocks to the ramp that let them drive their vehicles onto the Santa Monica Municipal Pier. There, from 1930 to 1955, Iowa-born "Captain" Orie Judson Bennett ran his notable Sea Food Grotto. As customers, motorists could even park their cars on the wharf for free at the time. Located on the first small rectangular extension on the north side of the pier, Bennett's grotto offered seafood specialties including swordfish, abalone, halibut, and rock bass, all initially served in natural shell "platters," as well as chilled shrimp and crab cocktails. California writer Sharon Thoreau reported in 1941, "The fish you eat at noon was caught that morning and what you eat for dinner was pulled out of the ocean in the afternoon." In the days prior to air conditioning, the cross-ventilation of sea breezes through Bennett's during the warm months, combined with spectacular views of the beach, ocean, and Santa Monica Mountains, made it an ideal location for festive meals, like celebrating the completion of

a trip along Highway 66. Some locals knew the eatery as an "open-air casino," where they enjoyed bridge parties and low-profile gaming at the seaside.

American food critic Duncan Hines discovered Orie J. Bennett sometime in the late 1930s, and Hines became a year-after-year repeat diner at the grotto. He later wrote for the *Saturday Evening Post* magazine that "in a little wharf-side eating place at Santa Monica . . . I had a hankering for something different in sea food." There "Captain Bennett broiled barracuda as I had never eaten fish before." The meal so impressed the writer that from 1945 to 1957 he included Bennett's personal instructions for frying ocean whitefish in his annual cookbooks of recipes from Duncan Hines–approved restaurants. After its founder's death in 1955, Bennett's Sea Food Grotto continued serving meals until its place at 301 Santa Monica Pier was taken by the Boathouse Restaurant in 1966. It has remained possible to eat fish in the same location on the pier, where at the time of this writing the Bubba Gump Shrimp Company Restaurant offered seafood with views matching those that Orie Bennett's diners enjoyed during the heyday of the Mother Road.[72]

Turning Around and Driving Back

Despite the general twentieth-century trend of people relocating to California, the majority of those who drove Highway 66 westbound ended up driving back east. This meant that they would again feel similar fatigue, discomfort, and uncertainty from road travel. Some of them already had had food experiences that they might want to repeat. African American motorists would likely be packing away staples to carry along,

Fried Fish, BENNETT'S SEA FOOD GROTTO,
SANTA MONICA, CALIFORNIA

Food critic Duncan Hines was very particular about seafood, and he really enjoyed fish prepared by Orie J. Bennett at his popular Sea Food Grotto on the Santa Monica Pier. He liked Bennett's preparation so much, in fact, that he asked him to share its details. The restaurateur did so with the disclaimer, "It is so simple that I can hardly call it a secret."

Fish for two or three
1 pound fresh white fish fillets
sprinkle of salt on one side of each fillet
sprinkle of black pepper on one side of each fillet
1 five-ounce can evaporated milk
1 egg (beaten)
½ cup soda (saltine) cracker crumbs (finely crushed)
2 cups cooking oil (to fill an iron skillet ½ inch deep)

Instructions in Orie J. Bennett's own words from 1944:

"I first dip the fish in a pan of milk (canned preferably, as it adheres to the fish better) then into a pan with eggs beaten up; season, then into a pan of fine cracker meal, which seals the fish up, keeping the oil out and the flavor in.

"I use an iron skillet with about one-half inch of Wesson Oil or other good oil. Have it hot when the fish is put in so it will form a crust. Then turn over, and you will have a nice golden brown piece of fish. Time the cooking according to the thickness of the fish."

Original recipe from O. J. Bennett, Santa Monica, California, to Duncan Hines, Bowling Green, Kentucky, November 6, 1944, typewritten letter, box 2, folder "1943 7th and 8th Printing," Duncan Hines Collection, Division of Rare and Manuscript Collections, Cornell University Library, Ithaca, New York.

A mother with three children from Tulsa, Oklahoma, stopped on a California roadside to eat while looking for agricultural work in November 1936. The mother declared, "We're making it all right here, all but for the schooling, 'cause that boy of mine, he wants to go to the University." Photograph by Dorthea Lange, Farm Security Administration, call number LC-USF34-009871-E [P&P] Lot 344, courtesy of Library of Congress, Washington, D.C.

for they did not know where they might or might not find welcome. As travelers made preparations for the eastbound return, some might recall the Monte Cristo sandwich at the Wagon Wheel in Needles. Others might consider the options of having freshly prepared Chicken in the Rough in its Oklahoma City birthplace or in one of the scores of privately owned roadside cafés that purchased franchises from its Sooner State inventors, Rubye and Beverly Osborne. Youthful travelers might long to revisit the frozen delights proffered by teenaged staff working the service windows at Ted Drewes Frozen Custard in Saint Louis. Farther ahead beckoned the multiple chili parlors of Springfield, Illinois, and their local competitors ladling savory Welsh rarebit sauce on top of ham steak and french fries in open-faced horseshoe sandwiches. Those wayfarers bound for the Windy City might very well have in mind returning for wurst and kraut at the Berghoff or maybe navy beans at the Bowl & Bottle at the very head of the highway. Whatever their thoughts, the bounty of America lay ahead of these Route 66 travelers, who would complete their sojourns and meal stops with their very own new memories.

NOTES

INTRODUCTION

1. Michael Wallis, in *Route 66: The Mother Road* (New York: St. Martin's Press, 1990), provides by far the most popular and widely read account of Route 66 history.

2. [James Agee], "The Great American Roadside," *Fortune* 10, no. 3 (September 1934): 53–63, 172, 174, 177; Catherine Gudis, *Buyways: Billboards, Automobiles, and the American Landscape* (New York: Routledge, 2004), 54–47, 150–60.

3. I. B. Holley Jr., *The Highway Revolution, 1895–1925: How the United States Got out of the Mud* (Durham, N.C.: Carolina Academic Press, 2008), 3–163.

4. C. H. Skip Curtis, ed., *Birthplace of Route 66: Springfield, Mo.* (Springfield, Mo.: Curtis Enterprises, 2001), 11–19; Susan Croce Kelly, *Father of Route 66: The Story of Cy Avery* (Norman: University of Oklahoma Press, 2014), 127–211.

5. Arthur Krim, *Route 66: Iconography of the American Highway* (Santa Fe, N.Mex.: Center for American Places, 2005), 73–173.

6. Peter B. Dedek, *Hip to the Trip: A Cultural History of Route 66* (Albuquerque: University of New Mexico Press, 2007), 63–128; Nick Gerlich, "America's Highway," *Route Magazine*, February–March 2021, pp. 22–30; Maria R. Traska, "Why Route 66? The Indelible Appeal of America's Classic Road Trip for Foreign and Domestic Travelers," pt. 1, *Illinois Geographer* 56, no. 1 (Spring 2014): 4–17; and pt. 2, *Illinois Geographer* 56, no. 2 (Fall 2014): 4–22.

7. T. Lindsay Baker, "Old Route 66 in a Model A: Driving the Full Length, Both Directions, between Chicago and Los Angeles," *Restorer* (Model A Ford Club of America, La Habra, Calif.) 63, no. 1 (May–June 2018): 14–19. For a helpful annotated bibliography of published first-person accounts of cross-country motoring in the United States, see Carey S. Bliss, *Autos across America: A Bibliography of Transcontinental Automobile Travel, 1903–1940*, 2nd ed., Contributions to Bibliography 7 (Austin, Tex.: Jenkins and Reese, 1982).

8. Charles S. Johnson, *Patterns of Negro Segregation* (New York: Harper and Brothers, 1943), 64–65; Gretchen Sorin, *Driving while Black: African American Travel and the Road to Civil Rights* (New York: Liveright Publishing, 2020), 62–63, 87–90, 93–94.

9. Robert Dirks, *Come and Get It! McDonaldization and the Disappearance of Local Food from a Central Illinois Community* (Bloomington, Ill.: McLean County Historical Society, 2011), 147–62, 170–85; Nancy Lamb, "Ozark Fruit Stands," *Ozarks Mountaineer* (Branson, Mo.) 25, no. 6 (July 1977): 23; Amy W. Osgood, "Lunching by the Roadside," *Good Housekeeping* 87, no. 2 (August 1923): 74–75; "Our Gastronomic Highways," *House and Garden* 44, no. 6 (December 1923): 50; "Wayside Eating-Stands," *Literary Digest* 103, no. 4 (October 26, 1929): 37; Terry P. Wilson, *The Cart That Changed the World: The Career of Sylvan N. Goldman* (Norman: Oklahoma Heritage Association by the University of Oklahoma Press, 1978), 77–92.

10. Dirks, *Come and Get It!*, 64–65, 101–3, 105–8, 188–95, 232–37; Andrew Hurley, "From Hash House to Family Restaurant: The Transformation of the Diner and Post–World War II Consumer Culture," *Journal of American History* 83, no. 4 (March 1977): 1282–1308; John A. Jakle and Keith A. Sculle, *Fast Food: Roadside Restaurants in the Automobile Age* (Baltimore: Johns Hopkins University Press, 1999), 25–32, 45–49, 54–62; Johnson, *Patterns of Negro Segregation*, 59–63, 71; Clare Patterson Jr., "Patterson's Route 66 Milk Run," in *Route 66 Remembered*, ed. Michael Karl Witzel (Osceola, Wisc.: MBI Publishing, 1996), 179; Jack D. Rittenhouse, *A Guide Book to Highway 66* (Los Angeles: privately printed, 1946; repr., Albuquerque:

University of New Mexico Press, 1989), 31; Keith A. Sculle, "Diners," *Historic Illinois* (Springfield, Ill.) 5, no. 6 (April 1983): 2–4; Jan Whitaker, "Quick Lunch," *Gastronomica* 4, no. 1 (Winter 2004): 69–73.

11. Dirks, *Come and Get It!*, 62–71, 107–8; Dave Hoekstra, *The Supper Club Book: A Celebration of a Midwest Tradition* (Chicago: Chicago Review Press, 2013), vii–xvi; Dave Hoekstra, "Supper Clubs and Roadhouses," in *The Chicago Food Encyclopedia* (Urbana, Ill.: University of Illinois Press, 2017), ed. Carlo Mighton Haddix, Bruce Kraig, and Colleen Taylor, 248–49; John A. Jakle and Keith A. Sculle, *America's Main Street Hotels: Transiency and Community in the Early Auto Age* (Knoxville: University of Tennessee Press, 2009), 119–36; Jakle and Sculle, *Fast Food*, 23–25, 49–50, 64; Johnson, *Patterns of Negro Segregation*, 59–63; Alice Foote MacDougall, *The Secret of Successful Restaurants* (New York: Harper and Brothers, 1929), 30–38; "The Origin of the Cafeteria—the Institution," *Journal of Home Economics* 17, no. 7 (July 1925): 390–93; Thyra Samter Winslow, "When You Order DINNER What Goes on behind the Scenes," *Illustrated World* 25, no. 3 (May 1916): 337–41.

12. Eleanor Alexander, "'Woman's Place Is in the Tea Room': White Middle-Class American Women as Entrepreneurs and Customers," *Journal of American Culture* 32, no. 2 (June 2009), 126–36; Cynthia A. Brandimarte, "'To Make the Whole World Homelike': Gender, Space, and America's Tea Room Movement," *Winterthur Portfolio* 30, no. 1 (Spring1995): 1–19; Dirks, *Come and Get It!*, 103–5; Jan Whitaker, *Tea at the Blue Lantern Inn: A Social History of the Tea Room Craze in America* (New York: St. Martin's Press, 2002), 1–184.

13. Dirks, *Come and Get It!*, 89–94; Hoekstra, "Supper Clubs and Roadhouses," 248–49; Walter C. Reckless, *Vice in Chicago*, University of Chicago Sociological Series (Chicago: University of Chicago Press, 1933), 120–36; Mary Ross, "Blowing on the Flame of Youth," *Survey* 63, no. 5 (December 1, 1929): 292–93, 308.

14. Dirks, *Come and Get It!*, 122–47, 156–58, 163–88, 201–23, 239–74; Harvey Levenstein, *Paradox of Plenty: A Social History of Eating in Modern America* (New York: Oxford University Press, 1993), 9–255; Elaine N. McIntosh, *American Food Habits in Historical Perspective* (Westport, Conn.: Praeger, 1995), 97–138; Waverley Root and Richard de Rochemont, *Eating in America: A History* (Hopewell, N.J.: Ecco, 1981): 276–457.

15. Dave Cathey, *Classic Restaurants of Oklahoma City* (Charleston, S.C.: American Palate, a Division of the History Press, 2016), 21–26, 67–70; Gail Driskill, "Beverly Osborne: From Shoeshine Boy to Millionaire," *Sunday Oklahoman* (Oklahoma City), March 18, 1979, the Oklahomans supplement, pp. 1, 4–7; Jakle and Sculle, *Fast Food*, 217–18.

16. Robert P. Cronin, *Selling Steakburgers: The Growth of a Corporate Culture* (Carmel: Guild Press of Indiana, 2000), 1–108.

17. John F. Love, *McDonald's: Behind the Arches* (New York: Bantam Books, 1986), 9–86.

18. Jakle and Sculle, *Fast Food*, 186–89, 195–96; Caroline H. Otis, *The Cone with the Curl on Top: The Dairy Queen Story* (Minneapolis: International Dairy Queen, 1990), 10–37.

19. Gustavo Arellano, *Taco USA: How Mexican Food Conquered America* (New York: Scribner, 2012), 60–66, 68–70; Debra Lee Baldwin, *Taco Titan: The Glen Bell Story* (Arlington, Tex.: Summit Publishing Group, 1999), 49–115.

CHAPTER 1. ILLINOIS

1. David G. Clark, "Driving US 66 in Chicagoland: Jackson Boulevard," pt. 2, *Route 66 Federation News* 10, no. 1 (Winter 2004): 19–25; David G. Clark, *Exploring Route 66 in Chicagoland: Journeys through History on the Mother Road in Cook County, Illinois*, 2nd ed. (Chicago: Windy City Road Warrior.com, 2008), 1–100; David C. Clark, "Where the Highway Began," *Route 66 Magazine* 14, no. 2 (Spring 2007): 32–35.

2. Christopher P. Adams, "Prosperity Menu: Fred Harvey Comes to Michigan Avenue," *Chicagoan* 13, no. 11 (June 1933): 35, 77; T. Lindsay Baker, "Fred Harvey Serves Route 66 in Chicago," *Route 66 Magazine* 24, no. 2 (Spring 2017): 30–32; David G. Clark, "An Affair of Character," *Route 66 Federation News* 11, no. 3 (Summer 2005): 24–32, 34; Stephen Fried, *Appetite for America: Fred Harvey and the Business of Civilizing the Wild West—One Meal at a Time* (New York: Bantam Books, 2010), 33–40; Fred Harvey Company,

[Kansas City, Mo.], "Announcing the Opening of the New Fred Harvey Bowl & Bottle Restaurant and Cocktail Room" (advertisement), *Chicago Daily Tribune*, May 22, 1951, sec. 1, p. 7; Fred Harvey Company, [Kansas City, Mo.], *Fred Harvey Bowl & Bottle Restaurant and Cocktail Room* ([Kansas City, Mo.]: Fred Harvey, 1951), printed menu, and Fred Harvey Company, *Soda Fountain Luncheonette* ([Kansas City, Mo.]: Fred Harvey, 1951), printed menu, both in Fred Harvey Company Collection, MS 208, series 3, box 2, folder 28, Special Collections and Archives, Cline Library, Northern Arizona University, Flagstaff (hereafter Fred Harvey Company Collection); "Newly Decorated Cafeteria," *Hospitality* (Fred Harvey Company, Chicago) 9, no. 2 (April 1959): 3; "A New Restaurant Marks Our Seventy-fifth Year," *Hospitality*, January 1951, p. [3]; "Presenting the Bowl & Bottle," *Hospitality*, Summer 1951, pp. [6]–7. Maillard's, a Chicago branch of a long-standing New York restaurant, occupied the ground level in the Straus Building from the mid-1920s to 1933. John Drury, *Dining in Chicago* (New York: John Day, 1931), 155–56; "Harvey, of Santa Fe Fame, Gets Maillard Restaurant," *Chicago Sunday Tribune*, February 26, 1933, pt. 1, p. 15.

3. Norma Brewton, "Visit the Gallios Brothers 3 Outstanding Restaurants at Wabash and Adams," *Chicago Tribune*, August 13, 1980, sec. 3, p. 10; Brown, "Wedding Ring—Lost" (advertisement), *Chicago Daily Tribune*, January 3, 1936, p. 29; Rudolph Busch, "Jimmy Gallios, 81: Owner Made Miller's Pub a South Loop Institution," *Chicago Tribune*, November 19, 2002, sec. 2, p. 8; Calvert [Distilling Company, Baltimore, Md.], "Calvert Chartered Dispensers" (advertisement), *Chicago Daily Tribune*, November 2, 1934, p. 23; David G. Clark, "Driving Route 66 in Chicagoland: Adams Street," pt. 3, *Route 66 Federation News* 10, no. 2 (Spring 2004): 10–12; Will Leonard, "On the Town: Elegance Lives on in Empire Room," *Chicago Tribune*, September 3, 1972, sec. 11, p. 11; John McCarron, "Parking Garage on Tap in the Loop Might Put a Popular Tavern on Ice," *Chicago Tribune*, July 10, 1987, sec. 2, p. 3; Sally McCormick, "Where the Celebrities Meet to Eat! Miller's Pub[,] 23 East Adams Street," *Chicago Tribune*, June 7, 1978, sec. 5, p. 4; Miller's Café, "Cashier" (advertisement), *Chicago Daily Tribune*, December 1, 1955, pt. 4, p. 21; Miller's Pub, "Now! New and Larger Miller's Pub" (advertisement), *Chicago Tribune*, July 2, 1963, sec. 1, p. 19; Miller's Pub, "Miller's Pub[,] 'Chicago's Friendliest Café'" (advertisement), *Chicago Tribune*, May 24, 1965, sec. 1, p. 6; James Quick Auctioneers, Naperville, Ill., "Building to Be Demolished-Complete Contents of 2 Restaurants to Be Auctioned" (advertisement), *Chicago Tribune*, July 23, 1989, sec. 7, p. 18; Beth Wicks, "Miller's Wabash Inn: The World's Finest Buffet at the Corner of Adams and Wabash Is Now Twice as Good!," *Chicago Tribune*, January 21, 1981, sec. 3, p. 8; Bob Wiedrich, "'Night People' Show Him the Human Side of a City," *Chicago Tribune*, May 23, 1976, sec. 1, p. 5. Though no corroboration has been found, folklore persists that Nat King Cole first sang Bobby Troup's "Route 66" song at the old Miller's Tavern in 1946. Frances Epstein, "A Nostalgic Trip to Yesteryear," *Route 66 Magazine* 1, no. 1 (Winter 1993–94): 50–51.

4. Greg Borzo, *Lost Restaurants of Chicago* (Charleston, S.C.: American Palate, 2018), 40, 42–44; "John R. Thompson Leases Jackson Blvd. Building," *Chicago Sunday Tribune*, April 19, 1925, pt. 2, p. 18; [John R.] Thompson [Company], "Here's What You Get: More for Your Money All-Ways" (advertisement), *Chicago Daily Tribune*, March 14, 1939, p. 7; "Thompson's Will Open Eat Shop at Franklin-Adams," *Chicago Sunday Tribune*, April 17, 1927, pt. 3, p. 6; Jan Whitaker, "Early Chains: John R. Thompson," Restaurant-ing through History, http://restaurant-ingthroughhistory.com/2010/06/10/early-chains-john-r-thompson/ (accessed September 15, 2012).

5. Carlyn Berghoff, Jan Berghoff, and Nancy Ross Ryan, *Berghoff Family Cookbook: From Our Table to Yours, Celebrating a Century of Entertaining* (Kansas City, Mo.: Andrews McMeel, 2007): 1–19; Berghoff Restaurant, *State and Adams Street 1898[,] the Berghoff in 1898[,] the Berghoff Today* (Chicago: Berghoff Restaurant, 1966), menu, author's collection; Berghoff Restaurant, *Berghoff[,] Established 1898[,] Dinner* (Chicago: Berghoff, 1955), menu, author's collection; Samantha Bomkamp, "Berghoff Restaurant Sold but Will Stay in the Family," *Chicago Tribune*, May 7, 2016, sec. 1, p. 8; Greg Borzo, *Lost Restaurants*, 64–65; John Drury, *Dining in Chicago* (New York: John Day, 1931): 103 (first quotation); "$500,000 Lease Closed in Loop: Thompson Property at 15 to 23 West Adams Street Secured by H. J. Berghoff," *Chicago Daily*

Tribune, December 25, 1912, p. 18; Leigh Haddix, "Savoring Place: Protecting Chicago's Sense of Place by Preserving Its Legacy Restaurants" (master's thesis, Goucher College, Baltimore, 2018), 73–88; Carol Mighton Haddix, Bruce Kraig, and Colleen Taylor Sen, eds., *The Chicago Food Encyclopedia* (Urbana: University of Illinois Press, 2017): 47–49; Mike Hughlett, "Historic Berghoff to Close," *Chicago Tribune*, December 29, 2005, sec. 1, pp. 1, 12 (second quotation); Blair Kamin, "Preservationists Wary over Future of Berghoff Buildings," *Chicago Tribune*, March 1, 2006, sec. MW2, pp. 1, 7; "Large Leases of the Year," *Chicago Daily Tribune*, January 1, 1898, p. 17; "Men-only Bar Bows to Women," *San Francisco Examiner*, November 21, 1969, p. 9; Joe Morang, "Women Again Invade 'For Men Only' Bar," *Chicago Tribune*, December 19, 1969, sec. 1, p. 1; "Old Time German Restaurant Is Being Enlarged," *Chicago Sunday Tribune*, May 24, 1936, pt. 1, p. 20; "Restaurant's Addition Will Mix Old, New," *Chicago Daily Tribune*, June 19, 1950, pt. 4, p. 6; Mike Royko, "The Battle for Maleness at Berghoff's Bar," *Des Moines (Iowa) Tribune*, December 30, 1969, p. 9.

6. T. Lindsay Baker, "Fred Harvey Serves Route 66," pp. 30–32; "City within a City: Chicago Union Station Marks Its First Quarter Century," *Hospitality*, March 1950, pp. 3–4; David G. Clark, "Architects of Chicago's 66: Daniel Burnham's Successors," *Route 66 Federation News* 14, no. 1 (Winter 2008): 32–33; John Drury, *Dining in Chicago*, pp. 219–20 (first quotation); "Fred Harvey, Caterer, Chicago Union Station," *Hotel Monthly* (Chicago) 33, no. 8 (August 1925): 38–73; Fred Harvey [Company, Kansas City, Mo.], *The Union Station: Chicago* (Kansas City, Mo.: Fred Harvey, [ca. 1925]), unpaged booklet; Duncan Hines, *Adventures in Good Eating* (Chicago: Adventures in Good Eating, 1938), 81; Eugene Koch, "Our Gold Lion Champagne Dinner Receives Raves," *Hospitality* 11, no. 4 (December 1959): 4–5; Katherine Loring: "Have You Heard? Your Temporary Job Can Become a Permanent One," *Chicago Sunday Tribune*, October 25, 1959, pt. 7, p. 7 (second quotation); R. Stephen Senott, "Chicago Architects and the Automobile, 1906–26," in *Roadside America: The Automobile in Design and Culture*, ed. Jan Jennings (Ames: Iowa State University Press, 1990), 161–63; "We Proudly Announce the Opening of One of Fred Harvey's Finest and Most Exciting Rooms: 'The Gold Lion,'" *Hospitality* 9, no. 5 (June–July 1957): 6–7. For a substantial collection of historic menus from the eating places in Chicago Union Station, see Fred Harvey Company Collection, series 3, box 2, folders 38, 39, 41, 42, 43, 44, and 50.

7. Jane Bernard and Polly Brown, *American Route 66: Home on the* Range (Santa Fe: Museum of New Mexico Press, 2003), 25 (fourth quotation); Robert Blau, "A Slice of Life (and of Toast, Too) in the Big, Sort of Cruel City," *Chicago Tribune*, September 18, 1985, sec. 7, p. 30; Phyllis Feuerstein, "'I Want People to Feel Good and Eat Here Again,'" *Chicago Tribune*, January 26, 1992, sec. SM, p. 29; Paul Galloway, "At Lou Mitchell's with Jimmy Carter," *Chicago Tribune*, January 18, 1994, sec. 5, pp. 1–2; Nick Gerlich, "Lou Mitchell's," *Route Magazine*, December–January 2020, pp. 20–25; Bob Goldsborough, "Heleen Thanasouras-Gillman 1952–2015: West Loop Restaurant's Co-owner and Hostess," *Chicago Tribune*, December 1, 2015, sec. 2, p. 6; Ron Grossman, "Lou Mitchell: Philosopher amid the Power Brokers," *Chicago Tribune*, September 13, 1987, sec. 5, p. 3; Leigh Haddix, "Savoring Place," pp. 1–3, 46; Judy Hevrdejs, "Du Jour: Restaurant Service, the State of the Art in Chicago," *Chicago Tribune*, March 10, 1980, sec. 6, pp. 1, 6 (third quotation); Judy Hevrdejs, "Where Good Meals Are Good Deals," *Chicago Tribune*, September 11, 1981, sec. 4, pp. 1, 4; Nick Kindelspurger, "Love Dinner Coffee? You Probably Just Like Weak Brew," *Chicago Tribune*, September 19, 2018, sec. 6, p. 2; Iris Krasnow, "America's Brave New Meal: Brunch," *Chicago Tribune*, June 30, 1980, sec. 4, pp. 1 (second quotation), 11; Lou Mitchell's Restaurant, "Presented the Golden Cup" (advertisement), *Chicago Daily News*, May 15, 1959, pt. 1, p. 10; Nomination to the National Register of Historic Places for Lou Mitchell's, Chicago, March 28, 2006, this and subsequent nominations in Office of the Keeper, National Register of Historic Places, National Park Service, Washington, D.C.; Carol Rasmussen, "Julia Childs Samples a Chicago-style Breakfast among Her Fans," *Chicago Tribune*, March 25, 1982, sec. 7, p. 2; Mimi Sheraton, "The Great American Breakfast," *Condé Nast Traveler* (New York) 24, no. 4 (April 1989): 110 (first quotation); Diane Struzzi, "Restaurateur Louis Mitchell, 90," *Chicago Tribune*, March 30, 1999, sec. 2, p. 7.

8. Judith Case, "Society to Take Many Guests to Opening at Arlington Park," *Chicago Daily Tribune*, June 20, 1933, pp. 17, 19; Art Institute [of Chicago], "Salad Maker—Experienced, for Small Cafeteria" (advertisement), *Chicago Daily Tribune*, September 20, 1921, p. 25; John Drury, *Dining in Chicago*, 154–55 (first quotation); Madeline Holland, "She Puts Imagination into Her Cooking," *Chicago Daily Tribune*, June 5, 1959, pt. 3, p. 1; Eleanor Jewett, "Art and Artists," *Chicago Sunday Tribune*, April 24, 1927, pt. 8, p. 4; Kay Loring, "Listing of Favorite Eating Places Brought up to Date," *Chicago Tribune*, August 6, 1967, sec. 5, p. 12; Ruth McKay, "White Collar Girl: She Builds Cafeteria Patronage from 300 to 3,000 in 8 years," *Chicago Daily Tribune*, February 24, 1950, pt. 2, p. 12; Lucy Key Miller, "Front Views and Profiles," *Chicago Daily Tribune*, May 4, 1953, pt. 3, p. 9; Evangeline Mistaras, "Chicago Restaurants and Night Life," *ALA Bulletin* (American Library Association) 57, no. 6 (June 1963): 565–70; "Mrs. Ludlow, Art Institute Café Head, Dies," *Chicago Tribune*, July 28, 1964, sec. 2, p. 6; Elizabeth Rannells, "Have You Heard?" *Chicago Sunday Tribune*, July 10, 1955, pt. 7, p. 4 (second quotation); William Rice, "Cheap Eats: Where to Eat for Less Than $13 an Entrée," *Chicago Tribune*, July 17, 2002, sec. 7, p. 3.

9. Clark, *Exploring Route 66*, pp. 12–21; John Kobler, *Capone: The Life and World of Al Capone* (New York: G. P. Putnam's Sons, 1971), 111–16, 151–57; James W. Loewen, *Sundown Towns: A Hidden Dimension of American Racism* (New York: New Press, 2005), 10–12, 203, 256, 399.

10. "In Circuit Court: Enjoin Cicero Drive-In," *Berwyn (Ill.) Life and the Berwyn Beacon*, July 17, 1955, p. 1; "Jeanette M. DeLegge, Henry's Waitress," *Berwyn (Ill.) Cicero Life*, June 7, 1992, p. 24; Bruce Kraig and Patty Carroll, *Man Bites Dog: Hot Dog Culture in America* (Lanham, Md.: Taylor Made Publishing, 2014), 132–33; Paul Lawrisuk quoted in Ted Giovanazzi and Larry Scinto, eds., "Tales from the Road," *66 News!* (Route 66 Association of Illinois), Summer 2003, p. 12; Tom Lohr, "A Real Wiener of a Road Trip," *Route 66 Magazine* 25, no. 1 (Winter 2017–18): 14–16; "Property Transfers," *Berwyn Cicero Life*, March 12, 2004, p. 32; "Teenaged Beer, Gin Drinker Fined $105," *Berwyn Life and the Berwyn Beacon*, March 24, 1965, p. 3.

11. "Building Gutted: Lightning Hits Town Structure," *Berwyn Life and the Berwyn Beacon*, August 29, 1965, p. 2; "Building Permits Total: $97,677," *Berwyn (Ill.) Life*, October 16, 1970, p. 3; Bunyon's, "Drive in Help Male or Female" (advertisement), *Berwyn Life*, May 29, 1966, p. 14; Bunyon's, "Bunyon's[,] 6150 Ogden Ave.[,] Cicero[,] 652–4616" (advertisement), *Berwyn Cicero Life*, March 22, 1996, p. 9; Bunyon's, "Serving Customers for 25 Years" (advertisement), *Berwyn Cicero Life*, June 7, 1991, p. 11; Haddix, Kraig, and Sen, *Chicago Food Encyclopedia*, 195; Bruce Kraig, *Hot Dog: A Global History* (London: Reaktion Books, 2009), 78, 116; Mark R. Madler, "Bunyon's Serves Last Hot Dogs," *Cicero Life* (Berwyn, Ill.), January 29, 2003, p. 3; "Now I Lay Me Down to Sleep," *Berwyn Life*, April 17, 1968, p. 9; Eileen Pech, "Japanese TV Crew Focuses on Route 66 Restaurant Owners," *Berwyn Cicero Life*, December 15, 1993, p. 14; "Property Transfers," *Berwyn Cicero Life*, April 23, 2003, p. 31; John Weiss and Lenore Weiss, *As the Story Goes . . . Trivia—Oddities—Folklore and Ghosts: A Unique Collection of Useless Information That Should Not Be Lost to Time* (Wilmington, Ill.: Historic 66, 2006), 24.

12. "Road News: Bunyon Giant Finds New Home," *Route 66 Magazine* 11, no. 4 (Fall 2004): 44; Ole Rolvaag, "Giants in the Road," *66 News!*, Spring 1997, p. 9; Bill Thomas, "Atlantans 'Own' a Bit of Route 66 History," *Pantagraph* (Bloomington, Ill.), December 28, 2010, sec. D, p. 3; John Weiss, "Bunyon Giant Dedication," *66 News!*, Fall 2004, p. 9; John Weiss, "The Buynon Giant," pt. 3, *66 News!*, Spring 2004, pp. 7–8; John Weiss, "Preservation Report: Happy 50 Years to Tall Paul, the Bunyon Giant!," *66 News!*, Winter 1966, pp. 8–9; John Weiss and Lenore Weiss, "The Bunyon Giant," pt. 1, *66 News!*, Summer 2003, pp. 5–6; John Weiss and Lenore Weiss, "Good-bye Bunyon," *66 News!*, Spring 2003, p. 17; John Weiss and Lenore Weiss, "The Moving of the Bunyon Giant," pt. 2, *66 News!*, Summer 2003, p. 7.

13. David G. Clark, "Driving US 66 in Chicagoland: Ogden Avenue," pt. 5, *Route 66 Federation News* 10, no. 4 (Autumn 2004): 25–27; Clark, *Exploring Route 66*, pp. 12–21; Irving Cutler, *Chicago: Metropolis of the Mid-Continent*, 4th ed. (Carbondale: Southern Illinois University Press, 2006), 96–105; Loewen, *Sundown Towns*, 211, 215, 267, 399; Patricia Stemper, "The Drive-In Restaurant Scene; or, How to Egress Gracefully," *Chicago Tribune*, July 23, 1970, sec. 2AN, p. 5.

14. "Clark's Custard a Sweet Memory," *Berwyn Cicero Life*, June 10, 1992, p. 19; Clark's Frozen Custard, "Grand Opening of Berwyn's Newest Refreshment Center" (advertisement), *Cicero Life*, May 17, 1940, p. 2; "Genevieve Clark, Owned Custard Shop," *Life* (Berwyn, Ill.), August 4, 2000, p. 5.

15. "Along the Street: 'Big Boy' Makes Debut Tomorrow at Frejlach's," *Berwyn Life and the Berwyn Beacon*, November 14, 1954, p. 5 (first quotation); "Along the Street: Mac's Drive-In Grand Opening Will Be Tomorrow," *Berwyn Life*, January 12, 1962, p. 3; David G. Clark, "The Reality of Change," *Route 66 Magazine* 18, no. 4 (Fall 2011): 14–16; Vince Iaccino III, "Twist of Fate: Frejlachs Remember Ice Cream, Kroc and Sanders," *Berwyn Cicero Life*, September 29, 1991, p. 8; "Issue Five Building Permits in Berwyn," *Berwyn Life*, February 13, 1972, p. 3; "James F. Frejlach, Ice Cream Firm Owner," *Berwyn Cicero Life*, November 24, 1996), p. 22; Ray Kroc and Robert Anderson, *Grinding It Out: The Making of McDonald's* (New York: St. Martin's Paperbacks, 1987), 79 (second quotation); Mac's Drive-In, "Big Mac Says" (advertisement), *Berwyn Life and Berwyn Beacon*, May 22, 1963, p. 16; Mac's Drive-In, "Mac's Grand Opening" (advertisement), *Berwyn Life and the Berwyn Beacon*, June 9, 1954, p. 6; "Started with 2nd Hand Freezer: From Jumbo Cone, Frejlach Built Jumbo Food Business," *Berwyn Life and the Berwyn Beacon*, May 7, 1961, p. 7; "Still Expanding: Frejlach Ice Cream Co. Began in Depression Era," *Berwyn Life and the Berwyn Beacon*, June 27, 1958, Berwyn Golden Jubilee Edition, sec. J, p. 47.

16. Rose Marie Benedetti and Virginia C. Bulat, *Portage, Pioneers, and Pubs: A History of Lyons, Illinois* (Chicago: Angel Guardian Orphanage Press, 1963), 83; "By-pass Cuts Time on U.S. Highway 66," *Belvidere (Ill.) Daily Republican*, January 6, 1940, p. 7; Clark, *Exploring Route 66*, 75–76; Carl Johnson, "Rediscovering It—Hidden Route 66: Early Route 66 through Lyons, Illinois," *66 News!*, Spring 2003, pp. 20–21; William Presecky and Ray Gibson, "Lyons Tries to Dim Honky-tonk Image," *Chicago Tribune*, April 22, 1984, sec. 3, pp. 1–2.

17. "Amusement Guide," *Berwyn Life*, July 21, 1950, p. 7; "Brite Spots," *The Berwyn Life*, October 27, 1949, p. 10; "Houdek[,] Joseph C. Houdek," *Chicago Tribune*, June 5, 1983, sec. 3, p. 15; "Houdek," *Chicago Daily Tribune*, October 18, 1935, p. 37; "Houdek's Hotel Opens Fall Season Next Week," *Berwyn Life*, October 13, 1933, p. 1; Houdek's Restaurant, "Houdek's Restaurant" (advertisement), *Cicero Life*, April 6, 1955, p. 8; Houdek [Tourist Hotel], "Barbecue Man—Charcoal" (advertisement), *Chicago Daily Tribune*, May 24, 1939, p. 29; "Joseph Houdek," *Berwyn Life and the Berwyn Beacon*, December 11, 1956, p. 13; Lyons Tourist Hotel Restaurant, "Announcing That the Lyons Tourist Hotel Restaurant" (advertisement), *Suburban Leader* (Cicero, Ill.), May 16, 1929, p. 5; John Weiss, "The Whoopee Ride," *66 News!*, Winter 2006–7, p. 8.

18. Clark, *Exploring Route 66*, 77–78; Thomas Arthur Repp, *Route 66: The Empires of Amusement* (Lynwood, Wash.: Mock Turtle Press, 1999), 6 (quotation); Jim Ross and Shellee Graham, *Secret Route 66: A Guide to the Weird, Wonderful, and Obscure* (St. Louis: Reedy Press, 2017), 128–29; Weiss and Weiss, *As the Story Goes*, 5; John Weiss and Lenore Weiss, "The Whoopee Ride," *Route 66 Federation News* 13, no. 3 (Summer 2007): 15–17. At least two other whoopee auto coasters operated in the Chicago area about the same time, one in the village of Franklin Park and another other about four miles west of Winnetka. Whoopee Auto Coaster, [Winnetka, Ill.], "Let's All Ride the Whoopee Auto Coaster" (advertisement), *Palatine (Ill.) Enterprise*, June 7, 1929, p. 6; "Whoopee Ride River Rd. Open," *DuPage County Register* (Bensenville, Ill.), August 8, 1929, p. 8.

19. "Arrest Bar Co-owner; Charge Gaming Devices," *Chicago Tribune*, December 3, 1964, sec. 16, p. 16; David G. Clark, "Of Romance and Finance, or Marriage and McCook," *Route 66 Federation News* 12, no. 2 (Spring 2006): 10, 12–14, 16–18; Clark, "Reality of Change," 14; "53 Bet Stamps Are Issued in Four Counties," *Chicago Tribune*, August 3, 1965, sec. 1, p. 16; "Gambling Tax Stamp Sales Show Increase," *Chicago Tribune*, December 1, 1964, sec. 2, p. 6; "Hall of Famer Snuffy's Now a Steak 'n Egger," *66 News!*, Summer 2012, p. 16; Lyn Rains, "Grill Becomes Scene for Formal Wedding," *Berwyn Life*, February 28, 1996, p. 10; "Sheriff's Raid Disperses 400 at Bingo Game," *Chicago Tribune*, May 16, 1963, sec. 1, p. 2; "2016 Hall of Fame Inductees," *66 News!*, Summer 2017, pp. 14–15.

20. "Chicken Basket Hatched from Gas Station: Route 66 Landmark Celebrates Fifty Years in Business," *Route 66 Magazine* 3, no. 3 (Summer 1996): 40–41; "Delbert F. Rhea," *Chicago Tribune*, October 19, 1992, sec. 2 Northwest, p. 7; Al Doyle, "Dell Rhea Chicken Basket," *Route 66 Magazine* 11, no. 3 (Summer 2004): 32–33; Vicky Gehrt, "History to Crow About," *Chicago Tribune*, November 7, 1993, sec. 18 Tempo Southwest, p. 10; "Hall of Fame Welcomes New Members," *66 News!*, Summer 1993, p. 7; "Erwin F. Kolarik," *Chicago Tribune*, May 27, 1993, sec. 2 Northwest, p. 10; Nomination to the National Register of Historic Places for Dell Rhea's Chicken Basket, March 28, 2006; Kevin Pang, "Get Your Fried-chicken Fix on Route 66," *Chicago Tribune*, September 8, 2011, sec. 5, pp. 1, 5; Patrick Rhea, telephone interview by T. Lindsay Baker, Willowbrook, Ill., to Wauconda, Ill., June 19, 2012, manuscript notes in author's collection; Patrick Rhea [Willowbrook, Ill.], email messages to T. Lindsay Baker [Rio Vista, Tex.], June 26, 2012, and June 28, 2012, author's collection; "Robbers Beat Tavern Owner; Flee with $3,500," *Chicago Daily Tribune*, August 16, 1950, p. 1; "Tire Purchaser Is Convicted of Ration Breach," *Chicago Daily Tribune*, April 27, 1943, p. 20. The current municipality encompassing the Chicken Basket is Willowbrook, which was incorporated from the mostly rural area south of Hinsdale in 1960 and subsequently developed as suburban housing. Rudolph Unger, "Willowbrook Has Come a Long Way in 30 Years," *Chicago Tribune*, October 18, 1990, sec. 2 DuPage, pp. 1, 6.

21. Neil Gale, "Illinois Historic Route 66 Icons: White Fence Farm in Romeoville, Illinois[,] on Route 66," *Route 66 Federation News* 25, no. 3 (Autumn 2019): 20–23; June Provines, "A Line o' Type or Two," *Chicago Daily Tribune*, March 25, 1938, p. 12; S[tuyvesant] Peabody, Chicago, Ill., to Duncan Hines, Bowling Green, Ky., June 12, 1939, typewritten letter, Duncan Hines Collection, box 2, folder P17, Division of Manuscript Collections, Cornell University Library, Ithaca, N.Y.; "S. Peabody Sr. Dies at 58; Head of Coal Empire," *Chicago Daily Tribune*, June 8, 1946, p. 14; "Vocational Society to Meet at White Fence Farm," *Chicago Daily Tribune*, June 6, 1939, p. 15; White Fence Farm, [Romeoville, Ill.], "White Fence Farm Catering to Luncheon Card Parties" (advertisement), *Chicago Sunday Tribune*, May 8, 1949, pt. 3, p. 12SW; "White Fence Farms Restaurant Leased to Ray MacFarland," *Chicago Sunday Tribune*, March 14, 1948, pt. 3, p. C.

22. Denise M. Baran-Unland, "White Fence Farm Celebrates Tradition," *Herald News* (Joliet, Ill.), March 5, 2014, p. 25; Meg McSherry Breslin, "White Fence Farm Owner R. C. Hastert," *Chicago Tribune*, October 24, 1998, sec. 1, p. 25; Harmony House, Aurora, Ill., "Dining at Its Very Best" (advertisement), *Chicago Daily Tribune*, December 6, 1956, pt. 7, p. 11; Hines, *Adventures in Good Eating* (1938), p. 86; Dave Hoekstra, *Ticket to Everywhere: The Best of Detours Travel Column as Seen in the Chicago Sun-Times* (Chicago: Lake Claremont Press, 2000), 273 (first quotation); Lynne Metcalfe Kornecki, "Pickin' the Right Chicken: Coin Flip Set Course of White Fence Farm," *Chicago Tribune*, May 30, 1993, sec. 18, pp. 1 (second quotation), 6; Kay Loring, "Front Views and Profiles," *Chicago Tribune*, October 11, 1963, sec. 2, p. 12; Thomas A. Repp, "Chicken Big," *Route 66 Magazine* 5, no. 4 (Fall 1998): 24–25, 29; Tom Teague, "The Class of 98," *66 News!*, Summer 1998, pp. 12–13; Patricia Trebe, "Doris Mae Hastert[,] 1913–2006[,] Longtime Lemont Restaurant Owner," *Chicago Tribune*, August 16, 2006, sec. 3MW, p. 8; "The Underground Gourmet," *Pantagraph*, June 11, 1983, Preview supplement, p. 23; White Fence Farm, [Romeoville, Ill.], "Now Open the Newly Enlarged, Completely Remodeled White Fence Farm" (advertisement), *Chicago Daily Tribune*, April 25, 1957, pt. 5, p. 1.

23. David G. Clark, "One Bridge Too Far," *Route 66 Magazine* 26, no. 3 (Summer 2019): 34–37; *Illinois: A Descriptive and Historical Guide*, American Guide Series (Chicago: A. C. McClurg, 1939), 342–46; Frank Norris, "Courageous Motorists: African American Pioneers on Route 66," *New Mexico Historical Review* 90, no. 5 (Summer 2015): 311; David Thompkins, "Joliet Kicks," *Route 66 Magazine* 25, no. 1 (Winter 2017–18): 36–38.

24. Dairy Queen, Joliet, Ill., "It's Time Again for Genuine Dairy Queen" (advertisement) *Chicago Sunday Tribune*, April 30, 1950, pt. 3, p. 12; Anne Cooper Funderburg, *Chocolate, Strawberry, and Vanilla: A History of American Ice Cream* (Bowling Green, Ky.: Bowling Green State University Popular Press, 1995), 144–53; John A. Jakle and Keith A. Sculle, *Fast Food: Roadside Restaurants in the Automobile Age* (Baltimore:

Johns Hopkins University Press, 1999), 186–89; City of Joliet, Joliet Historic Preservation Commission, Joliet Register of Historic Places, Local Landmark Application, Original Dairy Queen, typescript, 2010, "Dairy Queen" Vertical File, Joliet Area Historical Museum, Joliet, Ill.; Caroline H. Otis, *The Cone with the Curl on Top: The Dairy Queen Story* (Minneapolis: International Dairy Queen, 1990), 10–29; John Weiss, "The First Dairy Queen," *66 News!*, Winter 2005–6, pp. 9–10.

25. Walter C. Reckless, *Vice in Chicago*, University of Chicago Sociological Series (Chicago: University of Chicago Press, 1933), 120–36; Mary Ross, "Blowing on the Flame of Youth," *Survey* 63, no. 5 (December 1, 1929): 292–93, 308.

26. Ted Giovanazzi and Marilyn Giovanazzi, eds., "Stories from Illinois 66," *66 News!*, Summer 2000, pp. 17–18; George Knoop quoted in Ted Giovanazzi and Marilyn Giovanazzi, eds., "Stories from Illinois 66," *66 News!*, Fall 2000, p. 16.

27. Dari Delite, Wilmington, Ill., "Drive-In—Dari Delite" (advertisement), *Chicago Daily News*, June 2, 1952, pt. 3, p. 16; Amy Frerichs, "The Launching Pad Blasts Off with '50s Influence," *Chicago Tribune*, November 8, 1992, sec. 18 Tempo Southwest, p. 5; "Giant's Creator Dies at Age 87," *Route 66 Pulse* (Richfield Springs, N.Y.) 2, no. 7 (September 2007): 15; Hoekstra, *Ticket to Everywhere*, 257–59; Katy Spratte Joyce, "Reviving a Giant," *Route Magazine*, August–September 2020, pp. 18–24; Bob Okon, "Restoring Restaurant Is a Labor of Love for Couple," *Sunday Herald and Review* (Decatur, Ill.), March 11, 2018, sec. A, p. 4; Rolvaag, "Giants in the Road," 9; Tom Teague, "Route 66 Hall of Fame," *66 News!*, Summer 2000, pp. 12–13; David Tompkins, "Relaunching the Launching Pad," *Route 66 Magazine* 25, no. 4 (Fall 2018): 8–11; "$20,000 Blast in Fireworks Company Shed," *Chicago Daily Tribune*, June 26, 1952, sec. 1, p. 1; Carrie Wolfe, "Giant Gives Wilmington a Landmark," *Star* (Tinley Park, Ill.), January 23, 2003, sec. A, p. 17.

28. Hal Foust, "Bypass around Joliet Open," *Chicago Daily Tribune*, August 12, 1939, p. 12; "Route 66 Showing Modern Highways Benefit to Public," *Lemonter* (Lemont, Ill.), April 11, 1940, p. 1; John Weiss, *Traveling the New, Historic Route 66 of Illinois* (Frankfort, Ill.: A. O. Motivational Programs, 1997), 13–15.

29. "Molly's Ranch Sold," *Gibson Courier and Gibson City Enterprise* (Gibson City, Ill.), December 5, 1940, p. 2; "$100,000 Blaze Routs 50; Save 100 Big Trucks," *Chicago Daily Tribune*, November 10, 1950, sec. 3, p. 16; Repp, *Route 66: The Empires of Amusement*, pp. 10–13; Quinta Scott and Susan Croce Kelly, *Route 66: The Highway and Its People* (Norman: University of Oklahoma Press, 1988), 171–72; Welco Truckers Lodge, Lemont, Ill., "Two Experienced Waitresses in Well Known Restaurant and Truck Stop" (advertisement), *Daily Pantagraph* (Bloomington, Ill.), February 16, 1944, p. 8; Welco Truck Stop, Lemont, Ill., "Restaurant for Lease" (advertisement), *Chicago Tribune*, June 23, 1969, sec. 2, p. 26; Welco Truck Stop, "Welco Truck Stop" (advertisement), *Chicago Tribune*, October 26, 1984, sec. 6, p. 18; Welco's Truck Stop, Lemont, Ill., "Seeking Experienced Waitresses" (advertisement), *Tinley Park (Ill.) Times Herald*, October 30, 1974, p. 21.

30. "Charlie Reid," *Chicago Tribune*, August 1, 1982, sec. 3, p. 15; Mary Daniels, "Hitting the Mother Road," *Chicago Tribune*, September 19, 2004, sec. 15, pp. 1, 8; Marijo Gosselink, "'Montana Charlie's Bird Haven' Most Colorful Spot in Town," *Forest Park (Ill.) Review*, May 5, 1976, p. 15; Montana Charlies Flea Market, Lemont, Ill., "Montana Charlies Flea Market" (advertisement), *Berwyn Life*, May 25, 1973, p. 24; Repp, *Route 66: The Empires of Amusement*, pp. 10–13.

31. "Burglars Load up With Loot," *Streator (Ill.) Daily Times-Press*, December 18, 1958, p. 9; Peggy Gray Chase, Alice Gray Creech, Ruth Gray, and Mary Leona Provance, "The Gray's Station Way," *66 News!*, Spring 1994, pp. 6–9; *Illinois: A Descriptive and Historical Guide*, 588–89; Jack D. Rittenhouse, *A Guide Book to Highway 66* (Los Angeles: privately printed, 1946; repr., Albuquerque: University of New Mexico Press, 1989), 10–11; Shirley Yedlicka Skuban, "Circle Inn," *66 News!*, Summer 1995, p. 10.

32. "Crews Battle Fire at Historic Restaurant," *Herald and Review* (Decatur, Ill.), June 9, 2010, sec. A, p. 7; Hoekstra, *Ticket to Everywhere*, pp. 260–63; Offerman and Associates, Joliet, Ill., "For Sale[,] Riviera Restaurant[,] Gardner, IL" (advertisement), *66 News!*, Fall 1994, p. 5; Russell A. Olsen, *Route 66 Lost and Found: Mother Road Ruins and Relics—The Ultimate Collection* (Minneapolis: Voyageur Press, 2011), 18–19; Ted Giovanazzi and Marilyn Giovanazzi, "Hall of Famer Burt Parkinson on the Riviera," *66 News!*,

February 2001, p. 7; Repp, *Route 66: The Empires of Amusement*, pp. 20–25 (quotation p. 24); "Riviera a Classic Roadhouse," *66 News!*, Summer 1993, p. 8; Riviera, Gardner, Ill., "At the Riviera" (advertisement), *Streator Daily Times-Press*, January 13, 1936, p. 8; "Road News: Gardner[,] IL[,] Roadhouse & Supper Club Closes," *Route 66 Magazine* 16, no. 2 (Spring 2009): 50–51; John Weiss and Lenore Weiss, "Good Bye Riviera—We Sure Will Miss You," *66 News!*, Winter 2008–9, p. 16; John Weiss and Lenore Weiss, "The Riviera Says Goodbye," *Route 66 Federation News* 15, no. 2 (Spring 2009): 7–11.

33. Jeanne Millsap, "On Their Marks: County Filled with Well-known and Not-So-Known Landmarks," *Morris (Ill.) Daily Herald*, February 22, 2014, Hometown sec., p. 9; "Route 66 Preservation Project," *66 News!*, Winter 2000, p. 13; John Weiss, "Preservation Updates," *66 News!*, Fall 2003, pp. 15–16; John Weiss, "Riviera Streetcar Update," *66 News!*, Fall 2001, p. 10; John Weiss, "The 66 Streetcar Diner Restoration," *Route 66 Federation News* 8, no. 1 (Winter 2002): 13–14; John Weiss, "The Traveling Streetcar Diner," *Route 66 Federation News* 7, no. 1 (Winter 2001): 19–20; U.S. Census Bureau, Census of 1940, Population Schedules, Gardner, Grundy County, Ill., Enumeration District 32–15, page 10B, Roll m-t0627–00809, Microcopy T627, National Archives and Records Administration, Washington, D.C.; John Whiteside, "Treasure Lurks behind the Riviera near Gardner!" *66 News!*, Fall 1999, p. [16].

34. Marian Clark, "The Old Log Cabin—Pontiac, Illinois," *Route 66 Federation News* 3, no. 2 (Spring 1997): 15–17; "Four New Members Enter Hall of Fame," *66 News!*, Summer 1996, pp. 7–12; Chester D. Henry, *Route 66, My Home away from Home* (Charleston, S.C.: privately printed, 2014), 30; "Joseph R. Selotti," *Daily Pantagraph*, January 5, 1961, p. 7; Mark Kendall, "Then and Now: This '30s-Era Coffee Shop Still Percolates," *Press-Enterprise* (San Bernardino, Calif.), September 9, 2001, sec. A, pp. 1, 10; "Log Cabin Restaurant Reopens," *Daily Leader* (Pontiac, Ill.), October 11, 1973, p. 5; Russell Olsen, "Then & Now: Log Cabin Inn[,] c. 1939[,] Pontiac, Illinois," *Route 66 Magazine* 22, no. 2 (Spring 2015): 35; Repp, *Route 66: The Empires of Amusement*, pp. 26–29.

35. Marian Clark, "The Old Log Cabin," 16; "Death Takes Operator of Restaurant," *Streator Daily Times-Press*, July 28, 1965, p. 19; Lolita Driver, "It's a New Log Cabin," *Daily Pantagraph*, August 6, 1975, sec. C, p. 1; Charlotte Fleshman, "Pontiac Man Killed during Violent Storm," *Daily Pantagraph*, May 1, 1962, p. 2; M. K. Guetersloh, "Foreign Visitors Tour Route 66," *Pantagraph*, May 30, 1998, sec. A, p. 5; New Log Cabin Restaurant and Lounge, "New Log Cabin" (advertisement), *Daily Leader*, May 2, 1975, p. 9; Tony Parker, "Longtime Pontiac Restaurant for Sale," *Pantagraph*, February 10, 1988, sec. D, p. 2; Tony Parker, "Pontiac Eatery Changes Hands: Restaurant Owners Buying Lincoln Depot," *Pantagraph*, October 30, 1993, sec. C, pp. 1–2; "Paul Johnson Dies—Pontiac Restaurateur," *Daily Pantagraph*, July 28, 1965, p. 8; Tom Teague, *Searching for 66* (Springfield, Ill.: Samizdat House, 1991), 4–6; "Underground Gourmet," *Pantagraph*, November 2, 1985, Preview supplement, p. 21; "Virginia E. Johnson," *Pantagraph*, May 18, 1989, sec. D, p. 5.

36. Robert Dirks, *Come and Get It! McDonaldization and the Disappearance of Local Food from a Central Illinois Community* (Bloomington, Ill.: McLean County Historical Society, 2011), 195; "Elmer E. Wahls," *Daily Pantagraph*, January 18, 1984, sec. D, p. 4; Carolyn Parry, "New Wahls Café Opens Today on Route Four," typescript, [ca. 2000], unpaged, Chenoa Historical Society Museum, Chenoa, Illinois; "Orville Wahls," *Daily Pantagraph*, July 7, 1950, p. 3; "Steve's Café," *Chenoa Historical Society Newsletter* (Chenoa, Ill.) no. 26 (Spring 2005): 3–4; "2015 Hall of Fame Inductees," *66 News!*, Summer 2015, pp. 14–15; "Two Bandits Are Identified," *Streator Daily Times-Press*, May 28, 1934, p. 3; Orville Wahls, Chenoa, Ill., "Premier Pete Says" (advertisement), *Daily Pantagraph*, January 31, 1924, p. 12; Orville F. Wahls, Chenoa, Ill., "Stop at the Wahls' Café" (advertisement), *Sunday Pantagraph* (Bloomington, Ill.), January 28, 1934, p. 5 (quotation); "Zirkle Bros. Café Gains Popularity," *Daily Pantagraph*, April 13, 1938, p. 7.

37. *Chenowan* ([Chenoa, Ill.]: privately printed, 1955), high school yearbook, unpaged front matter, Chenoa Historical Society Museum, Chenoa, Illinois; Terri Ryburn-LaMonte, "Route 66, 1926 to the Present: The Road as Local History" (PhD diss., Illinois State University, 1999), 272; Don Schopp, "Steve's Café on Route 66[,] Interview with Don Schopp[,] Chenoa Historical Society, Inc.," typescript, unpaged, [ca. 2000], Chenoa Historical Society Museum, Chenoa, Illinois; "Steve's Café," 3–4; Fred Young, "Chenoa

Takes County Crown," *Sunday Pantagraph*, January 30, 1955, p. 8 (quotation); [Fred Young], "Young's Yarns," *Daily Pantagraph*, November 20, 1954, p. 6.

38. "Crash Kills Driver," *Pantagraph*, April 23, 1994, sec. A, pp. 1, 4; Dirks, *Come and Get It*, 195–96; Fred Murphy Auction Co., McLean, Illinois, "Public Auction" (advertisement), *Pantagraph*, June 22, 1994, sec. D, p. 7; Brad Genung, "Modern Tourists Still Look for Kicks on Route 66," *Pantagraph*, June 14, 1992, sec. A, p. 3; Brad Genung, "Route 66 Enthusiasts Travel Back in Time on Tour," *Pantagraph*, June 9, 1991, sec. A, p. 4 (second quotation); *Gourmet's Guide to Good Eating: A Valuable and Vital Accessory for Every Motorist and Traveler 1946–47* (New York: Gourmet, the Magazine of Good Living, 1946), 91; "Hoffman Partner in Chenoa Café," *Daily Pantagraph*, December 13, 1957, p. 8; Power Agency, Chenoa, Ill., "Rare Opportunity for a Good Restaurant Man" (advertisement), *Daily Pantagraph*, March 20, 1968, p. 44; "Price Panel Announces 4 Settlements," *Sunday Pantagraph*, June 16, 1946, p. 2; Schopp, "Steve's Café on Route 66," unpaged; "Steve's Café," 3–4 (first quotation); Steve's Café, Chenoa, Ill., "Finest Steaks between Chicago and St. Louis" (advertisement), *Daily Pantagraph*, August 7, 1953, p. 2; Steve's Café, "Fry Cook" (advertisement), *Decatur Daily Review* (Decatur, Ill.), April 19, 1945, p. 20; Steve's Café, "Steve's Café" (advertisement), *Daily Leader*, October 3, 1975, p. 12; "Steve Wilcox," *Daily Pantagraph*, January 29, 1958, p. 8. Highway 66 entered McLean County, Illinois, just before reaching Chenoa. For a guide to historic sites along the roadway across this central Illinois county, see Terri Ryburn-LaMonte, *Route 66: Goin' Somewhere: The Road in McLean County* (Bloomington, Ill.: McLean County Historical Society, 1995).

39. *Illinois: A Descriptive and Historical Guide*, 161–68; Rittenhouse, *Guide Book to Highway 66*, p. 13. For a guide to the Mother Road alignments through Normal and Bloomington, see Carl Johnson, "Hidden 66—Bloomington, IL: Navigating Original U.S. Route 66 Southbound (Despite Bloomington's Maze of One-way Streets)," *Route 66 Federation News* 12, no. 3 (summer 2006): 28–34.

40. Alene's Café, Normal, Ill., "305 Pine St." (advertisement), *Daily Pantagraph*, October 26, 1973, sec. B, p. 7; Col. "Bill" Sweeney Auctioneer, Bloomington, Ill., "Auction Pine Street Café" (advertisement), *Sunday Pantagraph*, August 16, 1970, sec. B, p. 2; Mary Ann Ford, "Roadside Assist: 1920s Route 66 Site Receiving Careful Restoration," *Pantagraph*, August 4, 2011, sec. A, pp. 1, 8; Nancy Gordon, "Make Your Wedding a Day to Remember," *Pantagraph*, June 22, 1994, sec. C, pp. 1–2; Greyhound [Corporation, Cleveland, Ohio], "Change in Agency at Normal" (advertisement), *Daily Pantagraph*, December 2, 1932, p. 15; "Hetzler's Cab Bid Wins Manager's Nod," *Daily Pantagraph*, December 18, 1954, p. 6; "Lunchroom Damaged $2,000 by Blaze," *Daily Pantagraph*, July 20, 1933, p. 12; Lusher's Station and Café, Normal, Ill., "Lusher's Station & Café" (advertisement), *Daily Pantagraph*, September 13, 1963, p. 3; Nomination to the National Register of Historic Places for Sprague's Super Service, March 7, 2008; Pine Street Café, Normal, Ill., "Restaurant Help Needed" (advertisement), *Daily Pantagraph*, August 18, 1967, p. 25; [Joseph E. Ruzic], Bloomington, Ill., "For Lease" (advertisement), *Daily Pantagraph*, June 6, 1941, p. 19; Terri Ryburn, "Sprague's Super Service, a 1930s Building with 'Much Historic Integrity and Significance,'" *66 News!*, Winter 2007–8, pp. 10–11; Terri Ryburn, "The Place at 305 East Pine Street," *Route 66 Magazine* 21, no. 1 (Winter 2013–14), pp. 28–30; Terri Ryburn, "Sprague's Super Service: Saving a Route 66 Icon in Normal, Illinois," *Illinois Geographer* 56, no. 1 (Spring 2014): 31–40; Ryburn-LaMonte, "Route 66," pp. 294–95; Joe Sonderman, "Ryburn Place," *Route 66 Magazine* 26, no. 1 (Winter 2018–19): 8–10; Sprague Service, Normal, Ill., "Bismarck Prince of Beers" (advertisement), *Daily Pantagraph*, July 7, 1934, p. 2; Triangle Café and Service, Normal, Ill., "Triangle Café and Service" (advertisement), *Sunday Pantagraph*, May 8, 1938, p. 20.

41. "Black Neighborhoods Go Back to 1850s," *Pantagraph*, February 11, 1990, sec. C, p. 2; Elaine Bux, "In 40 Years Delivers 12,000,000 Letters: Postman Anson Retires after Long Service," *Daily Pantagraph*, October 15, 1943, p. 11; "Court Notes," *Daily Pantagraph*, October 3, 1957, p. 3; "Flames Damage Chat 'n Chew," *Daily Pantagraph*, May 31, 1947, p. 9; "Luther B. Anson," *Daily Pantagraph*, July 29, 1957, p. 3; "Mrs. Clara Anson," *Daily Pantagraph*, March 8, 1969, sec. B, p. 9; "Mrs. Luther B. Anson Dies at Home Here," *Daily Pantagraph*, October 23, 1940, p. 5; John W. Muirhead, [Bloomington, Illinois], to Greg Koos, [Bloomington, Illinois], February 6, 2014 (second and third quotations), and February 12, 2014, email communications, "Chat 'n

Chew" Vertical File, Archives, McLean County Museum of History, Bloomington, Illinois; National Bank of Bloomington, Bloomington, Ill., "Public Auction" (advertisement), *Daily Pantagraph*, October 6, 1958, p. 9; Susan Sessions Rugh, *Are We There Yet: The Golden Age of American Family Vacations* (Lawrence: University Press of Kansas, 2008), 75 (first quotation).

42. Edith L. Belt, Bloomington, Illinois, to Dear Friends [location unidentified], February 22, 1955, mimeographed letter, Steak 'n Shake Collection, folder 2, Archives, McLean County Museum of History, hereafter cited as Steak 'n Shake Collection; "Business World: Hamburger Stand Grows into Big Business: Gus Belt Takes Partners, Plans National Chain," *Daily Pantagraph*, December 3, 1940, p. 14; Warren Chrisman, "I Remember Route 66," *66 News!*, Summer 1992, p. 10 (first quotation); Robert P. Cronin, *Selling Steakburgers: The Growth of a Corporate Culture* (Carmel: Guild Press of Indiana, 2000), 1–31 (second quotation p. 14; fifth quotation p. 9); Hoekstra, *Ticket to Everywhere*, pp. 47–50 (third quotation p. 48); *Polk's Bloomington (Ill.) City Directory 1932 Including Normal* (Chicago: R. L. Polk, 1932), 467; Terri Ryburn-LaMonte, "Route 66," pp. 303–5; Keith A. Sculle, "Art for Appetite: A Taste for Architecture," *Historic Illinois* 17, no. 5 (February 1995): 8–10 (fourth quotation); Keith A. Scully, "Learning to Eat Out: The Origins of Steak 'n Shake," *Mid-America* 81, no. 2 (Summer 1999): 147–68; Shell Inn, Normal, Ill., "Late Hour News" (advertisement), *Daily Pantagraph*, December 20, 1933, p. 5; Joe Sonderman, *Route 66 Then and Now* (London: Pavilion Books, 2018), 24; Steak 'n Shake, Bloomington, Ill., *In Sight[,] Steak n Shake[,] It Must Be Right[,] "It's a Meal" U.S. Trademark Registered[,] Specializing in Selected Foods with a Desire to Please the Most Discriminating* (Bloomington, Ill.: Steak 'n Shake, [ca. 1950]), menu, Steak 'n Shake Collection, folder 2; Steak 'n Shake Drive Inn, Normal, Ill., "Shell Inn Steak 'n Shake Drive Inn Now Open" (advertisement), *Daily Pantagraph*, March 6, 1939, p. 5; Michael Karl Witzel, *The American Drive-In Restaurant* (St. Paul, Minn.: MBI Publishing, 1994), 161–64.

43. Bill "Ace" Adams, *40 Years at the Lucca* ([Bloomington, Ill.: Lucca Grill, ca. 1976]), unpaged, and Bill "Ace" Adams and Chuck Williams, *1936–1986[,] 50 Years at the Lucca Grill* ([Bloomington, Ill.: Lucca Grill, ca. 1986]), unpaged, both in Locked Cabinets, Illinois Room, Bloomington Public Library, Bloomington; Bill Adams, "Lucca Grill Remains a Popular Stop," *ISU Today* (Normal, Ill.), Summer 1990, p. 7; Baldini Bro[ther]s, Bloomington, Ill., "Dine at Lucca's" (advertisement), *Daily Pantagraph*, December 28, 1936, p. 5 (first quotation); Dirks, *Come and Get It*, pp. 116–17; Karen Hansen, "Slice of History: Landmark Pizza Restaurant, Bar, Celebrity Stop Celebrating 75th Year in Downtown Bloomington," *Pantagraph*, December 4, 2011, sec. A, pp. 1, 12; [John F. Koch and Anthony Smith], Bloomington, Illinois, to T. Lindsay Baker, Rio Vista, Texas, [December 7, 2020], manuscript letter, author's collection; "Lucca Grill," typescript, 1937, unpaged, "Lucca Grill" Vertical File, Archives, McLean County Museum of History; Lucca Grill, Bloomington, Ill., "Get Some Pizza Today" (advertisement), *Daily Pantagraph*, February 11, 1953, p. 6; Lucca Grill, *Menu* ([Bloomington, Ill.]: Baldini's Lucca Grill, [ca. 1970]), menu, Menu Collection, Archives, McLean County Museum of History; Lucca's, *Lucca's Italian-American Food* ([Bloomington, Ill.: Lucca's, ca. 1950]), menu, "Lucca Grill" Vertical File, Archives, McLean County Museum of History; Ward Sinclair, "Definitely Old-timey Bar Thrives in the Plastic Era," *Washington Post*, July 29, 1980, sec. A, p. 4 (third quotation); Austin C. Wehrwein, "Bloomington: A Provincial Aristocracy," *New York Times*, July 19, 1965, p. 13; "Yanks Free Birthplace of 2 Bloomingtonians," *Daily Pantagraph*, September 8, 1944, p. 15. Two earlier documented eateries offering pizza in Bloomington before the Baldini brothers purchased their specialized oven in 1953 are Louie's Spaghetti House, 214 West Front Street, in 1944, and Streid's Restaurant, Highway 66 Beltway at Illinois Highway 150, in 1951. Louie's Spaghetti House, Bloomington, Ill., "Louie's Spaghettis House" (advertisement), *Daily Pantagraph*, May 17, 1947, p. 2; Streid's Restaurant, Bloomington, Ill., "Did You Know?" (advertisement), *Daily Pantagraph*, January 2, 1951, p. 2.

44. Dirks, *Come and Get It!*, pp. 200–201; Ryburn-LaMonte, "Route 66," pp. 299–301.

45. Chris Anderson, "'Sirup' Made in Outpouring of Tradition: Funk Business Flowing under Fifth Generation," *Pantagraph*, March 20, 2000, sec. C, pp. 1–2 (second quotation); T. Lindsay Baker, "Funk's Grove Maple Sirup," *Route 66 Magazine* 27, no. 1 (Winter 2019–20): 42–44; R. A. Barracks, "Sugarin' Time,"

Decatur (Ill.) Sunday Herald and Review, March 11, 1934, Illinois Magazine supplement, pp. [1, 3] (third quotation p. 3); Hazel Funk, "Making of Maple Syrup in County," *Daily Pantagraph*, Tuesday, May 4, 1926, p. 9 (first quotation); Funks Grove Pure Maple Sirup, Funks Grove, Ill., "Maple 'Sirup'" (advertisement), *Daily Pantagraph*, March 8, 1952, p. 5; Funks Grove Pure Maple Syrup, "Drive to the Country this Weekend for Funk's Grove Pure Maple Syrup" (advertisement), *Daily Pantagraph*, March 23, 1950, p. 2; Funks Grove Pure Maple Syrup, "Funk's Grove Pure Maple Syrup New 1934 Maple Syrup" (advertisement), *Daily Pantagraph*, February 17, 1934, p. 6; Steve Funk, "Funk's Grove Pure Maple Sirup," typescript, Feb[ruary] 17, 2007, Come and Get It Collection, folder 4, item 4, Archives, McLean County Museum of History, hereafter cited as Come and Get It Collection; Steve Funk and Gaida Funk, interview at Funk's Grove, near Shirley, Ill., September 6, 2006, typewritten transcript, pp. 1–16, Come and Get It Collection, folder 23, item 11; Hazel Funk Holmes, "Sugar Weather Comes to Funk[']s Grove," *66 News!*, March 1990, unpaged; Bob McCain, "Grove Produced 25,000 Gallons of Sap," *Daily Pantagraph*, April 16, 1951, p. 16; "Making and Selling Maple Syrup Still Paying Off," *Daily Chronicle* (DeKalb, Ill.), April 26, 1981, sec. E, p. 20; "Making Maple Syrup: It's an Interesting Business," *Daily Pantagraph*, April 12, 1933, p. 14; Richard Orr, "Tradition Carries On; Sap Flows," *Chicago Tribune*, March 15, 1964, sec. 1, p. 6; Jimmy Pack Jr., "Steeped in History," *Route Magazine*, February–March 2021, pp. 72–77; "Samuel Spaulding," *Daily Pantagraph*, January 23, 1981, sec. C, p. 3; Tom Teague, "Funk's Grove," *Route 66 Magazine* 8, no. 3 (Summer 2001): 13, 45; Tom Teague, "The Magic of Route 66: The Old Road Is Gone, but Its Character Lives on in the People," *Illinois Times* (Springfield, Ill.) 10, no. 48 (August 1–7, 1985): 4–11; Teague, *Searching for 66*, pp. 7–10; Mrs. H. G. Walter, "Describes Beauty of Nearby Woods," *Daily Pantagraph*, November 6, 1926, sec. B, p. 1.

46. Funks Grove [Park], "Dance at Funk's Grove, Ill." (advertisement), *Daily Pantagraph*, June 29, 1917, p. 3; Funks Grove Park, "Dance Tonite and Sunday Nite" (advertisement), *Daily Pantagraph*, July 26, 1924, p. 5; Funks Grove Park, "Dancing Saturday and Sunday Evenings" (advertisement), *Daily Pantagraph*, August 7, 1926, sec. A, p. 5; Chester D. Henry, *Route 66*, p. 104 (second quotation); Bill Kemp, "Jazz Age Dance Halls Looked upon as Menace to Society," *Pantagraph*, August 17, 2008, sec. B, p. 5; Terri Ryburn-LaMonte, "Route 66," p. 314 (first quotation).

47. "Cooksville Indees Trounce Shirley Dixie Oilers, 29–8," *Daily Pantagraph*, January 3, 1931, sec. B, p. 2; "Increases Capital Stock," *Sunday Pantagraph*, February 12, 1928, sec. A, p. 2; "J. P. Walters, Shirley Oil Co. Founder, Dies," *Daily Pantagraph*, May 27, 1950, p. 5; "New Incorporation," *Daily Pantagraph*, April 30, 1923, p. 5; Scott and Kelly, *Route 66*, 41–42; Shirley Oil and Supply Company, Shirley, Ill., "Attention Farmers!" (advertisement), *Daily Pantagraph*, March 29, 1930, sec. B, p. 5; "Standard Oil of Indiana Workers Get Stock at $62," *Chicago Daily Tribune*, May 12, 1925, p. 33; Tom Teague, "Seventy-Two and Still Truckin'," *Route 66 Magazine* 6, no. 4 (Fall 2000): 24–27; Tom Teague, "Still Trucking," *Illinois Heritage* (Illinois State Historical Society) 5, no. 5 (September–October 2002): 6–8; "3 Buildings in Shirley Burn—Loss Is $10,000: Fighters Save nearby House: Filling Station, Restaurant and Dwelling Quickly Destroyed," *Daily Pantagraph*, January 26, 1937, p. 2.

48. Brad Jay Bogart, "Love Notes of Ole 66," *66 News!*, Winter 1992, pp. 2–3 (third and fourth quotations); Dixie Truckers Home, McLean, Ill., "Restaurant Help Wanted" (advertisement), *Daily Pantagraph*, April 19, 1945, p. 15; Dixie Truck Stop, McLean, Ill., "1937 Packard '120'" (advertisement), *Sunday Pantagraph*, December 2, 1945, p. 19; Scott and Kelly, *Route 66*, pp. 41–42 (first and second quotations); Tom Teague, "Seventy-Two and Still Truckin'," 24–27; Tom Teague, "Still Trucking," 6–8; Truckers Dixie Home, McLean, Ill., "Curb Service[,] Truckers Dixie Home" (advertisement), *Daily Pantagraph*, August 15, 1940, p. 2; "Wide Area Served Best Oil Products," *Daily Pantagraph*, April 28, 1938, p. 9.

49. Ron Berler, "Truck Stop," *Chicago Tribune*, March 10, 1974, Chicago Tribune Magazine supplement, pp. 18–21, 46–47 (quotations p. 19); Dixie Truckers Home, *Relax . . . You're Almost Home . . . Dixie Truckers Home* (McLean, Ill.: Dixie Truckers Home, [ca. 2000]), folder, "Dixie Truckers Home" Vertical File, Archives, McLean County Museum of History; "Dixie Truckers Opens Today," *Daily Pantagraph*, May 22, 1967, p. 23; "Family Giving Up Dixie Truckers Home after 75 Years," *Southern Illinoisan* (Carbondale,

Ill.), August 1, 2003, sec. A, p. 3; Paul Garret Hendrickson, "Truckers' Home on U.S.-66, McLean's Dixie: Life on Open Road," *Chicago Tribune*, March 4, 1973, sec. 4, p. 2; Jeff La Follette, "Latest on the Dixie Truckers' Home and the Route 66 Association of Illinois Hall of Fame," *66 News!*, Fall 2003, p. 21; "Road News: What's New at the Dixie!," *Route 66 Magazine* 20, no. 2 (Spring 2013): 53; Tom Teague, "Seventy-Two and Still Truckin': The Finale of a Two Part Story," *Route 66 Magazine* 8, no. 1 (Winter 2000–2001): 24–27; Drew Williams, "Nation's Truck Drivers Still Whistling Dixie," *Pantagraph*, October 18, 1992, sec. E, p. 1.

50. J. R. Adams, Atlanta, Ill., "Best" (advertisement), *Sunday Pantagraph*, August 31, 1930, sec. D, p. 5; J. R. Adams, Beverly Hills, Calif., "Non-resident Will Lease Palm Grill, Atlanta, Ill." (advertisement), *Daily Pantagraph*, July 30, 1934, p. 9 (first quotation); J. R. Adams, Los Angeles, "'Palms Grill' Café" (advertisement), *Sunday Pantagraph*, April 5, 1936, p. 19; [J. R. Adams, Los Angeles], "Palms Grill Café, Atlanta" (advertisement), *Daily Pantagraph*, April 14, 1941, p. 11; "J. Robert Adams," *Daily Pantagraph*, February 28, 1951, p. 5; Nomination to the National Register of Historic Places for Downey Building, Atlanta, Ill., January 6, 2004, (second quotation sec. 8, p. 10); Palms Grill, Atlanta, Ill., "Don't Miss This Delicious Dinner Sunday $1.00" (advertisement), *Daily Pantagraph*, February 22, 1947, p. 2.

51. Kevin Barlow, "That's Pie You Smell in Atlanta: Baker's Work Honored by State," *Herald and Review*, March 10, 2013, sec. B, pp. 1–2; Bob Holliday, "Atlanta's Interest in Bunyon Statue Prompts Protest," *Pantagraph*, March 26, 2003, sec. A, p. 3; Bob Holliday, "Old-timey Palms Grill Reopens," *Pantagraph*, May 20, 2009, sec. C, pp. 1–2; Michelle Koetters, "New Palms Grill Aims for Old Feel," *Pantagraph*, March 13, 2009, sec. C, pp. 1, 3; Cheryl Eichar Jett, "A Small Town Experience," *Route Magazine*, October–November 2020, pp. 54–60; Nomination to the National Register of Historic Places for Downey Building; "Palms Grill Café Reopens to Fanfare," *Route 66 Federation News* 15, no. 3 (Summer 2009): 20–22; Weiss, "Bunyon Giant Dedication," 9.

52. "Albert Huffman," *Sunday Pantagraph*, January 8, 1978, sec. D, p. 15; Kevin Barlow, "The Mill Set to Reopen," *Pantagraph*, January 20, 2017, sec. A, p. 3; Kevin Barlow, "$10,000 Grand to Give Restoration of The Mill a Jump-Start," *Pantagraph*, August 4, 2009, sec. A, p. 4; Elizabeth Bettendorf, "Wheel Food: Road Food Flourished When the Highway Was the Destination," *State Journal-Register* (Springfield, Ill.), February 5, 1993, Heartland supplement, sec. A, pp. 6–9; "Blossom Huffman," *Pantagraph*, October 22, 1986, sec. B, p. 7; "George E. Huffman," *Pantagraph*, February 9, 1989, sec. C, p. 4; "Illinois Governor Rauner Attends Mill Museum Grand Opening," *Route 66 Federation News* 23, no. 2 (Summer 2017): 43; Jessica Lema, "Lincoln Route 66: Council Considers Donation to The Mill," *Courier* (Lincoln, Ill.), April 1, 2016, sec. A, pp. 1–2; "The Mill in Lincoln: Recent Developments," *66 News!*, Spring 2017, pp. 16–17; The Mill, Lincoln, Ill., "Schnitzel's, Schnitzel's, Schnitzel's" (advertisement), *Decatur Sunday Herald and Review*, January 28, 1951, p. 20 (quotation); "Paul Coddington," *Daily Pantagraph*, November 18, 1961, p. 16; Dan Tackett, "An Icon on Route 66 in Lincoln," *Courier*, October 5, 2013, sec. A, pp. 1–2; "Underground Gourmet," *Pantagraph*, September 13, 1986, Preview supplement, p. 23; John W. Usherwood, "Appropriations Package OK'd in Lincoln," *Pantagraph*, July 11, 2001, sec. A, p. 4; Jim Winnerman, "Dutch Themed Eatery in Lincoln, Illinois[,] Originally Featured Blue Trim with Waitresses Clad in Blue and White Aprons," *Route 66 Magazine* 17, no. 2 (Spring 2010): 22–24.

53. Greg Cima, "Fire Destroys Museum: Broadwell's Pig Hip Opened as Restaurant in 1937," *Pantagraph*, March 6, 2007, sec. A, p. 3; David G. Clark, "The Pig Hip and the Left Ham Sandwich," *Route 66 Magazine* 25, no. 1 (Winter 2017–18): 20–21; Marian Clark, "Blue Front Café—Amarillo, Texas," *Route 66 Federation News* 3, no. 4 (Autumn 1997): 10–12; Ernest L. Edwards, interview by Marian Clark, Broadwell, Ill., [ca. 1990], audio recording, Oklahoma Route 66 Association, Chandler, Okla., https://oklahomaroute66.com/marian-clark interviews/, accessed December 30, 2020; Ernie Edwards, "Ernie's Little Nanny Goats," *66 News!*, Spring 2001, pp. 4–7; Elaine Graybill, "Broadwell's Pig-Hip Restaurant Is a Slice of Life," *Pantagraph*, April 13, 1986, sec. D, pp. 1–2; Phil Luciano, "Remembering Ernie Edwards: One Hip Dude," *Courier*, April 18, 2012, pp. 1–2; John M. McGuire, "Passing Time at the Pig-Hip: Hungry Travelers Can Return to Another Age," *St. Louis Post-Dispatch*, August 20, 1989, sec. D, pp. 1, 15 (second quotation), reprinted

as John M. McGuire, "Look Back in Time," *Show Me Route 66* (Route 66 Association of Missouri) 16, no. 3 (Summer 2005): 9–11; Tony Parker, "Artifacts of Route 66 Eatery for Sale," *Pantagraph*, October 5, 1992, sec. A, p. 3; "Pig Hip Founder Edwards Dies at 94," *Pantagraph*, April 13, 2012, sec. A, p. 3; Pig-Hip Restaurant, Broadwell, Ill., *Pig-Hip Restaurant* (Broadwell, Ill.: Pig-Hip Restaurant, [ca. 1960]), menu, author's collection; Amanda Reavy, "Fire Guts Landmark Route 66 Museum," *State Journal-Register*, March 6, 2007, pp. 1, 5; Thomas Repp, "When Pigs Had Wings," *Route 66 Magazine* 5, no. 2 (Spring 1998): 24–26; Nancy Rollings Saul, "How 'bout a 'Pig Hip' Sandwich?" *Herald and Review*, June 12, 1985, Focus supplement, p. 1; Nancy Rollings Saul, "Monument Celebrates Former Pig Hip," *Pantagraph*, October 15, 2007, sec. A, p. 5; Dan Tackett, "Mother Road Loses a Son: Pig Hip Founder Edwards Dies at 94," *Courier*, April 13, 2012, pp. 1–2; Dan Tackett, "Pig-Hip Neon Has Faded; Edwards Still Going Strong," *Lincoln (Ill.) Courier* , June 9, 1990, Illinois US 66 supplement, 1–2; Tom Teague, "Route 66 Hall of Fame," *66 News!*, Summer 2000, pp. 12–13; Tom Teague, *Searching for 66*, pp. 11–13; "A Tribute from the Illinois Route 66 Preservation Committee—the Pig Hip Museum," *66 News!*, Summer 2007, pp. 6–8; "U.S. 66 Landmark Closes after 54 Years in Business: Travelers Still Find Their Way to Pig Hip Restaurant," *Sunday Dispatch* (Moline, Ill.), January 5, 1992, sec. C, p. 6. The Pig-Hip is one of only a handful of restaurants on Route 66 for which formal histories have been written. See William Kaszynski, *Pig-Hips on Route 66* (Lincoln, Ill.: Lincoln Printers, 2006), 1–92 (first quotation p. 27).

54. T. Lindsay Baker, "The Horseshoe Sandwich," *Route 66 Magazine* 25, no. 3 (Summer 2018): 12–14; Les Eastep, *Springfield, Illinois: A Chilli History*, 3rd ed. (Springfield, Ill.: Sangamon County Historical Society, 2014), 1–21; Julianne Glatz, "What Happened to Horseshoes? The History of Springfield's Iconic Food Shows the Original Was Nothing Like Today's Version," *Illinois Times*, February 2, 2012, pp. 12–16; Carolyn Harmon and Tony Leone, *Springfield's Celebrated Horseshoe Sandwich* (Charleston, S.C.: American Palate, 2019), 1–201; *Illinois: A Descriptive and Historical Guide*, pp. 282–96; Jakle and Sculle, *Fast Food*, pp. 296–321; Carl Johnson, "Rediscovering It—Hidden Route 66: Finding the Original Springfield Illinois, Alignments," *66 News!*, Fall 2003, pp. 5–6, 8; Rich Shereikis, "The Way We Were: Memories of Old Rt. 66 in Springfield," *Illinois Times*, August 3, 1989, pp. 11–13; Christine R. Toney, *The Magic of the Chilli: The Midwest Chilli History Cookbook* (St. Louis: Palmerston and Reed, 2000), 1–59.

55. Loewen, *Sundown Towns*, pp. 94–95; Frank Norris, "Courageous Motorists," pp. 311–12; William English Walling, "The Race War in the North," *Independent* 65, no. 3118 (September 3, 1908): 529–35 (quotation p. 529). For a general history of the Springfield race riot and its consequences, see Roberta Senechal de la Roche, *The Sociogenesis of a Race Riot: Springfield, Illinois, in 1908* (Urbana: University of Illinois Press, 1990).

56. Marian Clark, "Maldaner's Restaurant[,] Springfield, Illinois," *Route 66 Federation News* 9, no. 1 (Winter 2003): 12–13 (third quotation p. 12); Harmon and Leone, *Springfield's Celebrated Horseshoe Sandwich*, pp. 84–85; Tim Landis, "Maldaner's Quietly Marks 125th Anniversary," *State Journal-Register*, February 7, 2010, pp. 43, 46; "Maldaner's (from City Directories at the *State Journal and Register* Library)," typescript, [ca. 1978], 2 lvs., unpaged, "Springfield—Restaurants—Maldaner's" Vertical File, Sangamon Valley Collection, Lincoln Library (Springfield Public Library), Springfield, Illinois; Maldaner's Restaurant, Springfield, Ill., *Maldaner's* (Springfield, Ill.: Maldaner's, [ca. 1973]), menu, "Springfield—Restaurants—Maldaner's" Vertical File; Lizanne Poppens, "Saturday Gig," *State Journal-Register*, September 3, 1977, sec. A, p. 13; "State Capital Society," *Daily Inter Ocean* (Chicago), December 29, 1888, p. 16 (first quotation); [Untitled History of Maldaner's Restaurant], typescript, [ca. 1995], 1 lf., "Springfield—Restaurants—Maldaner's" Vertical File.

57. Joe [A. Bockelmann], "Springfield versus Texas," manuscript, 1969, 3 lvs., "Cookery—Springfield—Chilli" Vertical File, Sangamon Valley Collection; Joe Cooper, *With or Without Beans, Being a Compendium to Perpetuate the Internationally-Known Bowl of Chili (Texas Style) Which Occupies Such an Important Place in Modern Civilization* (Dallas, Tex.: William S. Henson, 1952), 210–14 (fourth and fifth quotations); "Dave Felts Column," *Southern Illinoisan*, April 2, 1959, p. 4 (first quotation); "Dew Chili Is 44 Years Old Today," *State Journal-Register*, March 29, 1953, p. 14; "Dew Chili Parlor No. 1 Closes Doors," *State Journal-Register*,

January 1, 1955, p. 8; Eastep, *Springfield, Illinois*, pp. 1–3, 8, 10; Fred Fernandez, "35 Years: Dew Chili Proprietor Tells of Bygone Days on Anniversary," clipping from unidentified newspaper rubber-stamped March 29, 1944, "Springfield—Restaurants—D" Vertical File, Sangamon Valley Collection (second and third quotations); Beulah Gordon, "Longest in State: Joe Bockelmann Member of Red Men over 50 Years," *Illinois State Journal* (Springfield, Ill.), November 11, 1954, p. 13 (second quotation); Thomas Morrow, "A Line o' Type or Two: Chili over the Counter," *Chicago Daily Tribune*, March 30, 1959, pt. 2, p. 18; Victoria Pope, "The Man Who Gave Chili Its Second 'L': He Always Did Like to Do Things a Little Differently," *Illinois Times*, February 5, 1976, pp. 4–5, 24–25; Toney, *The Magic of Chilli*, pp. 10–13, 41–46, 54–59.

58. "Champion Lamb Sells at $5 a Pound," unidentified newspaper clipping rubber-stamped June 21, 1953; Mike Clark, "3-Alarm Fire Destroys Mill Restaurant," unidentified newspaper clipping rubber-stamped April 25, 1972; "Mill Reopens Tonight After Remodeling," unidentified newspaper clipping rubber-stamped September 5, 1963; "Mill Tavern to Resume Serving Food Today," unidentified newspaper clipping rubber-stamped December 15, 1943; "Mill to Unveil Improvements," unidentified newspaper clipping hand marked November 9, 1948; "O.P.A. Suspension Order is Affirmed," unidentified newspaper clipping rubber-stamped September 7, 1943; and Pauline L. Telford, "Chit Chat," unidentified newspaper clipping rubber-stamped May 5, 1968 (second quotation), all of the above in "Springfield—Restaurants—Mill" Vertical File, Sangamon Valley Collection; Haddix, Kraig, and Sen, *Chicago Food Encyclopedia*, 248–49; Dave Hoekstra, *Supper Club Book*, vii–ix, xi–xvi; The Mill, Springfield, Ill., *The Mill*[,] *Corner Fifteenth and Matheny Ave.*[,] *Springfield*[,] *Illinois*[,] *Luncheon*[,] *Cocktails*[,] *Dinner*[,] *Dancing* (Springfield, Ill.: The Mill, [ca. 1950]), menu, "Springfield—Restaurants—Mill" Vertical File, Sangamon Valley Collection; Kathryn Rem, "Dinner and Dancing: Remembering the Nights When the Supper Club Reigned in Springfield," *State Journal-Register*, March 3, 2006, Heartland Magazine, sec. A, pp. 6–9 (first quotation).

59. Elizabeth Bettendorf, "Wheel Food," pp. 6–9 (fifth quotation); Heide Brandes, "Cozy in Springfield," *Route Magazine*, June–July 2021, pp. 30–36; Cozy Dogs, Inc., Springfield, Ill., "Cozy Dog—Exclusive Dealership Franchise Territory" (advertisement), *Belvidere Daily Republican*, April 16, 1947, p. 7; "Cozy to Relocate," *66 News!*, Spring 1996, p. 11; Cozy Drive-In, Springfield, Ill., *Menu*[,] *How Many Presidents Can You Identify?* Publication BF-110 500 9-64H 3155 N (Springfield, Ill.: Cozy Drive-In, [1964]), menu courtesy of Steve Rider; "Headed for the Hall of Fame," *66 News!*, May 1991, pp. 6–8 (first, second, and third quotations); Mark Kendall, "Serving up Down-home Eating," *Press-Enterprise*, September 9, 2001, sec. A, p. 11; David Knudson, "Bob, We'll Really Miss You: A Portrait of Bob Waldmire," *Route 66 Federation News* 4, no. 3 (Summer 1998): 18–21; Kraig, *Hot Dog*, 84, 95; Kraig and Carroll, *Man Bites Dog*, pp. 142–43; "New Custom Built Hot Dog Has Been Revealed," *DeKalb (Ill.) Chronicle*, June 17, 1946, p. 1; Olsen, *Route 66 Lost and Found*, 48–49; Charles Storch, "Birthplace (Maybe) of the Corn Dog: More Than Just a Wiener Tucked into a Cornmeal Blanket," *Chicago Tribune*, August 16, 2006, sec. 5, pp. 1, 8; Tom Teague, "The Cozy Family," *Route 66 Magazine* 2, no. 4 (Fall 1995): 4–7; Tom Teague, "Sign Here Please!," *Route 66 Magazine* 6, no. 1 (Winter 1998–99): 14–15 (seventh, eighth, and ninth quotations); Bob Waldmire, interview by David King Dunaway, Portal, Ariz., September 7, 2007, typewritten transcript, pp. 1–8 (fourth and sixth quotations p. 4), Route 66 Corridor Preservation Program, National Park Service, Santa Fe, N.Mex.; Buz Waldmire, interview by David King Dunaway, November 2010, typewritten transcript, pp. 1–10, 15–22, Route 66 Corridor Preservation Program; Buz Waldmire, Springfield, Ill., email communication to T. Lindsay Baker, Rio Vista, Tex., October 1, 2020, paper copy, author's collection; Ed Waldmire, interview by Clifford Keith Wilson III, Rochester, Ill., December 2, 1978, Ed Waldmire Memoir, Interview W146, audio recording and typewritten transcript, Archives/Special Collections, University of Illinois at Springfield, Springfield, Ill., available in Illinois Digital Archives, http://www.idaillinois.org/cdm/compoundobject/collection/uis/ud/4470/rec/1, accessed on October 28, 2019.

Edwin S. Waldmire II and wife Virginia had five sons, the one known most widely outside Springfield being Robert "Bob" Waldmire (1945–2009), who received national recognition as an artist using pen and ink to depict locations throughout the regions traversed by old Highway 66. David Knudson, "Bob, We'll

Really Miss You," pp. 18–21; Tom Teague, "Living Highway Icon Says 'Goodbye' to the Road," *Route 66 Magazine* 5, no. 3 (Summer 1998): 20–23; Tom Teague, "Where's Waldmire?," *66 News!*, Spring 1994, pp. 6–9; Dave Tompkins, "Celebration of a Road Scholar," *Route 66 Magazine* 18, no. 4 (Fall 2011): 34–35; Bob Waldmire, interview by David King Dunaway, September 7, 2007.

60. Automobile Club of Southern California, Los Angeles, *National Old Trails Road[,] New York City, New York[,] to Los Angeles, California[;] U.S. Highway 66[,] Chicago, Illinois[,] to Los Angeles, California[;] and Major Connecting Roads* (Los Angeles: Automobile Club of Southern California, 1932), p. 82; Dennis Garrels, *Then and Now: Macoupin County on Route 66* (Charleston, S.C.: Arcadia Publishing, 2007), 11–95; *Illinois: A Descriptive and Historical Guide*, pp. 594–99; Loewen, *Sundown Towns*, 94–95, 158–61; Rittenhouse, *Guide Book to Highway 66*, pp. 16–20; Weiss, *Traveling the New, Historic Route 66 of Illinois*, pp. 72–83.

61. "Benld's Coliseum Ballroom Destroyed in Weekend Fire," *Dispatch* (Moline, Ill.), August 2, 2011, sec. A, p. 8; "Body of Drowned Man Identified as That of Tarro," *Alton (Ill.) Evening Telegraph*, May 3, 1930, p. 1; David G. Clark, "Prohibition 1919: A Wet Nation Goes Dry," *Route 66 Magazine* 26, no. 1 (Winter 2018–19): 30–33; Coliseum Ballroom, Benld, Ill., "Dance All Nite" (advertisement), *Edwardsville (Ill.) Intelligencer*, December 23, 1929, p. 8; "Four Brothers, One Profession: New Hall of Fame Members for 2001," *66 News!*, Summer 2001, pp. 4–7; Cheryl Eichar Jett, "Memorable Women on Route 66," *Route 66 Magazine* 27, no. 1 (Winter 2019–20): 46–47; Jim Kulp, "Band Leader Points to Trends: Rock 'n' Roll Made Dances," *Alton Evening Telegraph*, February 15, 1958, p. 18 (quotation); "Two Former Residents Get Long Terms," *Decatur (Ill.) Herald*, July 27, 1976, p. 3; Rick Wade, "A Dance Hall, Al Capone, Brothels, and Bootleg Booze," *Route 66 Magazine* 21, no. 4 (Fall 2014): 48–51.

62. Automobile Club of Southern California, *National Old Trails Road*, p. 82; *Illinois: A Descriptive and Historical Guide*, pp. 594–599; Rittenhouse, *Guide Book to Highway 66*, pp. 16–20; Weiss, *Traveling the New, Historic Route 66 of Illinois*, pp. 62–71.

63. Bettendorf, "Wheel Food," sec. A, p. 9; Jim Hinckley, "News from the Road: Ariston Turns 90, Goes up for Sale," *Show Me Route 66* 25, no. 1 (Winter 2015): 6–7; Al Lopinot, "Litchfield's Ariston Café: A Route 66 International Travelers' Favorite," *66 News!*, Winter 2013, p. 11; Nomination to the National Register of Historic Places for the Ariston Café, March 28, 2006; "Road News: The Ariston Celebrates Eighty Years," *Route 66 Magazine* 12, no. 1 (Winter 2004–5): 50; Robert Rubright, *Breakfast, Lunch and Diner: Stories, Characters and Favorite Dishes from Fascinating Restaurants in St. Louis and Beyond* (St. Louis: RO Press, 2009), 123–25; Sonderman, *Route 66 Then and Now*, 31; Tom Teague, "The Ariston Eclectic," *Route 66 Federation News* 6, no. 3 (Summer 2000), pp. 21–22, 24; Rick Wade, "The Ariston Café," *Route 66 Magazine* 22, no. 1 (Winter 2014–15): 8–11.

64. Edward H. Aherns and Sons, Staunton, Ill., "Public Auction for: 66 Terminal Restaurant and Motels" (advertisement), *Edwardsville Intelligencer*, April 13, 1977, p. 15; "Felts," *Herald and Review*, February 6, 1996, sec. A, p. 11; Al Lopinot, "John Meckles and the 66 Terminal," *66 News!*, January 1992, p. 2; "Meckles," *Herald and Review*, July 19, 1990, sec. A, p. 9; Scott and Kelly, *Route 66*, pp. 76–77, 93 (quotations); "Sells 66 Café," *Edwardsville Intelligencer*, March 20, 1952, p. 9.

65. "Beautiful Hotz Home Transferred for $9,000," *Edwardsville Intelligencer*, November 13, 1922, p. [5]; George B. Cathcart, Edwardsville, Ill., "Notice" (advertisement), *Edwardsville Intelligencer*, October 21, 1938, p. 11; George B. Cathcart, Edwardsville, Ill., "Restaurant for Sale" (advertisement), *Edwardsville Intelligencer*, November 9, 1951, p. 2; "Cathcart's Café Popular Eating Place for Tourists," *Edwardsville Intelligencer*, August 30, 1938, p. 5; "George B. Cathcart," *Edwardsville Intelligencer*, March 5, 1952, p. 2; "George Cathcart Appeals Decision," *Edwardsville Intelligencer*, October 2, 1928, p. 1 (second quotation); R. Kenneth Evans, "Cathcart's Modern Café and Market Stands as a Monument to Hard Work and Fair Dealing," *Edwardsville Intelligencer*, October 11, 1933, p. 8; R. Kenneth Evans, "Cathcart's Modern Café Serves Just What you Want, When You Want It, for the Wanting Appetite," *Edwardsville Intelligencer*, February 13, 1934, p. 5 (first quotation); Cheryl Eichar Jett, "Cathcart's Café: Known from Coast to Coast,"

Show Me Route 66 23, no. 2 (Spring 2013): 25–28; "Planned Strike on Registration Day," *Houston Tex. Post*, October 9, 1917, p. 7.

66. "Fine of $100 Is Imposed," *Edwardsville Intelligencer*, February 28, 1933, p. 1; "H. A. Raffaelle Dies at Hospital," *Edwardsville Intelligencer*, May 24, 1937, p. 1; "Luna Café Makes Specialty of Cold Weather Dishes," *Edwardsville Intelligencer*, December 22, 1936, p. 6; Luna Café, Mitchell, Ill., "Luna Café" (advertisement), *Edwardsville Intelligencer*, June 23, 1936, p. 5 (quotation); Luna Café, "Luna Café" (advertisement), *Edwardsville Intelligencer*, October 12, 1938, p. 9; Luna Café, "Luna Café Announcement" (advertisement), *Edwardsville Intelligencer*, March 3, 1950, p. 3; Luna Café, "New Year's Eve Party" (advertisement), *Alton Evening Telegraph*, December 28, 1932, p. 5; "Luna Café Ownership History," typescript, 2010, 1 lf., "Route 66" Vertical File, Abraham Lincoln Presidential Library, Springfield, Ill.; Olsen, *Route 66 Lost and Found*, pp. 62–63; Gwen Podeschi, Springfield, Ill., email communications with Carol Dyson, Springfield, Ill., November 9–12, 2010, typescripts, "Route 66" Vertical File; Emily Priddy, "The Luna Café," *66 News!*, Winter 2004, pp. 23–24; "Raffaelle's Luna Café, Mitchell, Is Good Place to Eat," *Edwardsville Intelligencer*, September 16, 1936, p. 16; [Kid] Regan, "'Round the Town with Regan," *St. Louis Star-Times*, December 28, 1936, p. 17; Rubright, *Breakfast, Lunch and Diner*, pp. 264–66; Joe Sonderman, "The Chain of Rocks Bridge," *Show Me Route 66* 29, no. 3 (Summer 2019): 38–42; Joe Sonderman, "'Heart of Mitchell' Relighting Ceremony," *Route 66 Magazine* 19, no. 1 (Winter 2011–12): 8–11; Jim Thole, "The Luna's Dazzling Neon Scene Returns," *Show Me Route 66* 22, no. 1 (Winter 2012): 8–12.

67. John J. Archibald, "Update: Ed and Jack English," *St. Louis Post-Dispatch*, July 16, 1989, Magazine supplement, July 16, 1989, p. 4; Bush's Steak House, East St. Louis, Ill., "Bush's Steak House" (advertisement), *St. Louis Star-Times*, January 21, 1947, p. 5; Bush's Steak House, "Cook—Colored; Must be Neat" (advertisement), *St. Louis Post-Dispatch*, November 1, 1946, sec. D, p. 9; Bush's Steak House, "The Late-Late Club" (advertisement), *St. Louis Post-Dispatch*, June 24, 1960, sec. D, p. 7; "Fire Causes $50,000 Damage to Steak House," *St. Louis Globe-Democrat*, September 11, 1961, East Side News sec. A, p. 6; Bob Goddard, "At the Night Spots," *St. Louis Globe-Democrat*, sec. F, p. 2; Walter P. Grogan Jr., "English's New Owner Says Food, Style Will Remain," *St. Louis Post-Dispatch*, October 15, 1998, Metro Illinois Post sec., pp. 11, 13; "John T. 'Jack' English," *St. Louis Post-Dispatch*, March 19, 2000, sec. Metro C, p. 11; George Killenberg, "East St. Louis—the Sunday Oasis of Thirsty St. Louisans," *St. Louis Globe-Democrat*, June 19, 1949, sec. F, p. 1 (first quotation); Harrison Little, ed., *Where to Eat: 2,300 Restaurants Preferred by Businessmen* (Chicago: Dartnell Corporation, 1948), p. 79; Jake McCarthy, "A Personal Opinion: Checking 'Over There,'" *St. Louis Post-Dispatch*, December 28, 1979, sec. D, p. 2; "Razing Begins on Building in East St. Louis," *St. Louis Globe-Democrat*, November 29, 1962, sec. F, p. 3.

CHAPTER 2. MISSOURI

1. The distance from the Mississippi River bridges across St. Louis to the juncture of City 66 and Bypass 66 was about thirty miles. In contrast, motorists drove essentially the same twelve-mile alignment from the head of U.S. 66 Highway in downtown Chicago to its municipal boundary with Cicero throughout the history of the numbered highway. From South Pasadena in California, travelers made their way approximately sixteen miles across Los Angeles proper to West Hollywood on the way to Santa Monica. For particulars on the changing alignments in these three cities, see David G. Clark, *Exploring Route 66 in Chicagoland: Journeys through History on the Mother Road in Cook County, Illinois*, 2nd ed. (Chicago: Windy City Road Warrior.com, 2008), 32–67; Scott R. Piotrowski, *Finding the End of the Mother Road: Route 66 in Los Angeles County*, 2nd ed. (Pasadena, Calif.: 66 Productions, 2005), 32–89; Kip Welborn, *Things to Look Out for on Route 66 in St. Louis* (n.p.: privately printed, 2012), 3–57.

2. *Missouri, a Guide to the "Show Me" State*, American Guide Series (New York: Duell, Sloan and Pearce, 1941), 293–305.

3. Peter Aldrich, "California Here We Come!," *Route 66 Magazine* 12, no. 4 (Fall 2005): 32 (quotation); James R. Powell, "The History of U.S. Highway 66 in St. Louis," *Show Me Route 66* (Route 66 Association of

Missouri) 8, no. 4 (Winter 1966): 8–22; James R. Powell, "U.S. Highway 66 in St. Louis," *Show Me Route 66* 12, no. 4 (Fall 2001): 36–51; Jim Powell, "Which Came First?," *Route 66 Magazine* 5, no. 3 (Summer 1998): 48–50; Joe Sonderman, "Who's Lost? Simplifying Route 66 in St. Louis," *Show Me Route 66* 31, no. 2 (Spring 2021): 26–27, 29–32; Welborn, *Things to Look Out for on Route 66*, iii, 3, 8–9, 15–17, 26, 33, 38, 54–57.

4. Norma Maret Bolin, *Route 66 St. Louis from the Bridges to the Diamonds* (St. Louis: St. Louis Transitions, 2010), 42–43; Norma Maret Bolin, *The Route 66 St. Louis Cookbook: The Mother Lode of Recipes from the Mother Road* (St. Louis: St. Louis Traditions, 2009), 18; *Gourmet's Guide to Good Eating: A Valuable and Vital Accessory for Every Motorist and Traveler 1946–47* (New York: Gourmet, the Magazine of Good Living, 1946), 186 (quotations); Harrison Little, ed., *Where to Eat: 2,300 Restaurants Preferred by Businessmen* (Chicago: Dartnell Corporation, 1948), 149; "Mayfair Hotel Opens Doors to Public Tonight," *St. Louis Post-Dispatch*, August 29, 1925, p. 3; Nomination to the National Register of Historic Places for Hotel Jefferson, St. Louis, Mo., September 5, 2003, and for Mayfair Hotel, St. Louis, Mo., September 10, 1979, these and subsequent nominations in Office of the Keeper, National Register of Historic Places, National Park Service, Washington, D.C.

   According to St. Louis folklore, the Mayfair Hotel is where the practice began of luxury hotel staff placing wrapped chocolates on guests' pillows. Frequently told stories state that a Mayfair manager observed that Hollywood heartthrob Cary Grant had left a trail of chocolates from the parlor in his suite to the bedroom and onto the pillow of the bed, where he left a letter to a lady love. Tim Bryant, "Mayfair Work Signals Hotel Resurgence," *St. Louis Post-Dispatch*, June 20, 2014, sec. A, pp. 1, 6; Barbara Hertenstein, "Sweet Tradition at Refurbished Mayfair Hotel," *St. Louis Post-Dispatch*, August 24, 1997, sec. T, p. 3.

5. J. A. Baer, II, and Cecille K. Lowenhaupt, *Dining In—St. Louis* (Seattle: Peanut Butter Publishing, 1979), 147–57; Bolin, *Route 66 St. Louis*, 58–59; Bolin, *Route 66 St. Louis Cookbook*, 28–29; *Gourmet's Guide*, 185–86; Little, *Where to Eat*, 148, 150.

6. Paul A. Harris, "Charles Brown: A Star to the Stars," *St. Louis Post-Dispatch*, August 8, 1993, p. 25; Richard Jacobs, "Businesses Built on Negro Trade Suffer as Integration Spreads," *St. Louis Post-Dispatch*, April 5, 1964, sec. A, p. 5; Frank Norris, "Courageous Motorists: African American Pioneers on Route 66," *New Mexico Historical Review* 90, no. 5 (Summer 2015): 313; "7-Year-old Master of Boogie Woogie," *St. Louis Post-Dispatch*, June 6, 1946, sec. D, p, 3 (first quotation); Joe Sonderman, interview by Tom Peters, Hazlewood, Mo., May 18, 2015, p. 12 (second quotation), Greater Springfield Route 66 Oral History Project, Special Collections and Archives, Meyer Library, Missouri State University, Springfield, Mo., cited hereafter as Greater Springfield Route 66 Oral History Project; Gretchen Sorin, *Driving while Black: African American Travel and the Road to Civil Rights* (New York: Liveright Publishing, 2020), 81–90; W. Vernon Tietjen, "Louis, on Visit Here, Says Several Cities Are Bidding for Title Bout," *St. Louis Star-Times*, p. 12.

7. David Brown, "Miss Hulling's," *St. Louis Globe-Democrat*, November 12, 1961, clipping, "St. Louis Hotels, Taverns and Restaurants" Scrapbooks, 1:106–8, Library, Missouri Historical Society, St. Louis; Mary Kimbrough, "Food Is Her Business," *St. Louis Globe-Democrat*, August 2, 1973, clipping, "St. Louis Hotels, Taverns and Restaurants" Scrapbooks 2:62, Library, Missouri Historical Society; "New Cafeteria to Occupy Former Benish Location," *St. Louis Post-Dispatch*, January 28, 1934, sec. C, p. 1; Ellen Schlafly, "Miss Hulling's Recipe for Success," *St. Louis Post-Dispatch*, February 27, 1967, sec. D, p. 4; Jane Stern and Michael Stern, *Roadfood and Goodfood: Jane and Michael Stern's Coast-to-Coast Restaurant Guides Combined, Updated, and Expanded* (New York: Alfred A. Knopf, 1987), 371. For recipes prepared in Miss Hulling's Cafeterias, see Florence Hulling Apted, *Miss Hulling's Favorite Recipes* ([St. Louis]: Miss Hulling's Cafeteria, Inc., 1969), and Florence Hulling Apted, *Miss Hulling's Own Cook Book* (St. Louis: Miss Hulling's, 1962).

8. Richard Dudman, "St. Louis' Silent Racial Revolution: Newspapers Did Not Cover Campaign to Integrate Lunch Counters," *St. Louis Post-Dispatch*, June 11, 1990, sec. B, p. 3; Robert Joiner, "The Battle with Jim Crow: St. Louis CORE Won without Violence; Essayists Remind Us the Job's Not Done," *St. Louis Post-Dispatch*, February 4, 2001, sec. F, p. 8; Kenneth S. Jolly, *Black Liberation in the Midwest: The Struggle*

in St. Louis, Missouri, 1964–1970 (New York: Routledge, 2006), 24; Mary Kimbrough and Margaret W. Dagen, *Victory without Violence: The First Ten Years of the St. Louis Committee of Racial Equality (CORE), 1947–1957* (Columbia: University of Missouri Press, 2000), 32–104; "Negroes State Demands, Assail Sentences in Contempt Cases," *St. Louis Post-Dispatch*, November 22, 1963, Extra Edition, sec. A, pp. 1, 12; "Restaurants to Get Bid for Integration," *St. Louis Post-Dispatch*, October 22, 1960, sec. A, p. 9; "2 Negro Youths Arrested Twice in Café Sit-Ins," *St. Louis Post-Dispatch*, October 19, 1960, sec. A, p. 1.

9. Joseph Szalanski, *Boarding the Westbound: Journey of a Depression-Era Hobo* (Tarentum, Pa.: Word Association Publishers, 2010), 125 (second quotation); "Vanguard of Hoboes Here for Convention," *St. Louis Post-Dispatch*, April 11, 1937, sec. A, p. 11 (first quotation); "Wanderers Content at Transients' Camp," *St. Louis Post-Dispatch*, February 14, 1934, sec. B, p. 4.

10. "Century of Commerce Club Honors 13 New Members," *St. Louis (Mo.) Commerce* 51, no. 4 (April 1977): 26; "Curb Service Makes Life Easy and Simple for St. Louis Autoists," *St. Louis Star*, August 17, 1931, p. 2 (first quotation); "Funeral to Be Tomorrow for Henry J. Fabricius," *St. Louis Post-Dispatch*, December 4, 1959, sec. C, p. 3; "Hard Sell," *St. Louis Post-Dispatch*, December 9, 1976, sec. E, p. 1; John M. McGuire, "Twist and Shout," *St. Louis Post-Dispatch*, October 14, 1990, Magazine sec., pp. 8–11; "Neighborhood Tradition," *St. Louis Post-Dispatch*, June 20, 1991, sec. S, p. 3; "New Twist on Pretzel Bill Would Put Wraps on Project," *St. Louis Post-Dispatch*, July 21, 1967, sec. A, p. 12; "Pretzels, Pretzels!—30 Vendors Sell Them to Gravois Avenue Autoists," *St. Louis Star and Times*, September 27, 1932, p. 3 (second quotation); Tommy Robertson, "Vendors Are One Big, Happy Family," *St. Louis Post-Dispatch*, October 5, 1981, sec. A, p. 8; Nancy Shryock, "Pretzel People," *Profile St. Louis* (St. Louis, Mo.) 1, no. 30 (October 20, 1977): 3–5, 10; Dana L. Spitzer, "Pretzel Vendor Is St. Louis Institution," *St. Louis Post-Dispatch*, March 21, 1968, sec. W, pp. 4–5; Jane Stern and Michael Stern, *Roadfood: The Coast-to-Coast Guide to 500 of the Best Barbecue Joints, Lobster Shacks, Ice-cream Parlors, Highway Diners, and Much, Much More* (New York: Broadway Books, 2002), 314; "Street-Corner Pretzel Vendors a Fading Institution," *Springfield (Mo.) News-Leader*, December 8, 1996, sec. B, p. 4; Leah Thorsen, "Pretzel Vendor Collects Fans, City's OK," *St. Louis Post-Dispatch*, May 30, 2010, sec. B, p. 3; Theresa Tighe, "Pretzels? Pretzels? Pretzels? Street Vendors Are Institution," *St. Louis Post-Dispatch*, November 2, 1996, sec. A, p. 14.

11. Bolin, *Route 66 St. Louis*, 68–71; "Drive-Ins' Success Rests on Door Tray," *St. Louis Globe-Democrat*, May 6, 1951, clipping, "St. Louis Hotels, Taverns and Restaurants" Scrapbooks, 1:4, Library, Missouri Historical Society; Julie Stevenson, "Memories: The Corners of the Parkmoor Have Left Indelible Marks in Many Minds," *West End-Clayton Word* (St. Louis, Mo.), October 28, 1999, pp. 1, 8; Kip Welborn, "Ode to the Parkmoor," *Show Me Route 66* 15, no. 2 (Spring 2004): 25. For a book-length history of the Parkmoor Drive-Ins, see Lou Ellen McGinley and Stephanie Spurr, *Honk for Service: A Man, a Tray and the Glory Days of Drive-Ins* (Fredericksburg, Tex.: Tray Days Publishing, 2004). For original menus from the Parkmoor Drive-Ins, see Menu Collection, Library, Missouri Historical Society.

12. Bolin, *Route 66 St. Louis*, 109–10; Esley Hamilton, "Notes on the Eat-Rite Diner[,] 622 Chouteau, St. Louis," *Show Me Route 66* 20, no. 4 (Fall 2010): 7; "News from the Road: Classic Diner to Re-Open," *Show Me Route 66* 28, no. 2 (Spring 2018): 5; Joe Sonderman and Elizabeth Lauren, "The Melting Pot of St. Louis: The Eat-Rite Diner," *Show Me Route 66* 30, no. 1 (Winter 2020): 14–16, 18–19; "News from the Road: Eat-Rite Closes," *Show Me Route 66* 31, no. 1 (Spring 2021): 9; "South Side Raid Nets Gambling Machines," *St. Louis Post-Dispatch*, September 4, 1986, sec. A, p. 4; "Youth Gets 30 Years in Brick Killing," *St. Louis Post-Dispatch*, February 24, 1990, sec. C, p. 14.

13. T. Lindsay Baker, *Portrait of Route 66: Images from the Curt Teich Postcard Archives* (Norman: University of Oklahoma Press, 2016): 40–41; "Better Cookery Bureau, Star-Times," *St. Louis Star-Times*, July 5, 1935, p. 15; Bolin, *Route 66 St. Louis*, 80; Buckingham's, St. Louis, "Buckingham's Is Open for Luncheon at 12 Noon" (advertisement), *St. Louis Post-Dispatch*, December 15, 1967, sec. F, p. 7; Buckingham's, "You'll Like Our Chicken Dinners $1" (advertisement), *St. Louis Post-Dispatch*, May 17, 1942, sec. G, p. 10 (first quotation); "Clyde Buckingham," *St. Louis Globe-Democrat*, October 27, 1969, clipping, "Necrologies" Scrapbooks

28:122, Library, Missouri Historical Society; Duncan Hines, *Adventures in Good Eating* (Bowling Green, Ky.: Adventures in Good Eating, 1949), 191 (second quotation); "Lightning Hits Café; Flash Stuns Owner at Desk," *St. Louis Post-Dispatch*, July 7, 1949, sec. C, p. 4.

14. Bolin, *Route 66 St. Louis*, 83–84; Kate Godfrey, "Chow Biz," *St. Louis Post-Dispatch*, February 15, 1995, Seen Magazine sec., p. 22; Bill Helger, "The Route 66 'Rock Hill Food Corridor,'" *Show Me Route 66* 23, no. 2 (Spring 2013): 36–37; "Shot in the Hand," *St. Louis Post-Dispatch*, February 21, 1876, p. 1; Joe Sonderman, "Meet Me at the Trainwreck," *Show Me Route 66* 27, no. 2 (Spring 2017): 24–26, 28.

15. Russell Ainsworth, "Big Chief Revels in Reincarnation as '90s Grill: Restaurant Fed, Housed Travelers on Route 66," *St. Louis Post-Dispatch*, January 8, 1996, sec. W, pp. 1, 2, 5; Russell Ainsworth, "Big Chief Revival Serves up Memory of Route 66 Days," *St. Louis Post-Dispatch*, January 31, 1996, sec. SC, p. 2–3; Russell Ainsworth, "Ex-manager, 104, Shares Memories: 'Carefree Living,' Hard Work Blend," *St. Louis Post-Dispatch*, January 8, 1996, sec. W, p. 5; Big Chief Hotel, Pond, Mo., "Invite Your Friends to a Real Holiday Dinner at the Big Chief Hotel" (advertisement), *Meramec Valley Transcript* (Pacific, Mo.), May 25, 1934, p. 4; Bolin, *Route 66 St. Louis*, 94–97, 148–50; Joe Bonwich, "Dining Out: The Dakota Kids, New Steakhouse Is Family Friendly and at Home in the Mid-priced Range," *St. Louis Post-Dispatch*, November 26, 2003, Get Out supplement, p. 8; "First of Chain of Cabin Hotels Opens at Pond," *St. Louis Star-Times*, July 28, 1933, p. 22; "News a la Carte: Get Your Kicks, Again," *St. Louis Post-Dispatch*, January 4, 2007, Get Out supplement, p. 9; Nomination to the National Register of Historic Places for Big Chief Restaurant, 19 February 2003; "Something New in Hotels," *Pacific (Mo.) Transcript*, September 28, 1928, p. 1; Joe Sonderman, "The Big Chief Turns 90," *Show Me Route 66* 19, no. 4 (Fall 2019): 24–28; "Where H.E.E.C. Women Will Spend a Two-day Vacation," *Meramec Valley Transcript*, August 10, 1934, p. 1.

16. Bolin, *Route 66 St. Louis*, 143–45; David Gerard Hogan, *Selling 'Em by the Sack: White Castle and the Creation of American Food* (New York: New York University Press, 1997), 39–40; Marcia L. Koenig, "St. Louis Classic Culinary Traditions," *St. Louis Post-Dispatch*, September 2, 1981, sec. BN, p. 9; Kevin Meuhring, "Poor Man's Castle: Little Bitty Burgers Have Been Hanging in Since 1921," *St. Louis Post-Dispatch*, April 30, 1978, Pictures supplement, pp. 4, 6, 8–9, 11 (quotation); White Castle System, (Wichita, Kans.), "5 Hamburgers 10¢" (advertisement), *St. Louis Post-Dispatch*, December 5, 1937, sec. D, p. 8.

17. Marian Clark, "Ted Drewes Frozen Custard[,] St. Louis, Missouri," *Route 66 Federation News* 3, no. 1 (Winter 1997): 5–6; Brenda Enders, "Ted Drewes," *Show Me Route 66* 1, no. 1 (May 1990): 4–5; Harold Flaschbart, "Ted Drewes, at 61, Praises and Advises Earl Buchholz," *St. Louis Post-Dispatch*, January 25, 1959, sec. F, p. 4; Ellen Futterman, "The Custard King," *St. Louis Post-Dispatch*, July 10, 1988, Magazine sec., pp. 8–13; Jack Rice, "Christmas Tree Shopping in July," *St. Louis Post-Dispatch*, July 8, 1962, sec. J, p. 2; Robert Rubright, *Breakfast, Lunch and Diner: Stories, Characters and Favorite Dishes from Fascinating Restaurants in St. Louis and Beyond* (St. Louis: RO Press, 2009), 185–89; Stern and Stern, *Roadfood*, 319; Joe Sonderman, "The Scoop on a Route 66 Icon: Ted Drewes Frozen Custard Turns 90," *Route 66 Magazine* 26, no. 4 (Fall 2019): 8–10; Ted Drewes Frozen Custard, St. Louis, Mo., "1¢ Sale" (advertisement), *St. Louis Post-Dispatch*, June 14, 1957, sec. B, p. 2; Ted Drewes Frozen Custard, "Ted Drewes Frozen Custard" (advertisement), *St. Louis Star-Times*, May 11, 1934, p. 35; Tom Teague, *Searching for 66* (Springfield, Ill.: Samizdat House, 1991): 31–35; "Tennis Star Ted Drewes Dies at 70," *St. Louis Post-Dispatch*, January 29, 1968, sec. C, p. 4; "Tree Dealers Forego the Spirit of Giving," *St. Louis Post-Dispatch*, December 24, 1973, sec. A, p. 3; Elaine Viets, "Concrete and Custard," *St. Louis Post-Dispatch*, May 3, 1981, sec. K, p. 3; Michael Wallis, *Route 66: The Mother Road* (New York: St. Martin's Press, 1990), 49–52.

18. Anne Cooper Funderburg, *Chocolate, Strawberry and Vanilla: A History of American Ice Cream* (Bowling Green, Ky.: Bowling Green State University Popular Press, 1995): 149–50; Susan Manlin Katzman, "5 St. Louis Classics," *St. Louis Homes and Lifestyles* 4, no. 4 (May 1999), newcomers guide section, p. ng26; Stern and Stern, *Roadfood and Goodfood*, 377; Jerri Stroud, "Father of the Blizzard Is Dairy Queen Loyalist," *St. Louis Post-Dispatch*, September 15, 1986, sec. A, pp. 10, 13.

19. C. H. (Skip) Curtis, "Driving Missouri US 66 St. Louis County," *Show Me Route 66* 10, no. 4 (Winter 1998): 6–10, 15–17; Powell, "U.S. Highway 66 in St. Louis," pp. 43–44; Joe Sonderman, "City 66 in St. Louis," *Route 66 Magazine* 25, no. 2 (Spring 2018): 22–25; Joe Sonderman, "The Clover Leaf," *Show Me Route 66* 26, no. 1 (Winter 2016): 30–33; Welborn, *Things to Look Out for on Route 66*, 33–37; Jim Winnerman, "A Path across the Mississippi," *Route 66 Magazine* 12, no. 4 (Fall 2005): 14–15.

20. Bolin, *Route 66 St. Louis*, 276; Joe Bonwich, "It's Raining Hens! (Hallelujah!)," *St. Louis Post-Dispatch*, October 23, 2003, Get Out supplement, pp. 18–19; "Drug Ringleader Pleads Guilty," *St. Louis Post-Dispatch*, December 3, 1985, sec. A, p. 8; John T. Edge, *Fried Chicken: An American Story* (New York: G. P. Putnam's Sons, 2004), 30–31; *Gould's St. Louis (Missouri) City Directory 1930* (St. Louis: Polk-Gould Directory Co., 1930), 1265; Carolyn Olson, "Romine's: Fried Chicken Has Pleased Diners Here for 61 Years," *St. Louis Post-Dispatch*, June 25, 1992, sec. G, p. 12; Rose Polster, interview by [Tommy Pike], St. Louis, Mo., June 8, 2001, audio recording in Route 66 Oral History Collection (Missouri Route 66 Association), Special Collections and Archives, Meyer Library, Missouri State University, Springfield, Mo., hereafter cited as Route 66 Oral History Collection; Romine Sandwich Shop, St. Louis, Mo., "Cook—Experienced" (advertisement), *St. Louis Post-Dispatch*, August 16, 1940, sec. C, p. 4; Romine's Restaurant, St. Louis, Mo., "Business Men's Luncheon" (advertisement), *St. Louis Post-Dispatch*, January 8, 1967, sec. K, p. 20; Rebecca Roussell, "Why Did the Chicken Cross the Missouri River?," *St. Louis Post-Dispatch*, November 28, 2006, sec. C, pp. 1, 4; U.S. Census Bureau, Census of 1940, Population Schedules, St. Louis City, Mo., Enumeration District 96–781, page 1A, Roll m-t0627–02181, Microcopy T627, National Archives and Records Administration, Washington, D.C.

21. R. T. Bamber, "Spencer's Grill," *Kirkwood Historical Review* (Kirkwood Historical Society, Kirkwood, Mo.) 28, no. 1 (March 1989): 3; Bolin, *Route 66 St. Louis*, 303–9; Joe Pollack and Ann Lemons Pollack, *The Great St. Louis Eats Book* (St. Louis: Virginia Publishing, 2005), 195; Rubright, *Breakfast, Lunch and Diner*, 82–86; Kip Welborn, "End of the Plate Lunch Special," *Show Me Route 66* 15, no. 2 (Spring 2004): 16; Kip Welborn, "News from the Road: Spencers Grill," *Show Me Route 66* 16, no. 3 (Summer 2005): 8.

22. Gary A. Adlkins, "Pieces of the Road," *Show Me Route 66* 13, no. 4 (Fall 2002): 15; Greg Freeman, "Time Takes Its Toll on Howard Johnson's but Not on Memories," *St. Louis Post-Dispatch*, April 23, 2002, sec. B, p. 1; Margaret Gillerman, "Lights beneath the Orange Roof Blink Out," *St. Louis Post-Dispatch*, October 24, 2002, sec. W, p. 5; "Howard Johnson Chain to Acquire Third Place Here," *St. Louis Post-Dispatch*, December 5, 1954, sec. E, p. 2; "Howard Johnson's Comes to St. Louis with Restaurant, 28 Flavors of Ice Cream," *St. Louis Globe-Democrat*, June 21, 1953, clipping, "St. Louis Hotels, Taverns and Restaurants" Scrapbooks 1:13–14, Library, Missouri Historical Society; Howard Johnson's, Kirkwood, Mo., "Howard Johnson's New Restaurant" (advertisement), *St. Louis Post-Dispatch*, September 26, 1955, sec. B, p. 5; "Pieces of the Road," *Papa Joad's 66, the Independent News Journal of Route 66* 2, no. 4 (Winter 2002): 11; Kip Welborn, "Memories of Howard Johnson's," *Show Me Route 66* 13, no. 4 (Fall 2002): 16 (quotation).

23. John F. Bradbury Jr., Rolla, Mo., email to T. Lindsay Baker, Rio Vista, Tex., October 8, 2020, paper copy, author's collection; John F. Bradbury Jr., "'Good Water and Wood but the Country Is a Miserable Botch': Flatland Soldiers Confront the Ozarks," *Missouri Historical Review* 90, no. 2 (January 1996): 166–86; National U.S. 66 Highway Association, Clinton, Okla., *1600 Miles of 4 Lane Highway Chicago to Los Angeles[,] Main Street of America[,] Drive US 66[,] Shortest[,] Fastest[,] Year Round[,] Best Route across the Scenic West[,] the Will Rogers Highway[,] the Grand Canyon Route* (Clinton, Okla.: National U.S. 66 Highway Assn., 1964), booklet, Map File, History Department, Los Angeles Public Library, Los Angeles; Nomination to the National Register of Historic Places Nomination for Route 66 in Missouri; Frank Norris, "The Twilight of Route 66: Transitioning from Highway to Freeway, 1956–85," *Chronicles of Oklahoma* 93, no. 3 (Fall 2015): 312–27; Quinta Scott and Susan Croce Kelly, *Route 66: The Highway and Its People* (Norman: University of Oklahoma Press, 1988), 18–31, 178–89; Joe Sonderman, *Route 66 Missouri* (Atglen, Pa.: Schiffer Publishing, 2010), 4–128.

24. Baker, *Portrait of Route* 66, 42–43; Bolin, *Route 66 St. Louis*, 327–31; Pat Henderson, "Once-thriving Communities on Missouri's 66: Rock City and Sylvan Beach," *Route 66 Federation News* 13, no. 4 (Autumn 2007): 16–18; "Many Amusements at Sylvan Beach," *Meramec Valley Transcript*, June 8, 1934, p. 1; *Missouri, a Guide to the "Show Me" State*, 406; Sylvan Beach Amusement Park, Kirkwood, Mo., "Sylvan Beach Amusement Park" (advertisement), *Meramec Valley Transcript*, August 7, 1936, p. 5 (first quotation); Sylvan Beach Restaurant and Bar, Kirkwood, Mo., "Grand Opening Saturday, October 20th" (advertisement), *St. Louis Post-Dispatch*, October 18, 1945, sec. A, p. 17; Sylvan Beach Restaurant, "Chicken Dinner[,] Family Style" (advertisement), *St. Louis Star-Times*, October 16, 1937, p. 15; Sylvan Beach Restaurant, "Try Our Special 1-pound Steak" (advertisement), *St Louis Post-Dispatch*, November 3, 1940, sec. H, p. 2 (second quotation); "Sylvan Beach Restaurant Liquor License Suspended," *St. Louis Post-Dispatch*, April 8, 1960, sec. A, p. 17; "Sylvan Beach Tavern Burns Tuesday A.M.," *Meramec Valley Transcript*, June 8, 1934, p. 1; "Truck in Collision Crashes through Restaurant Wall," *St. Louis Post-Dispatch*, April 28, 1951, sec. A, p. 3. Although the Sylvan Beach Restaurant no longer exists, its neon sign is preserved in the Interpretive Center at the Route 66 State Park near Eureka, Mo., where at the time of writing it was exhibited illuminated.

25. Bolin, *Route 66 St. Louis*, 352–61; Skip Curtis, "The Beach," *Route 66 Magazine* 11, no. 1 (Winter 2003–4): 12–14; Michal Dale, "Ozarks Answers: Route 66 State Park on Site of Times Beach," *Springfield News-Leader*, March 20, 2000, sec. B, p. 8; Pat Henderson, "Once-thriving Communities on Missouri's 66: Times Beach," *Route 66 Federation News* 13, no. 2 (Spring 2007): 25–27; Marilyn Leistner, "The Times Beach Story," *Show Me Route 66* 23, no. 1 (Spring 2013): 36–39; John McGuire, "Times Beach: Dust to Dust," *St. Louis Post-Dispatch*, March 10, 1985, sec. D, pp. 3, 14; James R. Powell, "Route 66 State Park," *Route 66 Magazine* 5, no. 1 (Winter 1997–98): 48–49; Randy Smith, "Times Beach Invaded!," *66 News* (Route 66 Association of Illinois), Summer 2000, pp. 15–16.

26. Bolin, *Route 66 St. Louis*, 362–65; Bridge Head Inn, [Eureka, Mo.], *Good Food Is Good Health*[,] *Bridge Head "The Inn Beautiful"* ([Eureka, Mo.]: Bridge Head, 1938), menu, courtesy of Steven Rider; "Grand Opening of Bridge Head Inn Saturday Night," *Meramec Valley Transcript*, October 2, 1936, p. 1; "Inn 'Disorderly,' Says County, Asks Closure," *St. Louis Star-Times*, August 21, 1947, p. 30; "Inn Operators Buy Bridgehead across Meramec," *St. Louis Post-Dispatch*, September 21, 1947, sec. J, p. 1; [Kit] Regan, "Round the Town with Regan," *St. Louis Star-Times*, August 31, 1940, p. 7 (quotation); Russell A. Olsen, *Route 66 Lost and Found: Mother Road Ruins and Relics—The Ultimate Collection* (Minneapolis: Voyageur Press, 2011), 72–73; Steiny's Inn, Eureka, Mo., *Steiny's Inn* (Eureka, Mo.: Steiny's Inn, [ca. 1955]), menu, courtesy of Steven Rider; Steiny's Inn, "Steiny's Inn[,] a Delicious Filet Mignon or Fried Tenderized Milk Fed Chicken Full Course Dinner $1.00" (advertisement), *St. Louis Post-Dispatch*, April 5, 1942, sec. A, p. 11.

27. Bolin, *Route 66 St. Louis*, 410–13; Bonwich, "It's Raining Hens," p. 18 (quotation); Marian Clark, "Red Cedar Inn[,] Pacific, Missouri," *Route 66 Federation News* 2, no. 4 (Autumn 1996): 5–7; Valarie Kearney, "Red Cedar Gets High Marks for Blend of Atmosphere, History, Good Food," *Show Me Route 66* 6, no. 2 (December 1994): 4–5; [Missouri, Office of Historic Preservation], "Architectural/Historic Inventory Survey Form[,] Route 66 in Missouri[,] Reference No.: SL.019[,] Historic Name: Red Cedar Inn," Office of Historic Preservation, Jefferson City, Mo.; "News from the Road: What's New on Route 66," *Show Me Route 66* 20, no. 4 (Fall 2010): 39; Nomination to the National Register of Historic Places for Red Cedar Inn; "Something New[,] Get up a Party" (advertisement), *Washington (Mo.) Missourian*, November 17, 1949, sec. B, p. 3; Red Cedar Tavern, Pacific, Mo., "Every Wednesday and Thursday Dancing" (advertisement), *Meramec Valley Transcript*, October 18, 1935, p. 8; [Kit] Regan, "Round the Town with Regan," *St. Louis Star-Times*, November 24, 1938, p. 27; Joe Sonderman, "Red Cedar Inn: Where Past and Present Come Together," *Show Me Route 66* 29, no. 2 (Spring 2019): 10–12, 14; Joe Sonderman, "The Red Cedar Inn," *Route 66 Magazine* 26, no. 3 (Summer 2019): 30–32; Jim Winnerman, "The Red Cedar Inn," *Route 66 Magazine* 11, no. 4 (Fall 2004): 20–21.

28. Bolin, *Route 66 St. Louis*, 413–19; "Architectural/Historic Inventory Survey Form[,] Route 66 in Missouri[,] Reference No.: SL.020[,] Historic Name: Jensen Point," Office of Historic Preservation; Cheryl

Eichar Jett, "The Henry Shaw Gardenway," *Show Me Route 66* 29, no. 1 (Winter 2019): 21–26; "News from the Road: Jensen's Point Re-Opens," *Show Me Route 66* 26, no. 2 (Spring 2016): 6; "Pavilion Is Dedicated on Cliff on Meramec," *St. Louis Post-Dispatch*, May 31, 1939, sec. A, p. 8; Kip Welborn, "Cleanup Day at Jensen's Point," *Show Me Route 66* 26, no. 1 (Winter 2016): 10–11; Kip Welborn, "Jensen's Point, the Henry Shaw Gardenway and the Gateway to the West," *Route 66 Federation News* 21, no. 3 (Autumn 2015): 19–37.

29. Bolin, *Route 66 St. Louis*, 419; *Missouri: A Guide to the "Show Me" State*, American Guide Series (New York: Duell, Sloan and Pearce, 1941), 407.

30. Herb's Auction Service, Pacific, Mo., "Antique Auction" (advertisement), *St. Louis Post-Dispatch*, September 4, 1983, sec. 1, p. 25; "Men Reported Missing, Wounded and Prisoners of War from This Area," *St. Clair (Mo.) Chronicle*, November 4, 1943, p. 1; "Pacific's First War Casualty Reported," *Daily Capital News* (Jefferson City, Mo.), October 29, 1943, p. 14; Pacific Softball Association, Pacific, Mo., "Annual Valentine Dance" (advertisement), *Washington Missourian*, February 10, 1955, sec. B, p. 6; "St. Bridget's Annual Fall Festival Nov. 17," *Franklin County Tribune* (Union, Mo.), November 11, 1949, p. 1; "Tom Eagleton to Speak at Pacific," *Washington Missourian*, September 15, 1960, sec. A, p. 3; Williams' Shack, Pacific, Mo., "Dance Music from 9 'Till ? at Williams' Shack" (advertisement), *St. Louis Post-Dispatch*, February 29, 1940, sec. C, p. 4; Williams' Shack, "Williams' Shack Beer—Sandwiches" (advertisement), *Meramec Valley Transcript*, March 9, 1934, p. 4; Williams' Shack, "I'm on My Way to Williams' Shack" (advertisement), *Pacific Transcript*, July 14, 1933, p. 4; Williams Shack, *Williams Shack New Rathskeller*[,] *December 31, 1941*[,] *New Year Eve* (Pacific, Mo.: Williams Shack, 1941), advertising card, author's collection.

31. Bolin, *Route 66 St. Louis*, 397, 440–44; Skip Curtis, "The Banana Stand," *Show Me Route 66* 10, no. 3 (Fall 1998): 10–12 (first quotation); "Diamonds Is Destroyed Late Wednesday Night," *Washington (Mo.) Citizen*, February 27, 1948, p. 1; Gary W. Ferguson, "'Million Dollar a Mile' Becomes 'Death Valley,'" *St. Louis Post-Dispatch*, April 17, 1960, Pictures supplement, pp. 2–5 (third quotation); "Formal Opening of 'Diamonds' Set for July 10," *St. Louis Star-Times*, July 1, 1949, p. 27; Spencer Groff, *Diamond Dust* (Kansas City, Mo.: Brown-White Company, 1936), 56–96; Pat Henderson, "The Diamonds and Twin Bridges Café: A Route 66 Connection," *Route 66 Federation News* 11, no. 2 (Spring 2005): 10–13; Susan Croce Kelly and Quinta Scott, "Haven of the Road: It Caters to as Many as 1,000 Truckers a Day," *St. Louis Post-Dispatch*, September 30, 1979, Pictures supplement, pp. 6–7, 9, 11, 13; John A. Kofton, "My Girl Lou and Me: The Mother Road and East in 1952," *Newsletter of the Canadian Route 66 Association* 6, no. 3 (November 2002): 1 (second quotation); "Louis B. Eckelkamp Sr., 70; Was Banker and Businessman," *St. Louis Post-Dispatch*, March 9, 1983, sec. C, p. 23; Joe Sonderman, "The Diamonds," *Show Me Route 66* 24, no. 1 (Spring 2014): 18–25; Joe Sonderman and Kevin Krattli, "Ghosts of the Million Dollar Stretch," *Show Me Route 66* 30, no. 3 (Summer 2020): 36–38, 40–41.

32. Bolin, *Route 66 St. Louis*, 441; Pat Henderson, "The Diamonds and Twin Bridges Café," 10–13; "Key's Twin Bridge Café," *St. Clair Chronicle*, July 26, 1956, p. [7]; E. Knap, "Notes on Wildlife News," *Washington Missourian*, July 14, 1948, sec. 2, p. 3 (quotation); "Architectural/Historical Inventory Survey Form[,] Route 66 in Missouri[,] Reference No.: FR.009a[,] Historic Name: Key's Twin Bridge Café," 1993, Office of Historic Preservation; Sonderman and Krattli, "Ghosts of the Million Dollar Stretch," 41.

33. William Childress, "No Frills, Just Home-cooked Food," *St. Louis Post-Dispatch*, April 16, 1989, sec. C, p. 2; "Lewis Café Gets a New Front . . . by Accident," *St. Clair Chronicle*, July 3, 1952, p. 1; "Lewis Café Has 14th Anniversary," *St. Clair Chronicle*, October 16, 1952, p. 1; "Lewis Café Will Double Its Size," *St. Clair Chronicle*, October 19, 1961, p. 1; "Lewis, Vergil," *St. Louis Post-Dispatch*, April 16, 1984, sec. B, p. 9; *Missouri: A Guide to the " Show Me" State*, 407; Dorothy O. Moore, "St. Clair Sidelights," *St. Clair Chronicle*, July 16, 1953, p. [7] (third quotation); Rubright, *Breakfast, Lunch and Diner*, 54–57; Joe Sonderman, "Open for Business: Route 66 in St. Clair, Missouri," *Show Me Route 66* 25, no. 2 (Spring 2015): 11–16; "32 Years for Lewis Café," *St. Clair Chronicle*, October 8, 1970, p. 1; "Vergil Lewis Receives Honors That Conjure up Chicken Pickin'," *St. Clair Chronicle*, January 24, 1973, p. [5] (first and second quotations).

34. Hoyt Alden, "Persia's Gift to Backyard Chefs," *St. Louis Post-Dispatch*, July 5, 1956, sec. D, p. 2; Frances Dawson, "Favorite Dish: Guinea Hen Braised with Sherry Sauce," *St. Louis Post-Dispatch*, November 20, 1949, Pictures supplement, p. 4; "Funeral to Be Tomorrow for Louis Wurzburger," *St. Louis Post-Dispatch*, May 14, 1960, sec. A, p. 3; Duncan Hines, *Adventures in Good Eating* (Bowling Green, Ky.: Adventures in Good Eating, 1947), 176; "Obituary," *Sullivan (Mo.) Tri-County News*, December 2, 1965, p. [8]; Thomas Arthur Repp, *Route 66: The Empires of Amusement* (Lynnwood, Wash.: Mock Turtle Press, 1999), 46–51; Jack D. Rittenhouse, *A Guide to Route 66* (Los Angeles: privately printed, 1946; repr., Albuquerque: University of New Mexico Press, 1989), 23; Robert Ruark, "Wurzburgers Offer the Best in Vittles," *Detroit Free Press*, July 4, 1949, p. 18; Joe Sonderman, "Meramec Caverns," *Show Me Route 66* 23, no. 4 (Fall 2013): 10–16; "Stanton Restaurateur, Wurzburger, Dies," *Sunday News and Leader* (Springfield, Mo.), May 15, 1960, sec. A, p. 23; "Well Known Cook Dies at Stanton," *Sullivan Tri-County News*, November 25, 1965, p. [4] (quotation); Morrison Wood, "Report on Dining out on Trip West," *Chicago Daily Tribune*, June 24, 1951, pt. 7, sec. 3, pp. 1–2; Louis Wurzburger, Stanton, Mo., "Cook" (advertisement), *St. Louis Post-Dispatch*, February 9, 1919, sec. B, p. 12.

35. *Missouri, a Guide to the "Show Me" State*, 409–10; Cuba File, Missouri Place Names 1928–1945 Collection, State Historical Society of Missouri, Columbia, Missouri; Rittenhouse, *Guide Book to Highway 66*, 24 (first quotation); Diane Wood, *An Ordinary Adventure: Retracing Mom and Grandpa's 1934 Trip on Route 66—In a Model A* (Los Alamitos, Calif.: Life in the Dash, 2018): 52–53 (second quotation).

36. "Auto Accident near Cuba Fatal to Two," *St. Clair Chronicle*, April 21, 1932, p. 1; "Driving Missouri US 66 Crawford County," *Show Me Route 66* 9, no. 4 (Winter 1997): 13; "Fire Destroys Building at Cuba in Zero Weather," *St. Clair Chronicle*, January 11, 1940, p. 1; Emma Comfort Dunn, "The Lazy Y," *Show Me Route 66* 8, no. 3 (Fall 1996): 12–13 (quotations); Lazy Y Camp, Cuba, Mo., "Tourist Camp" (advertisement), *St. Louis Post-Dispatch*, October 29, 1933, sec. C, p. 9; "Local News of the Week," *Republican-Tribune* (Union, Mo.), October 21, 1927, p. 5; "Marshal Gets Robbers," *Washington Citizen*, August 29, 1930, p. [6]; "Missouri Weekly Industrial Review," *Macon (Mo.) Chronicle-Herald*, June 1, 1932, p. 3; "R. J. Horsefield Hurt in Auto Accident," *Republican-Tribune*, September 21, 1928, p. 1; "Three Robberies in Cuba during One Night," *St. Clair Chronicle*, July 20, 1933, p. 1.

37. Cherwyn Cole, "Still on the Road," *Route Magazine*, October–November 2020, pp. 18–24; Connie Echols, Wagon Wheel Motel, Cuba, Mo., to T. Lindsay Baker, Rio Vista, Tex., January 12, 2021, typewritten letter, author's collection; Riva Echols, *The Wagon Wheel Motel on Route 66* (Cuba, Mo.: South Fanning Ink, 2011): 23–30, 45–53, 61–97 (quotations, p. 49); Cheryl Eichar Jett, "'A Home Away from Home': The History of the Wagon Wheel Motel," *Show Me Route 66* 25, no. 3 (Summer 2015): 14–16; Nomination to the National Register of Historic Places for Wagon Wheel Motel; Joe Sonderman, "A New Era for the Wagon Wheel," *Show Me Route 66* 20, no. 1 (Winter 2010): 18; "Wagon Wheel in New Setting at Cuba," *St. Clair Chronicle*, August 30, 1956, p. [5]; "Wagon Wheel Motel Debuts New Shop and Restored Rooms," *Route 66 Federation News* 16, no. 3 (Summer 2010): 23; Jim Winnerman, "Wagon Wheel Rolls Again!," *Route 66 Magazine* 18, no. 1 (Winter 2010–11): 18–21.

38. John F. Bradbury Jr., "From Knobview to Rosati," *Newsletter of the Phelps County Historical Society* N.S., 15 (April 1997): 3–8; Leo Cardetti, "Rosati since 1935," *Newsletter of the Phelps County Historical Society* N.S., no. 15 (April 1979): 9–11; Echols, *Wagon Wheel Motel*, 46, 56; Angela Hancock, and Nancy Honssinger, eds., "'We Hardly Talk Italian Anymore': A Visit with Joe and Sophie Piazza," *Bittersweet* (Lebanon, Mo.) 7, no. 1 (Fall 1979): 4–13; William Kaszynski, *Route 66: Images of America's Main Street* (Jefferson, N.C.: McFarland, 2003), 38–40; Susan Croce Kelly, "Survival along Route 66: The People Who Live near Old Road Remember the Way It Was before I-44 Upstaged It," *St. Louis Post-Dispatch*, May 17, 1981, Sunday Magazine, p. 12; Robert Magnin, *Life on Old "66*," edited by Arlene Magnin (n.p.: Paul Magnin, 1995), 18–19 (quotation); *Missouri, a Guide to the "Show Me" State*, 410; John E. Rybolt, "The Story of Rosati, Missouri," *Vincentian Heritage* 13, no. 1 (Spring 1992): 69–74; Robert F. Scheef, "Prohibition Vineyards: The Italian Contribution to Viticulture in Missouri," *Missouri Historical Review* 88, no. 3 (April 1994): 279–300; Tom

Snyder, *The Route 66 Traveler's Guide and Roadside Companion* (New York: St. Martin's Press, 1990), 23; Teague, *Searching for 66*, 45–47; Kip Welborn, "Growing Grapes on Route 66: The Story of the People Who Brought Grapes to Rosati, Missouri[,] on Route 66," *Route 66 Federation News* 18, no. 3 (Autumn 2012): 32–41; Kip Welborn, "The Wine Producers in the Rosati-St. James Area: Missouri Grapes Are Not Only Used for Slathering on Toast," *Route 66 Federation News* 19, no. 1 (Spring 2013): 25–35.

Many local residents, as well as occasional Route 66 travelers who chanced to see advertisements, as early as the 1930s and 1940s enjoyed parish fundraiser spaghetti dinners organized by the predominately Italian members of St. Anthony Catholic Church in Rosati. "400 Attend Spaghetti Supper at Rosati," *Rolla (Mo.) Herald*, October 30, 1941, p. 1; Ladies Sodality, St. Anthony Catholic Church, Rosati, Mo., "Italian Spaghetti Dinner" (advertisement), *Rolla Herald*, October 23, 1952, p. 5; Ladies Sodality, St. Anthony Catholic Church, Rosati, Mo., "Spaghetti Dinner in the New Church Building" (advertisement), *Rolla Herald*, June 1, 1949, p. 2; [St. Anthony Catholic Church, Rosati, Mo.], "Spaghetti Dinner" (advertisement), *Rolla Herald*, May 4, 1944, p. 5.

39. "Architectural/Historic Inventory Survey Form[,] Route 66 in Missouri[,] Reference No.: PH:004[,] Historic Name: Rose Cafe," 1993, Office of Historic Preservation; Leann K. Arndt and John F. Bradbury, "The Route 66 Photographs of Rolla Photographer I. J. Baumgardner," *Newsletter of the Phelps County Historical Society* N.S., No. 45 (April 2012): 11–12; John Bullock, "My Corner of Route 66," *Show Me Route 66* 8, no. 2 (Summer 1996): 12–13; Commercial Café, St. James, Mo., "Fountain Service[,] Good Steak Dinners" (advertisement), in Keith McCanse, *Where to Go in the Ozarks*, 4th ed. (St. Louis, Mo.: Hotel Mayfair, 1931), 75; "News from the Road: What's New on Route 66," *Show Me Route 66* 20, no. 4 (Fall 2010): 41; "St. James Chamber of Commerce Organized with Dr. Breuer as President," *Rolla Herald*, March 8, 1928, p. [2].

40. Arndt and Bradbury, "Route 66 Photographs," 12; Kozy Kottage Kamp, St. James, Mo., "For Sale: House Trailer" (advertisement), *Rolla Herald*, June 24, 1937, p. 8; "Kozy Cottage" Vertical File, John F. Bradbury Jr. Files, State Historical Society of Missouri, Curtis Laws Wilson Library, Missouri University of Science and Technology, Rolla; Norris, "Courageous Motorists, 19, "St. James Man Drops Dead at Fire," *St. Clair Chronicle*, February 19, 1942, p. 1. Route 66 historian Joe Sonderman described the problems for African American travelers passing through small-town Missouri this way: "When you got out in the rural areas every time you stopped, you know, it was a chance for an encounter with a local that wouldn't go well." Joe Sonderman, interview by Tom Peters, Hazlewood, Mo., May 18, 2015, p. 12, audio recording and typewritten transcript, Greater Springfield Route 66 Oral History Project.

41. "Architectural/Historic Inventory Survey Form[,] Route 66 in Missouri[,] Reference No.: PH:007[,] Historic Name: Rock Haven Tourist Court and Restaurant," 1993, Office of Historic Preservation; D.R.B Realtors, St. Louis, Mo., "Tourist Court[,] Rock Haven Motor Court" (advertisement), *St. Louis Post-Dispatch*, October 2, 1949, sec. C, p. 6; "Liquor Licenses Suspended," *Springfield (Mo.) Daily News*, February 17, 1977, p. 28; "Ozarks Dental Group Has Dinner Meeting," *Rolla Herald*, November 29, 1951, p. 2; "Pete Smith to Manage Rock Haven," *Rolla Herald*, May 14, 1953, sec. A, p. 1; "Real Estate Transfers," *Bland (Mo.) Courier*, January 30, 1964, p. [5]; Rock Haven, St. James, Mo., "For Sale—Wind Charger" (advertisement), *Rolla Herald*, December 4, 1941, p. 8; "Waring's/Rock Haven" Vertical File, John F. Bradbury Jr. Files.

42. *Missouri: A Guide to the "Show Me" State*, 411–14; *Phelps County Tourist Map* (Rolla, Mo.: Rolla Chamber of Commerce, [ca. 1935]; repr., n.p., n.d.), map, author's collection.

43. Kaszynski, *Route 66*, 40–41; Kentucky-Tennessee Light and Power Company, Bowling Green, Ky., "Industrial Survey of Rolla, Missouri," typescript with photographs, 1931, p. 2, Archives, Curtis Laws Wilson Library, Missouri University of Science and Technology, Rolla, Mo.; Diane Mattes, "Tourists Got Their 'Kicks' on 66 in Rolla," *Rolla (Mo.) Daily News*, September 30, 1984, sec. B, p. 1; "Montgomery and Fagan Lease Sinclair Tavern," *Rolla Herald*, June 4, 1942, p. 1; "Outstanding New Year Observance," *Rolla Herald*, January 6, 1938, p. 1; "Pierce Company to Build Restaurant Chain on Highways," *St. Louis Globe-Democrat*, January 10, 1929, p. 1; "Pierce Pennant Hotel Open," *Rolla Herald*, November 7, 1929, p. 5; "Rolla (Mo.) Motel Burns, Damage Put at $100,000," *St. Louis Post-Dispatch*, August 19, 1953, sec. B, p. 2;

Keith A. Sculle, "'Our Company Feels That the Ozarks Are a Good Investment . . .': The Pierce Pennant Tavern System," *Missouri Historical Review* 93, no. 3 (April 1999): 293–307; Sinclair Refining Company, Tulsa, *Sinclair Pennant Hotels and Taverns* (Tulsa: Sinclair Refining Co., [ca. 1930]), 1–8, in "Pennant Tavern—Rolla, Mo." Vertical File, John F. Bradbury Jr. Files; "To Erect Bus Depot and Filling Station," *Rolla Herald*, November 3, 1927, p. 1.

44. "Architectural/Historic Inventory Survey Form[,] Route 66 in Missouri[,] Reference No.: PH:008[,] Historic Name: Bell Café and Bus Station," 1993, Office of Historic Preservation; "Bell's Café Changes Hands," *Rolla Herald*, June 17, 1943, p. 1; Bell's Café, Rolla, Mo., "Have You Ever Taken a Meal at Bell's Café" (advertisement), *Rolla Herald*, April 30, 1942, p. 5; Bell's Café, "Turkey Dinner, 50¢ Sunday at Bell's" (advertisement), *Rolla Herald*, November 23, 1933, p. 1; R. D. Hohenfeldt, "Last 66 Business Building Razed," *Rolla Daily News*, January 6, 2002, sec. A, p. 8; "Plans for Modern New Bus Depot Announced," *Rolla Herald*, October 30, 1947, p. 1; R. & M. Motor Company, Rolla, Mo., "Announcement" (advertisement), *Rolla Herald*, March 14, 1929, p. 5; "17-ton Truck Crashes into Café at Rolla," *St. Clair Chronicle*, May 20, 1943, p. 1; "Watermans Will Celebrate 60th Wedding Anniversary," *Rolla Daily News*, March 9, 1997, sec. A, p. 13.

45. Rich Dinklea II, "Farewell Zeno's," *Show Me Route 66* 22, no. 1 (Winter 2012): 14–15, 17; Vernelle Gasser, interview by John F. Bradbury Jr., May 18, 1993, manuscript notes with follow-up typewritten letter, "Route 66 Phelps County" Vertical File, John F. Bradbury Jr. Files; R. D. Hohenfeldt, "Landmark to Close: Zeno's Leaves behind Legacy of Over 50 Years," *Rolla Daily News*, October 21, 2011, 1, 13; Michael Scheffer, "A Golden Oldie: Zeno's Motel and Steak House Turns 50," *Show Me Route 66* 18, no. 3–4 (Summer–Fall 2007): 11; "Vernelle Vera Gasser 1917–2015[,] Hairdresser for Over 70 Years," *Rolla Daily News*, January 13, 2015, p. 3; Zeno's Steakhouse and Motel, Rolla, Mo., *Zeno's[,] Experience the Elegance* (Rolla, Mo.: Zeno's Steakhouse and Motel, [ca. 2010]), folder in "Zeno's" Vertical File, John F. Bradbury Jr. Files.

46. Leann K. Arndt, "From Centerville to Doolittle," *Newsletter of the Phelps County Historical Society* N.S., no. 48 (October 2013): 14–26; [Ruth Corder], "Starting at Martin Springs Store and Cabins," typescript, [1994], unpaged, in "Ruth Corder" Vertical File, John F. Bradbury Jr. Files; "Doolittle Dedicated by General Doolittle," *Rolla Herald*, October 17, 1946, p. 1; "Doolittle to Fly Back to Missouri to Dedicate Town Named for Him," *Rolla Herald*, October 10, 1946, p. 1; Joe Sonderman, "Doolittle, Missouri," *Show Me Route 66* 23, no. 2 (Summer 2016): 16–23.

47. "Architectural/Historic Inventory Survey Form[,] Route 66 in Missouri[,] Reference No.: PH:023 [,] Historic Name: Bennett's Catfish Cafe," 1993, Office of Historic Preservation; Pauline Badger, interview by John F. Bradbury Jr., May 11, 1993, manuscript notes in "Route 66 Phelps County" Vertical File, John F. Bradbury Jr. Files; John Bradbury, "Bennett's Catfish," *Show Me Route 66* 10, no. 2 (Summer 1998): 10–11; "Newburg News," *Rolla Herald*, June 19, 1941, p. 8; Paul Bennett Café and Camp Ground, Doolittle, Mo., "Camp Meeting" (advertisement), *Rolla Herald*, July 6, 1949, p. 2; Paul Bennett's Cabin Camp, Doolittle, Mo., "Victory Camp Meeting" (advertisement), *Rolla Herald*, July 12, 1945, p. 4 (first quotation); Paul Bennett Tabernacle, Doolittle, Mo., "Blackwood Brothers Quartet" (advertisement), *Rolla Herald*, July 6, 1950, p. 4; "Paul Bennett Will Open Revival Here," *Springfield (Mo.) Leader*, January 3, 1925, p. 2; "Rev. Paul Bennett Funeral Conducted Yesterday in Newburg," *Rolla Herald*, March 1, 1951, p. 1; Joe Sonderman, "The Fishing, Coon Hunting Preacher of the Ozarks: Paul Bennett and Bennett's Catfish," *Show Me Route 66* 31, no. 1 (Spring 2021): 36–38, 40–41; Edward W. Sowers, "The Editor Says," *Rolla Daily News*, April 24, 1981, sec. A, p. 4.

48. [Corder], "Starting at Martin Springs Store," unpaged; Eldomar Restaurant, Doolittle, Mo., "Restaurant" (advertisement), *St. Louis Post-Dispatch*, September 13, 1953, sec. D, p. 9; Elsie Hudgens, Doolittle, M[iss] o[uri], to [John F. Bradbury, Rolla, Mo.], April 5, 1994, manuscript letter with copy of registration of fictitious name form, "Eldomar Restaurant Doolittle" Vertical File, John F. Bradbury Jr. Files; "The Week Ahead," *Rolla Herald*, May 20, 1949, p. 1.

49. "Architectural/Historic Inventory Survey Forms[,] Route 66 in Missouri[,] Reference No.: PH:020a[,] Historic Name: Stonydell Cabin," 1993, and "Architectural/Historic Inventory Survey Form[,] Route 66

in Missouri[,] Reference No.: PH:020b [,] Historic Name: Stonydell Bus Station," 1993, both in Office of Historic Preservation; Arndt and Bradbury, "Route 66 Photographs," pp. 27–28; Van Beydler, "Stonydell," *Show Me Route 66* 8, no. 2 (Summer 1996): 9–11; Susan C. Dunn, "Gone but Not Forgotten," *Outlook on Geology, Land Survey, Water Resources, Dam Safety and the State Water Plan* (Jefferson City, Mo.) 9, no. 1 (Fall 1998): 1–2; Cheryl Eichar Jett, "The Ghost Town of Arlington," *Show Me Route 66* 24, no. 3 (Summer 2014): 27, 30–31, 33; Joe Sonderman, "Stonydell, Missouri," *Route 66 Magazine* 20, no. 2 (Spring 2013): 14–16; Stony Dell Pool, Arlington, Mo., "Let's Go to Stony Dell Pool" (advertisement), *Rolla Herald*, May 18, 1933, p. 1; "Stony Dell Swimming Pool and Park One of the Beauty Spots," *Rolla Herald*, June 13, 1935, p. 1 (quotation); Jerry W. T. Wilson, "George Grant Prewitt, a Man of Myth," *MST Alumnus* (Rolla, Mo.), October–November 1997, pp. 26–31.

50. "Architectural/Historic Inventory Survey Form[,] Route 66 in Missouri[,] Reference No.: PH:019[,] Historic Name: Beacon Hill Tourist Camp & Restaurant," 1993, and "Architectural/Historic Inventory Survey Form[,] Route 66 in Missouri[,] Reference No.: PH:021 [,] Historic Name: Happy Hill Café," 1993, both in Office of Historic Preservation; Gasser interview; [Missouri, Office of Historic Preservation], Route 66 Building Survey Work Sheet, Current Name of Building/Business: Vernelle's Motel," [ca. 1993], typescript, manuscript, photocopies, and photographs, John F. Bradbury Jr. Files; Arndt and Bradbury, "Route 66 Photographs," 25; Jeff Myers, "Way Back When," *Show Me Route 66* 13, no. 2 (Spring 2002): 21; Russell A. Olsen, *Route 66 Lost and Found*, 94–95; Powellville Café, Arlington, Mo., "Help Wanted" (advertisement), *Rolla Herald*, February 26, 1953, p. 5; Joe Sonderman, "The Missouri Maze," pt. 1, *Show Me Route 66* 26, no. 4 (Fall 2016): 32–33, 35–37.

51. Tom Chesser, "The Big Piney Basketmaker," *Ozarks Mountaineer* (Branson, Mo.) 25, no. 9 (October 1977): 19; Elbert I. Childers, "Basketville: Roadside Community on Route 66," *Newsletter of the Phelps County Historical Society* N.S., no. 13 (April 1996), unpaged; Elbert I. Childers and John F. Bradbury Jr., "Basketville and the Roadside Craftspeople on Route 66," *Missouri Historical Review* 91, no. 1 (October 1996): 24–34; Renee Cook, "Haunting Memories of Clementine," *Ozarks Mountaineer* (Tomball, Tex.) 58, no. 4 (July–August 2010): 5–12; Susan Croce Kelly and Quinta Scott, "Survival Along Route 66," 9–12; Mike O'Brien, "Retired Basket Maker Weaves If the Mood Strikes," *Springfield News-Leader*, April 6, 1980, sec. B, p. 1; Oral Potere, Rolla, Mo., to Skip Curtis, Lake St. Louis, Mo., June 6, 1996, typescript, "Basketville (via Oral Potere)" Vertical File, John F. Bradbury Jr. Files; Terry Primas, *Route 66 in Pulaski County, Missouri: A Local History* (Duke, Mo.: Big Piney Productions, 2017), 29–39; Repp, *Route 66: The Empires of Amusement*, 75–79; Rittenhouse, *A Guide Book to Highway 66*, 26.

52. Primas, *Route 66 in Pulaski County*, 40–49; Veterans Bar-B-Q, Hooker, Mo., "Eat at the Veterans Bar-B-Q" (advertisement), *Rolla Herald*, October 16, 1947, p. 6.

53. Kaszynski, *Route 66: Images of America's Main Street*, 42–43; McCanse, *Where to Go in the Ozarks*, 41; Nomination to National Register of Historic Places for Devil's Elbow District, Mo., 2017; Olsen, *Route 66 Lost and Found*, 98–101; Primas, *Route 66 in Pulaski County*, 50, 53–54; 66; Scott and Kelly, *Route 66: The Highway and Its People*, 178 (quotation); Joe Sonderman, "The Devils Elbow," *Route 66 Magazine* 19, no. 1 (Winter 2011–12): 36–39.

54. Arndt and Bradbury, "Route 66 Photographs," 29; John Bradbury and Terry Primas, *Old Pulaski in Pictures* (Duke, Mo.: Big Piney Productions, 2012), 73, 81–83, Primas, *Route 66 in Pulaski County*, 55–58; "Scrap Book" [of Journey by Rail from Portland, Oregon, to Detroit, Michigan, and Return by New Automobile via U.S. Highway 66, November–December 1938], unpaged, author's collection; "To Operate Filling Station at Devil's Elbow," *Rolla Herald*, March 2, 1933, p. 1.

55. Hank Billings, "Reader Remembers Resort/Café," *Springfield News-Leader*, October 24, 2005, sec. B, p. 2 (second quotation); Bradbury and Primas, *Old Pulaski in Pictures*, 80; George E. Branson, "Munger-Moss Sandwich Shop," *Show Me Route 66* 5, no. 2 (November 1993): 22–23; Olsen, *Route 66 Lost and Found*, 96–97; "Personals," *Rolla Herald*, September 21, 1939, p. 4 (first quotation); Primas, *Route 66 in Pulaski County*, 51–52; Katherine Rodeghier, "Route 66: Something of a Ghost, the Highway Still Provides Plenty

to See in Missouri," *Chicago Tribune*, September 5, 2010, sec. 5, p. 4; Scott and Kelly, *Route 66: The Highway and Its People*, 150–53; Sonderman, "The Devil's Elbow," 38–39; Joe Sonderman, "The Neon Still Shines Brightly at Munger Moss," *Route 66 Magazine* 18, no. 2 (Spring 2011): 8–11; Joe Sonderman, *Route 66 Then and Now* (London: Pavilion Books, 2018), 46, 50.

56. Brian L. Alexander, "Hooker Cut," *66 News!*, (Spring 2015): 18–19; "Fatalities Soar in Ft. Wood Area," *St. Louis Star-Times*, August 13, 1941, p. 3; "Huge Stone Cut to Provide Paving Material for Route 66 Pulaski County Improvement," *Rolla Herald*, September 11, 1941, p. 7; David Knudson, "Towns on Route 66 That Have Vanished," pt. 4, *Route 66 Federation News* 26, no. 4 (Fall 2020): 6–7, 12–13; Mrs. Joe Page, Devils Elbow, Mo., "For Rent—Veterans Bar-B-Cue and Café" (advertisement), *Rolla Herald*, October 24, 1949, p. 3; Primas, *Route 66 in Pulaski County*, 66, 70–96; Jim Ross and Shellee Graham, *Secret Route 66: A Guide to the Weird, Wonderful, and Obscure* (St. Louis: Reedy Press, 2017), 23–24; Sonderman, "The Devils Elbow," 38–39; Joe Sonderman, "Fort Lost in the Woods," *Route 66 Magazine* 18, no. 4 (Fall 2011): 18–21.

57. Mike Penprase, "Towns around Fort Wood Seek Own Identity," *Springfield News-Leader*, April 12, 1981, sec. A, p. 12; Primas, *Route 66 in Pulaski County*, 97–144; *St. Robert's News Magazine for the Fort Leonard Wood Area* 1, no. 1 (January 1957), unpaged, in John F. Bradbury Jr. Files.

58. "Meet Ft. Wood's Metropolis: You'd Never Know Waynesville since the Old Town 'Vanished,'" *Sunday News and Leader*, June 14, 1942, sec. A, pp. 1, 3 (quotations); Primas, *Route 66 in Pulaski County*, 156–57; "What the War's Done to Waynesville," *Sunday News and Leader*, June 14, 1942, sec. A, p. 7; Bill Wheeler, "Growing up on Route 66," *Show Me Route 66* 24, no. 4 (Fall 2014): 33–37; Jax Welborn, "Waynesville, Tucked in the Ozarks," *Show Me Route 66* 19, no. 4 (Fall 2019): 10–11, 13–15; Bill Wheeler, *A Kid Growing up on Route 66 (the Best of Times)* (Lebanon, Mo.: Hazell Arts, 2015), 9–10, 13–15.

59. Bell Hotel, Waynesville, Mo., "Bell Hotel and Resort on Highway 66" (advertisement), *St. Louis Post-Dispatch*, May 20, 1928, sec. A, p. 13; Bell Hotel, "For a Wonderful Recreation Stop at the Bell Hotel" (advertisement), *St. Louis Post-Dispatch*, May 25, 1930, sec. A, p. 13; Bradbury and Primas, *Old Pulaski in Pictures*, 112; "Expand Richland Funeral Business," *Sunday News and Leader*, January 4, 1976, sec. C, p. 2; "Judge Bell's Rites Monday," *Sunday News and Leader*, March 19, 1967, sec. D, p. 16; McCanse, *Where to Go in the Ozarks*, pp. 38 (second quotation), 44–45 (first quotation); Nomination to the National Register of Historic Places for Old Stagecoach Stop, Waynesville, Mo.; "Pulaski County Democrat," *Houston (Mo.) Herald* , January 30, 1936, p. [2]; Primas, *Route 66 in Pulaski County*, 152, 185–87; Joe Sonderman, "The Old Stagecoach Stop," *Route 66 Magazine* 24, no. 2 (Spring 2017): 18–20; Joe Sonderman, "The Old Stagecoach Stop," *Show Me Route 66* 17, no. 2 (Spring 2017): 34, 37; "Waynesville Hotel Destroyed by Fire," *Rolla Herald*, January 15, 1942, p. 2; "Waynesville, Mo., Progressive Town," *Springfield (Mo.) Republican*, October 25, 1925, sec. 2, p. 3.

60. Bradbury and Primas, *Old Pulaski in Pictures*, 121, 144–46; Jean Bybee, "Old Gascozark—an Appeal for Help," *Show Me Route 66* 12, no. 2 (Spring 2001): 16; Olsen, *Route 66 Lost and Found*, 106–107; Primas, *Route 66 in Pulaski County*, 224–26; Sonderman, *Route 66 Then and Now*, 48; Jim Winnerman, "36 Miles of Memories on Route 66 in Missouri," *Route 66 Magazine* 19, no. 2 (Spring 2012): 31–32.

61. Eden Resort, Hazelgreen, Mo., "Let's Fish!" (advertisement), *St. Louis Star-Times*, May 22, 1935, p. 26; Eden Resort, Hazelgreen, Mo., "Easy to Reach" (advertisement), *St. Louis Post-Dispatch*, July 14, 1946, sec. H, p. 11; Eden Resort, "Eden Resort" (advertisement), *St. Louis Post-Dispatch*, July 19, 1964, sec. A, p. 32; "Funeral Set for Ozarker: Eden Resort Owner Dick Dickinson, 69," *Springfield (Mo.) Leader and Press*, March 19, 1971, p. 20; Everett Kennell, "Glory Days Gone: Route 66 Style Lingers," *Springfield News-Leader*, August 8, 1988, sec. D, pp. 1, 4 (second quotation); Kirk Pearce, interview by David Dunaway, December 31, 2008, typescript, p. 4, National Park Service Route 66 Corridor Preservation Program, Santa Fe, N.Mex.; Kirk Pearce, "About Town—Hugh McClure Jr.," *Show Me Route 66* 13, no. 3 (Summer 2002): 13–17; Riley, "The Ozark Life," *The Sullivan Tri-County News*, May 15, 1952, p. [14] (first quotation); Rittenhouse, *Guide Book to Highway 66*, 28; Gary Sosniecki, "Eden Was Paradise on the Highway," *Show Me Route 66* 27, no. 4 (Fall 1917): 24, 26–29 (third quotation).

62. Blue Moon Camp, Lebanon, Mo., "Tourist Camp" (advertisement), *St. Louis Post-Dispatch*, July 17, 1943, sec. A, p. 10; El Rancho Motel, Lebanon, Mo., "Café, Completely Equipped" (advertisement), *Springfield Leader and Press*, July 31, 1962, p. 18; 4 Acre Court, Lebanon, Mo., "Sell or Rent Tavern and Café" (advertisement), *Sunday News and Leader*, November 17, 1963, sec. D, p. 17; "Driving Missouri US 66 Laclede County," *Show Me Route 66* 7, no. 4 (Winter 1995): 29; Cheryl Eichar Jett, "Our Town, Your Town: Lebanon's Hospitality History," *Show Me Route 66* 24, no. 2 (Spring 2014): 18–19, 22–23; Olsen, *Route 66 Lost and Found*, pp. [108–9]; Pearce interview, pp. 2–3, 5–6 (quotation); John T. Riley, "'Riley's Court and Snack Bar[,]' U.S. Route 66 9 Miles East of Lebanon, Mo.," *Show Me Route 66* 12, no. 2 (Spring 2001): 17; Satellite Café, Lebanon, Mo., *Menu[,] Meadow Gold* (Chicago: Excello Press, [ca. 1965]), printed menu, courtesy of Steve Rider; Satellite Café, *Menu[,] Made with Foremost Ice Cream* (St. Paul, Minn.: Brown-Blodgett, Inc., [ca. 1970]), printed menu, courtesy of Steve Rider; Scotty Tourist City, Lebanon, Mo., "Motel-Café" (advertisement), *St. Louis Post-Dispatch*, October 1, 1950, sec. C, p. 7; John Sellars, interview by Tom Peters, Springfield, Mo., March 11, 2015, p. 9, audio recording and transcript, Greater Springfield Route 66 Oral History Project; "Suspect Jailed in Lebanon: Shot at Tavern, Man, 24, Dies," *Springfield Daily News*, January 2, 1967, p. 27; Teague, *Searching for 66*, 50–52; Vesta Court, Lebanon, Mo., "Free Rent" (advertisement), *Springfield Leader and Press*, October 11, 1956, p. 46.

63. Jim Billings, "Building Boom Giving Lebanon Growing Pains," *Sunday News and Leader*, February 1, 1942, sec. B, pp. 8, 12; Jett, "Our Town, Your Town," 18–19, 22–23; *Missouri: A Guide to the "Show Me" State*, 418–20; *The Mullin-Kille and Page Lebanon[,] Missouri[,] ConSurvey Master Edition 1953* (Chillicothe, Ohio: Mullin-Kille ConSurvey Co., 1953), 25, 43; Gary Sosniecki, "End of the Road: 60 Years Ago, Route 66 Moved, Became I-44 in Lebanon," *Show Me Route 66* 27, no. 4 (Fall 2017): 30–31, 33–34.

64. "Carl G. Hudson," *Sunday News and Leader*, September 15, 1974, sec. D, p. 9; Pearce interview, pp. 6–7 (second quotation); "Lebanon Restaurant to New Ownership," *Sunday News and Leader*, April 17, 1977, sec. C, p. 2; Ramona Lehman, "The Munger Moss," *Show Me Route 66* 9, no. 1 (Spring 1999): 12–13; Munger Moss Motel, Lebanon, Mo., "Your Home Away from Home on Route 66: The Munger Moss Motel," http://www.mungermoss.com/history2.html, accessed July 5, 2014; "Ralph E. Lepp," *Springfield Daily News*, May 5, 1965, p. 19; Scott and Kelly, *Route 66: The Highway and Its People*, 150–53 (first quotation).

65. Bernard and Brown, *American Route 66*, p. 40; William Childress, "He Dispenses Food for Thought," *St. Louis Post-Dispatch*, October 30, 1988, sec. F, p. 2; Skip Curtis, "In Memoriam, Wrink: Wrink's Market a Route 66 Landmark," *Show Me Route 66* 16, no. 2 (Spring 2005): 8; Skip Curtis, "'Just Call Me Wrink,'" *Show Me Route 66* 11, no. 1 (Spring 1999): 8–9 (quotations); Downs Auctioneers and Associates, Springfield, Mo., "Grocery Store Liquidation Auction" (advertisement), *Springfield (Mo.) Sunday News-Leader*, June 7, 2009, sec. G, p. 13; "Glenn W. [*sic*] Wrinkle," *Springfield News-Leader*, March 18, 2005, sec. B, p. 5; Joan Hart, "Route 66 Fixture Wrink's Market to Reopen," *Springfield Sunday News-Leader*, July 15, 2007, sec. A, p. 4; Jimmy J. Pack Jr., "Wrink Wrinkle's Memory," *Route 66 Federation News* 16, no. 1 (Winter 2010): 13–15; "Pappa Joad's Road Kill, the Best Grub on '66: Searching for the Ultimate Bologna Sandwich," *Papa Joad's 66* (St. Louis, Mo.) 1, no. 1 (Summer 2001): 8–9; "Wrink's Food a Route 66 Staple: The Market, Owned and Operated by Glenn Wrinkle, Is a Lebanon Landmark," *Springfield News-Leader*, October 23, 1998, sec. B, p. 6.

66. "Driving Missouri US 66 Laclede County," 30; Jett, "Our Town, Your Town," 22–23; *The Mullin-Lille and Page Lebanon*, 25, 205; Pearce interview, 11–12.

67. "Driving Missouri US 66 Laclede County," 33; C. W. Johnson, "Talking Things Over," *Sunday News and Leader*, December 1, 1957, sec. B, p. 4; Gary Sosniecki, "News from the Road: Underpass Café Restoration Update," *Show Me Route 66* 19, no. 4 (Fall 2019): 8; Gary Sosniecki, "News from the Road: Underpass Café to Be Spruced Up," *Show Me Route 66* 28, no. 1 (Winter 2018): 7–8; Gary Sosniecki, "News from the Road: Unique Lodging Has Deep 66 Heritage," *Show Me Route 66* 30, no. 3 (Summer 2020): 8–9; Wood, *An Ordinary Adventure*, 53, 62 (quotations).

68. "Byron Harris," *Springfield Daily News*, June 19, 1969, p. 39; Marian Clark, *The Route 66 Cookbook* (Tulsa, Okla.: Council Oak Books, 1993), 43–44; "Driving Missouri US 66 Laclede County," 33; John McGuire, "A Love Affair with Route 66," *St. Louis Post-Dispatch*, August 20, 1989, sec. D, p. 15; Sarah Overstreet, "Boom Town Memories: Older Folks Recall Conway's Busier Days; Teens Say It's Still a Nice Town," *Springfield News-Leader*, June 18, 1985, sec. D, p. 1; Pearce interview, p. 21 (quotations).

69. Abbylee Court, Niangua, Mo., "Tourist Court" (advertisement), *St. Louis Post-Dispatch*, May 8, 1949, sec. C, p. 7; "Architectural/Historic Inventory Survey Form[,] Route 66 in Missouri[,] Reference No.: WB.001 [,] Historic Name: Abbylee Motel," 1993; "Architectural/Historic Inventory Survey Form[,] Route 66 in Missouri[,] Reference No.: WB.003a[,] Historic Name: Carpenter's Camp (Café/Service Station)," 1993; "Architectural/Historic Inventory Survey Form[,] Route 66 in Missouri[,] Reference No.: WB.002[,] Historic Name: Rockhaven Service Station," 1993; "Architectural/Historic Inventory Survey Form[,] Route 66 in Missouri[,] Reference No.: WB.008[,] Historic Name: Trask's Place," 1993; all in Office of Historic Preservation; "Driving Missouri US 66 Webster County," *Show Me Route 66* 7, no. 2 (Summer 1995): 20–24; Everett Kennell, "Highway through History: Memories Still Lure Travelers Back to 66," *Springfield News-Leader*, August 9, 1988, sec. D, p. 1; "Mary Martha Burtner Bresee," *Springfield Sunday News-Leader*, December 18, 2005, sec. B, p. 4; Olsen, *Route 66 Lost and Found*, 114–16; James Roderique, "Marshfield, Missouri: At the Top of the Ozarks," *Show Me Route 66* 25, no. 2 (Spring 2015): 26, 28, 30; "Route 66 in 1997: Then," *Springfield News-Leader*, February 28, 1997, sec. D, pp. 1, 8.

70. Homer Boyd and George Culp, interview by Tom Peters and Alex Primm, Springfield, Ill., September 9, 2014, p. 6, audio recording and transcript, Greater Springfield Route 66 Oral History Project (third quotation); "Café Operator Shoots at Would-be Burglars," *Springfield Leader and Press*, March 31, 1956, p. 4; Case Auction Company, Marshfield, Mo., "Closing Out Auction[,] Garbage Can Café" (advertisement), *Sunday News and Leader*, February 4, 1973, sec. C, p. 10; Clark, *Route 66 Cookbook*, 43–44 (first quotation); Leatha [*sic*] Lowery, "Remembering the Garbage Can Café," *Mother Road Journal* (Lakewood, Colo.), no. 10 (October 1993): 7; "Mrs. Victor Evans," *Springfield Daily News*, May 23, 1964, p. 15; John Sellars interview, audio recording and transcript, p. 9, Greater Springfield Route 66 Oral History Project (second quotation); Alf D. Smith, "In Search of the Garbage Can," *Show Me Route 66* 5, no. 1 (June 1993): 27; "Speeding Car Skids, Flips, Driver Killed," *Springfield Leader and Press*, June 4, 1963, p. 13.

71. C. H. Skip Curtis, *Birthplace of Route 66: Springfield, Mo.* (Springfield, Mo.: Curtis Enterprises, 2001), 11–20; J. N. Darling, *The Cruise of the Bouncing Betsy: A Trailer Travelogue* (New York: Frederick A. Stokes Company, 1937), 41 (quotations); "Glenstone Is Designated as State Highway," *Springfield Leader*, April 30, 1926, p. 1; *Missouri: A Guide to the "Show Me" State*, American Guide Series, rev. ed. (New York: Hastings House, 1954), 295, 329–36; Rittenhouse, *Guide Book to Highway 66*, 32, 34.

72. Kimberly Harper, *White Man's Heaven: The Lynching and Expulsion of Blacks in the Southern Ozarks, 1894–1909* (Fayetteville: University of Arkansas Press, 2010), 109–234; Katherine Lederer, *Many Thousand Gone: Springfield's Lost Black History* (Springfield, Mo.: Independent Printing, 1986): 2–46; Sarah Overstreet, "Sad History Revealed in 1958 Study of Eateries Off-limits to Blacks," *Springfield News-Leader*, March 21, 2002, sec. B, p. 1.

73. "Clearing Lot for Drive-In," *Springfield Daily News*, February 28, 1962, p. 15; Robert F. Cronin, *Selling Steakburgers: The Growth of a Corporate Culture* (Carmel: Guild Press of Indiana, 2000): 26–28; "Daily Record," *Springfield Leader and Press*, February 16, 1962, p. 14; "Eating Place," *Sunday News and Leader*, June 24, 1962, sec. D, p. 8; Jenny Fillmer, "Link to Route 66 Could Land Eatery on Historic Register," *Springfield News-Leader*, August 16, 2006, sec. B, pp. 1–2; Mark Marymount, "Cutout Your Kicks: A New Book of Route 66 Die-cuts and Decals Includes a Picture of a Springfield Steak n Shake," *Springfield News-Leader*, September 5, 1998, sec. B, p. 8; "Near 45 for Week: It's Holiday Season, Sales in Slight Dip," *Sunday News and Leader*, December 17, 1961, sec. D, p. 12; Dee Nilsen, "Local Steak 'n Shake Patriarch Dies: Herb Leonard, 90, Took Over the Chain in Springfield in 1973," *Springfield (Mo.) Business Journal*, February 13, 2006, p. 3; Nomination to the National Register of Historic Places for Route 66 Steak 'n Shake,

Springfield, Mo., 2012; Alan Rose, *Route 66 Souvenirs* (New York: St. Martin's Griffin, 1998), unpaged; "St. Louisans Plan a Second Drive-In," *Springfield Leader and Press*, June 13, 1962, p. 18; Steak 'n Shake, Springfield, Mo., "Grand Opening" (advertisement), *Springfield Daily News*, June 19, 1962, p. 2; Steak 'n Shake, "Steak 'n Shake Now Hiring" (advertisement), *Sunday News and Leader*, June 10, 1962, sec. D, p. 18.

74. "Architectural/Historic Inventory Survey Form[,] Route 66 in Missouri[,] Reference No.: GR.016[,] Historic Name: Kentwood Arms Motor Hotel," 1993, Office of Historic Preservation; Automobile Club of Southern California, Los Angeles, *National Old Trails Road[,] New York City, New York[,] to Los Angeles, California[;] U.S. Highway 66[,] Chicago, Illinois[,] to Los Angeles, California[;] and Major Connecting Roads* (Los Angeles: Automobile Club of Southern California, 1932): 88; Jim Billings, "A Million Cups of Coffee," *Bias* (Springfield, Mo.) 5, no. 24 (October 19, 1954): 14–16; Colonial Coffee Shop, Springfield, Mo., *The Colonial Luncheon[,] Dinner* ([Springfield, Mo.]: The Colonial, 1945), menu, author's collection; Colonial Hotel Rendezvous, [Springfield, Mo.], *The Colonial Hotel Rendezvous Beverages* ([Springfield, Mo.]: Colonial Hotel, [ca. 1950]), menu, author's collection; "Colonial Opens Its Dining Room in New 'Dress,'" *Springfield Leader and Press*, July 17, 1957, p. 17; Curtis, *Birthplace of Route 66*, 63–66, 125–26, 128, 117–21, 132, 135, 178–79; "Downtown Inn Shuttered," *Springfield Leader and Press*, January 11, 1965, pp. 11, 15; Hotel Ozarks, Springfield, Mo., *Hotel Ozarks of Springfield, Missouri: May We Suggest?* ([Springfield, Mo.]: Young-Stone Printing, [ca. 1950]), menu, author's collection; "Kentwood Arms Open to Public: Springfield's Newest Hotel Attracts Many Guests—Is One of City's Beauty Spots," *Springfield Republican*, July 25, 1926, sec. A, pp. 1, 8; Kentwood Arms Hotel, Springfield, Mo., "Kentwood Arms Anniversary" (advertisement), *Sunday News and Leader*, August 5, 1928, sec. A, p. 6; Mike O'Brien, "A Few More Memories from a Grand Hotel: The Colonial Houses Memories of a Holiday Haven, a Stellar Waiter and Political Posturing," *Springfield News-Leader*, December 1, 1997, sec. B, p. 2; Thomas A. Peters, *John T. Woodruff of Springfield, Missouri, in the Ozarks: An Encyclopedic Biography* (Springfield, Mo.: Pie Supper Press, 2016): 179–83, 191–201, 265–66; Traci Shurley, "The End of the Colonial Hotel: Reminiscing," *Springfield News-Leader*, November 28, 1997, sec. A, p. 28; Traci Shurley, "Landmark Leaves a Legacy: As the Colonial Comes Down Starting Today, Those Who Knew Its Glory Won't Forget," *Springfield News-Leader*, November 28, 1997, sec. A, pp. 1, 9.

75. "Architectural/Historic Inventory Survey Form[,] Route 66 in Missouri[,] Reference No.: GR.016[,] Historic Name: Kentwood Arms Motor Hotel," 1993, Office of Historic Preservation; *Gourmet's Guide to Good Eating*, 187; Duncan Hines, *Adventures in Good Eating* (Bowling Green, Ky.: Adventures in Good Eating, 1939), 148 (second quotation); Duncan Hines, *Adventures in Good Eating* (Bowling Green, Ky.: Adventures in Good Eating, 1945): 167; Little, *Where to Eat*, 150; Joseph (Joe) Jefferson, interview by Tom Peters, Springfield, Mo., January 13, 2015, audio recording and typewritten transcript, p. 7, Greater Springfield Route 66 Oral History Project (first quotation); Michael Kelley, "Kentwood Is Living Link to City's Past," *Springfield Leader and Press*, January 8, 1981, sec. B, p. 1; Kentwood Arms Hotel, Springfield, Mo., "Kentwood Arms Breakfast in the Garden Terrace" (advertisement), *Springfield Leader and Press*, June 12, 1972, p. 2; Kentwood Arms Hotel, *Menu[,] Excellent Cuisine[,] Kentwood Arms Hotel* (Springfield, Mo.: Inland, [ca. 1950]), menu, author's collection; "SMS Now Owns Hotel Property," *Springfield Leader and Press*, March 2, 1984, sec. B, p. 1.

76. T. Lindsay Baker, "No Room at the Inn," *Route 66 Magazine* 25, no. 2 (Spring 2018): 28; "Desegregation Movement Carried on Quietly Here," *Springfield Leader and Press*, September 20, 1960, p. 9; Harper, *White Man's Heaven*, 251–56; "Kentwood Arms, Heer's Ending Segregation: Issue Brought into Focus by Nixon Visit," *Springfield Daily News*, September 20, 1960, pp. 1, 15 (fourth and fifth quotations); Irv Logan, interview by Tom Peters, Springfield, Mo., March 13, 2015, audio recording and typed transcript, p. 12 (first quotation), Greater Springfield Route 66 Oral History Project; "Negroes Say They're Not Given Service," *Springfield Daily News*, December 23, 1969, p. 19; Mike O'Brien, "Tip Yields Surprise: Nixon Visit Spurred Integration Here," *Springfield News-Leader*, January 21, 2001, sec. G, p. 1; Overstreet, "Sad History," sec. B, p. 1 (third quotation); Springfield Chamber of Commerce, Springfield, Mo., "Report of Findings: Segregation-Integration Committee," typescript, September 27, 1958, pp. 1–8, Katherine G.

Lederer Ozarks African American Collection, Special Collections and Archives, Meyer Library, Missouri State University, Springfield, Mo. (second quotation).

77. "Bowlers' Money, Hams Are Stolen," *Springfield Leader and Press*, March 29, 1957, p. 4; "Chestnut Street Barbecue Stand Damaged in Fire," *Sunday News and Leader*, February 16, 1958, sec. D, p. 9; Elaine Graham Estes, interview by Tom Peters, Springfield, Mo., November 21, 2014, audio recording and typewritten transcript, pp. 1–21 (first and second quotations, pp. 3 and 6), Greater Springfield Route 66 Oral History Project; "Graham Death Is Heart Attack," *Springfield Daily News*, November 29, 1957, p. 33; "James M. Graham," *Springfield Leader and Press*, November 30, 1957, p. 5; Harold McPherson, interview by Tom Peters, Lee's Summit, Mo., February 23, 2015, audio recording and typewritten transcript, p. 12 (third quotation), Greater Springfield Route 66 Oral History Project; *Missouri: A Guide to the "Show Me" State* (1941), 330; *Official Negro Directory*[,] *Springfield and Greene County in Missouri* ([Springfield, Mo.]: privately printed, [ca. 1936], unpaged; "Pearl Bailey Here with Large Family," *Springfield Daily News*, July 21, 1962, p. 7; Karla Price, "Zelma and James Graham Were Cooking up a Tradition," *Springfield News-Leader*, February 9, 1995, sec. C, p. 1; Jackie Rehwald, "Remembering a Local Icon: Diner Survived the Great Depression and Was in Business for Some 60 Years," *Springfield News-Leader*, February 28, 2018, sec. A, pp. 1, 3; Angel Streeter, "Historic Oasis for Black Travelers Razed," *Springfield News-Leader*, March 15, 1996, sec. A, p. 1; "Zelma M. Graham," *Springfield Sunday News-Leader*, December 12, 2010, sec. B, p. 6.

78. "Burglars in Big Haul," *Springfield Daily News*, May 12, 1960, p. 23; "Daily Record," *Springfield Leader and Press*, March 8, 1960, p. 13; Estes interview, pp. 13–14; Victor H. Green, ed., *The Negro Travelers' Green Book: The Guide to Travel and Vacations* (New York: Victor H. Green, 1953): 39; Victor H. Green, ed., *Travelers' Green Book* (New York: Victor H. Green, 1963): 36; Logan interview, pp. 1–3, 5–14, 16; Irv Logan Jr., "Money Couldn't Buy," *Show Me Route 66* 8, no. 1 (Spring 1996): 16–17, also reprinted as Irv Logan, "Money Couldn't Buy," *OzarksWatch* (Springfield, Mo.) 11, no. 3–4 (1998): 54–56, and as Irv Logan Jr., "Money Couldn't Buy," *Route 66 Magazine* 10, no. 4 (Fall 2003): 20–22; Ora "Cricket" Logan and Bert Adams, interview by Alex Primm, St. Louis, October 22, 2014, audio recording and typewritten transcript, pp. 17–28, 37–42, 48–49, 62–66, 70–71, Greater Springfield Route 66 Oral History Project; Ora Logan, interview by Alex Primm, [at St. Louis, Mo.], October 23, 2014, audio recording and typewritten transcript, pp. 2–10, Greater Springfield Route 66 Oral History Project; "Mrs. Robert L. Ellis," *Springfield Leader and Press*, July 19, 1966, p. 12; Norris, "Courageous Motorists," 315; Denny Whayne, interview by Alex Primm, Springfield, Mo., October 1, 2014, audio recording and typewritten transcript, unpaged, Greater Springfield Route 66 Oral History Project.

79. Margaret Breen, "He's Practiced Art 'Like Forever,'" *Sunday News and Leader*, January 14, 1962, sec. C, p. 9; "Cook Maintains Casper's Chili Tradition for 46 Years," *Springfield News-Leader*, February 27, 2012, sec. B, p. 6; "Ex-owner of Cafes, C. Lederer, Dies," *Springfield Leader and Press*, October 19, 1972, p. 25; Patricia Fennewald, "Family Burger Tradition Dies with Casper's Son: Charles Lederer's Demise Ruled a Suicide," *Daily News* (Springfield, Mo.), August 13, 1985, sec. C, pp. 1–2; Kris Ann Hegle, "Casper's Diner Traces Its Roots back to 1909," *Springfield Business Journal*, September 24, 2001, p. 8; Sony Hocklander, "Casper's Restaurant, Old and New: A Springfield Institution Is Changing—Slowly," *Springfield News-Leader*, September 30, 2014, sec. A, pp. 1, 6; C. W. Johnson, "Talking Things Over," *Sunday News and Leader*, April 19, 1964, sec. B, p. 4; Lisa Langley, "Hot for Chili: Whether It's Spicy, Fancy or Home-style, a Hot Bowl of Chili Still Chases the Cold Away," *Springfield News-Leader*, November 15, 1995, sec. B, p. 1 (quotation); Casper Lederer, Springfield, Mo., "A Box of His Favorite Smokes" (advertisement), *Springfield*[,] *Missouri*[,] *Republican*, July 27, 1917, p. 4; Casper Lederer, "Casper Lederer" (advertisement), *Springfield*[,] *Missouri*[,] *Republican*, September 1, 1912, p. 6; C. C. Lederer, Springfield, Mo., "Buy Your Fruits, Nuts and Candy from C. C. Lederer" (advertisement), *Springfield*[,] *Missouri*[,] *Republican*, December 23, 1910, p. 4; "Lederer Store Has New Iceless Soda Fountain," *Springfield*[,] *Missouri*[,] *Republican*, November 15, 1914, p. 7; Mike O'Brien, "Parking Lots Chip Away at Springfield's Unique Eateries," *Springfield News-Leader*, June 23, 1985, sec. J, pp. 1, 8; Kathleen O'Dell, "A Century of Casper's: Chili Café Cooking up a Celebration

Later This Fall," *Springfield News-Leader*, September 7, 2009, sec. A, pp. 1, 9; Eula Mae Stratton, "Mr. Pioneer and Still Going Strong!," *Ozarks Mountaineer* 15, no. 7 (August 1967): 14–15, 22; Katie Tonarely, "Casper's Serves up Character, American Classics," *Springfield News-Leader*, March 9, 2017, Weekend supplement, pp. 8–9; "Town Talk," *Springfield Leader*, August 18, 1910, p. 4; Chris Whitley, "Casper's IV: Burger Hut Reopens Yet Again, This Time on Walnut Street," *Springfield News-Leader*, November 24, 1985, sec. C, pp. 1–2.

80. Julia Chaney, interview by Tommy Pike, Springfield, Mo., August 1, 2005, audio recording and typewritten transcript, pp. 6–23, 26 (fourth quotation p. 13; eighth quotation p. 14), Route 66 Oral History Collection; Julia E. Etter Chaney, *Prairies to Hamburgs: Julia's Story* (Virden, Ill.: Gold Nugget Publications, 2003), unpaged (first and fifth quotations); Skip Curtis, "Red's Giant Hamburg," *Show Me Route 66* 8, no. 1 (Spring 1996): 14–15; Steve Cusick, "Last Stand for Hamburg Finally Ends: Red Closes 'Sooper' Career to That Old Rockabilly Beat," *Springfield News-Leader*, December 15, 1984, sec. A, pp. 1–2; Kenneth Estes, interview by Tom Peters, Springfield, Mo., April 20, 2015, p. 21 (sixth quotation), Greater Springfield Route 66 Oral History Project; Rene Glass, interview by T. Lindsay Baker, Springfield, Mo., August 17, 2016, manuscript notes, author's collection; Sony Hocklander, "Remembering Red's: Route 66 Diner Gone, but Memory Lives On," *Springfield Sunday News-Leader,* December 8, 2013, sec. C, p. 5; Dave Hoekstra, "Red's Sails into the Sunset: Route 66 Drive-In Fades into Landscape," *Route 66 Magazine* 5, no. 1 (Winter 1997–98): 30–31; Kelly and Scott, *Route 66: The Highway and Its People*, 102, 153–54, 170–71 (second, third, and seventh quotations); Steve Koehler, "Bulldozer Gets Last Bite at Red's: Memories of Tasty Burgers Are All That's Left of Red Chaney's Nationally Known Eatery," *Springfield News-Leader*, May 20, 1997, sec. A, pp. 1, 9; Steve Koehler, "Fast-food Innovator Chaney Dies: The Owner of Red's Giant Hamburg 'Never Retired from Life,' a Friend Remembers," *Springfield News-Leader*, June 3, 1997, sec. A, pp. 1, 10; Mike O'Brien, "Inquiring Minds Want to Know about Red's Car and 'Blue Stuff,'" *News-Leader* (Springfield, Mo.), February 11, 1990, sec. F, p. 1; Sarah Overstreet, "Red's Giant Hamburg Sizzled with Food, Fun, Heart," *Show Me Route 66* 17, no. 2 (Spring 2006): 29–30; Joe Robles, interview by Samuel Knox, Springfield, Mo., October 16, 2015, audio recording and typewritten transcript, unpaged, Greater Springfield Route 66 Oral History Project; Martin W. Schwartz, "Red's Giant Hamburg: A City Landmark," *Springfield Business Journal*, December 5, 1983, p. 9; Joe Sonderman, "Red's Giant Hamburg," *Show Me Route 66* 22, no. 4 (Fall 2012): 28–32; Chris Whitley, "Bye-bye Burgers, Farewell French Fries: Home of the 1st Drive-up Window to Serve Last Meal as Owners Retire," *Springfield News-Leader*, December 9, 1984, sec. A, pp. 1–2; Chris Whitley, "He's Broken Most of the Rules, but Red's Hamburgers Still Sizzle," *Springfield Leader and Press*, June 24, 1982, sec. A, pp. 1–2; Chris Whitley, "Red's Tunes up for Frying Debut with Rock Band," *Springfield News-Leader*, May 29, 1983, sec. B, p. 9.

81. Dairy Town, Springfield, Mo., "Grand Opening" (advertisement), *Springfield Leader and Press*, July 11, 1964, p. 12; Dairy Town, "Waitress Needed" (advertisement), *Springfield Leader and Press*, June 25, 1964, p. 58; Karen Eicher, interview by Tommy Pike, Springfield, Mo., May 16, 2007, audio recording (second, third, and fourth quotations), Route 66 Oral History Collection; "Glen R. Eicher, 82," *Springfield Leader and Press*, June 26, 1985, sec. B, p. 2; "Johanna Eicher," *Springfield News-Leader,* February 28, 2002, sec. B, p. 4; Keith and Hopkins Auction Co., Branson, Mo., "Auction[,] Dairy Town Drive In" (advertisement), *Springfield Leader and Press*, February 2, 1973, p. 21; Sarah Overstreet, "Homey Motels Squashed by Steamroller of Progress," *Springfield Leader and Press*, November 11, 1985, sec. D, pp. 1, 4 (first quotation); Willis Talbot Auction Service, [Springfield, Mo.], "Auction[,] Cordova Motel" (advertisement), *Springfield Leader and Press*, October 14, 1972, p. 11.

82. "Architectural/Historic Inventory Survey Form[,] Route 66 in Missouri[,] Reference No.: LA.013[,] Historic Name: Gay Parita Store," 1993, Office of Historic Preservation; Cheryl Eichar Jett, "The New Caretakers: Barbara and George Bloom at Gary's Gay Parita," *Show Me Route 66* 27, no. 4 (Fall 2017): 14–15, 17; "Mrs. Fred Mason," *Springfield Leader and Press*, October 29, 1957, p. 15; Barbara Southwick, "Paris Springs: Once a Mecca for the Sick and Weary," *Sunday News and Leader*, October 5, 1975, sec. F, p. 3.

83. Barry Duncan, *The Crossroads of America: Carthage, Missouri: The Carl Taylor Years: 1955–1959* ([Carthage, Mo.]: privately printed, 2014), 66, 264, 268, 278; Barry Duncan, *The Crossroads of America: Carthage, Missouri: The Carl Taylor Years: 1960–1975* ([Carthage, Mo.]: privately printed, 2014), 9–10, 94, 138, 206, 218, 288–89, 318, 381; John Hacker, "The Jefferson Highway," *Route 66 Magazine* 18, no. 4 (Fall 2011): 36–37; Michele Hansford, *Images of America: Carthage, Missouri* (Chicago: Arcadia, 2000), 98–101; Pauline Masson, "Carthage: Missouri Town Celebrates Past with Artful Eye on the Future," *St. Louis Post-Dispatch*, June 4, 1998, sec. S, pp. 1, 3; *Missouri: A Guide to the "Show Me" State* (1941), 421; Rodeghier, "Route 66: Something of a Ghost," sec. 5, p. 4; Jim Ross, "Navigating Carthage," *Route 66 Federation News* 13, no. 1 (Winter 2007): 4–7.

84. "Architectural/Historic Inventory Survey Form[,] Route 66 in Missouri[,] Reference No.: JP.010[,] Historic Name: Boots Motel," 1993, Office of Historic Preservation; Baker, *Portrait of Route 66*, 62–63; Robert Boots, interview by Tommy Pike, Michelle Hansford, and Jerry Benner, Carthage, Mo., April 26, 2006, audio recording and typewritten transcript, pp. 1–5, 7–8, 22 (quotation), Route 66 Oral History Collection; Glenda Pike, "Ilda Boots November 25, 1906–January 2, 2009," *Show Me Route 66* 19, nos. 1–2 (Winter–Spring 2009): 33; Cheryl Eichar Jett, "The Sisters Who Saved the Boots," *Show Me Route 66* 30, no. 3 (Summer 2020): 16–17, 19–20; Susan Redden, "Neon Light to Brighten Boots Court," *Springfield Sunday News-Leader*, April 10, 2016, sec. A, p. 6; Alex J. Rodriguez, "Relighting History," *Route Magazine*, August–September 2020, pp. 60–65; Jim Thole, "The Boots Is Back—in All Its Glory," *Show Me Route 66* 26, no. 3 (Summer 2016): 14, 16–17; "Two Divorces Granted," *Joplin (Mo.) Globe*, September 13, 1945, sec. B, p. 3.

85. "Architectural/Historic Inventory Survey Form[,] Route 66 in Missouri[,] Reference No.: JP.011[,] Historic Name: Boots Drive-In," 1993, Office of Historic Preservation; Boots interview, pp. 2–3, 9–12, 20 (first, sixth, and seventh quotations); Robert A. Boots, "Boots Drive-In 'Added Definition to Its Time," *Carthage (Mo.) Press*, December 18, 2000, sec. A, p. 5; Al de Buhr, "Good Morning, Sir," *Washington Missourian*, September 23, 1948, p. 6 (second, third, fourth, and fifth quotations).

86. Boots interview, pp. 10–11 (quotations); "Carthage Drive-In Has New Ownership," *Sunday News and Leader*, March 13, 1966, sec. D, p. 10; Cheryl Eichar Jett, "Breakfast at the Crossroads of America: Carthage, Missouri," *Show Me Route 66* 24, no. 1 (Winter 2014): 34–39; "Leon Harvey 'Lee' Crocker," *Springfield News-Leader*, May 18, 2000, sec. B, p. 4; Russell Olsen, "Boots Drive-In[,] Carthage, Missouri[,] ca. 1946," *Route 66 Magazine* 25, no. 2 (Spring 2018): 41; "Ozark Briefs," *Sunday News and Leader*, March 24, 1963, sec. D, p. 12; "Then and Now on Route 66," *Show Me Route 66* 20, no. 4 (Fall 2010): 49.

87. *Missouri: A Guide to the "Show Me" State* (1941), 422–23; James W. Loewen, *Sundown Towns: A Hidden Dimension of American Racism* (New York: New Press, 2005), 389; Rittenhouse, *Guide Book to Highway 66*, 37–39.

88. Laura Betz, "So Long to Another Webb City Tradition: Last Chance Tomorrow to Get a Bill's Foot-Long," *Webb City Sentinel* (Webb City, Mo.), August 13, 1999, p. 1 (quotations); "Clem C. Benintendi of Webb City Is Dead," *Joplin Globe*, October 25, 1951, sec. B, p. 7; "Drive-In Providing a Slice of Americana Is Closing Its Doors," *St. Louis Post-Dispatch*, August 15, 1999, sec. C, p. 14; "New Ice Cream Store," *Joplin Globe*, October 3, 1954, sec. C, p. 6; "New Regime Takes Over at Webb City," *Joplin Globe*, April 20, 1954, p. 11; Southwestern Bell Telephone Company, Joplin, Mo., *Joplin—Webb City[,] Carl Junction, Carterville, Orongo, Missouri[,] Telephone Directory[,] January, 1958* (Joplin, Mo.: Southwestern Bell Telephone Company, 1958), 45, classified section 49; "Webb City Hot Spot Sold to Wendy's," *Springfield News-Leader*, August 12, 1999, sec. B, p. 3. An idea of the long hours Montie Benintendi devoted to her job in the laundry and dry cleaners before opening the Kreamy Kup comes from the manuscript census taken in 1940, the most recent tally available to researchers. During the week before enumerator Combs D. Logan interviewed her on April 18, 1940, Benintendi had worked fifty-five hours as a presser in the tailor shop. U.S. Census Bureau, Census of 1940, Population Schedules, Webb City, Jasper County, Mo., Enumeration District 49–38, page 10A, Roll m-t0627–02118, Microcopy T627, National Archives and Records Administration, Washington, D.C.

89. Imma Curl, "House of Lords: When Vice Was King," typescript, June 17, 1986, pp. 1–11, "Joplin History—House of Lords" Vertical File, Joplin Public Library, Joplin, Mo.; Terry Dickinson, "Joplin—a City with a Shady Past and a Sunny Future," *Midwest Motorist*, (Auto Club of Missouri, Maryland Heights, Mo.), February 1978, pp. 12–16; Victor H. Green, ed., *The Negro Motorist Green-Book* (New York: Victor H. Green, 1940), 19; Green, *Negro Travelers' Green Book*, 37; Harper, *White Man's Heaven*, 69–108; Thomas W. Johnson, "The House of Lords," *In Joplin* (Joplin, Mo.) 3, no. 8 (February 1987): 23–28; Loewen, *Sundown Towns*, 95–96, 389; *Missouri: A Guide to the "Show Me" State* (1941), 233–40; Norris, "Courageous Motorists," 215–16; Rittenhouse, *Guide Book to Highway 66*, 38–39.

90. "Add Two to Convictions in Jasper County Probe," *Sunday News and Tribune* (Jefferson City, Mo.), March 14, 1937, p. 3; Baker, *Portrait of Route 66*, 64–65; Broadway Bar, Joplin, Mo., "Broadway Bar" (advertisement), *Joplin Globe*, April 23, 1949, p. 10; "John Davenport's House of Lords in an Opening Today," *Joplin Globe*, January 10, 1958, sec. B, p. 7; John's Ringside Tavern, Joplin, Mo., "It's always Cool at John's Ringside Tavern" (advertisement), *Joplin Globe*, September 11, 1948, p. 6; "Joplin Area Labor Unions Will Open Private Club Soon," *Joplin Globe*, February 1, 1948, sec. A, p. 9; "Dick and John's Bar," Joplin Historical Postcards, Missouri Digital Heritage, Missouri Secretary of State, Jefferson City, Mo., http://cdm16795.contentdm.oclc.org/cdm/singleitem/collection/jplnpstcrds/id/902/rec/1, accessed November 19, 2018 (quotations); Pla-Mor Bar, Joplin, Mo., "Pla-Mor Bar" (advertisement), *Joplin Globe*, September 19, 1951, p. 6; "Purchase Metsker Bar," *Joplin Globe*, April 5, 1944, p. 6; 2 Johns Bar, Joplin, Mo., "'2' Johns Bar" (advertisement), *Joplin Globe*, July 12, 1947, p. 6; Victory Bar, Joplin, Mo., "Announcing the Opening of the Victory Bar" (advertisement), *Joplin Globe*, April 6, 1944, p. 8.

91. "Charges Dropped against 12 in Oklahoma Alcohol Case," *St. Louis Post-Dispatch*, March 9, 1934, sec. D, p. 1; "Druggists at Joplin Face Liquor Charges," *Miami (Okla.) Daily News-Record*, June 22, 1934, p. 4; "Possessing Parts of Still Charged Druggist," *Joplin Globe*, February 16, 1929, p. 10; "Quantity of Wine Is Seized in Raid," *Joplin Globe*, April 19, 1929, p. 5; "7 Indictments Are Returned by Federal Grand Jury; 22 Persons Are Sentenced by Judge Reeves," *Joplin Globe*, January 15, 1929, p. 2.

92. Brad Belk, "The Wilder's Restaurant Story," *Show Me Route 66* 28, no. 3 (Summer 2018): 12–13 (first and second quotations); *Polk's Joplin (Missouri) City Directory 1930* (Kansas City, Mo.: R. L. Polk, 1930), 330, 399; *Polk's Joplin (Missouri) City Directory 1931* (Kansas City, Mo.: R. L. Polk, 1930), 301, 363; *Polk's Joplin (Missouri) City Directory 1933* (Kansas City, Mo.: R. L. Polk, 1932), 281, 339; *Polk's Joplin (Jasper County, Mo.) City Directory 1935* (Kansas City, Mo.: R. L. Polk, 1935), 323, 384, 467; "7 District Firms Face OPA Charges," *Joplin Globe*, August 26, 1944, p. 3; Wilder's, Joplin, Mo., *Wilder's[,] 1216 Main Street, Joplin, Missouri* ([Joplin, Mo.]: Wilder's, [1942]), printed menu with typewritten insert (third and fourth quotations), "Restaurants" Vertical File, Baxter Springs Heritage Center, Baxter Springs, Kans.; Porter Wittich, "Globe Trotter," *Joplin Globe*, January 2, 1944, sec. A, p. 9.

93. Jim Ellis and Tom Osterloh, "Wilder's Buffet Dynamited; 6 Hurt: Isgrigg Believes Explosion Set in Murder Attempt," *Joplin Globe*, September 4, 1959, sec. A, pp. 1, 4; "Joplin Casino Closed Down in Hurry after Blair Comment," *St. Louis Post-Dispatch*, October 3, 1958, sec. A, pp. 1, 4 (quotations); "Joplin Jury Fixes Blame: Death Due to Blast by Unknown Persons," *Springfield Leader and Press*, September 10, 1959, p. 39; Ron Padgett, *Oklahoma Tough: My Father, King of the Tulsa Bootleggers* (Norman: University of Oklahoma Press, 2003): 145–47; "Prosecutor Asks Grand Jury Probe Bombing at Joplin," *Sunday News and Leader*, September 6, 1959, sec. A, p. 11; "6 Hurt in Blast at Restaurant-casino in Joplin," *St. Louis Post-Dispatch*, September 4, 1959, sec. B, p. 16.

94. Belk, "Wilder's Restaurant Story," 12–13 (quotation); "Joplin Firm Buys Kansas Outlet," *Sunday News and Leader*, April 16, 1972, sec. D, p. 2; "Joplin Wilder's Restaurant Sold," *Sunday News and Leader*, February 29, 1977, sec. E, p. 2; Wally Kennedy, "Wilder's Remains a Part of Joplin's DNA," *Joplin Globe*, April 18, 2015, https://www.joplinglobe.com/news/local_news/wilkder-s-remains-a-part-of-joplin-s-dna/article_c39be5fa-d585-5cd1-b946-46a51d568e81.html, accessed March 5, 2017; "Longtime Chef, Others Buy Joplin's Wilder's Restaurant," *Springfield Leader and Press*, November 5, 1970, p. 3; "New Wilder's for

Joplin," *Sunday News and Leader*, April 6, 1975, sec. B, p. 5; "Reopen Joplin Wilder Restaurant Nov. 15," *Sunday News and Leader*, October 29, 1972, sec. E, p. 2; Jim Thole, "Wilder's Rooftop Neon Sign Is Again Ablaze," *Show Me Route 66* 28, no. 3 (Summer 2018): 11–12; "12 Million in Building Here," *Joplin Globe*, May 12, 1946, sec. A, p. 1, sec. B, p. 7.

95. "Driving Missouri US 66 Jasper County," *Show Me Route 66* 11, no. 2 (Summer 1999): 19; "Fire Destroys Ozark Distilling Bottling Plant," *Joplin Globe*, February 21, 1948, p. 1; "Fred Archer Rites Will Be Saturday," *Joplin Globe*, August 19, 1955, sec. B, p. 5; "Harry C. Gray Estate Is Left to His Widow," *Joplin Globe*, September 21, 1951, sec. B, p. 7; *Missouri: A Guide to the "Show Me" State* (1941), 239, 423; Rittenhouse, *Guide Book to Highway 66*, 38–39; Joe Sonderman and Elizabeth Olwig, "The State Line," *Show Me Route 66* 31, no. 1 (Spring 2021): 24–26, 28; Southern Garage, Joplin, Mo., *For Your Convenience This Folder Contains Many of the Principal Highways out of Joplin* ([Joplin, Mo.]: McCann Printing Co., [ca. 1930]), map, unpaged, author's collection.

96. "Architectural/Historic Inventory Survey Form[,] Route 66 in Missouri[,] Reference No.: JP.030[,] Historic Name: Gillead's Barbecue," 1993; "Architectural/Historic Inventory Survey Form[,] Route 66 in Missouri[,] Reference No.: JP.031[,] Historic Name: Gray & Archer Filling Station," 1993; "Architectural/Historic Inventory Survey Form[,] Route 66 in Missouri[,] Reference No.: JP.032[,] Historic Name: Harry's Super Station," 1993; "Architectural/Historic Inventory Survey Form[,] Route 66 in Missouri[,] Reference No.: JP.033[,] Historic Name: State Line Restaurant," 1993, all in Office of Historic Preservation; "Bandit Robs State Line Liquor Store," *Joplin Globe*, July 20, 1955, p. 2; Harry H. Burge, Joplin, Mo., "For Sale—Package Liquor Store" (advertisement), *Joplin Globe*, March 30, 1952, sec. D, p. 9; "15 Years Handed Joplin Resident on Two Charges," *Springfield Daily News*, February 1, 1972, p. 15; "In Joplin Area Masked Men Strike Again," *Springfield Leader and Press*, January 5, 1963, p. 6; "Liquor Store Clerk Shoots at a 'Bandit,'" *Moberly (Mo.) Monitor-Index*, November 17, 1954, p. 10; Olsen, *Route 66 Lost and Found*, 130–31; Russell Olsen, "Then and Now: State Line Mercantile Company[,] Joplin, Missouri[,] Circa 1946," *Route 66 Magazine* 18, no. 3 (Summer 2011): 42; Conrad L. Ricker, "These Were My Kicks on Route 66," pp. 55–57 (quotation) in *Memories on Route 66 1991* (Bethany, Okla.: Oklahoma Route 66 Association, 1991); Sonderman, *Route 66 Then and Now*, 57; "State Line Liquor Store Is Held Up," *Joplin Globe*, January 6, 1946, sec. A, p. 5; State Line Mercantile, Joplin, Mo., "Agate Jewelry, Petrified Wood and Turquoise, Mounted in Silver" (advertisement), *Joplin Globe*, July 8, 1945, sec. B, p. 9. The modern street address for Paddoc Liquor is 7839 West Old 66 Boulevard, Joplin, Mo.

CHAPTER 3. KANSAS

1. Emily Fredrix, "Kansas Route 66 a Trip Back in Time," *Manhattan (Kans.) Mercury*, June 25, 2003, sec. B, p. 4; *Kansas: A Guide to the Sunflower State*, American Guide Series (New York: Viking Press, 1939), 439–40; Johnnie Meier, "Kansas Kicks," *Route 66 Magazine* 16, no. 3 (Summer 2009): 8–10; Nominations to the National Register of Historic Places for Historic Resources of Route 66 in Kansas, July 11, 2003, and for Kansas Route 66 Historic District, East of Galena, July 11, 2003, these and subsequent nominations in Office of the Keeper, National Register of Historic Places, National Park Service, Washington, D.C.; Jack D. Rittenhouse, *A Guide Book to Highway 66* (Los Angeles: privately printed, 1946; repr., Albuquerque: University of New Mexico Press, 1989), 38–39; Joe Sonderman and Cheryl Eichar Jett, "Route 66 in Kansas," *Show Me Route 66* 26, no. 2 (Spring 2016): 10–14; Beccy Tanner, "Effort Ongoing to Preserve Famed Route 66," *Salina (Kans.) Journal*, April 11, 2000, sec. A, p. 8; Herb Tappenbeck and Ellen Tappenbeck, "The Way It Was on the Route," *Route 66 Federation News* 5, no. 4 (Autumn 1999): 18 (quotation); Michael Wallis, *Route 66: The Mother Road* (New York: St. Martin's Press, 1990), 79–80.

2. "Fire Damages Edifice in Downtown Galena," *The Iola (Kans.) Register*, October 17, 1978, p. 1; "Galena City Treasury Has Balance of $13,408," *Joplin (Mo.) Globe*, January 6, 1944, p. 3; Greg Grisolano, "Owner, Patrons Recall Galena's Last Bar," *Joplin Globe*, September 28, 2007, https://www.joplinglobe.com/archives/owner-patrons-recall-galena-s-last-bar/article_15f5d712-c3bb-555c-ba44-f9b2a689ecdd.html, accessed

August 30, 2019; "James Roy Green, 55, of Galena Is Dead," *Joplin Globe*, March 7, 1952, sec. D, p. 3; Kansas, Legislature, Legislative Research Department, Topeka, Kans., "February 24, 2003: Kansas Liquor Laws," memorandum 33441(2/24/3(2:12PM)), KGI Online Library, https://cdm16884.contentdm.oclc.org/digital/collection/p16884coll8/id/300, accessed August 30, 2019; "Sinking Town Seeks Solutions," *Manhattan Mercury*, September 6, 2007, sec. A, p. 3; Larry Spahn, "Green Parrot Mine Collapse," *National Association of Abandoned Mine Land Programs Newsletter* (Harrisburg, Pa.) 28, no. 2 (Fall 2006): 14–15; Jerry Thomas, "Uncles, Outlaws, and Green Parrots," Cherokee County, Kansas, Genealogy, History and News of Today, https://www.tapatalk.com/groups/cherokeecountykansas/that-special-place-called-galena-2-t381-s20. html, accessed August 30, 2019 (quotations).

3. "Century-old Building Destroyed in Fire," *Council Grove (Kans.) Republican*, November 2, 1998, p. 2; Marian Clark, "Coffee Shops, Diners and Other Swell Places," *Route 66 Magazine* 2, no. 4 (Fall 1995): 30–31; Marian Clark, *The Route 66 Cookbook* (Tulsa: Council Oak Books, 1993), 57–59; Downs Auction Service, Springfield, Mo., "Restaurant and Lounge Liquidation Auction" (advertisement), *Springfield (Mo.) News-Leader*, March 23, 1997, sec. C, p. 30; Russell A. Olsen, *Route 66 Lost and Found: Mother Road Ruins and Relics—The Ultimate Collection* (Minneapolis: Voyageur Press, 2011), 128–29; Spring River Inn, Riverton, Kans., "Announcing" (advertisement), *Miami (Okla.) Daily News-Record*, April 6, 1958, p. 3; Spring River Inn, Riverton, Kans., "Open to the Public" (advertisement), *Miami (Okla.) News-Record*, July 12, 1967, p. 3; Spring River Inn, "When You Go out for Dinner" (advertisement), *Miami Daily News-Record*, April 17, 1959, p. 3; Spring River Inn, "World Famous Spring River Inn" (advertisement), *Neosho (Mo.) Daily News*, April 18, 1975, p. 3. The reinforced concrete arch bridges used several places on Highway 66 in Kansas are a design invented and patented by engineer James Barney Marsh. One of these survives over Brush Creek north of Baxter Springs. Michael Shulman, "James Barney Marsh, Builder of Bridges," *Route 66 Magazine* 26, no. 2 (Spring 2019): 46–48.

4. Marian Clark, "Coffee Shops, Diners and Other Swell Places," pp. 30–31; Kathleen Duchamp, "Kansas Kicks," *Route 66 Magazine* 11, no. 1 (Winter 2003 4): 48–49; Sarah E. Lookadoo, "Iconic Store Celebrates 90th Anniversary," *Route 66 Magazine* 22, no. 3 (Summer 2015): 48–49; Scott Nelson, interview by T. Lindsay Baker, Riverton, Kans., July 24, 2013, handwritten and typewritten transcription, author's collection; Nelson's Old Riverton Store, Riverton, Kans., *Nelson's Old Riverton Store[,] Home of the "Handcrafted Sandwich"* (Riverton, Kans.: Nelson's Old Riverton Store, [2013]), menu, author's collection; Nelson's Old Riverton Store, *Nelson's Old Riverton Store[,] Listed on the National Registry of Historic Places on Route 66* (Riverton, Kans.: Nelson's Old Riverton Store, [ca. 2013]), brochure, author's collection; Nomination to the National Register of Historic Places for Williams' Store, Riverton, Kans., July 11, 2003; Olson, *Route 66 Lost and Found*, pp. 140–41; "Papa Joad's Road Kill, the Best Grub on '66: Searching for the Ultimate Bologna Sandwich," *Papa Joad's 66* (St. Louis, Mo.) 1, no. 1 (Summer 2001): 8–9; Jon Robinson, *Route 66: Lives on the Road* (Osceola, Wisc.: MBI Publishing, 2001), 92–94; Cecil Stehelin, "Carrying on Tradition," *Route Magazine*, June–July 2019, pp. 38–43.

5. Blue Castle Café, Baxter Springs, Kans., *Menu[,] Blue Castle Café[,] Baxter Springs, Kansas* (Baxter Springs, Kans.: Blue Castle Café, [ca. 1960]), menu, "Menus" Vertical File, Baxter Springs Heritage Center, Baxter Springs, Kans. "Chas. Beavers Accidentally Shot," *Neosho (Mo.) Daily Democrat*, November 5, 1919, p. 1; "Dining Spots Reflect Originality, Quality of People," *Baxter Springs (Kans.) Citizen*, July 1, 1983, Horizon supplement, unpaged; "George Lewis of Kansas City, Mo., Has Purchased the Portland Café," *Baxter Daily Citizen* (Baxter Springs, Kans.), May 10, 1920, p. [4]; Cheryl Eichar Jett, "Kansas Route 66 Kicks It up Another Notch," *Show Me Route 66* 29, no. 2 (Spring 2019): 38–39, 40–42; "List of Citizens to Appear Thurs[day]," *Baxter Daily Citizen*, October 8, 1918, p. [4]; "Mrs. Loretta M. Lewis Dies at Baxter Springs," *Joplin Globe*, January 23, 1946, p. 3; Nomination to the National Register of Historic Places for Route 66 Historic District, North Baxter Springs, July 15, 2014; Portland Café, Baxter Springs, Kans., "Wanted—Experienced Cook" (advertisement), *Miami Daily News-Record*, October 16, 1944, p. 5; J. C. Smith, "Blue Castle Café: Good Food[,] Food People[,] Good Memories," *Route 66 Magazine* 6, no. 1 (Winter 1998–99):

46–47; "To Open Baxter Café," *Joplin Globe*, May 5, 1946, sec. B, p. 12; "Two Fire Calls," *Joplin Globe*, May 23, 1953, p. 2; Vitell Auction Service, Carthage, Mo., "Public Auction!" (advertisement), *Springfield News-Leader*, July 27, 1980, sec. C, p. 10.

6. Rittenhouse, *Guide Book to Route 66*, 40; Jim Ross, *Oklahoma Route 66*, 2nd ed. (Arcadia, Okla.: Ghost Town Press, 2011), 20–22.

CHAPTER 4. OKLAHOMA

1. Mary Ann Anders, ed., *Route 66 in Oklahoma: An Historic Preservation Survey* (Stillwater: Oklahoma Historic Preservation Survey, History Department, Oklahoma State University, 1984), 1–14; "General Information for Tourists," typescript, [ca. 1940], pp. 1–8, U.S. Works Progress Administration, Federal Writers' Project, Oklahoma, in Federal Writers' Project Collection, 1935–1942 (1981.105), box 73, folder 25, Research Center, Oklahoma Historical Society, Oklahoma City, cited hereafter as Federal Writers' Project Collection; Nomination for Route 66 and Associated Historic Resources in Oklahoma to the National Register of Historic Places, this and subsequent nominations in Office of the Keeper, National Register of Historic Places, National Park Service, Washington, D.C.; *Oklahoma: A Guide to the Sooner State*, American Guide Series (Norman: University of Oklahoma Press, 1941): 219–33; "Oklahoma Pioneered Western Pikes," *Sunday Oklahoman* (Oklahoma City), April 19, 1964, Trails to Turnpikes supplement, p. 12; Mark Potter, "Oklahoma's Twists and Turns in the 1950s Leave the Roadbed Intact," *Route 66 Federation News* 11, no. 4 (Autumn 2005): 10–14; Jim Ross, "'Proud of What It Means': Route 66, Oklahoma's Mother Road," *Chronicles of Oklahoma* 73, no. 3 (Fall 1995): 260–77. For a helpful overview of the geology of the route traversed by Highway 66 across Oklahoma, see *Highway Geology of Oklahoma: Road Logs of the Major Highways of the State with Notations on Oklahoma's Historic Sites* (Oklahoma City: Oklahoma City Geological Society, 1955), 48–61, 155–58.

2. Ida Belle Hunter, "Oklahoma's 'Jim Crow' Laws," typescript, January 6, 1939, pp. 1–2, "Jim Crow Law" Vertical File, Research Center, Oklahoma Historical Society; Harold McPherson, interview by Tom Peters, Lee's Summit, Mo., February 23, 2015, audio recording and typewritten transcript, p. 23, Greater Springfield Route 66 Oral History Project, Special Collections, Meyer Library, Missouri State University, Springfield, Mo., cited hereafter as Greater Springfield Route 66 Oral History Project; James M. Smallwood and Crispin A. Phillips, "Black Oklahomans and the Question of 'Oklahomaness': The People Weren't Invited to Share the Dream," in *The Culture of Oklahoma*, ed. Howard F. Stein and Robert F. Hill (Norman: University of Oklahoma Press, 1993), 48–67.

3. Ned DeWitt, "Tour 1 (Tour Introduction—Section A)," typescript, 1 lf., Federal Writers' Project Collection, box 82, folder 11 (first quotation); Zephine Humphrey, *Green Mountains to Sierras* (New York: E. P. Dutton, 1936), 51 (third and fourth quotations); Velma Nieberding, *The History of Ottawa County* (Marceline, Mo.: Walsworth, 1983), 36–38; Jack D. Rittenhouse, *A Guide Book to Highway 66* (Los Angeles: privately printed, 1946; repr., Albuquerque: University of New Mexico Press, 1989), 40 (fifth quotation); Diane Wood, *An Ordinary Adventure: Retracing Mom and Grandpa's 1934 Trip on Route 66—In a Model A!* (Los Alamitos, Calif.: Life in the Dash, 2018), 63 (second quotation).

4. Black Cat Café, Commerce, Okla., "Black Cat Café" (advertisement), *Miami (Okla.) Daily News-Record*, March 7, 1948, p. 9; Black Cat Café, "Black Cat Café[,] Commerce, Oklahoma" (advertisement), *Miami Daily News-Record*, March 23, 1956, p. 3; Black Cat Café, "Black Cat Café in Commerce for Sale or Trade for Acreage" (advertisement), *Miami Daily News-Record*, November 26, 1954, p. 11 (third quotation); Black Cat Café, "Dine in Air Conditioned Comfort" (advertisement), *Miami Daily News-Record*, July 7, 1954, p. 10; "Commerce," *Miami Daily News-Record*, September 4, 1947, p. 9; "Commerce[,] Black Cat Repairs," *Miami Daily News-Record*, August 19, 1948, p. 12; Ann DeFrange, "Dreams Still Roll along Aging Route 66 While Memories Collect by Roadside," *Sunday Oklahoman*, May 28, 1989, sec. A, p. 18; "Dorothy S. Howell," *Miami Daily News-Record*, March 24, 1958, p. 3; Norene Hale and Frances Anderson, "Commerce," *Miami Daily News-Record*, August 11, 1960, p. 8; Leonard Lyons, "Mantle Recalls Commerce

Days," *Daily Oklahoman* (Oklahoma City), September 11, 1961, p. 22 (second quotation); Mickey Mantle and Ben Epstein, *The Mickey Mantle Story* (New York: Henry Holt, 1953), 6; Mickey Mantle and Herb Gluck, *The Mick* (New York: Berkley Publishing Group, 1986), 24; "On the Business Front," *Miami Daily News-Record*, August 15, 1943, p. 5; "Riley Saffell, Operator of the Black Cat Café, Is Preparing for the Summer Heat," *Miami Daily News-Record*, April 19, 1933, p. 8 (first quotation).

5. T. Lindsay Baker, "The Miami, Oklahoma[,] Marriage Mill," *Route 66 Magazine* 26, no. 1 (Winter 2018–19): 26–28; "Ceremonies Open Turnpike," *Miami Daily News-Record*, June 28, 1957, p. 1; Ivy Coffey, "Ottawa County Reconstructs Economy on Diversification," *Daily Oklahoman*, May 27, 1962, sec. A, pp. 16–17; John Feen, "Lead and Zinc Find Started Miami Boom," *Daily Oklahoman*, October 20, 1957, sec. C, p. 6; Marguerite Hanbury, "Miami," typescript, May 5, 1936, pp. 1–4, and Marguerite Hanbury, "Miami (Mining Field) 820," typescript, April 21, 1936, 1 lf. (first quotation), in Federal Writers' Project Collection, box 39, folder 14; Joseph (Joe) Jefferson, interview by Tom Peters, Springfield, Mo., December 29, 2014, audio recording and typewritten typescript, p. 11 (second and third quotations), Greater Springfield Route 66 Oral History Project; Susan Croce Kelly, "Just for Kicks! Route 66," *Chicago Tribune*, May 22, 1983, sec. 11, p. 2; Nieberding, *History of Ottawa County*, 23–28, 113–16.

6. "City Properties Annexed; Board Hears a Protest," *Miami (Okla.) News-Record*, January 18, 1966, p. 1; Marian Clark, *The Main Street of America Cookbook: A Culinary Journey Down Route 66* (Tulsa: Council Oak Books, 1997), 124–25; Business Entity Search No. 1293331, Kansas Business Center, Secretary of State, Kansas, https://www.kansas.gov/bess/flow/main?execution=e1s4, accessed September 15, 2019; The Ku-Ku, Miami, Okla., "Grand Opening" (advertisement), *Miami News-Record*, April 3, 1966, p. 6; "Ku-Ku, Hamburgers Nearly Synonomous [*sic*]," *Miami News-Record*, April 3, 1966, p. 6; The Ku-Ku, "Register Now!" (advertisement), *Miami News-Record*, December 7, 1965, p. 7; The Ku-Ku., Inc., Salina, Kans., "Interested in Making $10,000 a Year and More?" (advertisement), *Moline (Ill.) Daily Dispatch*, September 23, 1964, p. 45; "A Living Legacy," *Route Magazine*, February–March 2020, 54; "Oklahoma Route 66 Business Spotlight: Waylan's Ku-Ku Burger," *On the Road* (Oklahoma Route 66 Association) [N.S.] 2, no. 3 (August 2010), 7; "On Corner of Ninth, Merchant: New Drive-In Restaurant Will have a Cuckoo Clock," *Emporia (Kans.) Gazette*, December 12, 1964, p. 3; Patrick Richardson, "Restaurant Destination for Tourists," *Miami News-Record*, May 2003, Route 66 supplement, p. 21 (quotation); Joe Sonderman and Jim Hinckley, *Route 66 Roadside Signs and Advertisements* (Minneapolis: Voyageur Press, 2016), 58–59.

7. Buffalo Ranch, Afton, Okla., "Grand Opening" (advertisement), *Miami Daily News-Record*, April 6, 1956, p. 5; Dairy Ranch, Afton, Okla., "Open for the Season" (advertisement), *Miami Daily News-Record*, March 13, 1959, p. 7; Dairy Ranch, "You're Invited to the Grand Opening" (advertisement), *Miami Daily News-Record*, May 14, 1954, p. 9; Laurel Kane, "Old Buffalo Ranch Torn Down, New One Emerges," *On the Road* 15, no. 1 (March 2003): 3–4; William Kaszynski, *Route 66: Images of America's Main Street* (Jefferson, N.Dak.: McFarland, 2003), 58–59; Steve Lackmeyer, "Buffalo Ranch, 66 Motel, Antique Cars Attracting Route Fans to Afton," *Oklahoman* (Oklahoma City), June 20, 2007, sec. B, pp. 1, 4; Russell A. Olsen, *Route 66 Lost and Found: Mother Road Ruins and Relics—The Ultimate Collection* (Minneapolis: Voyageur Press, 2011), 154; Thomas Arthur Repp, *Route 66: The Empires of Amusement* (Lynnwood, Wash.: Mock Turtle Press, 1999), 104–11; Thomas Arthur Repp, "That Wooly Bully Buffalo Ranch," *Route 66 Magazine* 4, no. 3 (Summer 1997): 52–54; "A Ribbon Runs through It," *Route Magazine*, October–November 2020), p. 72; Jim Ross, *Oklahoma Route 66*, 2nd ed. (Arcadia, Okla.: Ghost Town Press, 2011), 24–30; Quinta Scott and Susan Croce Kelly, *Route 66: The Highway and Its People* (Norman: University of Oklahoma Press, 1988), 154–55 (quotation); Joe Sonderman, *Route 66 Then and Now* (London: Pavilion Books, 2018), 63; Sheila Stogsdill, "Afton Ranch Restocked with Buffalo," *Sunday Oklahoman*, July 27, 2003, sec. A, p. 3; Sheila K. Stogsdill, "Buffalo Ranch Set for Restoration," *Sunday Oklahoman*, February 23, 2003, sec. A, p. 10.

8. "Boston Changes Hands," *Vinita (Okla.) Evening Sun-Herald*, August 17, 1916, p. 1; "Café Sign along Road," photograph, call number Lot 13087, no. 2, reproduction number LC-USZ62–127767 (b&w file copy neg.), Visual Materials from the National Association for the Advancement of Colored People Records, Library

of Congress, Washington, D.C.; Marian Clark, *The Route 66 Cookbook* (Tulsa: Council Oak Books, 1993), 68; Craig County Heritage Association, comps., *The Story of Craig County[,] Its People and Places* (Dallas: Curtis Media Corporation, 1984), 80, 91, 115–16; "Grand Café Is Vinita's Oldest Eating Place," unidentified newspaper clipping [ca. 1946], "Businesses" Vertical File, Eastern Trails Museum, Vinita, Okla.; "Grand Café Opened," *Vinita (Okla.) Journal*, September 11, 1919, p. [5]; Grand Café, Vinita, Okla., *Grand Café 37 Years the Leader—in Vinita* (Vinita, Okla.: Grand Café, [ca. 1952]), menu, (quotation), "Businesses" Vertical File, Eastern Trails Museum; James S. Hirsch, *Riot and Remembrance: The Tulsa Race War and its Legacy* (New York: Houghton Mifflin, 2002), 186–87; "Bing" Hooper, "Who's Who in Vinita?" *Vinita Journal*, February 14, 1918, p. [5]; "Hopton and Uptegraff [*sic*] of Plainview, Ark., Have Bought the Boston Café of J. E. Beeman," *Vinita (Okla.) Leader*, February 13, 1913, p. 5; Joseph E. Howell, "Vinita History to Fall for Business," *Tulsa Tribune*, September 4, 1989, sec. C, pp. 7–8; "Prominent Citizen Dies," *Craig County Gazette* (Vinita, Okla.), August 17, 1922, p. 1; Ripley, "Believe It or Not," *St. Louis Post-Dispatch*, July 10, 1933, sec. D, p. 2; Jim Sharp, interview by T. Lindsay Baker, Vinita, Okla., July 25, 2013, typewritten transcript, author's collection; "Updegraff Buys Grand Café," *Vinita Evening Sun-Herald*, September 19, 1916, p. 4; Updegraff's Grand Café, Vinita, Okla., *Upde Graff's Grand Café[,] "One of Oklahoma's Better Restaurants[,]" 32 Years the Leader—in Vinita* (Vinita, Okla.: Upde Graff's Grand Café, [ca. 1948]), menu, "Businesses" Vertical File, Eastern Trails Museum; Wilson's Grand Café, Vinita, Okla., *Wilson's Grand Café[,] Know Where You Eat[,] Know What You Eat[,] Mr. and Mrs. Archie Wilson* (Vinita, Okla.: Wilson's Grand Café, [ca. 1952]), menu, "Businesses" VerticalF, Eastern Trails Museum. For some length of time in the mid-1920s, Orvon Grover "Gene" Autry worked as a telegrapher for the St. Louis–San Francisco Railway in Vinita, and he rented a room from Mrs. Ella Updegraff of the Grand Café, later returning as a Hollywood film star to visit with her and other friends in the town. "Film Star Visits Vinita," *Miami Daily News-Record*, March 30, 1937, p. 3; "Gene Autry Visits Vinita," *Craig County Democrat* (Vinita, Okla.), April 23, 1936, p. [5].

9. Deborah Bouziden, *Off the Beaten Path Oklahoma: A Guide to Unique Places*, 8th ed. (Guilford, Conn.: Globe Pequot, 2015), 39; "Clanton-Long," *Miami Daily News-Record*, October 3, 1937, p. 6; Tom Long, interview by T. Lindsay Baker, Vinita, Okla., July 25, 2013, typewritten transcript (quotations), author's collection; Marian Clark, "Clantons Café[,] Vinita, Oklahoma," *Route 66 Federation News* 6, no. 2 (Spring 2000): 18–19; *Heritage of Craig County and Cooweescoowee and Delaware Districts, Indian Territory* (Vinita, Okla.: Craig County Genealogical Society, 2000) 3: 136; Elaine Kumin and Lyntha Wesner, *Word-of-Mouth Eating in Oklahoma* (n.p.: privately printed, 1980), 134; Johnnie Meier, "Having a Ball in the Calf Fry Capital of the World," *Route 66 Magazine* 17, no. 3 (Summer 2010): 34–36; Ami Reeves, "Today's Special," *Oklahoma Today* (Oklahoma City) 56, no. 4 (August 2006): 74–77.

10. Gene Campbell, "Pike Restaurant Real Eye-Catcher," *Daily Oklahoman*, December 1, 1957, sec. A, p. 2; Tom Clanton, interview by T. Lindsay Baker, July 25, 2013 (quotations); "Contract Given for 'Pike Work," *Miami Daily News-Record*, August 18, 1956, p. 1; Craig County Heritage Association, *Story of Craig County*, 91, 114–15; "Formal Opening of Vinita Pike Café Slated Feb. 18," *Miami Daily News-Record*, February 9, 1958, p. 7; Glass House Restaurant, Vinita, Okla., "Dine in the Sky" (advertisement), *Miami Daily News-Record*, September 25, 1959, p. 3; "Glass House Restaurant Exceptionally Significant," *Preservation Oklahoma News* 13, no. 4 (July 2007): 3; "Look Up! Turnpike Café Opens Tuesday," *Daily Oklahoman*, February 16, 1958, sec. D, p. 1; Michael McNutt, "Eatery Updates Set for Turnpike," *Oklahoman*, October 31, 2009, sec. A, p. 18; Richard Mize, "One Super-sized McDonald's," *Oklahoman*, August 12, 2000, sec. C, p. 3; Rhett Morgan, "Hundreds Join Celebration as Rebuilt Will Rogers Archway Is Unveiled," *Oklahoman*, December 23, 2014, sec. A, p. 11; "New McDonald's to Open," *Sunday Oklahoman*, November 29, 1987, Classified Advertising sec., p. 1; "Work to Start Monday on Will Rogers Turnpike Overhead Restaurant," *Daily Oklahoman*, August 16, 1956, p. 3.

11. Barbara Brackman, "Ed Galloway's Totem Pole: A Case Study in Restoration," in *Backyard Visionaries: Grassroots Art in the Midwest*, ed. Barbara Brackman and Cathy Dwigans (Lawrence: University Press

of Kansas, 1999), 94–112; Kean Isaacs, "The Foyil Texaco Station," *Route 66 Magazine* 24, no. 1 (Winter 2016–17): 28–29; Norman R. Martin, *Up on Route 66: A Time Remembered, Travelers along the Way, 1928 and Forward* (Searcy, Ark.: Martinian Press, 2000), 77 (quotation); Nomination to the National Register of Historic Places for Ed Galloway's Totem Pole Park, January 25, 1999; *Oklahoma: A Guide to the Sooner State*, 220–22. Foyil was the home for Andy Payne, the Oklahoman who won the 1928 Bunion Derby footrace across the United States. Tom Teague, *Searching for 66* (Springfield, Ill.: Samizdat House, 1991), 98–103.

12. *Claremore[,] Oklahoma[,] Famous for Its Natural Mineral Water* (Claremore, Okla.: n.p., [ca. 1945]), folder, "Oklahoma—Cities and Towns—Claremore" Vertical File, Oklahoma Collection, Downtown Library, Metropolitan Library System, Oklahoma City; Don Emrick, "When Healing Waters Flowed: Claremore's Radium Town Area Prospered during the Early Days of Statehood," *Tulsa World*, May 12, 1985, OK Magazine sec., pp. 10–11; Joseph E. Howell, "Mineral Water: It's Staging a Comeback[,] Claremore's Baths Attracting New Interest," *Tulsa Tribune*, June 21, 1978, sec. B, p. 1; Lucille Byerly Lackore, *To California on Route 66 in 1932* (n.p., 1998), 22 (quotation); *Oklahoma: A Guide to the Sooner State*, 222–23; *A Tourist Guide to Claremore[,] Oklahoma* (Claremore, Okla.: Claremore Chamber of Commerce, 1948), 17–29, "Claremore History" scrapbook, Will Rogers Library (Claremore Public Library), Claremore, Okla..

Not everyone who came to Claremore took away a positive impression. The elitist English traveler Sir Walter Citrine visited there on December 4, 1940, jotting down, "All I saw was a few single-storey [*sic*] shacks, a garage or two, a single main street and a mob of towsy children running about," though he later visited and enjoyed the Will Rogers Memorial. Sir Walter Citrine, *My American Diary* (London: George Routledge and Sons, 1941), 47–48.

13. Marian Clark, "Café Rene[,] Will Rogers Center[,] Claremore, Oklahoma," *Route 66 Federation News* 7, no. 1 (Winter 2001): 16–18; Don Emrick, "Taking the Waters," *Oklahoma Today*, January–February 1985, pp. 40–44; Duncan Hines, *Lodging for a Night* (Chicago: Adventures in Good Eating, 1938), 206; Hotel Will Rogers, Claremore, Okla., *Coffee Shop[,] Finest Foods Graciously Served[,] Smorgasbord Delightful Continental Buffet Every Sunday Evening* (Claremore, Okla.: Hotel Will Rogers, [ca. 1950]), folder, "Oklahoma Cities—Claremore" Vertical File, Tulsa and Oklahoma Collection, Tulsa City-County Library, Tulsa; Hotel Will Rogers, *Hotel Will Rogers Coffee Shop Menu[,] Hotel Will Rogers* (Claremore, Okla.: Hotel Will Rogers, [ca. 1940]), menu (third quotation), courtesy of Steven Rider; Hotel Will Rogers, *"Where the World Gets Well": Morton R. Harrison[,] Manager[,] Hotel Will Rogers[,] Claremore[,] U.S.A.* (Claremore, Okla.: Hotel Will Rogers, [ca. 1933]), folder, "Oklahoma Cities—Claremore" Vertical File, Tulsa and Oklahoma Collection, Tulsa City-County Library; Nomination to the National Register of Historic Places for the Will Rogers Hotel, December 24, 1994; Thomas A. Repp, "Paradise Regained," *Route 66 Magazine* 5, no. 4 (Fall 1998): 16–19; Repp, *Route 66: The Empires of Amusement*, 118–23; *Tourist's Guide to Claremore*, 23; "Will Rogers Looks over New Hotel in Claremore," *Daily Oklahoman*, February 16, 1930, sec. A, p. 4; "Will Rogers Remarks," *Los Angeles Times*, February 17, 1930, p. 1 (first and second quotations).

14. Carl Bakal, "The Ocean Comes to Oklahoma," *Reader's Digest* 97, no. 583 (November 1970): 121–24; "Catoosa[,] Population 364—Altitude 625," typescript, April 5, 1937, p. 6 (first and second quotations), Federal Writers' Project Collection, box 37, folder 5; "Closed for Business," *Route Magazine*, October–November 2020, p. 48; Lloyd A. Gilbert Sr., "These Were My Kicks on Route 66," in *Memories on Route 66 1991* (Bethany, Okla.: Oklahoma Route 66 Association, 1991), 50–51 (third and fourth quotations); Ed Montgomery, "Catoosa—Cowtown to Port City," *Sunday Oklahoman*, January 26, 1969, Oklahoma's Orbit supplement, pp. 6–9; *Oklahoma: A Guide to the Sooner State*, 222–24; Repp, *Route 66: The Empires of Amusement*, 124–31; Rittenhouse, *Guide Book to Highway 66*, 43–45; Ross, *Oklahoma Route 66*, 52–64; Michael Wallis, interview by David K. Dunaway, January 6, 2006, typewritten transcript, p. 15, Route 66 Corridor Preservation Program, National Park Service, Santa Fe, N.Mex.

15. Frank Norris, "Courageous Motorists: African American Pioneers on Route 66," *New Mexico Historical Review* 90, no. 3 (Summer 2015), 297, 316–17; *Oklahoma: A Guide to the Sooner State*, 204–215; Rittenhouse, *Guide Book to Highway 66*, 45; *Tulsa: A Guide to the Oil Capital* (Tulsa: Mid-West Printing, 1938), 6–75.

For the belated official state inquiry into the violent events of 1921, see Oklahoma Commission to Study the Tulsa Race Riot of 1921, *The Tulsa Race Riot: A Report* ([Oklahoma City]: Oklahoma Commission to Study the Tulsa Race Riot of 1921, 2001).

16. "Faculty Party and Dinner," *Jenks (Okla.) Times*, March 23, 1939, p. 1; Susan Croce Kelly, *Father of Route 66: The Story of Cy Avery* (Norman: University of Oklahoma Press, 2014), 72–74, 82, 243; "Kiwanians Elucidate on Progressive Farming," *Wagoner (Okla.) Tribune*, September 1, 1927, p. 3; "Three Stand Square," *Coweta (Okla.) Times-Star*, July 22, 1926, p. 4.

17. "The Big Parade," *Bristow (Okla.) Daily Record*, December 10, 1936, p. 1; Scott Cherry, "Venerable Chili House to Return—Delighting Longtime Customers," *Tulsa World*, September 1, 2006, pp. 17, 19; "Chililess Tuesday Appears in Offing," *Tulsa Democrat*, January 21, 1918, p. 9; Connie Cronley, "Fifth Generation of Tulsans Enjoying Chili from Ike's," *Tulsa Tribune*, October 30, 1981, sec. C, p. 2 (first and second quotations); Sharon Dowell, "100 Oklahoma Foods to Try before You Die," *Daily Oklahoman*, January 3, 2007, sec. E, pp. 2–3; "Ike Johnson Chili Parlor," *Tulsa Daily Democrat*, June 29, 1913, unpaged; "Ike's Chili Leaves Downtown Tulsa," *Daily Oklahoman*, May 1, 1996, p. 15; Ike's Chili Parlor, Tulsa, "Chili and Spaghetti" (advertisement), *Tulsa Daily World*, September 3, 1916, morning edition, p. 12; Ike's Chili Parlor, Tulsa, "Chili con Carne" (advertisement), *Tulsa Daily World*, November 16, 1913, morning edition, p. 18; Ike's Chili Parlor, "Ike Johnson is Back" (advertisement), *Tulsa Daily World*, August 15, 1914, morning edition, p. 2; "Ike's Grecian Grip Now about to Slip," *Tulsa Daily Democrat*, April 11, 1913, p. 8; Kumin and Wesner, *Word-of-Mouth Eating*, 131; "The Lookout," *Indian Journal* (Eufala, Okla.), April 10, 1969, p. 1 (third quotation).

18. Greg Broadd, "King of the Coneys Expanding Domain," *Tulsa World*, July 13, 1969, sec. B, pp. 1–2; Tom Carter, "Hot Dog: After 58 Years, It's Still Steamy Inside, Chili Outside," *Tulsa World*, June 24, 1984, sec. A, pp. 1, 4; Kyle Cermak, interview by T. Lindsay Baker, Tulsa, August 7, 2013, typewritten transcript, pp. 1–2, author's collection; "Coney I-Lander Founder[,] Tulsa Greek Leader, Restaurateur Dies" and "Patriarch of Tulsa's Greek Community Dies," newspaper clippings, "Tulsa Biography—Ea–El" Vertical File, Tulsa and Oklahoma Collection, Tulsa City-County Library; Coney Island, Tulsa, "Coney Island System" (advertisement), *Tulsa Daily World*, January 8, 1926, p. 3; Suzanne Holloway, "Downtown Dining: A Guide to Eating out in the Heart of the City," *Tulsa World*, December 18, 1988, sec. H, pp. 1, 7; Bruce Kraig and Patty Carroll, *Man Bites Dog: Hot Dog Culture in America* (Lanham, Md.: Taylor Trade Publishing, 2014), 75, 124; Bruce Kraig, *Hot Dog: A Global History* (London: Reaktion Books, 2009), 78–79; David C. MacKenzie, "One American Dream—with Everything," *Tulsa World*, March 25, 1979, sec. B, pp. 1, 4; *Polk's Tulsa City Directory 1926* (Kansas City, Mo.: R. L. Polk, 1926), 246; Georgia Economou Tsilekas, interview by T. Lindsay Baker, Tulsa, August 8, 2003, typewritten transcript, p. 1, author's collection; "Tulsa Good to Talented Greek—and Vice Versa," *Tulsa Daily World*, June 10, 1973, sec. B, p. 6; U.S., Department of Justice, District Court District of Northern Texas, Dallas, Tex., Declaration of Intention 2097, Christos Economou, August 6, 1925, Record Group 21, Records of District Courts of the United States, 1685–2009, National Archives and Records Administration, Fort Worth, Tex..

19. Bishop's Restaurant, Oklahoma City, "Announcing Our All Day and All Night 24 Hour Service" (advertisement), *Daily Oklahoman*, October 5, 1945, p. 9; Bishop's Restaurants, Inc., *Oklahoma City[,] the Central City of the Great Southwest[,] Bishop's Restaurants, Inc.[,] Oklahoma City—Tulsa[,] "Leaders of the Southwest"* (Oklahoma City: Bishop's Restaurants, Inc., 1945), menu, author's collection; Bishop's Restaurants, Inc., Tulsa, *Bishop's[,] Tulsa—Okla.[,]* © 1948 by Paul E. Corrubia (Tulsa: Bishop's Restaurants, Inc., 1950), menu, author's collection; Bishop's Restaurants, Inc., Tulsa, *Sky Line—Tulsa[,] Bishop's Restaurants Inc.[,] Tulsa and Oklahoma City* (Tulsa: Bishop's Restaurants Inc., [ca. 1935]), menu, "Restaurants" Vertical File, Tulsa Vertical Files, Tulsa and Oklahoma Collection, Tulsa City-County Library; Bob Foresman, "Bishop Restaurant Site to Become Parking Lot," *Tulsa Tribune*, March 1, 1969, sec. A, pp. 1, 4; Dave Cathey, *Classic Restaurants of Oklahoma City* (Charleston. S.C.: American Palate, 2016), 21–22; *Gourmet's Guide to Good Eating: A Valuable and Vital Accessory for Every Motorist and Traveler 1946–47* (New York: Gourmet,

the Magazine of Good Living, 1946), 272, 275; Katherine Hatch, "Bishop's Closing Ends an Era," *Daily Oklahoman*, August 16, 1969, p. 19; Effie S. Jackson, "FEC Tulsa (Restaurants) 520 References," typescript, March 11, 1936, p. 1–2 (first quotation), Federal Writers' Project Collection, box 41, folder 3; Kansas City Waffle House, Tulsa, "Opening Today at Noon: Kansas City Waffle House (Number Two)" (advertisement), *Tulsa Daily World*, May 18, 1916, morning edition, p. 3; Robert E. Lee, "Readers Offer Tales of Bishop's," *Daily Oklahoman*, January 18, 1999, Community sec., p. 1 (second quotation); Terrell Lester, "Good Times, Even Better Food," *Tulsa World*, August 10, 1997, sec. A, pp. 1, 3; Rhys A. Martin, *Lost Restaurants of Tulsa* (Charleston, S.C.: American Palate, 2018), 14–20; "Pioneer Tulsa Restaurant Folds," *Daily Oklahoman*, February 19, 1966, p. 2; Tri-Hard Auction, Tulsa, "Auction[,] Bishop's Restaurant" (advertisement), *Sunday Oklahoman*, March 27, 1966, p. 10; "Waffles Are Making Drumright Men Rich," *Tulsa Democrat*, July 18, 1917, p. 3.

20. Jenni Carlson, "Gautt Was a Sooner Trailblazer," *Sunday Oklahoman*, July 23, 2000, sec. B, p. 12; "Incident Is Explained by Coach," *Oklahoma Daily* (Norman, Okla.), November 3, 1956, p. 1.

21. Gustavo Arellano, *Taco USA: How Mexican Food Conquered America* (New York: Scribner, 2012), 246–49; Mark Brown, "The Hawk Is Howling: El Rancho Grande and the Birth of Tulsa Tex-Mex," *This Land* (Tulsa) 4, no. 12 (June 15, 2013): 6, 8–11, 15; Connie Cronley, "We Still Love El Rancho Grande," *Tulsa Tribune*, March 22, 1985, sec. C, p. 2; "Deaths Listed throughout Oklahoma," *Daily Oklahoman*, June 4, 1971, sec. 4, p. 9; Carol Mighton Haddix, Bruce Kraig, and Colleen Taylor Sen, eds. *The Chicago Food Encyclopedia* (Urbana: University of Illinois Press, 2017), 179–81; *Polk's Tulsa (Tulsa County) City Directory 1940* (Kansas City, Mo.: R. L. Polk, 1940), 501, 842; *Polk's Tulsa (Tulsa County) City Directory 1951*, 290, 780; *Polk's Tulsa (Tulsa County) City Directory 1953* (Dallas: R. L. Polk, 1953), 275, 771; *Polk's Tulsa (Tulsa County) City Directory 1955*, 283; *Polk's Tulsa (Tulsa County) City Directory 1957*, 382; David Pollard, "Another Historic Route 66 Sign in Tulsa Restored: Rancho Grande Mexican Food," *On the Road* 21, no. 3 (September 2009): 7; *Vintage Tulsa Neon Signs: A Few of Our Favorite Neon Treasures* (Tulsa: Tulsa Foundation for Architecture, 2010), 4; John Walden, interview by T. Lindsay Baker, Tulsa, August 7, 2013, typewritten transcript, author's collection (quotation); Jerry Weber, "El Rancho Grande Offers More Than Just Tacos," *Tulsa Tribune*, July 28, 1978, sec. C, p. 3. Railways provided employment for many Mexican American families like that of Frank and Ruby Rodriguez across much of the American West, and they consequently introduced traditional Mexican foodways to many new areas. Jeffrey Marcos Garcílazo, *Traqueros: Mexican Railroad Workers in the United States* (Denton: University of North Texas Press, 2012), 142–46.

   As early as 1956, Garin H. Ferguson opened the Old Mexico Restaurant, dishing up Tex-Mex food 180 miles up the road at 1929 South Glenstone Avenue in Springfield, Missouri. He had served during World War II as an aviator at Randolph Field in San Antonio, Texas, where he became fond of Mexican-style cookery. In 1961 he moved the café to 1408 South National Avenue and changed its name to the Mexican Villa. There and in other locations around Springfield it continues preparing foods using Ferguson's original handwritten recipes. Gregory J. Holman, "65 Years of Mexican Villa," *Springfield (Mo.) News-Leader*, September 16, 2016, sec. A, pp. 1, 4–5; Mexican Villa, Springfield, Mo., "Welcome Amigos" (advertisement), *Sunday News and Leader* (Springfield, Mo.), September 30, 1962, sec. B, p. 6; Old Mexico Restaurant, Springfield, Mo., "Free Money" (advertisement), *Springfield (Mo.) Daily News*, December 16, 1959, p. 16.

22. Kyle Arnold, "Frankoma Pottery Marks 75 Years," *Tulsa World*, September 26, 2008, sec. E, p. 2; Rex F. Harlow, "The First Oil City in Oklahoma," *Harlow's Weekly* (Oklahoma City) 20, no. 45 (November 11, 1922): 8–11, 15–16; Terrell Lester, "Frankoma Pottery: New Management Team Has Sapulpa Company Rolling, Again," *Tulsa World*, May 3, 1992, sec. G, pp. 1–2; Nomination for 11th Street Arkansas River Bridge to the National Register of Historic Places, October 14, 1996; *Oklahoma: A Guide to the Sooner State*, 224; Rittenhouse, *Guide Book to Highway 66*, 47–48; Jim Ross, *Route 66 Crossings: Historic Bridges of the Mother Road* (Norman: University of Oklahoma Press, 2016), 145; Lloyd "Shorty" Smith, "Are We

There Yet? Author Recalls His Childhood Journeys on the Mother Road," *Route 66 Magazine* 17, no. 2 (Spring 2010): 42–44 (quotation); Roy P. Stewart, "Sapulpa Pottery Triumph of Perseverance," *Daily Oklahoman*, March 7, 1962, p. 9.

23. Gary A. Adkins, "Papa Joad's Memory Lane: People and Places of Route 66," *Papa Joad's 66* (St. Louis) 1, no. 1 (Summer 2001): 5–8; Marian Clark, "Norma's Diamond Café[,] Sapulpa, Oklahoma," *Route 66 Federation News* 3, no. 3 (Summer 1997): 20–21; "Norma's Diamond 66 Café More Than a Jewel," *Sunday Oklahoman*, April 9, 2000, sec. C, pp. 1–2; Michael Wallis, *Route 66: The Mother Road* (New York: St. Martin's Press, 1990), 110 (quotation).

24. Rittenhouse, *Guide Book to Highway 66*, 48–49 (third quotation); Irene M. Roberti, "A-Traveling We Did Go," typescript in travel scrapbook, July 12–August 27, 1941, p. [4] (first quotation), author's collection; Herb Tappenbeck and Ellen Tappenbeck, "The Way It Was on the Route," *Route 66 Federation News* 5, no. 4 (Autumn 1999): 17–20 (second quotation).

25. "Negroes Driven Out: White Residents of Stroud, Okla., Expel All the Blacks," *St. Louis Globe-Democrat*, August 26, 1901, p. 2; *100 Years Stroud 1892–1992* (Stroud, Okla.: Stroud Centennial History Book Committee, 1992), 2–17; Michael Smith, "True-grit Town: A Year After a Devastating Tornado, Stroud Is Slowly Forging Ahead," *Tulsa World*, April 29, 2000, sec. A, pp. 1, 3. Following the 1901 race riot, the local press reported, "A sign was painted and stuck up on one of the prominent corners in this city which read as follows: '[N<—>], Don't let the sun go down on U.'" "The Stroud Mob: All Negroes Were Run out of Town Last Saturday, Their Property Burned," *Stroud (Okla.) Messenger*, August 30, 1901, p. 1.

26. "Beautiful New Rock Café Opened," *Stroud Messenger*, August 4, 1939, p. 1; Phoebe Billups, "Rockin' On," *Route Magazine*, June–July 2001, pp. 64–68, 70; David Cathey, "Rock On: Historic Café Reopens in Stroud," *Oklahoman*, May 30, 2009, sec. A, pp. 13, 18; Marian Clark, "Coffee Shops, Diners and Other Swell Places: The Rock Café[,] Stroud, Oklahoma," *Route 66 Magazine* 4, no. 1 (Winter 1996–97): 30–31; Ann DeFrange, "Route 66 Cruise Gets Main Streets Buzzing Again," *Daily Oklahoman*, June 11, 1990, pp. 1–2 (quotation); Jay Grelen, "Find Sweet Tea and Romance at Rock Café," *Daily Oklahoman*, August 10, 1999, pp. 1, 13; Ron Jackson, "Rock Solid: Fire-gutted Stroud Café Will Reopen," *Oklahoman*, May 22, 2008, sec. A, pp. 1–2; Jerry McClanahan, Jim Ross, and Shellee Graham, *Route 66 Sightings* (Arcadia, Okla.: Ghost Towns Press, 2011), 86–87; Nomination to the National Register of Historic Places for the Rock Café, June 14, 2001; *100 Years Stroud 1892–1992*, 180, 211–212; Emily Priddy, "Rock Café Returns to Its Roots," *On the Road* 15, no. 1 (March 2003): 4–6; "Route 66 Offers Toll-free Drive between Tulsa, City," *Daily Oklahoman*, July 6, 1993, p. 6; "Edgar Noel (Ed) Smalley," *Oklahoman*, April 19, 2005, sec. A, p. 15; Michael Wallis and Marian Clark, *Hogs on 66: Best Food and Hangouts for Road Trips on Route 66* (Tulsa: Council Oak Books, 2004), 70–73; Dawn Welch, "Rock Café," *Route 66 Preservation: Success through Partnerships*, 3 (Santa Fe: Route 66 Corridor Preservation Program, National Park Service, 2004); Dawn Welch and Raquel Pelzel, *Dollars to Donuts: Comfort Food and Kitchen Wisdom from Route 66's Landmark Rock Café* (New York: Rodale, 2009), viii. Rock Café owner Dawn Welch was the inspiration for the character Sally Carrera in the 2006 Pixar Animation Studios feature motion picture, *Cars*.

27. Paul English, "Her Life for the Cause: One Shot Transforms Woman's Life," *Sunday Oklahoman*, November 28, 1999, sec. A, pp. 1, 4; Howard Johnson's, [Quincy, Mass.], *Any Time Is Vacation Time in Oklahoma* ([Quincy, Mass.]: Howard Johnson's, [ca. 1957]), place mat, Menu Collection, Oklahoma Collection, Downtown Library, Metropolitan Library System, Oklahoma City; Steve Lackmeyer, "Fans Reminisce about Stop That Graced Turnpike, City," *Oklahoman*, May 7, 2006, sec. C, p. 2; Robert E. Lee, "Both Signs in Storage," *Daily Oklahoman*, February 6, 1987, sec. S, p. 1; Ed Montgomery, "Phillips' Contract for Turnpike Concessions Renewed," *Daily Oklahoman*, August 19, 1977, p. 33; Mary Jo Nelson, "Concessions Site to Replace Turnpike Skywalk," *Sunday Oklahoman*, March 30, 1986, sec. B, p. 1; Mary Jo Nelson, "Howard Johnson's Restaurants on Turnpike to Be Torn Down," *Daily Oklahoman*, September 23, 1986, p. 13; "Oklahoma Opens a Turnpike: 88-mile Road Parallels U.S. 66 between Tulsa and State Capital," *New York Times*, May 24, 1953, sec. 10, p. 20; *100 Years Stroud 1892–1992*, 15–16; "State Group Finds Stroud

Handy Spot," *Daily Oklahoman*, October 6, 1953, p. 7; "Welfare Office to Use Turnpike Landmark," *Daily Oklahoman*, May 19, 1987, p. 3.

28. Ben Berger, "Wellston Plugs the Gap," *Sunday Oklahoman*, June 6, 1965, Oklahoma's Orbit supplement, pp. 12–13; M. W. Gantt, "Wellston, a Worthy Town," *Western* (Fort Smith and Western Railway, Fort Smith, Ark.) 1, no. 9 (November 1935): 3–4; J. W. "Jim" Parker, interview by Rodger Harris, Yukon, Okla., September 24, 1992, audio recording and typewritten transcript, p. 15, Research Center, Oklahoma Historical Society; Ray Parr, "Still on the Map," *Daily Oklahoman*, January 8, 1939, sec. D, p. 1; Ross, *Oklahoma Route 66*, 99–105; Jim Ross and Shellee Graham, *Secret Route 66: A Guide to the Weird, Wonderful, and Obscure* (St. Louis: Reedy Press, 2017), 130–31.

29. Dave Cathey, "Butcher BBQ Conquers World Championship," *Oklahoman*, November 7, 2018, sec. C, p. 1; Dave Cathey, "Butcher BBQ Stand on Target to Become Dining Destination," *Oklahoman*, May 11, 2016, sec. D, pp. 1, 3; Susan Croce Kelly, "Just for Kicks! Route 66," *Chicago Tribune*, May 22, 1983, sec. 11, p. 2; "Local News," *Luther (Okla.) Register*, June 7, 1929, p. 1; J. C. Long and John D. Long, *Motor Camping* (New York: Dodd, Mead, 1923), 202–3; Pioneer Camp, Wellston, Okla., "For Sale by Owner" (advertisement), *Sunday Oklahoman*, July 24, 1994, Classified Advertising sec., p. 22; Pioneer Camp, "Happy New Year" (advertisement), *Wellston (Okla.) News*, January 1, 1959, p. [3]; Martha Engel Pitts, "Daily Jots," *Oklahoma County Register* (Luther, Okla.), December 13, 1945), p. 1; Rittenhouse, *Guide Book to Highway 66*, 50–51; Janette Cooper Rutledge, *How to Tour the United States in Thirty-one Days for One Hundred Dollars* (New York: Harlan Publications, 1939), 10–11; Terri Ryburn-LaMonte, "Route 66, 1926 to the Present: The Road as Local History" (PhD diss., Illinois State University, 1999), 154–60; "Shot Woman Saves Gunman's Life," *Daily Oklahoman*, September 29, 1999, sec. D, p. 7; "25 Years Ago," *Wellston News*, October 29, 1959, p. 1.

30. "Colored Folks' News," *Luther (Okla.) Citizen*, December 23, 1948, p. [5]; August 11, 1949, p. [5]; "Fire Destroys Barbecue Stand; Mill Has 2 Fires," *Luther Citizen*, October 7, 1948, p. 1; Carla Hinton, "'A Safe Haven': 'Green Book' Movie, Preservation Efforts Fuel Renaissance of Fueling Luther Station," *Oklahoman*, December 11, 2018, sec. A, pp. 1–2 (first and fourth quotations); "Holdup Spurs Bandit Search," *Daily Oklahoman*, September 29, 1946, p. 1; "Latest News Notes of Luther Colored Folks," *Luther Register*, July 18, 1935, p. 8; August 6, 1936, p. 8; December 30, 1937, p. 8; August 11, 1938, p. 8; April 6, 1939, p. 8; July 31, 1941, p. 8 (third quotation); "Luther Colored Folks," *Oklahoma County Register*, July 23, 1942, p. 8; Richard Mize, "Funds Go for Fixes on Route 66," *Oklahoman*, September 22, 2018, sec. C, p. 2; "Mrs. Jefferson at Threatt's Café," *Oklahoma County Register*, November 25, 1948, p. [8]; "Negro Democrats Schedule Rallies," *Oklahoma News* (Oklahoma City), June 15, 1936, p. 7; "News from Luther Colored Folks," *Oklahoma County Register*, September 7, 1944, p. [8]; August 28, 1947, p. [4]; April 8, 1948, p. 4; May 13, 1948, p. [4]; "N.H.A. News," *Oklahoma County Register*, October 23, 1947, p. [4]; Nomination to the National Register of Historic Places for Threatt Filling Station, December 19, 1994; Norris, "Courageous Motorists," 293–99; "Some Late Local News," *Luther Register*, May 21, 1936, p. 1; Threatt's Park, Luther, Okla., "Picnic!" (advertisement), *Oklahoma County Register*, August 8, 1940, p. 1; James J. West, M. Yeldell Jones, J. Z. Hunter, J. F. Moore, J. T. Armstrong, and C. C. Russell, "The Negro in Oklahoma: Luther, Oklahoma[,] and Vicinity," typescript, May 9, 1939, pp. 7–8 (second quotation), Federal Writers' Project Collection, box 22, folder 11.

31. Linda Jones, "The Night Arcadia Burned: 'Toodie' Teuscher Doesn't Remember It; She Wasn't Born until Later That Night," *Edmond (Okla.) Booster*, August 12, 1976, sec. 3, p. 3; Mike McCarville, "Young Town Rode Cotton Crest: Arcadia's History Eventful," *Oklahoma City Times*, August 22, 1963, p. 8N; Nominations to the National Register of Historic Places for Arcadia Round Barn, December 1977, and for Tuton's Drugstore, August 15, 1979; Perry Rogers, "Perry Rogers Tells This Story of the White Goose Café, on Route 66," in *Oklahoma Route 66 Arcadia, Okla.[,] Sept. 1994*, ed. Eula Teuscher, 4–5 (Arcadia, Okla.: Arcadia Historical Society, 1994); "Rogers," *Oklahoman*, August 21, 2007, sec. A, p. 13. The historic roadway less than a mile southwest of Arcadia is the site of a latter-day food-vending enterprise, Pop's, which specializes in a widely diverse range of bottled sodas and short-order foods including buffalo burgers. It opened in 2007 and continued serving the public at the time of this writing. Steve Lackmeyer, "Pops

Drink Shop: Rare Soda Sales Have Sparkled More Than Manager Expected," *Oklahoman*, September 20, 2006, sec. B, p. 1; Candacy Taylor, *Moon Route 66 Road Trip* (Berkeley, Calif.: Avalon Travel, 2016), 153–52.

32. Humphrey Bard, "Hear 'n There on the Rural Routes," *Edmond (Okla.) Enterprise*, November 24, 1953, p. 8; "Everett M. Bradbury," *Daily Oklahoman*, February 2, 1959, p. 9; Linda Jones, "'Crossroads of America': Bradbury Corner, Scene of History, and Tragedy," *Edmond (Okla.) Evening Sun*, June 25, 1984, sec. D, p. 6; Ray Parr, "$2 Million Four-lane Road Projects Urged for County Program," *Daily Oklahoman*, November 9, 1952, sec. 2, p. 1.

33. David King Dunaway, *Across the Tracks: A Route 66 Story* (Albuquerque: privately printed, 2001), 107–9, 114–17; "Edmond Editor Dies," *Miami Daily News-Record*, January 27, 1942, p. 5; Christopher P. Lehman, "West Edwards Days: African Americans in Territorial Edmond," *Chronicles of Oklahoma* 97, no. 2 (Summer 2019): 174–91; *Oklahoma: A Guide to the Sooner State*, 226–27; Rittenhouse, *Guide Book to Highway 66*, 51–52; Royce Café, Edmond, Okla., *"From Dawn to Dawn We're Never Gone" Air Conditioned*, publication A-2090 (Oklahoma City: American Stamp Co., [ca. 1940]), postcard (quotations); Joe Sonderman and Jim Ross, *Images of America: Route 66 in Oklahoma* (Charleston, S.C.: Arcadia Publishing, 2011), 76; Candacy Taylor, "Why Black Americans Are Not Nostalgic for Route 66," *Atlantic*, November 3, 2016, https://www.theatlantic.com/politics/archive/2016/11/the-roots-of-route-66/506255/ (accessed on November 7, 2016).

34. "Eugene Weldon Noe," *Daily Oklahoman*, December 14, 1963, p. 20; David Randall Fisk, *Legendary Locals of Edmond*[,] *Oklahoma* (Charleston, S.C.: Arcadia Publishing, 2014), 84; Stan Hoig, *Edmond: The First Century* (Edmond, Okla.: Edmond Historic Preservation Trust, 1987), 25, 32; "Know Your Neighbor: Mrs. Cleo Noe," *Edmond Enterprise*, February 17, 1953, p. 1; "Lamson," *Oklahoman*, December 29, 2010, sec. A, p. 15; "Mum Show Nov. 15–16 in Basement M. E. Church," *Edmond Enterprise*, November 7, 1929, p. [2]; Curt Munson, *Tales of the Wide-A-Wake Café* (Bloomington, Ind.: Author House, 2004), v–xi, 1–224; "Personals," *Edmond Enterprise*, December 1, 1942, p. 6; "T. Crawford Noe," *Daily Oklahoman*, April 16, 1953, p. 5; "Wide-A-Wake Goes Paris One Better," *Edmond Enterprise*, March 15, 1938, p. [4]; Wide A Wake Café, Edmond, Okla., "Delicious Sandwiches" (advertisement), *Edmond Enterprise*, January 12, 1932, p. [2] (second quotation); Wide-A-Wake Café, "Incoming Oil Field Workers . . . Eat Here" (advertisement), *Edmond Enterprise*, August 7, 1934, p. [2] (third and fourth quotations); Wide-A-Wake Café, "Wide-A-Wake Café" (advertisement), *Edmond Enterprise*, September 5, 1950, p. [5]; "Wide-A-Wake Café Opens Refreshment Garden for Summer," *Edmond Enterprise*, July 2, 1935, p. [2]; "Wide-A-Wake Café[,] Steaks—Chicken," *Oklahoma County News* (Jones, Okla.), January 22, 1959, p. 12; Wide A Wake Lunch, Edmond, Okla., "Wide A Wake Lunch Formerly Highway Café" (advertisement), *Edmond Enterprise*, October 27, 1931, p. [2].

35. "Announcing," *Edmond Enterprise*, July 4, 1933, p. 1; "Card of Thanks," *Edmond Enterprise*, February 10, 1942, p. [5]; "Edmond Editor Dies," p. 5; Fisk, *Legendary Locals*, 85; Hendenbrand and Anderson, Inc., Oklahoma City, "Royce Café (of Edmond) Auction" (advertisement), *Daily Oklahoman*, August 15, 1970, p. 24; Duncan Hines, *Adventures in Good Eating* (Bowling Green, Ky.: Adventures in Good Eating, 1941), 245 (quotation); Hoig, *Edmond*, 73; "Know Your Neighbor: Mrs. Royce B. Adamson," *Edmond Enterprise*, December 2, 1952, p. 1; "Longtime Owner Will Retire: Royce Café, City Landmark, Sold Outright to Jim Mills," *Edmond Booster*, January 9, 1958, p. 1; "Mrs. Adamson, Edmond Civic Leader, Dies," *Daily Oklahoman*, July 31, 1965, p. 17; "Nick Nacks," *Oklahoma County Register*, April 23, 1953, p. 1; "The Office Hound," *Oklahoma County Register*, January 31, 1957, p. 2; Royce Café, Edmond, Okla., "Heralding New Hours" (advertisement), *Edmond Enterprise*, December 25, 1945, p. [7]; Royce Café, "Royce Café" (advertisement), *Edmond Enterprise*, October 26, 1937, p. [6]; Royce Café, "Royce Café Announces New Hours" (advertisement), *Edmond Enterprise*, October 3, 1944, p. 3; "Royce Café Invites Friends and Patrons to Formal Open House October 9th," *Edmond Enterprise*, October 7, 1941, p. 1; "Royce Café Is Sold by Mills to R. R. McCoys," *Edmond Booster*, June 16, 1958, p. 1; "Royce Café Now Cool as Want [*sic*]; Is Air Conditioned," *Edmond Enterprise*, July 26, 1938, p. 1; "Royce Café Opens New Attractive Dining Room,"

Edmond Enterprise, June 2, 1936, p. 1; "Royce Café Payroll One of Largest in Edmond," *Edmond Enterprise*, October 7, 1941, p. [4]; "Royce Café's New Steaks Are Delicious," *Edmond Enterprise*, September 29, 1936, p. [4]; "Sipe," *Oklahoman*, April 11, 2006, p. 15.

36. Ann DeFrange, "Project Preserves the 'Kicks': Sprit of 66 Still Lives in Oklahoma City," *Sunday Oklahoman*, February 6, 1994, sec. A, pp. 1, 19; Debs Myers, "Oklahoma City: It Has Grown in a Little More Than Half a Century from Frontier Outpost to Modern Metropolis," *Holiday* 7, no. 5 (May 1950): 114–16, 119–22, 124–26, 128–29; *Oklahoma: A Guide to the Sooner State*, 164–80; Rittenhouse, *Guide Book to Highway 66*, 52–53, 55; Jim Ross, "Mapping the Metro," *Route 66 Magazine* 4, no. 3 (Summer 1997): 30–31, 48; Ross, *Oklahoma Route 66*, 114–25.

37. [Willie] Allen, "Hotels," typescript, December 12, 1935, pp. 1–2, Federal Writers' Project Collection, box 33, folder 30; Cathey, *Classic Restaurants of Oklahoma City*, 100–102; Norris, "Courageous Motorists," 317–18; Allen Saxe, "Protest and Reform: The Desegregation of Oklahoma City" (PhD diss., University of Oklahoma, 1969), 45, 49–50, 158, 162–76, 240–41; Rachel E. Watson, "An Unflinching Call for Freedom: Clara Luper's Pedagogy at the Center of Sit-Ins," *Chronicles of Oklahoma* 97, no. 3 (Fall 2019): 278–95. For listings of Black-operated businesses in Oklahoma City at the eve of World War II, see *Oklahoma City, Oklahoma[,] Negro City Directory 1941–1942* (Oklahoma City: Oklahoma City Negro Chamber of Commerce, [1941]).

38. Ilya Ilf and Eugene Petrov, *Little Golden America: Two Famous Soviet Humorists Survey These United States*, trans. Charles Malamuth (New York: Farrar and Rinehart, 1937), 160 (first quotation); *Oklahoma: A Guide to the Sooner State*, 166; Anne Merriman Peck and Enid Johnson, *Roundabout America* (New York: Harper and Brothers, 1933), 1:93; Ernie Pyle, *Home Country* (New York: William Sloane, 1935), 87 (second and third quotations); Roberti, "A-Traveling We Did Go," pp. [4 (fourth quotation), 24].

39. "Beer License Row Splits Partnership," *Daily Oklahoman*, July 22, 1933, p. 1; "Driver of Taxicab Left Tied to Tree," *Daily Oklahoman*, November 6, 1932, sec. A, p. 2; "Fray at Roadhouse," *Oklahoma News*, August 27, 1929, p. 5; Leavitt Co., Oklahoma City, "We Have the Oak Cliff Night Club" (advertisement), *Oklahoma News*, February 23, 1934, p. 14; Lincoln Inn, Oklahoma City, "Grand Opening" (advertisement), *Daily Oklahoman*, March 21, 1923, p. 9; Mitchell's Night Club, Oklahoma City, "Dining and Dancing Every Night at Mitchell's Oak Cliff Night Club" (advertisement), *Daily Oklahoman*, November 8, 1931, sec. C, p. 11; Mitchell's Oak Cliff Night Club, Oklahoma City, "Dine and Dance to a Real Band" (advertisement), *Daily Oklahoman*, October 5, 1932, p. 4; Mitchell's Oak Cliff Nite Club, Oklahoma City, "Mitchell's Oak Cliff Nite Club" (advertisement), *Daily Oklahoman*, July 15, 1933, p. 4 (second quotation); Mitchell's Oak Cliff, Oklahoma City, "Come out Sunday Afternoon and Eat an Old-fashioned Chicken Dinner" (advertisement), *Daily Oklahoman*, May 3, 1930, p. 7; Mitchell's Oak Cliff, "Cool! Breeze! Invigorating!" (advertisement), *Daily Oklahoman*, May 27, 1933, p. 9 (first quotation); Oak Cliff, Oklahoma City, "Mr. and Mrs. Mitchell" (advertisement), *Daily Oklahoman*, Sunday, April 28, 1929, sec. A, p. 18; Oak Cliff, "Oak Cliff" (advertisement), *Daily Oklahoman*, August 18, 1929, sec. C, p. 2; "Road House Burned," *Oklahoma News*, June 29, 1929, p. 1; Silver Club, Oklahoma City, "Chicken Dinner—Dancing" (advertisement), *Oklahoma News*, August 28, 1934, sec. 2, p. 4 (third quotation).

40. "Bell[,] Eva Lee Howard," *Daily Oklahoman*, December 15, 1998, p. 31; "Bell[,] John William Bell," *Daily Oklahoman*, May 20, 2003, sec. A, p. 11; "County Club Raided Again," *Daily Oklahoman*, March 8, 1948, pp. 1–2; Sharon Dowell, "Former Chef Recalls Years Working at Kentucky Club," *Sunday Oklahoman*, February 7, 1999, Travel and Entertainment sec., p. 8 (quotations); Sharon Dowell, "Oklahoma Menu: Restaurant's History Legendary," *Sunday Oklahoman*, February 7, 1999, Travel and Entertainment sec., p. 8; "50 Escape Fire," *Miami Daily News-Record*, December 13, 1945, p. 7; Kentucky Club, Oklahoma City, "Dine and Dance Nightly" (advertisement), *Daily Oklahoman*, October 1, 1949, p. 4; Kentucky Club, "Formal Opening" (advertisement), *Daily Oklahoman*, October 26, 1938, p. 9; Kentucky Club, "Re-opening Tonite[,] a Beautiful New Kentucky Club" (advertisement), *Daily Oklahoman*, May 1, 1946, p. 9; "Man Charged in Gun Fight," *Daily Oklahoman*, February 22, 1945, p. 4; "Marneres[,] Anthony A. (Tony)," *Daily*

Oklahoman, April 19, 1982, p. 18; "Raid Battle Won by Club's Owner," *Daily Oklahoman*, November 10, 1948, p. 16; J. Nelson Taylor, "Tony Marneres Faces Immigration Quiz," *Daily Oklahoman*, May 27, 1953, p. 1.

41. "Board's Stand on Annexation of Tract Eased," *Daily Oklahoman*, January 9, 1959, p. 5; Cathey, *Classic Restaurants*, 41; Dave Cathey, "Gabriella's Offers a Taste of Krebs in Historic Oklahoma City Setting," *Oklahoman*, July 26, 2012, sec. D, p. 6; Clark, *Route 66 Cookbook*, 92–93; Dowell, "Oklahoma Menu," p. 8; Joan Gillmore, "Ann Lynn Busy with Invitations for Lavish Black-Tie Party," *Daily Oklahoman*, June 17, 1979, Women's News sec., pp. 4, 10; Kentucky Club, Oklahoma City, "The Kentucky Club" (advertisement), *Daily Oklahoman*, April 4, 1980, p. 19; "Kentucky Club Opens Oct. 29," *Sunday Oklahoman*, October 21, 1979, sec. B, p. 1; "License Approved for Ramada Club," *Daily Oklahoman*, March 30, 1961, p. 2; Melba Lovelace, "Restaurant Review: Barbecue Featured at Oklahoma Line," *Sunday Oklahoman*, May 24, 1981, the Oklahomans supplement, p. 21; "$1.5 Million Inn Is Planned Here," *Daily Oklahoman*, August 16, 1959, sec. B, p. 5; Jennifer Palmer, "Legendary Barbecue Eatery Shuts Down after 29 Years," *Oklahoman*, November 10, 2010, sec. B, pp. 1, 6; Ross, *Oklahoma Route 66*, 119, 123; Ross and Graham, *Secret Route 66*, 1–2; Tom Snyder, *The Route 66 Traveler's Guide and Roadside Companion* (New York: St. Martin's Press, 1990), 46.

42. Anson B. Campbell, *Stalwart Sooners* (Oklahoma City: Paul and Paul, 1949), unpaged; Cathey, *Classic Restaurants*, 22–25; Ferdie J. Deering, "Youngsters with Resourcefulness, Ambition Can Succeed with Effort," *Daily Oklahoman*, November 30, 1976, p. 12; Gail Driskill, "Beverly Osborne from Shoeshine Boy to Millionaire," *Sunday Oklahoman*, March 18, 1979, the Oklahomans supplement, pp. 1, 4–7; "Hard Work Took Youth and Mate to Success," *Oklahoma News*, July 30, 1930, p. 14; Osborne Waffle Shops, Oklahoma City, "Eat at the Osborne Waffle Shops" (advertisement), *Oklahoma City Star*, August 7, 1931, p. 2; *Polk's Oklahoma City Directory for the Year Commencing May 1st[,] 1922* (Dallas: R. L. Polk, 1922), 701, 1255.

43. Campbell, *Stalwart Sooners*, unpaged (second quotation); Marian Clark, "Oklahoma City Is Home to a Route 66 Classic Eatery," *Route 66 Federation News* 1, no. 2 (Spring 1995): 15–16; Driskill, "Beverly Osborne," p. 6 (first quotation); John A. Jakle and Keith A. Sculle, *Fast Food: Roadside Restaurants in the Automobile Age* (Baltimore: Johns Hopkins University Press, 1999), 217–18; Bob Moore, "Chicken in the Rough: Road Food Supreme," *Route 66 Magazine* 3, no. 4 (Fall 1996): 28–29.

44. Beverly's Drive-In, Oklahoma City, "Announcing the Formal Opening" (advertisement), *Daily Oklahoman*, September 5, 1935, p. 3; Beverly's Drive-In, "Are You Going?" (advertisement), *Daily Oklahoman*, March 27, 1937, p. 7; Beverly's Drive-In, *Beverly's Drive In* (Oklahoma City: Beverly's Drive-In, [ca. 1940]), menu, courtesy of Steven Rider; Beverly's, Oklahoma City, *Welcome to . . . Beverly's[,] Home of the Original Chicken in the Rough[,] Copyright 1937 by Beverly Osborne* ([Oklahoma City]: Bowman Printing, [1958]), menu, Menu Collection, Oklahoma Collection, Downtown Library, Metropolitan Library System, Oklahoma City; Max Nichols, "Max Nichols," *Daily Oklahoman*, May 30, 1982, sec. B, pp. 1–2 (quotations); "One Grill Sells to Sit-in Group," *Daily Oklahoman*, April 9, 1961, sec. A, p. 7. For representative references to the use of the expression, "chicken in the rough," referring to people consuming hand-held pieces of fried chicken, see "A Des Moines River Steamboat Excursion in the Early Days," *Des Moines Register*, March 20, 1910, Magazine sec., p. 1; and "Sudye Cleckler, Visiting in California, Gives Our Readers Interesting Highlights of Trip," *Sand Springs (Okla.) Leader*, July 6, 1930, p. 1.

45. Cathey, *Classic Restaurants*, 26, 67–70; Chicken in the Rough, Oklahoma City, "Franchise Representative to Contact Restaurants and Drive Ins" (advertisement), *San Antonio Express*, November 19, 1939, sec. C, p. 6; Dave Dryden, "Franchising Trend Grows Apparent," *Sunday Oklahoman*, January 11, 1970, Forward Oklahoma sec., p. 20; Jakle and Sculle, *Fast Food*, 217; Michael Karl Witzel, *Route 66 Remembered* (Osceola, Wisc.: MBI Publishing, 1996), 109. As early as 1942, national columnist and inspirational writer Dale Carnegie was praising Beverly Osborne's diligence and business acumen. Dale Carnegie, "Dale Carnegie," *Joplin (Mo.) Globe*, February 12, 1942, p. 6.

46. Briana Bailey, "Recipe for Success," *Oklahoman*, July 25, 2014, sec. C, pp. 1, 6; "Chicken Franchise Sold," *Daily Oklahoman*, May 3, 1979, p. 59; "Drive-In Shuts Door for Good," *Daily Oklahoman*, December 30, 1960, p. 4; "Fried Chicken Franchise Sold," *Daily Oklahoman*, November 3, 1969, pp. 1–2; Kevan

Goff-Majors, "Summer Job Stretched into 50 Years," *Saturday Oklahoman and Times* (Oklahoma City), May 23, 1987, p. 12; Richard Mize, "Beverly's Pancake Moving," *Oklahoman*, December 27, 2007, sec. B, p. 4; "Old, Familiar Beverly's Site Closing Friday," *Daily Oklahoman*, August 24, 1972, p. 40; Ray Parr, "Site Approved for Two New State Capitol Buildings: 4-block Area Voted at Cost of $2 Million," *Daily Oklahoman*, October 27, 1960, pp. 1, 2, 10; "Restaurant Pioneer of 'Chicken in the Rough,' Beverly Osborne, Dies at 82," *Daily Oklahoman*, July 4, 1979, p. 34; "R. Osborne Services Scheduled," *Daily Oklahoman*, December 15, 1977, p. 11.

47. Cathey, *Classic Restaurants*, 99–100; Dave Cathey, "Florence's Restaurant Serves the Best of Our Past, Smothered or Fried," *Oklahoman*, February 25, 2015, sec. D, pp. 1–2 (second quotation); Dave Cathey, "Restaurateurs Keep Their Mission on a Roll," *Oklahoman*, February 28, 2016, sec. A, p. 12; Sean Ely, "City Official Dreams of New Life for NE 23," *Oklahoman*, July 21, 2009, sec. A, p. 11; Devona Walker, "Once upon a Time: Restaurateur Makes State History One Meal at a Time," *Oklahoman*, February 2, 2008, sec. B, pp. 1, 6 (first quotation).

48. "Business Firms and Residents Compiled," *Daily Oklahoman*, February 23, 1930, sec. A, p. 10; Cathey, *Classic Restaurants*, 27–29; Dave Cathey, "Recipe for Success: History Shows 'Secret Sauce' Has Made Many Comebacks in State, Elsewhere," *Oklahoman*, April 8, 2018, sec. S, pp. 7–10; Dolores Unusual Sandwich Mill, Oklahoma City, "Ralph A. Stephens Announces 'Dolores'" (advertisement), *Daily Oklahoman*, April 19, 1930, p. 7; "Free Music in Wee Hours of Night Irks 12," *Daily Oklahoman*, July 2, 1930, p. 13; Katherine Hatch, "Ride to Top Bit Bumpy, but Worth It," *Sunday Oklahoman*, January 21, 1969, pp. 7, 9; Stephens Restaurant, Oklahoma City, "State Fair Visitors" (advertisement), *Daily Oklahoman*, September 23, 1923, sec. E, p. 4.

49. Dolores Restaurant and Drive-In, Oklahoma City, *Dolores Personalized Foods* (Oklahoma City: Dolores Restaurant and Drive-In, [ca. 1945]), menu, Menu Collection, Oklahoma Collection, Downtown Library, Metropolitan Library System, Oklahoma City; Sharon Dowell, "Our Readers Speak," *Daily Oklahoman*, October 27, 1999, sec. B, p. 3; *Gourmet's Guide to Good Eating*, 274; Hines, *Adventures in Good Eating* (1938), 192; Duncan Hines, *Adventures in Good Eating* (Bowling Green, Ky.: Adventures in Good Eating, 1939), 208; Hines, *Adventures in Good Eating* (1941), 246 (second quotation); Duncan Hines, "Coconut Cream Dessert Tasty," *Daily Oklahoman*, October 20, 1950, p. 17; Roberti, "A-Traveling We Did Go," p. [4] (first quotation); Curt Teich and Company, Chicago, Production File D-3708 for Menu for Dolores Sandwich Mill, Oklahoma City, February 4, 1935, Curt Teich Postcard Archives Collection, Special Collections, Newberry Library, Chicago.

50. Cathey, *Classic Restaurants*, 30; "Drive-In Done in by California Progress," *Saturday Oklahoman and Times*, February 28, 1981, p. 5; "Extinction Threatening Drive-In of Ex-cityans' Tradition," *Sunday Oklahoman*, June 8, 1980, sec. A, p. 4; Mark Kurlansky, ed., *The Food of a Younger Land* (New York: Riverhead Books, 2009), 415–16; "Meet the Champ!," *Miami Daily News-Record*, April 22, 1941, p. 1. The curly french fries became such a hit at the Dolores that Amanda and Ralph even placed their picture on the front of one of their restaurant menus. Dolores Restaurant and Drive-In, Oklahoma City, *Dolores Restaurant and Drive-In[,] Oklahoma City* (Oklahoma City: Dolores Restaurant and Drive-In, [ca. 1940]), menu, Menu Collection, Oklahoma Collection, Downtown Library, Metropolitan Library System, Oklahoma City.

51. Dolores Restaurant, Oklahoma City, "Colored Girl for Dishwashing Machine" (advertisement), *Daily Oklahoman*, August 27, 1958, sec. B, p. 2 (sixth quotation); Dolores Restaurant, "Experienced Cashier" (advertisement), *Daily Oklahoman*, July 1, 1953, p. 26 (third quotation); Dolores Restaurant, "Lady from East Side for Salad Department" (advertisement), *Daily Oklahoman*, May 13, 1966, p. 39 (seventh quotation); Dolores Restaurant, "Need Attractive Lady for Hostess Job" (advertisement), *Daily Oklahoman*, October 16, 1969, p. 69 (second quotation); Dolores Restaurant, "Waitress" (advertisement), *Daily Oklahoman*, March 2, 1966, p. 18 (fourth quotation); Dolores Restaurant, "White Girl for Fountain Work" (advertisement), *Daily Oklahoman*, August 27, 1958, sec. B, p. 2 (fifth quotation); Dolores Sandwich Mill, Oklahoma City,

"Boys around 20 to Hop Cars and Wait Tables" (advertisement), *Daily Oklahoman*, May 2, 1937, sec. B, p. 7 (first quotation); Ray Parr, "Boy Wanted," *Daily Oklahoman*, January 4, 1942, sec. D, pp. 1–2.

52. "City Founder of Restaurant Is Dead at 75," *Daily Oklahoman*, January 12, 1966, p. 7; Dolores Restaurant, "Beginning January 14, Dolores Restaurants Blends Old Spain with Traditional Oklahoma" (advertisement), *Daily Oklahoman*, January 15, 1972, p. 18; "Dolores Shuts Doors in City after 44 Years," *Daily Oklahoman*, October 20, 1974, p. 6; "History on Auction Block: Sale Puts Curtain down on Dolores Restaurant," *Sunday Oklahoman*, February 2, 1975, sec. A, p. 17; Jack Money and Ellie Sutter, "Building 'Tickles' Residents," *Daily Oklahoman*, May 13, 1996, sec. B, pp. 1–2; "Restaurateur Dead at 91," *Daily Oklahoman*, November 19, 1983, p. 64.

53. "Certificate of Partnership," *Daily Record* (Oklahoma City), January 23, 1932, p. 8; "Grocery Burglary Suspect Captured," *Daily Oklahoman*, July 21, 1980, p. 15; Humpty Dumpty Supermarkets, Oklahoma City, "See Santa in Person" (advertisement), *Daily Oklahoman*, December 15, 1961, p. 35; Mary Jo Nelson, "Shopping Cart Inventor Sylvan Goldman Dies at 86," *Daily Oklahoman*, November 26, 1984, pp. 1, 9; Oklahoma City Advertiser, Oklahoma City, "Now You Can Buy the Advertiser at 40 Locations" (advertisement), *Oklahoma City Advertiser* (Oklahoma City), December 31, 1959, p. 15; *Polk's Oklahoma City (Oklahoma County) Directory 1935* (Kansas City, Mo.: R. L. Polk, 1935), pp. 666, 311; Praise Center, Oklahoma City, "Morris Chapman in Concert" (advertisement), *Saturday Oklahoman and Times*, December 3, 1983, p. 30; Standard Food Markets, Oklahoma City., "It's New—It's Sensational[,] No More Baskets to Carry" (advertisement), *Oklahoma City Times*, June 4, 1937, p. 7; Standard Food Markets, "Shoppers Came, Saw and Said 'It's a Wow!'" (advertisement), *Oklahoma City Times*, June 11, 1937, p. 23; Standard Food Markets, "We Thank You" (advertisement), *Daily Oklahoman*, January 26, 1932, p. 11; Sunshine Stores, Oklahoma City, "A New Sunshine Store!" (advertisement), *Daily Oklahoman*, November 1, 1930, pp. 24–25; Lawrence Van Gelder, "Shopping Carts: Carrying the Load across U.S.," *New York Times*, October 4, 1975, sec. C, p. 16; Terry P. Wilson, *The Cart That Changed the World: The Career of Sylvan N. Goldman* (Norman: Oklahoma Heritage Association by the University of Oklahoma Press, 1978), 77–93.

54. "Bandit Gets $300 in N Classen Raid," *Daily Oklahoman*, February 19, 1949, p. 2; "Chief Orders Police to End Robbery Wave," *Daily Oklahoman*, July 3, 1941, p. 18; Cooper Cleaners and Hatter, Oklahoma City, "Cooper Cleaners and Hatters" (advertisement), *Oklahoma City Star*, December 19, 1930, p. 1; "New Corporations," *Daily Record*, August 7, 1936, p. 5; Nomination to the National Register of Historic Places for Milk Bottle Grocery, January 23, 1998; "Polite Bandit Robs Grocery: Robber Flees with $165, Leaves Change," *Daily Oklahoman*, March 1, 1948, p. 1; Ross, *Oklahoma Route 66*, 118, 122–23; Kent Ruth, "'Milk Bottle' Grocery Once Housed Trade in Bootleg Whiskey: Historical Crooks, Crannies," *Sunday Oklahoman*, February 10, 1974, Showcase supplement, p. 18; "$35,000 Hospital Suit Trial Opens," *Oklahoma News*, March 5, 1935, p. 5; "Those Pie-shaped Buildings," *Sunday Oklahoman*, January 8, 1978, Oklahoma's Orbit supplement, pp. 8–9.

55. Phillip Morris, "Signs Grow Past Life-Size: City Takes a Cue from 'Pop' Artists," *Daily Oklahoman*, September 11, 1964, p. 29; Nomination to National Register of Historic Places for Milk Bottle Grocery; Sonderman, *Route 66 Then and Now*, 77; "Taking Inventory," *Daily Oklahoman*, April 18, 1997, p. 19.

56. Briana Bailey, "Guthrie Boutique to Breathe New Life into Local Landmark," *Oklahoman*, April 15, 2015, sec. C, pp. 1, 6; Briana Bailey, "Milk Bottle Empty Again, but Not for Long," *Oklahoman*, December 17, 2015, sec. C, p. 2; Briana Bailey, "Time in a Bottle: Iconic Oklahoma City Building Will Be Restored to Its Original Glory," *Oklahoman*, August 19, 2014, sec. C, pp. 1, 6; "Bandits Rob Store of $75," *Daily Oklahoman*, February 6, 1958, sec. A, p. 1; "Flower Shop to Open in Milk Bottle Building," *Sunday Oklahoman*, April 15, 1984, sec. B, p. 2; Stacy Smith Martin, "'Milk Bottle' Building Needs New Occupant," *Daily Oklahoman*, January 17, 1987, Real Estate Magazine sec., pp. 1, 9; "Milk Bottle Raises Classen Problem," *Daily Oklahoman*, August 29, 1951, p. 6; Nomination to National Register of Historic Places for Milk Bottle Grocery; "Oft-robbed Store Hit Once More," *Daily Oklahoman*, November 21, 1960, p. 1; Penny Owen, "Landmark Milk Bottle Building Survives Fire, Repairs to Start," *Sunday Oklahoman*, April 25, 1993, sec. A, p. 11;

"Popcorn Stand Robbed of $25," *Daily Oklahoman*, April 17, 1973, p. 13; Rib Shak, Oklahoma City, "A Fun Place to Work" (advertisement), *Daily Oklahoman*, February 1, 1989, p. 30; "Robbery Fails at Beer Store," *Daily Oklahoman*, September 30, 1975, sec. S, p. 2; "Route 66 Architecture at Its Finest," *Route Magazine*, December–January 2021, p. 64.

57. Lewis Gannett, *Sweet Land* (Garden City, N.Y.: Doubleday, Doran, 1934), 33 (quotation); *Oklahoma: A Guide to the Sooner State*, 227; Rittenhouse, *Guide Book to Highway 66*, 55; Ross, "Mapping the Metro," 30–31, 41; Ross, *Oklahoma Route 66*, 124–27.

58. "Bethany-Peniel College," typescript, pp. 1–3, [ca. 1940], Federal Writers' Project Collection, box 36, folder 9; Gregg Biggs, "Bethany Pioneer Says Town Must Stay Independent," *Bethany (Okla.) Tribune-Review*, January 11, 1983, p. 2; Mike Brake, "Gamblers Find Warr Acres Haven," *Oklahoma Journal* (Oklahoma City), May 15, 1976, p. 9; Brian Brus, "Road Map to Peace: After Bethany and Warr Acres Waged a Street War over Shoppers, They Found Peace in a Joint Chamber of Commerce," *Oklahoma Gazette* (Oklahoma City.), August 14, 2003, p. 11; Ed Wallace, "It Pays to Be Good, and the Little Town of Bethany Finds Peace in Faith—Pleasure in Doctrine—and Life in the Living," *Tulsa World*, November 1, 1936, sec. B, p. 7; Warr Acres Chamber of Commerce, Warr Acres, Okla., *"The Courteous City"*[:] *Warr Acres, Oklahoma—Suburban Paradise* (Warr Acres, Okla.: Warr Acres Chamber of Commerce, [ca. 1970]), folder, "Oklahoma—Cities and Towns—Warr Acres" Vertical File, Oklahoma Collection, Downtown Library, Metropolitan Library System, Oklahoma City.

59. *Czech Festival* ([Yukon, Okla.]: privately printed, [ca. 1969]), poster, "Oklahoma—Cities and Towns—Yukon" Vertical File, Oklahoma Collection, Downtown Library, Metropolitan Library System, Oklahoma City; *History of Canadian County*[,] *Oklahoma* (El Reno, Okla.: Canadian County History Book Association, Inc., 1991), 173–82; Stacy D. Johnson, "Yukon Residents Yearning to Relight Old Mill Sign," *Daily Oklahoman*, January 27, 1989, sec. S, p. 1; Sophia Lovette, "Yukon Mill and Elevator," typescript, September 11, 1936, 1 lf., Federal Writers' Project Collection, box 42, folder 14; "The Observer," *Yukon Oklahoma Sun*, January 9, 1930, p. 1; Mark Potter, "Oklahoma Route 66 Alignment Crosses Bridge, Skirts Lake," *Route 66 Federation News* 26, no. 2 (Summer 2020): 14–16; Mark Potter, "Yukon, Oklahoma[,] Owes Name to Canadian Territory," *Route 66 Federation News* 22, no. 1 (Spring 2016): 26–28; S. S. Sanger, "City of Yukon," typescript, March 17, 1936, pp. 1–2 (quotation), Federal Writers' Project Collection, box 42, folder 14; Jay Turk, "500 Dozen Kolaces Make Quite a Feast," *Sunday Oklahoman*, October 9, 1966, Oklahoma's Orbit supplement, p. 18.

60. "Belisle Promoted from P.F. Class to Corporal," *Yukon Oklahoma Sun*, January 28, 1943, p. 1; "Belisle's New Café to Open Here Soon," *Yukon Oklahoma Sun*, December 30, 1954, p. 1; "C. A. Newkirk Has Moved His Restaurant Business," *Yukon Oklahoma Sun*, March 5 1931, p. 6; "C. A. Newkirk Vet in Lunch and Café," *Yukon Oklahoma Sun*, November 9, 1933, p. 5; "Charley Newkirk Set for Hospital—Maybe," *Yukon Oklahoma Sun*, March 13, 1952, p. 9; "Down by the Silo," *Yukon Oklahoma Sun*, December 6, 1951, p. 1; November 27, 1952, p. 1 (second quotation); January 27, 1955, p. 1; "Former Mayor at Yukon Dies," *Daily Oklahoman*, January 5, 1970, p. 24; Newkirk Café, Yukon, Okla., "For Sale" (advertisement), *Yukon Oklahoma Sun*, March 12, 1953, p. 7; Newkirk's Café, Yukon, Okla., *Menu*[,] *Newkirk's Café*[,] *Yukon, Oklahoma*[,] *Phone 334* (Yukon, Okla.: Newkirk's Café, [ca. 1940]), menu, author's collection; Pete's Place, Yukon, Okla., "Announcing Bud Belisle Has Leased Pete's Place" (advertisement), *Yukon Oklahoma Sun*, January 17, 1952, p. 4; "Rites Are Held for Charles A. Newkirk," *Yukon Oklahoma Sun*, January 6, 1955, p. 1; "Seniors of 1927," *Yukon Oklahoma Sun*, March 8, 1928, p. 1 (first quotation); Sanitary Café, Yukon, Okla., "Sanitary Café" (advertisement), *Yukon (Okla.) Sun*, August 10, 1922, p. [8]; "Yukon Couple Buys Newkirk Café Here," *Yukon Oklahoma Sun*, September 24, 1953, p. 1.

61. Ernest O. Hill, "These Were My Kicks on Route 66," in *Memories on Route 66 1991*, 44–45; *History of Canadian County*[,] *Oklahoma*, 88–118, 300–304; *Oklahoma: A Guide to the Sooner State*, 228–30; Rittenhouse, *Guide Book to Highway 66*, 56–57; Tammy Sellers, "Blacks Recall Their History in Early El Reno: Life Was Often Difficult" (quotation), clipping from *El Reno (Okla.) Tribune*, February 27, 1983, in "African Americans—El Reno—Oklahoma" Vertical File, Research Center, Oklahoma Historical Society.

62. Heide Brandes, "Sunday at Sid's," *Route Magazine*, August–September 2020, pp. 54–58; Dave Cathey, "Celebrate Fried Onions on Burgers," *Oklahoman*, April 29, 2009, sec. E, p. 1; John T. Edge, *Hamburgers and Fries: An American Story* (New York: G. P. Putnam's Sons, 2005), 24–30; El Reno Main Street, El Reno, Okla., "Onion-fried Burger Day" (advertisement), *Daily Oklahoman*, May 2, 1990, sec. N, p. 9; Marty Hall, *A Burger Boy on Route 66: "Even God Loves Hamburgers"* (San Bernardino, Calif.: privately printed, 2017), 116–27; Stacy D. Johnson, "Festival Offers 100-pound Burger," *Daily Oklahoman*, May 5, 1989, sec. N, p. 4; Tom Snyder, *Route 66, Pioneering Highway: Stories from the Road* (n.p.: U.S. Route 66 Association, 1992), 40.

63. Edge, *Hamburger and Fries*, 26–27 (quotations); Hamburger Inn, El Reno, Okla., "Hamburger Inn" (advertisement), *Calumet (Okla.) Chieftain*, July 25, 1935, p. [11]; "Hamburger Inn," *Minco (Okla.) Minstrel*, July 25, 1957, p. 3; Stacy Johnson, "Festival Offers," sec. N, p. 4; "Rob Hamburger Inn," *El Reno (Okla.) Democrat*, January 18, 1929, p. 1.

64. Bob['s] White Rock Café, El Reno, Okla., "Bob['s] White Rock Café" (advertisement), *Calumet Chieftain*, August 3, 1933, p. [3]; Bob's Whiterock, El Reno, Okla., "Wanted—Boy at Bob's Whiterock" (advertisement), *El Reno (Okla.) Daily Democrat*, September 12, 1929, p. 6; Bob's White Rock, El Reno, Okla., "Welcome VIA Delegates" (advertisement), *Labor's Voice* (Oklahoma City), March 8, 1938, p. 3; Marian Clark, "Coffee Shops, Diners and Other Swell Places: Home of the Onion Burger[,] El Reno, Oklahoma," *Route 66 Magazine* 7, no. 4 (Fall 2000): 37; Sharon Dowell, "History Comes with Burgers at El Reno Diners," *Oklahoman*, May 4, 2005, sec. D, p. 3; Bill Kramer, "All about the Burger," *Oklahoman*, August 21, 2004, sec. A, pp. 19, 22; George Motz, *Hamburger America: One Man's Cross-Country Odyssey to Find the Best Burgers in the Nation* (Philadelphia: Running Press, 2008), 225–27 (first and second quotations); *Polk's El Reno (Canadian County, Okla.) City Directory 1965* (Dallas: R. L. Polk, 1966), 43, 130, 135; "Ross Grill," *Minco Minstrel*, June 18, 1959, p. 3; Jane Stern and Michael Stern, *Roadfood: The Coast-to-Coast Guide to 500 of the Best Barbecue Joints, Lobster Shacks, Ice-cream Parlors, Highway Diners, and Much, Much More* (New York: Broadway Books, 2002), 404–5 (third quotation).

65. Marian Clark, "Coffee Shops, Diners and Other Swell Places: Home of the Onion Burger," 36–37; Marian Clark, *Route 66 Cookbook*, 99–100; Dowell, "History Comes with Burgers," sec. D, p. 3; Edge, *Hamburgers and Fries*, 24–25; Hall, *Burger Boy on Route 66*, 51–67; Stacy Johnson, "Festival Offers," sec. N, p. 4; Sam Kann and Beth Mulinax, interview by T. Lindsay Baker, Johnnie's Grill, El Reno, Okla., July 17, 2014, typescript, author's collection; Jack Money, "El Reno to Accord Tasty Onion Burger Honor it Deserves," *Daily Oklahoman*, May 4, 1990, sec. N, pp. 1–2 (quotation); Motz, *Hamburger America*, 219–20; *1975 El Reno (Canadian County, Okla.) City Directory* (Dallas: R. L. Polk, [1975]), 19, 66, 80; Reeves, "Today's Special," 75; "State Pair Dies in Raging River," *Daily Oklahoman*, December 23, 1955, p. 1; Stern and Stern, *Roadfood*, 402–3.

When Oklahoma City journalist Gene Triplett assessed and asked his readers to rate places selling the tastiest cheeseburgers in the Sooner State in 2002, both he and his audience listed Johnnie's Grill in the top ten choices. Gene Triplett, "Out of This World Cheeseburgers," *Daily Oklahoman*, June 14, 2000, sec. B, pp. 1–2.

66. "Geary," typescript, [ca. 1940], pp. 1–3, Federal Writers' Project Collection, box 38, folder 15; *History of Canadian County*, 75–82, 124–27; Nora Lorrin, "Bridgeport," typescript, January 25, 1938, pp. 1–2 (quotations), Federal Writers' Project Collection, box 36, folder 13; Nomination to the National Register of Historic Places for Bridgeport Hill-Hydro Route 66 Segment, January 20, 2004; Parker interview, pp. 5, 12–13; Mark Potter, "Pony Bridge at South Canadian to Be Improved Retaining Original Trusses in $28 Million Project," *Route 66 Federation News* 27, no. 2 (Spring 2021): 28–29; Ross, *Oklahoma Route 66*, 135–50; Ross, *Route 66 Crossings*, xix, 37, 132; Quinta Scott and Susan Croce Kelly, *Route 66: The Highway and Its People* (Norman: University of Oklahoma Press, 1988), 28.

Henry Breeze's station, store, and tourist courts managed to stay in business after Highway 66 bypassed Calumet in 1934, the business passing through others' hands and the cabins disappearing but with an antique store operating in the station building at the time of this writing. Henry Breeze's Cash Cooperative Store, Calumet, Okla., "Attention Please!" (advertisement), *Calumet Chieftain*, October 29, 1931, p. 8; "Building Camp Houses," *Calumet Chieftain*, May 15, 1930, p. 1; "Building New Service Station," *Calumet Chieftain*, March 13, 1930, p. 1; Jay C. Grelen, *Race the Sun: Down the Road in Oklahoma* (Edmond, Okla.: Bigfoot Books, 2000), 49–51; "Henry Breeze," *Daily Oklahoman*, April 10, 1944, p. 17; "Increase in Business Demands More Room," *Calumet Chieftain*, January 24, 1935, p. 1.

67. Don Earney, "A Chat with the Editor," *Hinton (Okla.) Record*, August 8, 1957, p. 1; Kelly, "Just for Kicks," sec. 11, p. 23; Leon Little, Hinton, Okla., "Wanted—Immed., Man and Woman for Service Station and Café Work" (advertisement), *Daily Oklahoman*, July 11, 1948, sec. B, p. 7; Little's Café, Hinton, Okla., "Under New Management" (advertisement), *Hinton Record*, August 8, 1957, p. 3; "Oklahoma News Briefs," *Okemah Daily Leader* (Okemah, Okla.), August 2, 1962, p. 6; Ross, *Oklahoma Route 66*, 144–45; Scott and Kelly, *Route 66*, 57, 59, 62–64, 109, 156–57, 182 (quotations); "W. Leon Little," *Country Connection* (Eakly, Okla.), February 8, 1994, p. 9.

68. "Court House News," *Custer County Chronicle* (Clinton, Okla.), March 21, 1929, p. [6]; Ann DeFrange, "Lucille Wrote the Book on 66: Hydro Landmark Becomes Tourist Destination," *Sunday Oklahoman*, July 13, 1997, pp. 1–2; Ann DeFrange, "Moving on Down the Road," *Sunday Oklahoman*, September 17, 2000, sec. 2, pp. 1, 4; Ramona Duff, *Hydro, Oklahoma[,] 1901 to 1998: Photographs and Memories* (Hydro, Okla.: privately printed, 1998), 61–62, 188; Lucille Hamons, *Lucille: Mother of the Mother Road*, ed. Cheryl Hamons Nowka (Las Vegas: privately printed, [ca. 2000]), 3–32 (quotations p. 5); Ron Jackson, "Historic Gas Station's Sign to Find Home in Museum," *Daily Oklahoman*, January 22, 2002, sec. A, p. 4; Ron Jackson, "New Owner to Restore Landmark on Route 66," *Daily Oklahoman*, October 30, 2002, sec. A, p. 4; "Last Rites Held for Mrs. Carl Ethel at Methodist Church," *Hydro (Okla.) Review*, April 25, 1957, p. 1; "Men Arrested in Raids Are Taken to Oklahoma City," *Custer County Chronicle*, August 29, 1929, p. 1; Nomination to the National Register of Historic Places for Provine Service Station, May 19, 1997; Donna Rhoads Pearce, "Route 66 . . . the Ghost Road's Spirit Revived," *Country Connection*, January 25, 1994, p. 1; *Polk's Oklahoma City (Oklahoma County) Directory 1934* (Kansas City, Mo.: R. L. Polk, 1934), 657; Teague, *Searching for 66*, 104–8.

69. Roger Bromert, John K Hayden, Terry Magill, and Joyce Stofers, eds., *Weatherford: 1898–1998* (Weatherford, Okla.: Centennial History Book Committee, City of Weatherford, 1998), 56–59, 82–83, 120–22, 139–40; Clinton Chamber of Commerce, Clinton, Okla., *You'll Like Clinton[,] Oklahoma[,] the Ideal Location for Your Home and Business* (Clinton, Okla.: Chamber of Commerce, [ca. 1940]), folder, "Oklahoma—Cities and Towns—Clinton" Vertical File, Oklahoma Collection, Downtown Library, Metropolitan Library System, Oklahoma City; *Oklahoma: A Guide to the Sooner State*, 230–31; Russell Olsen, "Then and Now: Weatherford, Oklahoma," *Route 66 Magazine* 13, no. 3 (Summer 2006): 20–21; Mark Potter, "Clinton: Route 66's Hub City in Western Oklahoma," *Route 66 Federation News* 7, no. 2 (Spring 2001): 23–261; Mark Potter, "I-Day Comes to Clinton and Weatherford 50 Years Ago," *Route 66 Federation News* 26, no. 3 (August 2020): 18–21; Mark Potter, "Weatherford: Popular Tourist Stop on Route 66 for Decades," *Route 66 Federation News* 19, no. 1 (Spring 2013): 21–25.

70. Bradford Café, Clinton, Okla., *E. E. Hicks, Prop. Bradford Café[,] Hwy 66[,] Clinton, Okla.* (New York: Diamond Match Co., [ca.1940]), matchbook, "Introduction to Route 66 Matchcovers," Welcome to My Route 66, http://rt66x1ohost.com/matchcovers/introduction.html, accessed November 5, 2019; "Café Operator at Clinton Is Killed," *Weatherford (Okla.) News*, July 30, 1936, p. 1; "Clinton Killing in Self-Defense," *Oklahoma News*, July 26, 1936, p. 2; Carol Duncan, "A Salute to a Special Friend," *Oklahoma Route 66 Association, Inc.[,] Newsletter* 11, no. 3 (August 1999): 14–15; "Gary Expected to Give Paroles to Three Slayers," *Lawton (Okla.) Constitution*, June 26, 1957, p. 27; Hicks Welding Shop, Clinton, Okla., "Get It Done R-I-G-H-T" (advertisement), *Clinton (Okla.) Times-Tribune*, March 7, 1935, p. 2; Ron Jackson, "Clinton Fire Destroys Route 66 Landmark: Rebuilding Not Likely for Pop Hicks," *Daily Oklahoman*, August 3, 1999, pp. 1, 3 (quotations); "New Damage Estimate Put on Hicks Car in Fire," *Clinton Times-Tribune*, April 11, 1935, p. 1;

"New Officers of the Oklahoma Restaurant Association," *Daily Oklahoman*, January 24, 1960, sec. A, p. 15; "Open House Today for Glancy's Motel Addition," *Clinton (Okla.) Daily News*, March 1, 1959, p. 1; "Pop Hicks on 66, Restaurant—Clinton, Okla.," *Thomas (Okla.) Tribune*, July 31, 1958, p. [3]; Pop Hicks Restaurant, Clinton, Okla., "Let's Eat!" (advertisement), *Washita County Enterprise* (Colony, Okla.), February 7, 1957, p. [5]; Pop Hicks Restaurant, "New at Pop Hick's! [*sic*]" (advertisement), *Clinton Daily News*, July 22, 1960, p. 2; Pop Hicks Restaurant, "Pop Hicks Restaurant" (advertisement), *Country Connection*, July 19, 1994, p. 12; Pop Hicks Restaurant, "Presenting Our New Manager Johnny Murray" (advertisement), *Clinton Daily News*, September 4, 1960, sec. B, p. 6; Wallis and Clark, *Hogs on 66*, 76; "Welding Firm Is Opened in 1930: E. E. Hicks Shop Employs Three," *Clinton Daily News*, February 14, 1937, sec. A, p. 7.

71. Jim Etter, "Former Canute Motel on Old Route 66 Now Home for Family," *Sunday Oklahoman*, December 15, 1996, sec. A, p. 20; Bertha Killian, "Holy Land on the Prairie (Statue of Christ)," typescript, March 18, 1936, pp. 1–2, Federal Writers' Project Collection, box 82, folder 17; "Laying of Slab at Underpass Is Started," *Weatherford (Okla.) News*, August 4, 1932, p. 1; Irene McCombs, "Canute," typescript, March 7, 1936, pp. 1–2, Federal Writers' Project Collection, box 82, folder 17; Scott and Kelly, *Route 66*, 29.

72. James E. Bassett, "Dust Bowl Menace Checked: Oklahoma Town Thrives," *Los Angeles Times*, July 4, 1939, p. 4; John Dexter, "Elk City Harnesses the Boom," *Daily Oklahoman*, May 30, 1954, Magazine supplement, pp. 14–15; "Good Times, Bad Times in Elk City," *Tulsa Tribune*, April 23, 1986, sec. B, p. 5; Wood, *An Ordinary Adventure*, 69 (quotation).

73. "The Anadarko Basin Museum of Natural History," typescript, [ca. 1990], pp. 1–2, "Towns in Oklahoma—Elk City" Vertical File, Research Center, Oklahoma Historical Society; Anders, *Route 66 in Oklahoma*, 62; Casa Grande Hotel, Elk City, Okla., "This Is Your Invitation to Attend" (advertisement), *Elk City (Okla.) Daily News*, June 14, 1957, p. 4; Casa Grande Hotel, "Wanted: Nice Desk Clerk and Colored Maid" (advertisement), *Elk City Daily News*, June 24, 1960, p. 5; Carol Duncan, "Casa Grande: The Grand House," *On the Road*, no. 14 (July 2015): 1–2; Heldenbrand and Company, Inc., Oklahoma City, "Casa Grande Hotel" (advertisement), *Daily Oklahoman*, April 3, 1960, sec. B, p. 18; "Memorial Services for YMCA Health Director Planned Thursday," *Daily Oklahoman*, October 11, 1978, p. 7; Nomination to the National Register of Historic Places for Casa Grande Hotel, December 19, 1994; "Road Meeting Program Set: Parade Will Open Session at Elk City," *Daily Oklahoman*, April 12, 1931, sec. A, p. 4; "The Smoking Room," *Daily Oklahoman*, December 3, 1950, Magazine supplement, p. 3 (quotation).

74. "Carbon Plant in Sayre Pool," *Daily Oklahoman*, July 13, 1930, sec. B, p. 7; Carlton C. Cornels, *And That's the Way Sayre Was in the Twenties and Thirties with Spillage Fore and Aft* (Sayre, Okla.: Spitzer Publishing, 1997), 83–84; Hazel Martin, Sayre, Oklahoma, to Eula E. Fullerton, Oklahoma City, Oklahoma, May 16, 1940, typewritten letter, Federal Writers' Project Collection, box 82, folder 18; *Oklahoma: A Guide to the Sooner State*, 232; Rittenhouse, *Guide Book to Highway 66*, 60.

75. Ida Baldridge, "Description of Sayre," typescript, November 12, 1936, 1 lf. (quotation), Federal Writers' Project Collection, box. 42, folder 4; Cornels, *And That's the Way Sayre Was*, 59–61, 117; H. F. J., "Black," *Daily Oklahoman*, February 16, 1941, sec. D, p. 12; "L. Randle Rites to Be Friday," *Sayre (Okla.) Sun*, October 24, 1957, p. 1; "New Drug Store," *Sayre (Okla.) Standard*, November 26, 1908, p. [10]; "Owl Drug Is Bought by Robison," *Sayre Sun*, January 9, 1958, p. 1; "Owl Drug Store a Landmark in Sayre," *Sayre Record and Beckham County Democrat* (Sayre, Okla.), September 12, 2001, sec. C, p. 10; "Owl Drug Store Has Radio," *Sayre (Okla.) Headlight*, June 29, 1922, p. 1; "Road News: New Owner of OK Landmark," *Route 66 Magazine* 11, no. 4 (Fall 2004): 43.

76. Jim Hinckley, *Murder and Mayhem on the Main Street of America: Tales from Bloody 66* (Tucson: Rio Nuevo Publishers, 2019), 140–41; "Mob Leaders at Erick May Face Charges," *Miami Daily News-Record*, July 15, 1930, pp. 1, 6; "Negroes Driven from Homes by Mob at Erick," *Miami Daily News-Record*, July 14, 1930, p. 1; "Quiet Prevails at Erick Today," *Miami Daily News-Record*, July 16, 1930, p. 6; Rittenhouse, *Guide Book to Highway 66*, 61 (quotation); Snyder, *Route 66 Traveler's Guide*, 55; Floyd Yancy, *Driving Route 66 in a 46 Ford in 1954 and 2010* (n.p.: privately printed, 2012), 79–81.

77. Marian Clark, *The Main Street of America Cookbook: A Culinary Journey Down Route 66* (Tulsa: Council Oak Books, 1997), 176–79; Sharon Dowell, "Erick Beekeepers Stick to Honey Farm Business," *Daily Oklahoman*, September 12, 1990, p. 15; "Erick Residents Abuzz over Honey Festival," *Sunday Oklahoman*, November 8, 1987, Travel and Entertainment sec., p. 2; "Honey Festival to Sweeten Day," *Sunday Oklahoman*, November 4, 1984, Entertainment and Arts sec., p. 8; Ron Jackson, "Erick Honey Farm Has Sweet Past," *Daily Oklahoman*, July 8, 2002, sec. A, p. 4; Irene M. Lefebvre, "Bees Do the Work," *Sunday Oklahoman*, September 8, 1968, Oklahoma's Orbit supplement, p. 9; R. Claire Shannonhouse, "Making a Living Making 'Designer' Candles, Honey," *Daily Oklahoman*, May 23, 1983, p. 7; Lee Stevens, "Bee City," *Sunday Oklahoman*, July 11, 1965, Oklahoma's Orbit supplement, p. 7; Francis Thetford, "Couple Making Erick 'City of Bees,'" *Daily Oklahoman*, June 29, 1964, p. 17 (quotation).

78. "Change in Management at Market and Café," *Texola (Okla.) Tribune*, September 10, 1925, p. 1; "City Café Changed Hands on Last Saturday Night," *Texola Tribune*, November 5, 1925, p. 1; DeFrange, "Dreams Still Roll," sec. A, p. 18; DeLuxe Café, Texola, Okla., "Come to the Picnic" (advertisement), *Texola Tribune*, June 18, 1925, p. [2]; "Directory Reliable Business Firms of Beckham and Adjoining Counties," *Southwestern Elk City (Okla.) Press*, June 11, 1920, p. 5 (first quotation); H. D. Gottlieb and Company, [Los Angeles], "The New Whizz Bang Pin Game Machine" (advertisement), *Los Angeles Times*, May 8, 1932, pt. 4, p. 3; Hinckley, *Murder and Mayhem*, 140–41; "Keep Your Good Eye on Texola," *Texola (Okla.) Herald*, August 27, 1920, p. 1; Lackore, *To California on Route 66*, 25 (second quotation); [Irene] McCombs, "Texola," typescript, [ca. 1940], 1 lf., Federal Writers' Project Collection, box 42, folder 7; Rittenhouse, *Guide Book to Highway 66*, 61; Alvin Rucker, "Texola Mayor Orders All in City to Work or Move; Says Farm Labor Plentiful," *Daily Oklahoman*, October 17, 1930, pp. 1, 13; "Stubborn Operator Makes Collection from Motorist," *Daily Oklahoman*, July 15, 1956, sec. B, p. 6; "Texola Speed Trap May Mean Trouble for City Officials," *Daily Oklahoman*, February 1, 1941, p. 4; "We Thought He Needed Help and Went to the Rescue," *Texola Tribune*, April 30, 1925, p. 1.

CHAPTER 5. TEXAS

1. Peter Aldrich, "California Here We Come!," *Route 66 Magazine* 12, no. 4 (Fall 2005): 32–34 (first and second quotations); T. Lindsay Baker, "Eating up Route 66: Foodways of Motorists Crossing the Texas Panhandle," in *Folklore in Motion: Texas Travel Lore*, Publications of the Texas Folklore Society 64 (Denton: University of North Texas Press, 2007): 252–65; Jack D. Rittenhouse, *A Guide Book to Highway 66* (Los Angeles: privately printed, 1946, repr., Albuquerque: University of New Mexico Press, 1989), 61–69; Victor H. Schoffelmayer, "The High Plains of Texas," *Texas Geographic Magazine* 7, no. 1 (Spring 1943): 1–13; *Texas: A Guide to the Lone Star State*, American Guide Series (New York: Hastings House, 1940), 159–65, 489–92; Evelyn Tucker, "Diary—August 1938 Three Days on Highway 66 Tulsa to California," in *Memories on Route 66 1991* (Bethany, Okla.: Oklahoma Route 66 Association, 1991), 71–72 (third and fourth quotations).

2. T. Lindsay Baker, *Portrait of Route 66: Images from the Curt Teich Postcard Archives* (Norman: University of Oklahoma Press, 2016), 118–19; "The Mystery Texas Monument," *Old Route 66 Association of Texas Newsletter*, March 2009, pp. 6–7; Oliver E. Rooker, *Riding the Travel Bureau: Ghost Riders Network on Route 66 during the Great Depression* (Canton, Okla.: Memoir Publishing, 1994), 4; Joe Sonderman, *Images of America: Route 66 in Texas* (Charleston, S.C.: Arcadia Publishing, 2013), 9; U.S. Census Bureau, Census of 1940, Population Schedules, Precinct 1, Wheeler County, Tex., Enumeration District 242, page 10A, Roll m-t0627–02118, Microcopy T627, National Archives and Records Administration, Washington, D.C.; Masel Zimmerman, interview by T. Lindsay Baker, Texola, Okla., July 18, 2014, handwritten notes and typescript, author's collection.

3. Nomination to the National Register of Historic Places for Route 66 in Texas Multiple Property Submission, August 8, 2006, this and subsequent nominations in Office of the Keeper, National Register of Historic Places, National Park Service, Washington, D.C.; Mark Pepys, *Mine Host, America* (London: Collins,

1937), 152 (second, third, and fourth quotations); Irene M. Roberti, "A-Traveling We Did Go," typescript in travel scrapbook, July 12–August 27, 1941, unpaged (first quotation), author's collection.

4. Alwyn Barr, *Black Texans: A History of African Americans in Texas, 1528–1995*, 2nd ed. (Norman: University of Oklahoma Press, 1996), 184–96; Leonard Brewster Murphy, "A History of Negro Segregation Practices in Texas, 1865–1958" (PhD diss., Southern Methodist University, 1958), 48–60, 210–23; *The Negro Motorist Green Book* (New York: Victor H. Green, 1949), 67; *The Negro Travelers' Green Book* (New York: Victor H. Green, 1954), 63; *The Travelers' Green Book* (New York: Victor H. Green, 1962), 87; Joseph P. Sánchez, "Two Men on a Highway: A Political Legacy of New Mexico's Old East Highway 66," *Historic Route 66: A New Mexican Crossroads: Essays on the Hispanic Heritage of Old Highway 66*, ed. Joseph P. Sánchez and Angélica Sánchez-Clark (Los Ranchos, N.Mex.: Rio Grande Books, 2017), 144 (second quotation); Gregory Smith, "'Finest for Negroes': Lodgings in Jim Crow Era Texas," *Society for Commercial Archeology Journal* 23, no. 2 (Fall 2005): 12–19; Howard Suttle, *Behind the Wheel on Route 66* (Raton, N.Mex.: Data Plus! Printing and Publishing, 1993), 11 (first quotation).

5. "Another Texas Route 66 Icon Is Finished!" *Newsletter*[,] *the Old Route 66 Association of Texas*, December 2003, p. 6; "Buy Shamrock Café," *Pampa (Tex.) Daily News*, January 2, 1952, p. 10; Kerry Campbell, "Café Still a Landmark," *Amarillo (Tex.) Daily News*, March 11, 1991, sec. A, pp. 1–2 (first, second, and third quotations), also reprinted as an Associated Press feature as Kerry Campbell, "Panhandle Café Was Hot Spot during Route 66 Heyday," *Monitor* (McAllen, Tex.), March 17, 1991, sec. A, p. 25; Carrol's Bar-B-Que, Shamrock, Tex., "Catfish Fry" (advertisement), *Wellington (Tex.) Leader*, November 17, 1977, p. 11; "Clay Moved to Border Town of Texola in 1901," *Pampa Daily News*, October 22, 1933, p. 5; Jay Firshing, "The Incomparable U-Drop Inn/Tower Station to Be Restored," *Route 66 Federation News* 7, no. 1 (Winter 2001): 9–13 (fourth quotation); "J. L. Nunn Rites Set; Dies Sunday," *Pampa Daily News*, September 2, 1957, p. 2; Jerry Malin, "Panhandle People!" *Amarillo Daily News*, March 24, 1950, p. 29; "Much New Construction Past Two Years," *Shamrock Texan*, September 7, 1937, sec. 2, p. 1; Nomination to the National Register of Historic Places for U-Drop-Inn Café, August 12, 1997; "New Building to Hold Formal Opening," *Shamrock Texan*, March 31, 1936, p. 1; Sanborn Map Company, New York, N.Y., *Shamrock*[,] *Wheeler County*[,] *Texas*[,] *Oct. 1931* (New York: Sanborn Map Company, 1931), sheets 1–2, 4, and Sanborn Map Company, *Shamrock*[,] *Wheeler County*[,] *Texas*[,] *Oct. 1931* [rev. 1945] (New York: Sanborn Map Company, 1945), sheet 9, both in Sanborn Map Company Archives, New York, N.Y.; Quinta Scott and Susan Croce Kelly, *Route 66: The Highway and Its People* (Norman: University of Oklahoma Press, 1988), 65–66, 113; "Shamrock Café Leased," *Amarillo Daily News*, October 10, 1945, p. 3; Delbert Trew, "Trew Stories: Thirty-five Years on the Mother Road," *Route 66 Magazine* 12, no. 4 (Fall 2005): 28–29; "U-Drop Inn to Be Re-opened Soon," *Pampa Daily News*, April 7, 1946, p. 2; "U.S. Highway 66 Now Open to Shamrock," *Amarillo (Tex.) Globe*, June 24, 1931, p. 6; U-Drop Inn, Shamrock, Tex., "He Listed Our Café 'Extra Okay!'" (advertisement), *Shamrock Texan*, September 7, 1937, sec. 3, p. 8.

6. Ray Blount Jr., "Route 66: The Long and Lonesome Main Street of the West," *Sunday Denver Post*, June 20, 1982, Empire supplement, pp. 10–14, 16, 18–19, 27–29 (second quotation p. 13); Harry E. Hoare, "McLean Is the Trading Center for Citizens of Four Counties," *Amarillo Globe*, April 28, 1943, p. 6; Eloise Lane, "Memories Abound on McLean's Route 66," *Pampa News*, September 10, 1990, p. 7; Tom Matthews, "Route 66: The Long Unwinding Road," *Cara* (Aer Lingus, Dublin Airport, Ireland) 17, no. 4 (July–August 1984): 30–41; Nomination to the National Register of Historic Places for McLean Commercial Historic District, November 3, 2006; Rittenhouse, *Guide Book to Highway 66*, 63; Herb Tappenbeck and Ellen Tappenbeck, "The Way It Was on the Road," *Route 66 Federation News* 5, no. 4 (Autumn 1999): 17–20 (first quotation); B. H. Whitehead, "McLean: 'Where Opportunity Beckons,'" *Amarillo (Tex.) Sunday News-Globe*, October 31, 1926, sec. 3, p. 11.

7. Mrs. Jim Back, "Story of Notorious Jericho Gap Related on Eve of Fete," *Pampa Daily News*, October 7, 1936, pp. 1, 8; Harry E. Hoare, "Groom Never Had a Boom but Enjoyed Steady Business Growth: Town Became Famous for Its 'Jericho Gap,'" *Amarillo Daily News*. August 18, 1943, p. 4; "Jericho Gap, That

Bugaboo of Tourists, Is Completely Paved," *Amarillo Globe*, September 16, 1936, p. 1; Jerry McClanahan, "The Jericho Gap," *Route 66 Magazine* 1, no. 2 (Spring 1994): 18–19; Zachary S. Malham, "Jericho and the Gap," *Route 66 Magazine* 18, no. 2 (Spring 2011): 22–23; Rittenhouse, *Guide Book to Highway 66*, 63–65; Jim Ross, "Capturing the Past," *Route 66 Federation News* 3, no. 1 (Winter 1997): 3–5; "Scotts Buy Café," *Pampa Daily News*, December 18, 1949, p. 15; Shirley's Diner and Bob Faye's Texaco Stop, Jericho, Tex., "Shirley's Diner and Bob Faye's Texaco Stop[,] Route 66[,] Jericho, Texas," typewritten menu, n.d., courtesy of Steven Rider; Delbert Trew, "It's All Trew: Rockledge, Texas: Did Route 66 Pass This Way?," *Route 66 Magazine* 12, no. 3 (Summer 2005): 52; Delbert Trew, "Trew Stories: Why the Jericho Gap!," *Route 66 Magazine* 14, no. 2 (Spring 2002): 30.

8. Ken Brodnax, "Snow Losing Its Grip: Traffic Starts to Move," *Amarillo (Tex.) Globe-Times*, February 23, 1971, pp, 1, 12 (first quotation); "Golden Spread Closes," *Newsletter[,] the Old Route 66 Association of Texas*, March 2003, p. 5; [Golden Spread Grill, Groom, Tex.], *A la Carte* ([Groom, Tex.: Golden Spread Grill, ca. 1957]), menu, 2 lvs. unpaged, courtesy of Steven Rider; [Golden Spread Grill], *Good Morning! Always Stop at the Golden Spread and Be Among the Best Fed!* ([Groom, Tex.: Golden Spread Grill, ca. 1957]), menu, 2 lvs. unpaged, courtesy of Steven Rider; "'Golden Spread' to Promote New Weather Picture," *Canyon (Tex.) News*, February 17, 1954, p. 1; Kerry Haglund, "Route 66 Grill Keeps Rolling: Golden Spread Endures Changes," *Dallas Morning News*, October 10, 1993, sec. A, pp. 52–53 (second, third, and fourth quotations); Cheryl Eichar Jett, "Memorable Women of Route 66," *Route 66 Magazine* 27, no. 2 (Spring 2020): 42–43; Jerry McClanahan, "Ruby Denton: 43 Years at the Golden Spread Grill," *Route 66 Federation News* 6, no. 2 (Spring 2000): 20–22; "New Business in Groom," *Newsletter[,] the Old Route 66 Association of Texas*, September 2003, pp. 1–2; "New on the Road," *The Old Route 66 Association of Texas Newsletter*, June 2009, p. 2; Cynthia Puckett, "Home Cooking Keeps Customers Coming to Route 66 Restaurant," *Kerrville (Tex.) Daily Times*, May 6, 1990, sec. C, p. 7; Scott and Kelly, *Route 66: The Highway and Its People*, 115, 187–88 (fifth, sixth, and seventh quotations); "Steak Houses in Texas," *Old Route 66 Association of Texas Newsletter*, June 2006, pp. 4–5.

9. Larry BeSaw, "Ice, Sleet, Snow Due to Strike Centex," *Austin (Tex.) American-Statesman*, p. 1; *The New Handbook of Texas* (Austin: Texas State Historical Association, 1996), s.v. "Conway, Texas"; Mrs. H. A. Harbison, Conway, Tex., "For Lease" (advertisement), *Amarillo Globe-Times*, January 6, 1961, p. 21; C. M. Hudson, Conway, Tex., "Wanted: Man and Woman" (advertisement), *Amarillo Globe*, June 25, 1945, p. 11; Jerry McClanahan, Jim Ross, and Shellee Graham, *Route 66 Sightings* (Arcadia, Okla.: Ghost Town Press, 2011), 38–39; "Plains Speaking News Roundup: Pistol-whipping Victim Improves," *Amarillo Globe-Times*, June 19, 1963, p. 37; Bruce Romig, "Senator Schedules Busy Days on Plains," *Amarillo Globe-Times*, August 15, 1969, pp. 1–2; Delbert Trew, *Notes and Tales on Texas' Old Route 66* (Alanreed, Tex.: privately printed, 1990), 13 (quotations); "What They Write to Tack," *Amarillo Globe*, October 5, 1931, pp. 2–3.

10. "By-pass: State Puts Next Move up to City and County," *Amarillo Globe*, July 20, 1948, pp. 1–2; Beth Duke, "The Sign in Front of the Gas Station-Turned-Antique Shop Sums up Sixth Street's Message to Visitors: Second Time Around," *Route 66 Magazine* 1, no. 2 (Spring 1994): 38–39; "Marking the Change," *Amarillo Globe-Times*, November 1, 1963, p. 2; Nominations to the National Register of Historic Places for Route 66 in Texas Multiple Property Submission, August 8, 2006, and U.S. Route 66—Sixth Street Historic District, July 11, 1994; Glenn Oldham, "Amarillo's Forgotten 66," *Route 66 Federation News* 8, no. 1 (Winter 2002): 25–31; "One Street Makes a Building Boom—Amarillo's West Sixth," *Amarillo Globe-Times*, April 8, 1946, p. 13; Mark Potter, "Amarillo's Route 66," *Route 66 Magazine* 16, no. 2 (Spring 2009): 42–45; "Sixth Street, Amarillo's Commercial Artery," *Amarillo Daily News*, August 2, 1925, sec. 1, p. 8. Although Sixth is formally named an avenue, as followed by this author, many local residents from the 1920s onward have often dubbed it Sixth Street.

11. Air Terminal Restaurant, Amarillo, "What Better Way to Say 'Merry Christmas' to Mother" (advertisement), *Amarillo Globe-Times*, December 24, 1959, p. 10; "City Officials Firm on Annexing Base," *Amarillo Globe-Times*, November 4, 1959, p. 25; Bobby Lee, Danny Lee, Diana Lee Magill, and Hannah Jane, *The*

Story of the Free 72 oz Steak and the Big Texan Steak Ranch[,] *Legendary Steak House to the World and Route 66 Icon* (Amarillo: Big Texan Press, 2008), 9–14; "Man in M.U. Home Economics Class," *Joplin (Mo.) Globe*, June 6, 1953, p. 12; "Owner of Amarillo Steak House Dies," *Daily Oklahoman*, February 7, 1990, p. 6; Potter County, Tex., "Notice[:] the State of Texas[,] County of Potter[,] No. 15006" (advertisement), *Amarillo Globe-Times*, April 8, 1963, p. 25; Frank Ramirez, "The Biggest Steak in Texas: South Bend Native Mary Ann Lee Serves up 72-ounce Steaks in Amarillo," *South Bend (Ind.) Tribune*, June 12, 1994, sec. E, pp. 11, 13; Sonderman, *Images*, 57–58; "Underwood Cafeteria Opening Set," *Amarillo Globe-Times*, February 20, 1963, p. 2; Underwood's, Amarillo., "Delicious Barbecue Pit Cooked over Live Hickory Coals" (advertisement), *Amarillo Globe-Times*, January 3, 1956, p. 6.

12. Big Texan Western Style Cafeteria, Amarillo, "Yipee! Happy Birthday" (advertisement), *Amarillo Globe-Times*, February 4, 1964, p. 18; Lee, Lee, Magill, and Jane, *Story of the Free 72 ox Steak*, 14–17; R. J. Lee, Amarillo, "Big Texan Barbecue Cafeteria & Catering Service" (advertisements), *Amarillo Globe-Times*, May 21, 1964, p. 41, and August 26, 1964, p. 41; Laura Raitman, "The Best Little Steak House in Texas," *Route 66 Magazine* 9, no. 2 (Spring 2002): 24–27; Jean Simmons, "No Wimpy Burgers Served at Amarillo's Big Texan," *Dallas Morning News*, February 4, 1990, sec. G, p. 2; Thomas Thompson, "Turnstile," *Amarillo Globe-Times*, June 13, 1966, p. 2; Michael Wallis and Marian Clark, *Hogs on 66: Best Feed and Hangouts for Road Trips on Route 66* (Tulsa: Council Oak Books, 2004), 98–99.

13. Jane Bernard and Polly Brown, *American Route 66: Home on the Road* (Santa Fe: Museum of New Mexico Press, 2003), 89–91 (quotations); Big Texan, Amarillo, *The Big Texan: We're Glad You're Here!* (Amarillo: The Big Texan, [ca. 1985]), menu, author's collection; David Bowser, "Big Texan Fire Ruins $100,000 in Antiques," *Amarillo Globe-Times*, July 14, 1976, p. 1; Lee, Lee, Magill, and Jane, *The Story of the Free 72 oz Steak*, 17–149; Larry O'Brien, "Eatin' the (Big Texan) Steak," *Route 66 Magazine* 10, no. 1 (Winter 2002–3): 11; "Steak-Eating Shindig to Begin Thursday," *Amarillo Globe-Times*, September 4, 1973, p. 12.

14. Canton Café, Amarillo, "Announcing to Our Customers!" (advertisement), *Amarillo Daily News*, January 27, 1945, p. 9; "Chinese Bride Brings News from Homeland," *Amarillo Globe*, November 20, 1940, p. 2; Ding How Restaurant, Amarillo, "Announcing the Grand Opening of the Ding How Restaurant" (advertisement), *Amarillo Globe-Times*, August 15, 1957, p. 31; Ding How Restaurant, *Specializing in Chinese and American Dishes*[,] *Ding How Restaurant*[,] *2415 Northeast Eighth*[,] *Amarillo, Texas* (Amarillo: Ding How Restaurant, [ca. 1960]), menu, author's collection; Duck On Gee, You Yuen, and Joe Yon, Amarillo, Tex., "Public Notice" (advertisement), *Amarillo Globe-Times*, July 5, 1957, p. 7; Ben Fong-Torres, *The Rice Room: Growing up Chinese-American, from Number Two Son to Rock 'n' Roll* (New York: Plume, 1995), 70–81 (quotations); *1990 Amarillo*[,] *Texas*[,] *City Directory* (Dallas: R. L. Polk, [ca. 1990]), 215; Sonderman, *Images*, 67; "These Chinese Won't Wait for New Year," *Amarillo Globe*, February 17, 1939, p. 20; Bette Thompson, "All Around Town," *Amarillo Globe-Times*, November 27, 1961, p. 9; Thomas Thompson, "Business Briefs: Indefinite Future for Federal Taxes," *Amarillo Globe*, December 8, 1948, p. 28; Thomas Thompson, "Turnstile," *Amarillo Globe-Times*, August 5, 1966, p. 2, and October 2, 1968, p. 2. For a helpful overview of Chinese restaurant food prepared for American diners that places the Ding How into broader context, see Anne Mendelson, *Chow Chop Suey: Food and the Chinese American Journey* (New York: Columbia University Press, 2016).

15. Baker, *Portrait of Route 66*, 128–29; Duncan Hines, *Adventures in Good Eating*, (Ithaca, N.Y.: Adventures in Good Eating, 1955), 267 (third quotation); Long Champ Café, Amarillo, "Wanted: Experienced Cook" (advertisement), *Amarillo Globe*, January 9, 1945, p. 9 (first quotation); Long Champ Café, "Wanted: Two Dish Washers" (advertisement), *Amarillo Daily News*, November 11, 1943, p. 11; Longchamp Dining Salon, Amarillo, *If It Swims We Have It! Long Champ Dining Salon*[,] *AAA*[,] *on Hwy. 60 and 66, Amarillo, Texas*[,] *Recommended by Duncan Hines* (Amarillo: Long Champ Dining Salon, [ca. 1950]), menu (second quotation), author's collection; Long Champ [Dining Salon], "Pardon Our Popularity!" (advertisement), *Amarillo Daily News*, September 22, 1947, p. 9; Longchamp's Café, Amarillo, "Longchamp's Special Sea Food Suggestions with That 'Tang of the Sea' Flavor" (advertisement), *Amarillo Daily News*, May 18, 1945,

p. 23; "Homer Rice Is Home on Brief Furlough," *Amarillo Globe*, February 18, 1944, p. 2; Homer Rice Service Station, Amarillo, "Phillips 66 Service" (advertisement), *Amarillo Daily News*, April 14, 1943, p. 7; Homer Rice Used Cars, Amarillo, Tex., "'Special' 1940 Buick" (advertisement), *Amarillo Globe*, May 26, 1943, p. 13; Rice's Dining Salon, Amarillo, *Formerly Long Champ*[,] *Rice's Dining Salon Owned and Operated by Homer Rice since 1947 on Highways 60 and 66*[,] *Amarillo, Texas* (Amarillo: Rice's Dining Salon, [ca. 1953]), menu, author's collection; Rice's Motor Hotel and Restaurant Amarillo, "America's Most Electronic 50 Unit Motor Hotel with a Personal Touch" (advertisement), *Amarillo Globe-Times*, March 8, 1963, pp. 12–13; "Wilson Executive Stops in Amarillo on Business Tour," *Amarillo Globe*, June 5, 1939, p. 3; "You Can't Eat Atmosphere but You Pay Plenty for It," *Amarillo Globe-Times*, August 21, 1967, p. 4.

16. *Negro Motorist Green Book* (1949), 67; *The Negro Travelers' Green Book: The Guide to Travel and Vacations* (New York: Victor H. Green, 1955), 63; Frank Norris, "Courageous Motorists: African American Pioneers on Route 66," *New Mexico Historical Review* 90, no. 3 (Summer 2015): 297, 302, 318–19; Lesley Poling-Kempes, *The Harvey Girls: Women Who Opened the West* (Cambridge, Mass.: DaCapo Press, 1989), 87, 140; *Travelers' Green Book* (New York: Victor H. Green, 1963), 70.

17. "City May Hire Negro Police," *Amarillo Daily News*, April 7, 1948, p. 1; "College Doors Opened to Negroes," *Amarillo Daily News*, October 2, 1951, pp. 1–2; "Fete Planned for Old Bones," *Amarillo Globe*, April 21, 1948, p. 4; *Hudspeth Directory Company's Amarillo City Directory 1931*, 308; *Hudspeth Directory Company's Amarillo City Directory 1939–40* (El Paso, Tex.: Hudspeth Directory Co., 1939), 224, 370; *Hudspeth Directory Company's Amarillo City Directory 1941–42* (El Paso, Tex.: Hudspeth Directory Co., 1941), 231, 388; *Hudspeth's Amarillo (Potter and Randall Counties, Texas) City Directory 1957* (El Paso, Tex.: Hudspeth Directory Co., 1957), 436, 742, 768; *Hudspeth's Amarillo (Potter and Randall Counties, Texas) City Directory 1959* (Dallas: Hudspeth Directory Co., 1960), 346, 696, 727; *Hudspeth's Amarillo (Potter and Randall Counties, Texas) City Directory 1967* (Dallas: Hudspeth Directory Co., 1967), 450, 908, 947; *Hudspeth's Amarillo (Potter and Randall Counties, Texas) City Directory 1968* (Dallas: Hudspeth Directory Co., 1968), 274; *Hudspeth's Amarillo (Potter and Randall Counties, Texas) City Directory 1971* (Dallas: Hudspeth Directory Co., [ca. 1971]), 157; *Hudspeth's Amarillo (Potter County, Tex.) City Directory 1948* (El Paso, Tex.: Hudspeth Directory Co., 1948), 243, 473; *Hudspeth's Lubbock (Lubbock County, Texas) City Directory 1960* (Dallas: Hudspeth Directory Co., 1960), 320; "Hughes Rites Tuesday at 3," *Amarillo Globe-Times*, May 7, 1956, p. 7; "Integration Due in Summer," *Amarillo Globe-Times*, January 10, 1956, pp, 1, 6; "June'teenth Bond Sales: Lobo Club Organized for Drive," *Amarillo Daily News*, June 19, 1944, p. 1 (first quotation); Martin Herman Kuhlman, "The Civil Rights Movement in Texas: Desegregation of Public Accommodations, 1950–1964" (PhD diss., Texas Tech University, 1994), 209–10; "Man Charged in Burglary," *Amarillo Globe-Times,* June 12, 1970, p. 12; "Negroes of Amarillo to Hold Luncheon," *Amarillo Daily News*, May 1, 1940, p. 2; "Negroes Picket YMCA Meeting," *Amarillo Globe-Times*, July 13, 1964, p. 9; "Negroes Request Use of City Park," *Amarillo Daily News*, May 27, 1948, p. 3; "November Grand Jury Impanelled," *Amarillo Globe-Times*, November 12, 1956, p. 4; Nancy J. Pfister, "Supporters of Renovation Remember 'Flats' as Vital," *Amarillo Sunday News-Globe*, February 1, 1987, clipping in "Amarillo, Texas, Clippings 1987" Vertical File, Texas Collection, Baylor University, Waco, Tex. (second quotation); "Plates for Negro Benefit Luncheon Are Available," *Amarillo Daily News*, May 2, 1940, p. 3; "Record Vote Turnout Predicted This Year," *Amarillo Globe-Times*, January 22, 1964, p. 16; "Runaway Auto Causes Damage," *Amarillo Daily News*, August 14, 1950, p. 7; "Sheriff's Sale," *Amarillo Globe-Times*, October 13, 1976, p. 38; Bruce G. Todd, *Bones Hooks: Pioneer Negro Cowboy* (Gretna, La.: Pelican Publishing, 2005), 185; "Two Men Held for Burglary," *Amarillo Globe-Times*, June 10, 1970, p. 8; Clyde Walter, "City Adopts Policy on Tournaments Held at Ross Rogers Golf Course," *Amarillo Globe-Times*, April 17, 1963, p. 25.

18. The Aristocrat, Amarillo, "Announcing the Formal Opening of the Aristocrat" (advertisement), *Amarillo Daily News*, August 31, 1945, p. 9; "Aristocrat Café," *Canyon News*, September 19, 1946, p. [7] (first, second, and third quotations); Baker, *Portrait of Route 66*, 134–35; "Burglar Loots Coin Machines, Eats Hamburger," *Amarillo Globe-Times*, January 18, 1968, p. 11; "Culinary Workers Are Picketing Café," *Amarillo Globe*,

June 18, 1947, p. 1; *Hudspeth's Amarillo (Potter and Randall Counties, Texas) City Directory 1961* (Dallas: Hudspeth Directory Co., 1962), pp. 489, 515 (fourth quotation); *Hudspeth's Amarillo (Potter County, Tex.) City Directory 1945–46* (El Paso, Tex.: Hudspeth Directory Co., 1946), 237, 374; Mickey's Club, Amarillo, "Announcing the Opening of Mickey's Club," *Amarillo Daily News*, May 16, 1952, p. 16; "Nabs $1,000," *Amarillo Globe*, November 18, 1948, pp. 1, 14; "$220 Taken in 3 Thefts," *Amarillo Globe-Times*, May 30, 1973, p. 41.

19. Calf Stand, Amarillo, "The Calf Stand" (advertisement), *Amarillo Globe*, May 1, 1928, p. 5; *Hudspeth Directory Company's Amarillo City Directory 1926* (El Paso, Tex.: Hudspeth Directory Co., 1926), 316, 441, 738; *Hudspeth Directory Company's Amarillo City Directory 1928* (El Paso, Tex.: Hudspeth Directory Co., 1928), 205; *Hudspeth Directory Company's Amarillo City Directory 1931* (El Paso, Tex.: Hudspeth Directory Co., 1931), 181, 422, 504; Jim Matthews, "Historic Route 66 in Amarillo," *Route 66 Magazine* 5, no. 1 (Winter 1997–98): 46–47; Musical Pig Stand, Amarillo, "Free Beer All Day Saturday" (advertisement), *Amarillo Globe*, August 1, 1934, p. 9; "Ration Nerves Get Café Men," *Amarillo Daily News*, October 7, 1947, pp. 1, 12. The appeal of "pig sandwiches" made using freshly cut thin slices of baked ham entered American popular culture after entrepreneurs Jessie G. Kirby and Reuben W. Jackson introduced them in 1921 at their initial Pig Stand drive-in restaurant between Dallas and Fort Worth, Texas. Within a decade, their concept of "America's Motor Lunch" delivered to car windows by car hops spread from coast to coast. Randy Mallory, "Pig Stands: Pork (and Pop) on the Go," *Texas Highways* 44, no. 9 (September 1997): 4–9; Michael Karl Witzel, *The American Drive-In Restaurant* (St. Paul, Minn.: MBI Publishing, 1994), 24–30.

20. "All Around the Town," *Amarillo Globe*, October 5, 1937, p. 3 (quotation); *Hudspeth Directory Company's Amarillo City Directory 1931*, 223, 422; *Hudspeth Directory Company's Amarillo City Directory 1934* (El Paso, Tex.: Hudspeth Directory Co., 1934), 279; "Hugh Dinsmore Dies in Tulsa, Okla.," *Amarillo Globe*, January 6, 1947, p. 16; Jerry Graham, "Pig Hip May Get to Sell Beer by a Bare Foot," *Amarillo Globe-Times*, October 4, 1974, p. 35; Kim Johnson, "City's Oldest Drive-In Still Serving Famous Sandwich," *Amarillo Globe-Times*, January 15, 1971, p. 8; "Personal," *Alton (Ill.) Evening Telegraph*, October 24, 1928, p. 3; "Pig Hip King," *Amarillo Sunday News-Globe*, August 16, 1938, sec. E, p. 26; Pig Hip Sandwiches, Amarillo, "Pig Hip Sandwiches" (advertisement), *Amarillo Sunday News-Globe*, August 16, 1938, sec. D, p. 16. In the 1990s, Ernest Leo "Ernie" Edwards, longtime owner of the Pig-Hip Restaurant in Broadwell, Illinois, told food historian Marian Clark that Hugh and John Dinsmore, while working in Pittsfield, Illinois, developed the secret Pig Hip sauce that both he and they used on their pork sandwiches. Marian Clark, "Blue Front Café—Amarillo, Texas," *Route 66 Federation News* 3, no. 4 (Autumn 1997): 10–12. Edwards in Illinois used the same "They make their way . . ." sales slogan after the Tingleys introduced it in 1937.

21. "'Chisel's' Place Is Popular," *Amarillo Globe*, May 24, 1937, p. 6 (quotation); *Hudspeth Directory Company's Amarillo City Directory 1933* (El Paso, Tex.: Hudspeth Directory Co., 1933), 82, 248, 392; *Hudspeth's Amarillo (Potter County, Tex.) City Directory 1947* (El Paso, Tex.: Hudspeth Directory Co., 1947), 52, 377; Odom and Martin Co., Amarillo, "Once in a Lifetime Opportunity" (advertisement), *Amarillo Globe-Times*, May 23, 1957, p. 34; "Paramount Lunch Features Royal Pig," *Amarillo Globe*, July 26, 1937, p. 6; Royal Pig Café, Amarillo, "Chisel Benton Announces the Grand Opening" (advertisement), *Amarillo Daily News*, April 8, 1948, p. 15; Royal Pig Drive Inn, Amarillo, "Tuesday Special[,] Come in for a Delicious Pig Sandwich only 25¢" (advertisement), *Amarillo Globe-Times*, September 25, 1972, p. 15; Royal Pig Sandwich Shop, Amarillo, "Chisel Has Gone Back to Work!" (advertisement), *Amarillo Globe*, September 23, 1946, p. 5.

22. Marian Clark, "The Golden Light Is Amarillo's Oldest," *Route 66 Federation News* 2, no. 1 (Winter 1996): 5–6; "Dorothy Gaulden," *Amarillo Daily News*, August 3, 1998, sec. C, p. 2; Jim Foster, "Golden Light Café," *Route 66 Magazine* 8, no. 3 (Summer 2001): 28–30; *Hudspeth's Amarillo (Potter and Randall Counties, Texas) City Directory 1957*, 202, 370, 633; *Hudspeth's Amarillo (Potter and Randall Counties, Texas) City Directory 1960* (Dallas: Hudspeth Directory Co., 1962), 180, 299; *Hudspeth's Amarillo (Potter County, Tex.) City Directory 1947*, 176, 363; *Hudspeth Directory Company's Amarillo City Directory 1939–40*, 263–64; *Hudspeth Directory Company's Amarillo City Directory 1942–43* (El Paso, Tex.: Hudspeth Directory Co.,

1942), 84, 278; *Hudspeth's Amarillo (Potter and Randall Counties, Texas) City Directory 1971*, 179, 187; Martin's Drive-In, Amarillo, "A Merry Christmas and Happy New Year" (advertisement), *Amarillo Globe*, December 24, 1941, p. 19; Jim Matthews, "Croissants and Cowboys," *Route 66 Magazine* 5, no. 3 (Summer 1998): 38, 54–55, 62; Bob Moore, "The Golden Light Café: Good Road Food in the Middle of Town," *Mother Road Journal* (Lakewood, Colo.) no. 10 (October 1993): 19; June Naylor, *Texas Landmark Cafes* (Fort Worth: Great Texas Line Press, 2007), 70; Oldham, "Amarillo's Forgotten 66," p. 30 (quotation); San Jacinto Realtor, Amarillo, "Good Business Location: 2908 West 6th" (advertisement), *Amarillo Globe-Times*, January 30, 1956, p. 19; Sanborn Map Company, New York, N.Y., *Insurance Maps of Amarillo[,] Texas*, 2 vols. (New York: Sanborn Map Company, 1955) 2: 217, in Library of Congress, Washington, D.C.; Scott's Drive-In, Amarillo, "Good Hamburgers, 50¢ Dozen" (advertisement), *Amarillo Globe*, November 10, 1938, p. 10; Jane Stern and Michael Stern, *Roadfood: The Coast-to-Coast Guide to 500 of the Best Barbecue Joints, Lobster Shacks, Ice-cream Parlors, Highway Diners, and Much, Much More* (New York: Broadway Books, 2002), 415; "'Twice as Good II': Food and Music in Texas 2006," *Texas Music* (Austin) 7, no. 4 (Fall 2006): 40–52.

23. Charles S. Johnson, *Patterns of Negro Segregation* (New York: Harper and Brothers, 1943), 64–65; Marisue Pickering, "66 in '46: Finding Old Family Photos Recall a 1946 Journey on Route 66," *Route 66 Magazine* 13, no. 2 (Spring 2006): 24–26 (third and fourth quotations); Lloyd "Shorty" Smith, "Are We There Yet? Author Recalls His Childhood Journeys on the Mother Road," *Route 66 Magazine* 17, no. 2 (Spring 2010): 42–44 (first and second quotations). For a scholarly examination of the evolution from grocery stores to supermarkets in a Route 66 community, see Robert Dirks, *Come and Get It! McDonaldization and the Disappearance of Local Food from a Central Illinois Community* (Bloomington, Ill.: McLean County Historical Society, 2011), 147–62, 179–85.

24. Bradford Grocery, Amarillo, "Quality[,] Price" (advertisement), *Amarillo Globe*, December 8, 1939, p. 23; Bradford Grocery Stores, "We Complied Promptly with the NRA Code" (advertisement), *Amarillo Globe*, August 10, 1933, p. 21; "Cigaret [*sic*] Theft, Junior 'Crime Wave' Reported," *Amarillo Globe*, February 21, 1933, p. 2; *Hudspeth Directory Company's Amarillo City Directory 1927* (El Paso, Tex.: Hudspeth Directory Co., 1927), 208, 922; *Hudspeth Directory Company's Amarillo City Directory 1928*, 186; *Hudspeth Directory Company's Amarillo City Directory 1929* (El Paso, Tex.: Hudspeth Directory Co., 1929), 186; *Hudspeth Directory Company's Amarillo City Directory 1932* (El Paso, Tex.: Hudspeth Directory Co., 1932), 103, 192, 427–28, 473–74; *Hudspeth's Amarillo (Potter County, Tex.) City Directory 1947*, 64; Tom Snyder, *The Route 66 Traveler's Guide and Roadside Companion* (New York: St. Martin's Press, 1990), 62–63; Mary Kate Tripp, "New Book Recounts Chicken Follies of Old San Jacinto," *Amarillo Sunday News-Globe*, February 10, 1991, sec. D, p. 9; Mary Kate Tripp, "Plenty of Grocery Competition on West Sixth in 1930s," *Amarillo Sunday News-Globe*, February 17, 1991, sec. D, p. 8 (quotation).

25. Frances Epstein, "A Nostalgic Trip to Yesteryear," *Route 66 Magazine* 1, no. 1 (Winter 1993–94): 50–51 (second, third, and fourth quotations); Lewis Gannett, *Sweet Land* (New York: Doubleday, Doran, 1934), 206 (first quotation).

26. Marian Clark, *The Route 66 Cookbook* (Tulsa: Council Oak Books, 1993), 126–27; "Don 'Flying Dutchman' Krahn," *Amarillo Globe-News*, September 15, 2006, sec. B, p. 3; [Gene Howe], "The Tactless Texan," *Amarillo Globe*, April 11, 1946, p. 2; Krahn's Texaco Station and Café, Vega, Tex., "Café Station Help Wanted" (advertisement), *Amarillo Daily News*, September 9, 1963, p. 16; Krahn's Texaco Truck Stop and Café, Vega, Tex., "Help Wanted in Café" (advertisement), *Amarillo Globe-Times*, August 25, 1972, p. 40; David Rasco, "Jack Frost Deals Vega a Full House," *Amarillo Daily News*, February 12, 1948, pp. 1, 12 (quotations); "A Member of Our Hall of Fame Died Saturday, June 21," *Newsletter[,] the Old Route 66 Association of Texas*, June 2003, p. 8; Oldham County Chamber of Commerce, Vega, Tex., *Oldham County Remembers Route US 66: A Special Collection of Stories, Memories, and Recipes from Route 66 in Oldham County, Texas* (Vega, Tex.: Oldham County Chamber of Commerce, 1997), 31; Ruth [Trew], "Bits 'n' Pieces," *The Old Route 66 Association of Texas Newsletter*, September 2006, pp. 7–8; "Vega Man Hurt by Tire Blast," *Amarillo Globe-Times*, December 27, 1971, p. 24;

27. "Adrian Rancher Dies of Burns Suffered in Blast," *Amarillo Daily News*, June 10, 1947, p. 1; "Adrian's Project," *Old Route 66 Association of Texas* [*Newsletter*], March 1995, p. 9; "Bent Door Lives Again," *Old Route 66 Association of Texas* [*Newsletter*], June 1995, p. 14; "Café at Adrian Hit by Bandit," *Amarillo Globe-Times*, February 13, 1963, p. 1; "Café Steaks Pair to Fuel to Flee On [*sic*]," *Amarillo Globe-Times*, June 30, 1971, p. 34; "Explosion at Adrian Burns One," *Amarillo Globe*, June 9, 1947, p. 1; Joann Harwell, "Adrian, Texas," *Route 66 Magazine* 8, no. 4 (Fall 2001): 50–51; "Historic Bent Door for Sale," *Route 66 Federation News* 8, no. 2 (Spring 2002): 24–25; "Lotto Texas Winner Bought Ticket at Adrian Grocery Store," *Amarillo Globe-Times*, August 21, 1997, sec. C, p. 3; "Manuel F. Loveless," *Amarillo Globe-Times*, August 19, 1970, p. 12; Steve Rider, "Remember the Bent Door," *Route 66 Federation News* 7, no. 4 (Autumn 2001): 12–18; Tom Teague, "Preserving 66," *Route 66 Federation News* 1, no. 1 (Summer 1995): 15–18; Tommy's Restaurant, Adrian, Tex., "Cooks and Waitresses Needed" (advertisement), *Amarillo Globe-Times*, May 14, 1973, p. 24.

28. Bernard and Brown, *American Route 66*, 84; Cheryl Berzanskis, "Desserts Key to the Holidays," *Amarillo Globe-News*, November 15, 2006, sec. B, pp. 1, 3; Marian Clark, "Coffee Shops[,] Diners and Other Swell Places: The Adrian Café[,] Adrian, Texas," *Route 66 Magazine* 4, no. 2 (Spring 1997): 30–31; Nick Gerlich, "Halfway There," *Route Magazine*, June-July 2020, pp. 60–64, 66; Nick Gerlich, "News from Our Neighbors in Texas: Mid Point Café," *Route 66 New Mexico* 26, no. 1 (Spring 2018): 22; Jesse's Café, Adrian, Tex., "Wanted Man and Wife for Cook and Waitress" (advertisement), *Amarillo Globe-Times*, September 16, 1966, p. 29; Russell A. Olsen, *Route 66 Lost and Found: Mother Road Ruins and Relics—The Ultimate Collection* (Minneapolis: Voyageur Press, 2011), 220 (quotations); Joe Nick Patoski, "Three for the Road: This Route 66 Diner and Its Owners Do Hospitality More Than Just Halfway," *Texas Highways* 66, no. 8 (August 2019): 61–63; Jessica Raynor, "Adrian Café Owner Stays Busy Cooking for Storm-Stranded," *Amarillo Daily News*, December 30, 2000, sec. C, p. 1; Rick Storm, "Historic Café Adds Antique Shop," *Amarillo Daily News*, August 18, 1998, sec. B, p. 1.

29. T. Lindsay Baker, "Glenrio in Two States," *Eagle News* (Cleburne, Tex.), February 26, 1988, p. 6; T. Lindsay Baker, *More Ghost Towns of Texas* (Norman: University of Oklahoma Press, 2003), 64–66; Stanley Francis Louis Crocchiola [F. Stanley, pseud.], *The Glenrio[,] New Mexico[,] Story* (Nazareth, Tex.: privately printed, 1973), 3–23; Allen Ehresman, interview by T. Lindsay Baker, Texas Longhorn 2 (TL²) Truck Stop, Endee, N.Mex., February 6, 1987, pp. 1–3, manuscript notes, author's collection; Jake Fortenberry, Bea Fortenberry, and Linda Drake, interview by David K. Dunaway, Adrian, Tex., September 29, 2007, typewritten transcript, p. 7, Route 66 Corridor Preservation Program, National Park Service, Santa Fe, N.Mex.; Andy House, "Glenrio: A Ghostly Reminder of Where It All Begins," *Route 66 New Mexico* 17, no. 1 (Summer 2009): 4–5, 26; *The Land and Its People 1876–1981: Deaf Smith County[,] Texas* ([Hereford, Tex.]: Deaf Smith County Historical Society, Inc., 1982), 72–73; Nomination to the National Register of Historic Places for Glenrio Historic District, Tex./N.Mex., August 8, 2006; "13,250 Head of Cattle Moved from Glenrio, N.M.[,] and Vicinity in Week," *Santa Fe New Mexican*, May 1, 1916, p. 2; Michael Wallis, interview by David K. Dunaway, Taos, N.Mex., January 6, 2006, typewritten transcript, p. 19, Route 66 Corridor Preservation Program (quotation).

30. Fred Brownlee, Glenrio, Tex., "For Rent or Lease to Right Party, Diner Café, Glenrio, Texas" (advertisement), *Amarillo Sunday News-Globe*, November 7, 1954, sec. C, p. 11; "Glenrio Woman Wins in Canning Event," *Clovis[,] New Mexico[,] Evening News-Journal* (Clovis, N.Mex.), January 3, 1938, p. 8; Al Hall, "San Jon, Glenrio Folk Recall Stories of Rescue Mission," *Amarillo Daily News*, March 9, 1956, p. 7; "Mrs. Lillian S. Brownlee," *Amarillo Daily News*, April 26, 1974, p. 30; Nomination to the National Register of Historic Places for Glenrio Historic District, Tex./N.Mex.; Quinta Scott, *Along Route 66* (Noman: University of Oklahoma Press, 2000), 181.

31. "Another Hall of Famer Gone," *Old Route 66 Association of Texas* [*Newsletter*], March 1996, p. 2; Ehresman interview, pp. 1–3; John A. Kofton, "My Girl Lou and Me: The Mother Road and East in 1952," *Newsletter of the Canadian Route 66 Association* 6, no. 3 (November 2002): 1–4; Nomination to the National Register of Historic Places for Glenrio Historic District, Tex./N.Mex.; Oldham County, *Oldham County Remembers*,

23; Olsen, *Route 66 Lost and Found*, 222–23; Jim Ross and Shellee Graham, *Secret Route 66: A Guide to the Weird, Wonderful, and Obscure* (St. Louis: Reedy Press, 2017), 4–5; Scott and Kelly, *Route 66: The Highway and Its People*, 61, 66–67, 118–19; Texas Longhorn Café, Glenrio, Tex., "Wanted for Café Work" (advertisement), *Amarillo Daily News*, January 10, 1955, p. 8; Texas Longhorn No. 2, Endee, N.Mex., *Good Morning! TL²* (Endee, N.Mex.: Texas Longhorn No. 2, [ca. 1985]), menu, courtesy of Mike Ward; Delbert Trew, interview by David K. Dunaway, Shamrock, Tex., January 4, 2006, typewritten transcript, p. 7, Route 66 Corridor Preservation Program; U.S. Post Office Department, Records of Appointment of Postmasters, 1832–1971, New Mexico Quay-Valencia Counties, vol. 45, unpaged, Microcopy M841, reel 85, National Archives and Records Administration, Washington, D.C.; Wallis and Clark, *Hogs on 66*, 116–18.

CHAPTER 6. NEW MEXICO

1. Russ Davidson, "Route 66 in New Mexico: A Select Guide to Museum, Archival, and Library Resources" (2008), http://digitalrepository.com.edu/cswe_reference/6, accessed January 27, 2020; Martin Link, *New Mexico Kicks on Route 66* (Tucson: Rio Nuevo Publishers, 2016), 1–92; *New Mexico: A Guide to the Colorful State*, American Guide Series (New York: Hastings House, 1940), 309–27; New Mexico State Highway Department, State Tourist Bureau, *Welcome to the Land of Enchantment* ([Santa Fe]: New Mexico State Tourist Bureau, [1938]), folder, author's collection; Nomination to the National Register of Historic Places for Historic and Architectural Resources of Route 66 through New Mexico, October 4, 1993, this and subsequent nominations in Office of the Keeper, National Register of Historic Places, National Park Service, Washington, D.C.; Jack D. Rittenhouse, *A Guide Book to Highway 66* (Los Angeles: privately printed, 1946; repr., Albuquerque: University of New Mexico Press, 1989), 69–92; Don J. Usner, *New Mexico Route 66 on Tour: Legendary Architecture from Glenrio to Gallup* (Santa Fe: Museum of New Mexico Press, 2001), 1–108. When the New Mexico Tourist Bureau produced 100,000 brochures entitled "Welcome to the Land of Enchantment" in 1938, it began using this catchy long-term slogan to attract vacationers. Carrol W. Cagle, "A One-Man Tourist Bureau," *Sunday New Mexican* (Santa Fe), March 24, 1968, sec. D, pp. 1, 3; "250,000 Road Maps," *Santa Fe New Mexican*, March 18, 1939, pp. 1, 8.

2. Allen Ehresman, interview by T. Lindsay Baker, Texas Longhorn 2 (TL²) Truck Stop, Endee, N.Mex., February 6, 1987, pp. 1–3, manuscript notes, author's collection; Jake Fortenberry, Bea Fortenberry, and Linda Drake, interview by David K. Dunaway, Adrian, Tex., September 29, 2007, typewritten transcript, p. 7, Route 66 Corridor Preservation Program, National Park Service, Santa Fe; Andy House, "Glenrio: A Ghostly Reminder of Where It All Begins," *Route 66 New Mexico* (New Mexico Route 66 Association) 17, no. 1 (Summer 2009): 4–5, 26; Nominations to the National Register of Historic Places for Glenrio Historic District, Tex./N.Mex., August 8, 2006, and for Historic and Architectural Resources of Route 66 through New Mexico, October 4, 1993, E60; Usner, *New Mexico Route 66*, 2–3.

3. "Acquitted of Death," *Clovis (N.Mex.) News-Journal*, October 19, 1949, p. 1; "Bar Owner Makes Plea of Innocent to Manslaughter," *Farmington (N.Mex.) Daily Times*, October 1, 1949, p. 1; "Court Upholds Damage Award," *Albuquerque Journal* (Albuquerque), December 31, 1958, p. 7; "General Store Burns in Glenrio, N.M.," *Amarillo Daily News*, September 17, 1937, p. 1; Jim Hinckley, *Murder and Mayhem on the Main Street of America: Tales from Bloody 66* (Tucson: Rio Nuevo Publishers, 2019), 160–61; "Jury Finds Lee Guilty," *Clovis News-Journal*, November 1, 1973, pp. 1–2; Russell Olsen, "State Line Bar/Post Office[,] Glen Rio [sic], New Mexico[,] C. 1943," *Route 66 Magazine* 24, no. 1 (Winter 2016–17): 41; Owner, Glenrio, N.Mex., "For Sale by Owner" (advertisement), *Amarillo Daily News*, September 29, 1957, p. 23; "Slaying Suspect Sought," *Albuquerque Journal*, July 11, 1973, sec. A, p. 12; U.S. Post Office Department, Records of Appointment of Postmasters, 1832–1971, New Mexico Quay-Valencia Counties, vol. 45, unpaged, Microcopy M841, reel 85, National Archives and Records Administration, Washington, D.C.; Paul W. Zickefoose, *Economic Survey of Tourist-related Business along Highway 66 (Interstate 40) in New Mexico, 1956–1963*, New Mexico State Highway Department Planning Division Bulletin 27 ([Santa Fe]: New Mexico State Highway Department, 1963), 9.

4. "Farmer Hurt as Car Overturns," *Albuquerque Journal*, August 5, 1929, p. 3; Nathan Greene, "Cruising Route 66 in New Mexico," pt. 1, *Route 66 New Mexico* 19, no. 1 (Spring 2011): 4–5; Zephine Humphrey, *Green Mountains to Sierras* (New York: E. P. Dutton, 1936), 61–62; David Kammer, "Seven Wonders on Old Route 66," *New Mexico Magazine* 79, no. 2 (February 1989): 60, 63; "Killed When Truck Crashes," *El Paso (Tex.) Herald-Post*, May 14, 1939, p. 1; Jerry McClanahan, "Tangled Threads of Time," *Route 66 Magazine* 3, no. 3 (Summer 1996): 24–26; Stephen D. Mandrgoc, "La política y los caminos: Building Route 66 in New Mexico," in *Historic Route 66: A New Mexican Crossroads: Essays on the Hispanic Heritage of Old Highway 66*, ed. Joseph P. Sánchez and Angélica Sánchez-Clark (Los Ranchos, N.Mex.: Rio Grande Books, 2017), 45–46, 47; Johnnie Meier, "The San Jon Bypass," *Route 66* Magazine 13, no. 4 (Fall 2006): 30–32; Nominations to the National Register of Historic Places for Historic and Architectural Resources of Route 66 through New Mexico, E3–E4, E40–E41, E60; Locally Maintained Route 66: Glenrio to San Jon, April 10, 1993; and State Maintained Rt. 66: San Jon to Tucumcari, August 1996; Mark Potter, "New Mexico Battles Interstate Bypassing in 1960s," *Route 66 Federation News* 20, no. 1 (Spring 2014): 35–38; Mark Potter, "San Jon, NM: Toughing It out for Survival," *Route 66 Federation News* 10, no. 4 (Autumn 2004): 11–13; Jill Schneider, *Route 66 across New Mexico: A Wanderer's Guide* (Albuquerque: University of New Mexico Press, 1991), 199; "Soldier Killed in Car Crash," *Amarillo (Tex.) Globe-Times*, April 24, 1957, p. 10; "Texas Woman Fatally Hurt in Accident," *Las Vegas (N.Mex.) Daily Optic*, April 21, 1930, p. 1; "Tucumcari Leader Dies in Collision," *Clovis News-Journal*, April 7, 1970, p. 14; Usner, *New Mexico Route 66*, 3–5; Ed Vogel, "Interstate Truckers Won't Shed Any Tears for Death of Route 66," *Albuquerque Tribune*, April 30, 1976, sec. C, p. 6; Fred Wortham Jr., "Politics, Bureaucracy Keep 'Death Alley' Monster Alive," *Amarillo (Tex.) Sunday News-Globe*, November 16, 1969, sec. D, p. 1.

5. Marian Clark, *The Route 66 Cookbook* (Tulsa: Council Oak Books, 1993), 131; Nomination to the National Register of Historic Places for Historic and Architectural Resources of Route 66 through New Mexico, E59; "On the Cover," *Route 66 Federation News* 10, no. 4 (Autumn 2004): front cover, 2; Oliver E. Rooker, *Riding the Travel Bureau: Ghost Riders Network on Route 66 during the Great Depression* (Canton, Okla.: Memoir Publishing, 1994), 46, 48; Usner, *New Mexico Route 66*, 3–5; Michael Wallis, *Route 66: The Mother Road* (New York: St. Martin's Press, 1990), 148; Zickefoose, *Economic Survey of Tourist-related Business*, 9.

6. "Balanced Rock Is Preserved by Rerouting Highway," *Popular Mechanics* 53, no. 4 (October 1929): 615; "Road Detours by Monument Rock, near Tucumcari," *Amarillo Daily News*, March 11, 1929, p. 5; "Road Engineers Save Landmark," *Santa Fe New Mexican*, June 30, 1928, p. 7; Debra Ann Whittington, *In the Shadow of the Mountain: Living in Tucumcari* (Tucumcari, N.Mex.: Sundowner Gallery, 1997), 112–13.

7. Lucille Byerly Lackore, *To California on Route 66 in 1932* (n.p., 1998), 29 (second quotation); Thomas W. Pew Jr., "Tucumcari Tonight!," *The American West* 17, no. 1 (January–February 1980): 32–35, 62–63; Mark Potter, "Rt. 66 Still Glowing in Tucumcari: Endless Stretch of Neon, Vintage Motels, Restaurants," *Route 66 Federation News* 6, no. 2 (Spring 2000): 24–27; Rittenhouse, *Guide Book to Highway 66*, 70–71; Schneider, *Route 66 across New Mexico*, 190–93 (first quotation); *Tucumcari-Logan[-]Nara Visa-San Jon[,] Area Code 505[,] Mountain States Telephone[,] July 1962* (Albuquerque: Mountain States Telephone & Telegraph Company, 1962), yellow-page section 32–34; Whittington, *In the Shadow*, 72–78; Usner, *New Mexico Route 66*, 4–12; Paul W. Zickefoose, *Economic Survey of Tucumcari, New Mexico, 1950–1960*, New Mexico State Highway Department Planning Division Bulletin 23 ([Santa Fe]: New Mexico State Highway Department, 1962), 3, 5–26. Many travelers breathed sighs of relief as they pulled into roadside lodgings in Tucumcari after fatiguing driving, like an unidentified couple who motored there 524 miles from Emporia, Kansas, on U.S. Highway 54 on June 20, 1955, jotting down, "Dust storm and rain. What a Day." "West Again 1955" Scrapbook, June 18 to July 1, 1955, unpaged, author's collection.

8. "Banquet Closes State Restaurant Annual Parley," *Albuquerque Journal*, March 15, 1968, sec. A, p. 10; Clark, *Route 66 Cookbook*, 134; U.S. Selective Service, World War II Draft Card for Harry Elmer Garrison, Hereford, Tex., October 16, 1940, WWII Draft Registration Cards, Record Group 147, National Archives

and Records Administration, Washington, D.C., https://www.fold3.com/image/624704050?terms=garr ison,harry,elmer, accessed January 29, 2020; *Hudspeth's Tucumcari (Quay County, N.M.) City Directory 1948* (El Paso, Tex.: Hudspeth Directory Co., 1948), 43, 71, 182; *Mountain States Telephone[,] Tucumcari[,] Conchas Dam[,] Logan-Nara Visa[,] San Jon Telephone Directory[,] Area Code 505[,] March 1968* (Santa Fe: Mountain States Telephone, 1968), 16–17, yellow pages 37; *Polk's Tucumcari (Quay County, New Mexico) City Directory 1961* (El Paso, Tex.: R. L. Polk, 1961), 34, 40, 43; Denny Welch, telephone interview by T. Lindsay Baker, Tucumcari, N.Mex., July 16, 2017, typewritten transcript, author's collection.

9. "On the New Records—Old and New Tunes Turn up in Week's Listing of Discs," *Tampa (Fla.) Sunday Tribune*, April 4, 1948, sec. D, p. 10; Edith Kermit Roosevelt, "Southern Belle: Hillbilly Vocalist Pens Own Lyrics," *Arizona Republic* (Phoenix), November 28, 1952, p. 34; Jill Schneider [K. Hilleson, pseud.], "Roadside Attractions Give Character to 66 Towns," *New Mexico Magazine* 67, no. 2 (February 1989): 50–60, 62); Schneider, *Route 66 across New Mexico*, 193–98; "Singer Dorothy Shay Dies," *Chicago Tribune*, October 23, 1978, sec. 5, p. 7; Toby Smith, "Homeward Bound: The Magic and Memories of Railway Stations," *Albuquerque Journal*, February 3, 1987, pp. 4–9, 14; *Tucumcari[,] Conchas Dam[,] Logan[,] Nara Visa[,] San Jon[,] Telephone Directory[,] Area Code 505[,] Mountain Bell[,] March 1973* (Roswell, N.Mex.: Mountain Bell, 1973), 16–17.

10. Greene, "Cruising Route 66 in New Mexico," pt. 1, 7–8; Milt Loewe, "Bypasses to Nowhere Dot Highways," *Carlsbad (N.Mex.) Current-Argus*, April 23, 1963, pp. 1–2; Nominations to the National Register of Historic Places for Historic and Architectural Resources of Route 66 through New Mexico, E4–E5, E14–E15; Abandoned Route 66, Cuervo to SR 154, October 4, 1993; Metropolitan Park Bathhouse and Pool Historic District, Tucumcari, N.Mex., September 30, 1995; State Maintained Rt. 66: Montoya to Cuervo, August 1996; and State Maintained Route 66: Palomas to Montoya, October 4, 1993; Tracey Pierce, "Ghosts on the Road," *Route 66 New Mexico* 24, no. 2 (Fall 2016): 10–11; Rittenhouse, *Guide Book to Highway 66*, 71–73; Steven Rosen, "Get Your Kicks on US 66: Club Café Soaks in Nostalgia of America's Road," *Denver Post*, June 30, 1990, sec. E, pp. 1, 4 (quotations); Usner, *New Mexico Route 66*, 12–15; Zickefoose, *Economic Survey of Tourist-related Business*, 11–13.

11. Richard Delgado, "Blue Hole Road: Nature—No Neon on Historic Route 66," *Route 66 New Mexico* 14, no. 2 (Fall 2006): 7, 9; Sue Bohannan Mann, "Santa Rosa: A Diamond in the Desert," *New Mexico Magazine* 79, no. 2 (February 1989): 54–59; Johnnie V. [Meier], "A Look Back at Santa Rosa," *Route 66 New Mexico* 16, no. 1 (Spring 2008): 18–21; Nomination to the National Register of Historic Places for Park Lake Historic District, Santa Rosa, N.Mex., September 30, 1995; Donna Olmstead, "Diving in the Desert: Blue Hole Beckons Swimmers Deep into Mystical World," *Albuquerque Journal*, July 18, 1996, sec. B, pp. 1, 5; Mark Potter, "Santa Rosa a Must Stop on 66 through New Mexico," *Route 66 Federation News* 18, no. 2 (Summer 2012): 14–16; Schneider, "Roadside Attractions," 52–54; Schneider, *Route 66 across New Mexico*, 173–85; Usner, *New Mexico Route 66*, 15–19; Steve Winston, "Santa Rosa Gains Its Lifeblood from Passing I-40 Tourists," *Albuquerque Journal*, May 6, 1979, sec. C, p. 3; Paul W. Zickefoose, *Economic Survey of Santa Rosa, New Mexico, 1950–58: The 'Before' Portion of a Highway Relocation Impact Study*, New Mexico State Highway Department Planning Division Bulletin 10 ([Santa Fe]: New Mexico State Highway Department, 1959), 4, 6–20.

12. John A. Kofton, "My Girl Lou and Me: The Mother Road and East in 1952," *Newsletter of the Canadian Route 66 Association* 6, no. 3 (November 2002): 1–4 (quotations); Thomas Arthur Repp, "Long Live the Fat Man," *Route 66 Magazine* 5, no. 1 (Winter 1997–98): 50–53; Schneider, *Route 66 across New Mexico*, 178–79; Wallis, *Route 66: The Mother Road*, 149, 151, 153–58.

13. "Club Café Opened Doors Last Week," *Santa Rosa (N.Mex.) News*, November 20, 1936, p. 1; Club Café, Santa Rosa, N.Mex., *Club Café[,] Spend a Few Days in Friendly Santa Rosa* (Port Byron, Ill.: Mississippi River International Promotions, [ca. 1955]), menu (third and fourth quotations), courtesy of Mike Ward; Club Café, "Sunday Dinner . . . 60¢" (advertisement), *Santa Rosa News*, December 4, 1936, p. [3]; Davi Antonio (Davy) Delgado, "The Late Great Club Café," *Route 66 New Mexico* 10, no. 2 (Summer 2002): 13–17,

19–20 (first quotation); "Mr. and Mrs. Floyd Shaw Moved into the Sanford Apartments on Monday of This Week," *Santa Rosa News*, December 4, 1936, p. [3]; Bob Moore, "The Club Café: A Brief History," *Mother Road Journal* (Lakewood, Colo.) no. 6 (October 1992): 53; "Nute H. Epps, 51, Dies Suddenly," *Alamogordo (N.Mex.) Daily News*, August 18, 1958, p. 8; "Rancher P. N. Craig Dies at 66," *Albuquerque Journal*, March 1, 1980, sec. G, p. 12; "Remodeling of Club Café," *Santa Rosa News*, June 30, 1950, p. 1; Quinta Scott and Susan Croce Kelly, *Route 66: The Highway and Its People* (Norman: University of Oklahoma Press, 1988), 30 (second quotation); "Structures Are Being Remodeled," *Santa Rosa News*, February 27, 1948, p. 7; "Victor L. Epps," *Las Vegas Daily Optic*, March 8, 1960, p. 8.

14. "Café Owner Files Suit for Removal of Signs," *Albuquerque Journal*, July 25, 1976, sec. F, p. 2; Ronald P. Chávez, *Time of Triumph: Short Stories and Selected Poems* (n.p.: privately printed, 2007), [243–44]; Delgado, "The Late Great Club Café," 14–17, 19–20; "Epps—Charlie Epps," *Albuquerque Journal*, July 24, 1964, sec. A, p. 2; Keith Kofford, "The Building Has Left the Fat Man," *Route 66 Magazine* 24, no. 1 (Winter 2016–17): 38–39; Fred McCaffrey, "Biscuits and Billboards," *New Mexican* (Santa Fe), September 6, 1979, sec. D, p. 4; Scottie King, "Homecoming in Puerto de Luna," *New Mexico Magazine* 57, no. 8 (August 1979): 54–61; Dave Nidel, "Club Café Closes," *New Mexico Route 66 Association Newsletter* 2, no. 4 (Spring 1993): 3; Linda Quintana, "Live Entertainment: The New Club Café Is Real Different, Elegant, Informal," *Santa Rosa News*, March 31, 1977, sec. 2, p. 3; Rick Romancito, "Author-Poet Ronald P. Chávez, 78, Dies," *Taos (N.Mex.) News*, October 23–29, 2014, sec. A, p. 2; Rosen, "Get Your Kicks," sec. E, pp. 1, 4; Tom Teague, *Searching for 66* (Springfield, Ill.: Samizdat House, 1991), 138–45; Wallis, *Route 66*, 151, 153 (quotations). Santa Rosa restaurateur and mayor Joseph Campos acquired rights to the fat man logo long used by the Club Café, and he and his wife, Christina, employ it an promoting their Joseph's Bar and Grill just down Parker Avenue from the old site. Sue Bohannan Mann, "Reprisal of a Famous Favorite in Santa Rosa," *New Mexico Route 66 Association Newsletter* 6, no. 1 (Winter 1999): [10–11].

15. "Complete Road in New Mexico," *Amarillo Globe*, November 12, 1937, p. 1; Nathan Greene, "Cruising Route 66 in New Mexico Part," pt. 4 [5], *Route 66 New Mexico* 22, no. 1 (Spring 2014): 4–8; Jerry McClanahan, "The Lost Highway," *Route 66 Magazine* 1, no. 1 (Winter 1994–95): 25–30.

16. Greene, "Cruising Route 66 in New Mexico Part," pt. 4 [5], 4–6; Jim Hinckley, *Ghost Towns of Route 66* (Minneapolis: Voyageur Press, 2011), 107; Elrond Lawrence, *Route 66 Railway: The Story of Route 66 and the Santa Fe Railway in the American Southwest* (Alhambra, Calif.: Los Angeles Railroad Heritage Foundation, 2008), 142–43; McClanahan, "The Lost Highway," 26–30; Dallas Lore Sharp, *The Better Country* (Boston: Houghton Mifflin, 1928), 140; C. K. Shepherd, *Across America by Motor-cycle* (New York: Longman, Green, 1922), 144–45; Maud Younger, "Alone across the Continent: Adventures of a Woman Motorist on the Road from Coast to Coast," *Sunset* 52, no. 6 (June 1924): 26–27. Emily Post rode as a passenger on a westbound cross-country auto trip in 1915, a decade before the designation of Highway 66, crossing over Glorieta Pass. Distastefully she recounted, "Between Las Vegas and Santa Fe, the going was the worst yet." Emily Post, *By Motor to the Golden Gate* (New York: D. Appleton, 1917), 149.

17. T. Lindsay Baker, "Oldest Well in the U.S.: A Historic Route 66 Tourist Attraction," *Route 66 Magazine* 23, no. 3 (Summer 2016): 38–40; T. Lindsay Baker, *Portrait of Route 66: Images from the Curt Teich Postcard Archives* (Norman: University of Oklahoma Press, 2016), 148–49; Ray T. Bohacz, "Blowing in the Wind: The Automotive Radiator," *Hemmings Classic Car* 3, no. 1 (October 2006): 84–87; "Glorieta Features 'Old-Timer,'" *Sunday New Mexican* (Santa Fe), May 30, 1965, Pasatiempo supplement, p. 8; Thos. L. Greer, El Paso, Tex., "Riding and Roping Contest" (advertisement), *El Paso Daily Times*, May 2, 1907, p. 8; "Historic Spot on Santa Fe Trail: Glorieta Pass and Pecos Ruins Make Unusually Interesting Trip," *Albuquerque Journal*, September 30, 1928, sec. 3, pp. 1, 3; H. S. Hunter, "Around Here," *El Paso Times*, May 30, 1934, p. 4; Ilya Ilf and Eugene Petrov, *Little Golden America: Two Famous Soviet Humorists Survey These United States*, trans. Charles Malamuth (New York: Farrar and Rinehart, 1937), 174 (third and fourth quotations); *Interior View of One of Old Rooms with Old Fire Place—Mr. Thos. L. Greer, a Real Western Cowboy*, publication 2755–29 (Chicago: Curt Teich, [1929]), postcard (first quotation), author's collection;

Oldest Well in U.S.A.: Most Historic and Wonderful Old Indian Spanish Well, publication 114921 (Chicago: Curt Teich, [1927]), postcard (second quotation), author's collection; "Old Well Owner Dies in Santa Fe," *Las Vegas Daily Optic*, May 7, 1964, p. 1; Joe Sonderman, *Route 66 Then and Now* (London: Pavilion Books, 2018), 91; Robert L. Spude, *Pigeon's Ranch Historic Structures Report: Historical Data Section*, Intermountain Cultural Resource Management Professional Paper no. 74 (Denver: Cultural Resources Management Intermountain Regional Office, National Park Service, 2008), 1–21. For a scholarly study of Thomas and Nate Greer's Cowboy Park venture, which played a significant role in the development of commercial rodeo competition, see John O. Baxter, *Cowboy Park: Steer-Roping Contests on the Border* (Lubbock: Texas Tech University Press, 2008).

18. W. C. Clark, *Touring the West with Leaping Lena*, 1925, ed. David Dary (Norman: University of Oklahoma Press, 2016), 242–45; George Fitzpatrick, "The Inn at the End of the Trail," *New Mexico Magazine* 28, no. 10 (October 1950): 23–25, 43, 45, 47, 49; [Fred Harvey Company, Kansas City, Mo.], *Harveycar Courier Service*[,] *May We Take You? Indian-Detour Harveycar Motor Cruises*[,] *La Fonda in Old Santa Fe*, publication 1-1-29 (100M) (Chicago: Rand McNally, [1929]), folder, "Harvey, Fred—Businessman" Vertical File, Center for Southwest Research, Zimmerman Library, University of New Mexico, Albuquerque; Stephen Fried, *Appetite for America: Fred Harvey and the Business of Civilizing the Wild West—One Meal at a Time* (New York: Bantam Books, 2010), 281–84, 286–87, 310–12; Lewis Gannett, *Sweet Land* (Garden City, N.Y.: Doubleday, Doran, 1934), 52 (quotation); David Gebbard, "Architecture and the Fred Harvey Houses: The Alvarado and La Fonda," *New Mexico Architecture* 6, nos. 1–2 (January–February 1964): 18–25; Greene, "Cruising Route 66 in New Mexico Part," pt. 4, 6; For two recent overviews of La Fonda Hotel history, see *La Fonda on the Plaza: From Every Window a Glimpse of the Past* (Santa Fe: La Fonda on the Plaza, 2011) and *La Fonda Then and Now* (Santa Fe: La Fonda Holdings, 2016).

19. Fred Harvey [Company, Kansas City, Mo.], *La Fonda in Old Santa Fe*[,] *Fred Harvey*[,] *Dinner on the Indian Detour* ([Kansas City, Mo.:] Fred Harvey, 1940), menu, and [Fred] Harvey Company, [Kansas City, Mo.], *New Mexican Room*[,] *La Fonda in Old Santa Fe*[,] *the Harvey Company* ([Kansas City, Mo.]: The Harvey Company, [ca. 1943]), menu, both in Fred Harvey Company Collection, MS 208, series 3, box 3, folder 70, Special Collections and Archives, Cline Library, Northern Arizona University, Flagstaff (hereafter Fred Harvey Company Collection); Fried, *Appetite for America*, 311–12, 380–82; Duncan Hines, *Adventures in Good Eating* (Chicago: Adventures in Good Eating, 1938), 154 (quotation); "Konrad Allgaier Retires," *Hospitality* (Fred Harvey Company), September 1949, unpaged; Oliver LaFarge, "Oliver La Farge, Santa Fe Birdwatcher: Hotel Progressively Succumbs to the Bland and Synthetic," *New Mexican*, August 12, 1961, sec. 1, p. 10; Ernie Pyle, "Life Goes On: 'Steak and Potatoes' Ernie Stumped by Exquisite Meal," *Knoxville (Tenn.) News-Sentinel*, January 26, 1937, p. 6. After enjoying a meal at La Fonda on Sunday, July 20, 1941, Irene M. Roberti penned in a motor trip diary, "We had dinner at the 'La Fonda,' which besides being a Fred Harvey and Duncan Hines place was the swankiest place in the city. And did it have atmosphere!" Irene M. Roberti, "A-Traveling We Did Go," typescript in travel scrapbook, July 12–August 27, 1947, unpaged, author's collection.

20. Simone de Beauvoir, *America Day by Day*, trans. Carol Cosman (Berkeley: University of California Press, 1999), 186; James Montgomery Flagg, *Boulevards All the Way—Maybe: Being an Artist's Truthful Impression of the U.S.A. from New York to California and Return, by Motor* (New York: George H. Doran, 1925), 106–7; Fried, *Appetite for America*, 404–5; Ernie Pyle, "Life Goes On: Santa Fe—Population 15,000—Has 20 Interesting Persons," *Knoxville News-Sentinel*, January 21, 1937, p. 6 (quotations); Nate Skousen Jr., "Road Contracting and the Santa Fe Mystique," *New Mexico Route 66 Association Newsletter* 5, no. 1 (Winter 1998): 1–2.

21. Guy K. Austin, *Covered Wagon, 10 H.P.: Being the Further Adventures of an English Family in Its Travels across America* (London, England: Geoffrey Bles, 1936), 67 (quotations); "Beautiful New Woolworth Store Opens Friday," *The Santa Fe New Mexican*, August 24, 1939, p. 5; F. W. Woolworth Company, Santa Fe, "F. W. Woolworth Co." (advertisement), *Santa Fe New Mexican*, August 24, 1939, p. 7; "Step Ahead," *Santa*

Fe New Mexican, August 22, 1939, p. 4; "Woolworth Sets Grand Opening in Expanded, Remodeled Store," *Sunday New Mexican*, May 10, 1964, sec. B, p. 4.

22. Baker, *Portrait of Route 66*, 158–59; Richard Chang, "Woolworth's Is Officially a Memory, but Legacy Endures," *Sunday Santa Fe New Mexican*, October 26, 1997, sec. B, pp. 1–2; Kaleta Doolin, *Fritos Pie: Stories, Recipes and More* (College Station: Texas A&M University Press, 2011), 105–10; Gregory McNamee, *Tortillas, Tiswin and T-Bone: A Food History of the Southwest* (Albuquerque: University of New Mexico Press, 2017), 182–83; Deborah Potter, Five & Dime General Store, Santa Fe, email communication to T. Lindsay Baker, Rio Vista, Tex., October 8, 2020, paper copy, author's collection; Bob Quick, "Five-and-Dime Coming Back to the Plaza," *Santa Fe New Mexican*, September 26, 1997, sec. A, pp. 1, 6; Bob Quick, "Plaza Business Still a Hot Summer Item," *New Mexican*, July 1, 1985, sec. A, p. 7 (second quotation); Bob Quick, "Woolworth's on the Plaza Closing Shop," *Santa Fe New Mexican*, July 18, 1997, sec. A, pp. 1, 6; Sandra Rector, "Summer in the City," *New Mexican*, June 27, 1986, Events sec., p. 36; Judy Wiley-Williams, "'Perfect' Frito Pies at Plaza Landmark," *New Mexican*, July 18, 1983, sec. A, p. 1 (first quotation).

23. T. Lindsay Baker, "La Bajada Hill," *Route 66 Magazine* 23, no. 3 (Summer 2016): 22–24; Andy House, "A Visit to a Highway Legend: La Bajada Hill," *Route 66 New Mexico* 10, no. 4 (Winter 2003): 11, 14–15, 18–19; Vernon McGill, *Diary of a Motor Journey from Chicago to Los Angeles* (Los Angeles: Grafton Publishing, 1922), 60, 62 (quotations); Nomination to the National Register of Historic Places for New Mexico State Highway 1, El Camino Real Highway (La Bajada Hill), September 2002; Charles Ralph, "La Bajada Still out There, Recalling Bygone Journeys," *Albuquerque Journal*, May 10, 1970, Color supplement, pp. 8, 24; "Road News: La Bajada Hill Closed to Public," *Route 66 Magazine* 24, no. 4 (Fall 2017): 50; Usner, *New Mexico Route 66*, 37–39.

24. "Auto Plunges off la Bajada: 4 Escape Death by a Miracle," *Albuquerque Journal*, December 28, 1929, p. 1; Andy House, "The Big Cut," *Route 66 New Mexico* 9, no. 3 (Fall 2001): 4–5, 10; Nomination to the National Register of Historic Places for New Mexico State Highway 1; "Personal News Items," *Evening Herald* (Albuquerque), September 10, 1917, p. 8; "Herbert C. Walden," *Albuquerque Journal*, November 30, 1969, sec. F, p. 16; "Walden Rites Today; Early Motel Operator," *Albuquerque Journal*, December 31, 1982, sec. C, p. 8; W. E. Walden, Domingo, N.Mex., "For Sale" (advertisement), *Albuquerque Morning Journal*, June 13, 1925, p. 9; W. E. Walden, Domingo, N.Mex., "Young Woman for General House Work" (advertisement), *Albuquerque Journal*, September 23, 1929, p. [6].

25. James Albert Davis, *From Coast to Coast via Auto and Tent* (Federalsburg, Md.: J. W. Stowell Printing, 1922), 34 (quotation).

26. Cindy Lopez, "Fourth Street Regarded as Distinctive Piece of Automotive History," *New Mexico Route 66 Association Newsletter* 8, no. 1 (Winter 2001): 1–2; Mark Pepys, *Mine Host, America* (London: Collins, 1937): 176 (quotation); Mark Potter, "Historic Motels Plentiful on 66 through the Duke City," *Route 66 Federation News* 8, no. 2 (Spring 2002): 11–13; Polly Summar, "Central Avenue: Albuquerque's Main Drag Rekindles Spirit of 66," *New Mexico Magazine* 67, no. 2 (February 1989): 32–37, 39; Usner, *New Mexico Route 66*, 43–80. For a recent inventory and analysis of historic architecture in the corridor of consumption that Highway 66 created across Albuquerque, see Donatella Davanzo, "Tangibility and Symbolism along Historic Highway 66 in Albuquerque" (PhD diss., University of New Mexico, 2018).

27. "Funeral Rites Will Be Held Saturday Morning for Nestor R. Padilla," *Albuquerque Journal*, April 13, 1962, sec. D, p. 14; *Hudspeth Directory Company's Albuquerque City Directory 1922* (El Paso, Tex.: Hudspeth Directory Co., 1922), 145, 409; "Man Gets Ribs Broken in Auto Car Smashup," *Albuquerque Morning Journal*, May 19, 1925, p. 3; "Padilla—Mrs. Aurora C. Padilla," *Albuquerque Journal*, June 21, 1989, sec. D, p. 11; Red Ball Café, Albuquerque, "Red Ball Café" (advertisement), *Albuquerque Journal*, April 6, 1944, p. 14; Red Ball Café, "The Red Ball Café Will Be Closed Two Weeks for Vacation" (advertisement), *Albuquerque Journal*, September 18, 1955, p. 45; Red Ball Café, "Rolled Enchiladas 5¢" (advertisement), *Albuquerque Journal*, August 24, 1935, p. 7; "Pilar Rubi de Padilla, Aged 75 Years, Dies Here," *Albuquerque Journal*, March 14, 1944, p. 4.

28. For representative examples in New Mexico of Atchison, Topeka and Santa Fe Railway employee use of the term "Red Ball" in referring to high-priority, express freight trains, see "McNally's Orders," *Albuquerque Daily Citizen*, January 8, 1902, p. [3]; "Railroad Notes," *Las Vegas Daily Optic*, November 25, 1905, p. [3]; "Switchman Woods under Arrest," *Albuquerque Evening Citizen*, December 16, 1905, p. 11.

29. Alan Carlson, "Restaurant Reviews: The Red Ball Café," *Route 66 New Mexico* 18, no. 1 (Spring 2010): 8–9, 11; John Randolph Kent, "The Red Ball Is Bouncing Back," *Route 66 Magazine* 5, no. 2 (Spring 1998): 40–41; John R. Kent, "Return of the Red Ball," *Albuquerque Journal*, December 29, 1997, Business Outlook sec., pp. 1, 9; Keith Kofford, "The Red Ball Bounces Back," *Route 66 Magazine* 26, no. 2 (Spring 2019): 8–11; Keith Kofford, "Red Ball Is Still Cooking," *Route 66 New Mexico* 27, no. 3 (Fall 2019): 22; Robert Rodriguez, "Old-Timers Breathe Life into Tales of Barelas," *Albuquerque Journal*, November 24, 1989, sec. B, p. 1 (quotations); Katherine Saltzstein, "Voices, Photographs Add Flesh to the Memories of Barelas," *Albuquerque Journal*, April 29, 1990, sec. G, pp. 1–2; Andrew Webb, "Red Ball Reopened to Line," *Albuquerque Journal*, December 10, 2005, sec. E, p. 2.

30. "Complete Road in New Mexico," *Amarillo Globe*, November 12, 1937, p. 1; Greene, "Cruising Route 66 in New Mexico," pt. 4 [5], 4–8; Nomination to the National Register of Historic Places for Historic and Architectural Resources of Route 66 through New Mexico, E47–E48; Roger M. Zimmerman, "The Junction of Route 66 and Route 66: A Memorial to New Mexico's Political Past and Albuquerque's Future," *Route 66 New Mexico* 25, no. 2 (Winter 2017–18): 25–27.

31. "Bankruptcy Case Closed; Others Await Hearings," *Albuquerque Journal*, May 25, 1932, p. 8; O. O. Boren, Bernalillo, N.Mex., "Café for Rent by Owner," *Albuquerque Journal*, June 6, 1953, p. 15; "Café and Filling Station of U.S. Highway 66, East of Albuquerque, New Mexico," catalog number LC-USF34–037074-D, photograph by Russell Lee, July 1940, in Farm Security Administration Office of War Information Photograph Collection, Library of Congress, Washington, D.C.; "Daily Record," *Albuquerque Journal*, September 23, 1961, sec. A, p. 5; Glen W. Driskill, "Horn Brothers Gasoline," in *Route 66 Remembered*, by Michael Karl Witzel (Osceola, Wisc.: MBI Publishing, 1996), 167–70; "East Central Café Damaged by Fire," *Albuquerque Journal*, September 27, 1948, p. 2; Iceberg, Albuquerque, "Announcing the Opening Thursday at 1 P.M. Iceberg under New Management," *Albuquerque Journal*, May 18, 1933, p. 8; Iceberg, "Café for Sale" (advertisement), *Albuquerque Journal*, December 12, 1940, p. 14; Iceberg, "Iceberg For Sale" (advertisement), *Albuquerque Journal*, January 16, 1938, p. 10; Iceberg Café, Albuquerque, "Eat at the Iceberg Café" (advertisement), *Albuquerque Journal*, February 22, 1947, p. 10; Iceberg Café, "Iceberg Café" (advertisement), *Albuquerque Journal*, October 14, 1949, p. 22 (second quotation); Iceberg Café, "Under New Management[,] Old Iceberg Café" (advertisement), *Albuquerque Journal*, June 5, 1945, p. 8; Iceberg Café and Service Station, Albuquerque, "22-Month Lease: Café and Service Station at a Bargain" (advertisement), *Albuquerque Journal*, October 19, 1951, p. 26; "Iceberg Draws Crowd at Opening," *Albuquerque Journal*, May 28, 1931, p. 3; Iceberg Inn, Albuquerque, "The Iceberg Inn" (advertisement), *Albuquerque Journal*, June 26, 1932, p. 10; "Iceberg Is Sold," *Albuquerque Journal*, June 7, 1932, p. 3; "Iceberg, Long Landmark on Central, Gone for Good," *Albuquerque Journal*, May 10, 1953, p. 19; "Iceberg's Passing Still Mourned," *Albuquerque Journal*, May 17, 1953, p. 21; "Journal Action Line," *Albuquerque Journal*, February 17, 1969, sec. B, p. 8; Mac's Iceberg, Albuquerque, "Announcing the Opening of 'Mac's Iceberg'" (advertisement), *Albuquerque Journal*, May 27, 1931, p. 5; [Mac's] Iceberg, "Did You Know That We Serve the Best Sandwiches and Coffee in Town?" (advertisement), *Albuquerque Journal*, August 9, 1931, 2 (first quotation); Johnnie Meier, "Retro Cool—Chillin' at the Iceberg Café," *Route 66 New Mexico* 27, no. 4 (Winter 2019–20): 15–18; "Out of Albuquerque's Past," *Albuquerque Tribune*, May 13, 1977, sec. B, p. 16; Thomas Arthur Repp, *Route 66: The Romance of the West* (Lynwood, Wash.: Mock Turtle Press, 2002), 21; A. B. Schmidt, Bernalillo, N.Mex., "Massey-Harris Tractor, Almost New" (advertisement), *Albuquerque Journal*, June 22, 1660, sec. D, p. 2; Shaw Motor Company, Albuquerque, N.Mex., "We Buy, Sell or Trade" (advertisement), *Albuquerque Journal*, September 26, 1952, p. 34; Sonderman, *Route 66 Then and Now*, 98; Usner, *New Mexico Route 66*, 57–79.

32. Robert Archibald, "'Albuquerque's Alvarado': The Life and Death of an Institution," typescript, [ca. 1970], Fred Harvey Company Collection, MS 280, series 4, box 12, folder 286; Melville F. Ferguson, *Motor Camping on Western Trails* (New York: Century, 1925), 270–72; Fred Harvey Company, [Kansas City, Mo.], *Alvarado Hotel*[,] *Albuquerque*[,] *New Mexico*, publication no. 3—1955 ([Kansas City, Mo.]: Fred Harvey, [1955]), folder, Special Collections, University of Arizona Library, Tucson; Gerhard, "Architecture and the Fred Harvey Houses," 18–25; Fried, *Appetite for America*, 187–92, 327–28, 405; Bob O'Sullivan, "It's 55 Years Late, but Thanks, Mr. Harvey, for the Memory," *Chicago Tribune*, December 11, 1988, sec. 12, p. 3; Lesley Poling-Kempes, *The Harvey Girls: Women Who Opened the West* (Cambridge, Mass.: Da Capo Press, 1989), 100, 156–65, 185–87, 199–201, 207–8; Miss Pugsley, "Stepping Westward: The Log of a Spinster's Transcontinental Trip," travel album with transcript, unpaged, item HM 81399, Huntington Library, San Marino, Calif.; Deborah C. Slaney, *Jewel of the Railroad Era: Albuquerque's Alvarado Hotel* (Albuquerque: Albuquerque Museum, 2009), 3–111; Toby Smith, "Those Harvey Girls," *Albuquerque Journal*, August 11, 1981, Impact supplement, pp. 8–10; "Stopping at the Alvarado," *Hospitality*, January 1950, pp. 3–4; Usner, *New Mexico Route 66*, 53–72. For a critical examination of the lives of waitresses in the American West including Harvey employees, see Mary Lee Spence, "Waitresses in the Trans-Mississippi West: 'Pretty Waiter Girls,' Harvey Girls and Union Maids," in *The Women's West*, ed. Susan Armitage and Elizabeth Jameson (Norman: University of Oklahoma Press, 1987), 219–34.

33. Central Drug Store, Albuquerque, "Pete Duran Announces the Grand Opening of the Central Drug Store New Location" (advertisement), *Albuquerque Journal*, November 30, 1945, p. 16; Central Drug Store, "Save Time and Tires" (advertisement), *Albuquerque Journal*, July 18, 1942, p. 10; E. Clair, "Dining Out: A Guide to Albuquerque Restaurants," *Albuquerque Journal*, July 16, 1985, Impact magazine, p. 4; Tracy Dingman, "Duran Family Goes Way Back," *Albuquerque Journal*, September 10, 2005, sec. E, p. 2; "Drug Store Making Room for Highway," *Albuquerque Journal*, November 25, 1958, p. 26; "Duran—Pedro (Pete) G. Duran," *Albuquerque Journal*, August 17, 1984, sec. E, p. 11; "Duran Pharmacy Ownership Goes to R. N. Ghattas," *Albuquerque Journal*, October 10, 1965, sec. E, p. 8; Duran's Central Pharmacy, Albuquerque, "Duran's Central Pharmacy" (advertisement), *Albuquerque Journal*, September 8, 1975, sec. D, p. 8; Mona Ghattas, Albuquerque, to T. Lindsay Baker, Rio Vista, Tex., email communication, October 12, 2020, paper copy, author's collection; Charlotte Balcomb Lane, "Duran Pharmacy Has New Station Sibling," *Albuquerque Journal*, November 25, 2005, Venue supplement, p. 12; Dinah Long, "Pharmacy Fare Could Become Habit-forming: Comfort Tastes Great at Duran's," *Albuquerque Journal*, July 19, 1996, Venue supplement, sec. E, p. 11; Pete Duran Central Pharmacy, Albuquerque, "Duran's Pharmacy Back-to-school Get Acquainted Sale" (advertisement), *Albuquerque Journal*, September 2, 1959, sec. A, p. 5; "Pete Duran, Founder of Duran Pharmacy, Dead at 87," *Albuquerque Tribune*, August 17, 1984, sec. D, p. 8; "Pete Duran Heads Pharmacy Board," *Albuquerque Journal*, June 15, 1949, p. 2; "Pete Duran Named as Postmaster in Old Albuquerque," *Albuquerque Journal*, January 10, 1926, p. 7; "Pete Duran, Veteran Pharmacist, Opens Store," *Albuquerque Journal*, August 15, 1941, p. 3; Charles Peters, "To My Taste," *Albuquerque Journal*, July 18, 1986, sec. F, p. 28; Jane Stern and Michael Stern, *Roadfood and Goodfood: Jane and Michael Stern's Coast-to-Coast Restaurant Guides Combined, Updated, and Expanded* (New York: Alfred A. Knopf, 1987), 433–34 (quotation); Jane Stern and Michael Stern, *Roadfood: The Coast-to-Coast Guide to 500 of the Best Barbecue Joints, Lobster Shacks, Ice-cream Parlors, Highway Diners, and Much, Much More* (New York: Broadway Books, 2002), 392.

34. Casa de Armijo, Albuquerque, "Casa de Armijo Artistic Studio Apartments" (advertisement), *Albuquerque Journal*, December 31, 1938, p. 10; Bette Dickson Casteel, *Old Town Albuquerque in the 1940s and a Little Beyond* (Corrales, N.Mex.: privately printed, 1996), 7–8, 11–12, 23, 29–32, 34–35, 46; "Daily Record," *Albuquerque Journal*, January 8, 1935, p. 7; La Placita, Albuquerque, "Dine Where It's Restful and Cool—in the Patio at La Placita" (advertisement), *Albuquerque Journal*, August 15, 1937, p. 9; La Placita Coffee Shop, Albuquerque, "La Placita Coffee Shop" (advertisement), *Albuquerque Journal*, March 16, 1933, p. 8; La Placita Coffee Shop, Albuquerque, "Public Opening—Friday, Oct 4th" (advertisement), *Albuquerque*

Journal, October 4, 1935, p. 9; La Placita Patio Tea Garden, Albuquerque, "Public Opening Wednesday[,] La Placita Patio Tea Garden" (advertisement), *Albuquerque Journal*, May 22, 1935, p. 5; "Moorhead—Nelda Sewell Moorhead," *Albuquerque Journal*, December 7, 1986, sec. H, p. 8; "Nelda Sewell and Patio Market Featured in Woman's Magazine," *Albuquerque Journal*, August 20, 1950, p. 19; Ellie Phillips, *La Placita Historical Notes[,] Famous Recipes* (Albuquerque: La Placita Dining Rooms, 1973), 9–28, booklet, author's collection; "Rites Held for Nelda Moorhead, Old Town's Preservation 'Mother,'" *Albuquerque Journal*, December 9, 1986, sec. B, p. 4; "Sherman-Sewell Saturday Rites Are Disclosed," *Albuquerque Journal*, June 20, 1942, p. 8; "Society," *Albuquerque Journal*, September 20, 1931, p. 8, and May 2, 1936, p. 9; "Society Flashes," *Albuquerque Journal*, February 15, 1939, p. 7.

35. "Brown—Marie Brown," *Albuquerque Journal*, May 25, 1991, sec. H, p. 9; "Cyrus F. Brown, Owner of La Placita, Dies at Hospital Here," *Albuquerque Journal*, October 6, 1944, p. 6; *Gourmet's Guide to Good Eating: A Valuable and Vital Accessory for Every Motorist and Traveler 1946–47* (New York: Gourmet, the Magazine of Good Living, 1946), 215 (quotations); Hacienda Dining Rooms, Albuquerque, "Hacienda Dining Rooms (Formerly La Placita)" (advertisement), *Albuquerque Journal*, December 22, 1951, p. 9; "Hacienda Dining Rooms Buys Old Town Property," *Albuquerque Journal*, August 1, 1952, p. 4; La Placita, Albuquerque, "Announcing the Opening! Friday and Saturday La Placita Patio" (advertisement), *Albuquerque Journal*, April 27, 1940, p. 14; La Placita, Albuquerque, "La Placita Is Now Open" (advertisement), *Albuquerque Journal*, March 9, 1940, p. 14; "La Placita Now the Hacienda," *Albuquerque Journal*, December 21, 1951, p. 2; La Placita, Albuquerque, *La Placita on the Plaza in Old Albuquerque, New Mexico[,] Recommended by Duncan Hines* (Albuquerque: La Placita, [ca. 1947]), menu, author's collection; La Placita, Albuquerque, "La Placita Restaurant for Lease" (advertisement), *Albuquerque Journal*, October 28, 1940, p. 6; "La Hacienda to Move June 8," *Albuquerque Journal*, June 2, 1954, p. 9; Rick Nathanson, "La Hacienda Rubble Probed for Fire's Cause," *Albuquerque Journal*, January 25, 1981, sec. A, p. 2; "A New Building for Hacienda Dining Rooms," *Albuquerque Journal*, March 28, 1954, p. 18; Lorraine Peterson, "Fear of Indian Attacks Dictated the Structure of Early Old Town Home," *Albuquerque Journal*, January 11, 1952, p. 7.

36. "Civic Leader E. D. Elliott Dies," *Albuquerque Journal*, March 9, 1980, sec. A, p. 4; Clark, *Route 66 Cookbook*, 154–55; "Court Enterprises to Run La Placita," *Albuquerque Journal*, October 12, 1954, p. 16; "Elliott—Elmer D. Elliott," sec. F, p. 14; La Placita Dining Room[s], Albuquerque, "Announcing the Reopening of Albuquerque's Famous La Placita Dining Room" (advertisement), *Albuquerque Journal*, January 14, 1955, p. 44; La Placita Dining Rooms, *La Placita Dining Rooms[,] Old Albuquerque[,] New Mexico* (Albuquerque: La Placita Dining Rooms, [ca. 1965]), menu, "Albuquerque—Restaurants—La Placita—Old Town—Ambrosio Armijo House" Vertical File, Center for Southwest Research, Zimmerman Library, University of New Mexico, Albuquerque; La Placita Dining Rooms, Albuquerque, "While in Albuquerque Visit the La Placita Dining Rooms" (advertisement), *Albuquerque Journal*, May 5, 1963, sec. E, p. 11; Paul Logan, "West Side Eatery Serves La Placita Fare and More," *Albuquerque Journal*, May 1, 1996, sec. M, p. 3; "Mr. and Mrs. Elmer Elliott," *Childress (Tex.) Index*, April 12, 1970, pp. 4–5; "Old Town Restaurant Owner Dies," February 12, 1994, sec. D, p. 11; Jason K. Watkins, "Old Town Charm: La Placita Offers New Mexican Favorites in Historic Atmosphere," *Albuquerque Journal*, October 13, 2017, Venue supplement, pp. 16–17.

37. Steve Brewer, "The Spirit of 66," *Albuquerque Journal*, June 28, 1992, sec. C, pp. 1–2; Arnold Carlson, "Keeping Pace with Bobby Unser," *Route 66 Magazine* 24, no. 1 (Winter 2018–19): 38–40; *Hudspeth's Albuquerque (Bernalillo County, New Mexico) City Directory 1949* (El Paso, Tex.: Hudspeth Directory Co., 1949), 517, 584; Paul McLaughlin, "Unser Racing Museum," *Route 66 New Mexico* 13, no. 1 (Spring 2005): 18–19; Johnny Meier, "The Unser Racing Museum," *Route 66 Magazine* 18, no. 3 (Summer 2011): 22–25.

38. Blake de Pastino, "Understanding Diners: A Trip to West Central and the Golden Age of the Coffee Shop," *Weekly Alibi* (Albuquerque), 4–10 February 1993, pp. 14–15; Desert Vu Restaurant, Albuquerque, "Cooks, Waitresses, and Dishwashers" (advertisement), *Albuquerque Journal*, September 8, 1968, sec. C, p. 17; Desert Vu [Café], Albuquerque, "Dishwasher Wanted" (advertisement), *Albuquerque Journal*, April

23, 1957, p. 30; "Peter I. Kellis," *Albuquerque Journal*, October 8, 2001, sec. D, p. 11; Charlotte Balcomb Lane, "Diner's Wide Menu Seasoned with Nostalgia," *Albuquerque Journal*, March 24, 2000, Venue supplement, p. E-10; Andrea Lin, "Diner Serves up Comfort with a View," *Albuquerque Journal*, January 1, 2010, Venue supplement, p. 12; Sharon Niederman, "Just Plain Good: Diner Offers Hearty, Home-style Cooking Straight out of the '50s," *Albuquerque Journal*, April 8, 2016, Venue supplement, pp. 12–13; Rory McClannahan, "Neon Arch Will Adorn West Central: Steel Structure to Stretch 110 Feet," *Albuquerque Journal*, June 16, 2004, Rio Rancho Journal supplement, p. 3; "Narcotics Dealer Given Suspended Prison Sentence," *Albuquerque Journal*, May 9, 1969, sec. E, p. 8; "Pappas—Tasia Pappas," *Albuquerque Journal*, July 28, 1992, sec. D, p. 11; Jill Schneider [K. Hilleson, pseud.], *Route Sixty-six Revisited: A Wanderer's Guide to New Mexico, a Collection of Trips and Memories along Route 66* (Albuquerque: D. Nakii Enterprises, 1988), 2 (quotation); Steve Suttle, "Restaurant Review: The Western View Diner & Steakhouse," *Route 66 New Mexico* 9, no. 4 (Fall 2001): 20–21; Western View Diner & Steakhouse, Albuquerque, "Now Open!" (advertisement), *Albuquerque Journal*, December 18, 1969, sec. E, p. 6; Western View Diner & Steakhouse, "For the Most Elegant Dining Visit Western View Diner & Steakhouse" (advertisement), *Albuquerque Tribune*, April 27, 1974, sec. A, p. 11.

39. "Arrogant Warning," *Santa Fe New Mexican*, May 20, 1949, p. 4; "Roy Cline Jr.," *Albuquerque Journal*, December 15, 2004, sec. D, p. 6; Clines Corners, Encino, N.Mex., "*Indian Jewelry*[,] *Moccasins*[,] *Curios*[,] *Pottery*[,] *Beaded Belts*[,] *Here It Is! Elevation 7200 Ft. Welcome Amigo*[,] *Clines Corners*" (Encino, N.Mex.: Clines Corners, [ca. 1955]), placemat, author's collection; "Clines Corners Founder's Wife Dies at Age 76," *Albuquerque Journal*, January 23, 1971, sec. D, p. 8; Spencer Crump, *Route 66: America's First Main Street* (Corona del Mar, Calif.: Zeta Publishers, 1994), 88–89; "Feds OK Special Side Roads in NM," *New Mexican*, April 23, 1959, p. 15; Kofton, "My Girl Lou and Me," 1–4 (fourth and fifth quotations); Susie McComb, "Famous 'Cool' Clines Corners Worth Stopping For," *New Mexico Route 66 Association Newsletter* 6, no. 3 (Summer 1999): 1, 3; Chuck McCutcheon, "You Want It? They've Got It," *Albuquerque Journal*, August 21, 1988, sec. C, pp. 1, 6; Johnnie V. [Meier], "Howdy from Clines Corners[,] N.M.," *Route 66 New Mexico* 24, no. 1 (Spring 2016): 10–11; Jenna Naranjo, "Small Town's Travel Center Serves as Community Hot Spot," *Albuquerque Tribune*, June 12, 2003, sec. A, p. 7; J. V. Pigg, "Restaurant Review: Clines Corners Is Cooking," *Route 66 New Mexico* 11, no. 1 (Spring 2003): 20–21; "Roy E. Cline Is Dead at 92; Founder of Clines Corners," *Albuquerque Journal*, March 26, 1982, sec. B, p. 4; Scott and Kelly, *Route 66*, 67–69, 163–64 (first, second, and third quotations); Toby Smith, "Clines Corners: The 'Rubber Tomahawk' Trade," pt. 2, *Albuquerque Journal*, August 9, 1983, Impact magazine, p. 13; Howard Suttle, *Behind the Wheel on Route 66* (Raton, N.Mex.: Data Plus! Printing and Publishing, 1993), 29–31, 88, 235–37.

40. Robert V. Beier, "New Mexican Heads Revival of Stuckey's," *Albuquerque Journal*, August 11, 1985, sec. F, p. 1; "Fire Destroys Tourist Ranch," *Albuquerque Journal*, July 10, 1976, sec. A, p. 12; Flying C Ranch Café, Santa Rosa, N.Mex., "Wanted—Waitress $20 Weekly, Board and Room" (advertisement), *Albuquerque Journal*, April 16, 1948, p. 14; Flying C Ranch, Palma, N.Mex., "Flying C Ranch" (advertisement), *Albuquerque Journal*, June 18, 1950, p. 28; Flying C Ranch, "For Sale" (advertisement), *Albuquerque Journal*, April 3, 1955, p. 51; "Flying C Ranch Sold to New Corporation," *Albuquerque Journal*, April 2, 1961, sec. A, p. 6; "Liquor License Changes Asked," *Albuquerque Journal*, January 29, 1964, sec. A, p. 5; "Roy E. Cline Is Dead," p. 4; "Stuckey Store Opens Saturday," *Albuquerque Journal*, August 25, 1961, sec. A, p. 6; "Work Starts on I-40 Interchanges," *Albuquerque Journal*, April 30, 1972, sec. A, p. 9.

41. "Adams—Frank Adams," *Albuquerque Journal*, November 14, 1990, sec. D, p. 9; Lynn Chambers, "Household Memos," *Santa Rosa News*, December 22, 1950, p. [13]; George King, Albuquerque, "Wanted: At Once, Two Married Men" (advertisement), *Albuquerque Journal*, March 2, 1941, p. 10; Geo. S. King, Edgewood, N.Mex., "Wanted—Married Couple or Single Woman" (advertisement), *Albuquerque Journal*, May 7, 1940, p. 12 (second, third, and fourth quotations); Geo. S. King, Glencoe, N.Mex., "Wanted—Two Reliable People" (advertisement), *Clovis*[,] *New Mexico*[,] *Evening News-Journal* (Clovis, N.Mex.), April 18, 1935, p. 6; "King's Cherry Cider," *Albuquerque Journal*, April 30, 1940, sec. D, p. 4; "Public Health Nurse," *Santa*

Fe New Mexican, August 30, 1928, p. 7; "Public Health Nurse," *Windsor (Mo.) Review*, November 8, 1923, p. 5; Schneider, *Route 66 across New Mexico*, 146–47 (first quotation); "War, Floods and Epidemics Is Life History of 73-year-old Resident of Ruidoso Valley," *Ruidoso (N.Mex.) News*, October 23, 1964, p. 1. Cyrus and Florence Sanders ran a roadside cider stand called the Kickapoo Corral next to their daughter's store on Route 66 in Elk City, Oklahoma, but their apple- and cherry-flavored "cider" beverage came as a mix to be diluted in water. Wanda Queenan, the daughter, explained, "You got the concentrate . . . in jars and you mixed water with it." Wanda Queenan, interview by Rodger Harris, Elk City, Okla., October 29, 1992, audio recording and typewritten transcript, p. 7, Research Center, Oklahoma Historical Society, Oklahoma City; Thomas Arthur Repp, *Route 66: Empires of Amusement* (Lynnwood, Wash.: Mock Turtle Press, 1999), 149.

42. Greene, "Route 66 in New Mexico Beckons," 18; Kammer, "Seven Wonders," 61, 63–64; Keith Kofford, "Rock Stars," *Route 66 New Mexico* 20, no. 2 (Summer 2012): 12–13, 22; Keith Kofford, "Tale of the Ale," *Route 66 New Mexico* 23, no. 1 (Spring 2015): 6–9; Keith Kofford, "'Zuzax': The Last Word on '66," *Route 66 New Mexico* 22, no. 2 (Summer 2014): 14–17; Ted Raynos, "Tijeras Rises from Spanish Grant, Becomes Mountain Hub," *Albuquerque Journal*, July 13, 1958, p 36; Rittenhouse, *Guide Book to Highway 66*, 77–78; Schneider, *Route 66 across New Mexico*, 140–43.

43. "Grants Manager Sues Assailants," *Albuquerque Journal*, November 22, 1958, p. 17; National Register of Historic Places Nominations for State Maintained Route 66: Albuquerque to Rio Puerco, August 1996; and State and Locally Maintained Rt. 66: Correo to Laguna, August 1996; Repp, *Route 66: The Romance of the West*, 28 (quotation); Rittenhouse, *Guide Book to Highway 66*, 81–82; Schneider, *Route Sixty-six Revisited*, 30–31.

44. Nathan Greene, "Cruising Route 66 in New Mexico," pt. 4, *Route 66 New Mexico* 21, no. 1 (Spring 2013): 12–13 "Hugh Crooks Is Dead at 73," *Albuquerque Journal*, September 9, 1981, sec. D, p. 10; R. G. Allen Jackson, "Miscellaneous Odds and Ends[,] Thoughts and True Experiences of the Original Stumblebum," in *A Trilogy: Miscellaneous Odds and Ends, Thoughts and True Experiences of the Original Stumblebum[;] a Cab Driver's Conception of the Ten Commandments of God[;] a Cab Driver's Diary: On the Spot[;] the Above Trilogy (Three Books) Represents an Effort of Twenty-five Years by Yours Truly*, ([Amarillo]: privately printed, 1966), 83–84 (quotation); Keith Kofford, "Laguna Camp[,] New Mexico," *Route 66 Magazine* 22, no. 3 (Summer 2015): 22–25; Nominations to the National Register of Historic Places for Pueblo of Laguna, N.Mex., January 19, 1973, and for Historic and Architectural Resources of Route 66 through New Mexico, E8–E9; Repp, *Route 66: The Romance of the West*, 28; Schneider, *Route Sixty-six Revisited*, 36–39; "Three Indians Accused of Robbery at Paraje," *Albuquerque Journal*, July 12, 1945, p. 14; Usner, *New Mexico Route 66*, 83–86; Zickefoose, *Economic Survey of Tourist-Related Business*, 18.

45. Bendix Aviation Corporation, [Los Angeles], "Everywhere Acclaimed" (advertisement), *Albuquerque Journal*, November 28, 1947, p. 12; "Budville's Bud Rice Would Rather Put Motorists to Bed," *Albuquerque Journal*, July 4, 1954, p. 19; "California Man Blasts Justice," *Albuquerque Journal*, February 18, 1954, p. 17; "Father, Brother Battle for Policy," *Albuquerque Journal*, December 13, 1949, p. 15; Sue Bohannan Mann, "Budville-Cubero Villages Stand as Living Links to Mother Road," *New Mexico Magazine* 76, no. 10 (October 1998): 56–60; Johnnie V. Meier, "Once upon a Time in Cubero," *New Mexico Route 66 Association Newsletter* 8, no. 2 (Spring–Summer 2001): 28–29; Johnnie Meier, "Law West of the Rio Puerco," *Route 66 New Mexico* 9, no. 3 (Fall 2001): 12–15; Johnnie Meier, "Who Killed Bud Rice?" *Route 66 New Mexico* 10, no. 1 (Spring 2002): 16–19; John Millrany, "Flossie, Bud, and Budville," *Route 66 Magazine* 6, no. 4 (Fall 1999): 27, 30–31; "NM Police Try to End Road Slaughter[;] Motor Club Scoff 'Speed Trap' Claim," *Las Vegas Daily Optic*, December 21, 1953, p. 1; Nomination to the National Register of Historic Places for Route 66 Rural Historic District: Laguna to McCarty's, November 18, 1993; Purdy Bakeries, Albuquerque, "Purdy Bakeries Serve" (advertisement), *Albuquerque Journal-Herald* (Albuquerque), April 11, 1926, p. 9; "Rites Planned Sunday for Cubero Marine," *Albuquerque Journal*, July 27, 1946, p. 5; "Roscoe Rice," *Sacramento (Calif.) Bee*, June 14, 1959, sec. A, p. 2; Schneider, *Route Sixty-Six Revisited*, 47–48; Fritz Thompson, "Murderous

Past: Tiny Route 66 Town Tight-lipped about '67 Double Slaying," *Albuquerque Journal*, March 5, 1995, sec. B, pp. 10, 12; U.S. Post Office Department, Records of Appointment of Postmasters, 1832–1971, New Mexico Quay-Valencia Counties, vol. 90, pp. 395–96, Microcopy M841, reel 85, National Archives and Records Administration; "Valencia Settles 66 Rift: Right-of-Way for Projects Bought by County," *Gallup (N.Mex.) Independent (and Evening Herald)*, January 23, 1936, p. 1; "Woman Kills Self as Her Son Did," *Albuquerque Journal*, October 23, 1946, p. 1; Zickefoose, *Economic Survey of Tourist-Related Business*, 20–21.

46. Michael A. Amundson, *Yellowcake Towns: Uranium Mining Communities in the American West* (Boulder: University Press of Colorado, 2002), 77–103, 117–18, 154–55; Chamber of Commerce, Grants, N.Mex., *Grants[,] New Mexico[,] the Lava City[,] Where Industry, Scenery and Sports Combine to Provide Pleasant Living in "the Land of Enchantment"* (Grants, N.Mex.: Chamber of Commerce, [ca. 1950]), folder, author's collection; Greene, "Cruising Route 66 in New Mexico," pt. 4, 14; Keith Kofford, "Exit #100: San Fidel, New Mexico," *Route 66 Magazine* 28, no. 1 (Winter 2020–21): 26–30; Gertrude E. Metcalfe-Shaw, *English Caravanners in the Wild West: The Old Pioneers' Trail* (Edinburgh, Scotland: William Blackwood and Sons, 1926), 168–74; Nomination to the National Register of Historic Places for State Maintained Rt. 66: McCartys to Grants, August 1996; Cy Rouse, "F.O.B. Grants," *New Mexico Magazine* 22, no. 4 (April 1944): 14–15, 30 (quotation); Schneider, *Route Sixty-six Revisited*, 62–65; Usner, *New Mexico Route 66*, 90–92; Paul W. Zickefoose, *Economic Survey of Grants, New Mexico, 1950–58: The "Before" Portion of a Highway Relocation Impact Study*, New Mexico State Highway Department Planning Division Bulletin 9 ([Santa Fe]: New Mexico State Highway Department, 1959), 7–18, 33–36.

47. "Grants Hotel, Store Burn," *Albuquerque Journal*, September 17, 1936, p. 1; "Grants Resident Dies in California," *Albuquerque Journal*, May 13, 1958, p. 11; "Inquest Brings to Light Details of Toltec Case," *Albuquerque Morning Journal*, March 15, 1919, p. 3; Paul Milan, Grants, N.Mex., email communication to T. Lindsay Baker, Rio Vista, Tex., January 20, 2021, paper copy, author's collection; Mohawk Rubber Company, Akron, Ohio, *Guide No. 3[,] Mohawk Hobbs Grade and Surface Guide[,] Price 20¢[,] Santa Fe Trail Los Angeles-Denver[,] Western Division National Old Trails*, 4th ed., publication Hworow 30851 (Akron, Ohio: Mohawk Rubber Company, 1929), 22 (third quotation), booklet, author's collection; "'Mother' Whiteside, a Pioneer, Surprised with Birthday Visit," *Gallup (N.Mex.) Independent*, May 9, 1953, p. 6 (first and second quotations); "Municipal Library, Financed by Texan, to Honor Venerable Grants Midwife," *Albuquerque Journal*, September 20, 1954, p. 13; Cecilia Perrow, "The Importance to Our Community of Lucy Jane Ross Whiteside," Mother Whiteside Memorial Library, Grants, N.Mex., accessed March 20, 2020, http://www.youseemore.com/whiteside/about.asp?=13; Schneider, *Route Sixty-Six Revisited*, 65; Whiteside Hotel and Café, Grants, N.Mex., "Whiteside Hotel and Café" (advertisement), *Gallup Independent*, August 10, 1940, sec. 5, p. [6].

48. Bohacz, "Blowing in the Wind," 84–87; Chevrolet Motor Company, Detroit, *Instructions for the Operation and Care of Chevrolet Motor Cars[,] Universal Series AD*, 8th ed. (Detroit: Chevrolet Motor Co., 1930), 43–46, author's collection; Ford Motor Company, Detroit, *Ford Manual for Owners and Operators of Ford Cars and Trucks*, publication 300M-1-15-18 (Detroit: Ford Motor Company, [1918]), 19–21, author's collection; Greene, "Cruising Route 66 in New Mexico," pt. 4, 15; *New Mexico: A Guide to the Colorful State*, 316–22; Nomination to the National Register of Historic Places for State Maintained Rt. 66: Milan to Continental Divide, August 1996; Rittenhouse, *Guide Book to Highway 66*, 87–88.

49. "Daily Record," *Albuquerque Journal*, July 7, 1938, p. 9; "Defendants Bound over in Slaying of Littleton," *Independent* (Gallup, N.Mex.), January 6, 1966, p. 1; Gallup Realty, Gallup, N.Mex., "Business Opportunities" (advertisement), *Gallup (N.Mex.) Daily Independent*, May 3, 1957, p. 1; William Kaszynski, *Route 66: Images of America's Main Street* (Jefferson, N.C.: McFarland, 2003), 110, 112; "Legal Notice," *Gallup Daily Independent*, August 3, 1959, p. 7; and November 28, 1960, p. 7; "Mrs. Alma Crow of the Top of the World," *Gallup Independent*, December 10, 1940, p. [4]; "Notice of Foreclosure Sale," *Gallup Independent (and Evening Herald)*, May 29, 1936, p. [2]; "Notice of the Pendency of Suit," *Gallup Independent*, October 17, 1946, p. 4; "Off and on the Highway East," *Gallup Independent*, October 8, 1942, p. 2 (second quotation);

"Real Estate Transfers," *Gallup Independent*, August 29, 1944, p. 2; Repp, *Route 66: The Romance of the West*, 54–58; Rittenhouse, *Guide Book to Highway 66*, 88; Alma Rosenberg, [Continental Divide, N.Mex.], "Notice" (advertisement), *Gallup Independent and Evening Herald*, May 6, 1930, p. 4; Sharp, *Better Country*, 156–57 (first quotation); "Three Accused in Confidence Game," *Las Cruces Sun-News* (Las Cruces, N.Mex.), July 9, 1946, p. 2; Top o the World Café, [Continental Divide, N.Mex.], "Can Use Manager or Will Lease Café" (advertisement), *Albuquerque Journal*, May 29, 1946, p. 10; Top o' the World, Continental Divide, N.Mex., "Top 'o the World Bar—Hotel—Café under New Management" (advertisement), *Gallup Independent*, August 9, 1949, sec. 7, p. 3; Top o' the World, "Top 'o the World[,] 'It's the Food'" (advertisement), *Gallup Independent*, April 22, 1947, p. 6; Top-o-the World Hotel and Café, Continental Divide, N.Mex., "Top-o-the World Hotel and Café" (advertisement), *Gallup Independent*, February 2, 1946, p. 4; Top of the World Hotel, [Continental Divide, N.Mex.], "Greetings Ceremonial Visitors from Top of the World Hotel" (advertisement), *Gallup Independent*, August 9, 1955, sec. 2, p. 8.

50. Big Horn Café, Continental Divide, N.Mex., "Welcome Visitors" (advertisement), *Gallup Daily Independent*, August 7, 1956, sec. A, p. [6]; Buck & Squaw Trading Post, Continental Divide, N.Mex., "Furnished Store" (advertisement), *Gallup Independent*, April 2, 1953, p. 5; Continental Trading Company, Continental Divide, N.Mex., "Genuine Hand Made Indian Jewelry" (advertisement), *Gallup Independent*, March 1, 1945, p. 3; Distant Drums Trading Post and Western Club, Continental Divide, N.Mex., "Welcome Visitors" (advertisement), *Gallup Daily Independent*, August 12, 1958, sec. D, p. 8; "Eckles Given Term," *Independent*, November 13, 1965, p. 1; "Fire Destroys Tourist Cabins at Top of World," *Gallup Independent*, April 29, 1944, p. 1; G & H Café, Continental Divide, N.Mex., "Welcome Ceremonial Visitors" (advertisement), *Gallup Independent*, August 9, 1955, sec. [2], p. 5; Great Divide Café, Continental Divide, N.Mex., "Dinner Cook, Male or Female" (advertisement), *Gallup Independent*, May 15, 1953, p. 7; Great Divide Trading, Continental Divide, N.Mex., "Dance at Great Divide Trading" (advertisement), *Gallup Independent*, September 9, 1944, p. 4; Haller's Great Divide Camp, [Continental Divide, N.Mex.], *Gallup Independent*, August 14, 1940, p. [4]; Sigmund Hass, [Continental Divide, N.Mex.], "I Will Not Be Responsible" (advertisement), *Gallup Daily Independent*, August 23, 1956, p. [8]; "Legal Notice," *Gallup Daily Independent*, October 22, 1956, p. 5; Leslie Linthicum, "Trucker Converts Shuttered Stuckey's into Dream Home," *Carlsbad Current-Argus*, December 16, 2004, sec. A, p. 7; "Man Bests Coyote with Bare Fists," *Gallup Independent*, December 5, 1944, p. 1; Repp, *Route 66: The Romance of the West*, 56–58; Zickefoose, *Economic Survey of Tourist-Related Business*, 22.

51. Repp, *Route 66: The Romance of the West*, 55–58; Schneider, *Route Sixty-six Revisited*, 104–6 (quotations).

52. Harold S. Colton and Frank C. Baxter, *Days in the Painted Desert and the San Francisco Mountains: A Guide*, Northern Arizona Society of Science and Art Bulletin no. 2 (Flagstaff: Museum of Northern Arizona, 1932), 33; Gerald M. Knowles, *Route 66 Chronicles*, vol. 1, *Shadows of the Past over Route 66, Arizona–New Mexico* (Winfield, Kans.: Central Plains Book Manufacturing, 2002), 120–21; Johnnie V. [Meier], "Hollywood Goes Gallup," *Route 66 New Mexico* 13, no. 3 (Fall 2005): 8, 10; Sally W. Noe, *Greetings from Gallup: Six Decades of Route 66* (Gallup, N.Mex.: Gallup Downtown Development Group, 1991), 1–86; Nomination to the National Register of Historic Places for State Maintained Rt. 66: Iyanbito to Rehobeth, August 1996; Usner, *New Mexico Route 66*, 95–96, 99–100, 107; Paul W. Zickefoose, *Economic Survey of Gallup, New Mexico, 1950–1960: The "Before" Portion of a Highway Relocation Impact Study*, New Mexico State Highway Department Planning Division Bulletin 24 ([Santa Fe]: New Mexico State Highway Department, 1962), 5–8, 25–26.

53. "Griffiths Run 187 Theaters in Southwest," *Oklahoma News* (Oklahoma City), October 13, 1937, sec. B, p. 7; "New Theater Opens on West 66 Avenue," *Gallup Independent (and Evening Herald)*, July 17, 1936, p. 1.

54. El Rancho Hotel, Gallup, N.Mex., "Dance Sunday Nite El Rancho" (advertisement), *Gallup Independent*, December 9, 1937, p. 4; El Rancho [Hotel], "We Announce Informal Opening" (advertisement), *Gallup Independent*, November 23, 1937, p. 4; "Gambling Devices Seized in Raids," *Albuquerque Journal*, July 11, 1946, p. 6; Hotel El Rancho, Gallup, N.Mex., *Hotel El Rancho[,] Gallup[,] New Mexico[,] World's Largest*

Ranch House[,] *Capacity: 400 Guests*[,] *with the Charm of Yesterday and the Convenience of Tomorrow! Menu* (Gallup, N.Mex.: Masons, 1946), menu, courtesy of Mike Ward; "In New Mexico," *Albuquerque Journal*, December 5, 1937, p. 8; Kirk Littlefield, "Hotel El Rancho: 'World's Largest Ranch House[,]' Gallup, New [Mexico]," *Route 66 Magazine* 9, no. 2 (Spring 2002): 40–41; Armand Ortega, interview by David K. Dunaway, Gallup, N.Mex., June 28, 2007, typewritten transcript, p. 2 (quotation), Route 66 Corridor Preservation Program, National Park Service, Santa Fe; "Two Gambling Raids in Gallup: State Police Seize Hotel, Café Devices," *Albuquerque Journal*, February 18, 1943, p. 9; Usner, *New Mexico Route 66*, 96–99. Meals were not cheap at the El Rancho. After spending a night on the road there in 1952, motorist Lou Kofton had breakfast in the coffee shop, paying $1.50. She later noted, "I remember the cost of breakfast, because it was pretty high." Kofton, "My Girl Lou and Me," 2.

55. "California Man Takes over Hotel El Rancho July 1," *Gallup Independent*, June 16, 1945, p. 1; "Complete $750,000 Deal," *Albuquerque Journal*, May 4, 1946, p. 6; El Rancho Hotel, "Rooms Kitchenettes and Some Furnished Apts." (advertisement), *Independent*, October 5, 1967, p. 11; El Rancho Hotel, "Wanted Waitress White Only" (advertisement), *Gallup Independent*, August 9, 1945, p. 3; "Film Industry Helps New Mexico," *Deming (N.Mex.) Headlight*, July 11, 1941, p. 1; "Gallup Men Purchase El Rancho," *Albuquerque Journal*, December 23, 1961, sec. A, p. 1; "Griffith Purchases Night Club Ranch," *Gallup Independent*, November 11, 1943, p. 4; "Hotel Expansion 'in the Future,'" *Albuquerque Journal*, July 3, 1948, p. 8; "In New Mexico," *Albuquerque Journal*, May 2, 1950, p. 6; Noe, *Greetings from Gallup*, 44–46; "Personal Mention," *Gallup Independent*, July 10, 1939, p. [4]; "R. Griffith, Owned 345 Film Theatres," *New York Times*, November 26, 1943, p. 23; Schneider, *Route Sixty-Six Revisited*, 112–14 (quotation); "Show Owner Is against Bill," *Gallup Independent*, January 5, 1940, p. 1; Toby Smith, "When Reagan Rode the Range," *Albuquerque Journal*, December 9, 1980, Impact supplement, pp. 4–8. As least since the 1960s, a myth has arisen that the El Rancho Hotel was constructed by "R. E. Griffith," a brother of famous film director D. W. Griffith. As early as 1990 writer Tom Snyder accurately pointed out that filmmaker Griffith had no brothers with this name. Despite the fact that the hotel builder, Rupert Earl Griffith, was instead an unrelated operator of movie theaters, the myth persists. "Noted Gallup Hotel Sold," *New Mexican*, December 24, 1961, p. 19; Tom Snyder, *The Route 66 Traveler's Guide and Roadside Companion* (New York: St. Martin's Press, 1990), 79, 81.

56. American Automobile Association, *Western Tour Book* (Washington, D.C.: American Automobile Association, 1940), 253; Baker, *Portrait of Route 66*, 174–77; "California Limited Makes Meal Stops Again," *Hospitality* (April 1950), 7; Fred Harvey Company, [Kansas City, Mo.], *El Navajo*[,] *Gallup, New Mexico*[,] *"the Heart of the Indian Empire,"* publication no. 4601 ([Kansas City, Mo.]: Fred Harvey, [1946]), folder, author's collection; Fred Harvey Company, [Kansas City, Mo.], *El Navajo Hotel* ([Kansas City, Mo.]: Fred Harvey, 1951), menu, Fred Harvey Company Collection, MS 280, series 3, box 3, folder 69; Noe, *Greetings from Gallup*, 56–61; Pepys, *Mine Host, America*, 181 (quotations); Poling-Kempes, *Harvey Girls*, 172–75; "Two Operations Closed—Newton Restaurant[,] El Navajo Hotel," *Hospitality* 9, no. 4 (May 1957): 9; Usner, *New Mexico Route 66*, 101–2.

57. "Attractive Ranch Kitchen Catching on in Farmington," *Albuquerque Journal*, October 18, 1953, p. 17; Bentley and Associates, [Albuquerque], "Auction[,] Commercial Real Estate and Restaurant Auction" (advertisement), *Albuquerque Journal*, December 14, 2005, sec. C, p. 7; Crocodile Lile, "The Prez Sez," *Old Route 66 Association of Texas Newsletter*, September 2005, pp. 1–2; Doug Mattson, "'Easterner-Turned-Cowboy' Dies from Parkinson's Disease Complications," *Santa Fe New Mexican*, July 13, 2004, sec. B, p. 1; "Notice of Dissolution," *Gallup Independent*, January 7, 1955, p. 7; J. V. Pigg, "Best Eats on 66," *Route 66 New Mexico* 10, no. 2 (Summer 2002): 11; J. V. Pigg, "Restaurant Review: The Ranch Kitchen, Doing It Right for 50 Years," *Route 66 New Mexico* 12, no. 2 (Summer 2004): 12–17 (quotation); Ranch Kitchen, Gallup, N.Mex., "The Ranch Kitchen" (advertisement), *Gallup Independent*, May 18, 1954, p. 5; Ranch Kitchen, *Ranch Kitchen*[,] *Indian Crafts*[,] *Welcome*[,] *Home Cooking* (Gallup, N.Mex.: Ranch Kitchen, [ca. 1996]), menu, author's collection; Ranch Kitchen, *The Ranch Kitchen*[,] *Thunderbird Motel*[,] *Gallup*[,] *New Mexico* (Gallup, N.Mex.: Ranch Kitchen, [ca. 1965]), menu, courtesy of Steve Rider; Thunderbird Lodge,

Gallup, N.Mex., "The Thunderbird Lodge and the Ranch Kitchen" (advertisement), *Gallup Independent*, August 1, 1954, p. 5.

58. Ida Bailey Allen, "4-H Club Changing Image," *Alton (Ill.) Evening Telegraph*, January 4, 1968, sec. B, p. 4; "Bitters Entertain at Navajo Dinner," *The San Juan Record* (Monticello, Utah), May 6, 1965, p. [4]; "Daniels Described as Friend of Indian in Shiprock Visits," *Albuquerque Journal*, October 24, 1972, sec. A, p. 13; Jen Miller, "Frybread: This Seemingly Simple Food Is a Complicated Symbol in Navajo Culture," *Smithsonian Magazine*, July 2008, http://www.smithsonianmag.com/arts-culture/frybread-79191/, accessed February 2, 2017; Schneider, *Route Sixty-Six Revisited*, 101; Arch Napier, "A Paleface Guide to Navajoland," *Los Angeles Times*, August 30, 1970, West Magazine supplement, pp. 25–26, 28–29; Ranch Kitchen, *"Navajo Tacos"* (Gallup, N.Mex.: George C. Hight, [ca. 1995]), postcard, author's collection; Ranch Kitchen, "Pauline Invites You to Try Our Navajo Taco" (advertisement), *Independent*, June 3, 1977, sec. 2, p. 7; Kent Ruth, "Navajo Scenes Changing," *Sunday Oklahoman* (Oklahoma City), October 9, 1966, Home and Leisure sec., p. 7; John Waliczek, "Gallup Lions Rated Tops," *Independent*, June 11, 1970, pp. 1, 8; Window Rock Lodge and Restaurant, Window Rock, Ariz., "Worth the Drive to Window Rock!" (advertisement), *Gallup Independent*, April 13, 1966, p. 4.

59. Ilf and Petrov, *Little Golden America*, 174; *New Mexico: A Guide to the Colorful State*, 327; "NM Sign Recalls Early Route 66 Passage," *Route 66 Magazine* 17, no. 4 (Fall 2010): 51; Nomination to the National Register of Historic Places for State Maintained Route 66: Manuelito to the Arizona Border, October 4, 1993; Repp, *Route 66: The Romance of the West*, 80–93; Rittenhouse, *Guide Book to Highway 66*, 89–92; Norman C. Wallace, "Some Hills along the Highways: Motoring through and over a Few of Arizona's Mountain Ranges," *Arizona Highways* 10, no. 6 (June 1934): 3–5, 21–22, 24–25.

CHAPTER 7. ARIZONA

1. *Arizona: A State Guide*, American Guide Series (New York: Hastings House, 1940), xix–xxi; Richard Mangum and Sherry Mangum, *Route 66 across Arizona: A Comprehensive Two-Way Guide for Touring Route 66* (Flagstaff: Hexagon Press, 2001), 4–110; Roger Naylor, *Arizona Kicks on Route 66* (Tucson: Rio Nuevo Publishers, 2011), 1–89; Nomination to the National Register of Historic Places for Historic US Route 66 in Arizona, August 2, 1988, this and subsequent nominations in Office of the Keeper, National Register of Historic Places, National Park Service, Washington, D.C.; Dallas Lore Sharp, *The Better Country* (Boston: Houghton Mifflin, 1928), 180–81 (quotations); C. K. Shepherd, *Across America by Motor-Cycle* (New York: Longmans, Green, 1922), 166–67; Anne Stephenson, "Family of the Mother Road: Fans of Route 66 Relive Highway's Glory Days," *Arizona Republic* (Phoenix), July 22, 1990, sec. E, pp. 1, 4.

2. Mary Bassent, "West to East on Route 66," *Roadsigns* (California Historic Route 66 Association) 2, no. 1 (January–February 1992): 10–11; Norman R. Martin, *Up on Route 66: A Time Remembered, Travelers along the Way, 1928 and Forward* (Searcy, Ark.: Martinian Press, 2000), 8; Armand Ortega, interview by David K. Dunaway, Gallup, N.Mex., June 28, 2007, typewritten transcript, 8–11, Route 66 Corridor Preservation Program, National Park Service, Santa Fe; Mark Pepys, *Mine Host, America* (London: Collins, 1937), 182–83; Irene Poindexter, "Irene Poindexter's Trip on Route 66 to California, in 1930," *Roadsigns* 2, no. 2 (March–April 1992): 9; Jack D. Rittenhouse, *A Guide Book to Highway 66* (Los Angeles: privately printed, 1946; repr., Albuquerque: University of New Mexico Press, 1989), 91–92; Oliver E. Rooker, *Riding the Travel Bureau: Ghost Riders Network on Route 66 during the Great Depression* (Canton, Okla.: Memoir Publishing, 1994), 48–49; Evelyn Tucker, "Diary—August 1938[,] Three Days on Highway 66 Tulsa to California," in *Memories on Route 66 1991* (Bethany: Oklahoma Route 66 Association, 1991), 75; "Westbound Traffic Stops at Lupton Station for Inspection against Diseased Plants," *Arizona Republic*, May 30, 1954, Arizona Days and Ways magazine, p. 33; "Western Tour Yields Interest to 18 Boys of Panhandle: Wonders of New Mexico and Arizona Viewed," *Amarillo (Tex.) Sunday News-Globe*, August 10, 1930, sec. 2, p. 5; William H. Windes, "Plant Control Inspection," *Arizona Highways* 13, no. 7 (July 1937): 12–13, 17–19.

3. Ron Dungan, "Navigating the Open Road during Jim Crow," *Arizona Republic*, February 21, 2016, sec. A, pp. 1, 14; Irv Logan, interview by Tom Peters, Springfield, Mo., March 13, 2015, audio recording and typewritten transcript, p. 25, Greater Springfield Route 66 Oral History Project, Special Collections, Meyer Library, Missouri State University, Springfield, Mo.; Frank Norris, "Courageous Motorists: African American Pioneers on Route 66," *New Mexico Historical Review* 90, no. 3 (Summer 2015): 298, 320–21; Johnny Otis, "Let's Talk," *Los Angeles Sentinel*, September 15, 1960, sec. A, p. 4 (quotation); Norma Jean Richards Yount, *Goldroad[,] Arizona[,] on Historic Route 66: The Golden Years 1937–1943*, 4th ed. (n.p.: Aardvark Global Publishing, 2009), 182–83. The "Negro Motorist Green Book" guides published by Victor H. Green from the 1930s to 1960s only started listing Arizona locations that welcomed Black customers in the 1950s and none are known that include any Route 66 eating places in Arizona. For an overview of auto travel for African Americans, see Gretchen Sorin, *Driving while Black: African American Travel and the Road to Civil Rights* (New York: Liveright Publishing, 2020).

4. *Arizona State Business Directory 1928* (Denver: Gazetteer Publishing and Printing, 1928), 246; George Baird, Lupton, Ariz., "For Sale—Lupton Café" (advertisement), *Gallup (N.Mex.) Independent*, April 12, 1947, p. 3; Charles J. Finger, *Adventure under Sapphire Skies* (New York: William Morrow, 1931), 165–68; E. A. Frick and Sons, Lupton, Ariz., "E. A. Frick and Sons" (advertisement), *Arizona Republic*, May 30, 1954, Arizona Days and Ways magazine, p. 33; Jim Hinckley, *Ghost Towns of Route 66* (Minneapolis: Voyageur Press, 2011), 116; W. R. Hutchins, "From Flagstaff, through Scenic Wonderland, to Arizona–New Mexico Boundary Line," *Arizona Highways* 2, no. 4 (April 1926): 9–10, 19 (quotation); Ellen Klinkel and Nick Gerlich, *A Matter of Time: Route 66 through the Lens of Change* (Norman: University of Oklahoma Press, 2019), 172–75; Ena Middleton, interview by David K. Dunaway, August 3, 2007, typewritten transcript, pp. 2–4, 7–8, 20–22, Route 66 Corridor Preservation Program, National Park Service, Santa Fe; Roger Naylor, "Trading Places: Frontier-Era Practices of Bartering Goods and Exchanging Customs Live On," *Arizona Republic*, September 6, 2014, sec. D, pp. 1, 6; Thomas Arthur Repp, *Route 66: The Romance of the West* (Lynwood, Wash.: Mock Turtle Press, 2002), 80–94; Rittenhouse, *Guide Book to Highway 66*, 92; Herb Tappenbeck and Ellen Tappenbeck, "The Way It Was on the Route," *Route 66 Federation News* 5, no. 4 (Autumn 1999): 17–20 (quotation); Tomahawk Trading Post, Lupton, Ariz., "The Tomahawk Trading Post" (advertisement), *Arizona Republic*, 30 May 1954, Arizona Days and Ways magazine, p. 32; Michael Karl Witzel, *Route 66 Remembered* (Osceola, Wisc.: MBI Publishing, 1996), 42, 168–70.

5. "Cassidy Ordered Held for Trial," *Tucson (Ariz.) Daily Citizen*, May 14, 1947, p. 1; Log Cabin Trading Post, Sanders, Ariz., "The Buried City" (advertisement), *Gallup Independent*, August 14, 1940, p. [4]; Bill Nixon, "Highway's Approach Routs Justice from Tiny Sanders," *Arizona Republic*, March 23, 1963, p. 17; Repp, *Route 66: The Romance of the West*, 95–113; Rittenhouse, *Guide Book to Highway 66*, 92–93; "Sanders-Chambers-Lupton: Area Abounds in Trading Posts, and Unique Open Pit Clay Mine," *Arizona Republic*, May 30, 1954, Arizona Days and Ways magazine, pp. 30–32; Mark Shaffer, "Your Essay Can Win Trading Post: Couple Struggle to Sell Property," *Arizona Republic*, December 27, 2004, sec. B, pp. 1, 9.

6. "Abandoned to Time," *Route Magazine*, February–March 2021, p. 48; E. A. Frick and Sons, "E. A. Frick and Sons," p. 33; "Flames Destroy Big Trading Post," *Arizona Republic*, August 11, 1942, sec. 2, p. 3; [Frontier West, Yellowstone National Park, Wyo.], *Fort Courage[,] Home of "F Troop[,]" Houck, Arizona* ([Yellowstone National Park, Wyo.: Frontier West, ca. 1970]), menu, courtesy of Steve Rider; Frontier West, Houck, Ariz., "General Maintenance Man" (advertisement), *Albuquerque (N.Mex.) Journal*, August 13, 1967, sec. H, p. 2; Repp, *Route 66: The Romance of the West*, 96; Rittenhouse, *Guide Book to Highway 66*, 92; "Robert B. 'Bill' Gipe," *Great Falls (Mont.) Tribune*, December 4, 1997, sec. M, p. 2; Tom Varner, "A Scorpion, a Horse, and a Hat Thief," *Route 66 Magazine* 26, no. 4 (Fall 2019): 12–13.

7. Edward D. Dunn, *Double-Crossing America by Motor: Routes and Ranches of the West* (New York: G. P. Putnam's Sons, 1933), 90; "Julia Miller, Apache County Figure, Dies," *Arizona Republic*, December 1, 1956, p. 31; Zilpha Pallister Main, *Come Travel along to South America and to Panama: A Sampler of Motor Trips Decades Apart* (Los Angeles: University Publishers, 1978), 27 (quotation); Lillian Makeda, "A Fly in the

Amber: Route 66 Architecture at Petrified Forest National Monument," *Buildings and Landscape: Journal of the Vernacular Architecture Forum* 17, no. 1 (Spring 2010): 63–65, 66–69; Mohawk Rubber Company, Akron, Ohio, *Guide No. 3*[,] *Mohawk Hobbs Grade and Surface Guide*[,] *Price 20¢*[,] *Santa Fe Trail Los Angeles-Denver*[,] *Western Division National Old Trails*, 4th ed., publication Hworow 30851 (Akron, Ohio: Mohawk Rubber Company, 1929), 21; "Pet Lion Batters Owner, He May Die," *Arizona Daily Star* (Tucson), July 24, 1931, p. 1; Charles J. Smith, "Petrified Forest National Monument," *Arizona Highways* 8, no. 12 (December 1932): 7–8, 26; Nomination to the National Register of Historic Places for Painted Desert Inn, Petrified Forest National Park, 1986; Repp, *Route 66: The Romance of the West*, 88, 107–8, 118–31.

8. Harold S. Colton and Frank C. Baxter, *Days in the Painted Desert and the San Francisco Mountains: A Guide*, Northern Arizona Society of Science and Art Bulletin no. 2 (Flagstaff: Museum of Northern Arizona, 1932), 28; Dunn, *Double-Crossing America*, 90–91; JoLynn Fox, "Holbrook, Arizona: The Early Years," *Route 66 Magazine* 20, no. 4 (Fall 2013): 32–35; Russell Olsen, "Then and Now: Holbrook, Arizona," *Route 66 Magazine* 12, no. 3 (Summer 2005): 20–21; *The Story of the Arizona Unit*[,] *U.S. Highway 66 Association*[,] *and a Roster of the Membership and Officers as of April 1st, 1949* (n.p.: Arizona Unit[,] U.S. Highway 66 Association, 1949), unpaged booklet, Special Collections, Cline Library, Northern Arizona University, Flagstaff; Tappenbeck and Tappenbeck, "The Way It Was," 19 (quotation); Harold C. Wayte Jr., "A History of Holbrook and the Little Colorado Country (1540–1962)" (master's thesis, University of Arizona, 1962), 248–308, 326; "What the Folks Are Thinking about—in Holbrook, Arizona," *Collier's* 71, no. 18 (May 5, 1923): 23.

9. "Aurelia B. Tafoya," *Arizona Republic*, November 15, 1990, sec. B, p. 15; Jane Bernard and Polly Brown, *American Route 66: Home on the Range* (Santa Fe: Museum of New Mexico Press, 2003), 131; "Forest Unit Maps Plans," *Arizona Republic*, September 6, 1947, p. 13; "Fuchs Heads HHH Group," *Arizona Republic*, October 5, 1968, p. 8; Steve Gallegos interview by T. Lindsay Baker, Holbrook, Ariz,, July 28, 2015, manuscript notes (quotation), author's collection; William Kaszynski, *Route 66: Images of America's Main Street* (Jefferson, N.C.: McFarland, 2003), 115; "Over 300 Attend Montoya Family Reunion," *Holbrook Tribune-News and Snowflake Herald* (Holbrook, Ariz.), August 28, 1975, p. 3; Rick Paul, "In Search of Route 66: 'The Main Street of America' Is Hip Again, but What's All the Fuss about, Anyway?," *Motor Trend* 45, no. 7 (July 1993): 74–78; "Thomas Smithson," *Arizona Daily Sun* (Flagstaff), March 3, 2006, sec. A, p. 2.

10. *Arizona State Business Directory 1928*, 425–28; *Business and Professional Directory of Arizona* (Phoenix: Arizona Directory Co., 1939), 285–89; Vada F. Carlson and Joe Rodriguez, *A Town Is Born: A Pictorial Review of Winslow, Arizona*[,] *First Fifty Years* (Winslow, Ariz.: County Printers, 1981), 137–62; Colton and Baxter, *Days in the Painted Desert*, 28; Rittenhouse, *Guide Book to Highway 66*, 97–98.

11. James Montgomery Flagg, *Boulevards All the Way—Maybe: Being an Artist's Truthful Impression of the U.S.A. from New York to California and Return, by Motor* (New York: George H. Doran, 1925), 123–31; Caroline Rittenberg, *Motor West* (New York: Harold Vinal, 1926), 40 (quotation); "Winslow Is Booming," *Arizona Republican*, July 7, 1897, p. 4.

12. Roger W. Birdseye, "La Posada Brings Harveycars to Winslow," *Winslow (Ariz.) Daily Mail*, June 2, 1930, La Posada supplement, pp. 2–3; Fred Harvey Company, [Kansas City, Mo.], *A Refreshing Oasis on the Way to and from Grand Canyon National Park: La Posada*[,] *Winslow*[,] *Arizona*, publication 4708 ([Kansas City, Mo.]: Fred Harvey, [1947]), folder, author's collection; Stephen Fried, *Appetite for America: Fred Harvey and the Business of Civilizing the Wild West—One Meal at a Time* (New York: Bantam Books, 2010), 321–23; C. L. Giragi, "Why 'La Posada'—The Finest on the Line," *Winslow Daily Mail*, 2 June 1930, La Posada supplement, p. 12; Janice Griffith, "La Posada Catered to Route 66 and Santa Fe Crowd," *Route 66 Magazine* 1, no. 1 (Winter 1993–94): 30–33; Gertrude Henson, "'La Posada[,]' a Typical Spanish Rancho," *Winslow Daily Mail*, June 2, 1930, La Posada supplement, pp. 1, 16–17; "La Posada—'The Resting Place,'" *Hospitality* (Fred Harvey Company), April 1949, unpaged; Elrond Lawrence, *Route 66 Railway: The Story of Route 66 and the Santa Fe Railway in the American Southwest* (Alhambra, Calif.: Los Angeles Railway Heritage Foundation, 2008), 108–9; Nomination to the National Register of Historic Places for La Posada

Historic District, Winslow, Ariz., February 20, 1992; Lesley Poling-Kempes, *The Harvey Girls: Women Who Opened the West* (Cambridge, Mass.: Da Capo Press, 1989), 65–68, 87, 189–90, 204–5, 206; "They Have Green Thumbs around La Posada," *Hospitality* 5, no. 4 (June 1953): 9.

13. Fred Harvey Company, [Kansas City, Mo.], *The Origin of the Term "Sub-Rosa" Signifying the Confidence of the Dinner Table* ([Kansas City, Mo.]: Fred Harvey, 1940), menu, Fred Harvey Company Collection, MS 208, series 3, box 1, folder 13, Special Collections and Archives, Cline Library, Northern Arizona University (hereafter Fred Harvey Company Collection); Janice Henling, "Being a Harvey Girl Was a Fulltime [*sic*] Job in Early Days," *Winslow (Ariz.) Mail*, March 31, 1995, Navajo County Centennial supplement, sec. C, p. 11 (quotation).

   American humorist Will Rogers occasionally passed through La Posada in travel by a short-lived air-and-train connection between California and New York, which, starting in 1929, used Santa Fe Railway sleeping cars at night and Transcontinental Air Transport aircraft landing at the Winslow airport during the day. From there in his May 12, 1931, newspaper column, Rogers lauded Fred Harvey for his contributions: "I reckon wild buffalo fed the early traveler in the West and for doing so they put his picture on a nickel. Well, Fred Harvey took up where the buffalo left off. For what he has done for the traveler one of his waitress' pictures with an arm load of ham and eggs should be placed on both sides of every dime." Neal Davis Sr., "The Lindberg Line," *Route 66 Magazine* 17, no. 2 (Spring 2010): 34–37; Will Rogers, "Will Rogers' Dispatch," *Boston Daily Globe*, May 13, 1931, p. 1 (quotation).

14. Don Dedera, "Good Morning! Winslow Mourns as Fred Harvey Café Bows out at End of an Era," *Arizona Republic*, December 2, 1956, sec. 2, p. 1; Rachel Fernandez, "Winslow Warriors," *Route Magazine* (December 2018–January 2019): 5–54; Fried, *Appetite for America*, 392, 398, 405–6; La Posada, Winslow, Ariz., *La Posada Hotel, Restaurant[,] Museum and Grounds—1930* (Winslow, Ariz.: La Posada, [ca. 2013]), 1–28, author's collection; Sam Lowe, "Rosy Outlook for Historic Harvey House: The La Posada," *Route 66 Magazine* 5, no. 2 (Spring 1998): 20–22; Poling-Kempes, *Harvey Girls*, 194–95; "Santa Fe Acquires Hotel in Winslow," *Arizona Daily Star*, September 16, 1960, sec. C, p. 7; Opal Singer, "World-famed La Posada Hotel in Winslow to Close up Shop This Thursday Midnight," *Arizona Daily Sun*, January 14, 1959, p. 1.

15. James Albert Davis, *From Coast to Coast via Auto and Tent* (Federalsburg, Md.: J. W. Stowell Printing Company, 1922), 40 (quotation); *Arizona State Business Directory 1929* (Denver: Gazetteer Publishing and Printing, 1929), 699.

16. *Arizona State Business Directory 1936* (Denver: Gazetteer Publishing and Printing, 1936), 655; Coney Island Café, Winslow, Ariz., "Drop in Anytime" (advertisement), *Winslow Mail*, April 13, 1934, p. 8 (second quotation); Coney Island Lunch Room, Winslow, Ariz., "Announcing the Opening of the Coney Island Lunch Room" (advertisement), *Winslow Daily Mail*, November 27, 1931, p. 3 (first quotation); "Coney Island White Café Opens Saturday," *Winslow Mail*, May 12, 1944, p. 3; "George T. Cheros," *Arizona Republic*, April 2, 1990, sec. B, p. 5; Thelma Bonney Hall, "Winslow Fines Bars as 40 Indians Jailed," *Arizona Republic*, May 11, 1954, p. 1; "Marriage of Winslow Man Is Announced," *Winslow Mail*, April 22, 1938, p. 2; "Officers Unable to Get Safe out of Clear Creek," *Arizona Daily Star*, December 13, 1953, sec. A, p. 9; Bob Thomas, "Family Keeps Famous Eatery Soaring High: Nostalgia on Menu in Winslow," *Arizona Republic*, April 26, 1992, sec. T, p. 2; Bob Thomas, "Touched by the Mother Road," *Route 66 Magazine* 1, no. 3 (Summer 1994): 6–7; White Café, Winslow, Ariz., "Merry Christmas" (advertisement), *Winslow Mail*, December 26, 1952, p. 11; White Coney Island Café, Winslow, Ariz., "The White Coney Island Café" (advertisement), *Winslow Mail*, May 12, 1944, p. 3.

17. "Building Here Shows Decline," *Winslow Mail*, January 25, 1957, pp. 1, 5; Falcon Restaurant and White Café, Winslow, Ariz., "Season's Greetings to All Our Friends and Patrons" (advertisement), *Winslow Mail*, December 23, 1955, p. [5]; "Falcon Restaurant Open for Business," *Winslow Mail*, July 15, 1955, p. 4; Falcon Restaurant, Winslow, Ariz., "Season's Greetings from the Falcon Restaurant" (advertisement), *Winslow Mail*, November 29, 1957, p. 7; "George N. Kretsedemas," *Arizona Republic*, September 5, 2018, p. 20; "Greek Orthodox Wedding Is Held for Yiota Lycouria and Nicholas Stathis October 9," *Winslow Mail*, October

14, 1955, p. 12; "Konstantina N. Kretsedemas," *Arizona Daily Sun*, April 2, 2004, sec. A, p. 2; Bob Moore, "The Falcon: Thirty-Seven Years and Still Doing It Right," *Mother Road Journal* (Lakewood, Colo.) no. 4 (April 1992): 17; "P. A. Kritsidimas, 85," *Arizona Daily Sun*, March 11, 1983, p. 2; "Panagiotis Kretsedemas," *Arizona Daily Sun*, December 22, 2010, sec. A, p. 2; "Personality of the Week: Peter Kretsedemas," *Winslow Mail*, April 10, 1975, p. 2; Mark Shaffer, "Rte. 66 Still Kickin': 66-Year-Old Trail's Adventures Recalled," *Arizona Republic*, May 11, 1992, sec. A, pp. 1–2 (quotations); Thomas, "Family Keeps Famous Eatery," sec. T, p. 2; Thomas, "Touched by the Mother Road," 6–7; "Winslow Hearing Set on Shift of La Posada Liquor License," *Arizona Daily Sun*, October 21, 1959, p. 10; "Winslow Man Hurt in Auto Accident," *Arizona Daily Sun*, June 12, 1956, p. 4; "Winslow News: Rotary Hears Restauranteur [*sic*], Sees Film about Development," *Arizona Daily Sun*, February 15, 1960, p. 10.

18. "Burglars Enter Filling Station," *Arizona Republic*, October 11, 1936, sec. 2, p. 2; "Cattle Theft Cases against 'Rimmy Jim' Giddings and Dave Joy Are Dismissed," *Coconino Sun* (Flagstaff), February 21, 1919, pp. 1, 6; "Charles Harp Takes over Rimmy Jim's," *Winslow Mail*, November 26, 1943, p. 1; Platt Cline, "News and Views: More Sketches of Our Flagstaff Fire Boys," *Arizona Daily Sun*, August 3, 1977, p. 4; Jerry Kammer, "A Life from Post to Post," *Arizona Republic*, June 3, 1979, Arizona supplement, pp. 12, 14; Jerry McLain, "Oddities in Arizona's News," *Arizona Republic*, October 16, 1938, sec. 2, p. 1; Martin, *Up on Route 66*, 26–27; Repp, *Route 66: The Romance of the West*, 148–57; "'Rimmy Jim' Giddings Is Heart Victim," *Winslow Mail*, June 25, 1943, p. 1; Rimmy Jim's Trading Post, Winslow, Ariz., "At Meteor Crater Junction" (advertisement), *Arizona Republic*, August 17, 1952, sec. 5, p. 5; Rittenhouse, *Guide Book to Highway 66*, 99; Paul Schweitzer, "Sunlight on Sports," *Arizona Daily Sun*, September 29, 1976, p. 7; "Sid Griffin Badly Hurt in Mishap," *Arizona Daily Sun*, July 2, 1966, p. 2; "'Sid' Griffin, 77, Dies," *Arizona Daily Sun*, November 11, 1987, p. 2; Tom Snyder, *Route 66, Pioneering Highway: Stories from the Road* (n.p.: U.S. Route 66 Association, 1992), 19–20; Clay Thompson, "Cowboy Rimmy Jim and the Case of His Missing Roadside Stop," *Arizona Republic*, March 9, 2008, sec. B, p. 8; Witzel, *Route 66 Remembered*, 24–25.

19. *Arizona: A State Guide*, 187–92, 315–19; Colton and Baxter, *Days in the Painted Desert*, 28–29; James E. Cook, "We Called Ourselves the Joy Boys," in *Route 66 Remembered* by Michael Karl Witzel (Osceola, Wisc.: MBI Publishing, 1996), 164–67 (quotations); "Flagstaff, Pinnacle City of Wonders, Where Winter Plays with Summer," *Arizona Highways* 4, no. 6 (June 1928): 19, 45; Hutchins, "From Flagstaff, through Scenic Wonderland," 9–10, 19; Mangum and Mangum, *Route 66 across Arizona*, 21–26, 79–84; Rittenhouse, *Guide Book to Highway 66*, 99–102. For a view of Flagstaff from the perspective of a child in an impoverished migrant family in the mid-1930s, see Louella Murphy, *Thumbs Up: A Child[']s Journey on Route 66* (n.p.: privately printed, 2019), 33–68.

20. Dean Eldredge Museum, Flagstaff, "Deer Heads and All Other Trophies of the Hunt Mounted True to Life" (advertisement), *Williams(Ariz.) News*, October 17, 1930, p. 3; "Dean M. Eldredge," *Wausau (Wisc.) Daily Record-Herald*, May 19, 1937, p. 4; Bonnie Holmes, "The Museum Club," *Route 66 Magazine* 8, no. 1 (Winter 2000–2001): 28–30; Nomination to the National Register of Historic Places for the Dean Eldredge Museum, Flagstaff, March 9, 1994; Russell Olsen, "Then and Now: Dean Eldredge Museum and Taxidermy AKA: The Museum Club," *Route 66 Magazine* 14, no. 1 (Winter 2006–7): 20–21; Jim Ross, *Route 66 Crossings: Historic Bridges of the Mother Road* (Norman: University of Oklahoma Press, 2016), 80, 109–10, 137; Snyder, *Route 66, Pioneering Highway*, 15–16.

21. Barker Village Museum Club, Flagstaff, "Come One . . . Come All . . . Tonight, Tomorrow, Any Night" (advertisement), *Arizona Daily Sun*, October 29, 1947, p. 5; Bill Cameron, "Doc Williams Has Been Making Saddles for Cowpokes Ever Since Spanish-American War," *Arizona Daily Sun*, January 27, 1949, p. 2; Doc Williams' Museum Club, Flagstaff, "We Dance 5 Nites" (advertisement), *Arizona Republic*, July 4, 1937, sec. A, p. 2; "Don Scott Sehulster, 62," *Arizona Daily Sun*, February 13, 1975, p. 14; Frank's Museum Club, Flagstaff, "Frank's Museum Club—Flagstaff" (advertisement), *Arizona Republic*, May 27, 1945, sec. 2, p. 7; "Gracie Cooney Added to Museum Club Show," *Arizona Daily Sun*, January 21, 1947, p. 6; Sam Lowe, "66 Reasons Flag Loves the 'Zoo,'" *Arizona Republic*, January 27, 1997, sec. C, pp. 1–2; Hal Mattern,

"High-country Clubs," *Arizona Republic*, August 4, 1991, sec. F, pp. 1, 4; Museum Club, Flagstaff, "Appearing Tonight One Nite Only Hank Thompson with his Brazos Valley Boys" (advertisement), *Arizona Daily Sun*, January 7, 1971, p. 2; Museum Club, "Flagstaff's 'Nashville, Arizona'" (advertisement), *Arizona Daily Sun*, July 1, 1974, Pow Wow supplement, p. 3; Museum Club, "For Your Dining and Dancing Pleasure" (advertisement), *Arizona Daily Sun*, September 23, 1947, p. 6; "Museum Club Reopens Tonight," *Arizona Daily Sun*, April 11, 1977, p. 12; Nomination to the National Register of Historic Places for the Dean Eldredge Museum, Flagstaff, March 9, 1994; "Pathways of Memories," *Arizona Daily Sun*, November 12, 1987, p. 2; "Pathways of Old Memories," *Arizona Daily Sun*, March 13, 1957, p. 4; May 2, 1957, p. 4; "Pathways of Old Memories (from the Files of the *Sun*)," *Arizona Daily Sun*, February 26, 1947, p. 2; Quirk's Museum Club, Flagstaff, "Quirk's Museum Club" (advertisement), *Arizona Daily Sun*, January 21, 1947, p. 4; Christina Stephens, "Club Hot Spot Highlights Route 66," *Arizona Daily Sun*, April 1, 1995, p. 5; Jacquie Villa, "Car and Driver Features Unique Flagstaff Roadhouse," *Arizona Daily Star*, April 12, 1992, sec. H, p. 3.

22. Suzanne Adams-Ockrassa, "New Owners Call It Quits: Bare Winter, Wage Hike, New Food Too Much All at Once," *Arizona Daily Sun*, June 14, 2018, sec. A, pp. 1, 10; "Albert D. Wong," *Arizona Daily Sun*, June 8, 1995, p. 2; "Alfred Wong, 74," *Arizona Daily Sun*, February 5, 1986, p. 3; "Edward F. Wong Dies Here at 60," *Arizona Daily Sun*, May 4, 1966, p. 2; "Gourmet Corner," *Arizona Daily Sun*, February 2, 1962, Entertainment Roundup sec., p. 8; Grand Canyon Café, Flagstaff, "Grand Opening of the Grand Canyon Café" (advertisement), *Arizona Daily Sun*, March 14, 1950, p. 7 (quotation); Maury Herman, "The Building at 112 East Route 66," *Arizona Daily Sun*, April 15, 1994, Flagstaff's First Century supplement, sec. A, p. 39; "Negro Soldier Killed during Flagstaff Row," *Tucson Daily Citizen*, July 11, 1942, pp. 1, 11; "Newly Remodelled [*sic*] Café Announces Opening Today," *Arizona Daily Sun*, March 14, 1950, p. 7; "Pathways of Old Memories (from the Files of the *Sun*)," *Arizona Daily Sun*, March 1, 1949, p. 2; April 7, 1952, p. 4; August 4, 1952, p. 2; "Stove on Wooden Floor Starts Fire in Café Tuesday," *Arizona Daily Sun*, July 5, 1950, p. 2; Corina Vanek, "GC Café Owners Pick Local Buyers: Two Husband-wife Teams to Keep Charm," *Arizona Daily Sun*, September 4, 2016, sec. A, pp. 1, 10; Corina Vanek, "Grand Canyon Café Reopens with New Owners, Same Feeling," *Arizona Daily Sun*, July 16, 2017, sec. C, pp. 1–2; John S. Westerlund, *Arizona's War Town: Flagstaff, Navajo Ordnance Depot, and World War II* (Tucson: University of Arizona Press, 2003), 205–6; John S. Westerlund, "In a War Town, a Soldier Dies," *Arizona Daily Sun*, May 24, 2015, sec. A, pp. 1, 9; "William (Bill) Yee," *Arizona Daily Sun*, July 3, 2015, sec. A, p. 4; "William J. Dokos, 81," *Arizona Daily Sun*, May 16, 1978, p. 3. For comprehensive overviews of Chinese restaurants in the United States, placing the Grand Canyon Café into broader context, see Haiming Liu, *From Canton Restaurant to Panda Express: A History of Chinese Food in America* (New Brunswick, N.J.: Rutgers University Press, 2005) and Anne Mendelson, *Chow Chop Suey: Food and the Chinese American Journey* (New York: Columbia University Press, 2016).

23. "Downtown Café to Be Part of Documentary," *Arizona Daily Sun*, February 22, 2013, sec. B, p. 4; "Julia Ann Sartor," *Arizona Daily Sun*, January 21, 2000, p. 2; Malcolm Mackey, "More Tales of a Flagstaff Institution," *Arizona Daily Sun*, April 27, 2013, sec. A, p. 6 (quotation); Roger Naylor, "Get Dining Kicks on Route 66," *Arizona Republic*. April 3, 2011, sec. E, pp. 3, 5; Dana Prom Smith, "The Grand Canyon Café," *Arizona Daily Sun*, April 13, 2013, sec. A, p. 8; Paul Sweitzer, "Farewell to a Tough-as-Nails Waitress," *Arizona Daily Sun*, January 28, 2000, p. 2; Al Wheelock, "Showing Thanks," *Arizona Daily Sun*, December 8, 1982, p. 4.

24. Susannah Carney, "Flagstaff History," *Arizona Daily Sun*, December 2, 2018, sec. A, p. 8; Susan Eberle, "Ordnance News," *Arizona Daily Sun*, October 17, 1946, p. 4; "Miss Rachel Apodaca and Louis DeMiguel Jr. Wed in Fall Rites Here," *Arizona Daily Sun*, October 21, 1946, p. 3; "Pathways of Memories," *Arizona Daily Sun*, October 6, 1992, p. 4; "Pathways of Old Memories," *Arizona Daily Sun*, January 11, 1955, p. 5; "Purely Personal," *Arizona Daily Sun*, November 19, 1952, p. 3; Jackie Richard, "A Family Effort at Nena's Led to These Recipes," *San Bernardino County (Calif.) Sun*, December 11, 1983, sec. E, p. 2; "Society," *Arizona Daily Sun*, September 21, 1948, p. 5; Spanish Inn, Flagstaff, "Enchiladas[,] Tacos],] Tamales],] Tostados by the Dozen" (advertisement), *Arizona Daily Sun*, March 24, 1947, p. 6; Spanish Inn, "Special

Friday and Saturday" (advertisement), *Arizona Daily Sun*, March 28, 1947, p. 3; April 11, 1947, p. 8; April 18, 1947, p. 4; "Spanish Inn Reopens Next Monday Evening," *Arizona Daily Sun*, October 24, 1946, p. 2.

25. Jane Lloyd, "Ernest A. Castro Retires after 32 Years of Teaching," *Arizona Daily Sun*, May 18, 1977, p. 6; Spanish Inn, "Our Appreciation" (advertisement), *Arizona Daily Sun*, July 10, 1952, p. 8; Spanish Inn, "Spanish Inn Now under Management of Mrs. Ernest Castro" (advertisement), *Arizona Daily Sun*, July 10, 1951, p. 8; Spanish Inn,, "The Spanish Inn Open for Business" (advertisement), *Arizona Daily Sun*, February 5, 1954, p. 8; Spanish Inn, "Under New Management" (advertisement), *Arizona Daily Sun*, April 30, 1953, p. 6.

26. Bob Boze Bell, *The 66 Kid Raised on the Mother Road* (Minneapolis: Voyageur Press, 2014), 139 (second and third quotations); Betsey Bruner, "Keeping It in the Family: Southside Stalwarts Gilbert and Carlotta Montoya Pass the Torch at the 55-Year-Old El Charro Café to Daughter Petra," *Arizona Daily Sun*, July 25, 2011, sec. A, pp. 1, 6; Elias Butler, "Good Food, Great Music at El Charro Café," *Arizona Daily Sun*, August 26, 1999, sec. A, pp. 6, 19; Kathy Lozania (Castillo), "Earlier Generation Built El Charro," *Arizona Daily Sun*, October 27, 2013, sec. A, p. 4; "Clara M. Castillo," *Arizona Daily Sun*, January 16, 1991, p. 3; "Coconino Daily Record," *Arizona Daily Sun*, January 22, 1963, p. 2; "D. B. Castillo Funeral Mass Said Monday," *El Paso (Tex.) Times*, September 23, 1970, sec. B, p. 5; El Charro Café, Flagstaff, "Announcement" (advertisement), *Arizona Daily Sun*, April 16, 1948, p. 3; El Charro Café, "Beginning April 14th" (advertisement), *Arizona Daily Sun*, April 5, 1958, p. 2; El Charro Restaurant, Flagstaff, "Grand Opening" (advertisement), *Arizona Daily Sun*, March 2, 1966, p. 7; El Charro Café, "Spanish and American Dishes Served Here" (advertisement), *Arizona Daily Sun*, August 5, 1946, p. 4 (first quotation); Sally Evans, "El Charro Restaurant Will Be Missed," *Arizona Daily Sun*, September 22, 2013, sec. A, p. 4; "Five Weekend Blazes Keep Firemen Hopping," *Arizona Daily Sun*, November 29, 1965, p. 1; "For Fine Mexican Food," *Arizona Daily Sun*, January 24, 1975, sec. B, p. 6; "Gilbert Lomeli Montoya," *Arizona Daily Sun*, October 14, 2012, sec. A, p. 2; "Local Café's Transfer to New Owner Told," *Arizona Daily Sun*, January 20, 1948, p. 4; Marie Remiss, "Northland Neighbors: Church, El Charro Dan Castillo's Interests," *Arizona Daily Sun*, May 31, 1960, p. 8; Spanish Inn, "Change of Name" (advertisement), *Arizona Daily Sun*, December 19, 1956, p. 6; Spanish Inn, "Grand Opening of the Spanish Inn" (advertisement), *Arizona Daily Sun*, May 25, 1956, p. 5.

27. "Flagstaff Paving Will Be Started," *Arizona Republic*, March 24, 1940, sec. 2, p. 2; "Modern Engineering along Arizona Highways," *Arizona Highways* 12, no. 5 (June 1936), 11; "New Flagstaff Underpass to Open for Two-way Traffic on Saturday," *Arizona Daily Sun*, September 5, 1958, p. 1; "$248,596 Bid for Underpass," *Arizona Daily Sun*, November 14, 1957, p. 1.

28. Betsey Bruner, "An Independent Spirit Behaves Herself at 100 Years Old," *Arizona Daily Sun*, February 5, 2006, sec. C, p. 5; "Café Here Sold to Couple from Williams," *Arizona Daily Sun*, June 4, 1956, p. 3; "$50,000 Dining Place Open to Public Thurs.," *Arizona Daily Sun*, October 1, 1946, p. 7 (first quotation); "Former Flagstaff Business Owner, Booster Souris Dies," *Arizona Daily Sun*, December 20, 1987, p. 2; "GOP Candidates Here for Rally," *Arizona Daily Sun*, October 2, 1956, p. 3; "Notice of Sale in Bulk," *Arizona Daily Sun*, October 24, 1959, p. 10; "Pathways of Memories," *Arizona Daily Sun*, December 19, 1988, p. 18; Sportsman's Steak House, Flagstaff, "To Our Many Friends and Patrons" (advertisement), *Arizona Daily Sun*, February 19, 1957, p. 3; Paul Sweitzer, "Harvey's Girls Get Together," *Arizona Daily Sun*, October 22, 1993, p. 2; Tony's Steak House, Flagstaff, "For Consistently Good Food" (advertisement), *Arizona Daily Sun*, October 25, 1946, p. 7 (second quotation); Tony's Steak House, "Now . . . Ready for You . . . Northern Arizona's Finest Dining Establishment" (advertisement), *Arizona Daily Sun*, October 1, 1946, p. 5.

29. "Articles of Incorporation of Lumberjack Café, Inc.," *Arizona Daily Sun*, August 21, 1965, p. 5; "Big Hunk of Man!," *Arizona Daily Sun*, June 18, 1963, p. 3; "Bob Morison, Operator of the Lumberjack Café," *Arizona Daily Sun*, May 27, 1963, p. 5; "Bronc's Beat," *Arizona Daily Sun*, May 13, 1966, Northlander supplement, p. 2; Brian Butko and Sarah Butko, *Roadside Giants* (Mechanicsburg, Pa.: Stackpole Books, 2005), 15–16; Abbie Gripman, "Around Town: Last Chance at a Treasure from the Closet," *Arizona Daily Sun*, April 27, 2017, sec. A, p. 2; John Kofton, "My Girl Lou: The Roads We've Been on, Have You Been There Too?," *Roadsigns* (Winter–Spring 2003), p. 13 (quotation); Lumberjack Café, Flagstaff, "For Your Dining Pleasure"

(advertisement), *Arizona Daily Sun*, December 4, 1959, TV and Entertainment Round-Up supplement, p. [3]; Lumberjack Café, *Lumberjack Café[,] Flagstaff, Arizona* (Flagstaff: Northland Press, [ca. 1965]), menu, courtesy of Steven Rider; Lumberjack Café, "Something New! Something Different! Our Big Special $1.66 Dinners" (advertisement), *Arizona Daily Sun*, December 6, 1963, p. 3; "Paul Creates a Problem," *Arizona State College Lumberjack* (Flagstaff), September 24, 1963, p. 3; "Robert O. Morison," *Arizona Daily Sun*, September 10, 1985, p. 2.

30. Suzanne Adams-Ockrassa, "Face of Route 66 Changing," *Arizona Daily Sun*, September 17, 2017, sec. A, pp. 1, 5; "Frank (Ferdinando) Zanzucchi," *Arizona Republic*, October 12, 2003, sec. B, p. 6; "Fun Stored in Granny's Closet," *Arizona Daily Sun*, December 6, 1974, sec. B, p. 10; Nick Gerlich, "American Giants," *Route Magazine*, December–January 2021, pp. 44–60; "Granny's Closet Closed," *Arizona Daily Sun*, November 16, 2016, sec. A, pp. 1, 7; Granny's Closet, Flagstaff, "Granny's Closet Now Open!" (advertisement), *Arizona Daily Sun*, October 24, 1974, p. 3; "Guardians of Flagstaff," *Route Magazine*, December–January 2021, p. 42; Connie Cone Sexton, "Flagstaff Milkman Zanzucchi Leaves Legacy of Diligence," *Arizona Republic*, February 22, 2004, sec. B, p. 10; Jan Stevens, "Making Pies Sure Beats Milking Cows," *Arizona Daily Sun*, March 1, 1994, p. 14; "The Story of the Famous Lumberjacks," *Arizona Daily Sun*, August 28, 1996, sec. B, p. 2.

31. B. M. Atwood, "From Ash Fork over the Arizona Divide to Flagstaff and the Snow Capped Peaks of the San Francisco Mountains," *Arizona Highways* 2, no. 3 (March 1926): 12–15; Colton and Baxter, *Days in the Painted Desert*, 29–30; James R. Fuchs, *A History of Williams, Arizona 1876–1951*, Social Science Bulletin 23, University of Arizona Bulletin 24, no. 5 (Tucson: University of Arizona, 1955): 124–26, 145–46, 155–56; Pepys, *Mine Host, America*, 195–96; Jack Raymer, "Boy Scouts' Trip to the Grand Canyon, Arizona," *Eagle Rock Reporter-Sentinel* (Los Angeles), May 2, 1930, p. 2, and May 9, 1930, p. 2; Steve Rider, "October 13, 1984[,] Revisited," *Route 66 Federation News* 20, no. 3 (Summer 2014): 27–33; Tom Teague, *Searching for 66* (Springfield, Ill.: Samizdat House, 1991), 176–79; Town of Williams, Ariz., "Let's Give the Tourist Parking Space" (advertisement), *Williams News*, April 17, 1947, p. 8; Michael Wallis, *Route 66: The Mother Road* (New York: St Martin's Press, 1990), 196–97.

32. American Automobile Association, *Western Tour Book* (Washington, D.C.: American Automobile Association, 1940), 23; "California Limited Makes Meal Stops Again!" *Hospitality* (April 1950), 7; "Close Hotel and Other Units," *Hospitality* 6, no. 1 (April 1954), p. 5; "Fray Marcos Fills Community Need," *Williams News*, November 21, 1963, sec. 3, p. 1; "Fray Marcos to Be Closed This Sunday, January 31," *Williams News*, January 28, 1954, pp. 1, 7; "The Grand Canyon: Santa Fe Is Rushing Work on the New Line to the Great Gorge," *Williams News*, August 10, 1901, p. 2; "Hotel Fray Marcos Open," *Williams News*, March 14, 1908, p. 1 (first quotation); Al Richmond, "Harvey Girls Brought Touch of Class to Western Travelers on the Santa Fe," *Route 66 Magazine* 1, no. 2 (Spring 1994): 6–7; Irene M. Roberti, "A-Traveling We Did Go," typescript in travel scrapbook, July 12-August 27, 1941, unpaged (second quotation), author's collection; "Stopping at the Fray Marcos," *Hospitality* (April 1950), p. 15; Scott Walters, "Grand Decade on the Rails: After 10 Years of Trial and Error, Grand Canyon Railway Has Found a Smooth Line," *Arizona Daily Sun*, November 7, 1999, pp. 23–24.

33. Marian Clark, "Rod's Steak House," *Route 66 Federation News* 4, no. 3 (Summer 2000): 13–14; "Cowboy Bosses Famous Eating House," *Williams News*, March 22, 1956, sec. 2, p. 3; "Grand Canyon Tavern Changes Ownership," *Williams News*, June 29, 1939, p. 1; "Helen E. Graves," *Arizona Daily Sun*, April 4, 2006, sec. A, p. 2; Kaszynski, *Route 66*, 122–24; "Notice of Sale in Bulk," *Williams News*, November 29, 1945, p. 6; "Rod Graves Lauded by Laredo Writer," *Williams News*, October 23, 1952, p. 3; "Rod's Steak House Builds Reputation throughout Country as One of Southwest's Best," *Williams News*, August 12, 1948, pp. 1, 8 (quotation); Rod's Steak House, Williams, Ariz., *Rod's Steak House[,] Williams, Arizona[,] "Gateway to the Grand Canyon"* (Flagstaff: Rod's Steak House, [ca. 1950]), menu, author's collection; Lawrence Sanchez and Stella Sanchez, interview by David King Dunaway, August 2, 2007, typewritten transcript, p. 25, Route 66 Corridor Preservation Program, National Park Service, Santa Fe; "Successful Opening of Rod's

Steak House," *Williams News*, August 29, 1946, p. 1; "Walls Going up for Graves' Steak House," *Williams News*, April 11, 1946, p. 10; Frances Esther Wells, "Along the Avenue," *Williams News*, September 19, 1946, pp. 1, 5, and October 2, 1947, p. 1.

34. "Bubbling Brew Balm or Bane; Solons Seeking Soothing Sip," *Arizona Daily Star*, March 24, 1933, p. 1; "'Casey at the Bat,'" *Williams News*, May 11, 1967, p. 7; "Charles Proctor Plays Big Part in Wms. Progress," *Williams News*, November 21, 1963, sec. 3, p. 8; "City Hall Is to Be Very Much Enlarged," *Williams News*, January 9, 1931, p. 2; "Famous Sultana Featured in Beverage Journal," *Williams News*, July 10, 1952, pp. 1, 3; "Final Rites Held for Raymond (Gov.) Mowrey," *Williams News*, June 21, 1973, pp. 1, 6; "Frank G. Satrustegui," *Arizona Daily Sun*, June 9, 1988, p. 2; "Joe McDonald Killed While Making Arrest," *Williams News*, April 17, 1947, pp. 1, 8; "Legal Beer Goes on Sale Today," *Williams News*, April 7, 1933, pp. 1, 5; "Local Sultana Bar and Buffet Leased," *Williams News*, January 6, 1938, p. 1; "Mrs. John Rogers Opens Delicatessen in Williams," *Williams News*, May 1, 1931, p. 6; Roger Naylor, "Spirited Finish: Toast to Summer's End with These 10 Road Trips," *Arizona Republic*, August 17, 2019, sec. C, p. 3; David G. Price, "Along the Avenue," *Williams News*, August 24, 1950, pp. 1, 3; "Rolla M. Reese Former Williams Resident Dies," *Williams News*, December 21, 1967, p. [5]; W. J. Rorabaugh, *Prohibition: A Very Short Introduction* (New York: Oxford University Press, 2018), 106; Joe Sonderman and Jim Hinckley, *Route 66 Roadside Signs and Advertisements* (Minneapolis: Voyageur Press, 2016), 120; "Sultana Buffet Pleases Folks for Many Years in Williams," *Williams News*, December 1, 1938, p. 3; "Sultana Buffet Refurnishes Interior," *Williams News*, October 23, 1941, p. 1; "Sultana Building Provides Entertainment, Office Rooms," *Williams News*, March 22, 1956, sec. 3, p. 12; "The Sultana Opera House," *Williams News*, November 9, 1912, p. 1; "Sultana Proprietor to Take Rest," *Williams News*, November 8, 1945, p. 1; "Unique Watering Holes Draw the Curious," *Arizona Republic*, December 5, 2004, sec. T, p. 10; "Welcome to New Sunny Home of Williams Weekly News on Bill Williams Avenue," *Williams News*, July 19, 1913, p. 1 (quotation).

35. Atwood, "From Ash Fork over the Arizona Divide," 12–14; James E. Cook, "Mile for Mile, America's 'Main Street' Was a Dull Route," *Arizona Republic*, April 12, 1987, sec. B, p. 4 (quotations); Douglas E. Kupel, "Ash Fork: Transportation and Town-building in Northern Arizona," *Journal of Arizona History* 39, no. 2 (Summer 1998): 155–74; Rittenhouse, *Guide Book to Highway 66*, 104; Michael Karl Witzel and Gyvel Young-Witzel, *Legendary Route 66: A Journey through Time along America's Mother Road* (Minneapolis: Voyageur Press, 2007), 202–5.

36. Centennial Committee '82, *Ash Fork, Arizona[,] 1882–1982: A Pictorial History* (n.p., 1982), 9–11; Joie Davidson, "Ash Fork Harvey 'Boy' Retires after 42 Years of Service," *Arizona Republic*, May 21, 1950, sec. 2, p. 1; Fred Harvey [Company, Kansas City, Mo.], *Lunch Room Service[,] Luncheon[,] Hotel Escalante[,] Ash Fork, Ariz.[,] Aug. 29, 1940* ([Kansas City, Mo.]: Fred Harvey, 1940), menu, typewritten on preprinted cardstock, Fred Harvey Company Collection, MS 208, series 3, box 1, folder 1; "Harvey House Building Now Pile of Rubble," *Williams News*, October 18, 1973, p. [3]; Larry Hendricks, "Museum Tells Ash Fork's History," *Arizona Daily Sun*, July 24, 2012, sec. A, pp. 1, 6; Kupel, "Ash Fork," 158, 161, 165, 169–70; Vernon McGill, *Diary of a Motor Journey from Chicago to Los Angeles* (Los Angeles: Grafton Publishing, 1922), 80 (second quotation); "Magnificent Hotel for Ash Fork," *Weekly Arizona Journal-Miner* (Prescott, Ariz.), November 15, 1905, p. 5; Ralph Mahoney, "Ash Fork's Flagstone Rates High on Market," *Arizona Republic*, Arizona Days and Ways magazine, pp. 16, 19–20; "Newsstand and Rooms at Ash Fork Closed," *Hospitality* 5, no. 4 (June 1953), p. 9; Poling-Kempes, *Harvey Girls*, 204–5; "President E. P. Ripley," *Williams News*, October 20, 1906, p. [2]; Santa Fe, [Prescott and Phoenix Railway, Phoenix], "Travel Sense" (advertisement), *Arizona Republic*, April 11, 1907, p. 7; Jeanie Lippitt Weeden, *Rhode Island to California by Motor: September–October, 1916* (Santa Barbara: Pacific Coast Publishing, [1917]), 32, 34 (first quotation).

37. Guy K. Austin, *Covered Wagon, 10 H.P.: Being the Further Adventures of an English Family in Its Travels across America* (London: Geoffrey Bles, 1936), 93–103; Bernard and Brown, *American Route 66*, 140 (third and fourth quotations); W. C. Clark, *Touring the West with Leaping Lena, 1925*, ed. David Dary (Norman: University of Oklahoma Press, 2016), 229–30 (first and second quotations); Angel Delgadillo, interview by

Sean Evans, Seligman, Ariz., February 19, 2007, audio interview and unpaged typewritten transcript, NAU. OH.2006.115.3, item 78541, Special Collections and Archives, Cline Library, Northern Arizona University, http://archive.library.nau.edu/cdm,ref,collection/cpa/id/64446, accessed January 27, 2015; Gertrude E. Metcalfe-Shaw, *English Caravanners in the Wild West: The Old Pioneers' Trail* (Edinburgh, Scotland: William Blackwood and Sons, 1926), 86–87; Nomination to the National Register of Historic Places for Seligman Commercial Historic District, November 2004; Rittenhouse, *Guide Book to Highway 66*, 104–5; Fred Smith, "Quiet Seligman Outlives Its Epitaphs," *Arizona Republic*, February 21, 1988, sec. MS, p. 36.

38. T. Lindsay Baker, "Overnite at the Seligman Havasu Hotel," *Route 66 Magazine* 26, no. 4 (Fall 2019): 18–20; Jim Belshaw, "An Old Flame Still Flickers," *Albuquerque Journal*, August 6, 1991, sec. B, p. 1; Robert J. Farrell, "Route 66: The Melody Lingers On," *Arizona Highways* 64, no. 3 (March 1988): 37; "Fred Harvey Hotel Billboard," photograph NAU.PH.95.44.59.2, Special Collections and Archives, Cline Library, Northern Arizona University (first and second quotations); Fred Harvey Company, [Kansas City, Mo.], *Seligman, Arizona*[,] *Passengers Will Receive Ample Notice before Departure of Train*[,] *Breakfast* ([Kansas City, Mo.]: Fred Harvey, [ca. 1945]), menu, typewritten on preprinted cardstock, Fred Harvey Company Collection, MS 208, series 3, box 1, folder 1; "Harvey's Closed in Seligman," *Arizona Republic*, November 14, 1954, sec. 3, p. 15; Lee Griffin, "Letters," *Route 66 News* (Historic Route 66 Association of Arizona), Fall 1998, p. 8 (third quotation); Henling, "Being a Harvey Girl," sec. C, p. 11; Mohawk Rubber Company, *Guide No. 3*, 18 (fourth quotation); Sonu Munshi, "Protecting the Past: Seligman Residents Try to Save the Town's Historic, Decaying Harvey Hotel," *Arizona Daily Sun*, November 3, 2007, sec. A, pp. 1, 8; National Register of Historic Places Nomination for Seligman Commercial Historic District; Poling-Kempes, *Harvey* Girls, 96; "Saying Goodbye to Another Route 66 Icon," *Route 66 East to West* (Historic Route 66 Association of Arizona) no. 3 (2008): 19–20; Bob Thomas, "Hostesses Helped Tame Wild West," *Arizona Republic*, May 25, 1992, sec. C, pp. 1, 4; Jeremy Thomas, "Old Seligman Harvey House: End Is Near," *Arizona Daily Star*, April 16, 2008, sec. B, p. 4.

39. Delgadillo's Snow Cap, Seligman, Ariz., "Delgadillo's Snow Cap" (advertisement), *Williams News*, October 4, 1962, Business Directory sec., p. 4; Steve Morris, "Historic Highway Brought Tourists, Prosperity to City and Many Believe It Still Has That Ability," *Winslow Mail*, January 19, 1990, sec. 2, p. 5; Snow Cap Drive-In, Winslow, Ariz., "Try Our Foot Long Hot Dogs 40¢" (advertisement), *Winslow Mail*, August 16, 1963, p. 4; Snow Cap [Ice Cream, Company, Phoenix], "Everybody Loves Ice Cream!" (advertisement), *Arizona Republic*, August 13, 1951, p. 21 (quotations); Snow Cap [Ice Cream Company], "Want Your Own Business?" (advertisement), *Arizona Republic*, June 13, 1952, p. 41; "T&H Diner Stages Successful Opening with Free Ice Cream," *Williams News*, July 2, 1953, pp. 1, 5.

40. David Howell, "Route 66 Icon Delgadillo Is Sorely Missed by Travelers," *Arizona Republic*, December 29, 2004, Sun Cities/Surprise sec, p. 2; "Juan Delgadillo," *Route 66 News*, Spring 2000, p. 5; Luz Miller, "Who Was Juan?," *Route 66 News*, Fall 2004, pp. 13–16; Thomas Arthur Repp, "Faces of Route 66: America's Clown," *Route 66 Magazine* 4, no. 4 (Fall 1997): 12–14 (quotations); Repp, *Route 66: The Romance of the West*, 198, 201–2, 204, 206; Jon Robinson, *Route 66: Lives on the Road* (Osceola, Wisc.: MBI Publishing, 2001), 19–20; Mark Schaffer, "Town Still Drawing Tourists 2 Decades After Its Heyday," *Arizona Republic*, July 26, 2003, sec. B, pp. 1–2; Fred Smith, "No Strings Attached: Noteworthy Family Stays in Tune with Seligman," *Arizona Republic*, September 19, 1986, sec. D, pp. 1–2; Fred Smith, "Seligman Restaurateur Takes a Zany Approach to Corral His Customers," *Arizona Republic*, December 22, 1987, sec. B, pp. 1–2.

41. "Cavern, Extras Lure Crowd off Fast Track," *Arizona Republic*, May 4, 1986, sec. S, pp. 46–47; Caverns Inn, Grand Canyon Caverns, Ariz., "Caverns Inn Restaurant Now Opening for the Season" (advertisement), *Arizona Republic*, March 6, 1975, sec. E, p. 19; "Coconino Caverns to Be Added to Maps," *Williams News*, January 5, 1939, p. 5; "Dinosaur Caverns to Be Dedicated," *Arizona Republic*, May 11, 1962, p. 23; "Expansion of Facilities Planned for Cavern," *Arizona Republic*, February 23, 1963, p. 17; Jim Hinckley, *Jim Hinckley's America: Kingman, Arizona and 160-miles of Smiles* (n.p.: privately printed, 2015), [51]–52; Jim Hinckley, "News from Our Neighbors in Arizona," *Route 66 New Mexico* 26, no. 3 (Fall 2018): 24–25; 27, and no. 3

(Fall 2019): 24–25; "Just-Opened Motel Has Own Airport," *Arizona Republic*, July 28, 1963, sec. E, p. 6; Lonesome Lulu, "Along the Avenue," *Williams News*, May 17, 1962, sec. 2, pp. 1, 4; "Old Route 66 Roadside Attraction Still Operating," *Route 66 News*, January 1991, p. 17; "Plans Set to Boom Coconino Caverns," *Arizona Republic*, November 15, 1960, p. 11; Pam Powers, *Recollections of the Grand Canyon Caverns* (Peach Springs, Ariz.: Grand Canyon Caverns & Inn, [ca. 2006]), 11–34 (quotation p. 18); Repp, *Route 66: The Romance of the West*, 174–80; "Restaurant Ratings," *Arizona Daily Sun*, September 23, 1993, p. 4.

42. *Arizona State Business Directory 1936*, 228, 650; *Business and Professional Directory of Arizona*, 112, 448; T. Lindsay Baker, Baker, *Portrait of Route 66: Images from the Curt Teich Postcard Archives* (Norman: University of Oklahoma Press, 2016), 195–99; "Bion Elliott, 77; Peach Springs Motel Ex-Owner," *Arizona Republic*, September 30, 1972, p. 59; "Board Revokes Liquor Licenses," *Arizona Daily Sun*, March 15, 1972, p. 7; "Clara E. Linn," *Southern Utah News* (Kanab, Utah), February 2, 2000, p. 8; E. V. Durling, "On the Side," *San Francisco Examiner*, September 1, 1949, p. 13 (second and third quotations); "Eight Spring Tours from Qumacho Inn to Supai Village," *Williams News*, April 2, 1953, p. 6; "Elect R. V. Stewart Vice-President State Highway 66 Assn.," *Williams News*, October 8, 1953, p. 3; "Ethel J. Rutherford," p. 23; "Ex-Area Resident Dies in Arizona," *Morning Call* (Allentown, Pa.), December 29, 1958, p. 23; Jim Hinckley, "Peach Springs," *Route 66 Magazine* 16, no. 2 (Spring 2009): 14–16; R. G. Allen Jackson, "Miscellaneous Odds and Ends[,] Thoughts and True Experiences of the Original Stumblebum," in *A Trilogy: Miscellaneous Odds and Ends, Thoughts and True Experiences of the Original Stumblebum[;] A Cab Driver's Conception of the Ten Commandments of God[;] A Cab Driver's Diary: On the Spot[;] The Above Trilogy (Three Books) Represent an Effort of Twenty-Five Years by Yours Truly* ([Amarillo, Tex.]: privately printed, 1966), 93–95 (first quotation); Qumacho Café and Motel, Peach Springs, Ariz., "Qumacho Café and Motel" (advertisement), *Gallup Independent*, August 10, 1940, sec. 5, p. [6]; Qumacho Café and Motel, "Qumacho Café and Motel at Peach Springs" (advertisement), *Arizona Republic*, February 13, 1943, sec. 2, p. 5; Qumacho Café and Mot[e]l, "Wanted, Man and Wife and Dinner Cook and Waitress" (advertisement), *Arizona Republic*, September 22, 1945, p. 7; "Seligman Café Will Be Opened," sec. 2, p. 8.

43. "Arizona's Route 66 Communities," *Route 66 News*, September–October 1993, p. 13; "Business Spotlight: Frontier Café & Motel," *Route 66 News*, January–February 1996, p. 16; *Historic Route 66 Association of Arizona Welcomes You to the 7th Annual Fun Run[,] April 22nd–24th[,] 1994[,] I Traveled Route 66 in Arizona* (Kingman: Historic Route 66 Association of Arizona, 1994), booklet, p. 14, Library, Historic Route 66 Association of Arizona, Kingman, Ariz.; Scott Johnston, "An Old Highway Town Turns Quiet," *Arizona Daily Sun*, May 13, 1992, sec. A, p. 28; Klinkel and Gerlich, *A Matter of Time*, 208–9; David Lamb, "Romancing the Road," *National Geographic* 192, no. 3 (September 1997): 43, 46; Jim Michalec, "Frontier Motel: The Real Frontier, Long Time Proprietors Ray and Mildred Barker," *Route 66 Advertiser* (*Joplin [Mo.] Globe*) 1, no. 1 (April–May 2007): 28–29; Kathy Register, "Restoring the Frontier's Neon Sign," *Route 66 Federation News* 9, no. 2 (Spring 2003): 24–25; Stephenson, "Family of the Mother Road," sec. E, pp. 1–4 (quotations); Wallis, *Route 66: The Mother Road*, 202–3.

44. B. M. Atwood, "From the Colorado River East through Gold Fields of Mohave County to the Parting of the Ways," *Arizona Highways* 2, no. 2 (February 1926): 20–22, 28; Tom Carpenter, "Road Taken Holds Warm Memories," *Arizona Daily Sun*, December 29, 1996, p. 2; "Damage Suit Transferred," *Arizona Republic*, October 5, 1941, p. 9; Mohawk Rubber Company, *Guide No. 3*, 18; Russell A. Olsen, *Route 66 Lost and Found: Mother Road Ruins and Relics—The Ultimate Collection* (Minneapolis: Voyageur Press, 2011), 336–[337]; "Only Three Miles of Gravel Road Left on '66' in Arizona," *Williams News*, October 8, 1936, See Northern Arizona magazine supplement, p. 1; "Purchase Ranch," *Mohave County Miner* (Kingman, Ariz.), November 4, 1916, p. 3; Rittenhouse, *Guide Book to Highway 66*, 106–7; "Surveying Crozier Canyon Road," *Mohave County Miner and Our Mineral Wealth* (Kingman, Ariz.), August 19, 1921, p. 4.

45. William Ascarza, "Mine Tales: Bad News Turns Good as Horse Theft Leads to Discovery of Big Silver Lode," *Arizona Daily Star*, January 16, 2017, sec. A, pp. 2–3; "Board to Open Highway Bids," *Arizona Republic*, October 31, 1933, sec. 2, p. 1; *Business and Professional Directory of Arizona*, 71, 447; Alan Carlson,

"Goodbye to a Legend," *Route 66 New Mexico* 18, no. 1 (Spring 2010): 14–17; Scott Craven, "At Home on the Mother Road," *Arizona Republic*, May 6, 2018, Valley and State sec. E, pp. 1–2; Amy Franklin, Hackberry, Ariz., email communication to T. Lindsay Baker, Rio Vista, Tex., December 2, 2020, paper copy, author's collection; Kaszynski, *Route 66*, 127–28; Mohawk Rubber Company, *Guide No. 3*, 18; Rittenhouse, *Guide Book to Highway 66*, 107; Robinson, *Route 66: Lives on the Road*, 109–11; Quinta Scott and Susan Croce Kelly, *Route 66: The Highway and Its People* (Norman: University of Oklahoma Press, 1988), 20; Joe Sonderman, *Route 66 Then and Now* (London: Pavilion Books, 2018), 122; Carol Sowers, "Restless Artist Drawn to Settled Life," *Arizona Republic*, May 31, 1994, sec. B, pp. 1–2; "Spotlight on Hackberry and the Hackberry General Store," *Route 66 East to West* no. 4 (2009): 19–22; Tom Teague, "Living Highway Icon Says 'Goodbye!' to the Road," *Route 66 Magazine* 5, no. 3 (Summer 1998): 20–23; Bob Waldmire, interview by David King Dunaway, Portal, Ariz., September 7, 2007, typewritten transcript, pp. 14–19, Route 66 Corridor Preservation Program, National Park Service, Santa Fe.

46. Jim Hinckley, "Road to Victory," *Route 66 News*, Winter 2002, pp. 20–22; "Kingman Incorporation Stirs Major Controversy," *Arizona Republic*, November 21, 1951, p. 9; "Kingman's Graveyard Airfield Had Brief Post-war Fame," *Arizona Republic*, September 14, 1952, sec. 5, p. 7; Mary Lou Leichsenring Herridge, transcription of interview extracts in exhibit gallery, Arizona Route 66 Museum, Powerhouse Visitors Center, Kingman, Ariz. (third quotation), accessed by the author July 9, 2016; Mohawk Rubber Company, *Guide No. 3*, 18 (fourth quotation); "Nagel-Crome Trip," *Clinton (Mo.) Eye*, August 7, 1947, sec. A, p. 4 (first and second quotations); Mark Potter, "Kingman, AZ: Great Stopping Point on Route 66 East or West," *Route 66 Federation News* 20, no. 3 (Autumn 2014): 6–10; Rittenhouse, *Guide Book to Highway 66*, 107; *Story of the Arizona Unit*, unpaged.

47. *Arizona State Business Directory 1927* (Denver: Gazetteer Publishing and Printing, 1927), 628; Bell, *66 Kid*, 78–79, 133–35 (quotation); "'China' Jack, Pioneer of County, Dies in China," *Mohave County Miner*, June 7, 1935, p. 13; Steve Daniels, "Crowning 100 Years: Faded Glory Still Clinging to Kingman," *Arizona Republic*, October 24, 1982, sec. B, pp. 1–2; Jo Gray, "Charlie Lum: A Successful Man Remembers 'His Town,'" *Kingman (Ariz.) Daily Miner*, July 17, 1983, sec. B, p. 1; Jade Restaurant, Kingman, Ariz., "Jade Restaurant" (advertisement), *Arizona Republic*, November 27, 1960, Arizona Days and Ways magazine, p. 23; Jade Restaurant, "Kingman's Newest" (advertisement), *Arizona Republic*, September 14, 1952, sec. 5, p. 5; "Jeane Lum," *Arizona Republic*, June 19, 1957, p. 11; *Kingman City Directory 1939–1940* (Kingman, Ariz.: Mohave County Miner, 1939), 44, 103–4; "Kingman Rotary Club Installs Charlie Lum as President," *Mohave County Miner*, July 5, 1973, p. 8; Charlie Lum, interview by James Miller, Glenn Johnson, and Sharolyn Root, Kingman, Ariz., January 20, 1981, typewritten transcript, unpaged, "Lum—Charlie Family" File, Biographical Files, Library, Mohave Museum of History and Arts, Kingman, Ariz.; Mohawk Rubber Company, *Guide No. 3*, 18; Poling-Kempes, *Harvey Girls*, 123–25; *Story of the Arizona Unit*, unpaged.

48. Louise Benner, interview by T. Lindsay Baker, Kingman, Ariz., July 10, 2016, typewritten notes, author's collection; Denny's #96, Kingman, Ariz., "Fry Cook Wanted" (advertisement), *Arizona Republic*, June 21, 1965, p. 38 (fourth quotation); John A. Jakle and Keith A. Sculle, *Fast Food: Roadside Restaurants in the Automobile Age* (Baltimore: Johns Hopkins University Press, 1999), 53, 80–81; *Kingman[,] Bullhead City[,] Lake Havasu City[,] Chloride[,] Peach Springs[,] Hackberry[,] Topock[,] Lake Mohave Ranchos[,] Truxton[,] Mohave Valley[,] Valentine[,] Oatman[,] Wikieup[,] Yucca[,] October 1966[,] Telephone Directory[,] Citizens Utilities Company* (Kingman, Ariz.: Citizens Utility Company, 1966), 10, 89–90; *Kingman Chamber of Commerce 1995 Membership Directory and Buyers Guide Celebrating 70 Years of Service* (Kingman, Ariz.: Kingman Chamber of Commerce, 1995), 63; Philip Langdon, *Orange Roofs, Golden Arches: The Architecture of American Chain Restaurants* (New York: Alfred A. Knopf, 1986), 115–16, 136–37, 173–76 (first, second, and third quotations); Brady MacDonald, "Mother Road with No Plan," *Los Angeles Times*, June 11, 2017, sec. S, pp. 26–27; "No Injuries: Kingman Cook Seized after Shooting Spree," *Arizona Republic*, June 16, 1977, sec. B, p. 16; *Polk's Kingman (Mohave County, Ariz.) City Directory 1968* (Dallas: R. L. Polk, 1968), 27; Tammy Rutherford, interview by T. Lindsay Baker, Kingman, Ariz., July 9, 2016, manuscript notes,

author's collection; Rutherford's 66 Family Diner, Kingman, Ariz., *Rutherford's 66 Family Diner*[,] *2011 E. Andy Divine*[,] *Kingman, AZ. 86401*[,] *(928) 377–1660* (Kingman, Ariz.: Rutherford's 66 Family Diner, [2016]), menu, author's collection; Silver Spoon Family Restaurant, Kingman, Ariz., "Experienced Line Cooks" (advertisement), *Needles Desert Star* (Needles, Calif.), October 1, 2003, sec. A, p. 12; Silverspoon [*sic*] Family Restaurant, Kingman, Ariz., "Route 66 Special" (advertisement), *Kingman Daily Miner*, April 21, 1993, Route 66 supplement, p. 3; *Telephone Directory*[,] *October 1965*[,] *Kingman*[,] *Bullhead City*[,] *Lake Havasu City*[,] *Chloride*[,] *Hackberry*[,] *Lake Mohave Ranchos*[,] *Mohave Valley*[,] *Oatman*[,] *Peach Springs*[,] *Topock*[,] *Truxton*[,] *Valentine*[,] *Wikieup*[,] *Yucca*[,] *Citizens Utilities Company* (Kingman, Ariz.: Citizens Utility Company, 1965), 10, 76.

49. T. Lindsay Baker, "Making the Goldroad Grade: Drivers' Experiences Crossing Sitgreaves Pass," *Route 66 Magazine* 28, no. 1 (Winter 2020–21): 22–25; T. Lindsay Baker, "Notes on Climbing and Descending Passes on Route 66 in a 1930 Ford[,] July 2017," typescript, 2017, 1 lf., author's collection; Ray T. Bohacz, "Blowing in the Wind: The Automotive Radiator," *Hemmings Classic Car* 3, no. 1 (October 2006): 84–87; Patricia R. Buckley, *Route 66: Remnants* (n.p.: 1988), 35–37; Hinckley, *Jim Hinckley's America*, 33–37; Bonnie Jean Hoerner, *Pioneering on Route 66 and Beyond: The Story of Evangeline Hoerner McCoy* (Clovis, Calif.: privately printed, 2005), 12 (quotation); Roger Naylor, "Swimming with Goldfish, Braying with Burros," *Route 66 Magazine* 25, no. 1 (Winter 2017–18): 32–34; Rittenhouse, *Guide Book to Highway 66*, 107–11; Tom Snyder, *The Route 66 Traveler's Guide and Roadside Companion* (New York: St. Martin's Press, 1990), 97, 99–101; Norman C. Wallace, "Some Hills along the Highways: Motorists through and over a Few of Arizona's Mountain Ranges," *Arizona Highways* 10, no. 6 (June 1934): 3–5, 21–22, 24–25; Floyd Yancy, *Driving Route 66 in a 46 Ford in 1954 and 2010* (n.p.: privately printed, 2012), 142–45. Early-twentieth-century American novelist Thomas Wolfe crossed Sitgreaves Pass on June 23, 1938, and left his own poetic description of the oven-hot experience. Thomas Wolfe, *A Western Journal: A Daily Log of the Great Parks Trip June 20–July 2, 1938* (Pittsburgh: University of Pittsburgh Press, 1951), 13–15.

50. "Action by Duncan: 24 Applications for Transfer of License Ownership Approved," *Arizona Republic*, August 17, 1953, p. 2; Cool Springs Station, Kingman, Ariz., *Cool Springs Station Route 66 Gift Shop & Museum* (Kingman, Ariz.: Cool Springs Station, [2014]), folder, author's collection; Hinckley, *Jim Hinckley's America*, 32–33; Kaszynski, *Route 66*, 133–34; Rob Morris, Charles Crisman, and Mary Walter Crisman, "Cool Springs," *Route 66 Magazine* 7, no. 3 (Summer 2000): 26–27, 30–31, 62 (quotation); Olsen, *Route 66 Lost and Found*, 346–47; Rittenhouse, *Guide Book to Highway 66*, 110; Paul Taylor, "Cool Springs," *Route 66 Magazine* 13, no. 4 (Fall 2006): 8–10; Tucker, "Diary—August 1938," 76; Witzel and Young-Witzel, *Legendary Route 66*, 242–43.

51. *Arizona State Business Directory 1928*, 273; Arizona, State Department of Health, Division of Vital Statistics, Death Certificate for Osman Snell, February 23, 1942, Arizona Department of Health Services, Phoenix; Hinckley, *Jim Hinckley's America*, 36; Hoerner, *Pioneering on Route 66*, 125–26; "Juror to Be Held When Grazing Case at Kingman Closes," *Arizona Republican*, May 24, 1925, p. 1; Kara Hewson Nelson, "Route 66 Revisited," *Roadsigns* 5, no. 2 (Spring 1995): 12 (quotations); Russell Olson, "Then and Now: The Summit, Sitgreaves Pass[,] c. 1940," *Route 66 Magazine* 23, no. 2 (Spring 2016): 41; Rittenhouse, *Guide Book to Highway 66*, 110; U.S. Census Bureau, Census of 1940, Population Schedules, Rural, Mohave County, Arizona, Enumeration District 8–1, page 19A, Roll 110, Microcopy T627, National Archives and Records Administration, Washington, D.C.; "'Why Travel 66?' Theme of Association Meeting," *Williams News*, April 11, 1946, pp. 1, 4.

52. W. C. Clark, *Touring the West with Leaping Lena*, 227–30; Davis, *From Coast to Coast*, 47 (third and fourth quotations); Hinckley, *Ghost Towns of Route 66*, 128–33; Hinckley, *Jim Hinckley's America*, 37–39; Metcalfe-Shaw, *English Caravanners*, 77–80; Mohawk Tire Company, *Guide No. 3*, 17; Rittenhouse, *Guide Book to Highway 66*, 110–11; "A Sentimental Journey," *Arizona Highways* 57, no. 7 (July 1981): 36–42; Sharp, *Better Country*, 220 (first and second quotations); Willard S. Wood, "Circling through Arizona over Fine Dirt Roads," *Arizona Highways* 2, no. 11 (November 1926): 6–7.

53. Hinckley, *Ghost Towns*, 134–35; Hinckley, *Jim Hinckley's America*, 33; John Hurst, "There's Much to Gaze upon in Yucca, Ariz.," *Los Angeles Times*, August 20, 1982, pt. 1, pp. 3, 19; Roman Malach, *Oatman Gold Mining Center*, 2nd ed. (Kingman, Ariz.: privately printed, 1975), 38–48; "New Road Eliminates Old Grade," *Arizona Republic*, September 14, 1952, sec. 5, p. 4; R. H. Ring, "Boondocks," *Arizona Daily Star*, June 24, 1987, sec. EE, p. 2; Linda Stelp, "Yucca: A Town in Transition," *Kingman Daily Miner*, April 19, 2002, sec. B, p. 1; "Yucca Cut-Off on Highway 66 Open," *Arizona Daily Sun*, September 17, 1952, p. 1.

54. "Alonzo Williams," *Arizona Republic*, August 22, 1974, sec. C, p. 3; Nancy Carmody, interview by T. Lindsay Baker, Yucca, Ariz., July 11, 2016, manuscript notes, author's collection; Del Norte County, Calif., Index to the Affidavits of Registration[,] Del Norte County[,] California[,] 1942[,] to and Including July 16, 1942, unpaged, California State Library, Sacramento; Bob Drummond, "Once Bustling U.S. 66 Now a Phantom Road West," *Sunday Oklahoman* (Oklahoma City), August 30, 1981, sec. A, pp. 1, 22 (third quotation); "Eleven Liquor Permits Given," *Arizona Republic*, October 2, 1937, p. 11; "Father, Son Both Sued for Divorce in Same Day," *Arizona Republic*, April 12, 1979, sec. B, p. 9; "Fire at Oatman Causes Damage of Over $50,000," *Needles (Calif.) Nugget*, March 27, 1936, p. 1; Flagg, *Boulevards All the Way*, 140 (first and second quotations); Bill Freiday, interview by Mim Hoover, February 28, 2000, typewritten transcript, p. 19 (fourth quotations), Library, Mohave Museum of History and Arts; "J. W. Walden Surprised at Dinner Dance," *Arizona Republican*, December 25, 1927, sec. 23, p. 2; Kaszynski, *Route 66*, 132; Mohave County, Ariz., General Register of Voters 1916, unpaged, Mohave County Courthouse, Kingman, Ariz.; "Oatman Couple to Be Wed on Coast," *Needles Nugget*, July 28, 1939, p. 1; "Oatman, Ariz.," *Brooklyn (N.Y.) Daily Eagle*, August 18, 1935, magazine sec., p. 15; "Oatman News," *Needles Nugget*, April 2, 1937, p. [6]; July 30, 1937, p. [3]; August 13, 1937, p. [4]; and June 24, 1938, p. [2]; Ruth Rausch, "Illinois Valley: School Has Visitors," *Medford (Ore.) Mail Tribune*, October 3, 1958, p. 8; "Rich Los Angeles Oil Operator Given Credit for Discovery and Development of New El Dorado," *San Bernardino Daily Sun*, July 25, 1930, p. 17; Kate Smith, "Oatman News," *Needles Nugget*, September 3, 1937, p. [3]; February 28, 1938, p. [3]; July 15, 1938, p. [2]; and October 6, 1939, p. [3]; U.S. Census Bureau, Census of 1930, Population Schedules, School District 16 (Oatman), Mohave County, Ariz., Enumeration District 8–20, page 2A, Roll 55, Microcopy T626, and Census of 1940, Population Schedules, Crescent Twp., Del Norte County, California, Enumeration District 8–5, page 3A, Roll 199, Microcopy T627, National Archives and Records Administration, Washington, D.C.; "Well-remembered Boom Days Haunt Ghost-shadowed Town," *Arizona Republic*, September 14, 1952, sec. 5, p. 2; Yount, *Goldroad*, 31.

At least between 1932 and 1934, James and Dorothy Boyd owned a satellite roadhouse likewise called Honolulu Jim's on the Mother Road at Lenwood, five miles southwest of Barstow, California. Automobile Club of Southern California, Los Angeles, *National Old Trails Road*[,] *New York City, New York*[,] *to Los Angeles, California*[,] *U.S. Highway 66*[,] *Chicago, Illinois*[,] *to Los Angeles, California*[;] *and Major Connecting Roads* (Los Angeles: Automobile Club of Southern California, 1932), 64; "One O'clock Dance Law Invoked by Supervisors," *San Bernardino Daily Sun*, December 5, 1933, p. 7; "Rain Fails to Halt Visitors," *San Bernardino Daily Sun*, January 2, 1934, p. 10.

55. Matt C. Bischoff, *Life in the Past Lane: The Route 66 Experience: Historic and Management Contexts for the Route 66 Corridor in California*, vol. 1, *Route 66 in the California Desert*, Technical Series 86 (Tucson: Statistical Research, 2005), 44–46; "Extensive Developments in Lake Needles Resort District Scheduled," *San Bernardino Daily Sun*, August 14, 1938, p. 13; "Frontier Days," *Desert Star* (Needles, Calif.), January 24, 1957, p. 2; "Jack Crinklaw Will Reopen at Topock," *Needles (Calif.) Desert Star*, September 1, 1960, p. 1; Metcalfe-Shaw, *English Caravanners*, 73–75; "Novel Method of Erection Adopted in Raising Longest Highway Arch Span," *Engineering Record* 74, no. 20 (November 11, 1916): 580–81; "Topock Is Famous for Its Bridges and Gateway to Famed Marsh," *Needles Desert Star*, August 19, 1965, p. 2; "Topock Man Killed by No. 7 Sunday Noon," *Desert Star*, October 19, 1950, p. 1; Topock Store and Café, Topock, Ariz., "Arizona Fishing Licenses Can Now Be Had" (advertisement), *Needles Nugget*, July 16, 1937, p. [2]; "Workmen Are Razing the Old Crinklaw Tavern at Topock," *Needles Desert Star*, June 14, 1973, p. 7.

56. Russell Byrd, *Russ's Bus: Adventures of an American Bus Driver* (Los Angeles: Wetzel Publishing, 1945), 22–23 (quotations); "Novel Method," 580–81.

CHAPTER 8. CALIFORNIA

1. Bob Boze Bell, *The 66 Kid Raised on the Mother Road* (Minneapolis: Voyageur Press, 2014), 90 (quotations); Jack D. Rittenhouse, *A Guide Book to Highway 66* (Los Angeles: privately printed, 1946; repr., Albuquerque: University of New Mexico Press, 1989), 112–23.

2. T. Lindsay Baker, "Motorists Remember the Mojave Desert," *Route 66 Magazine* 24, no. 4 (Fall 2017): 18–21; L. Burr Belden, "History in the Making: Pioneer Motor Travelers Faced Trying Ordeals," *Sun-Telegram* (San Bernardino, Calif.), October 10, 1954, p. 40; Hoffman Birney, *Roads to Roam* (Philadelphia: Penn Publishing Company, 1930), 105–6 (first quotation); Vivian Davies and Darin Kuna, *California's Route 66: Landmarks, History, Mileage and Maps—1994[,] Needles to Santa Monica—East to West*, 3rd ed. (La Verne, Calif.: California Historic Route 66 Association, 1994), 1–48; Lewis Gannett, *Sweet Land* (New York: Doubleday, Doran, 1934), 212–13 (second and third quotations); Nomination to the National Register of Historic Places for U.S. Highway 66 in California, November 16, 2011, E6–E14, E25–E30, this and subsequent nominations in Office of the Keeper, National Register of Historic Places, National Park Service, Washington, D.C.; Nina Wilcox Putnam, "A Jitney Guide to the Santa Fe Trail," *Saturday Evening Post* 194, no. 50 (June 10, 1922): 26, 28, 30, 76–77.

3. Charlotta A. Bass, *Forty Years: Memoirs from the Pages of a Newspaper* (Los Angeles: Charlotta A. Bass, 1960), 70–71; Glen Campbell and Tom Carter, *Rhinestone Cowboy: An Autobiography* (New York: St. Martin's Paperbacks, 1995), 45–46 (fourth quotation); Irv Logan, interview by Tom Peters, Springfield, Mo., March 13, 2015, audio recording and typewritten transcript, p. 24, Greater Springfield Route 66 Oral History Project, Special Collections and Archives, Meyer Library, Missouri State University, Springfield, Missouri; Carey McWilliams, *Southern California Country: An Island on the Land* (New York: Duell, Sloan and Pearce, 1946), 324–26; Frank Norris, "Courageous Motorists: African American Pioneers on Route 66," *New Mexico Historical Review* 90, no. 3 (Summer 2015): 298, 321–26; Frank Norris, "Racial Dynamism in Los Angeles, 1900–1964: The Role of the *Green Book*," *Southern California Quarterly* 99, no. 3 (Fall 2017): 251–89; Arthur C. Verge, *Paradise Transformed: Los Angeles during the Second World War* (Dubuque, Iowa: Kendall/Hunt Publishing, 1993), 39–65, 144–45. In 1936 British observer Guy K. Austin concisely described white Californians' attitudes toward race when, as an outsider, he observed, "As negroes are to the south so are Chinese and Japanese to California." Guy K. Austin, *Covered Wagon, 10 H.P.: Being the Further Adventures of an English Family in Its Travels across America* (London: Geoffrey Bles, 1936), 108–9.

4. *California: A Guide to the Golden State*, American Guide Series (New York: Hastings House, 1939), 608–10; Dan Harlow, "Route 66 Journal: Places of Note[,] Needles, California," *Route 66 Federation News* 4, no. 4 (Autumn 1998): 16–19; Maggie McShan, "Rediscovery of Route 66 Roadside Park," *Roadsigns* (California Historic Route 66 Association) 5, no. 4 (Fall 1995): 4; Nomination to the National Register of Historic Places for U.S. Highway 66 in California, E4–E19, E41–E42; Rittenhouse, *Guide Book to Highway 66*, 112–13; Walter C. Schuiling, *San Bernardino County: Land of Contrasts* (Woodland Hills, Calif.: Windsor Publications, 1984), 61–69; Paul Taylor, "A Camp Born of the Southern Pacific," *Route 66 Magazine* 12, no. 4 (Fall 2005): 22–25; Paul Taylor, "Competitive Rails Meet at the Needles," *Route 66 Magazine* 19, no. 1 (Winter 2011–12): 26–29; David G. Thompson, *The Mohave Desert Region California: A Geographic, Geologic, and Hydrologic Reconnaissance*, U.S. Department of the Interior, Geological Survey, Water Supply Paper 578 (Washington, D.C.: Government Printing Office, 1929), 728–30.

5. T. Lindsay Baker, "Overnight at the El Garces," *Route 66 Magazine* 23, no. 4 (Fall 2016): 50–52; "El Garces a Splendid Hotel," *San Bernardino (Calif.) Daily Sun*, May 2, 1908, p. 7; James Montgomery Flagg, *Boulevards All the Way—Maybe: Being an Artist's Truthful Impression of the U.S.A. from New York to California and Return, by Motor* (New York: George H. Doran, 1925), 141–44, 47 (quotations); "Flashing Fire Takes

Lives: The Harvey House at Needles Goes up in Flames," *Los Angeles Times*, September 7, 1906, pt. 2, p. 10; Fred Harvey Company, [Kansas City, Mo.], *Lunch Room Service*[,] *El Garces Hotel*[,] *Fred Harvey*[,] *Needles, Calif. Special Luncheon* ([Kansas City, Mo.]: Fred Harvey, 1939), menu, typewritten on preprinted cardstock, Fred Harvey Company Collection, MS 208, series 3, box 1, folder 23, Special Collections and Archives, Cline Library, Northern Arizona University, Flagstaff; "Fred Harvey Hotel at Needles Closes," *Sun-Telegram*, September 18, 1949, p. 13; Vernon McGill, *Diary of a Motor Journey from Chicago to Los Angeles* (Los Angeles: Grafton Publishing, 1922), 84; Nomination to the National Register of Historic Places for El Garces, Needles, Calif.; Mark Pepys, *Mine Host, America* (London: Collins, 1937), 202–3; Lesley Poling-Kempes, *The Harvey Girls: Women Who Opened the West* (Cambridge, Mass.: Da Capo Press, 1989), 78, 125–27.

6. *Arizona State Business Directory 1927* (Denver: Gazetteer Publishing and Printing, 1927), 628; Austin, *Covered Wagon*, 108–9; C. K. Shepherd, *Across America by Motor-Cycle* (New York: Longmans, Green, 1922), 206 (quotation).

7. "Basil's Ramblings," *Needles (Calif.) Desert Star*, August 3, 1961, p. 2; "Certificate of Business Fictitious Firm Name," *Desert Star* (Needles, Calif.), August 28, 1958, p. 3; "Coombs Gives Ramp Story," *Needles Desert Star*, July 12, 1973, p. 1; "Fictitious Business Name Statement File No. FBN 25492," *Needles Desert Star*, July 19, 1978, p. 15; "Fire Monday Afternoon Gutted the Wagon Wheel Restaurant near the Westside Offramp [sic]," *Needles Desert Star*, August 16, 1978, p. 1; Garrett's Restaurant, Needles, Calif., "Garrett's Restaurant Formerly Lynn's" (advertisement), *Desert Star*, May 18, 1972, p. 8; "Jack Richey Passes Away," *Needles Desert Star*, September 10, 1980, p. 18; "Jack Richey Works on Café," *Desert Star*, January 14, 1971, p. 1; Dennis M. Kasum, "The Progressive Message," *Needles Desert Star*, July 28, 1976, p. 4; Lynn's Broiler, Needles, Calif., "Good Food" (advertisement), *Desert Star*, December 9, 1971, p. 14; Lynn's Broiler, "Now for the First Time" (advertisement), *Needles Desert Star*, December 8, 1966, p. 7; "Lynn's Restaurant Being Razed," *Desert Star*, September 3, 1970, p. 10; Maggie McShan, "Chit-Chat," *Needles Desert Star*, May 29, 1969, p. 2; "Margaret J. Bemish," *Needles Desert Star*, October 14, 1998, p. 2; "New Year Shows Progress," *Desert Star*, December 28, 1970, pp. 1–2; "Notice of Intention to Engage in the Sale of Alcoholic Beverages," *Needles Desert Star*, May 30, 1974, p. 7; "Notice to Creditors (Division 6 of the Commercial Code) Escrow No.: 4557–563-CCP Date: December 18, 1987[,] 52334," *Needles Desert Star*, January 27, 1988, sec. B, p. 11; "Owner Fights Seizure," *Needles Desert Star*, July 11, 1968, pp. 1, 4; "Request," *Needles Desert Star*, July 18, 1974, p. 11; Robin Richards, "Alexis Named Colorado River Round Up Rodeo Grand Marshal," *Needles Desert Star*, March 28, 2018, pp. 1, 9; "State Explains Status of Off-ramp Project," *Needles Desert Star*, July 26, 1973, p. 5; Wagon Wheel Restaurant, Needles, Calif., "A Truly Western Atmosphere" (advertisement), *Needles Desert Star*, December 3, 1980, p. 4; Wagon Wheel Restaurant, "Wanted: Cooks, Waitresses and Dishwashers!" (advertisement), *Needles Desert Star*, June 28, 1978, p. 15.

8. Belden, "History in the Making," p. 40; Matt C. Bischoff, *Preparing for Combat Overseas: Patton's Desert Training Center* (n.p.: LULU.COM, 2016), 1–113; Patricia R. Buckley, *Route 66: Remnants* (n.p., 1988), 40–41; *California: A Guide to the Golden State*, 608–10 (quotation); Gertrude E. Metcalfe-Shaw, *English Caravanners in the Wild West: The Old Pioneers' Trail* (Edinburgh, Scotland: William Blackwood and Sons, 1926), 70–71; Russell Olson [sic], "Then and Now: Essex, California[,] Circa 1942," *Route 66 Magazine* 23, no. 1 (Winter 2015–16): 41; Fremont Rider, *Rider's California: A Guide-Book for Travelers* (New York: Macmillan, 1925), 626–29; Thompson, *Mohave Desert Region*, 676.

9. Mohawk Rubber Company, Akron, Ohio, *Guide No. 3*[,] *Mohawk Hobbs Grade and Surface Guide*[,] *Price 20¢*[,] *Santa Fe Trail Los Angeles-Denver*[,] *Western Division National Old Trails*, 4th ed., publication Hworow 30851 (Akron, Ohio: Mohawk Rubber Company, 1929), 16; Paul E. Vernon, *Coast to Coast by Motor* (London: A. & C. Black, 1930), 82–83 (quotation); "Well Known Hotel at Goffs Is Burned," *San Bernardino Daily Sun*, February 5, 1929, sec. 2, p. 1; Thompson, *Mohave Desert Region*, 132–43; "We Understand That the Wayside Inn at Goffs Is Now Serving Meals," *Needles (Calif.) Nugget*, May 22, 1925, p. 4.

10. Dennis Casebier, interview by David K. Dunaway, Goffs, Calif., March 18, 2006, typewritten transcript, p. 9, Route 66 Corridor Preservation Program, National Park Service, Santa Fe; "Essex Reveler Pays Fifteen Dollar Fine," *Needles Nugget*, April 30, 1937, p. 1; "Fire Destroys Essex Café on Monday Night," *Desert Star*, June 26, 1958, p. 1; "Fire Destroys Essex Wayside Inn Sunday," *Needles Nugget*, December 12, 1944, p. 1; "Kingman Rites Unite Couple," *San Bernardino Daily Sun*, January 21, 1936, p. 12; "Legal Notice of Intention to Engage in the Sale of Alcoholic Beverages," *Desert Star*, July 22, 1948, p. [5]; "Mr. and Mrs. O. B. Chambers of San Bernardino Recently Purchased the Store and Buildings at Essex," *Desert Star*, January 25, 1945, p. 1; Chuck Mueller, "Desert Hamlets' Future Unsure," *San Bernardino County (Calif.) Sun*, April 3, 1995, sec. A, pp. 1, 4; "Non-Responsibility," *Needles Desert Star*, April 4, 1968, p. 4; "Notice of Intended Sale," *San Bernardino Daily Sun*, May 27, 1964, Classified Advertising sec., p. A; "Notice of Sale of Stock in Bulk and Fixtures and Equipment," *San Bernardino Daily Sun*, May 10, 1957, p. 18; "Notice of Intention to Engage in the Sale of Alcoholic Beverages," *Needles Nugget*, July 5, 1940, p. [6]; and February 23, 1945, p. [6]; Russell A. Olsen, *Route 66 Lost and Found: Mother Road Ruins and Relics—The Ultimate Collection* (Minneapolis: Voyageur Press, 2011), 374–75; "Passes," *Needles Desert Star*, May 31, 1978, p. 5; "Sheriff's Deputies Raid Desert Cafes," *San Bernardino Daily Sun*, March 2, 1949, city edition, p. 13; Bob Smith, "Bilking of Motorists in Desert Is Claimed," *Sun* (San Bernardino, Calif.), December 9, 1971, pp. 1–2; Wayside Camp, Essex, Calif., "Wanted—2 Women General Help, Café and Cabin Camp in Desert" (advertisement), *San Bernardino Daily Sun*, August 26, 1946, p. 9; "Wayside Inn at Essex Leased to Phoenix Men," *Desert Star*, July 22, 1948, p. 1; C.E. Wiley, Essex, Calif., "For Sale or Lease Store, Garage, Café and Auto Camp" (advertisement), *San Bernardino Daily Sun*, December 28, 1932, p. 14.

11. "Amboy Items," *Desert Star*, March 14, 1946, p. 6; "Amboy News," *Desert Star*, November 15, 1945, p. 3; March 21, 1946, p. 3; and April 18, 1946, p. 6; "Arrest Man for Shooting-Up Café," *Needles Desert Star*, October 20, 1960, p. 1; Matt C. Bischoff, *Life in the Past Lane: The Route 66 Experience: Historic and Management Contexts for the Route 66 Corridor in California*, vol. 1, *Route 66 in the California Desert*, Technical Series 86 (Tucson: Statistical Research, 2005), 77–78; "C. F. Hunt Buys Mobil Station," *Desert Star*, July 27, 1950, p. 1; "Child Burns to Death in Automobile," *San Bernardino Daily Sun*, November 10, 1954, p. [17]; "Crazed Man Dies on Desert," *Desert Star*, July 10, 1947, p. 1; Joe de Kehoe, "Cadiz Summit: 'Just Sagebrush and Rattlesnakes,'" *Route 66 Magazine* 25, no. 3 (Summer 2018), 22–24; Joe de Kehoe, *The Silence and the Sun: An Historical Account of People, Places and Events on Old Route 66 and the Railroad Communities in the Eastern Mojave Desert, California* (Bakersfield, Calif.: Trails End Publishing, 2007), 14–42 (second quotation p. 23); Ellen Klinkel and Nick Gerlich, *A Matter of Time: Route 66 through the Lens of Change* (Norman: University of Oklahoma Press, 2019), 228–30; Jerry McClanahan, Jim Ross, and Shellee Graham, *Route 66 Sightings* (Arcadia, Okla.: Ghost Town Press, 2011), 52–53; Cenovia (Martinez) Navarro, Sally (Martinez) Garcia, and Angie Martinez, telephone interview by Joe de Kehoe, Victorville, Calif., August 4, 2004, typewritten transcript, pp. 61–62 (first quotation), Joe de Kehoe Collection, Mojave Desert Archives, Mojave Desert Heritage and Cultural Association, Goffs, California, hereafter cited as Joe de Kehoe Collection; "Notice of Intention to Engage in the Sale of Alcoholic Beverages," *Desert Star*, January 12, 1950, p. [5]; "Sheriff's Deputies Raid Desert Cafes," p. 13; Thompson, *Mohave Desert Region*, 689–90.

12. "Bandit Suspect Taken in Wild Chase," *San Bernardino Daily Sun*, October 12, 1937, sec. 2, p. 1; Bischoff, *Life in the Past Lane*, 1:78–81; "Certificate of Partnership—Fictitious Firm Name," *San Bernardino Daily Sun*, March 30, 1941, p. 23; Marian Clark, *The Route 66 Cookbook* (Tulsa: Council Oak Books, 1993), 200; "Fire [sic] Year Sentence for Highway Gunman," *Needles Nugget*, October 22, 1937, p. [10]; "Hold Up Victim Reversed Roles and Nabs Thug," *Needles Nugget*, October 15, 1937, p. 1; Joe de Kehoe, "Chambless, California," *Route 66 Magazine* 25, no. 4 (Fall 2018): 12–14; de Kehoe, *Silence and the Sun*, 44–55; "A Fair Statement of the Proceedings of the Board of Supervisors," *San Bernardino Daily Sun*, 8 July 8, 1921, p. 15; Wiley Ford, interview by Joe de Kehoe, Daggett, Calif., September 6, 2003, typewritten transcript, p. 22, Joe de Kehoe Collection; "Last Rites for Mrs. Chambless," *Needles Desert Star*, May 19, 1966, p. 7; Maggie McShan, "Centennial '83 . . . Needles Celebrates," *Needles Desert Star*, June 15, 1983, p. 2; Maggie McShan,

"From the Desk of Maggie McShan: William E. Riddle Celebrates 100th Birthday," *Needles Desert Star*, September 16, 1987, sec. A, p. 2; Mohawk Rubber Company, *Guide No. 3*, 16; "Notice for Publication," *Needles Nugget*, December 24, 1926, p. 3; and January 24, 1930, p. 5; "Notice of Trustee's Sale No. 196-F-3906," *Sun*, January 15, 1969, sec. B, p. 9; "Notice to Creditors No. 12479," *The San Bernardino Daily Sun*, April 11, 1940, p. 31; Olsen, *Route 66 Lost and Found*, 380–81; Rittenhouse, *Guide Book to Highway 66*, 115 (quotation); "Three Liquor Permits Revoked by Board," *San Bernardino Daily Sun*, May 7, 1957, p. 27.

13. Ruben and Mary Arizaga, interview by Joe de Kehoe at Bullhead City, Ariz., October 7, 2006, typewritten transcript, pp. 52–53, and Carmen (Limon) Molina, interview by Joe de Kehoe, Twentynine Palms, Calif., June 13, 2004, typewritten transcript, p. 45, both in Joe de Kehoe Collection; Alan Ashby, "L.A. Man Arrested on Desert after Auto Runs into Tourist," *Sun*, February 5, 1969, sec. B, p. 1; Bischoff, *Life in the Past Lane*, 1:81–83; Micah Bohmker, "Seven Miles out of Bagdad," pt. 3, *Route 66 Federation News* 8, no. 1 (Winter 2002): 31–35; "Certificate of Partnership Transacting Business under Fictitious Name," *Needles Desert Star*, September 12, 1963, p. 6; "Crash Kills *Sun-Telegram* Executive," *Sun*, December 13, 1968, sec. B, p. 1; Joe de Kehoe, "The Roadrunner's Retreat," *Route 66 Magazine* 26, no. 2 (Spring 2019): 20–21; "Eckley Arrests Robbers," *Needles Desert Star*, November 16, 1972, p. 16; "Helen Tull an Amboy Housewife and Business Woman," *Needles Desert Star*, November 9, 1972, p. 11; Road Runner Retreat, East of Amboy, Calif., "Waitresses, Cooks and Station Attendants" (advertisement), *Desert Star*, October 12, 1967, sec. A, p. 5; Roadrunner [*sic*] Retreat, East of Amboy, Calif., "Wanted—Service Station Attendant" (advertisement), *Desert Star*, June 29, 1972, p. 14; "Roy H. Tull, Amboy," *Sun-Telegram*, July 6, 1977, Victor Valley sec. B, p. 1.

14. Mike Anton, "Destiny in the Desert," *Los Angeles Times*, January 17, 2007, sec. A, pp. 1, 14; Bischoff, *Life in the Past Lane*, 1:83–84; James Albert Davis, *From Coast to Coast via Auto and Tent* (Federalsburg, Md.: J. W. Stowell Printing, 1922), 49 (second quotation); de Kehoe, *Silence and the Sun*, 183–220; Roberta LeGrand, "Amboy: The Busiest Ghost Town on Route 66," *Route 66 Magazine* 14, no. 4 (Fall 2007): 22–24; Mohawk Rubber Company, *Guide No. 3*, 16 (first quotation); Chuck Mueller, "Amboy, Pop. 14, Is Becoming a Big-Time Destination," *San Bernardino County Sun*, October 17, 1997, sec. A, pp. 1–2; Thompson, *Mohave Desert Region*, 690–96; Tom Teague, *Searching for 66* (Springfield, Ill.: Samizdat House, 1991), 206–7.

15. "Amboy News," *Desert Star*, August 16, 1945, p. 4; "Amboy Resident Taken by Death," *San Bernardino Daily Sun*, April 11, 1940, p. 14; T. Lindsay Baker, *Portrait of Route 66: Images from the Curt Teich Postcard Archives* (Norman: University of Oklahoma Press, 2016), 214–15; "Bender, Joseph Michael," *Valley Times Today* (North Hollywood, Calif.), December 22, 1960, p. 23; "Blaze Destroys Third of Buildings in Amboy," *Los Angeles Times*, December 11, 1964, pt. 2, p. 2; "Conn Pulos[,] Amboy Postmaster," *San Bernardino County Sun*, May 9, 1990, sec. B, p. 6; de Kehoe, *Silence and the Sun*, 198–203; Luther Friend, Amboy, Calif., "Experienced Fry Cook, Single" (advertisement), *Sun*, August 3, 1966, Classified Advertising sec., p. B; Luther Friend, Amboy, Calif., "Single College Girls Preferred. Summer Work in Frosty Snack Bar" (advertisement), *Sun*, June 30, 1967, Classified Advertising sec., p. C; Bob Houchin and Gloria Houchin, eds., "Dear Editor," *Roadsigns* 7, no. 3 (Fall 1997): 7 (first quotation); Della (Foulenfont) Inglis, interview by Joe de Kehoe, Granite Bay, Calif., June 25, 2002, typewritten transcript, p. 9 (second quotation), Joe de Kehoe Collection; "Lillie Pulos, Rialto," *Sun*, December 23, 1971, sec. B, p. 6; "Mission Count Shows Errors," *San Bernardino Daily Sun*, September 12, 1922, p. 3; "Motorist Who Hit Sleeping Man Held," *San Bernardino Daily Sun*, July 22, 1936, p. 10; "Notice of Automobile Sale," *Needles Nugget*, August 12, 1938, p. [4]; "Notice of Constable's Sale of Real Property," *Needles Nugget*, August 26, 1938, p. [8]; "Notice of Primary Election," *San Bernardino Daily Sun*, August 8, 1922, pp. 12–13; "Notice of Sale," *Needles Nugget*, February 22, 1924, p. 3; Leonard Purdy, "Amboy? All's A-Okay There," *Sun-Telegram*, April 8, 1972, sec. B, p. 16; Roy's Café, Amboy, Calif., *Roy's Café[,] P.O. Box 12[,] Amboy, California* (Amboy, Calif.: Roy's Café, [ca. 1995]), printed menu, courtesy of Steven Rider and Mike Ward; Bob Smith, "Bilking of Motorists in Desert Is Claimed," sec. A, pp. 1–2.

16. Arizaga and Arizaga interview pp. 57, 59–62; "Betty May Burris, San Bernardino County," *Sun*, October 26, 1979, sec. C, p. 5; Danny Castro, "The First Time I Met Buster," *Roadsigns*, Winter–Spring 2001, pp. 3–4;

"The Crowls Have Spent Twenty Years at Amboy," *Desert Sun* (Palm Springs, Calif.), July 29, 1948, p. 1; de Keho, *Silence and the* Sun, 195–98; David Knudson, "Towns on Route 66 That Have Vanished," pt. 1, *Route 66 Federation News* 26, no. 1 (Spring 2020): 4–15; Andrea Arizaga Limon, interview by Joe de Kehoe, Twentynine Palms, Calif., August 6, 2004, typewritten transcript, pp. 52–53, Joe de Kehoe Collection; Elaine Marable, "It's Quieter Now, in Amboy, but the Town's Far from Dead," *Sun-Telegram*, October 6, 1977, Barstow-Yucca Valley-29 Palms sec. B, p. 1; "Notice to Creditors of Bulk Transfer," *San Bernardino Daily Sun*, September 18, 1965, Classified Advertising sec., p. A; "Roy I. Crowl, Cherry Valley," *Sun-Telegram*, September 13, 1977, sec. B, p. 5; Roy's Café, Amboy, Calif., "Cooks, Waitresses and Service Station Operators" (advertisement), *San Bernardino Daily Sun*, May 13, 1949, Classified Advertising sec., p. A; "Township Ballots to List 110 Justice, Constable Candidates," *San Bernardino Daily Sun*, June 26, 1938, pp. 13, 23.

17. Lowella Anne (McLain) Parker, interview by Joe de Kehoe, Twentynine Palms, Calif., February 1, 2008, typewritten transcript, 9, 19–20 (quotations), Joe de Kehoe Collection; Quinta Scott and Susan Croce Kelly, *Route 66: The Highway and Its People* (Norman: University of Oklahoma Press, 1988), 80, 140–41, 159–60; Michael Wallis, *Route 66: The Mother Road* (New York: St. Martin's Press, 1990), 217–19, 221, 223.

18. Melissa Lea Beasley, "News from the Road: Roy's Relighting," *Route 66 New Mexico* 28, no. 1 (Winter 2020): 30; Bohmker, "Seven Miles out of Bagdad," 32–33; Sheryl Kornman, "After 50 Years in Amboy, Again Proprietor Puts His Town Up for Sale," *Los Angeles Times*, October 1, 1989, pt. 8, pp. 1, 22–23; Albert Okura, interview by T. Lindsay Baker, San Bernardino, Calif., July 14, 2016, manuscript notes, author's collection; Albert Okura, *The Chicken Man with a 50 Year Plan*, 2nd ed. (Fontana, Calif.: LCM Publishing, 2015), 175–82; "Road News: Fast Food Entrepreneur Buys Amboy," *Route 66 Magazine* 12, no. 3 (Summer 2005): 51; Stephan Stern, "A Desert Gift for That Someone Who Has Everything," *Sunday Sun* (San Bernardino, Calif.), December 25, 1983, Inland Empire East Valley sec B, pp. 1, 4; "You Can Be Mayor: Town in Mojave Offered for Sale," *Los Angeles Times*, September 7, 1975, pt. 7, p. 11.

19. Bischoff, *Life in the Past Lane*, 1:85–90; de Kehoe, *Silence and the Sun*, 56, 69, 72; Stephen Fried, *Appetite for America: Fred Harvey and the Business of Civilizing the Wild West One Meal at a Time* (New York: Bantam Books, 2010), 428; Claudia Heller, "Bagdad, California[,] and the Graveyard," *Route 66 Magazine* 24, no. 2 (Spring 2017): 26–28; Bob Moore, "Bagdad," *Route 66 Magazine* 2, no. 4 (Fall 1995): 62–63; Bob Moore, "Bagdad Café," *Route 66 Magazine* 7, no. 4 (Fall 2000): 8–10; Russell Olsen, "Then and Now: Bagdad, California[,] with Bill Bergee," *Route 66 Magazine* 16, no. 2 (Spring 2009): 22–23; 16, no. 3 (Summer 2009): 22–23; Rittenhouse, *Guide Book to Highway 66*, 115–16; Joseph Szalanski, *Boarding the Westbound: Journey of a Depression-era Hobo* (Tarentum, Pa.: Word Association Publishers, 2010), 102 (quotations), 106, 134, 179–80, 182–87; Thompson, *Mohave Desert Region*, 71–73, 690–91.

20. Baker, *Portrait of Route 66*, 216–21; Bischoff, *Life in the Past Lane*, 1:93–96; Bob Butcher, "Ludlow, California," *Route 66 Magazine* 3, no. 1 (Winter 1995–96): 30–31; Lucille Byerly Lackore, *To California on Route 66 in 1932* (n.p.: 1998), 56; Metcalfe-Shaw, *English Caravanners*, 63–65; Mueller, "Desert Hamlets' Future," sec. A, p. 4; Roberta Ramsdell, "Diary" [of trip by automobile from Alhambra, California, to Washington, D.C., June 3 to June 13, 1935], manuscript, unpaged (quotation), "Route 66" Vertical File, Gilb Museum of Arcadia Heritage, Arcadia, Calif.; Thompson, *Mohave Desert Region*, 656–59.

21. In his 1942 conscription registration, Lee Yim saw that his wife's name transliterated from Chinese was clearly hand printed in block letters as "Ginswa Yim." The enumerators in the U.S. census hand wrote her name "Ginshu" in 1920, as "Ginshu" or "Ginshee" in 1930, and as "Guishee" in 1940. The local press referred to her as "Mrs. Lee Yim" or "Mrs. Yim." When Lee Yim registered for the military draft in World War I in 1918, he identified his wife as being "Mrs. Lee Yim" with her address as "China," indicating that she had not yet immigrated. "Ludlow Notes," *San Bernardino Daily Sun*, May 5, 1940, p. 21; U.S. Census Bureau, Census of 1920, Population Schedules, Ludlow Township, San Bernardino County, Calif., Enumeration District 160, page 1A, Roll 129, Microcopy T625; U.S. Census Bureau, Census of 1930, Population Schedules, Ludlow Township, San Bernardino County, Calif., Enumeration District 36-31, page 6A, Roll 188, Microcopy T626; and U.S. Census Bureau, Census of 1940, Population Schedules, Ludlow Twp., San Bernardino County,

California, Enumeration District 36–52, p. 3A, Roll 289, Microcopy T627, all in National Archives and Records Administration; U.S. Selective Service, World War I Draft Registration Cards, for Lee Yim, Stagg Post Office, San Bernardino County, Calif., September 12, 1918, https://search.ancestry.com/cgi-bin/sse.dll?dbid+6482&h+30008638&indiv+try&o_vc+Record:OtherRecord&rhSource+2442, accessed on July 4, 2020; U.S. Selective Service, World War II Draft Cards (4th Registration), April 27, 1942, for Lee Yim, Ludlow, San Bernardino County, Calif., https://search.ancestry.com/cgi-bin/sse.dll?bid=1002&h=13260906&indiv=try&o_vc=Record:OtherRecord&rhSource=2442, accessed on July 4, 2020.

22. "Amend Ruling on New County Road Program," *San Bernardino Daily Sun*, December 10, 1929, p. [12]; "County Warrants," *San Bernardino Daily Sun*, July 30, 1916, p. 12; de Kehoe, *Silence and the Sun*, 191, 221; Stephanie Lee Jordan, interview by Joe de Kehoe at Spring Valley, Calif., July 23, 2005, typewritten transcript, 21–22, 34 (quotation); and Tom R. Morgan, telephone interview by Joe de Kehoe, Escondido, Calif., November 30, 2005, typewritten transcript, 27–28, both in Joe de Kehoe Collection; "38 Applicants File Requests to Sell Beer," *San Bernardino Daily Sun*, May 28, 1933, p. 5; "Three Fined for Slot Machines: Sheriff's Men Raid Colorado River Area," *San Bernardino Daily Sun*, April 20, 1949, p. 19.

23. "Chinese Files on Ore Claims near Ludlow," *San Bernardino Daily Sun*, August 23, 1933, p. 4; "Chinese Miner Victorious in Two Lawsuits," *San Bernardino Daily Sun*, February 22, 1936, p. 13; "Chinese Victor in Suit to Hold Rich Gold Mine," *San Bernardino Daily Sun*, February 9, 1935, p. [11]; "Heirs Sought to $1,000,000 Ludlow Mine," *San Bernardino Daily Sun*, August 10, 1938, pp. 13, 23; "Lee Receives Degree in Hawaii Exercises," *San Bernardino Daily Sun*, June 28, 1951, p. 17; "Lee Yim Mine Ships Car of Rich Gold Ore," *Los Angeles Times*, March 13, 1933, p. [13]; "Ludlow Notes," *Desert Star*, September 6, 1945, p. 6; "Mine Activity near Barstow Forges Ahead," *San Bernardino Daily Sun*, March 7, 1933, p. 10; "Real Estate Diplomas Given," *San Bernardino Daily Sun*, April 14, 1960, sec. C, p. 3; U.S. Social Security Administration, Social Security Death Index for Lee Yim, 1969, https://www/fold3.com/record/7462949-lee-yim?terms+lee%20yim, accessed July 4, 2020; "Yim Risks Grub on Gold Quest: Promising Find near Ludlow Outcome of Pact with Prospector," *Los Angeles Times*, May 22, 1933, p. [13].

24. Bischoff, *Life in the Past Lane*, 1:96–98; "First Aid Demonstrated by Red Cross in Newberry," *San Bernardino Daily Sun*, February 13, 1937, p. 13; Bonnie Jean Hoerner, *Pioneering on Route 66 and Beyond: The Story of Evangeline Hoerner McCoy* (Clovis, Calif.: privately printed, 2005), 121–31, 134–39, 147–57, 162–66, 170–72, 175, 202–13, 216, 380–81, 414–20 (quotations); "Mojave Mining Group to Meet in Barstow Friday," *San Bernardino Daily Sun*, March 3, 1936, p. 13; "New Trial for Mine Suit Lost," *San Bernardino Daily Sun*, August 5, 1938, p. 14; "Oscar L. Hoerner," *San Bernardino Daily Sun*, October 4, 1964, sec. B, p. 10; "Quiet Title to County Land Sought as Complaint Filed," *San Bernardino Daily Sun*, March 22, 1931, p. 5.

25. "Burglars Seem to Want TVs," *Sun-Telegram*, Barstow, sec. B, p. 2; "Desert Gas Station Destroyed by Fire," *San Bernardino Daily Sun*, April 18, 1957, p. 15; "Desert Oasis Fire Destroys 4 Buildings," *San Bernardino Daily Sun*, February 18, 1955, p. 26; Charles K. Dooley, "Safety Valve," *Colton (Calif.) Courier*, May 25, 1945, p. 1; July 10, 1951, p. 1; "Jauss Named to School Board at Newberry," *San Bernardino Daily Sun*, July 13, 1963, sec. B, p. 4; "Missing Gardenia Divorcee's Broken Down Auto Located," *Valley Times* (North Hollywood, Calif.), November 13, 1958, p. 23; Joe Sonderman, *California Dreamin' along Route 66* (Charleston, S.C.: Arcadia Publishing, 2019), 30; "Route 66 Real Photo Postcards from California," http://rt66.x10host.com/rppc/caeast.html, accessed July 2, 2020; "Trio Held for Burglary of Two Stations," *San Bernardino Daily Sun*, March 11, 1965, sec. D, p. 2; "Vital Records," *San Bernardino Daily Sun*, August 21, 1948, p. 9; "Waitress Signs Rape Complaint," *San Bernardino Daily Sun*, September 11, 1952, p. 17. At least one writer has asserted that half a mile separated the site of the second Mojave Water Camp from the later Poe's Café/ Desert Inn. "Sign of the Times," Never Quite Lost, http://neverquitelost.com/2017/07/24/sign-of-the-times/, accessed July 2, 2020.

26. L. Burr Belden, "History in the Making: Once Main Road to Phoenix Has Years of Neglect," *Sun-Telegram*, April 20, 1958, sec. D, p. 6; Bischoff, *Life in the Past Lane*, 1:96–98; *California: A Guide to the Golden State*, 612; Metcalfe-Shaw, *English Caravanners*, 61–63; Mohawk Rubber Company, *Guide No. 3*, 15; Rider, *Rider's*

California, 626–27; Rittenhouse, *Guide Book to Highway 66*, 116; Dallas Lore Sharp, *The Better Country* (Boston: Houghton Mifflin, 1928), 232 (quotations).

27. "Barstow Folk Enjoy Outings," *San Bernardino Daily Sun*, June 2, 1933, p. 15; Belden, "History in the Making: Pioneer Motor Travelers," p. 40; Bischoff, *Life in the Past Lane*, 1:98–105; Cliff House, Newberry, Calif., "Middle Age Couple, No Children, Grocery Store and Restaurant Experience" (advertisement), *San Bernardino Daily Sun*, August 10, 1960, Classified Advertising sec., p. B; "Doris J. Sischo[,] Redlands Resident," *San Bernardino County Sun*, December 20, 1994, sec. B, p. 4; Burton Frasher Sr., "Swimming Pool at Cliff House, Newberry, Calif.," real photo postcard, 1934, index no. E1832, Frasher Foto Postcard Collection, Pomona Public Library, Pomona, Calif.; Betty Clack Grounds and Ollie Clack Bond, transcription of interview extracts in exhibit gallery, Arizona Route 66 Museum, Powerhouse Visitors Center, Kingman, Ariz. (quotations), accessed by the author July 9, 2016; Jack Hartsfield, "Victim Beaten, Possibly Shot; Youth Gives Up," *San Bernardino Daily Sun*, November 28, 1964, sec. A, pp. 1–2; Hoerner, *Pioneering on Route 66 and Beyond*, 157–59; Patricia Jernigan Keeling, ed., *Once upon a Desert: A Bicentennial Project* (Barstow, Calif.: Mojave River Valley Museum Association, 1976), 153–55; Metcalfe-Shaw, *English Caravanners*, 57–59; Mohawk Rubber Company, *Guide No. 3*, 15; Chuck Mueller, "Hidden Oasis Is a Paradise of 400 Lakes," *Sun*, July 14, 1981, sec. B, p. 1; "Newberry: Water Place Becomes Town," *Sun-Telegram*, September 29, 1957, sec. D, p. 14; "Notice of Primary Election," *San Bernardino Daily Sun*, August 18, 1930, p. 10; Olsen, *Route 66 Lost and Found*, 390–91; "Only Spring Board Is at Newberry," *Desert Star*, August 8, 1946, p. 8; "Possession of Auto Camp Issue in Suit," *San Bernardino Daily Sun*, April 6, 1934, p. 15; Rittenhouse, *Guide Book to Highway 66*, 117; Thompson, *Mohave Desert Region*, 437–38, 498–99; "Woman Pilots Good Maxwell to Oasis over Desert Trail," *Sunday Long Beach (Calif.) Press*, September 16, 1923, sec. 3, pp. 1, [8].

28. Bischoff, *Life in the Past Lane*, 1:106–8; Jim Hinckley, *Ghost Towns of Route 66* (Minneapolis: Voyageur Press, 2011), 152; John Kofton, "My Girl Lou from Knott's to Daggett to Calico," *Roadsigns*, June 2004, pp. 5–6; Rittenhouse, *Guide Book to Highway 66*, 117–18; Thompson, *Mohave Desert Region*, 437–38.

29. Peter Aldrich, "California Here We Come!," *Route 66 Magazine* 12, no. 4 (Fall 2005): 32–34 (first quotation); Birney, *Roads to Roam*, 108–9; Bischoff, *Life in the Past Lane*, 1:105–6; Glen Duncan and the California Route 66 Preservation Foundation, *Images of America: Route 66 in California* (Charleston, S.C.: Arcadia Publishing, 2005), 28–29; Gannett, *Sweet Land*, 119–24; James N. Gregory, *American Exodus: The Dust Bowl Migration and Okie Culture in California* (New York: Oxford University Press, 1989), 80–81; Claudia Heller, "Thumbin' on Route 66," *Route 66 Magazine* 21, no. 4 (Fall 2014): 40–41 (second and third quotations); Claudia Heller and Alan Heller, *Life on Route 66: Personal Accounts along the Mother Road to California* (Charleston, S.C.: History Press, 2012): 23–24; William Kaszynski, *Route 66: Images of America's Main Street* (Jefferson, N.C.: McFarland, 2003), 145–46; Nomination to the National Register of Historic Places for U.S. Highway 66 in California, E33–E34, E37; Olsen, *Route 66 Lost and Found*, 392; Pepys, *Mine Host, America*, 206–7; Rittenhouse, *Guide Book to Highway 66*, 117–18; Oliver E. Rooker, interview by Roger Harris, Canton, Okla., October 19, 1993, audio recording and typewritten transcript, pp. 14–21, Research Center, Oklahoma Historical Society, Oklahoma City; Orville Rooker, *Riding the Travel Bureau: Ghost Riders Network on Route 66 during the Great Depression* (Canton, Okla.: Memoir Publishing, 1994), 8, 11, 46–65, 68–70; Elizabeth Strickland, *Route 66 to the Fields in California* (Tallahassee, Fla.: Clark Publishing House, 2002), 54–60; Evelyn Tucker, "Diary—August 1938[,] Three Days on Highway 66 Tulsa to California," in *Memories on Route 66 1991* (Bethany: Oklahoma Route 66 Association, 1991), 76–77.

30. Bischoff, *Life in the Past Lane*, 1:108–14; *California: A Guide to the Golden State*, 612; Elmer Long, interview by David K. Dunaway, Oro Grande, Calif., July 2008, typewritten transcript, pp. 11–12, Route 66 Corridor Preservation Program, National Park Service, Santa Fe; Mohawk Rubber Company, *Guide No. 3*, 15; Rittenhouse, *Guide Book to Highway 66*, 119; Scott and Kelly, *Route 66: The Highway and Its People*, 73–74; Thompson, *Mohave Desert Region*, 372–73, 423–24, 430.

31. Helen Baker, "The Barstow Harvey House," *Roadsigns*, September 2004, pp. 7, 11–12; "Barstow Proud of New Hotel," *Los Angeles Times*, February 21, 1911, p. 13; Tom E. Donia, "Barstow Harvey House Threatened,"

Preservation News (Washington, D.C.) 17, no. 1 (December 1976): 1, 7; Kevin Hansel, "The Mother Road Museum," *Roadsigns*, Winter–Spring 2003, pp. 8–9, 14; Dan Harlow, "Tracing Railroad Preservation on Route 66: California Railroad Stations," pt. 2, *Route 66 Federation News* 6, no. 1 (Winter 2000): 19–23; "Hotel Name Is Cause of a Protest," *San Bernardino Daily Sun*, August 14, 1910, p. 10; "Huge Viaduct Dedicated at Gala Program," *San Bernardino Daily Sun*, April 27, 1930, p. 14; Keeling, *Once upon a Desert*, 65–66, 161–63, 166–67; Elaine Marable, "Ex-Harvey Girl Tells about a By-Gone Era," *Sun*, January 5, 1971, sec. B, p. 3; Elaine Marable, "Harvey House Rich in Memories of Past," *Sun-Telegram*, October 13, 1976, Barstow-Desert sec. B, p. 1; Metcalfe-Shaw, *English Caravanners*, 50–51; Germaine L. Ramounachou Moon, *Barstow Depots and Harvey Houses* (Barstow, Calif.: Mojave Valley Museum Association, 1980), 1–36; Nomination to the National Register of Historic Places for Harvey House Railroad Depot, Barstow, Calif., April 3, 1975; "Plaque Dedicated," *Sun*, May 3, 1983, Desert-Mountain sec. B, p. 3; Poling-Kempes, *Harvey Girls*, 165–67, 196–97, 202–3; Letitia Stockett, *America: First, Fast and Furious* (Baltimore, Md.: Norman-Remington, 1930), 213–15 (quotations); Paul Taylor, "When Harvey Came to Barstow," *Route 66 Magazine* 8, no. 2 (Spring 2001): 50–51.

32. Bischoff, *Life in the Past Lane*, 1:116–22; *California: A Guide to the Golden State*, 612–23; Rider, *Rider's California*, 626; Rittenhouse, *Guide Book to Highway 66*, 120–21; *Southern California at a Glance: History[,] Romance[,] Maps[,] Facts[,] Statistics* (Los Angeles: States Publishing, 1930), 82–83; Thompson, *Mohave Desert Region*, 371–76, 427–28.

33. Bischoff, *Life in the Past Lane*, 1:122; Jim Ross, *Route 66 Crossings: Historic Bridges of the Mother Road* (Norman: University of Oklahoma Press, 2016), 67; "Route 66 Museums: California Route 66 Museum—Victorville, California," *Route 66 Federation News* 20, no. 3 (Summer 2014): 17–21; Shell Oil Company [New York, N.Y.], *Shell Finger-Tip Tours: U.S. 66 60–70–91 89–85 Santa Monica to Amarillo* ([New York]: Shell Oil Company, 1949), 5; "Victor Growth Seen Since '12," *Mountaineer* (San Bernardino, Calif.), October 15, 1937, p. 2; Thompson, *Mohave Desert Region*, 373–74, 403–8, 414–16, 420–23.

34. "Eats on Rt 66: Hollandburger Café," *Roadsigns* 7, no. 3 (Fall 1997): [8–9]; "Get Your Kicks at Emma Jean's: Holland Burger Café Owner Remembers Route 66," *Daily Press* (Victorville, Calif.), August 10, 2012, sec. B, pp. 1, 6; Martial Haprov, "Enormous Eats at Emma Jean's," *Daily Press*, July 19, 2016, sec. D, p. 1; R. R. Holland, Victorville, Calif., "Café in Victorville for Lease" (advertisement), *Independent* (Long Beach, Calif.), October 8, 1957, sec. C, p. 9; Kara Hewson Nelson, "Hollandburger: Serving up the Best Biscuits and Gravy," *Roadsigns* 7, no. 1 (Spring 1997): 7; Registration Records for Catherine L. Holland and Robert L. Holland, San Bernardino County, Calif., Voter Registration, November 1958, San Bernardino 51 to Yucca Valley, Victorville p. 2, California State Library, Sacramento, Calif.

35. "Brown Bomber's Orange Juice Tops Training Diet," *San Bernardino Daily Sun*, March 15, 1939, p. 15; Leona Thomas Griner, interview by Richard D. Thompson, September 3, 2002, typewritten transcript, Mohahve Historical Society Oral Histories, pp. 12–14, http://mojavehistory.com/interviewgriner.html, accessed by the author August 23, 2007; "Joe Louis Camp Opened to Public," *San Bernardino Daily Sun*, March 11, 1939, p. 15; "Joe Louis Enjoys Guest Ranch Visit," *Mountaineer*, October 22, 1937, p. 4; "Life Goes to Murray's Ranch," *Mountaineer*, November 26, 1937, p. 3; "Murray's Dude Ranch Has Many Visitors," *Los Angeles Sentinel*, July 28, 1938, sec. A, p. 5; Murray's Dude Ranch, Victorville, Calif., "Murray's Dude Ranch for You[r] Week End" (advertisement), *Los Angeles Sentinel*, October 10, 1940, p. 2; Murray's Dude Ranch, "Vacation of Your Life[,] Murray's Dude Ranch" (advertisement), *Los Angeles Sentinel*, June 7, 1951, sec. A, p. 4; "Murray's Ranch—Desert Playground," *Los Angeles Sentinel*, September 8, 1938, p. 7; "Murray's Ranch Entertain Crowd," *Mountaineer*, June 3, 1938, p. 2; "Murray's Ranch Host to Hollywood Picture Group," *Mountaineer*, October 21, 1938, p. 1; "Negro Dude Ranch Opens in California: Word's Heavyweight Champion Is a Guest There," *Life* 3, no. 20 (November 15, 1937): 116–17; Cecilia Rasmussen, "L.A. Then and Now: In Prejudiced Era, Ranch Welcomed Dudes of All Colors," *Los Angeles Times*, February 22, 2004, sec. B, p. 4; "Seven File Notices for Liquor Permits," *San Bernardino Daily Sun*, September 8, 1937, p. 5; Lee Shippey, "The Lee Side o' L.A.," *Los Angeles Times*, October 1, 1937, pt. 2, p. 4; Richard D.

Thompson, *Murray's Ranch: Apple Valley's African-American Dude Ranch* (Apple Valley, Calif.: Desert Knolls Press, 2002), 1–25. For a scholarly examination of African American settlement in the high desert around Victorville including Murray's Ranch, see Jennifer L. Thornton, "Remembering Bell Mountain: African American Landownership and Leisure in California's High Desert during the Jim Crow Era" (PhD diss., University of California, 2018).

36. "California Dude Ranch," *Ebony* 2, no. 4 (February 1947), 5–11 (quotations); "Easter Rites on Catholic Peak," *Los Angeles Sentinel*, April 10, 1952, sec. A, p. 6; *Five Views: An Ethnic Site Survey for California* (Sacramento: Office of Historic Preservation, Department of Parks and Recreation, 1988), 89–90; "Jack Benny on Location with Film Company," *San Bernardino Daily Sun*, November 15, 1939, p. 12; Rasmussen, "L.A. Then and Now," sec. B, p. 4; Thompson, *Murray's Ranch*, 10–16, 18–25; "Thousands to Greet Dawn of Easter at Sunrise Services," *San Bernardino Daily Sun*, April 8, 1939, pp. 13, 23.

37. Matthew Cabe, "'The World's Only Negro Dude Ranch,'" *Daily Press*, May 12, 2017, sec. C, pp. 1, 6; Florence Cadrez, "Mostly 'bout Musicians," *Los Angeles Sentinel*, June 16, 1955, sec. A, p. 11; "Lela Murray of Victorville Taken by Death," *Los Angeles Sentinel*, March 24, 1949, sec. A, p. 1; "Pearl Bailey Buy's Murray's Desert Ranch," *Los Angeles Sentinel*, June 23, 1955, sec. A, p. 3; Rasmussen, "L.A. Then and Now," sec. B, p. 4; Thompson, *Murray's Ranch*, 25–34.

38. Birney, *Roads to Roam*, 105, 109 (first quotation); *California: A Guide to the Golden State*, 613–14; Davis, *From Coast to Coast*, 48 (second quotation); Elrond Lawrence, *Route 66 Railway: The Story of Route 66 and the Santa Fe Railway in the American Southwest* (Alhambra, Calif.: Los Angeles Railway Heritage Foundation, 2008), 53–55; Rider, *Rider's California*, 624–25; Rittenhouse, *Guide Book to Highway 66*, 122.

39. Ray T. Bohacz, "Blowing in the Wind: The Automotive Radiator," *Hemmings Classic Car* 3, no. 1 (October 2006): 84–87; J. W. Bush, Summit, Calif., "For Sale—Mountain Ranch Five Miles from Summit Station" (advertisement), *San Bernardino Daily Sun*, January 18, 1920, p. 4 (quotation); Chevrolet Motor Company, Detroit, Mich., *Instructions for the Operation and Care of Chevrolet Motor Cars[,] Universal Series AD*, 8th ed. (Detroit: Chevrolet Motor Co., 1930), 43–46, author's collection; Ford Motor Company, Detroit, *Ford Manual for Owners and Operators of Ford Cars and Trucks*, publication 300M-1-15-18 (Detroit: Ford Motor Company, [1918]), 19–21, author's collection.

40. Jack Booth, Pomona, Calif., "For Sale or Lease Summit Inn, Cajon Pass" (advertisement), *San Bernardino Daily Sun*, October 1, 1941, p. 18; "Grewsome [*sic*] Find May Solve Mystery in Ontario," *Bulletin* (Pomona, Calif.), September 14, 1923, sec. 2, p. 1; "Heavy Truck Rams into Bus in Cajon Pass," *San Bernardino Daily Sun*, November 30, 1951, p. 13; "Notice of Intention to Engage in the Sale of Alcoholic Beverages," *San Bernardino Daily Sun*, September 30, 1938, p. 14; "Notice of Sale of Stock in Bulk," *Pomona (Calif.) Progress Bulletin*, October 25, 1940, sec. 2, p. 5; Jon Robinson, *Route 66: Lives on the Road* (Osceola, Wisc.: MBI Publishing, 2001), 21–24; "Old Trails Is to Be Widened through Cajon," *San Bernardino Daily Sun*, September 14, 1926, p. [11] (quotation); Standard Oil Company (California), [San Francisco], "These Dealers in San Bernardino Sell Red Crown Gasoline" (advertisement), *San Bernardino Daily Sun*, June 10, 1924, p. [16]; Summit Inn, Cajon Pass, Calif., "Family Style Dinner" (advertisement), *San Bernardino Daily Sun*, November 5, 1939, p. 4; Summit Inn, "Wanted—Middle Age Couple" (advertisement), *San Bernardino Daily Sun*, May 22, 1926, p. 18; Union Pacific Stages, [Omaha, Neb.], "Big Modern Buses" (advertisement), *San Bernardino Daily Sun*, May 11, 1932, p. 15.

41. Colin Agagi and Gabby Ferreira, "Blue Cut Fire Grows, Evacuations Continue," *Desert Sun*, August 18, 2016, sec. A, pp. 1, 6; Alan Ashby, "Victorville Service Station Fined $15,000 as Fraud Curb," *Sun*, March 9, 1973, sec. B, p. 6; Jack Blue, "San Bernardino—in Retrospect," *Sun-Telegram*, July 31, 1975, sec. C, p. 2; Larry Bohannan, "Americana at 4,190 Feet. Gone," *Desert Sun*, August 18, 2016, sec. A, pp. 1, 6; "Boy Firebug Has Date with Smokey," *Los Angeles Times*, October 10, 1959, pt. 1, p. 6; Matthew Cabe, "Summit Inn R.I.P.," *Route 66 Federation News* 22, no. 3 (Autumn 2016): 4–5; Jan Cleveland, "Heavy Snowstorm Closes Schools, Blankets Roads," *Sun-Telegram*, January 7, 1977, sec. C, pp. 1, 4; "Former Mayor, Owner of Summit Inn Dead at 88," *San Bernardino County Sun*, March 30, 1993, sec. B, p. 4; Mike Gordon, "After

30 Years of Waiting, She's Home," *San Bernardino County Sun*, May 26, 1991, sec. A, p. 1 (quotation); Claudia Heller, "Memories of the Summit Inn," *Route 66 Magazine* 24, no. 1 (Winter 2016–17): 52–53; Bob Moore, "Inn at the Top," *Route 66 Magazine* 5, no. 2 (Spring 1998): 14–15; Jim Munding, "Summit Inn," *Roadsigns* 4, no. 3 (Summer 1994): 12; "Push Work on New Cajon Pass Freeway," *San Bernardino Daily Sun*, March 10, 1955, p. 18; Robinson, *Route 66: Lives on the Road*, 21–24; "San Bernardino Blaze Rages on; 2 L.A. County Fires Controlled," *Los Angeles Times*, September 9, 1968, pt. 1, pp. 1, 3; Joe Sonderman, *Route 66 Then and Now* (London: Pavilion Books, 2018), 136; Summit Inn, "Experienced Waitress, 30 Years or Over" (advertisement), *San Bernardino Daily Sun*, August 20, 1962, Classified Advertising sec., p. A.

42. *California: A Guide to the Golden State*, 614–23; Mohawk Rubber Company, *Guide No. 3*, 13–14; Rider, *Rider's California*, 507–11, 524–27; Rittenhouse, *Guide Book to Highway 66*, 122–24. Guidebook author Candacy Taylor brutally described the present-day landscape along former U.S. Highway 66 from San Bernardino westward as "little more than a concrete slab of suburbia and a gateway to the sprawling metropolis of Los Angeles." Candacy Taylor, *Moon Route 66 Road Trip* (Berkeley, Calif.: Avalon Travel, 2016), 312. For representative historic motorists' accounts of the descent from the Cajon Summit into the formerly lush agricultural area, see Birney, *Roads to Roam*, 109–10; Davis, *From Coast to Coast*, 49–51 (third quotation); McGill, *Diary of a Motor Journey*, 89–90 (first quotation); Pepys, *Mine Host, America*, 210–11; Sharp, *Better Country*, 234–37; Tucker, "Diary—August 1938," 79 (second quotation).

43. "Airdome Drive-In License Suspended," *Monrovia (Calif.) Daily News-Post*, November 22, 1938, p. 1; John A. Jakle and Keith A. Sculle, *Fast Food: Roadside Restaurants in the Automobile Age* (Baltimore: Johns Hopkins University Press, 1999), 139–62; Todd S. Jenkins, "Fast Feud: The Bitter Battle for a Drive-thru Empire," *Route 66 Magazine* 10, no. 4 (Fall 2003): 14–15, 23; "Kickoff Breakfast for Days of Gold Set for Today," *San Bernardino Daily Sun*, September 23, 1948, p. 17; Ray Kroc and Robert Anderson, *Grinding It Out: The Making of McDonald's* (New York: St. Martin's Paperbacks, 1987), 6–12, 69–73; John F. Love, *McDonald's: Behind the Arches* (New York: Bantam Books, 1986), 9–47; McDonald's Drive-In, San Bernardino, Calif., "Car Hop" (advertisement), *San Bernardino Daily Sun*, May 24, 1947, p. 15; McDonald's Drive-In, San Bernardino, "Did You Know That" (advertisement), *San Bernardino Daily Sun*, November 29, 1945, p. 5 (quotation); McDonald's Drive-In, San Bernardino, "Wanted! Girl Car Hop" (advertisement), *San Bernardino Daily Sun*, March 10, 1942, p. 18; Okura, *Chicken Man*, 93–96, 151–56; Geoffrey Willis, "McMemories Served Here," *Roadsigns* 9, no. 2 (Spring 1999): 8–10; Michael Karl Witzel, *The American Drive-In Restaurant* (St. Paul, Minn.: MBI Publishing, 1994), 34–36, 37, 90–92, 106, 110, 113, 116, 120, 123.

44. "Ceremonies Last Night: Salvador Rodriguez Installed President of Mexican Chamber," *Sun-Telegram*, January 10, 1960, sec. C, p. 5; "Co-Founder of Mitla[,] Lucia Rodriguez Dies," *Sun*, January 13, 1981, sec. A, p. 1; Julie Farren, "Now This Is Mexican Food," *San Bernardino County Sun*, May 7, 1997, sec. D, pp. 11, 3; "Notice of Intention to Engage in the Sale of Alcoholic Beverages," *San Bernardino Daily Sun*, April 27, 1941, p. 21; "Owner of Mitla's Café, Salvador Rodriguez, Dies," *Sun-Telegram*, October 13, 1974, p. 14; Denice A. Rios, "Mitla Café Boss, Vera Lopez, Dies," *Sun*, December 5, 1984, sec. B, p. 2; *San Bernardino Directory Co.'s City Directory 1940 Including Colton and Rialto* (San Bernardino, Calif.: San Bernardino Directory Co., 1940), 257, 317, 578; U.S. Census Bureau, Census of 1940, Population Schedules, Ward 5, San Bernardino, San Bernardino County, Calif., Enumeration District 36–132, page 2A, Roll 289, Microcopy T627, National Archives and Records Administration; "Vital Records," *San Bernardino Daily Sun*, April 5, 1941, p. 16.

45. Gustavo Arellano, *Taco USA: How Mexican Food Conquered America* (New York: Scribner, 2012), 52–59; Earl E. Buie, "They Tell Me," *Sun-Telegram*, October 2, 1960, sec. B, pp. 1, 5; Fabiloa Cabeza de Baca Gilbert, *The Good Life: New Mexico Traditions and Food*, 2nd ed. (Santa Fe: Museum of New Mexico Press, 1982), 71; Mitla Café, San Bernardino, Calif., *Mitla Café[,] 602 Mr. Vernon Av.[,] San Bernardino, California* (Mexico: Mitla Café, [ca. 1940]), menu, author's collection; Mitla Café, "Mitla Café[,] Tostados—Tacos[,] Enchiladas" (advertisement), *San Bernardino Daily Sun*, March 1, 1942, p. 28; "News of Food," *New York Times*, May 3, 1952, p. 24; Jeffrey M. Pilcher, "Was the Taco Invented in Southern California?," *Gastronomica*

8, no. 1 (Winter 2008): 26–34; U.S. Patent No. 2,506,305, Juvenico Maldonado, Form for Frying Tortillas to Make Fried Tacos, Filed July 21, 1947, Granted May 2, 1950, and U.S. Patent No. 2,570,374, Joseph P. Pompa, Machine for Frying Tortillas, Filed January 5, 1949, Granted October 9, 1951, both at U.S. Patent and Trademark Office, Washington, D.C. For articles reporting the preparation of crispy tacos in the San Bernardino area starting in the 1950s, see "Eagles Serve Spanish Dinner Friday," *Colton Courier*, May 10, 1950, p. 3; "Funtime's in Swing Now at Padua Hills," *Sun-Telegram*, July 8, 1956, p. 23; Dolores Heywood, "Many Events Planned for Mexican Fiesta," *San Bernardino Daily Sun*, September 12, 1957, pp. 40–41.

46. Arellano, *Taco USA*, 58–70 (quotation); Debra Lee Baldwin, *Taco Titan: The Glen Bell Story* (Arlington, Tex.: Summit Publishing, 1999), 49–115; "Building Figure for October Shows Drop under Last Month," *San Bernardino Daily Sun*, November 4, 1952, p. 15; "Business Briefs: 2 Former S.B. Residents Make Good with Taco Firm," *Sun*, February 24, 1967, sec. C, p. 7; "Detectives Investigate City Business Break In," *Sun-Telegram*, April 12, 1953, p. 47; Jakle and Sculle, *Fast Food*, 257–61; Gregory McNamee, *Tortillas, Tiswin and T-Bone: A Food History of the Southwest* (Albuquerque: University of New Mexico Press, 2017), 186–87; Jim Munding, "Mitla Café," *Roadsigns* 4, no. 4 (Fall 1994): 11; Sarah Parvini, "On a Taco Bell Run: Chain's Original Eatery Is Moved from Downey to Irvine," *Los Angeles Times*, November 21, 2015, sec. B, pp. 1, 6; Chuck Perlee and Virginia Perlee, "Place in the Sun," *Sun-Telegram*, May 11, 1958, sec. C, p. 2; Pilcher, "Was the Taco Invented in Southern California?," 34–37; Janet Zimmerman, "Founder of Taco-Tia Restaurant Dies at 82," *San Bernardino County Sun*, August 20, 1991, sec. B, p. 1.

47. Birney, *Roads to Roam*, 110 (third quotation); "Fontana: a Complete, Productive, Beautiful Community in Process of Creation," *San Bernardino Daily Sun*, October 1, 1914, sec. 5, p. 5; "Fontana Ready to Build City: Nucleus of New Valley Town Extension Already Raised on Site," *Los Angeles Times*, June 19, 1927, pt. 5, p. 6; Erwin Hein, "Fontana: Pittsburgh of the West?," *Westways* (Automobile Club of Southern California) 34, no. 9 (September 1942): 8–9; Ted Salmon [Salmon Fred Champion], *From Southern California to Casco Bay* (San Bernardino, Calif.: San Bernardino Publishing, 1930), 50–51; Sharp, *Better Country*, 235 (first quotation); *Southern California at a Glance*, 88–89; Tucker, "Diary—August 1938," 78 (second quotation); Walter Woehlke, "Fontana Story One of Success," *Los Angeles Times*, July 25, 1926, pt. 5, p. 4.

48. Joe Bono, interview by T. Lindsay Baker, Fontana, Calif., July 28, 2014, manuscript notes, unpaged, author's collection; Clark, *Route 66 Cookbook*, 206–7 (quotations); "Exonerate Fontana Man in Fire Case," *San Bernardino Daily Sun*, November 23, 1943, p. 11; "Federal Men Impound Wine," *San Bernardino Daily Sun*, February 21, 1936, p. 14; "Final Rites Planned for Joe Bono, Fontana," *San Bernardino Daily Sun*, December 14, 1944, p. 14; Hobby Nobby Market, Fontana, Calif., "Hobby Nobby Market" (advertisement), *San Bernardino Daily Sun*, April 29, 1947, p. 19; Nomination to the National Register of Historic Places for Bono's Restaurant and Deli, November 28, 2007.

49. Bono's Hobby Nobby Italian Market, Fontana, Calif., "Bono's Hobby Nobby Italian Market" (advertisement), *San Bernardino Daily Sun*, August 30, 1958, sec. B, p. 3; Bono's Hobby Nobby Market, Fontana, Calif., "Hello Paisanos" (advertisement), *Sun-Telegram*, December 14, 1958, sec. B, p. 3; Bono's Italian Market, Fontana, Calif., "Bono's Italian Market Home Cooked Dinners" (advertisement), *Sun-Telegram*, January 31, 1971, sec. D, p. 15; Bono's Italian Market, "Come to Bono's Italian Market" (advertisement), *San Bernardino Daily Sun*, May 5, 1960, sec. D, p. 8 (quotation); Bono interview, unpaged; Clark, *Route 66 Cookbook*, 206–7; "Frances Bono[,] Restaurant Owner," *San Bernardino County Sun*, August 4, 1994, sec. B, p. 4; Renee Hernandez, "Fontana: Restaurant to Reopen[,] Owner Plans Route 66 Theme," *San Bernardino County Sun*, May 5, 1995, sec. B, pp. 1, 3; Hobby Nobby Market, "Here's a Suggestion for Lenten Menus" (advertisement), *San Bernardino Daily Sun*, March 9, 1955, p. 18; "Road News: An Icon Returns," *Route 66 Magazine* 12, no. 3 (Summer 2004): 43; Nomination to the National Register of Historic Places for Bono's Restaurant and Deli; "Services for Bono Held," *Sun*, March 6, 1982, West Valley sec. B, p. 2.

50. "About Our Cover," *Roadsigns* 8, no. 1 (Spring–Summer 1998), inside front cover; Patricia R. Buckley, *Those Unforgettable Giant Oranges* (n.p.: privately printed, 1987), 6–21; Jerry Carroll, "Where Did the Giant Orange Go?," *San Francisco Examiner* (San Francisco), July 29, 1973, Sunday Punch supplement, p. 2;

Duncan, *Images of America: Route 66 in California*, 52; Jerry Gilliam and Howard Seelye, "New Law Puts the Squeeze on Roadside Juice Stands," *Los Angeles Times*, June 29, 1971, pt. 2, pp. 1, 4; Lorraine Bellwood Hunt, interview transcription extracts in exhibit gallery, Arizona Route 66 Museum, Powerhouse Visitors Center, Kingman, Ariz. (first quotation), accessed by the author July 9, 2016; Bob O'Sullivan, "Vacation Memories: On the Road West during the Depression," *Los Angeles Times*, April 24, 1988, pt. 7, p. 3 (second and third quotations); Thomas Arthur Repp, *Route 66: The Romance of the West* (Lynwood, Wash.: Mock Turtle Press, 2002), 192; Cerise A. Valenzuela, "Restoration: Historic Juice Stand Moves to New Site," *San Bernardino County Sun*, January 15, 1993, West Valley sec. B, p. 1; Carl Yetzer, "Route 66 Traces There if You Look," *San Bernardino County Sun*, November 18, 1985, sec. A, pp. 1, 3.

51. Marian Clark, "Coffee Shops, Diners and Other Swell Places: Sycamore Inn Dining House," *Route 66 Magazine* 5, no. 3 (Summer 1998): 36–37; Clark, *Route 66 Cookbook*, 208; Barbara Deters, "Restaurant Purchase Friendly Affair: Don't Mess with Success, Owners Say of Sycamore Inn," *San Bernardino County Sun*, July 25, 1989, sec. B, pp. 7, 10; "Establish Resort Inn near Upland," *San Bernardino Daily Sun*, December 2, 1920, p. 11 (quotation); "$500,000 Expansion Project Scheduled at Sycamore Inn," *Sun-Telegram*, February 14, 1954, p. 27; Phil Townsend Hanna, ed., *"Let's Dine Out" in Southern California: A Guide to Worthwhile Restaurants, Cafes, Inns, Taverns, Etc.* (Los Angeles: Automobile Club of Southern California, 1940), 87; "Plan Social Events for Sycamore Inn," *San Bernardino Daily Sun*, November 27, 1931, p. 13; Sycamore Inn, Rancho Cucamonga, Calif., *Sycamore Inn* ([Rancho Cucamonga, Calif.]: Sycamore Inn, 1990), menu, Menu Collection, Rare Books Room, Los Angeles Public Library, Los Angeles; Sycamore Inn, Upland, Calif., "The Liveliest and Most Beautiful Night Club East of Los Angeles" (advertisement), *San Bernardino Daily Sun*, July 26, 1940, p. 4; Sycamore Inn, Upland, Calif., "Sycamore Inn" (advertisement), *San Bernardino Daily Sun*, November 26, 1925, p. 4; John Weeks, "Café Couture Is Come as You Are," *Sun-Telegram*, February 28, 1975, sec. C, p. 1; Yetzer, "Route 66 Traces," sec. A, p. 3.

52. *California: A Guide to the Golden State*, 618–23; "Ethel M. Maskey," *The Palm Beach Post* (West Palm Beach, Fla.), May 23, 1963, p. 2; Hanna, *"Let's Dine Out,"* 21; Harrison Little, ed., *Where to Eat: 2,300 Restaurants Preferred by Businessmen: A Dartnell Directory* (Chicago: Dartnell Corporation, 1948), 25; *Los Angeles Directory Co's Monrovia (California) City Directory 1935 Including Arcadia and Duarte* (Los Angeles: Los Angeles Directory Co., 1935), 314, 361; "News of the Cafes," *Los Angeles Times*, October 20, 1933, pt. 2, p. 7; Passenger List of S.S. Patria Arriving in New York from Marseilles, France, June 12, 1920, U.S. Immigration and Naturalization Service, Passenger and Crew Lists of Vessels Arriving at New York, New York, 1897–1957, Microcopy T 714, reel 2780; and Passport Application for Ethel May Maskey, Certificate 41799, Approved October 26, 1918, U.S. Department of State, Passport Applications 1795–1925, Microcopy M 1490, reel 614, both in National Archives and Records Administration, Washington, D.C.; *Southern California at a Glance*, 85–88; S[haron] T[horeau], "'Let's Dine Out!' Valley and Foothill Boulevards," *Westways* 27, no. 11 (November 1935): 30–31 (quotations); "War Service Group Conducts Reunion," *Los Angeles Times*, February 26, 1933, pt. 2, p. 6; Alma Whitaker, "Fried Chicken? Not So—She Serves Guinea Hen," *Los Angeles Times*, October 16, 1933, pt. 2, p. 8.

53. Bernice, "After Dark," *Daily News-Post and Monrovia Daily News-Post* (Monrovia, Calif.), June 26, 1954, magazine sec., p. 6; "Certificate of Business Fictitious Firm-Name," *Daily News-Post* (Monrovia, Calif.), December 1, 1950, p. 2; Price Ferguson, "Wild Fowl Excellent at Sportsman's," *Independent Star-News* (Pasadena, Calif.), December 13, 1959, Scene magazine, p. 31; "Fictitious Business Name Statement," *Daily News-Post*, June 21, 1971, sec. A, p. 8; *Gourmet's Guide to Good Eating: A Valuable and Vital Accessory tor Every Motorist and Traveler 1946–47* (New York: Gourmet, the Magazine of Good Living, 1946), 29; Duncan Hines, *Adventures in Good Eating* (Bowling Green, Ky.: Adventures in Good Eating, 1941), 39; "Letter-type Will of Mrs. Adeline E. Baker, Unique in Form and Content, Admitted to Probate," *Monrovia News-Post* (Monrovia, Calif.), March 16, 1949, pp. 1, 12; "Lillian Wadsworth," *Monrovia News-Post*, July 5, 1979, sec. D, p. 1; "Mrs. Adeline E. Baker," *Los Angeles Times*, February 7, 1949, pt. 3, p. 6; "Notice of Intention to Engage in the Sale of Alcoholic Beverages," *Monrovia News-Post*, March 3, 1949, p. 14; "Notice to Creditors

of Bulk Transfer and of Intention to Transfer Alcoholic Beverage License (Secs. 6101–6107 U.C.C. and/or 24073 B&P)," *Monrovia News-Post*, February 2, 1978, sec. A, p. 6; "Resort Notes," *Los Angeles Times*, March 6, 1927, pt. 6, p. 13; Sportsman's Tavern, Duarte, Calif., *Just a Little Different: Sportsman's Tavern* (n.p.: Sportsman's Tavern, [ca. 1945]), postcard, author's collection; Sportsman's Tavern, "Sportsman's Tavern Dinners" (advertisement), *Monrovia Daily News-Post*, December 24, 1942, sec. 2, p. 3; Sharon Thoreau, "'Let's Dine Out!,'" *Westways* 31, no. 10 (October 1939): 28–29; "The Way It Was Opens with Turn-of-Century Look," *Monrovia News-Post*, June 22, 1978, sec. A, p. 2.

54. "Bakery Built to Look Like a Windmill," *Progressive Grocer* 1, no. 12 (December 1933): 31; "Death Takes L. L. Frank, Restaurateur," *Pasadena (Calif.) Independent Topics*, September 23, 1970, p. 1; "Old Dutch Windmill Model for Los Angeles Store," *Popular Mechanics* 37, no. 1 (January 1922): 85; George Purcell, "Maintaining Chain Identity: The Problem Was Intensified for Van de Kamp When It Set up Leased Baked Goods Departments," *Chain Store Age* 25, no. 11 (November 1948): 16, 43; Van de Kamp's Holland Dutch Bakeries, Los Angeles, *Van de Kamp's Coffee Shops and Twin Drive-In* ([Los Angeles]: Van de Kamp's, [ca. 1960]), menu, author's collection; "Western Restaurants: Van de Kamp's Drive-In," *Pacific Coast Record* (Los Angeles) 30, no. 9 (September 1939): 14–16. Although Van de Kamp coffee shops generally served customers of all races, civil rights activists in the 1960s did not hesitate to point out what they saw as their discrimination against hiring African Americans. "Bakery Sit-In Group Arrested," *Independent Press-Telegram* (Long Beach, Calif.), March 22, 1964, sec. A, p. 5; "Farmer among Pickets in L.A.," *Redlands Daily Facts* (Redlands, Calif.), April 27, 1964, p. 1; "200 Stage Sit-In at Van de Kamp," *Independent Star-News*, March 15, 1964, p. 3.

55. "Councilmen Express Concern over Proposed Sign Ordinance," *Arcadia Tribune* (Arcadia, Calif.), December 22, 1968, p. 1; "Ground Is Broken for Van de Kamp," *Arcadia Tribune*, June 4, 1967, p. 4; Dan Harlow, "Rotterdam on Route 66," *Route 66 Magazine* 3, no. 1 (Winter 1995-96): 28–29; Dan Harlow, "Winds of Change Blow in Vain," *Route 66 Magazine* 6, no. 4 (Fall 1999): 24–26; "Restaurant Planned for Sunfair Spot," *Arcadia Tribune*, December 18, 1966, p. 1; "Route Report: The Blades on Route 66's One of a Kind Denny's Are Spinning Once Again," *Route Magazine*, February–March 2019, p. 12; Van de Kamp's Coffee Shop, Buena Park, Calif., "Van de Kamp's Coffee Shop" (advertisement), *Arcadia Tribune*, June 4, 1967, p. 6; "Van de Kamp Windmill Gets Planners OK," *Arcadia Tribune*, January 26, 1967, pp. 1, 4; JoAnne Willis, "Rally Saves Windmill," *Roadsigns* 9, no. 3 (Summer 1999): 7.

56. Austin, *Covered Wagon*, 115 (first and second quotations); R. E. L. Farmer, *From Florida to the Far West* (Bartow, Fla.: privately printed, 1936), 61–62; *Fortnight*, January 5, 1955, quoted in Gwen Torges, "Pasadena a Dining Town? Westside, Beware!," *Los Angeles Times*, June 9, 1990, Pasadena Today advertising supplement, pp. 1, 10, 12 (third quotation); *Southern California at a Glance*, 84–85, 89–92.

57. "Buffet Breakfast," *Pasadena (Calif.) Post*, December 24, 1931, p. 5; John R. Crossland, ed., *The Modern Marvels Encyclopedia* (London: Collins Clear-type Press, 1938), 317; Jim Heimann, "California Crazy: Roadside Guide to Our Architecture of the Absurd," *Los Angeles Herald Examiner*, April 12, 1981, California Living supplement, pp. 18–21; Jim Heimann and Rop Georges, *California Crazy: Roadside Vernacular Architecture* (San Francisco: Chronicle Books, 1980), 20, 23, 57, 122; "Mother Goose, Inc., Gets Stock Permit," *Los Angeles Times*, March 13, 1927, pt. 1, p. 8; Mother Goose Market, Pasadena, Calif., "Mother Goose Market" (advertisement), *Pasadena (Calif.) Evening Post*, September 5, 1927, p. 5 (second and third quotations); "Mother Goose Pantry Opens in City Today," *Pasadena Evening Post*, September 1, 1927, p. 3; Mother Goose Pantry, Pasadena, Calif., "Announcing the Opening Thursday, Friday, Saturday of the First Mother Goose Pantry" (advertisement), *Pasadena Evening Post*, August 31, 1927, p. 6; Mother Goose Pantry, "Pasadena's Unique Eating Place" (advertisement), *Pasadena Evening Post*, October 11, 1928, p. 15 (first quotation); "New Chain of Stores Organized," *Los Angeles Times*, November 16, 1926, pt. 2, p. 24.

58. Big Shoe Toyland, Pasadena, Calif., "Sale! Sale! Sale!" (advertisement), *Pasadena (Calif.) Independent*, October 31, 1952, p. 19; Big Shoe Toyland, "There's New Life in the Big Shoe" (advertisement), *Pasadena Independent*, November 11, 1949, p. 6; [Mother Goose Pantry], "Drive-In for Lease, Fixtures Furnished,"

Pasadena Post, December 31, 1940, p. 9; Mother Goose Pantry, "Girl Car Hops" (advertisement), *Pasadena Post*, October 7, 1936, p. 8; "Notice of Intended Mortgage," *Pasadena (Calif.) Star-News*, September 6, 1947, p. 10; "Notice of Intended Sale," *Pasadena Independent*, February 28, 1951, p. 26; "Notice of Intended Sale," *Pasadena Star-News*, January 24, 1947, p. 6; *Polk's Pasadena (Los Angeles County, California) City Directory 1954 Including Altadena and Lamanda Park* (Los Angeles: R. L. Polk, 1954), 59; *Thurston's Pasadena (California) City Directory 1937 Including Altadena, Lamanda Park, and San Marino* (Los Angeles: Los Angeles Directory Co., 1937), 750; *Thurston's Pasadena (California) City Directory 1938 Including Altadena, Lamanda Park, and San Marino* (Los Angeles: Los Angeles Directory Co., 1938), 435, 738, 982; *Thurston's Pasadena (California) City Directory 1939 Including Altadena, Lamanda Park and San Marino* (Los Angeles: Los Angeles, Directory Co., 1939), 520, 564, 722, 962; *Thurston's Pasadena (California) City Directory 1940 Including Altadena, Lamanda Park and San Marino* (Los Angeles: Los Angeles Directory Co., 1940), 56, 771, 1014; *Thurston's Pasadena (California) City Directory 1943 Including Altadena, Lamanda Park and San Marino* (Los Angeles: Los Angeles Directory Co., 1943), 783; Tiny Tot's Shoe, Pasadena, Calif., "Tiny Tot's Shoe" (advertisement), *Pasadena Star-News*, January 13, 1945, p. 13.

The Mother Goose Pantry served as inspiration for novelist Nathanael West in writing *The Day of the Locust* in 1939. There he created a fictional Cinderella Bar set in 1930s Los Angeles, "a little stucco building in the shape of a lady's slipper" in which the "floor show consisted of female impersonators." Karal Ann Marling, *The Colossus of Roads: Myth and Symbol along the American Highway* (Minneapolis: University of Minnesota Press, 1984), 78; Nathanael West, *Novels and Other Writings*, ed. Sacvan Bercovitch (New York: Library of America, 1997), 339 (quotations).

59. Raymond Pharmacy, South Pasadena, Calif., "For Exchange—My Equity" (advertisement), *Los Angeles Times*, January 17, 1909, pt. 5, p. 14; Raymond Pharmacy, "For Sale—Soda Fountain" (advertisement), *Los Angeles Times*, August 31, 1913, pt. 5, p. 13 (quotation); Raymond Pharmacy, "Wanted Girl—to Learn Drug Trade" (advertisement), *Los Angeles Times*, April 24, 1910, pt. 4, p. 3; "Ready to Begin," *Los Angeles Times*, January 10, 1910, pt. 2, p. 10; "Thieves Rob a Pharmacy," *Los Angeles Times*, April 21, 1913, pt. 2, p. 8; "Thomas Edward Barrett," *Kansas City (Mo.) Times*, May 22, 1952, p. 19; *Thurston's Residence and Business Directory of Pasadena[,] South Pasadena, Altadena and Lamanda Park 1909–10* (Pasadena, Calif.: Thurston, 1909), 462, 475.

60. "About People," *Pasadena Evening Post*, July 14, 1928, p. 8; "Buy at South Pasadena," *Daily Telegram* (Long Beach, Calif.), May 4, 1922, p. 15; "Cleverness: Original Trap Catches Thief," *Los Angeles Times*, September 24, 1916, pt. 2, p. 13; "Credit to City," *Los Angeles Times*, June 28, 1914, pt. 6, p. 2; Fair Oaks Pharmacy Coffee Shop, South Pasadena, Calif., "Merry Christmas" (advertisement), *South Pasadena Review* (South Pasadena, Calif.), December 22, 1955, sec. 3, p. [2]; Fair Oaks Fountain Lunch, South Pasadena, Calif., "Fair Oaks Fountain Lunch" (advertisement), *South Pasadena Review*, February 28, 1968, sec. 1, p. 4; "Fair Oaks Pharmacy Is Remodeled," *South Pasadena Review*, November 6, 1961, pp. 1, 7; Fair Oaks Pharmacy, South Pasadena, Calif., "Fountain and Lunch Counter in Drug Store" (advertisement), *Los Angeles Times*, January 23, 1952, pt. 2, p. 13; Fair Oaks Pharmacy, "Valuable Coupon" (advertisement), *Pasadena Independent*, December 8, 1950, p. 8; Gaskill Pharmacy, South Pasadena, Calif., "Experienced Fountain Girl" (advertisement), *Pasadena Independent*, January 25, 1948, p. 53; Gaskill's Raymond Pharmacy, South Pasadena, Calif., "Gaskill's Raymond Pharmacy" (advertisement), *Pasadena Post*, April 30, 1942, p. 7; "Harry C. Libby Recovering from Major Operation," *South Pasadena Review*, October 18, 1961, sec. 1, p. 6; "New Owner for Local Coffee Shops," *South Pasadena Review*, February 2, 1966, sec. 3, p. 3; "New Store," *Pasadena Evening Post*, September 8, 1919, p. 3; "Noteworthy Project: Large Block for South Pasadena," *Los Angeles Times*, October 26, 1913, pt. 6, p. 1; "Notice of Bulk Transfer Escrow No. 3486," *South Pasadena Review*, December 15, 1971, sec. 2, p. 2; "Notice of Intended Sale," *Independent* (Pasadena, Calif.), February 28, 1964, p. 29; Skewer & Skillet Coffee Shop, South Pasadena, Calif., "Skewer & Skillet Coffee Shop" (advertisement), *South Pasadena Review*, February 2, 1966, sec. 3, p. 4; "Will Build Laundry," *Los Angeles Times*, January 25, 1914, pt. 6, p. 3.

61. Nicole Campos, "Fair Oaks Pharmacy and Soda Fountain," *LA Weekly*, September 25–October 1, 1998, p. 126; Marian Clark, "Coffee Shops, Diners and Other Swell Places: Fair Oaks Pharmacy and Soda Fountain[,] South Pasadena, California," *Route 66 Magazine* 5, no. 2 (Spring 1998): 36–37; "Eats on Rt 66: Fair Oaks Pharmacy and Soda Fountain," *Roadsigns* 7, no. 3 (Fall 1997): [9]; Fair Oaks Pharmacy and Soda Fountain, South Pasadena, Calif., *Fair Oaks Pharmacy and Soda Fountain[,] Soda Fountain and Lunch Counter Menu*, publication 3/99 (South Pasadena, Calif.: Fair Oaks Pharmacy and Soda Fountain, [1999]), menu, Menu Collection, Rare Books Room, Los Angeles Public Library; Michelle Huneven, "Of Soda Fountains and Soda Jerks," *Los Angeles Times*, June 27, 1991, sec. H, p. 31; "Lined up for Ice Cream at Fair Oaks Pharmacy," *South Pasadena Review*, February 27, 1991, p. 2; "Soon at Fair Oak Pharmacy: Genuine Old-Fashioned Soda Fountain for SoPas," *South Pasadena Review*, May 16, 1990, pp. 1, 3.

62. Automobile Club of Southern California, Los Angeles, *Principal Automobile Routes in and out of Los Angeles* (Los Angeles: Automobile Club of Southern California, [ca. 1935]), map, author's collection; Scott Garner, "Americana, Pleasantly Preserved," *Los Angeles Times*, March 18, 2017, sec. J, pp. 12–13; James W. Loewen, *Sundown Towns: A Hidden Dimension of American Racism* (New York: New Press, 2005), 75, 282; Scott R. Piotrowski, *Finding the End of the Mother Road: Route 66 in Los Angeles County*, 2nd ed. (Pasadena, Calif.: 66 Productions, 2005), 28–33, 44–51, 53–57; Scott R. Piotrowski, "Hidden Gems: A Maze in the Arroyo, Part Two—from Pasadena to Los Angeles," *Route 66 Federation News* 8, no. 4 (Autumn 2002): 27–30; *Southern California at a Glance*, 84; "Tale of Two Cities," *Pacific Citizen* (Japanese American Citizens League, Salt Lake City, Utah), January 4, 1947, p. 4.

63. "Assaults on Calles Denounced," *Los Angeles Times*, November 20, 1927, pt. 1, p. 2; Casa la Golondrina, Los Angeles, "Senora Consuelo Castillo de Bonzo Announces That the Original Mexican Cafes" (advertisement), *Los Angeles Times*, July 12, 1930, pt. 2, p. 6; "H. L. Suydam Reports Recent Realty Deals," *Los Angeles Times*, July 1, 1923, pt. 5, p. 10; "News of the Cafes," *Los Angeles Times*, November 7, 1925, pt. 2, p. 8; November 20, 1925, pt. 2, p. 7; July 11, 1930, pt. 2, p. 5; April 18, 1934, pt. 2, p. 18; Lee Shippey, "Lee Side o' L.A.," *Los Angeles Times*, September 17, 1929, pt. 2, p. 4; Ann Vierhus, "Sustains Tradition: Café on Olvera Street Rubs Elbows with Poignant Past," *Los Angeles Times*, April 15, 1955, pt. 3, p. 2; Matt Weinstock, "Some Strange Turns Taken by the Twist," *Los Angeles Times*, April 25, 1962, pt. 2, p. 6.

64. Fred Beck, "Bearing Up," *Los Angeles Times*, December 28, 1943, pt. 1, p. 2; Casa la Golondrina, Los Angeles, *La Golondrina Restaurant and Historic Landmark* (Los Angeles: Casa la Golondrina, [ca. 1990]), menu, Menu Collection, Rare Books Room, Los Angeles Public Library; Casa la Golondrina, "La Mision [*sic*] Café of Los Angeles and Hollywood Announces the Opening of a New Establishment" (advertisement), *Los Angeles Times*, April 19, 1930, pt. 2, p. 8; Casa la Golondrina, "Senora Consuelo Castillo de Bonzo Begs to Announce the Enlargement of Casa La Golondrina" (advertisement), *Los Angeles Times*, June 19, 1930, pt. 2, p. 8; Celeste Durant, "'Queen of Olvera Street' Dies at 87," *Los Angeles Times*, October 24, 1977, pt. 1, pp. 3, 22; Hanna, *"Let's Dine Out,"* 40 (quotations); Marian Manners, "Southland Cafes," *Los Angeles Times*, April 19, 1940, pt. 4, World's Kitchen supplement, p. 25; "Mexican Food Expert Coming: Feminine Culinary Authority Will Appear on Celebrity Program," *Los Angeles Evening Express*, October 23, 1930, p. 16; "Mexicans Open Café with Rites," *Los Angeles Times*, April 17, 1930, pt. 2, p. 5; Pat Morrison, "Pat Morrison Asks Olvera's Anchor," *Los Angeles Times*, June 5, 2010, sec. A, p. 25; "News of the Cafes," *Los Angeles Times*, April 25, 1930, pt. 2, p. 10; "Permits Issued," *Los Angeles Times*, August 7, 1930, pt. 1, p. 17; Lee Shippey, "The Lee Side 'o L.A.," *Los Angeles Times*, June 28, 1937, pt. 2, p. 4; Sharon Thoreau, "'Let's Dine Out!' Metropolitan Los Angeles," *Westways* 27, no. 2 (February 1935): 27, 32; "Throng Inspects El Paseo: Several Hundred Invited Guests at Festivities on Eve of Public Opening of Thoroughfare," *Los Angeles Times*, April 20, 1930, pt. 2, pp. 1, 3; Vierhus, "Sustains Tradition," pt. 3, p. 2.

65. T. Lindsay Baker, "Early Route 66 Travelers Discover Clifton's Cafeterias," *Route 66 Magazine* 24, no. 1 (Winter 2016–17): 14–16; Baker, *Portrait of Route 66*, 232–35; Charles Bukowski, *Ham on Rye* (New York: Ecco, 2002), 218 (fourth quotation); Clifton's Cafeterias, Los Angeles, *About Clifton's[,] November, 1937—Information* (Los Angeles: Clifton's, 1937), folder (first and second quotations), Menu Collection,

Rare Books Rooms, Los Angeles Public Library; Clifton's Cafeterias, Los Angeles, *Views of Clifton's*[:] *Pay What You Wish*[,] *Dine Free Unless Delighted* (Los Angeles: Pictorial California, [ca. 1945]), booklet, "Clifton's Cafeterias" Vertical File, California Vertical Files, History and Genealogy Department, Los Angeles Public Library; Larry Dietz, "A Gourmand's Guide to Downtown L.A.," *Los Angeles Times*, February 7, 1971, West magazine, pp. 20–21, 23; Elisabeth Webb Herrick, *Curious California Customs*, Los Angeles ed. (Los Angeles: Pacific Carbon and Print, 1935), 53–55 (third quotation); Sylvia F. Johnson, "Cafeterias of the Golden Rule: Clifton's Cafeterias," typescript, [ca. 1960], pp. 1–26, "Clifton's Cafeterias" Vertical File, California Vertical Files, History and Genealogy Department, Los Angeles Public Library; "'Let's Dine Out!,'" *Westways* 45, no 8 (August 1953): 35–37; Mary MacVean, "Where L.A. Finds Itself," *Los Angeles Times*, February 4, 2009, sec. F, pp. 1, 4; Cecilia Rasmussen, "L.A. Scene: The City Then and Now," *Los Angeles Times*, May 11, 1992, sec. B, p. 3; Art Sidenbaum, "A Slice of L.A. History on Toast," *Los Angeles Times*, July 28, 1976, pt. 4, pp. 1, 18; Alan Zarembo, "Nostalgia Is Main Dish: Reopening of Clifton's Cafeteria after a Five-Year Remodel Brings Back Customers from Earlier Eras," *Los Angeles Times*, October 5, 2015, sec. B, p. 3.

66. "'Baby-Faced' Gunman Robs Hollywood Café," *Los Angeles Times*, April 5, 1950, pt. 2, p. 11; Lois Dwan, "Roundabout," *Los Angeles Times*, April 16, 1978, Calendar supplement, pp. 102–5; "Fire Damages Café," *Los Angeles Times*, April 4, 1940, pt. 2, p. 12; Formosa Café, Los Angeles, "Formosa[,] Cantonese Food by Quon Lem, Your Host Jimmy Bernstein" (advertisement), *Los Angeles Times*, September 19, 1962, pt. 4, p. 6; Lynell George, "Memory Palace: A Visit to the Rehabbed Formosa Café Takes You Deep into Hollywood's Past," *Preservation* (National Trust for Historic Preservation, Washington, D.C.) 72, no. 1 (Winter 2020): 18–27; Nita Lelyveld, "Landmark Stands in Changing Neighborhood," *Los Angeles Times*, September 9, 2003, sec. B, pp. 1, 9; "'Let's Dine Out!,'" *Westways* 46, no. 11 (November 1954): 44–45 (first quotation); "Liquor Raiders Rout 75 in Café at 3 A.M.," *Los Angeles Times*, October 23, 1944, pt. 1, p. 12; Myrna Oliver, "Lem Quon: Hollywood Flocked to His Formosa Café," *Los Angeles Times*, December 10, 1993, sec. A, p. 40 (second quotation); "Picketed Café Gets Restraining Order," *Los Angeles Times*, April 12, 1939, pt. 1, p. 2; "Pickets Picketed by Elderly Woman," *Los Angeles Times*, April 8, 1939, pt. 1, p. 6; Michael Quintanilla, "Stars Still Shine on Fabled Formosa Café," *Los Angeles Times*, March 29, 1991, sec. E, pp. 1, 7; Christopher Reed, "Holding Court at the Confucian Café: Lem Quon," *Guardian* (London), December 14, 1993, sec. 2, p. 18; Margy Rochlin, "A Dim Future for Venerable Café to the Stars," *Los Angeles Times*, January 30, 1991, sec. F, pp. 1, 4, 5; William Scholl, "Roundup at the Formosa," *Westways* 71, no. 1 (January 1979): 47–49, 65; Gene Sherman, "Cityside," *Los Angeles Times*, November 25, 1956, pt. 1, p. A.

67. "Berkleyan Dies in Fall from Roof," *Oakland (Calif.) Tribune*, July 12, 1927, p. 25; "Championship Finals in Oakland Boy's League Sunday," *San Francisco Examiner*, November 3, 1922, sec. P, p. 4; Mark Coverly, "The Bad Man of the Campus," *Oakland Tribune*, October 15, 1922, Sunday Magazine supplement, p. 4 (first quotation); the Knave, "The Knave," *Oakland Tribune*, November 1, 1925, Society sec. S, p. [8]; "Maj. Gen. Dean to Be Marshal for Rose Parade," *Santa Cruz (Calif.) Sentinel-News*, December 29, 1953, p. 4 (second quotation); *Oakland Berkeley Alameda City Directory 1924* (Oakland, Calif.: Polk-Husted Directory Co., 1924), 282, 2173; *Polk's Oakland Berkeley Alameda City Directory 1927* (Oakland, Calif.: R. L. Polk, 1927), 290, 2131.

68. David Barry, "A Night in at Barney's Beanery," *Los Angeles Times*, March 13, 1977, Calendar supplement, p. 80; Hailey Branson-Potts, "Major Changes Are on the Menu: Barney's Beanery Project Worries West Hollywood," *Los Angeles Times*, September 30, 2016, sec. B, pp. 1, 8; Stephen Braun, "Barney's Bar Gives up Its 'Fagots' Sign," *Los Angeles Times*, January 16, 1985, pt. 2, p. 14; "Chatterbox," *Los Angeles Times*, October 9, 1936, pt. 2, p. 7; Clark, *Route 66 Cookbook*, 217; Chris Epting, *Marilyn Monroe Dyed Here: More Locations of America's Pop Culture Landmarks* (Santa Monica, Calif.: Santa Monica Press, 2004), 187; Jimmie Fidler, "In Hollywood," *Los Angeles Times*, April 17, 1940, pt. 1, p. 13 (first quotation); Rick Fry, "Barney's Beanery," *Route 66 Magazine* 9, no. 3 (Summer 2002): 24–27; P[hil] T[ownsend] H[anna], "Fine Food in California," *Westways* 31, no. 4 (April 1939): 21–22 (second quotation); Hanna, *"Let's Dine*

Out," 24; Hedda Hopper, "Hedda Hopper's Hollywood," *Los Angeles Times*, December 11, 1939, pt. 2, p. 11; "John Anthony, 70," *Los Angeles Times*, November 28, 1968, pt. 2, p. 8; "Notice of Intention to Engage in the Sale of Alcoholic Beverages," *Los Angeles Times*, May 27, 1966, pt. 5, p. 1; Scott Piotrowski, "A Straight Shot to Santa Monica," *Route 66 Federation News* 9, no. 2 (Spring 2002): 20–23; Cecilia Rasmussen, "L.A. Then and Now: Hip but Controversial Hangout," *Los Angeles Times*, March 19, 2006, sec. B, pp. 1–2; "Rock Singer Janis Joplin, 27, Found Dead in Hollywood Motel," *Los Angeles Times*, October 5, 1970, pt. 1, p. 3; Gene Sherman, "Cityside," *Los Angeles Times*, September 8, 1953, pt. 1, p. 2; January 24, 1954, pt. 1, p. A; July 12, 1954, pt. 1, p. 2; Joan Winchell, "Bit of Paris in Westwood," *Los Angeles Times*, May 11, 1962, pt. 4, p. 8.

69. Brown Derby, Los Angeles, *The Brown Derby Coffee Shop*[,] *Wilshire at Alexandria*, publication No. 1—9-52 (Los Angeles: Brown Derby, [1952]), menu, Menu Collection, Rare Books Rooms, Los Angeles Public Library; *The Brown Derby Cookbook* (Garden City, N.Y.: Doubleday, 1949), 1–11, 22, 68–69, 240–42; Brown Derby Service Corporation, [Los Angeles], *Dinner* ([Los Angeles]: Brown Derby Service Corp., 1948), menu, author's collection; Sally Wright Cobb and Mark Willems, *The Brown Derby Restaurant: A Hollywood Legend* (New York: Rizzoli International Publications, 1996), 12–20, 84; Edward D. Dunn, *Double-Crossing America by Motor: Routes and Ranches of the West* (New York: G. P. Putnam's Sons, 1933), 133; Hanna, *"Let's Dine Out,"* 11, 27–38; "Herbert K. Somborn Dies," *Los Angeles Times*, January 3, 1934, pt. 2, p. 12; Herrick, *Curious California Customs*, 14–15; "'Let's Dine Out!,'" *Westways* 46, no. 6 (June 1954): 44–45; Cecilia Rasmussen, "L.A. Then and Now: Once in Fashion, the Brown Derby Became Old Hat," *Los Angeles Times*, November 27, 2005, sec. B, p. 2; Ruth Ryon, "Brown Derby to Crown New Shopping Plaza," *Los Angeles Times*, May 19, 1985, pt. 8, pp. 1, 12; Sharon Thoreau, "'Let's Dine Out!,'" *Westways* 29, no. 11 (November 1937): 30, 32; Sharon Thoreau, "'Let's Dine Out!' Beverly Hills," *Westways* 30, no. 4 (April 1938): 24–25; Sharon Thoreau, "'Let's Dine Out!' Care-Free and Cosmopolitan Hollywood," *Westways* 26, no. 10 (October 1934): 33–34; Sharon Thoreau, "'Let's Dine Out!' 'Hollywood and Vine' I," *Westways* 29, no. 12 (December 1937): 28; "Wilshire Blvd. Café Declared Flagrant Violation of Building Laws," *Los Angeles Evening Express*, March 8, 1928, pp. 3, 5.

70. *California: A Guide to the Golden State*, 417, 623–24; Harry Carr, *Los Angeles: City of Dreams* (New York: Grosset and Dunlap, 1935), 307; Thos. D. Murphy, *On Sunset Highways: A Book of Motor Rambles in California* (Boston: Page, 1915), 19–23; Piotrowski, *Finding the End of the Mother Road*, 87–92; Jessica Slating, "The End of the Trail," *Route 66 Federation News* 16, no. 1 (Winter 2010): 16–18; *Southern California at a Glance*, 67; James Thole, "Santa Monica: Picture the End of the Mother Road," *Route 66 Federation News* 12, no. 1 (Winter 2006): 20–22. Unlike many locations along Highway 66, African Americans throughout the Route 66 years had their own designated recreational area on the Santa Monica beach south of Pico Boulevard between Bay and Bicknell Streets. Alison Rose Jefferson, "African American Leisure Space in Santa Monica: The Beach Sometimes Known as the 'Inkwell,' 1900s–1960s," *Southern California Quarterly* 91, no. 2 (Summer 2009): 155–89; Alison Rose Jefferson, *Living the California Dream: African American Leisure Sites during the Jim Crow Era* (Lincoln: University of Nebraska Press, 2020), 71–103.

71. Belle-Vue French Restaurant, Santa Monica, Calif., *Belle-Vue French Restaurant*[,] *Cocktail Lounge*[,] *Dinner*[,] *Where Santa Monica Boulevard Meets the Sea*, Publication 6-68 (Santa Monica, Calif.: Santa Monica Printers, [1968]), menu, author's collection; "Bouillabaisse Featured," *Valley News and Valley Green Sheet* (Van Nuys, Calif.), October 23, 1970, sec. A, p. 28; "Eats 250 Bowls of Bouillabaisse," *Van Nuys News and Valley Green Sheet*, May 3, 1968, Central Valley Edition, sec. A, p. 32; P[hil] T[ownsend] H[anna], "Fine Food in California," *Westways* 30, no. 8 (August 1938): 25–26; Hanna, *"Let's Dine Out,"* 83–84; Michelle Huneven, "Restaurant Review: Santa Monica's Belle-Vue Lets in the Light," *Los Angeles Times*, April 19, 1991, sec. F, p. 11; Kathie Jenkins, "Restaurants See Green in the Valley: Doin' the Chinois-Spago-Eureka Shuffle," *Los Angeles Times*, January 19, 1992, Calendar supplement, pp. 93, 98; "'Let's Dine Out,'" *Westways* 46, no. 7 (July 1954): 29; *Los Angeles Directory Co's Bay Cities Directory 1938 Including Santa Monica, Ocean Park, Venice, West Los Angeles and Brentwood Heights* (Los Angeles: Los Angeles Directory Co., 1938), 545; *Los Angeles Directory Co's Santa Monica (California) City Directory 1940 Including*

Brentwood Heights, Ocean Park and West Los Angeles (Los Angeles: Los Angeles Directory Co., 1940), 454, 559, 660; Jean McMurphy, "About," *Los Angeles Times*, June 5, 1966, Calendar supplement, pp. 43–45; "Pilloni, Edward L.," *Los Angeles Times*, July 9, 1976, pt. 3, p. 15; Stanley Ralph Ross, "Good Tastes: Fish Story," *LA Weekly*, August 3–August 9, 1979, p. 38; Art Ryon, "About," *Los Angeles Times*, February 6, 1966, Calendar supplement, pp. 41–43; Art Ryon, "Roundabout," *Los Angeles Times*, November 8, 1963, pt. 5, p. 8; U.S. Census Bureau, Census of 1940, Population Schedules, Santa Monica City, Los Angeles County, Calif., Enumeration District 19–766, page 14A, Roll 257, Microcopy T627, National Archives and Records Administration; "Wallace, Anne," *Los Angeles Times*, September 8, 2000, sec. B, p. 8; "Wallace, James J.," *Los Angeles Times*, June 27, 1982, pt. 2, p. 2.

72. Baker, *Portrait of Route 66*, 250–51; O. J. Bennett, Santa Monica, Calif., to Duncan Hines, Bowling Green, Ky., November 6, 1944, typewritten letter, box 2, folder "1943 7th and 8th Printing," Duncan Hines Collection, Division of Rare and Manuscript Collections, Cornell University Library, Ithaca, N.Y.; James Harris, *Santa Monica Pier: A Century on the Last Great Pleasure Pier* (Santa Monica, Calif.: Santa Monica Pier Restoration Corporation, 2009), 109–10; Jim Harris, interview, n.d., Santa Monica, Calif., "Authors@Google: Jim Harris," http://www.allreadable.com/63297ZHP, accessed on August 12, 2014; Duncan Hines, *Adventures in Good Cooking (Famous Recipes) and the Art of Carving in the Home* (Bowling Green, Ky.: Adventures in Good Eating, 1945), recipe 153 unpaged; Duncan Hines, *Adventures in Good Cooking (Famous Recipes) and the Art of Carving in the Home* (Ithaca, N.Y.: Duncan Hines Institute, 1957), recipe 207 unpaged; Duncan Hines, *Adventures in Good Eating* (Chicago: Adventures in Good Eating, 1938), 48; Hines, *Adventures in Good Eating* (1941), 51; Duncan Hines, "How to Find a Decent Meal," *Saturday Evening Post* 219, no. 43 (April 26, 1947): 18–19, 97, 99–100, 102 (second and third quotations); Al Martinez, "Waterfront Fixture Is Losing Its Moorings," *Los Angeles Times*, April 1, 2002, sec. E, pp. 1, 4; Carolyn Sackarison, "Boathouse Lawsuit Asks for $50 Million," *Santa Monica Daily Press* (Santa Monica, Calif.), May 22, 2002, pp. 1, 5; Sharon Thoreau, "'Let's Dine Out!,'" *Westways* 33, no. 9 (September 1941): 28 (first quotation).

INDEX OF RESTAURANTS AND OTHER EATERIES

GENERAL INDEX